Religion on the American Frontier
1783-1840

Vol. II
The Presbyterians

Religion on the American Frontier · 1783–1840

Vol. II
The Presbyterians

A Collection of Source Materials

By
WILLIAM WARREN SWEET

COOPER SQUARE PUBLISHERS, INC.

New York · 1964

CONTENTS

RELIGION ON THE AMERICAN FRONTIER
1783-1832

VOLUME II
THE PRESBYTERIANS

v

MAPS

PREFACE

This volume of Sources illustrating how Presbyterianism functioned on the early American frontier is the second in the series, *Religion on the American Frontier,* planned by the Department of Church History in the University of Chicago. The plan for the series originally called for the publication of both Presbyterian and Congregational materials in this volume, since the two churches, throughout the period covered, coöperated under the Plan of Union in those regions where the two denominations came together. But the materials collected became so voluminous that it was necessary to divide it. It is therefore the intention to devote volume three of the series to the Congregationalists.

As in the first volume, *The Baptists,*[1] I have been assisted in the editing of several of the manuscripts by successive seminars of graduate students. Among my former students who have rendered valuable service of this kind I should mention Dr. Paul H. Eller, Mr. Herbert Hatt, Mr. G. A. Riegler, Dr. Don W. Holter, Dr. R. L. Hightower, Dr. H. L. Lennox, Mr. Reid Wall, Dr. Marvin H. Harper, Mr. Eugene M. Harrison, Mr. Eric G. Hawkinson and Mr. Charles T. Thrift. Mr. Eugene Tilleux has not only rendered assistance as a member of two of my graduate seminars, but has also given much time and painstaking care to the making of the maps which appear in the volume. Mr. Charles T. Thrift and Dr. Marvin H. Harper have rendered valuable assistance in the making of the bibliography as has also Mr. H. R. Greenholt.

Thanks are due to many others in various parts of the country for generous assistance in helping me secure copies and photostats of manuscripts. I am especially indebted

[1] Henry Holt & Co., 1931.

PREFACE

for this type of assistance to Dr. S. M. Tenney, curator
of the Historical Foundation at Montreat, North Carolina, and to Mrs. Tenney, the assistant curator; to Rev.
Thomas C. Pears, Jr., secretary of the Presbyterian Historical Society in Philadelphia; Mr. H. M. Brimm, libra-
rian of the Spence Library of the Union Theological Seminary, Richmond, Virginia; to Miss Elizabeth Rutledge of
the Presbyterian Theological Seminary, Louisville, Kentucky; Dr. Joseph Schafer, secretary of the State Historical
Society of Wisconsin; and also to the officials of the Indiana State Library, of the Missouri Historical Society,
the Western Reserve Historical Society and to my cowork-
ers at the University of Chicago. Professor Robert
Hastings Nichols of the Auburn Theological Seminary not
only made possible the securing of manuscripts in the Library at Auburn, but has also read a part of the manuscript
and has offered valuable suggestions and criticisms. Professor A. C. Zenos of the Presbyterian Theological Seminary in Chicago has also read parts of the manuscripts and
has likewise offered valued suggestions. Many whose
names I have not mentioned have helped in one way or
another, to all of whom I wish to express my deep appre-
ciation.

WILLIAM WARREN SWEET

University of Chicago
    May 1, 1935

PART I
GENERAL INTRODUCTION

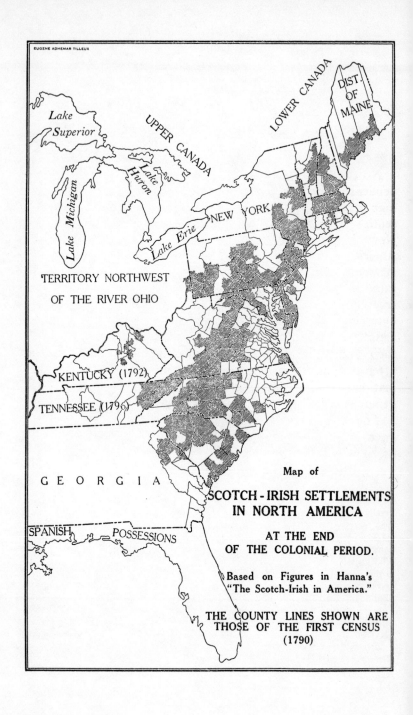

EUGENE ADHEMAR TILLEUX

Map of

SCOTCH-IRISH SETTLEMENTS
IN NORTH AMERICA

AT THE END
OF THE COLONIAL PERIOD.

Based on Figures in Hanna's
"The Scotch-Irish in America."

THE COUNTY LINES SHOWN ARE
THOSE OF THE FIRST CENSUS
(1790)

CHAPTER I

AMERICAN PRESBYTERIANISM AT THE CLOSE OF THE REVOLUTION

No church in America, at the close of the War for Independence, was in a better position for immediate expansion than was the Presbyterian. Representing the large eighteenth century Scotch-Irish immigration as well as a growing New England element, especially in Connecticut,[1] the American Presbyterians had supported the cause of independence with almost one hundred percent unanimity, and came through the Revolution with a united front and increased prestige. Briggs states that in 1775 "the Presbyterians and Congregationalists combined had the ecclesiastical control of the American colonies," and that "upon their action the destinies of America depended."[2] Even after discounting this statement as one colored by denominational pride, careful investigation will show that this generalization is not far from the truth.

The year the treaty of peace was signed (1783) which gave independence to the American Colonies, the Synod of New York and Philadelphia, which contained the largest

[1] Since their adoption of the Saybrook Platform in 1708 Connecticut Congregationalism had tended more and more toward Presbyterianism and by the opening of the American Revolution the names Congregational and Presbyterian were used interchangeably in that colony. For ten years, from 1766 to 1775, the "consociated" Congregational churches of Connecticut and the Presbyterian Synod of New York and Philadelphia held annual conventions at which plans of union and coöperation were discussed and an intimate relationship developed between them, which culminated after independence in the Plan of Union of 1801. See Chapter II of this volume; also *Records of the Presbyterian Church in the United States of America*, etc., 1706-1788 (Philadelphia, 1904), for 1783, hereafter cited as *Records of the Presbyterian Church*, appendix pp. 1-41; also *Extracts from the Itineraries and Other Miscellanies of Ezra Stiles, 1755-1794*, etc., edited by F. B. Dexter (New Haven, 1916), pp. 427; 458-459; 466-468; 591-593.

[2] Briggs, Charles A., *American Presbyterianism, Its Origin and Early History* (New York, 1885), p. 343.

3

proportion of the Presbyterian churches in America, congratulated the churches through its pastoral letter on "the general and almost universal attachment of the Presbyterian body to the cause of liberty and the rights of mankind." The address pointed to "our burnt and wasted churches, and our plundered dwellings" as an "earnest of what we must have suffered, had they [the enemy] finally prevailed." The Synod therefore request that Presbyterian people throughout the land "render thanks to Almighty God, for all his mercies, spiritual and temporal, and in a particular manner for establishing the Independence of the United States of America."[3]

No patriotic leader in the colonies had been more influential or useful to the cause of independence than John Witherspoon. He had come from Scotland in 1768 to assume the presidency of the College of New Jersey, in the very midst of the excitement over the passage of the Stamp Act, and had immediately identified himself with the cause of the American colonies. He had also become, almost at once, the recognized leader of American Presbyterianism, and at the close of the War for Independence was the directing spirit in organizing his church on a national scale. He was a member of the Continental Congress, being one of five members elected to represent New Jersey in that body, and became an influential member of the committee on finance, and was the only clergyman to sign the Declaration of Independence. His numerous writings abound in reasoned patriotic utterances, and so calm were his statements and so reasonable his position that through his influence the American cause gained respect on both sides of the Atlantic.[4] George Duffield, the Presby-

---

[3] Briggs, *op. cit.*, p. 357; also *Records of the Presbyterian Church* for the year 1783.

[4] Rogers, John, *Works of John Witherspoon, D.D., LL.D., to which is prefixed an account of the author's life.* 9 Vols. (Edinburgh, 1815). For an excellent summary of Witherspoon's influence in the Revolution see Humphrey, E. F., *Nationalism and Religion in America, 1774-1789* (Boston, 1924), pp. 83-96.

terian pastor of the third Presbyterian Church of Philadelphia and one of the chaplains of the Continental
Congress, was another of the influential leaders in Revolutionary America among the American Presbyterians.   John
Adams often sat under his preaching during the war years,
and in reporting a sermon of Duffield's to his wife he states,
"He filled and swelled the bosom of every hearer."[5]   Rank-
ing next in influence to Witherspoon in American Presbyterianism was John Rodgers, pastor of the Wall Street
Presbyterian Church of New York, who throughout the
War was engaged in numerous patriotic activities.[6]

While Witherspoon, Duffield and Rodgers were perhaps
the outstanding Presbyterian leaders of the time, yet as a
whole the Presbyterian leadership of the new nation was a
well-educated and forceful body of men. The ministers were
largely American educated and trained and were generally
thoroughly imbued with the American spirit.

At the opening of the War for Independence there were
543 Presbyterian congregations in the American colonies,
the largest number being found in New York, New Jersey,
Pennsylvania, western Maryland and Virginia.   Wherever
the Scotch-Irish had gone, however, and they were to be
found in every colony, in sufficient numbers to make their
influence felt, there was to be found at least a nucleus of
a Presbyterian church, for if the Scotch-Irish had any
religious leanings at all they were sure to be in the direction
of Presbyterianism.   These 543 congregations were organized into the following synods and presbyteries with the
number of ministers in each:

The Synod of New York and Philadelphia consisted of
eleven presbyteries and had 132 ministers; the Synod of
New England[7] consisted of three presbyteries and thirty-two

---

[5] Humphrey, *op. cit.*, pp. 96-98.

[6] See Rodgers, John, *The Divine Goodness Displayed in the American Revolution, A Sermon Preached December 11th, 1783, A Day of Public Thanksgiving* (New York, 1783), Reprinted in *Patriotic Preachers of the American
Revolution*, pp. 312-343. For a summary of Presbyterian activity during the
Revolution see Briggs, *op. cit.*, pp. 352-353.

[7] For these figures see Briggs, *op. cit.*, p. 342. "Synod of New England

ministers; the Presbytery in South Carolina had six ministers; while there were two Associate presbyteries and thirteen ministers, and one Reformed presbytery with three ministers.

The growth of the Presbyterians had been especially rapid since the Great Colonial Awakenings,[8] which had occurred first in the Middle Colonies under the leadership of the sons of William Tennent in the seventeen thirties and forties, and had spread southward into Virginia and North Carolina by the middle of the century under the leadership of Samuel Davies. As a result of opposition to the revival which had developed among the older ministers, especially in New Jersey and Pennsylvania, a schism occurred in 1745 and the church had been divided into Old Side and New Side Synods, but fortunately these differences had been composed by 1758 and the two synods had united to form the Synod of New York and Philadelphia. From 1758 to the formation of the General Assembly in 1789, 250 new ministers had been ordained, and seven new presbyteries had been organized; the Orange Presbytery in 1770; the Redstone in 1781; the South Carolina in 1784; the Abingdon in 1785; and the Transylvania, the Lexington and the Carlisle in 1786.[9]

Besides the regular Presbyterians by the opening of the Revolution there had come to be two groups of dissenting Scotch Presbyterians established in the colonies. The first were those who regarded the settlement of 1689 as failing

was formed May 31, 1775, by the forming of three Presbyteries of Londonderry, Salem, and Palmer. It met only once or twice; and in 1782 only the Presbytery of Salem remained, with barely a quorum."

Webster, Richard, *A History of the Presbyterian Church in America* (Philadelphia, 1857), p. 666. There was an earlier Presbytery formed in Maine, called the Presbytery of Eastward, which was never connected with the Synod of New England. Gillett, E. H., *History of the Presbyterian Church in the United States* (Philadelphia, 1864), II, p. 102 note.

[8] Maxson, C. H., *The Great Awakening in the Middle Colonies* (Chicago, 1920); and Gewehr, W. M., *The Great Awakening in Virginia* (Durham, N. C., 1930), especially Chapters III and IV.

[9] *Records of the Presbyterian Church*, pp. 491, 504, 510, 523. See also various references in Gillett, *op. cit.*, I.

to give proper recognition to the national covenants of 1638 and 1643 and renounced both church and state. For a number of years they were without ministers and the sacraments but by 1743 they were able to form the Reformed Presbytery of Scotland. Some of these "Covenanter" families migrated to the colonies, and in 1774 a Reformed or Covenanter Presbytery was organized in America. The other conservative Presbyterian body was the Associate Synod. This represented the first formal secession from the Church of Scotland which had taken place in 1733. Their secession was due to the growing centralization of power in the hands of the General Assembly and their protest against the strange and questionable doctrines which they claimed were being taught by professors of theology. It was in 1753 that the first Associate synod was formed in America, which by the opening of the War for Independence had increased to two presbyteries and thirteen ministers.[10]

During this period of rapid growth, however, the educational standards for the ministry had been maintained in the face of the greatly increased demands. The College of New Jersey, which had been established by the New Side Presbyterians in 1747 to train young men for the ministry, had turned out a long line of earnest and successful ministers. No college in the colonies had drawn its students from such wide areas. Indeed, the College of New Jersey was the only truly intercolonial educational institution. Harvard, Yale and the College of William and Mary were largely local institutions, drawing their students from the colonies in which they were located, which was likewise true to a large extent of King's College in New York and the College of Philadelphia. This wide geographical distribution of the Princeton students was due to the fact that Presbyterian people and churches were as widely scattered throughout the colonies as were the Scotch-Irish settlers. When James Madison entered the College of New Jersey,

[10] Scouller, J. B., *A History of the United Presbyterian Church*, American Church History Series, Vol. XI (New York, 1894), pp. 145-173.

of the eighty-four students in attendance only nineteen were from New Jersey, and every colony was represented in the student body.[11]   Of the twelve students who were in the graduating class of 1771 only one was from New Jersey. Of the 250 Presbyterian ministers who had received ordination between 1758 and 1789, 120 had come from the College of New Jersey; twenty from Yale; while the College of Philadelphia, Newark Academy, Hampden Sydney College and Washington Academy had furnished the remainder.[12]

At every meeting of the Synod of New York and Philadelphia throughout the Revolution there were calls from the back country for ministers, and the action taken by the Synod of 1779 records the fact that the church was fully conscious of the importance of the west.   A call had come from the Hanover Presbytery asking that missionaries be sent into western Virginia.   They state that, "it is greatly for the interest of the church to pay particular attention to the Southern and Western parts of this continent," for the reason that "congregations that will be formed there will be permanent," and that "it is not desirable, nor to be expected that the most extensive country should continue long without some form of religion; that this Synod has now an opportunity of promoting the interest of religion extensively, which in a few years may be utterly lost by the prevalency and preoccupying of many ignorant and irreligious sectaries."   The Synod therefore recommended that all the presbyteries turn their attention to this subject, "as peculiarly interesting and important" and urged the sending of missionaries who would be particularly adapted to the directing of the education of youth.[13]

But in spite of these increased demands the Synod refused in 1783 to permit the licensing of persons to preach the gospel who did not have a liberal education, and again

[11] Hunt, Gaillard, *The Life of James Madison* (New York, 1902), pp. 14-15.

[12] Humphrey, *op. cit.*, p. 267.

[13] *Records of the Presbyterian Church,* pp. 484-485.

in 1785 they reaffirmed the upholding of educational standards by answering in the negative "by a great majority" the
question as to,

Whether in the present state of the Church in America and the
scarcity of ministers to fill our numerous congregations, the Synod
or Presbyteries, ought to relax, in any degree, the literary qualifications required of intrants into the ministry.

It was even proposed to raise the standards and to require
both a liberal arts education and a two-year divinity course,
but this was laid over and rejected the following year.[14]

The Presbyterian emphasis upon the importance of education in general is well set forth in a resolution passed at
the meeting of the Synod of New York and Philadelphia in
1785, in which all congregations are "enjoined" to give
special attention "to the good education of children, as being
intimately connected with the interests of morality and religion."   The session of each congregation is therefore
urged to see that one or more schools be established in
places most convenient to the people, and this shall be considered as a part of congregational business, for they hold
that "schools under bad masters, and a careless management, are seminaries of vice rather than of virtue."   Presbyteries are also instructed to appoint special committees
to establish schools in vacant congregations, and that when
the presbyteries appoint supplies for vacant congregations
they shall require that a part of their duty is to visit the
schools at stated intervals, and that they shall be required
to report to the presbytery as to "their fidelity in this respect."   The net result of this emphasis was to make almost
every Presbyterian preacher in the west a school master.[15]

Of large importance in the development of American
Presbyterianism was the fact that immediately following the
achievement of independence steps were taken to organize
the church nationally.[16]   This meant that the church con-

[14] *Ibid.*, pp. 499, 511.
[15] *Ibid.*, p. 513.
[16] *Ibid.*, p. 212.   Also Humphrey, *op. cit.*, for a discussion of the whole subject of the organization of the Church, pp. 269-282.

ceived of its task as one of national scope. The first steps to form a national organization were taken at the meeting of the Synod of New York and Philadelphia in 1785. A committee was appointed, headed by Dr. Witherspoon, to compile a system of general rules for the government of the Synod and presbyteries, "and the people in their communion," which was to report at the next meeting of the Synod. At this session an overture was introduced providing for the formation of three synods and a general synod or assembly, and a definite day was fixed for its discussion at the next meeting of the Synod. A committee was also appointed to consider "modes of Divine Worship" and were instructed to compose a "version more suitable to our circumstances and tastes than any we yet have."

The following year, 1786,[17] it was determined to increase the number of presbyteries from twelve to sixteen and to group them into four synods to be "subordinate to a General Assembly to be constituted out of the whole." The Presbyteries of Dutchess County, Suffolk, New York and New Brunswick were to be gathered into the Synod of New York and New Jersey; the Synod of Philadelphia was to be composed of the Presbyteries of Philadelphia, Lewestown, New Castle, Baltimore and Carlisle; a third synod was constituted of Redstone, Hanover, Lexington and Transylvania Presbyteries and was to be called the Synod of Virginia; the fourth, the Synod of the Carolinas, was to be composed of the Presbyteries of Abingdon, Orange and South Carolina. The Synod of 1786 took further steps in the preparation of a "book of discipline and government . . . accommodated to the state of the Presbyterian Church in America."

The process of constitution making was somewhat retarded by an attempt to bring together the several Presbyterial sects in the United States into one body, and a committee was appointed to confer with the committees from the Dutch Synod and the Associate Reformed Synod. This occupied much of the attention of the Synod of 1786, but

[17] *Records of the Presbyterian Church*, pp. 523-524.

the smaller bodies were too tenacious of their independence for the plan to succeed.[18]

The following year the Synod discussed the reports of their several committees. Among the things which concerned them was the alteration of the plan of government and discipline in the Westminster Confession so as to eliminate the principle of an established church and religious persecution, "and to proclaim the religious liberty and legal equality of all Christian denominations."[19]   The original text of the Confession stated that the civil magistrate had the authority and duty to preserve the peace of the church and to see that "all blasphemies and heresies be suppressed, all corruption and abuses in worship and discipline prevented or reformed." This was revised so as to read, the civil magistrates were "to protect the church of our Common Lord, without giving the preference to any denomination of Christians above the rest."   Thus the American principle of religious liberty was incorporated in the fundamental law of the Presbyterian Church in America.

When the Synod met in Philadelphia in May, 1788 the new form of government and discipline, as well as the directions for worship, after some alteration, were ready for adoption, and this was accomplished on the twenty-ninth of the month. After selecting May 3, 1789, as the date of the convening of the first General Assembly, and Philadelphia as the place of meeting, and Dr. Witherspoon to preside until a moderator was selected, the Synod adjourned. When the first General Assembly met in Philadelphia the first Congress of the United States under the Constitution was in session in New York and a committee was appointed by the Assembly to bear to President Washington an appropriate address. In his reply Washington thanked the Assembly for their favorable opinion and their approbation of his conduct, and he desires them to accept his gratitude for their endeavors to render men sober, honest, and good citizens, and the obedient subjects of lawful government, as well as for their prayers for the country and himself.

---

[18] Humphrey, *op. cit.*, pp. 271-272.   Also Briggs, *op. cit.*, pp. 357-361.
[19] *Records of the Presbyterian Church*, p. 539.

APPENDIX TO CHAPTER I
A LIST OF THE MINISTERS AND CONGREGATIONS, WHETHER SETTLED OR VACANT, BELONGING TO THE REV. SYNOD OF NEW YORK AND PHILADELPHIA[1]

PRESBYTERY OF NEW YORK

Ministers Names	Names of Their Respective Congregations
Dr. Rodgers,	New York
Joseph Treat,	Ditto
Nathan Kerr,	Goshen
Abner Bruth,	Newburgh
Alex. McWhorter,	New-Ark
James Caldwell,	Elizabeth Town
Aaron Richards,	Raway
Azel Row,	Woodbridge
Benjamin Woodraft,	Westfield
Jonathan Elmore,	New Providence
Benjamin Hait,	Connecticut Farms
Jedediah Chapman,	Newark Mountains
Jacob Green,	Hanover
Azariah Horton,	South Hanover
Timothy Jones,	Morris Town
William Woodhull,	Sucka Sunny and Roxbury
Simon Horton,	West-Indies
Amizai Lewis,	{ Warwick Florida
Alexander Miller,	Schenectady
Thomas Lewis,	Mendum
Oliver Deming,	Bermudas
Hugh Knox,	St. Croix
Samuel Sackett,	Crump Ponds

Vacant

Newton	Persepanny
West Windsor and Bethlehem	I. of Saba, West-Indies
Blooming Grove	Richmond Town

[1] This list is taken from *Aitken's General American Register, and the Gentleman's and Tradesman's Complete Annual Account Book and Calendar, etc.* (Philadelphia, Joseph Cruickshank for R. Aitken, 1774), pp. 182-191.

Aitken was a Presbyterian Elder and printed the first English Bible in America in 1782.

Vacant

West Church on Staten-I.	Walkil
New Hempstead	Springfield
Smith's Clove	Hardyston

PRESBYTERY OF SUFFOLK, LONG-ISLAND, EAST HAMPTON

Ministers Names	*Names of [Their Respective]* Congregations
Samuel Buell,	East Hampton
James Brown,	Bridge Hampton
Sylvanus White,	
Benjamin Goldsmith,	Hockaboque
David Rose,	South Haven
Benjamin Talmadge,	Brook Haven
Ebenezer Prime,	Huntington
William Mills,	Jamaica

Vacant

Mattatana	Hempstead
Smith Town	Middletoun
Wading River	Oldman's

PRESBYTERY OF DUTCHESS COUNTY

Wheeler Case,	Pokepsie and Charlotte
Chauncey Graham,	Fish Kill
Elisha Kent,	Philip's Precinct
Solomon Mead,	Salem
Ichabod Lewis,	Sing Sing and White Plains
Samuel Dunlop,	Cherry Valley
Eliphalet Ball,	Kayderosies Patent
—— Mills,	Bedford

Vacant

Crump Ponds	Still Water
Albany	Pound Ridge
Fredericksburgh	

PRESBYTERY OF NEW-BRUNSWICK

Ministers Names	*Names of Congregations*
Dr. J. Witherspoon, President of the College, New Jersey	Princeton
⌐William Tennent,	Freehold
Charles McKnight,	Shrewsbury, Shark River, and Middle Town Point

PRESBYTERY OF NEW-BRUNSWICK—(Continued)

Ministers Names	*Names of Congregations*
Thomas Smith,	Cranbury and Penn's Neck
Israel Read,	Bound Brook and Brunswic
John Hanna,	Bethlehem and Kingwood
John Guild,	Hopewell
Samuel Kennedy,	Barnard's Town
Job Pruden,	Milford
Jeremiah Halsey,	Bedminster
James Lyon,	
Francis Peppard,	Upper Hardwick and Lower Hardwick
Jacob Van Arsdalen,	Kingston
Elihu Spencer,	Trenton, First Church / Second ditto
William Sebenck,	Allentown

Vacant

First and Second Church in Amwell	Oxford and Greenwich
	Mansfield Woodhouse
New-Brunswick	Bedminster
Leesburgh	Maidenhead

FIRST PRESBYTERY OF PHILADELPHIA

James Sprout,	Second Presbyterian church in Philadelphia
George Duffield,	Third ditto
Richard Treat,	Abington
Alexander Mitchell,	Tinecom
— Andrew Hunter	Greenwich
William Hollinshead,	Fairfield
Enoch Green,	Deerfield
Nehemiah Greenman,	Pilesgrove
— Benjamin Chesnut,	Timber Creek and Woodbury
John Brainard,	Brotherton
James Boyd,	Newtown
Samuel Eaken,	Penn's Neck and Salem
James Watt,	Cape May

Vacant

Neshamminy	Bensalem
Great Valley	Allen's Town
Mount Bethel	Egg Harbour, &c.
New-Providence	

SECOND PRESBYTERY OF PHILADELPHIA

Francis Allison, Vice Provost of the College of Philadelphia, and John Ewing, — First and third Presbyterian churches of Philadelphia

John Simonton, — Tridyfferin

John Steel, — Carlisle and lower Pensbury

John Elder, — Paxton Derry

Joseph Tate, — Donnegal

Patrick Allison, — Baltimore

Robert McMordic,

Vacant

Deep Run   Norrington

PRESBYTERY OF NEW-CASTLE

Thomas Smith, — St. George's

John McCrery, — Christiana and White Creek

William McKenman, } Joseph Smith, } — Wilmington

James Finley, — Elk

William Forrester, — Upper Octoraroa and Doe Run

John Carmichael, — Upper Brandywine

Robert Smith, — Pequea

John Clark, — Bethel

Alex. McDowell,

Joseph Montgomery, — { New-Castle / Christiana Bridge / Deer Creek

James Lata, — Chestnut Level

James Wilson, — Fogg's Manor

James Anderson, — { Middletown

Thomas Read, — { Drawyer's

Nodd Forres

John Woodhull, — Lancaster and Leacock

Vacant

Lower Brandywine   West Nottingham, first Church

George's Town   Apoquinimy

Pencader   Little Britain

West-Nottingham, second Church   Middle Octoraro

PRESBYTERY OF DONNEGAL

Samuel Thompson,	Cannawaga
John Rowan,	Derry, &c.
— John Strain,	Chancefoord and Slate Ridge
John Slemons,	Lower Marsh Creek
Robert Cooper,	Middle Spring
John Craighead,	Rocky Spring
Amos Thomson,	Leesburgh
James Lang,	East Connogocheague and Falling Spring
James Reak,	Piney Creek
James Hunt,	
Hugh Vance,	Tuscorora
John King,	West Connogocheague

Vacant

Cedar Creek and Opceken   Kishaco Quillap
Carlisle   Shrewsbury
Upper Marsh Creek   Round Hill
Managhon   Big Spring
Hanover   Upper and Lower churches of
Upper Paxton   W. Connogocheague
Center   Standing Stone
Dick's Gap   Path Valley
Upper Church in Sherman's   Great Cove
   Valley   Bedford
Cedar Spring

Vacancies in Maryland

Tom's Creek   Capt. John
Piney Creek   Blandensburgh
Jerusalem

Vacancies in Virginia

Falling Waters   Patterson's Creek
Cape Capen   Bullskin
Elk Branch   South Branch Potowmack

PRESBYTERY OF LEWIS

Jacob Kerr,	Monokin and Wicomoco
John Miller,	Dover and Duck Creek
—Alexander Huston,	{Murder Kill Three Runs
Matthew Wilson,	Lewis Town, &c.

Vacant

Snow Hill and Pitt's Creek	Vienna and Fishing Creek
Rehoboth and Accomac	Buckingham and Black Water
Broad Creek	Queen Ann's

PRESBYTERY OF HANOVER

—John Craig,	Tickling Spring —
John Brown,	New Providence
Charles Cummings,	Brown's Settlement
Thomas Jackson,	Peaked Mountains, Cook's, Linwell's and Mosly Creeks
Samuel Leake,	Rich Cove and Garden
David Rice,	Peaks of Otter, Ready Spring, Hatt Creek
John Todd,	Louisa, Goochland, Hanover, Upper counties
⌐ James Waddel,	Lancaster and Richmond counties
Richard Sankey,	Buffalo Creek
William Irwin,	Lower Hico

Vacant

Upper Hico	North Buffelo, Aldman's
Hawfield, E[.,] & Otille River	Sugar Creek

ORANGE PRESBYTERY IN NORTH AND SOUTH CAROLINA

Hugh McAden,	Upper Hico and Hogan's Creek
—David Caldwell,	North Buffalo
Henry Patillo,	Bute county
Joseph Alexander,	
⌐ Hezekiah Jas. Balch,	— Rocky River and Poplar Tent
Hezekiah Balch,	Bethel

ORANGE PRESBYTERY IN NORTH AND SOUTH CAROLINA
—(*Continued*)

John Harris,	Long Cane
— James Criswell,	Ninety Six
—— Campbell,	Bullocks Creek
_ John Simpson,	Lower Fishing Creek

Vacant Congregations
In Virginia

Upper Reed Creek	Tinkling Springs
Lower Reed Creek	Rock-Fish
New River Settlement	Mountain Plains
Higher Forks of Roanoke	Dyess
Fort Lewis	Sandy River
Stone House of Roanoke	Cub Creek
Catawaba Creek	Briary Creek
Craig's Creek	Halifax county
Lower Cow Pasture	Harris's Creek
Middle Cow Pasture	Cumberland county
Upper Cow Pasture	Amelia county
Jackson's River	Goochland county
Upper Calf Pasture	Orange county
Lower Calf Pasture	Spotsylvania county
Upper Forks of James Riv.	Carlisle county
Lower Forks of ditto	Hanover county
Timber Bridge	Henrico county
South Mountain	New Kent
North Mountain	Mecklenburgh county

In North Carolina

Bute county	Fourth Creek
Upper Dan River	Center Congregation
The Hollow	Coddle Creek
Upper Haw River	Hopewell
Lower Haw River	Rocky River
Deep River	Steel Creek
Duplin county	New Providence
Hitchcock Creek on Pedee	Quaker Meadows
Bryan's Settlement	Waker's Settlement
Mulberry Fields	Wilson's Settlement, on Cawtaba
Salisbury	Goshen
Carthy's Settlement	Bethel

In North Carolina

Fishing Creek	Union Congregation
Bullock's Creek	Fair Forest
Beersheba	Forks of Tyger River

In South Carolina

Indian Creek	Bull Town
Duncan's Creek	Fort Boon
Bush River	Turkey Creek
Upper Bush River	Wiahaas
Long Cane	Upper Fishing Creek
Wilson's Creek	Sugar Creek
Capt. Reed's	

In Georgia

Bryar Creek

Preachers

Joshua Hart
John Close   } Suffield New-England
Elam Potter

Nathaniel Irwin
Robert Davidson
——— Power   } New-Castle Presbytery
——— Dougall

Thomas McPherrin
——— Phrizby   } Donnegal Presbytery
——— McClure

Caleb Wallace,   Virginia

Joseph Periam,   New-England

Robert Keith, upon Trial
Israel Evans ditto   } First Presbytery

Moses Allan ditto
Oliver Rice ditto   } Brunswick ditto
John Debeau ditto

A LIST OF THE MINISTERS AND CONGREGATIONS BELONGING TO THE
ASSOCIATE PRESBYTERY OF PENNSYLVANIA, WHICH IS SUBORDI-
NATED TO THE ASSOCIATE SYNOD OF EDINBURGH, IN SCOTLAND

The associate Synod consists of upwards of an hundred Ministers,
and near an hundred thousand people under their inspection.

In the Province of Pennsylvania

James Proudfoot, of Pequea and Forks of Brandywine.
Matthew Henderson, of Oxford and Pencader.
William Marshall, of Philadelphia.
John Rodger, of Big Spring and Conogocheague.
John Smith, of Middle-Octorara and Mount Nebo.
James Clarkson, of Muddy Creed. [k]

In the Province of New York

John Mason, of New-York City.
Robert Annan, of Little-Britain and Wallkill.
Thomas Clark, of New Perth, a Corres. Mem.

Vacant Congregations in This Province under the Inspection of Said Presbytery

Deep-Run and Neshameny		Bucks county
Hanover and Raphoe		Lancaster do.
Marsh Creek & Conawago		York do.
Buffeloe Valley	in	Northumberland do.
Shearman's Valley, Juniata, Kishicocolas Valley		Cumberland do.
Redstone Chartiers, Monongahela & Youhageny		Westmoreland do.

CHAPTER II

THE PRESBYTERIANS AND WESTWARD EXPANSION

The last great wave of immigration to the English colonies previous to the American Revolution was that from northern Ireland. Unlike all other immigration movements to America the Scotch-Irish formed settlements in every one of the thirteen colonies and everywhere they were numerous and aggressive. Unlike others also, they had one uniform religion, Presbyterianism, and having come last to America, they were compelled to push further west than any other racial or religious group. Altogether by 1776 they constituted more than 500 communities,[1] and since their form of worship and church government were uniform in all of these communities, a spirit of solidarity was developed, more pronounced, perhaps, than that of any other single religious body in colonial America. Mr. Roosevelt has stated that the two facts of most importance in attempting to understand our pioneer history are, first, that the western portions of Virginia and the Carolinas were settled by an entirely different stock from that which had settled the tidewater region; and second, that western Pennsylvania was the great breeding ground for the earliest settlers who pushed their way into the valley of the Ohio. And constituting a most important element in these two regions were the Scotch-Irish.

By the middle of the eighteenth century a new society had been born in America, as well as a new section created. Geographically this new section lay "between the falls of

[1] Hanna, Charles A., *The Scotch-Irish or the Scot in North Britain, North Ireland, and North America*, 2 vols. (New York, 1902), II, pp. 2-5. There were nearly seventy communities of Scotch-Irish in New England; from forty to fifty in New York; fifty to sixty in New Jersey; over 130 in Pennsylvania and Delaware; more than a hundred in Virginia, Maryland and eastern Tennessee; about fifty in North Carolina; about seventy in South Carolina and Georgia (*Ibid.*, p. 2).

the rivers of the south Atlantic colonies on the one side and the Allegheny Mountains on the other," a kind of peninsula thrust down from Pennsylvania southward.[2] In numerous essentials this new society differed from the older colonial society of the seaboard. "It was a democratic, self-sufficing, primitive, agricultural society, in which individualism was more pronounced than in the community life of the lowlands."[3]

Mr. Roosevelt further states that these "Irish representatives of the Covenanters were in the West almost what the Puritans were in the Northeast, and more than the Cavaliers were in the South," and he characterizes them as "the pioneers of our people in their march westward, the vanguard of the army of fighting settlers, who with ax and rifle won their way from the Alleghenies to the Rio Grande and the Pacific." Many of these descendants of the Scotch Covenanters, in their fight for life and livelihood on the early American frontier, lost much of their religious interest, "but what few meetinghouses and schoolhouses there were on the border were theirs," and by 1760 there had been formed "a zone of Scotch-Irish Presbyterian churches" extending from the frontiers of New England to the frontiers of South Carolina.

With the close of the Revolutionary War, the western movement of population over the Allegheny Mountains, which had already begun, following the close of the French and Indian War in 1763, became increasingly important year by year. Kentucky in 1779 had but 176 white men, but by 1784 the population was numbered by the thousands, and each month brought hundreds of new settlers over the mountains from Virginia and the Carolinas, or down the Ohio from Pennsylvania and New Jersey. The southwestern section of Pennsylvania, known as the Redstone country, already contained a numerous population, and the vil-

---

[2] Turner, F. J., *The Frontier in American History* (New York, 1920), pp. 103, 104.

[3] Roosevelt, Theodore, *The Winning of the West,* 4 vols. (Homeward Bound edition, New York, 1900), I, pp. 124-128.

lage of Pittsburgh boasted a hundred cabins. "Cornfields and wheatfields and orchards began to spring up in every direction, and already the wagons that brought out merchandise from Philadelphia went back laden with grain."[4]

The Presbyterians had the best chance at this time of becoming the greatest of all the American churches both in point of numbers and in influence. For we now know that those churches which were destined to become the most influential bodies in America were those which most successfully followed population westward, and which most adequately ministered to the religious and cultural needs of the West. At this early period the Presbyterians, most certainly, were in the best position to meet both these requirements. Already their presbyteries, their churches and their ministers were to be found farthest west, and their leaders were imbued with the sturdy spirit of the pioneers. One of the purposes of this volume is to show, through the documents illustrating the frontier methods of Presbyterians, why they failed to take full advantage of their frontier opportunities.

As has already been noted, the American Presbyterians were early conscious of the importance of the West. In 1758 the Synod of New York and Philadelphia appointed a solemn fast in behalf of the frontier settlements, which were then engaged in war with the Indians and French. Two years later two ministers were permitted to go as chaplains with the Pennsylvania forces, and in 1763 the Synod recommended to all the presbyteries that they send one or more of their candidates for the ministry to the frontier settlements, and the same year they appointed Reverends Charles Beatty and John Brainerd to go as missionaries to the frontier settlements, and it is stated that the Synod has the "Mission to the frontiers much at heart."[5]

---

[4] McMaster, J. B., *History of the People of the United States*, 8 vols. (New York, 1900), I, pp. 147, 149.

[5] *Records of the Presbyterian Church*, p. 326; also Smith, Joseph, *Old Redstone, or Historical Sketches of Western Presbyterianism, Its Early Ministers, Its Perilous Times and Its First Records* (Philadelphia, 1854), pp. 113, 116.

Again in 1766 Mr. Beatty with Mr. Duffield was appointed to visit the West. They arrived at Fort Pitt where they conducted services, and visited the Delaware Indians on the Muskingum, 130 miles beyond. They reported numbers of people earnestly desirous of forming themselves into congregations, and found the Indians "waiting upon the preaching of the gospel with peculiar attention."[6] Again the following year, 1767, the Synod commissioned two of its members, Brainerd and Cooper, to visit the frontier settlements and the Indians, and directed that they spend at least three months on their mission, and forbad them to accept any money from the frontier people.[7] It was at this synod also, that a systematic plan for carrying on mission work on the frontier was adopted and the churches directed to take annual offerings for that purpose.

The principal burden of supplying the Pennsylvania frontier during these years was naturally placed upon the Donegal Presbytery in the Susquehanna valley, which had been formed in 1732, since its location was farther west than any other. From 1768 onward, year by year, increasing attention was given to the West, through the appointment of supplies to be sent to the frontier settlements, during the summer and autumn months. Thus in 1768 the Donegal Presbytery was directed to supply the western frontier with ten Sabbaths of ministerial labor; in 1771 Mr. Finley was appointed to spend at least two months over the Allegheny mountains; in 1772 the Donegal Presbytery was instructed to send either Mr. Craighead or Mr. King to "Monongahela and other places adjacent to stay as long as they can."[8]

Of particular interest was the work of Reverends David McClure and Levi Frisbie, who spent nearly ten months west of the mountains from August, 1772 to June, 1773.

---

[6] *Records of the Presbyterian Church,* pp. 375, 376.

[7] *Ibid.,* pp. 364-377.

[8] Smith, *op. cit.,* pp. 114-118. *Also Records of the Presbyterian Church* and *Minutes of the Donegal Presbytery,* for the appropriate years, quoted in Pears, Thomas C., "The Foundations of Our Western Zion," in the *Journal of the Department of History of the Presbyterian Church in the U. S. A.,* XVI, No. 4 (December, 1934), pp. 145-162.

They established headquarters at Pittsburgh and made numerous visits to the surrounding settlements in which the earliest trans-Allegheny churches were later organized. McClure and Frisbie seem to have been the first to establish regular preaching in these settlements and their work was the most important of any of the early missionaries. Both McClure and Frisbie bore commissions from the *Society in Scotland for Propagating Christian Knowledge* and had been ordained at Dartmouth College. In their contacts with the rigid Presbyterians in the frontier settlements they found their "Congregationalism" under suspicion, and at once sought admission into the Donegal Presbytery, and were received. The Synod of New York and Philadelphia, however, at its meeting in 1773 reversed this action on the ground that they had not been dismissed by the "ecclesiastical council by which they were ordained in New England," though the Synod favored the Presbytery's "taking them under their care" while they are laboring "occasionally in the bounds of the Presbytery."[9]

The relative slowness with which the Presbyterians proceeded to form frontier churches is well illustrated in the account of what took place in southwestern Pennsylvania, and helps explain why the Presbyterians failed to take full advantage of their frontier opportunities. For ten years, from 1766 to 1776, regularly assigned Presbyterian missionaries labored in this region before a single congregation was fully formed or a regular ministry established. The deliberation of Presbyterian procedure in this respect may well be contrasted with the usual rapidity with which church and circuit organization went forward among frontier Baptists and Methodists.[10]

The first Presbyterian minister to be settled over a con-

[9] An excellent summary of the activities of McClure and Frisbie is found in Pears, *op. cit.*, based upon *Diary of David McClure, with notes by Franklin B. Dexter* (New York, 1899).

[10] See Sweet, W. W., *Religion on the American Frontier*: Vol. I, The Baptists (New York, 1931); also Sweet, W. W., *Rise of Methodism in the West* (Cincinnati, 1920); Posey, W. B., *The Development of Methodism in the Old Southwest, 1783-1824* (Tuscaloosa, Ala., 1933).

gregation west of the Allegheny mountains was John Mc-
Millan,[11] who accepted the pastoral supervision of the two
congregations of Chartiers and Pigeon Creek in the Red-
stone country, in 1776. McMillan was a native of Pennsylvania and a graduate of the College of New Jersey.
Having received his preparation for college under the
Reverend Robert Smith at Pequea, on graduation from
Princeton he returned to Pequea for his theological study.
He was licensed by the Presbytery of Newcastle in 1774 and
from that time until his call to Chartiers and Pigeon Creek
he traveled through the frontier settlements of Virginia.
On receiving his call he was dismissed from the Presbytery
of Newcastle to join the Donegal Presbytery and was ordained in April, 1776 and in August of the same year was
married. He was prevented from removing his family to
his field of labor until 1778, due to Indian disturbances,
though he visited his churches as often as possible in the
meantime, ordained elders and baptized their children.
McMillan remained the outstanding Presbyterian leader in
western Pennsylvania throughout his long life. His influence, particularly in the education of young ministers, is especially noteworthy, a large majority of the young men
entering the ministry during the first generation having received their theological training under his instruction.

Thaddeus Dod,[12] the second minister to be settled west of
the mountains, was a native of New Jersey, a graduate of
Princeton, and had begun his ministry in the Presbytery of
New York in 1775. In 1777 he determined to cast in his
lot with the trans-Allegheny pioneers and was ordained

[11] Sprague, W. B., *Annals of the American Pulpit,* 7 vols. (New York,
1858), III, pp. 353-355, for letter from John McMillan to Reverend James
Carnahan, dated Chartiers, March 26, 1832. MS Journal of John McMillan
from October 26, 1774 to his marriage August 6, 1776; Smith, *op. cit.,* pp. 166-
215, "Sketch of the Life of John McMillan." James Power, also a native of
Pennsylvania and a graduate of Princeton, was the first ordained Presbyterian minister to settle in western Pennsylvania, though he did not become
the settled pastor of a congregation until 1779. *Ibid.,* pp. 225-250, for biographical sketch of Reverend James Power.

[12] Sprague, *op. cit.,* III, pp. 356-359; Smith, *op. cit.,* pp. 139-151. *Dictionary
of American Biography* (New York, 1930), V, p. 340.

sine titulo by his presbytery with that end in view. He began his work among a company of New Jersey settlers farther south in what is now Washington County, bordering on an unbroken wilderness. He succeeded in forming a church in August, 1781, though the first house of worship was not erected until 1785. In 1782 Dod opened a "classical and mathematical school" in a log building erected near his own house, which continued in operation for more than three years. Later he served for one year as head of the academy at Washington, Pennsylvania, which began operations in 1789.

James Power,[13] a native of Pennsylvania and also a graduate of the college at Princeton, and a member of the Presbytery of Newcastle, began his missionary labors in western Virginia in 1774. Two years later he determined to settle in the West, after receiving ordination *sine titulo* at the hands of the Presbytery of Newcastle. For the next three years he itinerated through the western settlements but in 1779 accepted a call to the congregations of Sewickley and Mount Pleasant.

A fourth member of the heroic band of Presbyterian preachers who helped to lay the foundations of society in the wilderness of Transappalachia was Joseph Smith,[14] a native of Maryland and like the others a graduate of the Presbyterian "school of the prophets" at Princeton. He was much older than the other three and came to western Pennsylvania in 1779 after a number of years' experience in the ministry. He received a call to the United Congregations at Buffalo and Cross Creek in June, 1779 which was signed by 204 names, and the amount subscribed for his support was £197 5s. 6d, though the amount promised was but £150 in Pennsylvania currency.

There were now four settled ministers in western Pennsylvania and according to Presbyterian practice the next step was the formation of a presbytery. This was accom-

---

[13] See Smith, *op. cit.,* pp. 225-250, for biographical sketch of James Power; also Sprague, *op. cit.,* III, pp. 326-330.

[14] Smith, *op. cit.,* "Life and Times of Rev. Joseph Smith," pp. 51-92.

plished on May 16, 1781 at a meeting of the Synod of New York and Philadelphia as a result of a request signed by the four western ministers. The name "Redstone" which was given the new presbytery was doubtless suggested by the petitioners, as the name "Redstone settlement" had come to be employed to designate the country which lay west of the mountains. The name "Redstone" is derived from the name of a creek which enters the Monongahela, the name being due to the red color of the outcroppings of coal, so abundant in the region.

With the close of the Revolution the new settlements in western Pennsylvania grew rapidly at the expense of the eastern and central portions of the state. The total population of the state increased from 1800 to 1810 at the rate of thirty-three percent, and from 1810 to 1820 at the rate of twenty-five percent. The growth was most rapid in the region around Pittsburgh, and population was rapidly pushing along the Ohio valley and out the tributaries of that great river. The rate of Presbyterian increase was proportionate to that of the population, and in the first twenty years of the new century the number of ministers increased from 82 to 135 and the congregations from nearly 180 to 280.[15]

The rapid development of Presbyterianism in the western country just east of the mountains is indicated by the rise of new presbyteries. In 1786 the Presbytery of Carlisle, located in the Valley, had been formed with twenty-six ministers and forty-five churches; it in turn was divided in 1794 to form the Presbytery of Huntington. In 1793 the Redstone Presbytery was divided to form the Ohio Presbytery, made up of the settlements farthest west, including several in or near the Western Reserve.[16] In 1801 the Erie Presbytery was erected by action of the Synod of Virginia, and was the third presbytery formed west of the Allegheny mountains. Up to this time this western region had been included in the Synod of Virginia and the journeys to the

---

[15] Gillett, *op. cit.*, I, pp. 471-472.
[16] *Ibid.*, I, pp. 322-324, 333, 471.

meetings of the synod were necessarily long and burdensome. In order to obtain a synod west of the mountains a third presbytery was a necessity, since Presbyterian law required that a synod must contain at least three presbyteries. Thus by the erection of the Presbytery of Erie[17] that requirement had been met, and the next year, 1802, the Synod of Pittsburgh was formed by action of the General Assembly. By 1820 the Synod of Pittsburgh consisted of eight presbyteries as follows: Redstone, with twenty-one ministers and forty congregations; Erie, with thirteen ministers and forty-nine congregations; Hartford, with ten ministers and twenty-two congregations; Grand River, twelve ministers and twenty-three congregations; Portage, nine ministers and thirty-three congregations; Washington, ten ministers and nineteen congregations; Steubenville, seven ministers and twelve congregations; and Ohio with about twelve ministers and eighteen congregations.[18] The entire Synod contained ninety-four ministers and 216 congregations.

So far we have been principally concerned with the expansion of Presbyterianism on the Pennsylvania frontier. Let us now turn to a consideration of the expansion westward from Virginia and the Carolinas. It will not be necessary to recount the story of the beginnings of settlement in Kentucky and Tennessee, other than to say that by the close of the Revolution numerous settlements had been formed along the banks of the streams flowing northward into the Ohio, constituted largely by people from Virginia and the Carolinas. Among these early Kentuckians were some who had been members of Presbyterian churches east of the mountains. The McAfees[19] are examples of this type of

[17] Eaton, S. J. M., *History of the Presbytery of Erie; embracing in its ancient boundaries the whole of northwestern Pennsylvania and northeastern Ohio, with biographical sketches of all its ministers, etc.* (New York, 1868), pp. 27-28. *Records of the Synod of Pittsburgh, Sept. 29, 1802-Oct., 1832* (Pittsburgh, 1852).

[18] Gillett, *op. cit.*, I, pp. 530-534.

[19] McAfee, Robert B., Clerk, *The History of the Rise and Progress of the first settlements on Salt River, and Establishment of the New Providence Church,* MS Draper Collection 14CC102 State Historical Society of Wis-

settler. In 1773 James, George and Robert McAfee with several others came to Kentucky from Botetourt County, Virginia, and after several visits, finally in 1779 crossed the mountains with their families and established themselves at McAfee's station in the vicinity of Harrodsburg, which soon became one of the prominent centers in the new country. Many of this company were stanch Presbyterians and a few years later were the leaders in the formation of the first Presbyterian churches in Kentucky.

The first Presbyterian minister to be settled in Kentucky was David Rice, a native of Virginia and a graduate of Princeton, who came first from Virginia to Kentucky in 1783 in search of land for his children. For thirteen years he had been the minister of a congregation at the Peaks of Otter in Bedford County, Virginia. While on this exploring tour he had preached where opportunity had offered and had been received with joy by the Presbyterian settlers, some of whom had known him personally east of the mountains. Urged to remove to the West by the settlers he had finally stated that if a written invitation were drawn up and signed by such only as were permanent settlers really desirous of constituting themselves into a church, he would take it into serious consideration. Accordingly some time later a paper was placed in his hands with some 300 signatures, entreating him to plant a Presbyterian church among them. With this petition he presented himself at the meeting of the Hanover Presbytery, which recommended his acceptance of the petition and in October of 1783 he removed to the region of Danville, Kentucky. We will let Robert McAfee tell the story of the formation of the first Kentucky Presbyterian churches:

In the year 1783 in the fall the Revd. David Rice came to Kentucky and settled near Danville then a small village and next spring collected a church called Concord, and next spring 1784 collected another church on Salt River & Cane Run three miles S.E. of Harrodsburgh and built a log cabin on John Haggins land for a school

consin; Davidson, Robert, *History of the Presbyterian Church in the State of Kentucky, etc.* (New York, 1847), pp. 58-63.

house and meeting house and in March 1785, twelve of the Salt River people viz James McAfee James Buchanan John McAfee George Buchanan Saml McAfee James McCoun Sr John Armstrong George McAfee Joseph Lyon William Armstrong Rob't McAfee James McCoun Jr met near the present N. Providence church and agreed to build another house near that place to be used for the double purpose of a school and for preaching. . . . N. Providence was called after a church of same name in Virginia of which my uncle Geo. Buchanan was a member.

The Revd David Rice preached at Providence once a month until about 79 [89]. In the fall 1789 the N. Providence people met and agreed to build a large house of Hewed logs and in the year 1790 a double hewed log house fifty feet by thirty was erected by subscription each person furnishing a portion of the logs and other materials. This was again enlarged on the south side in 1805 and finally pulled down in 1821 and the present brick house erected in its place. . . .[20]

The year following Rice's removal to Kentucky the Presbyterian settlers near Lexington called Reverend Adam Rankin of Augusta County, Virginia, to form a church among them. Rankin also took charge of a congregation called Pisgah.[21] The same years also churches were formed in Gerrard and Clarke Counties.

Two conferences were held in the spring and summer of 1785, made up of the ministers and licentiates and representatives of the several Kentucky congregations, and in the fall of that year two clergymen, Edward Crawford and Charles Cummings, visited Kentucky by order of the Presbytery of Hanover. With David Rice the visiting ministers were constituted a commission of Presbytery and examined and ordained James Crawford and Terah Templin as evangelists or to use the usual expression *sine titulo*. Crawford was a graduate of Princeton and Templin of Liberty Hall, the latter having received his preparatory education under David Rice in Virginia. The next year the Presbytery of

[20] McAfee, *op. cit.*, MS in Draper Collection.
[21] Davidson, *op. cit.*, pp. 73-74. Also Bishop, R. H., *An Outline of the History of the Church in the State of Kentucky during a period of forty years, etc.* (Lexington, 1824), pp. 67-69.

Transylvania[22] was formed, which included all of Kentucky, the settlements on the Cumberland in Tennessee, and also the settlements on the Miamis in the present state of Ohio. The first meeting of the new Presbytery was held in the Court House in Danville, October 17, 1768, with David Rice presiding. All the Kentucky Presbyterian preachers up to this time had come from Virginia.

In 1790 the General Assembly sent two missionaries to Kentucky, and from 1791 to 1800 the Synod of Virginia sent eight missionaries[23] to further the work across the mountains. Besides Virginia, North Carolina and western Pennsylvania as well as Scotland contributed to the ranks of the early Kentucky Presbyterian preachers.[24]

By 1799 the Transylvania Presbytery had grown to such an extent that with the consent of the Synod of Virginia it was divided into three presbyteries: the Transylvania embraced the central part of Kentucky west of the Kentucky River and south to the Cumberland, with ten ministers; the West Lexington Presbytery lay to the east of the Kentucky River, with nine ministers; (while the Washington Presbytery covered the territory northeast of the Licking and the settlements on the northwest side of the Ohio, with a membership of seven ministers.) Three years later (1802) the Synod of Kentucky was constituted by the General Assembly.

Kentucky Presbyterianism was from the beginning sorely afflicted with controversies and consequent divisions. The first arose over a dispute in regard to psalmody led by Rev. Adam Rankin of Lexington. This led finally to the trial of Rankin and his deposition by the Presbytery in 1792.[25] The following year Rankin was admitted into the Associate Re-

[22] MS *Minutes of the Transylvania Presbytery.* Davidson, *op. cit.,* pp. 79-82.

[23] For short biographies of each of these missionaries see Davidson, *op. cit.,* pp. 105-120.

[24] For brief biographies of these early members of the Transylvania Presbytery see *ibid.,* pp. 120-128; also Bishop, *op. cit.*

[25] MS *Minutes of the Transylvania Presbytery* for 1792. Davidson, *op. cit.,* pp. 88-98.

formed Church, and carried with him the majority of his congregation as well as the church edifice. The early history of the Associate Reformed Presbyterian Church in Kentucky is one of constant strife, leading to a series of trials, which because of the bitterness engendered eventually destroyed that Church in Kentucky. In 1818 Rankin was expelled from the ministry, and soon afterwards a group of the younger and more progressive ministers withdrew and joined the Presbyterian Church. Among the latter were Robert H. Bishop, later to become first president of Miami University. Later Kentucky Presbyterianism was torn asunder both by the Cumberland and by the New Light movement and several congregations were lost to the Shakers. Though gaining large numbers of members through the revivals of the early nineteenth century, they lost many by these divisions, so that by 1820 the total Presbyterian membership in Kentucky was only 2,700 besides about 1,000 belonging to the Cumberland group. At the same time the Baptists and Methodists numbered more than 20,000 each.[26]

In 1830 the population of Kentucky was about 700,000, and of this number 7,610 were members of the Presbyterian church. "Making all due allowances for deficiencies in the reports," states a contemporary, "there cannot be reckoned more than 10,000 regular members of the Presbyterian church in this State."[27] The churches numbered 120, while the number of ministers including licentiates did not exceed seventy.

From the beginning of settlement Tennessee attracted numerous Scotch-Irish settlers from Pennsylvania, Maryland, Virginia and the Carolinas, and in 1773 two Presbyterian congregations on the Holston River, Ebbing

---

[26] Bishop, op. cit., pp. 256, 306-307. Lathan, Robert, History of the Associate Reformed Synod in the South, etc. (Harrisburg, Pa., 1882), p. 242. For Robert H. Bishop's relation to the Associate Reformed Church in Kentucky, see Rodabaugh, James H., Robert Hamilton Bishop (Columbus, Ohio, The Ohio State Archaeological and Historical Society, 1935), pp. 29-35.

[27] From a letter in The Home Missionary, April, 1830. The population of Kentucky in 1830 was 687,917.

Spring and Sinking Spring, sent a call to the Hanover
Presbytery for the services of Rev. Charles Cummings.[28]
The petition was signed by 130 heads of families. Cummings accepted the call and for more than thirty years was
indefatigable in laying the foundations of Presbyterianism
in eastern Tennessee. The early years were full of dangers
because of Indian hostility, and people and preacher alike
went to church fully armed.[29] Five years later another
Scotch-Irish preacher, Samuel Doak, from Augusta County,
Virginia, came to the Holston country. He had graduated
from Princeton in 1775 and had been licensed to preach in
1777 by the Hanover Presbytery. He first labored in
Sullivan County, where Joseph Rea of Donegal Presbytery
had already preached, but in 1780 he settled in Washington
County where he established Salem church, near Jonesboro,
the first town in Tennessee that was not a mere stockade.
Doak was possessed of the true pioneering spirit and determined to cast in his lot with the frontier folk. Driving an
old "flea-bitten grey" horse loaded with books, he "crossed
the Alleghenies and came down along blazed trails to the
Holston settlements." Here Doak remained "and became
a most powerful influence for good throughout the whole
formative period of the southwest."[30] Doak built a log
school house on his farm which was incorporated in 1785
as Martin Academy; this was the first educational institution in the Mississippi valley. In 1795 it became Washington College and Doak continued to preside over it
until 1818.

In 1785 the third pioneer Presbyterian preacher arrived
in eastern Tennessee in the person of Hezekiah Balch.
Balch was also a graduate of the College of New Jersey
and had served for several years as a missionary in the
Hanover Presbytery. For twenty years Balch labored on
the Tennessee frontier and exerted an influence only second

---

[28] Gillett, *op. cit.*, I, p. 425.

[29] *Ibid.*, I, pp. 424-426.

[30] Roosevelt, *op. cit.* (Standard Library Edition, New York, 1905), II,
p. 222. Gillett, *op. cit.*, pp. 426-427.

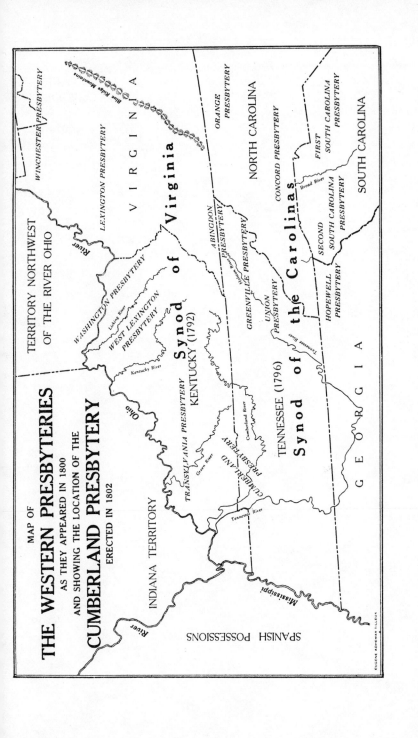

MAP OF
THE WESTERN PRESBYTERIES
AS THEY APPEARED IN 1800
AND SHOWING THE LOCATION OF THE
CUMBERLAND PRESBYTERY
ERECTED IN 1802

TERRITORY NORTHWEST
OF THE RIVER OHIO

INDIANA TERRITORY

SPANISH POSSESSIONS

WINCHESTER PRESBYTERY

LEXINGTON PRESBYTERY

VIRGINIA

Synod of Virginia

WASHINGTON PRESBYTERY

WEST LEXINGTON PRESBYTERY

TRANSYLVANIA PRESBYTERY

KENTUCKY (1792)

CUMBERLAND PRESBYTERY

TENNESSEE (1796)

ABINGDON PRESBYTERY

GREENVILLE PRESBYTERY

UNION PRESBYTERY

ORANGE PRESBYTERY

NORTH CAROLINA

CONCORD PRESBYTERY

Synod of the Carolinas

HOPEWELL PRESBYTERY

SECOND SOUTH CAROLINA PRESBYTERY

FIRST SOUTH CAROLINA PRESBYTERY

SOUTH CAROLINA

GEORGIA

Blue Ridge Mountains

Ohio River

River

Licking River

Kentucky River

Green River

Cumberland River

Tennessee River

Tennessee River

Mississippi River

Broad River

Synod of

EUGENE ASHEMAN TILLEUX

to that of Doak, likewise establishing a school which developed into Greenville College. With Balch's coming a petition was sent to the Synod of New York and Philadelphia asking that a presbytery be formed across the mountains, which resulted in the erection of the Abingdon Presbytery in 1785. The following year the Transylvania Presbytery took the northern part of its vast territory. By 1799 two presbyteries had been formed in eastern Tennessee besides the Abingdon: the Union Presbytery in 1797 and the Presbytery of Greenville in 1799, the latter being dissolved in 1804. In 1810 the Presbytery of West Tennessee was created, with boundaries described as "extending from the Cumberland Mountains to the Rockies and from the Ohio to the Gulf."[31]

Since a large proportion of the settlers in eastern Tennessee were of Scotch-Irish stock many of them were religiously minded and were church members. Theodore Roosevelt thus describes the early Tennessee Presbyterian preachers:

Their preachers, all Presbyterians, followed close behind the first settlers, and shared their fields rifle in hand, and fought the Indians valorously. They felt that they were dispossessing the Canaanites, and were thus working the Lord's will in preparing the land for a race which they believed were more truly his chosen people than was that nation which Joshua led across the Jordan. They exhorted no less earnestly in the bare meeting-houses on Sunday, because their hands were roughened with guiding the plow and wielding the axe on week-days; for they did not believe that being called to preach the word of God absolved them from earning their living by the sweat of their brows.[32]

Ohio Presbyterianism first took root in the Miami country. Columbia and what is now Cincinnati were laid out in 1788, Columbia being the first settlement in the Symmes purchase. The site of Cincinnati was purchased from John Cleves Symmes by Mathias Denman, Robert

---

[31] Gillett, op. cit., I, pp. 426-427; II, pp. 212-213. Little, D. D., History of the Presbytery of Columbia Tennessee (Columbia, Tenn., 1928 Pamphlet).
[32] Campbell MS quoted in Roosevelt, op. cit., I, pp. 167-169.

Patterson and John Filson. When the latter was killed by
the Indians his place in the company was taken by Israel
Ludlow. Denman's wife, both Patterson and his wife, and
Ludlow's parents were all Presbyterians, and when the
town was laid out in 1788 a lot was set aside for a Presbyterian church, although there was no minister in the
group.[33]   David Rice made a visit to the place in the fall
of 1790, but previous to his coming prayer-meetings were
held.[34]   Rice organized a church consisting of eight members, and in the following year, James Kemper, who was
"reading theology" under Rice, was sent as a supply to the
joint congregation of Columbia and Cincinnati. He was
called and ordained in 1792, but the congregation was too
small to have a session and all the male members acted
as an examining board for the admission of new members.
When on September 5, 1793 they chose the first Presbyterian session in Ohio, the church contained nineteen
heads of families.[35]   In 1792 steps were taken for the
erection of a house of public worship in the village of
Cincinnati to be used by the Presbyterians and 105 names
were placed on the subscription paper, probably the majority of the male inhabitants of the village as well as some
from Fort Washington. A crude building was erected from
timber on the reserved lots. From this time until the
coming of Joshua L. Wilson to the pastorate of the Cincinnati Church in 1808 there was little growth. In 1800
the town had about 750 inhabitants and in 1805 less
than 1,000.[36]

Among the other early southern Ohio Presbyterian
churches were those at Dayton, Chillicothe and Springfield.
A church had been formed at Columbus in 1806, of thirteen members, and there were other early congregations

---

[33] Cincinnati was called Losantville until the coming of Governor St. Clair.
History of Cincinnati and Hamilton County, Ohio (Cincinnati, 1894), p. 196.
[34] Testimony of David E. Wade on March 5, 1833. *Joshua L. Wilson
Papers,* Durrett Collection, University of Chicago.
[35] MS *Minutes of the United Congregation of Cincinnati and Columbia*
for September 5, 1793.
[36] Gillett, *op. cit.,* II, pp. 124-125.

along the two Miamis, the Mad and Scioto Rivers. Until 1799 these southern Ohio churches were in the bounds of the Transylvania Presbytery, but in that year the Presbytery of Washington was formed including these Ohio churches. In 1802 the Presbytery had five ministers and thirty-two congregations, on both sides of the Ohio River. The early churches in central Ohio were largely established by preachers from Pennsylvania, a number of them graduates of Dickinson College, then a Presbyterian institution.

The church at Lancaster was established in 1805 by John Wright, a graduate of Dickinson college. On a missionary tour in 1804 he came upon a little band of Presbyterians located on the Hock Hocking river and after visiting them several times decided to settle among them. Here he remained for thirty-two years, and many of the churches in that region were organized through his instrumentality. In 1808 the Presbytery of Lancaster was erected with five ministers and twenty-two churches, a majority of them being without pastors.[37] In 1810 the Miami Presbytery was formed, which in 1814 embraced six ministers and twenty congregations, and in the same year the Synod of Ohio was created of the three presbyteries of Washington, Lancaster and Miami. It covered southern and central Ohio and at its organization had twenty-nine ministers and eighty-one congregations.

The story of the planting of Presbyterianism in northern Ohio differs greatly from that in the southern and central part of the state and requires a knowledge of the movement of population westward from New England, as well as an understanding of the trend of Connecticut Congregationalism, especially, in the direction of Presbyterianism.

From the beginning of the eighteenth century Congregationalism in Massachusetts and Connecticut developed along different lines at least as far as polity was concerned. In 1708 the Connecticut Congregationalists adopted what is known as the Saybrook Platform which provided that all

[37] *Ibid.*, pp. 127-128. *MS Record—First Presbyterian Church, Lancaster, Ohio, 1806-1822.* Also Historical Essay by Benj. F. Paist.

churches should be grouped in "consociations" or standing councils which were to function in much the same way as the Presbytery among Presbyterians, each church being under the standing council in such matters as ordinations, installations and dismissions.[38] From this time forward for more than a hundred years the sympathies of Connecticut Congregationalism went out "increasingly toward fellowship with the Presbyterian Church of the Middle States." Massachusetts, on the other hand, developed an increasingly independent type of Congregationalism.

In 1766 there began a regular correspondence between the Presbyterian Synod (New York and Philadelphia) and the General Association of Connecticut which resulted in an annual convention of Congregational and Presbyterian ministers "in order to promote objects of common interest to both denominations."[39] These conventions met annually until 1775 when the outbreak of hostilities between England and the colonies put a stop to them. Among the matters discussed at these conventions was a plan of union between the Congregational Consociated churches and the Presbyterian churches, and there developed an intimate relationship between the two bodies.[40] Meanwhile in Massachusetts and New Hampshire the Presbyterian churches which had been established there by the early Scotch-Irish immigrants were dying out or were being absorbed by Congregationalism, for never were Congregationalism and Presbyterianism identified in Massachusetts.[41] On the other hand, by the time of the Revolution the names Congregational and Presbyterian were used interchangeably to denote the Connecticut churches.

[38] For a clear statement of the provisions of the *Saybrook Platform* see Walker, Williston, *A History of Congregational Churches in the United States* (New York, 1894), pp. 200-213, 315-320.

[39] Gillett, *op. cit.,* I, p. 163.

[40] *Records of the Presbyterian Church,* pp. 398, 399. The Minutes of these conventions are printed in *Records of the Presbyterian Church,* with an Introduction by Rev. William H. Roberts, Appendix, pp. 1-41.

[41] Hopkins, S. M., *Period from War to Organization: Centennial Historical Addresses* (Philadelphia, 1876). See also Blaikie, A., *History of Presbyterianism in New England* (Boston, 1881).

With the close of the Revolution and the formation of the General Assembly by the Presbyterians, steps were taken to renew the relationship with Connecticut Congregationalists. The General Assembly of 1791 proclaimed its desire "to renew and strengthen every bond of union" between the Congregational and Presbyterian churches, and recalled "with much satisfaction the mutual pleasure and advantage produced and received by their former intercourse. . . ."[42] Accordingly steps were taken at once to bring about this result and a committee was appointed for that purpose. In 1792 a plan was adopted whereby fraternal delegates were to be exchanged, and in 1793 Reverend Matthias Burnet, Jonathan Edwards the Younger, and Timothy Dwight sat as Congregational delegates in the Presbyterian General Assembly. The following year it was proposed that "the delegates from these bodies respectively, shall have a right not only to sit and deliberate, but also to vote in all questions which may be determined by either of them."[43] This was adopted by the General Association of Connecticut and the General Assembly, the following year.

Such is the story of the gradual drawing together of Connecticut Congregationalism and Presbyterianism, when the problems presented by the frontier settlements were responsible for a new *rapprochement* between them in what is known as the "Plan of Union."

The processes by which the Presbyterian organizations attempted to keep pace with the westward movement of population over the mountains have been set forth in the first part of this chapter. The Congregationalists were faced with the same problem when New Englanders began to push across the Hudson. The fertile valleys of central and western New York became veritable El Dorados to young New Englanders accustomed to the stony fields and

[42] *Minutes of the General Assembly of the Presbyterian Church in the United States of America from its Organization A.D. 1789 to A.D. 1820 inclusive* (Philadelphia, 1847), pp. 29, 52.

[43] *Ibid.*, 1794, p. 80.

thin soil of their native farms, and the tide of immigration became especially strong after the treaty of 1794, between the United States and the Six Nations, by which the danger of Indian depredations was removed.[44]   The staid Dutch citizens of Albany were astounded at the number of loaded sleighs and ox-sleds which passed through the streets of their town during the winter of 1795. "Twelve hundred of the former passed through the city within three days, and on the 28th of February five hundred were counted" on their way west, "between sunrise and sunset."[45]   This vast movement of New England population westward resulted, by the end of the century, in pushing settlement to the western boundary of New York and along the southern shore of Lake Erie into the region then known as New Connecticut or the Western Reserve of Connecticut.

The Connecticut Congregationalists were particularly active in carrying on missionary work among these new settlements, and the Connecticut Association took the initiative in New England in forming the first State Missionary Society in 1798.   The purpose of the "Missionary Society of Connecticut," as announced in their address to the "Good People of Connecticut" was "to extend the blessings of the gospel to the utmost of their power"; and especially they wish "to be instrumental in diffusing its glad tidings among the inhabitants of the newly settled frontiers of our country, and among the heathen tribes."

The founding of Union College in 1795 at Schenectady, New York, is an early example of interdenominational coöperation in the west, the Presbyterians and Dutch Re-

[44] For the process of the early settlement of New York see Higgins, Ruth, *Expansion in New York, with especial reference to the eighteenth century* (Columbus, 1931).

[45] From *Munsell's Annals of Albany*, quoted in Gillett, *op. cit.*, I, pp. 394-395. A more detailed account of the settlement of central and western New York and its significance to Congregationalism will be discussed in the volume on the Congregationalists. See Hotchkin, James H., *A History of the Purchase and Settlement of Western New York, etc.* (New York, 1848). Gillett, *op. cit.*, Chap. XVIII.

formed being largely responsible for its establishment. Its first president was John Blair Smith, the son of the founder of the Log "College" at Pequea, Pennsylvania, and an ardent advocate of coöperation. Soon after his inauguration a young Congregational missionary, Eliphalet Nott, on his way west, was entertained in his home, and President Smith took the opportunity to impress upon him the necessity of coöperation between Congregationalists and Presbyterians in the western settlements, since they were "substantially of the same faith." He asked:

> Is it wise, is it Christian, to divide the sparce population holding the same faith, already scattered, over the vast new territory, into two distinct ecclesiastical organizations, and thus prevent each from enjoying those means of grace which both might sooner enjoy but for such division? Would it not be better for the entire Church that these two divisions should make mutual concessions, and thus effect a common organization on an accommodation plan, with a view to meet the condition of communities so situated?[46]

President Smith's arguments convinced young Nott of the wisdom of such a plan and led, through the influence of other Congregational ministers whom he induced to coöperate, to the formation of numerous Presbyterian churches on the "accommodation plan." Nott became the pastor of the Presbyterian Church in Albany, and in 1801 Jonathan Edwards the Younger, then the President of Union College, sitting as a delegate in the General Assembly of the Presbyterian Church, proposed the adoption of a "Plan of Union" for the general coöperation of the two churches in the west.[47]

The plan consists of four parts: the first enjoins all missionaries to the new settlements "to promote mutual forbearance, and a spirit of accommodation" between the

---

[46] For Eliphalet Nott's account of this incident see his letter in Sprague, *op. cit.*, III, pp. 403-404.

[47] For satisfactory accounts of the adoption of the Plan of Union see Gillett, *op. cit.*, I, pp. 396-398; Walker, *op. cit.*, pp. 316-317; Baird, Samuel J., *A Collection of the Acts, Deliverances, and Testimonies of the Supreme Judicatory of the Presbyterian Church*, etc. (Philadelphia, 1856), Part III, pp. 554-564. Documents presented and arranged with an Old School bias.

adherents of both churches; the second directs that if a
Congregational church should settle a Presbyterian minister, they shall conduct their internal affairs, if they so
desire, according to Congregational usage, but if trouble
arises between the minister and the church it can either be
referred to the presbytery to which the minister belongs or
to a council made up of equal numbers from each group.
The third provision lays down rules for the regulation of a
situation where a Presbyterian church calls a Congregational minister, in which case Presbyterian regulations were
to prevail but in case of internal disagreement between
pastor and people it was to be referred to the association
to which the minister belonged or might be settled by a
council. The fourth provision suggests certain regulations
for the direction of churches made up of both Congregationalists and Presbyterians. In this case a church was to
choose a standing committee which should have oversight
of all members. In case of a Presbyterian member he was
to have the right of appeal to the Presbyterian judicatories;
if a Congregationalist he should have the right to appeal
to all the male members of the church. While the Plan
says nothing as to the formation of presbyteries and associations in the territory where it was to function, yet the
inference would seem to be that it contemplated that both
associations and presbyteries would be formed.

When the Plan of Union was adopted, Presbyterian and
Congregational missionaries were, in several instances,
working in the same territory in central and western New
York, though Congregational churches were naturally far
more numerous, since the majority of the people had come
from New England. Thus in 1809 there were five Congregational associations in existence in central and western
New York; the Oneida, the Ontario, the Middle, the Susquehanna and the Union.[48] Between 1800 and 1815 sixty

---

[48] Dill, J. H., "Congregationalism in Western New York," in *Congregational Quarterly*, Vol. i, pp. 151-158. See also Punchard, George, *History
of Congregationalism*, 5 vols. (Boston, 1881), V, p. 49.

Congregational churches were organized in this region, and only twenty-two Presbyterian.

With the adoption of the Plan of Union the Presbyterians seem to have become at once more aggressive in New York. In 1802 the Albany Presbytery was divided into three presbyteries: the Albany, the Columbia and Oneida, and the next year the Synod of Albany was formed. Two years later the Presbytery of Oneida was divided and the Presbytery of Geneva organized. At the same time a movement of population from New Jersey and Pennsylvania into central New York set in, which soon modified the prevailing New England character of that region. In 1803 the Presbytery of Oneida decided that a minister belonging to an association might be received as a constituent member of the presbytery, without discontinuing his relationship to the association. All these were influences balancing the scales in New York in the direction of Presbyterianism.

The largest of the Central New York associations was the Middle Association, occupying what was known as the Military tract and its vicinity, which had been formed in 1804. In 1807 this association made overtures to the Synod of Albany to become an integral part of that body. The Synod replied most cordially, inviting it to become "a constituent branch of our body, by assuming the characteristics and scriptural name Presbytery." However, they deemed the name of little importance and stated that if they desired to retain the name Association it would be no bar to a desirable union. They further stated:

Knowing the influence of education and habit, should the churches under your care prefer transacting their internal concerns in their present mode of Congregational government, we assure them of our cheerfulness in leaving them undisturbed in the administration of that government, unless they should choose to alter it themselves.[49]

By 1810 the union with the Albany Synod was completed and in 1811 the Middle Association lost its separate exist-

[49] Hotchkin, *op. cit.,* pp. 80, 83. See extracts from the Records of the Presbytery of Cayuga to which is appended an account of the Middle Association.

ence and was merged into the presbyteries of Cayuga and Onondaga. In 1810 an attempt had been made by the several Congregational associations in New York State to form a State Association and delegates gathered in a convention at Clinton to discuss its advisability. The net result of this convention, instead of strengthening Congregationalism, was to further the union between the two churches, for it was the opinion of the Convention that:

The terms under which the Middle Association had been received into connection with the Synod of Geneva, laid a foundation for the general union of the Congregational and Presbyterian churches throughout the State of New York.[50]

By 1822 the last of the New York associations had dissolved, though a few Congregational churches refused to unite with any presbytery.

The operation of the Plan of Union in the Western Reserve of Ohio was similar to that which we have observed in New York. Since the first settlers in the region were largely New Englanders, and especially from Connecticut a majority of the first churches formed were naturally Congregational. In 1805 the Congregational missionaries sent out by the Missionary Society of Connecticut formed themselves into "The Ecclesiastical Convention of New Connecticut," but by the end of 1806 all the New England missionaries had departed and the Missionary Society found it necessary to appeal to the Presbyterian Synod of Pittsburgh for men. For the next four years or to 1812 the missionaries to the Reserve were appointed by the Presbyterians while their salaries were paid by the Connecticut Missionary Society.[51] These young Presbyterian missionaries are described as:

Good pious men, of sound doctrine, and laborious habits, but not

[50] The Synod of Geneva was formed in 1811 as a result of the action of the absorption of the Middle Association. See Hotchkin, *op. cit.*, pp. 85-86, 100.

[51] "Furnish us with suitable men, and we will pay them as we pay our missionaries from this quarter" ($6.00 a week). Kennedy, W. S., *The Plan of Union: or A History of the Presbyterian and Congregational Churches of the Western Reserve, etc.* (Hudson, Ohio, 1856), p. 15.

as thoroughly educated nor perhaps generally as energetic and enter-
prising as the New England missionaries. Yet occupying the field
during a period when the churches were taking form and complexion
their influence was very important. The Presbyterian features of
polity were derived from them, as also somewhat of that decided
Calvinism which has ever characterized the Presbyteries and Synod
of the Reserve.[52]

In 1812 New England missionaries were again working
in the Reserve and an attempt was made to form another
Congregational association. That such an association was
not formed was due to the opposition of Thomas Barr,
the Presbyterian minister at Euclid, who objected on the
ground that such an association would keep him "ecclesiastically separated from them," an isolated Presbyterian,
connected with a presbytery sixty or eighty miles away.
Finally Barr's opposition was successful in persuading his
Congregational brethren to form a presbytery instead of an
association, and on November 8, 1814 the Grand River
Presbytery was organized on the compromise Plan of
Union.[53] All ministers were to become members of the
presbytery, though the churches were to retain their local
congregational form of church organization if they so desired.[54] Barr further stated that the Church at Tallmadge,
then the largest in the Reserve, refused to join the presbytery, and several others reserved the right to withdraw
if they later felt so disposed, and this in several instances
was what occurred.[55]

In 1818 there were three presbyteries in the region of
the Western Reserve; the Hartford, which had been
formed from the Erie in 1808; the Grand River, estab-

---

[52] Kennedy, *op. cit.*, p. 35. Most of these Presbyterian missionaries were
graduates of Canonsburg Academy, later to become Jefferson College, and
received their theological training under John McMillan. See Eaton, *op.
cit.*, for biographies of these early missionaries.

[53] See Barr's description of what took place, in Kennedy, *op. cit.*, pp. 162-
166.

[54] Dickinson, C. E., "Congregationalism in Ohio before 1852," in *Ohio
Church History Society Papers*, VII, p. 41. *Records of the Grand River Presbytery*, April 5, 1815.

[55] Kennedy, *op. cit.*, p. 166.

lished in 1814; and the Portage, organized in 1818. Five years later the Huron Presbytery was created and in 1825 these presbyteries were united into the Synod of the Western Reserve. Thus Presbyterianism had become completely triumphant in those regions where the Plan of Union had been most fully in operation.

There are many factors which help account for this development. In the first place there was an undoubted feeling among the Congregationalists themselves at this period that the Presbyterian form of government could more effectively meet the needs of the frontier. Many thought that, while Congregationalism might be well adapted "for a people homogeneous in character, orderly in habits, intelligent, cultivated, and independent in spirit" such as the people of New England, on a rough frontier, where there were many varieties of people and conflicting intellectual currents, Congregationalism was ill-suited to cope with such a situation.[56] Hotchkin states that:

> Many of the Congregational brethren, especially among the ministry, thought that the general principles of Presbyterial government were better calculated to preserve unity of action, and purity of doctrine in the church, while in a forming state, and to a great extent destitute of a stated ministry, than the Congregational form.

Nathanael Emmons (1745-1840) was one of the most decided opponents of the Plan of Union among the Massachusetts Congregationalists. He believed that the more rigid government of the Presbyterians would eventually prevail in such a union. He did not condemn the Presbyterians "for their attachment to their own system of government"; but he roundly "condemned the Congregationalists for their want of attachment to their own." He believed that a sect which had an imposing machinery of rules and orders would, in the very nature of the case, absorb one not thus barricaded. "He believed it is easier to swallow a naked babe than a babe encased in steel."

[56] Kennedy, op. cit., p. 145; Evens, Estwick, Pedestrious Tours, 1818, in Thwaites, R. G., Western Travels, VIII, p. 251. Hotchkin, op. cit., p. 101.

He held that, when the lion and the lamb lie down to- ✓
gether, "the lion has little to fear."[57]

Another factor of large importance was the tenacity with
which the Presbyterian ministers clung to their form of
polity in contrast to the willingness with which the Congregational clergy gave way. The young New England missionaries sent out by the Connecticut Society were instructed
to do all in their power to promote harmony between the
two denominations. Thus the tenacity of the Presbyterians
for their form of polity led the harmony-seeking Congregationalists to abandon their own in the interest of Presbyterian government.

The net result of the working of the Plan of Union
throughout central and western New York, northern Ohio,
southern Michigan and northern Illinois, especially was the
formation of many Presbyterian churches in which strong
Congregational elements were present. These churches
were sometimes described as "Presbygational," and as the
century wore on this New England influence in American
Presbyterianism was to have far-reaching effects.

Presbyterianism in Ohio was never brought into a state-
wide unit. In 1837 there were three synods lying wholly
within the state while the Pittsburgh Synod contained two
Ohio presbyteries. The synods within state boundaries
were the Ohio, the Cincinnati and the Western Reserve.
The Ohio contained six presbyteries, sixty-nine ministers,
138 churches and 9,442 members; the Synod of Cincinnati
had five presbyteries, eighty-six ministers, 118 churches and
8,426 members; the Synod of Western Reserve was composed of eight presbyteries, with 123 ministers, 140
churches with a membership of 7,743. The Ohio presbyteries in the Synod of Pittsburgh, the Steubenville and
Beaver, had twenty-five ministers, fifty-two churches and
4,897 members. The total Presbyterian strength in Ohio
in this critical year in Presbyterian history was twenty-one

[57] Park, E. A., *Memoir of Nathanael Emmons, etc.* (Boston, 1861); for
Emmons' views on the Plan of Union see pp. 166-172.

presbyteries, 301 ministers, 448 churches, and 30,509 communicants.[58]

The beginnings of Presbyterianism in Michigan date from the coming of John Monteith to Detroit in 1816 commissioned by the Assembly's Board of Missions. With Detroit as a center Monteith made frequent missionary excursions, visiting numerous neighboring settlements.[59] For several years following 1818 the Assembly's Board sent out other missionaries for longer or shorter periods, and other boards, the United Domestic Missionary Society, the United Foreign Missionary Society and the Western Missionary Society of Pittsburgh also sent workers into the territory both to labor among the settlers, in the military posts and with the Indian tribes. The well-known Indian agent Henry R. Schoolcraft gave encouragement to the work of the missionaries. In 1827 the Synod of the Western Reserve authorized the formation of the Presbytery of Detroit consisting of five churches. In 1833 two new presbyteries were formed, the St. Joseph's and the Monroe, which three years later (1836) had thirty-two ministers and fifty-nine churches.

The first Presbyterian church to be formed in the present state of Indiana was at the old French town of Vincennes in 1806. Previous to this (1805), however, the General Assembly had sent Thomas Williamson on a tour through the lower part of the territory, and the following year the West Lexington Presbytery had sent Samuel Holt on a similar errand. Samuel T. Scott of Kentucky became the first resident minister. When Indiana was admitted to the Union in 1816 there was but one settled pastor and five or six missionaries within the state. Two years later (1818) there was not a single settled pastor although by that time a number of churches had been organized. In

[58] Moore, William E., *History of Presbyterianism in Ohio to the Year 1870* (typed), University of Chicago Library, pp. 20-21. Moore was the stated clerk of the Synod of Ohio from 1882 to 1889 and permanent clerk of the General Assembly from 1884 to 1899.

[59] *The Christian Herald*, III, p. 320, quoted in Gillett, *op. cit.*, II, pp. 438-439.

1825 there were forty-three churches and ten ministers, five of whom were settled pastors.[60] This increase was due to the activities of missionaries sent out by the Connecticut, the New York Missionary Societies and the Assembly's Board of Missions.

The first Indiana presbytery was the Salem, formed under the Synod of Kentucky in 1824, and the following year two other presbyteries were organized, the Madison and the Wabash, and in 1826 the Synod of Indiana was erected.[61] In 1837 the strength of Indiana Presbyterianism was represented by six presbyteries and a portion of a seventh, as follows: Salem, Vincennes, Madison, Crawfordsville, Indianapolis, Logansport and a portion of the Oxford. There was an aggregate of 122 churches, sixtynine ministers and about 5,000 members.[62]

John Evans Finley, a Presbyterian preacher from Chester County, Pennsylvania, made a missionary tour down the Ohio and up the Mississippi as far as Kaskaskia in 1797. Samuel J. Mills and John F. Schermerhorn made their famous tour of the West in 1812-1813 and reported that: "In the Illinois Territory containing more than 12,000 people, there is no Presbyterian, or Congregational minister. There are a number of good people in the territory who are anxious to have some ministers among them."[63] Mills, with Daniel Smith, made a second tour of the West in 1814 and again reported: "There is no Presbyterian minister stationed, or laboring in this Territory." Near Kaskaskia he found numerous people who were either Methodists or Baptists, but had formerly been Presby-

---

[60] *Reed's Christian Traveller*, pp. 121, 139, 218, quoted in Gillett, *op. cit.*, II, pp. 395-414.

[61] Gillett, *op. cit.*, II, pp. 410, 412.

[62] For a summary of the growth of Indiana Presbyterianism in comparison with the population growth of the state see *The Home Missionary*, July, 1828, p. 51; Edson, H. A., *The Presbyterian Church in Indiana* (Indianapolis, 1908).

[63] Schermerhorn, John F., and Mills, Samuel J., *A Correct View of that part of the United States, which lies west of the Alleghany mountains, with regard to religion and morals* (Hartford, Conn., 1814).

terian, "and would have been so still . . . had they not been neglected by their eastern brethren."[64]

It was not until 1816 that any attention was given to Illinois by the Presbyterians, when two men were assigned to devote three and six months respectively to Illinois Territory.[65] In 1818 two other Presbyterian missionaries were sent to Illinois, Samuel Graham and Benjamin Low. Low reported that at Edwardsville, among its two or three hundred people there was not a single soul that "made any pretensions to religion," and "their shocking profaneness was enough to make one afraid to walk the street; and those who on the Sabbath were not fighting and drinking at the taverns and grog-shops were either hunting in the woods or trading behind their counters."[66]

Year by year the Board of Missions and other eastern missionary societies sent out men to Illinois, but as late as 1825 there were only two Presbyterian ministers in the state who were acting as regular pastors of congregations. These were Benjamin F. Spilman at Carmi and Charles Philips at Shawneetown.[67] In 1826 the American Home Missionary Society began to send men into the state and from that time forward, under the Plan of Union, Presbyterianism in Illinois went forward more rapidly. Of particular importance was the work of John M. Ellis who was sent out by the American Home Missionary Society in the year 1826, and was largely responsible for the founding of Illinois College and the coming to Illinois of what came to be known as the Illinois Band from the Theological Seminary at New Haven.[68]

[64] Mills, Samuel J., and Smith, Daniel, *Report of a Missionary Tour through that part of the United States which lies west of the Alleghany Mountains; performed under the direction of the Massachusetts Missionary Society* (Andover, 1815), pp. 16-17.

[65] Gillett, *op. cit.,* II, pp. 414-422.

[66] *Christian Herald,* IV, p. 329; V, p. 753.

[67] Norton, A. T., *History of the Presbyterian Church, in the State of Illinois* (St. Louis, 1879). For short biography of Spilman see pp. 23-33.

[68] The account of the Illinois Band will be told in greater detail in the following chapter. See MSS A. H. M. S. Letters, Illinois, 1826-1840.

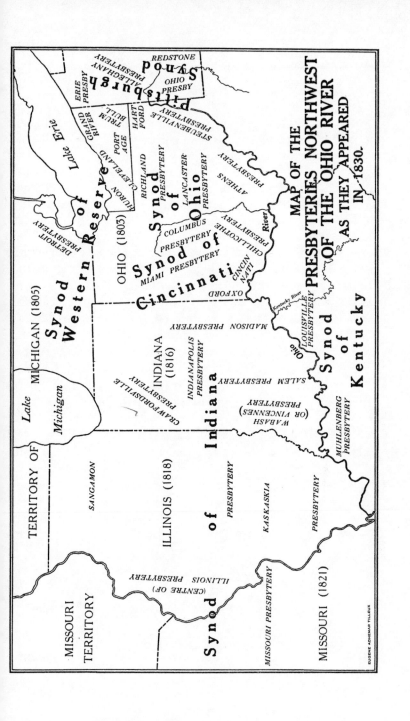

MAP OF THE PRESBYTERIES NORTHWEST OF THE OHIO RIVER AS THEY APPEARED IN 1830.

Pittsburgh Synod

REDSTONE

OHIO PRESBY

ALLEGHANY PRESBYTERY

ERIE PRESBY

GRAND RIVER

TRUM BULL

PORT AGE

HART FORD

STEUBENVILLE PRESBYTERY

CLEVELAND

HURON

RICHLAND PRESBYTERY

LANCASTER PRESBYTERY

ATHENS PRESBYTERY

Synod of Ohio

OHIO (1803)

COLUMBUS PRESBYTERY

CHILLICOTHE PRESBYTERY

River

Synod of Cincinnati

MIAMI PRESBYTERY

CINCIN NATI

OXFORD

Lake Erie

DETROIT PRESBYTERY

Synod of Western Reserve

MICHIGAN (1805)

Lake MICHIGAN

Michigan

TERRITORY OF Michigan

Kentucky River

Ohio

LOUISVILLE PRESBYTERY

Synod of Kentucky

MADISON PRESBYTERY

INDIANA (1816)

INDIANAPOLIS PRESBYTERY

CRAWFORDSVILLE PRESBYTERY

Synod of Indiana

SALEM PRESBYTERY

WABASH (OR VINCENNES) PRESBYTERY

MUHLENBERG PRESBYTERY

SANGAMON

ILLINOIS (1818)

PRESBYTERY

KASKASKIA

PRESBYTERY

Synod of

ILLINOIS PRESBYTERY (CENTRE OF)

MISSOURI TERRITORY

MISSOURI (1821)

MISSOURI PRESBYTERY

EUGENE ADHEMAR TILLEUX

In 1831 Aratus Kent began work at Galena and in 1833 Jeremiah Porter, who had spent the previous year in Michigan, came to Chicago, where he remained two years, during which period he established the first Presbyterian Church of that city. The Chicago church was organized with twenty-six members, all of whom, save one, were Congregationalists. Porter was also one of the founders of the Ottawa Presbytery, the first formed in northern Illinois.[69] Both Kent and Porter were New Englanders.

By 1837 there were eight Presbyteries in Illinois, with nearly 100 churches under their care, while the ministers, many of whom had been sent out by the American Home Missionary Society, numbered more than sixty.[70]

Samuel J. Mills, whose missionary tours west of the Alleghenies have been mentioned, was responsible for bringing Salmon Giddings, a graduate of Williams College, to the Mississippi Valley. He was sent out by the Connecticut Missionary Society and arrived in St. Louis on April 16, 1816. Gideon Blackburn had preached in St. Louis several times earlier in the year, and Giddings found two or three Presbyterians in the place. Giddings organized a church at Bellevue in Washington County, in August of that year, made up of some thirty members, around a nucleus of several lay elders who had migrated from North Carolina in 1807. Later in the same year he established another church at Bonhommie with sixteen members.[71] Soon Giddings was joined by other missionaries, among them Timothy Flint, who was sent out by the Connecticut Missionary Society. Flint's headquarters were at St. Charles, Missouri, but he extended his preaching to numer-

---

[69] MSS *Journals of Jeremiah Porter*; also MSS Jeremiah Porter Letters in the A. H. M. S. collection in Chicago Theological Seminary.

[70] Gillett, *op. cit.*, II, p. 422.

[71] Gillett, *op. cit.*, II, pp. 423-435. Hill, T., "Historical Discourse," in *Presbyterian Quarterly Review*, July, 1861. Norton, *op. cit.*, Chapter XXI, "The Rev. Aratus Kent of Galena," pp. 709-726. Reigler, Gordon A., "Aratus Kent, First Presbyterian Minister in Northern Illinois," in *Journal of Presbyterian Historical Society*, Vol. XIII (December, 1929), pp. 363-380; MSS A. H. M. S. Letters, 1827-1839.

ous settlements round about. Flint tells us that previous to his coming to St. Charles, "there was not a professor of our form of religion." The first Sabbath that he preached in the town there was a horse race directly opposite the place where the service was held. Giddings states that while in most of the principal settlements Methodist and Baptist churches had been formed and some of them were in a flourishing condition; "yet the state of moral feeling and the tone of piety was low throughout the country. Little attention had been paid to education and not more than one in five can read."[72]

In October, 1817, by order of the Synod of Tennessee a Presbytery of Missouri was constituted, made up of four ministers, John Matthews, Salmon Giddings, Timothy Flint and Thomas Donnell.[73] Missouri Presbyterianism grew slowly, however, and in 1825 there were but eighteen churches, at least half of which were in Illinois, and all of them were small. By 1837 there were three presbyteries in Missouri: the Missouri, the St. Charles and the St. Louis, with about forty churches and some thirty ministers, but of the thirty ministers only three were settled pastors, the others being stated supplies, or without charges.

In the lower valley of the Mississippi Rev. James Hall of North Carolina was sent as a missionary by the General Assembly of 1800. It was fifteen years before the Presbytery of Mississippi was formed from the Presbytery of West Tennessee. Two years later the presbytery had five ministers and eight churches. In 1822 there were not more than ten Presbyterian ministers in Mississippi and Louisiana. In 1825 the Presbytery of Mississippi which extended over a region of a quarter of a million people, had only thirteen congregations and thirteen ministers, most of whom were missionaries. By 1837 this region had been divided into three presbyteries with twenty-nine ministers,

[72] Kirkpatrick, J. E., *Timothy Flint* (Cleveland, 1911); Gillett, *op. cit.,* II, pp. 431-432.

[73] MSS *Records of the Missouri Presbytery* (Original in Missouri Historical Society, Columbia).

only three of whom were settled pastors, and with a total membership of not more than 1,000.[74]

[74] In 1833 Absalom Peters, the secretary of the American Home Missionary Society, made the following report of the work of the Society in Indiana, Illinois, Missouri, Mississippi, Tennessee, Arkansas and Louisiana in a series of letters published in *The American Home Missionary and Pastor's Journal*, V, p. 142; III, p. 194. In Indiana in 1826 there were twelve ministers and about forty-five churches, at the latter date there were 102 churches and fifty-three ministers, thirty-six of whom had been sent there or aided in their support by the Society. In Illinois and Missouri there were in 1826 eight Presbyterian churches, five of which were in Missouri and two in Illinois; in 1833 there were in these two states fifty-one Presbyterian ministers, of whom thirty-seven had been sent there or were aided in their support by the Home Missionary Society. In Tennessee, with a population of about 700,000, there were only sixty-eight Presbyterian ministers, less than one to 10,000 of the population. Mississippi, with a population of about 145,000, had only twenty Presbyterian ministers, or one to 7,000 of the population. Arkansas Territory, with an estimated population of 40,000, had but one minister of "our denomination," except such as were engaged in missionary work among the Indians. Louisiana, with a population of not less than 230,000, had not more than seven or eight Presbyterian ministers within its bounds. C. F. Letter of Absolom Peters to Benj. H. Rice, February 28, 1833, Chap. XIV.

CHAPTER III

CULTURAL AND EDUCATIONAL INFLUENCE OF THE PRESBYTERIANS IN THE EARLY WEST

It is now a generally recognized fact, at least among students of American history, that the great majority of the people who colonized the Atlantic seaboard came from the lower stratum of European society, and only a comparatively few represented the best in education and culture. Throughout the entire colonial period, at least until the eighteenth century Awakenings, the great mass of the people were little influenced by organized religion, and only a small proportion of the total population of the thirteen colonies were members of the colonial churches.[1]

It is also a well-known fact that the latter eighteenth century was a period of religious and moral deadness throughout the United States. This general decadence in religion and morals was due to a combination of causes, among them being the influences flowing from the French Revolution and the general political, social and intellectual upheavals which attended it. In America also Deism of the Tom Paine type was widely accepted, especially by the rising generation, causing orthodox views of religion to lose their appeal. The eight years of the War for Independence through which the country had just passed was another of the influences undermining religion and morals. To quote Benjamin Trumbull, the old historian of Connecticut:

A state of war is peculiarly unfriendly to religion. It dissipates the mind, diminishes the degree of instruction, removes great numbers almost wholly from it, connects them with the most dangerous company, and presents them with the worst examples. It hardens

[1] Sweet, W. W., "The Churches as Moral Courts of the Frontier," in *Church History*, March, 1933, pp. 3-21.

and emboldens men in sin; is productive of profaneness, intemperance, disregard to propriety, violence and licentious living.

The Revolutionary War, said Timothy Dwight, in a letter to a contemporary, "unhinged the principles, the morality, and the religion of this country more than could have been done by a peace of forty years."[2]

The pastoral letter sent out by the General Assembly of the Presbyterian Church in the United States of America in 1798, and similar letters sent out both before and after that date present an alarming picture of the general moral and religious decay of the time. They declare that they are "filled with concern and awful dread" at conditions which they behold on every hand, and express the solemn conviction "that the eternal God has a controversy with this nation."[3] In a sermon preached in 1801 at New Haven, Timothy Dwight, then President of Yale College, summarized the general moral and religious situation in the nation and declared that "profaneness of language, drunkenness, gambling and lewdness" were exceedingly increased while at the same time there was "a cold and contemptuous indifference toward every moral and religious subject."[4]

Such was the general moral and religious situation in the nation as a whole at the close of the Revolution, at the very time increasing waves of population were beginning to surge westward. If general moral, cultural and religious conditions were at low ebb in the older settled regions of the country, what could be expected in the new and raw communities rapidly springing up in almost every valley

[2] Trumbull, Benjamin, *History of Connecticut* (New Haven, 1818), 2 vols., II, p. 13; Osborn, *History of Connecticut*, 2 vols., II, p. 377. For a recent discussion of the general religious situation in the country following the Revolution, see Koch, G. A., *Republican Religion: The American Revolution and the Cult of Reason* (New York, 1933), pp. 239-284.

[3] *Minutes of the General Assembly of the Presbyterian Church in the Church in the United States of America from the organization A.D. 1789 to A.D. 1820 Inclusive* (Philadelphia, 1847), pp. 152-153. See also action taken in 1796, p. 116.

[4] Dwight, Timothy, *A Discourse on Some Events of the Last Century, delivered in the Brick Church in New Haven . . . January 7, 1801* (New Haven, 1801), p. 18.

west of the Allegheny Mountains? Cut off from the soften-
ing and restraining influences of the old communities, where
churches and schools were accepted institutions and where
a strict observance of the Sabbath was a commonly recognized practice, a vast majority of the early pioneer communities west of the Alleghenies became notorious for law-
lessness, rowdyism, Sabbath breaking, gambling, swearing,
drinking and fighting.[5]

The greatest single task which the American churches
faced at the beginning of the national period of our history
was that of following the westward moving population over
the Alleghenies into the valleys of the rivers which flowed
westward into the Mississippi or northward into the Great
Lakes, and southward into the Gulf of Mexico. Frontier
populations, are, as a rule, like colonizing populations, primarily concerned from necessity with the material things
of life. Homes must be built, farms must be carved out of
the forests or the virgin prairies, fences, and barns and
roads and bridges must be constructed, while the things of
the mind and the spirit must wait. Like the common people
of the colonial period, the nineteenth century frontiersmen
were largely unchurched; many had left their church membership behind in the older communities from which they
had migrated.

The policy adopted by the Presbyterians in reaching the
new communities rising in the West was to send ministers
on preaching tours through the new settlements. Some of
these men were commissioned by the General Assembly
from its organization in 1789, to give their whole time to
this type of work[6]; others were sent into more or less defi-

---

[5] For a summary of moral conditions in the early West see Sweet, W. W.,
"The Churches as Moral Courts of the Frontier," *op. cit.,* pp. 8-10. For a
portrayal of similar conditions in Canada see McNeill, J. T., "Religious
and Moral Conditions Among the Canadian Pioneers," in *Papers of the
American Society of Church History,* Second Series (New York, 1928),
VIII, pp. 67-122.

[6] In 1794 the General Assembly passed a resolution "That all the missionaries ordered to itinerate on the frontiers, be allowed for their services and
expenses at the rate of forty dollars per month; that the Treasurer pay
in advance, to each of them, the sum of sixty dollars, and that they account

nitely assigned regions for a limited time. Thus in 1814 the General Assembly commissioned fifty-one men to work on the frontier.[7] Besides the men commissioned to frontier work by the General Assembly, the presbyteries and synods likewise sent men to supply vacant churches. Thus in 1808 the Transylvania Presbytery appointed:

Messrs Templin and Dickey . . . to supply one sabbath each at Blue Lick fork of Pond River; Messrs Bowman & Donald to supply one sabbath each in Murray county; Messrs Rice and Howe to supply one sabbath each at Bay's fork of Big Barren; Mr. Balch to supply 2 sabbaths at Smyrna, likewise one sabbath & one week day at Concord; Messrs Wilson & Cleland to supply each one sabbath on Bear Creek, Harden County; Messrs Finley & Robertson to administer the sacrament of the Lord's supper at Paint Lick church; Mr. Finley to administer the ordinance at Silver Creek; Mr. McGready to supply one sabbath in Jones' settlement, Henderson county; Messrs Balch & McGready to supply one sabbath each at Mt. Carmel; Messrs McGready & Dickey to supply one sabbath each at Mt. Zion; Messrs Robertson & Wilson to supply one sabbath each at Danville.[8]

With the organization of the General Assembly in 1789 a permanent fund for missionary work was obtained by collections taken throughout the churches.[9] In 1799 the General Assembly was incorporated as a missionary society, and three years later a standing committee on missions was created which reported annually to the Assembly.[10]

The missionaries appointed by the General Assembly or its Board of Missions, were, up to the year 1829, itinerant missionaries, each covering an extensive territory, remaining

to the Assembly for all the moneys which they shall receive from the different congregations on their tour." *Minutes General Assembly 1794*, p. 87.

[7] *Journal of the General Assembly*, 1814, pp. 563-565. In 1812 there were thirty-nine missionaries employed by the General Assembly. *Ibid.*, 1812, pp. 505-506.

[8] MS *Minutes of Transylvania Presbytery*, April 6, 1808. See Part II, *Diaries of Preaching Tours*, 1813, 1814, Chapter XVII.

[9] In 1795-1796 the sum of $1,226.50 was spent for missionary purposes. *Minutes of the General Assembly of the Presbyterian Church*, 1795.

[10] Green, Ashbel, *Presbyterian Missions* (New York, 1893 reprint), p. 6.

but a short time in any one place, and receiving their entire support from the Assembly funds. In 1830 this mode of conducting missions was changed, the missionary being usually appointed to remain in one region for at least a year, serving as a pastor or as a stated supply over one, two or three congregations, and receiving his support, or a large share of it, from the people to whom he ministered.

The work of Gideon Blackburn among the Cherokee Indians in Blount County, Tennessee, is an early example of Presbyterian missionary effort among the Indians. Blackburn[11] had come to Tennessee at an early age where he had been placed in Martin Academy, established by Rev. Samuel Doak, and studied theology under Rev. Robert Henderson. He was licensed to preach by the Abingdon Presbytery in 1792, and began his ministry, traveling from stockade to stockade, on the Tennessee frontier, often under military escort. After establishing several churches, he proposed to establish a school for the Cherokee Indians. In 1803 he appealed to the General Assembly for funds and $200 was contributed, to which Blackburn through his own effort added $430. The school, known as the Highwassee Indian School, was opened in 1804 and Blackburn continued in charge until 1810, when local disagreements and broken health caused him to resign.[12]

Beginning in 1802 synodical missionary societies began to be formed, the first such society being that of the Pittsburgh Synod, called the *Western Missionary Society*.[13] In 1804 four missionaries were sent to the River Raisin in Michigan Territory and to the Wyandot Indians in Ohio. In like manner the Synods of Virginia, Kentucky and the Carolinas formed missionary societies and in the early years of the century sent out missionaries, either to carry on work

[11] For the best biography of Gideon Blackburn see Sprague, *op. cit.*, IV, pp. 43-58. *Dictionary of American Biography* (New York, 1929), IV, pp. 314-315.

[12] For contemporary accounts of Blackburn's Indian School see *Assembly's Missionary Magazine*, February, 1805; *Panoplist*, 1807, 1808.

[13] See Extracts from the MS *Minutes of the Western Missionary Society*, Part II. Chapter XIII.

among the Indians, or in the new settlements.[14]   Besides
these purely Presbyterian missionary agencies, there were
numerous missionary societies some of Congregational
origin, such as the Connecticut, the Massachusetts, the New
Hampshire and the Vermont Missionary Societies, and
later the United Domestic Missionary Society and the
American Home Missionary Society, the latter two largely
Presbyterian in origin,[15] which made large contributions to
frontier Presbyterianism, since a majority of their frontier
missionaries were primarily engaged in forming Presbyterian churches.

The instruction given the Presbyterian frontier missionaries and interim preachers by the General Assembly in
1795 was:

In discharge of the trust committed to you, much must be left to
your discretion. But the General Assembly, viewing with concern
the state of our frontiers, and other settlements destitute of the regular administration of the worship and ordinances of God, and desirous to do all in their power to extend the blessing to be derived
from the means of grace, confidently expect that you will faithfully
preach the gospel, administer the ordinances, organize churches, and
ordain elders, all these things according to the word of God, and the
standards of our Church, contained in our Confession of Faith,
Larger and Shorter Catechisms, the Government and Discipline, and
Directory of the worship of God. . . . Of your diligence wherein,
of the state of religion and of society, of the most probable means
of establishing the gospel in these parts, with every useful and

[14] Green, *op. cit.*, pp. 40-41; Elsbree, O. W., *The Rise of the Missionary
Spirit in America, 1790-1815* (Williamsport, Pa., 1928), pp. 71-75.
[15] The United Domestic Missionary Society was largely Presbyterian in
its origin and was formed to consolidate Presbyterian home missionary work
in New York State (Gillett, *op. cit.*, II, pp. 229-230). The American Home
Missionary Society was formed at a convention of delegates from thirteen
states, meeting in the Brick Presbyterian Church in New York City in 1826.
Though representing four denominations it was largely Presbyterian in
origin and management until 1833. Up to this date more than half its funds
came from New York State alone. "Its officers were Presbyterians. Its
Board of Directors in New York was exclusively Presbyterian." (*Ibid.*, II,
pp. 448-449; also *Personal Reminiscences of the Life and Times of Gardiner
Spring*, 2 vols. (New York, 1866), I, pp. 265ff.)

necessary information, you will give an account to the next General Assembly.[16]

If one is to judge from the records of the early preaching tours extant, it would seem that it was understood that the first task of the frontier Presbyterian minister was to find those localities where Presbyterians had settled, and with them as a nucleus to begin regular preaching, and when enough members had been gathered, to form a church. There were few instances where frontier Presbyterian churches were formed entirely of the raw material on the frontier. In other words the Presbyterian missionary went out looking for Presbyterians, and Presbyterianism prospered best where there was to be found the largest numbers of Presbyterian settlers, as was the case in western Pennsylvania.[17] On the other hand, to the Methodist circuit rider all communities were alike. He did not expect to find Methodists in the early settlements, but he was sent out to make Methodists of the raw materials which the frontier presented. This difference in approach is doubtless partially responsible for the relatively slow progress of frontier Presbyterianism, in comparison to the more rapid growth of the Methodists and Baptists. The average size of early frontier Presbyterian churches was small, a church often being formed with less than twenty members. Thus the churches formed at Columbus and Wabash, Indiana, had but fifteen members at the time of organization, while Crawfordsville had but nine; Indianapolis and Rushville numbered but twenty-five each, and Bloomington thirty.[18]

Rev. Jedidiah Chapman, a missionary of the General Assembly in western New York, in 1805 thus describes the organization of a church in a Scotch settlement, an interesting incident though not typical of the usual procedure:

[16] *Minutes of the General Assembly,* 1795, p. 103.

[17] In 1798 the General Assembly withdrew its restriction passed the previous year that the Sacrament of the Lord's Supper could only be administered where there were clerical officials regularly appointed. *A Digest of the Acts of the Supreme Judicatory of the Presbyterian Church, etc.* (Philadelphia, 1818), p. 127.

[18] Gillett, *op. cit.,* II, p. 411.

I preached in Caledonia in a large school house, which was full, and large numbers out of the door. The people are chiefly Highlanders from Scotland; they appear not only decent and attentive, but very solemn. They expressed a desire if I thought proper to be organized as a Presbyterian church.

Having appointed a conference on Monday for that purpose, the missionary after an exhortation, proceeded to receive and examine certificates. Numbers were from various parts of Scotland, and several who had never before joined the church were examined and approved, and some were not approved. This having been done they were organized into a church by the adoption of the Confession of Faith and the Directory for Church Government and Discipline. Three elders were then chosen, and after a sermon were ordained.[19]

The following story of the erection of a Presbyterian Church in Mercer County, Pennsylvania, in 1800 illustrates the method by which many a frontier community secured its first house of worship. The Rev. Samuel Tait, a graduate of the Canonsburg Academy and John McMillan's "Theological School," was sent out by the Ohio Presbytery to preach where he could find hearers. In the spring of 1800 he came to Cool Spring, in Mercer County, Pennsylvania, where he preached on the Sabbath. The interest manifested led him to propose that if they would secure a lot and build a church he would come and preach to them. The following Thursday was appointed as the day to build the meeting house. Men and boys came with their axes, and soon they were "lifted up against thick trees." Logs were cut off at proper lengths, but they were too heavy to be brought into position without a yoke of oxen, and alas the only team of oxen in all the settlement belonged to a professed infidel, and no one wanted to approach him on the subject. "Just as the necessity became pressing," who should appear approaching through the woods but the "infidel" with his yoke of sturdy oxen, shouting in a merry

[19] From the *Journal* of Jedidiah Chapman, quoted in Hotchkin, *op. cit.*, pp. 78-79.

voice, "Here comes the devil with his oxen to help you build your meeting house," and the work went gaily forward. "The next important thing was the appearance of Thomas McLean with a flat keg of whiskey under his arm." This was placed in the minister's hands, and beginning with the minister and ending with the donor, all took a drink, after which there were three cheers for Thomas McLean, with the promise that when the church was organized he should be the first elder. And this promise was fulfilled. By sundown the church was completed, "covered with clapboards, floored with puncheons, and round logs rolled in for seats. The house was so located that a huge stump answered the purpose of a pulpit, with two puncheons set upright in front and one across secured to the uprights with pins, on which the Bible might be placed. A puncheon seat for the minister completed the arrangement."[20]

During the summer months, and especially "on sacramental occasions" it became customary to hold the services out of doors. The sacrament of the Lord's Supper was administered much less frequently than is now customary, usually not more than once or twice a year, and these occasions attracted large numbers of people, not only from the two or three churches under one pastor's supervision, but from neighboring churches as well. Generally a hillside was selected for these out-door meetings, and a platform with a roof erected for the preacher, which was called a tent, and seats made of logs, hewn on one side, were arranged for the hearers. Long log tables were also constructed, with appropriate seats about them, which were covered with snowy cloth on which were placed the vessels containing the "sacred symbols." Joseph Smith in his *Old Redstone* has thus described the gathering of the people on one of these sacramental occasions:

The people are assembling from all directions—many on horseback, more on foot . . . some are seen on the ground, or on the logs,

[20] Eaton, S. J. M., *op. cit.*, pp. 31-32; for a brief sketch of the life of Samuel Tait, see *ibid.*, pp. 185-191.

putting on their stockings or shoes—for they have walked many miles barefoot, carrying these articles wrapped in their kerchiefs, in their hands. . . . He hears the neighing of horses, some near, and some far off. Perhaps he distinguishes, especially, the louder and peculiar tone of some old equine Nestor, that approaches, in its depth and grandeur, to the sublime.[21]

At length the people are sufficiently gathered for the service to begin. First is the short prayer with the people standing, followed with the singing of a psalm. Then the long prayer is followed by the singing of another psalm; then the sermon, after which comes the filling of the tables and the approaching and retreating crowd of communicants.

The administration of the Lord's Supper on the Sabbath was, however, but the culmination of a series of meetings which generally began on Thursday, which was observed as a day of fasting and prayer. There were usually services also on Saturday and the Monday following. The families residing in the vicinity of the meeting were usually thronged with lodgers, and people came from relatively long distances and remained for several days together, which gave them an opportunity for pleasant social intercourse, and the young people a chance to become acquainted. Indeed we are told that such meetings paved the way for many a happy marriage.

To make sure that only those who were properly prepared should receive the sacrament tokens were distributed on Saturday or Sunday morning. These were bits of lead with the initial of the name of the congregation stamped upon them, and were given only to those who were in good standing in the church, and were collected by the elders after the communicants had seated themselves at the tables.[22]

[21] Smith, *op. cit.*, pp. 152-165. Also Eaton, *op. cit.*, pp. 21-24.
[22] This practice of using tokens was brought from Scotland and Ireland, and its object was to exclude unworthy communicants. Large collections of tokens are in the possession of the Presbyterian Historical Society of Philadelphia and also of the Historical Foundation of the Presbyterian and Reformed Churches, Montreat, North Carolina. For an account of the origin and history of tokens and other communion practices of Presbyterians, see Burns, Thomas, *Old Scottish Communion Plate* (Edinburgh, R. & R. Clark, 1892); also Tenney, Mary McWhorter, *Communion Tokens, their*

The communion sermon or action sermon was preached by the resident minister, and this was followed by what was called *fencing the tables*. This was a long process by which members guilty of breaking any of the ten commandments were debarred from the sacrament. Its object was to aid the people in self-examination, and was undoubtedly effective in upholding high standards of life and conduct in frontier communities.

Presbyterianism was no easy-going religion, but the regular Presbyterians were mild in comparison to the more conservative "Psalm Singing" bodies. A young seceder minister in Indiana in 1838 described in his Diary a communion occasion, in which the *action sermon* lasted two and a half hours, and which he characterized as "the most tedious piece of work I ever listened to."[23]

Not least among the salient influences exercised by the churches on the rough and rude frontier was the fact they stood wholeheartedly for decency and order. Presbyterianism in itself is an orderly system of government and its introduction into any frontier community would at once tip the scales in favor of those forces which make for a better society. A study of the session records of frontier churches reveals the fact that the administration of discipline made up a large share of the business transacted. The trials were conducted with dignity and dispatch and the officials were careful to follow the regulations as to procedure laid down in the Form of Government.[24] There were two ways in which an offence could be brought before a judicatory; either

Origin, History and Use, etc., MS in the possession of the Hist. Foundation, Montreat, N. C. Also Smith, "Old Redstone," *op. cit.,* pp. 158-161; MacLennan, George A., *The Story of the Old Time Communion Service,* etc. (Toronto, 1924).

[23] *Diary of Professor T. A. Wylie,* August 12, 1838, quoted in Woodburn, J. A., "United Presbyterian Beginnings," in *Bloomington United Presbyterian Church Centennial* (Bloomington, Indiana, 1934), mimeographed. For *Seceder* practice see also Smith, *op. cit.,* p. 158.

[24] *The Form of Government and Forms of Process of the Presbyterian Church in the United States of America: as amended and ratified by the General Assembly, in May, 1821,* in *The Constitution of the Presbyterian Church in the United States of America,* etc. (Utica, 1822). See especially Book II, Chapter IV, "Of Actual Process," pp. 395ff.

by an individual or individuals, or by common fame. Citations were issued and signed by the moderator or clerk and the judicatory was to see that the citation was duly served. Witnesses were to be examined in the presence of the accused, and the accused was to be permitted to question the witnesses, but no professional counsel was permitted to appear and plead.

It will not seem strange to those familiar with the amount of raw whiskey consumed on the early frontier to learn that the principal cause of discipline among the members of frontier Presbyterian churches was intoxication. As Mr. Beveridge tells us, the offer of a dram from a bottle or jug was the first gesture of welcome to almost every cabin, and to refuse to drink was an "unpardonable incivility." Whiskey was considered with meat and bread as one of the necessities. In almost every country store there was a whiskey pail or barrel with cups attached and all comers were at liberty to help themselves. When Lincoln clerked in Offut's store at New Salem, Illinois, on the Sangamon, "everybody came on Saturdays to trade, gossip, wrestle, raffle, pitch horseshoes, run races, get drunk, maul one another with their fists, and indulge generally in frontier happiness, as a relief from the week's monotonous drudgery on the raw and difficult farms."[25]

Whiskey was commonly found on subscription papers for ministers' salaries. Such a paper containing subscriptions for the salary of Joshua L. Wilson of the first Presbyterian Church of Cincinnati for the year 1807 lists over 100 gallons.[26] And with a part of their salary quite commonly paid in whiskey it will not be surprising to learn that the most frequent cause for the discipline of ministers by the pres-

[25] Beveridge, Albert J., *Abraham Lincoln* (New York, 1929), I, pp. 110, 497. Also Faux, William, *Memorable Days in America; being a Journal, 1823,* in Thwaites, R. G., *Early Western Travels,* XI, pp. 212, 213. See also Sweet, W. W., *The Churches as Moral Courts of the Frontier,* pp. 8-10, 18-20.

[26] *Wilson Papers,* MS (Durrett Collection, University of Chicago), No. 36. For examples of trials of members of Presbyterian churches where the charge is intoxication see Part II, Chapter X.

byteries was their too copious use of ardent spirits. A famous case of this kind is that of Rev. William Mahan[27] of the Transylvania Presbytery. Several charges were brought against him in 1803 and he was brought to trial the following year. The testimony introduced presents a tragic picture of ministerial deterioration, due to drink. One of the specific charges against him was that he had "whipped his negro woman unmercifully," the implication being that he had done so while intoxicated. One witness, who signed her testimony with her mark, told of several visits Mahan had made to her cabin, in which he had "smelled very strong of whiskey." Another bore witness that on another occasion Mahan had used "unbecoming and scandalous language" due to the fact that he had taken too much whiskey at the tavern. Another stated that once when Mahan was conducting family worship in their home, he went to sleep while they were singing, and "once or twice slept a minute or two with the book in his hands," and even "nodded once or twice during prayer." The trial resulted, as might have been expected, in his expulsion, and though he attempted on several occasions to regain his ministerial standing, the presbytery steadfastly refused his requests. Like many other frontier Presbyterian ministers Mahan also taught a school which was attended by Joshua L. Wilson. Wilson characterized Mahan as "an able teacher and a drunken preacher."

The record of the trial of Rev. John Gillespie of the Shiloh Presbytery in Tennessee in the year 1821 covers twelve pages of the *Minute Book*. He was charged with having been drunk on three different occasions, once at a corn-husking in 1817; at a school entertainment in 1818; and at a social gathering at his own home in 1820. At the corn-husking, a witness stated that the minister, having been asked to serve the chicken, was so intoxicated that he missed the chicken and stuck the fork into the table. This trial, however, resulted in the acquittal of the minister and his

[27] *Minutes of the Transylvania Presbytery,* 1803, Part II, Chapter VI.

accusers were censured for bringing the case before the presbytery.[28]

By action of the General Assembly in 1812 it was recommended that all ministers in the Presbyterian Church deliver public discourses, "as often as circumstances may render it expedient on the sin and mischiefs of intemperate drinking," and all church sessions were urged to exercise special diligence and care over the conduct of members "with regard to this sin."[29]   The Synod of Pittsburgh was especially concerned with the growing use of intoxicants and the havoc it was causing in the churches, and in 1816 took the following action:

The excessive use of ardent spirits produces sickness, poverty and wretchedness; it destroys health and reputation; introduces discord into families and larger communities; it enervates the strong and changes many of the wise into idiots; it threatens to sweep our land as with the besom of destruction, and calls loudly on all friends of religion, order, science and humanity to exert their influence in checking an evil, so alarming in its progress and so various in its effects.

For these reasons the Synod resolved that:

. . . ardent spirits ought never be used, except as a medicine—that the free and common use of them at the raising of buildings, military musters, weddings and other public and social occasions, is unnecessary and pernicious—that the habitual use of ardent spirits in families and by laborers is training up thousands for poverty, disgrace, the prison, the gallows, and eternal misery.

And they further recommend:

. . . to all the ministers and professors of religion within their bounds to abstain from the unnecessary use of ardent spirits, and to endeavor both by precept and example to check the progress of the growing and destructive vice.[30]

But discipline was by no means confined to sins of intemperance.   Cases involving sexual immorality were often be-

[28] Little, *op. cit.*, p. 11.
[29] *Minutes of the General Assembly*, 1812.
[30] *Minutes of the Synod of Pittsburgh*, 1816, pp. 121, 122.

fore church sessions and presbyteries. Such a case came before the Presbytery of Missouri in 1819, appealed from the session of Union Church of Richwoods and Dry Creek. The accusation was for carrying "slanderous tales" involving attempted seduction and adultery. The slander accusation was not sustained, but the one who brought the action was suspended from all the church privileges until he had cleared himself of the charges. Another case involving immorality of a minister is found in the minutes of the Transylvania Presbytery for October 11, 1824.[31] The minister, J. Abbell, was charged with taking indelicate liberties with three female members of his congregations. On one occasion he took advantage of the crowded sleeping conditions in a cabin where he was a guest, and on another occasion compelled one of the married sisters to sit on his knee, assuring her that he "had the same anxiety for her temporal and spiritual welfare as for that of his own children." As a result of the trial, he was suspended from the ministry, but the following year he was restored, but later was again suspended and finally expelled.[32]

An interesting case of confessed immorality was that of James Mandy, who in 1807 presented a certificate of transfer of membership to the Lancaster, Ohio, church. On his appearance before the session he informed them that he did not wish to take advantage of his certificate, since he had been guilty of fornication previous to his obtaining the transfer. He manifested such sorrow for his wrongdoing, however, that the session admitted him to membership.[33]

Some of the cases tried before the session of the Presbyterian church at Franklin, Ohio, in the Western Reserve, between the years 1819 and 1839, were as follows: consenting to an illegal and unchristian marriage; departing from the church; dealing unjustly in the sale of dried fruit; publishing faults before the first and second steps were taken;

[31] See Part II of this volume, Chapter VI.
[32] *Minutes of the Transylvania Presbytery,* October 11, 1824.
[33] MS *Records of the Lancaster, Ohio, Presbyterian Church,* August 14, 1807.

refusing to commune because of difficulties with another man; attending places of vain amusement and allowing their children to attend; refusing to walk with the church in regard to the use of intoxicating liquors; obstinate refusal to hear the church; dancing; being destitute of piety; and imprudent and unchristian conduct. An American Home Missionary at Euclid, Ohio, in 1826, refused to administer the sacrament to his congregation because many members had gone to a party, and "had countenanced the gaiety and folly of the ball room with their presence." The following year the same minister reported that he had five cases of discipline on hand at once in his church.[34]

The various agencies, which have been noted, engaged in establishing Presbyterianism on the early frontier undoubtedly exerted the principal cultural and educational influence in that region for at least a third of the nineteenth century. Some of the factors which made for the large cultural and educational influence of frontier Presbyterianism were chiefly responsible for their failure to gain large numbers. One such factor was their insistence upon maintaining a relatively high educational standard for their clergy, in spite of the fact that numerous communities were calling for the services of ministers on every frontier, and in many instances there were three times as many churches as ministers available in a Presbytery.[35] The frontier Presbyterian minister seldom or never ministered regularly to more than three congregations, and usually to not more than two, with the result that Presbyterian influence tended to be more or less localized, whereas Methodist influence, through their circuit system, was spread broadcast throughout the fron-

[34] MS *Records of the Presbyterian Church, Franklin, Ohio,* 1819-1839. Photostat copies in the Library, University of Chicago. Letters of *Stephen Peet,* April 1, 1826; January 10, 1827. American Home Missionary Society Collection in Chicago Theological Seminary.

[35] In 1818 the Presbytery of Hartford, Ohio, contained thirteen ministers, but the field required "at least twice or thrice the number of laborers"; by 1818 a number of Presbyterian congregations had been formed in Indiana but not one of the churches had the services of a settled minister. Gillett, *op. cit.,* II, pp. 142, 399.

tier, one minister often serving as many as twenty-five communities.

It was a requirement of Presbyterian law that all candidates for the ministry must have a diploma of bachelor or master of arts from some college or university, or at least testimonials of having gone through a regular course of learning. To further test educational qualifications of candidates before admission to presbyteries they were examined by a regularly constituted committee.[36] Most of the early Presbyterian ministers west of the Alleghenies, as John McMillan, David Rice, Samuel Doak, Hezekiah Balch and Thaddeus Dod, and numerous others, were graduates of the College at Princeton. Thus Presbyterianism was responsible for sending to the frontier the first body of college-trained men, and in the very nature of the case, the vast educational need about them, as well as the necessity of increasing their means of livelihood, would naturally lead the average college-trained minister to become also a school master. And with few exceptions this is what happened.

The story of William Tennent's "Log College" at Neshaminy, Pennsylvania, is not alone important because it was the precursor of Princeton, but also because it was the seed which produced a large crop of other Presbyterian "log colleges" as Presbyterian influence extended westward.[37] Thus Samuel Blair, a graduate of Tennent's "Log College" established another such institution at Fagg's Manor in Chester County, Pennsylvania, and from this school came Samuel Davies, later president of Princeton, besides John Rogers, James Finley and Robert Smith, all of whom became educational and religious leaders of distinction. Samuel Finley established another "log college" at Nottingham, Pennsylvania, the most famous of whose graduates was Dr. Benjamin Rush, who as an influential

[36] For list of studies upon which candidates were examined see *Minutes of Presbytery of Cayuga*, 1810. They were: "Latin, Greek, English Grammar, Mathematics, Logic, Rhetoric, Geography and Natural Philosophy."

[37] For the best recent account of the "Log College" at Neshaminy and its influence in producing other such "Colleges" see Maxson, *op. cit.*, pp. 26-30.

Presbyterian layman was active in establishing Dickinson College. Another such school was that at Pequea in Lancaster County, Pennsylvania, from which came John McMillan, who in turn established a "log college" in the Redstone country in southwestern Pennsylvania.

Washington and Jefferson Colleges[38] will serve to illustrate how full-fledged colleges developed out of these "log colleges" founded by Presbyterian ministers. John McMillan and Thaddeus Dod were the first settled ministers in western Pennsylvania, and as has been noted, both established schools at about the same time. The third minister in the region, Joseph Smith, also opened a school. These schools were within a few miles of one another, and at times their sessions were held in turn, which enabled students to go from one to another, affording them a greater variety of instruction. As population in the region increased, the several Presbyterian ministers interested in education united, and with a Baptist minister and several laymen organized Washington Academy, which opened in 1789 with Dod as the first principal. The upper rooms of the Court House were used for the school, but when the Court House was burned in 1790, the school was closed, and when attempts failed to reopen it, as no suitable building was available, John McMillan and others turned their attention to the establishment of an academy at Canonsburg, fourteen miles away. This school opened in 1791 and received the approval of the Presbytery of Redstone and the Synod of Virginia. Activity at Canonsburg stimulated the people at Washington to reopen their institution, and 5000 acres of public lands were secured. Canonsburg Academy was rechartered as Jefferson College in 1802, in honor of President Thomas Jefferson, and four years later Washington

[38] *Washington and Jefferson College Bulletin*, 1932; Moffatt, J. D., *Historical Sketch of Washington and Jefferson College* (Washington, Pennsylvania, 1890), Pamphlet; Smith, J., *History of Jefferson College* (Pittsburgh, 1857). For the part played by McMillan, Dod and Smith in the founding of Washington and Jefferson Colleges, see Smith, *op. cit.*, Biographical and Historical Catalogue of Washington and Jefferson College, 1889, pp. 7, 263 ff.

Academy became Washington College, and though both institutions professed to be non-sectarian, in each the Presbyterian influence predominated.[39]

The University of Pittsburgh had its origin in another Presbyterian Academy, chartered by the Legislature of Pennsylvania, 1787. The incorporators were five Presbyterian ministers, four of them graduates of Princeton, the fifth educated in Scotland, and fourteen laymen. The most prominent of the early principals was Joseph Stockton, a descendant of Francis Makemie, the father of American Presbyterianism. In 1819 the Academy was reincorporated as the University of Pittsburgh, with a provision in the charter that persons of every denomination were capable of serving as trustees, and that no religious tests were to be applied to either faculty or students.[40]

The Great Revival in Virginia, beginning about 1750 and continuing for ten years, had not only served to establish Presbyterianism on a firm footing in central and western Virginia, but it also gave rise to two educational institutions for the training of ministers. The first was Hampden-Sydney College, the other Liberty Hall,[41] later to become Washington College, and after the Civil War, Washington and Lee. Both of the institutions grew out of academies conducted by Presbyterian ministers. Hampden-Sydney was established by the Presbytery of Hanover in 1776 in Prince Edward County, Virginia, with a Rector, Samuel S. Smith, and two graduates of Princeton, John Blair Smith and Samuel Doak, as teachers. The same year Hampden-Sydney Academy opened its doors, a second academy in Augusta County was taken under the patronage of the Presbytery. The Revolution, however, so depleted its student body that it was compelled to close in 1779, but in

[39] The two colleges naturally became rival institutions and though attempts to unite them were made from time to time, this was not accomplished until 1865.

[40] *Celebration of the One Hundred and Twenty-fifth Anniversary, University of Pittsburgh Bulletin* (Pittsburgh, 1912), pp. 108, 111, 114.

[41] For a most satisfactory recent account of the development of these two institutions see Gewehr, *op. cit.*, pp. 225-232.

1782 it reopened and was incorporated as Liberty Hall. Later it received an endowment from George Washington, and thereafter took the name Washington College.[42] Between 1786 and 1788 both colleges were visited with a remarkable revival which was responsible for turning numerous students toward the ministry. This resulted in the Synod of Virginia adding a theological department to Liberty Hall and in 1794 a separate building was erected for the carrying on of that work. This was the first theological school in connection with a college in America. It was maintained, however, but two years, and closed its doors with the resignation of William Graham, the theological instructor, in 1796.[43]

These early Presbyterian colleges established in Virginia are important for the trans-Allegheny frontier in that they furnished the training for many of the early preachers who crossed the mountains into Kentucky and Tennessee. In 1777 Samuel Doak, who the year before had taught at Hampden-Sydney Academy in Virginia, crossed the mountains into Tennessee and established a "log college" called Martin Academy which in 1795 was chartered as Washington College.[44] Other early Tennessee Presbyterian ministers such as Thomas B. Craighead, Hezekiah Balch and Samuel Carrick all established schools. In 1794 Carrick's school was chartered as Blount College, with Carrick as the first president, and the same year Balch became the first president of the newly chartered Greenville College.

Another of the early Presbyterian educational leaders of Tennessee was Philip Lindsley, a graduate of the College of New Jersey. After preaching for several years he entered upon an educational career in 1812, becoming senior tutor at Princeton in that year, and the following year

[42] Foote, W. H., *Sketches of Virginia* (Philadelphia, 1850), pp. 479-485. Washington's gift consisted of 100 shares of James River Canal stock. See Davidson, *op. cit.,* p. 46.

[43] For an account of this revival and the establishment of the theological department see Gillett, *op. cit.,* I, pp. 353-355.

[44] Sanford, E. T., *Blount College and the University of Tennessee,* 1879, Pamphlet.

professor of languages. After declining several college presidencies in Ohio and Kentucky he accepted the presidency of Cumberland College at Nashville in 1824. Here he labored until 1850 when he resigned to become a professor in the New Albany Theological Seminary. He exercised a wide educational influence throughout the West, and especially in Tennessee, and was one of the principal factors in making Nashville one of the chief educational centers in the south.[45]

The educational history of Kentucky likewise begins with the schools conducted by Presbyterian ministers. Transylvania Seminary, incorporated in 1783 and granted 20,000 acres of land by Virginia, was begun under Presbyterian influence. Rev. David Rice, the father of Kentucky Presbyterianism, was the first chairman of its board of trustees, and the school was opened in Rice's house near Danville. Later when the school was moved to Lexington (1788) the liberal element gained control and for a time Presbyterian influence waned and a new school was formed in 1797 called Kentucky Academy. The following year the Presbyterians regained control of the Transylvania Seminary and the two institutions were merged into one and given the imposing name of Transylvania University, with twenty-three trustees, a majority of whom were Presbyterians and some of them clergymen. In 1799 law and medical departments were added, the first gesture toward professional training west of the Alleghenies.[46]

The election of the Rev. Horace Holley of Boston to the presidency, in 1818, soon brought estrangement between the institution and the Presbyterians. Holley was a liberal in his theology and by legislative action the old trustees were turned out and a new board elected. The Presbyterians, now convinced that their control of Transylvania

[45] Sprague, *op. cit.*, Vol. IV; also *Dictionary of American Biography*, Vol. XI, article by Robert Hastings Nichols.

[46] Peter, R., and Peter, J., *Transylvania University: Its Origin, Rise, Decline and Fall* (Louisville, Kentucky, 1896). For an interesting though biased account of the beginnings of Transylvania University and Centre College see Davidson, *op. cit.*, Chap. XII, pp. 288-323.

was at an end formed a new college at Danville which in 1823 opened as Centre College.

The influence of Presbyterianism in the establishment of state institutions in the new states west of the Alleghenies is significant.   The Presbyterian influence in the establishment of Transylvania University in Kentucky has already been noticed.   Transylvania from the beginning was a state institution.   In Tennessee, Blount College was rechartered as East Tennessee College in 1807, and became an institution under state control, later developing into the University of Tennessee.[47]   In Ohio, Ohio University at Athens was chartered by the legislature in 1804 as a state institution, but like the early Kentucky and Tennessee state colleges, it was likewise under Presbyterian influence and control.   From its opening in 1818 for more than sixty years, Miami University's presidents without exception were Presbyterian ministers.[48]   The Indiana State Seminary at Bloomington, established in 1820, became Indiana College in 1828, and Indiana University in 1838.   From its beginning it was surrounded by Presbyterian influence, there being at one time in the little town of Bloomington, the seat of the institution, six Presbyterian churches.   Its early presidents were Presbyterian ministers and all the first teachers were likewise Presbyterians.[49]

Of the forty permanent colleges and universities established in the United States between the years 1780 and 1829, in all sections of the country, thirteen were established by Presbyterians, four by Congregationalists, one by Congregationalists and Presbyterians in coöperation, six by Episcopalians, one by Catholics, three by Baptists, one by the German Reformed and eleven by the states.   Of

[47] *University of Tennessee Record,* July, 1898, pp. 219ff., 267ff.

[48] Tobey, W. L., and Thompson, W. O., *The Diamond Anniversary Volume of Miami University* (Hamilton, Ohio, 1899) ; Knight, G. W., and Commons, J. R., *The History of Higher Education in Ohio* (United States Bureau of Education, Cir. 1891), No. 5, p. 15; Martzolff, C. L., *Ohio University: the Historic College of the Old Northwest* (Athens, Ohio, 1910).

[49] *Indiana University, 1820-1920: Centennial Memorial Volume* (Indiana University, 1921).

these forty institutions, fourteen were located west of the Alleghenies, and of the fourteen, seven were founded by Presbyterians, one by Congregationalists and Presbyterians together, one by Baptists, one by Episcopalians, while the remaining four were established by the states. And all of these four state institutions were begun under Presbyterian influence. These facts establish without further comment the dominance of Presbyterianism in the educational development of the early West.[50]

In the region north of the Ohio where the Presbyterian and Congregational streams came together a number of colleges were established as coöperative institutions. Ten such colleges were founded before the Civil War. Western Reserve University had its origin in societies organized by the Presbyteries of Grand River and Portage to promote the education of "indigent pious young men for the ministry within the limits of the presbyteries." In 1822 these Societies appointed a committee to establish a literary and theological institution on the Reserve. This resulted in the establishment of a college at Hudson which opened its doors for students in 1826.[51] Illinois College, established at Jacksonville, Illinois, is an interesting example of Congregational and Presbyterian coöperation in frontier

[50] Tewksbury, Donald G., *The Founding of American Colleges and Universities before the Civil War with particular reference to the Religious Influences bearing upon the College Movement* (New York, 1932), pp. 93-94. The following institutions were established by Presbyterians between 1782 and 1850: Liberty Hall (Washington and Lee) 1782; Transylvania, 1783; Hampden-Sydney, 1783; Dickinson, 1783; Tusculum, Greenville, Tennessee, 1794; Blount College (University of Tennessee) 1794; Jefferson College, 1802; Washington College, 1806; Hamilton, 1812; Allegheny, 1817; Centre College, Kentucky, 1823; University of Pittsburgh, 1819; Lafayette College, 1826; Hanover College, Indiana, 1833; Wabash College, Indiana, 1834; Oglethorpe University, Georgia, 1835; Muskingum College, 1837; Davidson College, North Carolina, 1838; Marysville College, Tennessee, 1842; Mississippi College, 1830; Cumberland University, Tennessee, 1833; Carroll College, Wisconsin, 1846; University of Buffalo, 1846; Austin College, Texas, 1849; Bethel College, Tennessee, 1850; Geneva College, Pennsylvania, 1850; Waynesburg College, Pennsylvania, 1850; Erskine College, South Carolina, 1850.

[51] Cutter, C., *History of Western Reserve College* (1826-1876) (Cleveland, 1876). *Western Reserve University Catalogue,* 1893-1894, pp. 16-17.

education. It grew out of the efforts of Rev. John M. Ellis, who was working in Illinois under the American Home Missionary Society. In 1828 he had been sent to the East by the Presbytery of Illinois to solicit funds for the establishment of a seminary at Jacksonville, which they hoped would grow into a college. Meanwhile a young man attending the newly established Theological Seminary at New Haven came upon a letter of Ellis in the *Home Missionary Journal* in which he told of the contemplated institution at Jacksonville. This young man, Mason Grosvenor, determined to offer himself for missionary work in Illinois. This plan he unfolded to several members of the senior class at Yale Divinity School, with the result that seven young men pledged themselves to devote their lives to missionary and educational work in Illinois.[52] All of these young men except Grosvenor, who was detained by ill health, on the completion of their theological studies, migrated to Illinois. Sturtevant became the first instructor in the college which was opened at Jacksonville in 1829, while Edward Beecher, the second son of Lyman Beecher, resigned the pastorate of the Park Street Church in Boston to become its first president. Though Sturtevant and Beecher were Congregationalists, both on removing to Illinois became members of the Presbytery, and Illinois College became eventually a Presbyterian institution.[53]

The first centers of theological instruction in the West were the homes of such ministers as John McMillan, who during the course of his long ministry in southwestern Pennsylvania had under his instruction about 100 young men. There was scarcely a minister, however, in the early western Presbyteries, who at one time or another did not have

[52] These men were Mason Grosvenor, Theron Baldwin, John F. Brooks, Elisha Jenney, William Kirby, Asa Turner, and J. M. Sturtevant.

[53] Rammelkamp, C. H., *Centennial History of Illinois College* (New Haven, 1928). Barton, C. E., *The Founders and Founding of Illinois College* (Jacksonville, Illinois, 1902), Pamphlet. Other institutions founded by Presbyterians and Congregationalists coöperating were Beloit College, 1846; Rockford College, 1847; Knox College, 1837; Ripon, 1851; Grinnell, 1847; Pacific, 1854; and California, 1855. Tewksbury, *op. cit.*, pp. 93-95, 121-122.

young men in training in their households.[54] Of the first
twenty-eight members of the Erie Presbytery, twenty-two
received their theological instruction from John McMillan.
McMillan's method of instruction was by written lectures
arranged in the form of questions and answers. These the
students transcribed and they were expected to recite, word
for word, what they had written. McMillan's system of
theology has been characterized as "concise, condensed,
multum in parvo, lucid, and forceful," though such a method
doubtless tended to create a lifeless and stereotyped
theology.[55]

Throughout the early years of the nineteenth century
there was an urgent demand for an increase in the number
of ministers among all the revivalistic churches. It was
largely due to the lack of adequately prepared ministers
that the Presbyterians suffered two serious schisms in the
West during these years, and the lack of men fitted for
pastoral and missionary work was considered a serious and
growing evil. At the General Assembly of 1805 Dr. Ashbel Green, then President of Princeton, prepared a moving
overture on the question. It declared:

Give us ministers is the cry of the missionary field; give us ministers is the importunate entreaty of our numerous and increasing
vacancies; give us ministers is the demand of many large and important congregations in our most populous towns.

Weak and illiterate ministers, he stated, could not supply
the want or meet the emergency. Pious but educated men
were needed, and the problem of first importance was
"How can such ministers be secured?"

Out of this general demand for an increasing number
of ministers came the establishment of the first Presbyterian Theological Seminaries. Princeton Theological
Seminary opened in 1812 and six years later Auburn Theological Seminary was incorporated for the purpose of train-

---

[54] Smith, *op. cit.,* pp. 209-210; Eaton, *op. cit.,* pp. 94-95.
[55] Many copies of McMillan's theological lectures are extant.

ing a ministry for the rapidly growing church in central and western New York.[56] The expansion of Presbyterianism westward and the policy adopted by the General Assembly of permitting the synods and the presbyteries to establish their own theological seminaries soon led to the founding of other theological institutions in the West. The third Presbyterian theological seminary established, however, grew out of action by the General Assembly. This action was taken in 1825 and a board of directors of the contemplated Western Seminary was elected. Thirteen locations were proposed for the new institution, nine in Ohio, one in Indiana and three in Pennsylvania. Joshua L. Wilson, minister of the First Presbyterian Church in Cincinnati, was the leader of a group urging that the new institution be established at Walnut Hills near Cincinnati. Allegheny-town, opposite Pittsburgh, however, offered the largest financial inducements and secured its location, and the new Western Theological Seminary opened its doors for students in 1827.[57]

The establishment of Western Theological Seminary in Pennsylvania was considered with disapproval by the more western synods and immediately steps were taken to open other theological institutions farther westward. In 1829 the Synod of Indiana formed a Theological Seminary in connection with their academy at South Hanover, which received the name in 1830 of Indiana Theological Seminary. In 1839 it was moved to New Albany, Indiana, and in 1859 on removal to Chicago it became the Presbyterian Theological Seminary of the Northwest; in 1886 it became McCormick Theological Seminary and more recently it has become the Presbyterian Theological Seminary of

[56] Adams, J. Q., *A History of Auburn Theological Seminary, 1818-1918* (Auburn, 1918). See also Hotchkin, *op. cit.,* Chapter XVII.

[57] *Bulletin of the Western Theological Seminary*, October, 1927, containing an account of *The Founding and Early History of the Western Theological Seminary* by Rev. A. D. Campbell. See also *ibid.,* April, 1928, Centennial Number. MS Letters of Joshua L. Wilson regarding the founding of a Theological Seminary in the West, Part II.

Chicago.[58] Other seminaries for the training of ministers were established at Danville, Kentucky, in connection with Centre College (1828); at Marysville, Tennessee, under synodical care, and in west Tennessee at Nashville, but by far the most important of the western seminaries of these early years was that founded at Walnut Hills, near Cincinnati.

The Synods of Kentucky, Ohio and Indiana had refused to coöperate with the new seminary at Allegheny and under the leadership of Joshua L. Wilson had urged that a western seminary be placed at or near Cincinnati. This was soon to be accomplished through the initiative of the Lane brothers, wealthy Baptist merchants of Boston. They had become convinced, as a result of their observations on a trip to New Orleans, that a school for the training of ministers in the West was sorely needed, and they resolved to found such an institution. Having failed to secure Baptist coöperation they presented their offer to the Presbyterians, which was at once accepted. Under the leadership of Joshua L. Wilson a literary department was first established, later moved to Miami University, and in 1832 Dr. Lyman Beecher was called from his Boston pulpit to take the presidency of the Theological Seminary, the wealthy New York merchant and philanthropist Arthur Tappan having agreed to found a professorship provided Lyman Beecher should be the incumbent.[59]

From the beginning Lane Seminary attracted large numbers of students, many of whom, as Charles G. Finney[60] states, having come out of the great revivals in which he had had a part in central and western New York, were imbued with evangelical fervor. The story of Lane Theo-

[58] Johnson, Jesse, "Early Theological Education West of the Alleghanies," in *Papers of the American Society of Church History*, Second Series, Vol. V, pp. 121-130; Gillett, *op. cit.*, II, pp. 348-354.

[59] Halsey, L. J., *A History of the McCormick Theological Seminary of the Presbyterian Church* (Chicago, 1893). For the early years at Hanover and New Albany see Chapters II and III. *McCormick Theological Seminary, Historical Celebration* (Chicago, 1910). *History of Lane Seminary* (Cincinnati, no date).

[60] *Memoirs of Charles G. Finney* (New York, 1896), p. 332.

logical Seminary and its part in the great Presbyterian schism of 1837 and 1838 will be told in the following chapter.

In 1835 Lyman Beecher traveled extensively through the Atlantic states in the interests of Lane Theological Seminary, and in numerous eastern cities delivered a *Plea for the West*. His first point in that address was "What is required to secure the civil and religious liberty of the West?" This, he stated, could not be done by prayers and supplications; nor by tracts, Bibles or itinerant missions, but rather by education; by establishing "permanent, powerful, literary and moral institutions." The great body of western teachers must be educated in the West, and the type of minister demanded in the West must be talented and eloquent as well as pious, for nowhere on earth is "talent, and learning, and argument, and popular eloquence" more "highly appreciated, and regarded." "We must educate! We must educate! or we must perish by our own prosperity." He was particularly concerned about the activities of the Roman Catholics in establishing educational institutions in the West, stating that his object in touching upon them was not to repudiate them, but to appeal to the nation, "whether it will sustain its own institutions for the education of its own people, or depend on the charity of the Catholic despotic governments of Europe." "Education," he stated, "intellectual and religious, is the point on which turns our destiny, of territorial glory and power, or of shame and everlasting contempt, and short is the period of our probation."[61] And I think it can be said without fear of overstatement that the Presbyterians stood first among those who answered that challenge.

[61] Beecher, Lyman, *A Plea for the West* (Third edition, Cincinnati and New York, 1836), pp. 22, 23, 27, 141.

CHAPTER IV

REVIVALISM AND PRESBYTERIAN CONTROVERSY

The first forty years of the nineteenth century witnessed the most serious controversies and schisms which American Presbyterianism has experienced throughout the whole course of its history, with the possible exception of that division which was caused by the Civil War. That the frontier was a large, if not the largest, factor in these controversies and divisions there can be no doubt. It was during the period from 1800 to about 1840 that the frontier was exercising perhaps its largest influence in the political, economic, social and religious life of the nation. It was during this period also that the great American churches were developing their peculiar frontier techniques, which were to be used over and over again, with variations, on succeeding frontiers. The methods developed by the Presbyterians in their attempt to follow settlement westward have been described in the previous chapter. In the present chapter it is planned to discuss some of the principal difficulties and disadvantages which Presbyterianism faced in its westward expansion.

In devising adequate frontier techniques Presbyterianism was handicapped by the rigidity of both its creed and polity. The numerous frontier controversies and divisions were largely the result of the lack of elasticity in Presbyterianism. The great Westminster Confession holds Presbyterians to a very definite credal statement, and any deviation from it is easily detected, and often resulted in controversy. Presbyterians of that period also held that the Christian Church was a society created by divine institution, with a form of organization based upon scriptural models, and that any change in credal statement or organization was therefore unscriptural and erroneous.[1] The fact that the

[1] See Moffatt, James, *The Presbyterian Churches* (New York, 1928),

Presbyterians believed that there was a definitely prescribed form of church government to be found in Scripture meant that any suggestion of change in polity to meet new situations would, in the very nature of the case, meet with resistance.[2]   These facts must be kept in mind if we are to understand the controversies and schisms which wrought such havoc in frontier Presbyterianism during the first half of the nineteenth century.   The Methodists, on the other hand, held to the view of John Wesley that there is no form of church government prescribed in Scripture, therefore to them church government was man-made, and subject to change.   It therefore possessed an elasticity which gave it a great advantage over the organization holding to a rigid creed and polity.   In view of these facts it will not be surprising, therefore, to learn that the most serious church divisions which took place on the early frontier were Presbyterian schisms.

The first serious problems faced by frontier Presbyterianism were those which grew out of the great Revival which swept over the western country in the latter years of the eighteenth and the early years of the nineteenth centuries. It is an interesting fact that most of the great American

Chap. VII, "The Doctrine of the Church."   Jonathan Dickinson clearly expresses this view of Church Government in a sermon preached before the Synod at Philadelphia in 1722, in which he said:

"We are hence instructed that the Man of God has no Power or Authority to make any new Laws or Constitutions in the Affairs of God's House; or to make any Additions unto or Alterations of those Laws, that Christ has left us in the Divine Order."

Further he stated:

"All the substantials of Government are left upon Record in the Word of God and are unalterable by any Humane Authority—As Christ is sole *King* & *Legislature* to his church, it is an uncommunicable Jewel in his Crown, to give all the *Laws* and all the Ordinances thereof; and it would therefore be an egregious Reflection on his Faithfulness, to suppose any Case that can possibly occur unprovided for."

Sermon preached at the opening of the Synod of Philadelphia, September 19, 1722, by Jonathan Dickinson, A. M., Minister of the Gospel in Elizabeth Town (Boston, 1723), pp. 11, 13-14, 15.

[2] "The rigid Presbyterians of the Old School felt that the entire system of Presbyterian government in the church was highly important, and in the estimation of some, nearly indispensable to the existence of a well-organized church." Hotchkin, *op. cit.,* p. 241.

revival movements have come largely through Presbyterianism, and the great Revival in the West is no exception. It
had its beginning in the little frontier Presbyterian churches
under the care of James McGready in Logan County,
Kentucky, in the year 1797.

James McGready was born of Scotch-Irish parents in
Pennsylvania, but removed with his parents to North Carolina at an early age. Here as a youth he developed such
interest in religion that an uncle encouraged him to think
of the ministry. Accordingly he returned to western Pennsylvania where he attended Joseph Smith's Academy and
had the privilege of studying theology under John Mc-
Millan, and in 1788 was licensed to preach by the Redstone Presbytery.[3] He now decided to return to North
Carolina and on his way spent some time at Hampden-
Sydney College then in the midst of a great revival, and
was there deeply impressed with the value of evangelical
preaching.

At the time of his return to North Carolina religion was
at low ebb, but McGready's preaching soon brought about
a sweeping religious awakening, and among the converts
were ten or twelve young men who eventually entered the
ministry, among them Barton W. Stone. McGready now
became pastor of a church in Orange County, where he was
so vehement in his denunciation of sin and hypocrisy that
the community was divided into factions, one made up of
his hearty supporters and the other of his bitter enemies.
Partly because of the threats of his enemies and partly because he wished to follow his converts in their migration
over the mountains, McGready came to Kentucky in 1796
and almost immediately took charge of three small congregations in Logan County. His preaching, which had been
so effective in North Carolina, was equally effective in Ken-

[3] Sketches of the life of James McGready may be found in Smith, *op. cit.*,
pp. 360-364; Sprague, W. B., *op. cit.*, III, p. 278. See also sketch in the
Dictionary of American Biography, XII, pp. 56-57, and attached bibliography.
McDonnold, B. W., in his *History of the Cumberland Presbyterian Church*
(Nashville, 1888), p. 47, states that the western revival began under Gideon
Blackburn and Samuel Doak in eastern Tennessee.

tucky and soon great revivals were in progress in each of his congregations, which proved to be the forerunners of the Great Revival of 1800. In a letter to the *New York Missionary Magazine* McGready compared the beginning of the revival to a "few scattering drops before a mighty rain" as contrasted with the "overwhelming floods of salvation" which "poured out like a mighty river" in the year 1800.[4] What is called the Logan County revival reached its culmination in the summer of 1800, and in the words of McGready, exceeded anything his eyes had ever beheld on earth. Other Presbyterian ministers besides McGready were active in the work and simultaneous movements were under way among Methodists and Baptists.

These meetings reached such proportions that of necessity they were held out of doors, and due to the fact that people attended from such great distances many came prepared to remain several days. Some came in wagons loaded with provisions and fitted up for temporary lodging; others built temporary shelters. Such, according to Davidson, was the beginning of the Camp Meeting, which thus owes its origin to Presbyterianism.[5] The first planned camp meeting was that held at the Gasper River Church in July, 1800. Invitations were sent out by McGready through the whole country, and a great concourse assembled "from distances of 40, 50 and 100 miles." A regular encampment was arranged in the form of a hollow square, the interior of which was fitted up for worship, with parallel rows of hewn logs designed as seats, and with the stand in the center. Some of the people occupied tents while others slept in covered wagons.

Camp meetings once introduced spread like wild fire through the frontier, and one after another was held in adjoining communities. Davidson thus describes the vast appeal which the camp meeting had upon frontier society:

---

[4] For descriptions of the Logan County revival see the *New York Missionary Magazine*, April, 1803, p. 156; Cleveland, C. C., *The Great Revival in the West* (Chicago, 1916), pp. 63-69.
[5] Davidson, *op. cit.*, pp. 134, 135, 136-137.

The woods and paths seemed alive with people, and the number reported as attending is almost incredible. The laborer quitted his task; Age snatched his crutch; Youth forgot his pastime; the plow was left in the furrow; the deer enjoyed a respite upon the mountains; business of all kinds was suspended; dwelling houses were deserted; whole neighborhoods were emptied; bold hunters and sober matrons, young women and maidens, and little children, flocked to the common center of attraction; every difficulty was surmounted, every risk ventured, to be present at the camp-meeting.

Soon the Methodists were joining with the Presbyterians in these great outdoor gatherings, and great General Camp Meetings were held, in which all denominations participated. During the year 1800 ten camp meetings were held in the Cumberland and Green River settlements, and as a result 340 converts were added to the Presbyterian churches. Between May and August, 1801, in upper Kentucky no less than six camp meetings were held, continuing from four days to a week each.[6]

Thus the revival fire spread far and wide and people came from long distances to behold for themselves the remarkable manifestations of divine power. Among those who came to Logan County to see for himself what was going on was Barton W. Stone, one of McGready's converts in North Carolina, who had now become the pastor of two Presbyterian congregations at Concord and Cane Ridge in Bourbon County. He returned to his churches fully convinced that what he had beheld in Logan County was the genuine work of God, and immediately the revival broke out under his preaching.[7] We will let Stone tell of the earlier meeting at Concord:

The effects of this meeting through the country were like fire in dry stubble driven by a strong wind. All felt its influence more or less. . . . The whole country appeared to be in motion to the place, and multitudes of all denominations attended. All seemed heartily

---

[6] Davidson, *op. cit.*, pp. 136-137; also McNemar, Richard, *The Kentucky Revival* (Cincinnati, 1808).

[7] Stone related the occurrences in his *Autobiography* printed in Rogers, James R., *The Cane Ridge Meeting-house* (Cincinnati, 1910), pp. 113-204.

to unite in the work and in Christian love.   Party spirit, abashed, shrunk away.   To give a true description of this meeting cannot be done; it would border on the marvelous.   It continued five days and nights without ceasing.[8]

The most remarkable of all the meetings in Kentucky was the General Camp Meeting held at Cane Ridge, which began on August 6, 1801.   It was exceptional not only because of what took place there, but also because of the vast numbers present.   Stone had made great preparations for the meeting, and a large area had been cleared, in the center of which a large tent had been erected, while the adjoining ground was laid off in regular streets along which the tents and lodges of the people were to be placed.   One statistically inclined person counted the number of conveyances on the ground and found that there were 143 carriages and wagons, 500 sleighs or sledges, and 500 without covers, making in all 1,143 vehicles, while there were 500 candles, besides lamps to illuminate the camp at night.[9]   John Lyle, one of the Presbyterian ministers on the ground, stated in his *Diary* that according to the calculation of one of the elders, there were from 800 to 1,100 communicants present, though the total number of people in attendance has been variously estimated at from ten to twenty thousand.   When the meeting was at its height numerous ministers carried on preaching simultaneously at various parts of the ground, and the effects produced upon the people were awe inspiring.[10]   Richard McNemar, one of the Presbyterian ministers present, stated that "the various operations and exercises on that occasion were indescribable."   Of these strange "exercises" that known as the "falling exercise" was the most notable.   One of the oldest and most reliable of the ministers, James Crawford, kept as accurate an ac-

[8] *Ibid.,* p. 157.

[9] Davidson, *op. cit.,* p. 138, quoted from the *Gospel Herald,* II, p. 200.

[10] The number of communicants referred to above were evidently Presbyterian communicants only, as we know from Lyle's *Diary* that "Mr. Marshall preached the action sermon."

count as possible and reported that those who fell numbered about 3,000.[11]

Davidson in his *History of Kentucky Presbyterianism*
has summarized the extravagances and disorders of the
revival, listing them under the following headings: undue
excitement of animal feeling; disorderly proceedings in
public worship; too free communication of the sexes; the
promulgation of doctrinal errors; and the engendering of
spiritual pride and censoriousness.[12]

The undue excitement of animal feeling produced strange
bodily manifestations which are listed as the *falling, jerk-
ing, rolling, running, dancing and barking exercises and
visions and trances*. As has been stated the falling exercise was the most common, and affected old and young,
men and women. Lyle notes that on one day at the Cane
Ridge meeting almost all who fell were men. Some fell
suddenly as if struck with a bullet; others were first seized
with a bodily tremor before falling. Some fell shrieking,
and continued to shriek and groan during the whole period
of prostration; others lay motionless as if dead. Another
characteristic of the revival particularly distasteful to those
who believed that decency and order should prevail in public worship was the noise and confusion which everywhere
attended the camp meeting revivals. The vast crowds
which assembled in the woods, in which the dissolute and
the irreligious were always more numerous than the professing Christians and the serious minded; the disorder
which always accompanied every gathering, often greatly
increased by the effect of raw whiskey sold by hucksters
from wagons about the camp grounds; the strange physical phenomena often seizing large numbers at once; the
shouting and perspiring preacher in the stand; these were
the common spectacles on the camp grounds which now

---

[11] These facts are from McNemar, Richard, *op. cit.* (New York, 1846),
pp. 26-27. The Presbyterian historians, such as Davidson, are inclined to
disparage the McNemar account of the revival since he later withdrew from
the Presbyterians and joined the Shakers.

[12] Davidson, *op. cit.*, Chap. VI, pp. 142-169. See also the discussion of
the "Phenomena of the Revival," in Cleveland, C. C., *op. cit.*, pp. 87-127.

sprang up in every direction. It was impossible to handle the vast crowds which attended these meetings, and people talked and walked about during the services. Often a dozen different hymns or songs were sung at once in the same assembly; often as many prayers were being offered at the same time. Preachers were interrupted in the midst of their discourses by bursts of singing and praying, while wild "shrieks, whoops and outcries and hysterical laughter, and the repetition of their words in louder accents, constituted a combination of annoyances to which the waves of the sea harangued by the Athenian orator must have been a mere trifle."[13]

There is an abundance of evidence that every camp meeting was largely attended by the dregs of frontier society. Davidson speaks of "wild fellows from adjoining towns frequenting the camps to take advantage of the opportunities afforded by the prevailing license and disorder." Lyle in his *Diary* states that the dissolute of both sexes resorted to the camp meetings, and records the tragic aftermath of some of those who professed conversion. "Becca Bell,—who often fell, is now big with child to a wicked trifling school master of the name of Brown who says he'll be damned to hell if he ever marries her." Further he continues, "Raglin's daughter seems careless . . . Kitty Cummings got careless. . . . Polly Moffitt was with child to Petty and died miserably in child bed."[14]

More reprehensible, perhaps, to the strict Calvinists among the frontier ministers, than any of the excesses already described, was the tendency on the part of the Presbyterian revivalists to accept "the doctrine of grace as held by the Methodists," and otherwise dilute the "excellent standards" of the Confession. Thus Richard McNemar

---

[13] An excellent account of the camp meeting as it existed in the early part of the nineteenth century will be found in Posey, *op. cit.*, Chap. II, pp. 17-34. Also Davidson, *op. cit.*, pp. 138, 156. McNemar, *op. cit.*, p. 34, speaks of "those who came with barrels of whiskey, to retail out to the multitude."

[14] Davidson, *op. cit.*, pp. 163, 164; Lyle, John, *Diary* (MSS), pp. 47-48.

describes the attitude of those ministers who soon began to resist the revival:

The people among whom the revival began, were generally Calvinists; and although they had been long praying in words, for the outpouring of the Spirit; and believed that God had "fore-ordained whatsoever comes to pass"; yet, when it came to pass that their prayer was answered, and the spirit began to flow like many waters, from a cloud of witnesses; and souls were convicted of sin, and cried for mercy and found hope and comfort in the news of a Saviour; they rose up and quarreled with the work, because it did not come to pass that the subjects of it were willing to adopt their soul-stupefying creed.[15]

It was inevitable that out of this general situation there should arise two parties among the Presbyterian ministers on the frontier, those favoring and defending the revival, called *Revival* men and those opposing it known as *Anti-Revival* men. Eventually there developed three distinct schisms as a result of the cleavages which now began to appear: the Cumberland Presbyterian Schism; the New Light Schism; and the Shaker Schism.

Due to the widespread influence of the Logan County or Cumberland revival, the beginnings of which have already been described, many people professed conversion and joined the church, and many new congregations were formed. Accordingly there was a large demand for additional ministers. To help meet this situation the Transylvania Presbytery in October, 1801, accepted four men: Alexander Anderson, Finis Ewing, Samuel King and Ephraim McClain, who were authorized to exhort and catechize in vacant congregations.[16] All of these men were somewhat advanced in years, had families and were without a college education. At a subsequent meeting of the Presbytery in April, 1802, a number of petitions having been received from places where they had acceptably sup-

---

[15] McNemar, *op. cit.*, p. 27.
[16] *Minutes of the Transylvania Presbytery*, October 9, 1801; Davidson, *op. cit.*, pp. 224-225; McDonnold, *op. cit.*, pp. 20-25ff.

plied, Anderson, Ewing and King were licensed, though three ministerial members and two elders dissented from this procedure.[17]

At the first session of the Synod of Kentucky, which met at Lexington on October 14, 1802, application was made for the division of Transylvania Presbytery, and the formation of a new presbytery to be known as the Cumberland was voted.[18] The new presbytery consisted of ten ministers, the majority favoring the revival, with the result that the policy of licensing educationally deficient candidates was continued. Anderson and Ewing were also ordained, and Davidson tells us that: "Illiterate exhorters, with Arminian sentiments were multiplied, till they soon numbered seventeen."[19] Candidates for the ministry were examined on experimental religion and on their motives in entering the ministry, but there was little attention given their educational qualifications. That the standards for receiving candidates were very much relaxed, the documents printed in this volume give abundant testimony.[20] Some were received as candidates after the delivery of a single discourse, while Davidson stresses the fact that none were "required to adopt the Confession of Faith, save so far only as they believed it to agree with the word of God."[21] And perhaps more distressing than any of the foregoing indications of growing laxity was the fact that these licensed exhorters, "burning with zeal," traveled through their "circuits," a term which they borrowed from the Methodists, and many converts were being won, and new churches established;

[17] *Minutes of the Transylvania Presbytery*, October 8, 1802. The dissenting ministers were Thomas B. Craighead, Sam'l Dannel and James Balch.

[18] See action of the Synod of Kentucky, *Minutes*, Part II, Chap. VII, October 15, 1802.

[19] Davidson, *op. cit.*, p. 229; *Minutes of the Synod of Kentucky. Minutes of the Cumberland Presbytery*, October 5, and 7, 1803.

[20] "James Farr, expressing his desire to join presbytery as a candidate for the holy ministry, delivered a discourse as a specimen of his abilities. The presbytery judging thereof received him as a candidate and appointed him to prepare a discourse on Mark 8:34 to be delivered at the intermediate presbytery." *Minutes of the Cumberland Presbytery*, October 3, 1804.

[21] Davidson, *op. cit.*, p. 229.

in short, the revivalists were growing so rapidly that there was grave danger that they would soon dominate the synod.

That the conservative and anti-revival men should do something about this situation was inevitable. The first action taken was at the meeting of the Synod of Kentucky in 1804, when a letter of protest was presented, signed by Craighead and two others, which resulted in the appointment of a committee to attend "the earliest meeting of the Cumberland Presbytery" to investigate the situation and report at the next meeting of the synod. David Rice headed this committee.[22] Only one of the committee, Archibald Cameron, however, attended. At the next meeting of the Synod, in October, 1805, the Records of the Cumberland Presbytery were examined by a committee which reported numerous irregularities. Among the matters cited were: their mode of conducting business is "various and discordant"; James Haw[e] a "regular minister of the Methodist Republican Church" is permitted to take a seat in presbytery, without recanting certain sentiments which he had publicly espoused, though they were inimical to the faith of the Presbyterian Church; persons were licensed to exhort "wherever God in his providence called them," a proceeding they considered disorderly, the number of these exhorters being seventeen; men living within the bounds of the Transylvania Presbytery were taken under the care of the Cumberland Presbytery and licensed to exhort, and afterwards appointed "subjects for trial"; the phrase "Finis Ewing's Circuit" was used; a letter was authorized recommending people to contribute for the support of exhorters, which was deemed illegal; Farr, an illiterate man, was licensed with approbation.[23]

After receiving this report it was voted to appoint a Commission made up of ten ministers and six elders, with full synodical[24] powers, to confer with the members of the

[22] *Minutes of the Synod of Kentucky,* October 20, 1804.

[23] *Ibid.,* October 17, 1805.

[24] The ministerial members of the Commission were John Lyle, J. P. Campbell, Archibald Cameron, Joseph P. Howe, Samuel Rannals, Robert

Cumberland Presbytery and "to adjudicate upon their Presbyterial proceedings." The Commission was instructed to meet at Gasper Meeting House in Logan County the first Tuesday in the following December.

The Commission accordingly met at the appointed time and place and after a three-hour sermon by John Lyle on the call and qualifications necessary to the Gospel ministry, proceeded to the business in hand.[25] The whole region was decidedly prejudiced in favor of the Cumberland Presbytery; the members of the Commission remained in session for nine days taking up each of the complaints against the Presbytery in turn. Those men who had been licensed and ordained by the Presbytery were summoned before the Commission to be reëxamined as to their fitness to preach, but they unanimously refused to submit, claiming that under Presbyterian law the Presbytery possessed the exclusive right to examine and license their own candidates. Thereupon the Commission prohibited the "said persons" from exhorting, preaching and administering the ordinances, while the older members of the Cumberland Presbytery who had supported the so-called irregular licensing and ordaining were cited to appear before the next regular session of the Synod.

Immediately on the adjournment of the Commission the revival members of the Cumberland Presbytery organized themselves into a *Council*, with representatives from all their congregations, and drew up a long letter of remonstrance to the next General Assembly, reviewing the events of the past several years, upholding their doctrinal soundness and their attachment to an educated ministry. Meanwhile at the next session of the Synod of Kentucky the

Stuart, Joshua L. Wilson, Robert Wilson, Thomas Clelland and Isaac Tull. *Minutes of Synod of Kentucky,* October 18, 1805.

[25] The minutes of the proceedings of the Commission are found in the *Minutes of the Synod of Kentucky,* Part II, Chap. VII. For an account of the proceedings from the anti-revivalistic angle, see Davidson, *op. cit.* pp. 234-253; from the Cumberland Presbyterian angle see McDonnold, *op. cit.,* pp. 77-81.

Cumberland Presbytery was dissolved and the members re-annexed to the Transylvania Presbytery.

It will be impossible to give in detail here the whole story of the next few years of controversy. The General Assembly of 1808 was inclined to uphold the Cumberland Presbytery, and to condemn the Synod of Kentucky, on the ground that a synod cannot deal with individual members except in case of appeal. It also expressed the hope that the Synod would reëstablish the Cumberland Presbytery and restore some of the former members to ministerial usefulness.[26] The following year (1809), however, under the influence of a strong emotional appeal of John Lyle, who was present to defend the action of the Synod, the General Assembly upheld without a dissenting vote, the action of the Synod of Kentucky, and thereby made impossible any reconciliation. The Council of the Cumberland group now decided by a large majority to organize as an independent presbytery, though a number of their most influential members and supporters, among them James McGready, had returned to the "bosom" of the Presbyterian church by submitting to its demands, while several others had withdrawn from Presbyterianism entirely and had joined the Shakers.

While the Cumberland Presbyterian controversy was in process in southern Kentucky and north central Tennessee, a second controversy was under way in northern Kentucky which finally developed into what came to be known as the New Light Schism. In 1799 the Synod of Virginia had divided the Transylvania Presbytery into three presbyteries: Transylvania, West Lexington, and Washington, in all of which the great revival had created definite cleavages. In northern Kentucky the revivalists early developed a decided anti-Calvinistic emphasis, and at the second meeting of the Synod of Kentucky in 1803, two members of the Presbytery of Washington, Richard McNemar and John Dunlavy, having already been condemned by their presby-

---

[26] For other documents relating to the Cumberland Schism see Baird, *op. cit.* (Philadelphia, 1855), pp. 640-647.

tery for holding unorthodox views, it was proposed that
the Synod enter into their examination and trial. To this
procedure five of the revival ministers, Robert Marshall,
John Dunlavy, Richard McNemar, Barton W. Stone and
John Thompson, at once entered their formal protest, and
declared their withdrawal from the jurisdiction of the
Synod.[27]

Their reasons for so doing they set forth in a letter to
the Synod in which they stated that the Minute sanctioned
by the Synod gave a distorted and false representation of
McNemar's views; that they claimed for themselves the
privilege of interpreting the Scriptures by themselves without restriction from the Synod; that they held to the doctrine of grace which had "been mighty in every revival since
the Reformation," doctrines which they believed were
darkened "by some expressions in the Confession of Faith,"
and since their attempt to uphold these doctrines was inter-
preted as departing from the Standards they therefore felt
under the necessity of relieving the Synod of the disagreeable task of prosecuting them. By this action, however,
they did not separate from "their communion, or exclude
you from ours," but bade them adieu "until through the
providence of God it seem good to your Revd Body to
adopt a more liberal plan respecting human Creeds & Confessions."

This precipitate withdrawal on the part of the seceders
aroused the Synod to immediate action and a committee
was appointed to "seriously and affectionately" converse
with the seceders in order "to bring them back to the standards and doctrines" of the church. The seceders agreed
to confer with the Synod in a body and to answer any questions on points of doctrine which were stated in writing.
The next day, however, the five "rebels" appeared before
the Synod and announced their withdrawal and the organ-

[27] Minutes of the Synod of Kentucky, September 8-10, 1803. See also the
account of Davidson, *op. cit.*, pp. 190-196. For Stone's account of the proceedings of the Synod see his "Autobiography" in Rogers, *The Cane Ridge
Meeting-house*, pp. 163-170. McNemar, *op. cit.*, pp. 42-75.

ization of a separate presbytery, which they called the Springfield. Whereupon the Synod suspended them from the ministry and declared their pulpits vacant.[28]

The next several months were occupied with a pamphlet warfare between the two parties. The first pamphlet to appear was the *Apology*[29] of the *New Lights* for their action in withdrawing from the Synod, in which is set forth their doctrinal position, maintaining that all creeds and confessions should be rejected, and that the Bible alone should be the bond of Christian fellowship. To this a committee of Synod replied in a *Circular Letter*, which was an exposition of the Synod's position, containing an account of all that had taken place up to that time. In reply to the *Apology* Robert H. Bishop issued his *Apology for Calvinism* while other pamphlets were issued back and forth.[30]

Meanwhile the "protestants" were busy preaching and establishing new congregations, and by 1804 there were fifteen regular societies under their direction in Kentucky and Ohio. By the spring of 1804 Stone and his associates had decided that their Presbytery was a handicap to the carrying forward of their work, and accordingly they agreed to disband it, which they announced to the world in a little publication called *The Last Will and Testament of the Springfield Presbytery*. In this interesting document, which Davidson characterizes as a "sorry attempt at wit," they announced in the legal language of a will, their abjuration of this and all other similar organizations; they also renounced the title of Reverend, written calls, salaries by subscription; affirmed the complete independence of each individual congregation; and acknowledged no other confession of faith except the Bible. Thus was launched a new denomination in the West. The seceding ministers had carried their congregations with them into the new church.

---

[28] *Minutes of the Synod of Kentucky,* September 13, 1803.

[29] *Apology for Renouncing the Jurisdiction of the Synod of Kentucky,* etc., by the Presbytery of Springfield (Lexington, 1805).

[30] For a recent account of the happenings of these years see Ware, C. C., *Barton Warren Stone, Pathfinder of Christian Union,* etc. (St. Louis, 1932), Chap. X.

In southwestern Ohio where Richard McNemar was the pastor of the Turtle Creek Church, every Presbyterian church with their ministers were swept into the new organization except two.[31] The name *Christian*, which had been adopted in 1804, was well calculated to win the allegiance of frontier people and the substitution of the Bible for manmade creeds found also ready support. But the very region where their greatest early successes were achieved was soon to witness the defection of several of their most influential leaders.

During the early years of the nineteenth century the newspapers in the eastern states had been filled with accounts of the great revival, then under way in Kentucky, Tennessee and Ohio. Among those to whom this information came as "good news" were the *Shakers*,[32] a small communistic sect which had recently established several communities in the New England states and in New York. The founder of the sect was Ann Lee (or Lees), who came to America from England with a small band of her followers in 1774 and established a community across the Hudson from Albany. Meanwhile "Mother Ann," as she was known by her disciples, continued to have visions in regard to the organization of the church, though the Shaker Church was not actually formed until after her death in 1783. The church on its formation took the name of *The United Society of Believers in Christ's Second Appearing*, holding that Ann Lee was the second appearing of Christ. The aversion which Ann Lee had developed against sexual relations caused the Shakers to adopt celibacy as one of their principal tenets, though among other beliefs they opposed

---

[31] MacLean, J. P., *The Kentucky Revival and its Influence on the Miami Valley* (No date), Pamphlet, pp. 18-19.

[32] Green, Calvin, and Wells, S. Y., *A Summary View of the Millennial Church, or United Society of Believers* (Commonly called Shakers) (Albany, N. Y., 1823), pp. 68-72. The "Mother Church" was established at New Lebanon, southeast of Albany, N. Y. Besides this community there were ten other communities in 1805; one in New York; four in Massachusetts; one in Connecticut; two in New Hampshire; two in Maine. See *Dictionary of American Biography*, XI, pp. 95-96, for brief biography of Ann Lee by Herbert W. Schneider.

war, and believed in direct revelation. Their leaders at
New Lebanon had been looking toward the West because
of a prophecy of "Mother Ann" that there was to be a
great opening for the new gospel in the western country.
Accordingly on the first day of January, 1805, three
Shaker missionaries[33] set out from New Lebanon at three
o'clock in the morning for the West. After a journey of
more than sixty days, traveling mostly on foot, they arrived
in the revival country. Their first stop was at Paint Lick
where Matthew Houston was the Presbyterian minister,
and from thence they proceeded to Cane Ridge where Barton W. Stone, according to Shaker testimony, "sucked in
our light as greedily as ever an ox drank water." Crossing the Ohio River they came to Malcolm Worley's,[34] who
was soon won to Shakerism and who contributed the first
land to the great 4,500-acre estate which became the chief
Shaker center west of the Alleghenies. Richard McNemar
was the next ministerial convert and finally John Dunlavy
and Matthew Houston were won. McNemar became the
outstanding leader of the Shaker Society in the West and
his account of *The Kentucky Revival* was their first bound
volume.[35]

Stone and his associates were naturally greatly stirred by
the large Shaker defection and were soon denouncing the
Shakers as wolves in sheep's clothing. But in the long run
perhaps the Shakers performed a real service for the
"Christians" in that the more fanatical element in the Stone
movement were drained off into the Shaker colonies.[36]

[33] The Shaker missionaries were Benjamin Seth Youngs, thirty-one years
of age and the ablest of the three; Issachar Bates and John Meacham.
MacLean, J. P., *Shakers of Ohio,* p. 41.

[34] MacLean, *op. cit.,* p. 41; Worley accepted Shakerism on March 27.
Purviance, Levi, *The Biography of Elder David Purviance* . . . written
by himself (Dayton, Ohio, 1848), p. 287.

[35] MacLean, J. P., *A Sketch of the Life and Labors of Richard McNemar.*
(Pamphlet, n.d.)

[36] There were eventually established six Shaker communities in the West
three in Ohio, the first near Lebanon, a second near Dayton, a third near
Cleveland; two in Kentucky, one near Harrodsburg, the other in Logan
County; and one community in Indiana, on the lower Wabash sixteen miles
above Vincennes. Green and Wells, *op. cit.,* pp. 75-76.

CHAPTER V

THE OPERATION OF THE PLAN OF UNION AND FRONTIER CONTROVERSY

In spite of the controversies and divisions, as the result of Revivalism, which have been occupying our attention in the previous chapter, the Presbyterian church in America during the first third of the nineteenth century grew with amazing rapidity. At the close of the year 1829 there were in the Presbyterian Church in the United States of America nineteen synods, ninety-eight presbyteries, 149 ministers and a membership of 173,329. The great expansion and growth had been largely to the westward, and although there had been local defections as a result of the Great Revival, yet as a whole there had been harmony, especially in the meetings of the General Assembly. Ashbel Green, the editor, writing in the *Christian Advocate* for June, 1830 stated:

Never have we seen a General Assembly—and we have seen the most that have met—in which there was apparently so much brotherly love, so much mutual concession, and so little in the speeches that were made to give offence to opponents in argument.[1]

This harmony, which so impressed Dr. Green in 1830, was soon to give place to a whole series of discords, to which Ashbel Green himself was to contribute not a few of the jarring notes, and between 1834 and 1837 the rapid increase in the church membership was to be largely offset by an actual decrease.

This new series of controversies, coming to a head in the eighteen thirties, which wrought such havoc in the church and which finally resulted in bisecting it, grew very largely

[1] *The Christian Advocate* (Philadelphia, 1830), VIII, p. 313. In 1837 the membership was 233,580; from 1834 to 1837 there was a loss of over 18,000. Gillette, *op. cit.*, II, pp. 443-445. Ashbel Green was one of the principal Old School leaders. *Dict. of Am. Biography,* vol. VII, article by R. H. Nichols.

out of conditions which arose in the newer sections of the country. These causes of controversy may be listed under the following heads: (1) the operation of the Plan of Union; (2) the conflict between the American Home Missionary Society and the Assembly's Board of Missions in attempting to work in the same field; (3) the doctrinal controversy; and (4) the question of slavery. All of these controversies came in large measure from the New England stream flowing into Presbyterianism as a result of the working out of the Plan of Union.

The Plan of Union[2] as it operated in central and western New York, and in northern Ohio and Illinois, and other places in the West has already been treated in Chapter II. It remains, however, to be considered here how the working of the Plan of Union brought controversy and final division in the Presbyterian church. It has been stated that "over two thousand churches, which were in origin and usages Congregational"[3] eventually became Presbyterian churches. Though these figures are doubtless incorrect, yet there had come to be by 1830 a great many Presby-

[2] The Plan of Union was first adopted by the General Assembly and the General Association of Connecticut in 1801; in 1803 a similar agreement had been reached between the General Assembly and the Congregational Convention of Vermont; in 1811 a Plan of Union was entered upon between the General Assembly and the General Association of Massachusetts. See Baird, *op. cit.* (Philadelphia, 1859), pp. 570-581; also Woods, H., *The History of the Presbyterian Controversy with Early Sketches of Presbyterianism* (Louisville, 1843), pp. 41-44.

[3] This statement is from Ross, A. H., *The Church-Kingdom: Lectures on Congregationalism . . . in Andover Theological Seminary, 1882-1886* (Boston and Chicago, 1887), pp. 360-361. I have been unable to discover any definite support for these figures, which seem to have been based on a loose estimate rather than upon any careful study of the facts. The late Rev. W. T. Thayer, after a careful investigation based upon the large collection of local church histories in the library of Auburn Theological Seminary, concluded, that of the churches of the twenty new school presbyteries of central and western New York which were in existence in 1850, besides the 105 churches which by that time had gone out of existence, making 525 churches in all, only 145 had originally been congregational. Mr. Thayer makes no claim of absolute accuracy, but even if only approximate his findings are sufficient to establish the fact that the figures given by Ross are grossly inaccurate.

terian churches which had Congregational or Plan of
Union origins, in which the Presbyterial form of local organization was not complied with. It was stated in 1831
that in the Synod of the Western Reserve many churches
had no ruling elders connected with them, and that this
office had been allowed to go into disuse throughout the
Synod.[4]

Since many churches had no ruling elders the presbyteries had sent members of standing committees[5] as delegates to the General Assembly, which the General Assembly
of 1831 declared "inexpedient and of questionable consti-
tutionality, and therefore ought not in the future to be
made." This question began to agitate the General Assembly as early as 1820,[6] and continued until 1833. At the
General Assembly of 1832 there were several committee-
men among the delegates who submitted their commissions,
but finally withdrew them. A resolution was then introduced stating that the Plan of Union "truly construed, does
not authorize any committeeman to sit and act in any case
in any Synod or in the General Assembly."[7]

These revelations of looseness in adhering to Presbyterian standards in polity began increasingly to alarm the
stiffbacked Presbyterian element. In 1826 the Synod of
Pittsburgh had memorialized the General Assembly over
the matter in which they expressed their growing concern
for the "constitutional standards, ecclesiastical institutions,
and doctrinal purity of the Church," in the light of these
revelations of laxity. In 1831, writing in the *Christian
Advocate*, Dr. Green thought that the church faced "a very
fearful crisis—a crisis in which it is soon to be decided

---

[4] *Minutes of the General Assembly,* 1832, p. 367.

[5] *Ibid.,* 1831, pp. 340-341. A protest was entered by thirty-one members
of the Assembly against this action. See Baird, *op. cit.,* (1859), p. 579.

[6] Several cases of this kind are cited in Baird, *op. cit.,* pp. 574-581. See
the case of Daniel W. Lathrop of the Presbytery of Hartford, in the General Assembly of 1820; the case of Josiah Bissell of the Presbytery of
Rochester, 1826; the case of Clement Tuttle, 1831, of the Presbytery of
Grand River; the case of Erastus Upson, of the Presbytery of Oswego.

[7] Baird, *op. cit.,* pp. 579-581. Gillett, *op. cit.,* II, p. 456.

whether changes, effecting materially her doctrinal purity, her ecclesiastical order, and all her institutions and endowments, shall or shall not take place." In view of this fact he calls upon all who have the welfare of "our beloved Church" at heart to speak out.[8]

A second cause of controversy, growing more or less also out of the Plan of Union, was the increasing rivalry between the American Home Missionary Society and the Assembly's Board of Missions. Previous to the formation of the American Home Missionary Society in 1826 there had been numerous local and state missionary organizations working in the West. In 1822 the United Domestic Missionary Society, a Presbyterian organization, had been formed to consolidate home missionary activities in the State of New York.[9] All of these agencies, more or less, were coöperative, in that they were supported both by Congregationalists and Presbyterians, and carried on their work under the Plan of Union. In 1828 the Assembly's Board of Missions, (formed in 1816) had been reorganized in order to carry on more effectively in the West, and at the same time the Assembly's Board of Education, which had been formed by the General Assembly in 1819, was also in the field and both were pressing their claims upon the church with increasing urgency.[10] In 1830 the *Missionary Reporter and Education Register* began publication in their interest and numerous auxiliary societies were formed, in sessions, presbyteries and synods. From 1829 to 1831 there was a large increase both in funds and number of missionaries employed by the Assembly's Board of Missions. Thus there came to be two active home missionary agencies, both supported by Presbyterians and carrying on the same type of work in the same territory. Such a situation could not fail to bring eventual discord.

Attempts were made in 1830 by the Assembly of that year to unite the operations of the two societies in the

[8] *The Christian Advocate* (Philadelphia), IX (July, 1831), p. 363.
[9] See Introduction to Chapter XIII.
[10] Gillett, *op. cit.*, II, p. 446.

West, and a committee reported favorably upon it, but the plan was rejected. Again in 1831 another effort was made to solve the serious problem, and a resolution was passed recommending that the western synods with their presbyteries agree upon some plan of conducting missions, which was to be reported at the next session of the Assembly. Continued agitation of the question led a number of presbyteries to pass resolutions declaring that it was the duty of the Presbyterian church to conduct its own Christian missions, both domestic and foreign, the Presbytery of Louisville stating that "the transaction of the missionary business of the Church in her distinctive character" is "too sacred to be safely committed to any irresponsible and self-created body."[11]

As a result of the recommendation of the General Assembly of 1831 a convention of the western synods was held in Cincinnati in November of that year. Of the forty-eight presbyteries entitled to send delegates only twenty were so represented, though twelve registered their positions by letters. Various plans were suggested, among them the formation of a Western Board, but none was adopted, and the adjournment of the convention left the situation in even greater confusion than it was before.[12]

An interesting illustration of the swing of Presbyterian opinion from support to condemnation of the American Home Missionary Society is that furnished by Joshua L. Wilson, pastor of the First Presbyterian Church of Cincinnati. Wilson had been a supporter of the American Home Missionary Society for several years after its organization, but the rivalry of the two societies in the region of Cincinnati had convinced him by 1830 of the improb-

[11] *Minutes of the Presbytery of Louisville,* 1831, as quoted in Gillett, *op. cit.,* II, p. 450.

[12] Gillett, *op. cit.,* II, p. 451, states that only fifteen presbyteries were represented. *The Standard* (Cincinnati), January 6, 1832, ff. published the proceedings of the Cincinnati convention. For a recent and excellent account of the mission situation see Hightower, R. L., *Joshua L. Wilson: Frontier Controversalist* (typed Ph.D. Thesis, University of Chicago, 1933), pp. 160-170: also Baird, "History of the New School," *op. cit.,* Chap. XXIV.

ability of their coöperation, and before the end of that year
he had reached the conclusion that the American Home
Missionary Society was "aiming to overthrow the Presbyterian Church."[13]   By 1831 Wilson had become active in
his opposition and in an address published in March of that
year set forth his views on the question. He stated that
the peace and unity of the church were threatened by a
voluntary society, which drew its support largely from
Presbyterians and yet was not subject to the control of the
church. If, he stated, the Society is Presbyterian, as it
claims, let it yield to the control of the church and become
auxiliary to the Assembly's Board. Those who favored the
Society, he asserted, were not Presbyterians and ought to
be regarded as schismatics.[14]

Another of the charges against the American Home Missionary Society as set forth in the *Western Memorial*[15]
presented to the General Assembly of 1834, was that the
Society in its own name and on its own authority commissioned men, nominally Presbyterian, whom it sent to labor
for months in the bounds of other Presbyteries, without
putting themselves under their care. Thus a voluntary society was permitted to do that which would have brought
a rebuke if done by a presbytery. The Society ordained as
Presbyterian ministers eight or ten young men at a time,
men who had been reared from infancy in Congregationalism, and before it was possible for them to have any clear
conception of what Presbyterianism was, they were sent
forth into presbyteries and Presbyterian churches in the
West. It was charged that many of these young missionaries received ordination at the hands of eastern presbyteries noted for their laxity when there were presbyteries

[13] MS Letter of R. Cushman to A. Peters, A. H. M. S. Correspondence,
December 17, 1830.

[14] This address is entitled *Four Propositions Sustained against the American Home Missionary Society*, excerpts published in *The Standard*, March
30, 1832. Hightower, *op. cit.*, p. 166.

[15] Baird, *op. cit.* (1859), pp. 670-679. This *Memorial* was adopted by
nine presbyteries and eight sessions, and was signed by eighteen ministers
and ninety-nine elders. *Ibid.*, p. 679.

in the fields to which they are being sent, citing particularly the Third Presbytery of New York and Newburyport Presbytery as frequent offenders in this respect.

These and similar abuses of the power of Presbyteries [it states], are great evils, and a gross infringement of the rights of those Presbyteries to which, and into whose churches, these men are immediately sent. Such a practice occasions just offence and inevitably creates jealousies, suspicions, and divisions, where otherwise they might never have existed.[16]

That the American Home Missionary Society found many able defenders goes without saying. In 1831 it had 463 missionaries in the field ministering in 577 congregations and missionary districts, and its work was increasing year by year. That it did foster a liberal attitude and was supported by the more liberal minded is, of course, true. These New School men, as they began to be called by the eighteen thirties, explained the opposition of the Old School men, by saying that as far as the Old School party was concerned it was simply a struggle for power. As such men as Ashbel Green and other conservative leaders witnessed the rapid growth of the church, largely furthered in the West by the operations of the American Home Missionary Society and those who favored voluntary societies, and as they saw their power slipping from them, they raised the cry that the church was being exposed to "impending ruin."[17] This fear of the Old School leaders of losing control of the church is well set forth in Joshua L. Wilson's *Standard* in 1831. The New School, he states:

. . . (unless God of his infinite mercy arrest the evil) will in a short time be able to control every existing judicatory and institution of learning belonging to the Presbyterian Church throughout the whole land.

It was inevitable that the opposition which had devel-

---

[16] *Ibid.*, pp. 671-672.

[17] In October, 1836, the Synod of Kentucky requested the American Home Missionary Society "to retire without delay, from our bounds, and attempt to make no future collections within our churches." MS Letter of R. Davidson to Absalom Peters, A. H. M. S. Collection.

oped to the American Home Missionary Society and to voluntary societies in general, on the part of the Old School party, would eventually be extended to the American Board of Commissioners for Foreign Missions. In the General Assembly of 1835[18] a resolution was passed appointing a committee to arrange with the Synod of Pittsburgh to transfer their Western Missionary Society, which the Synod had formed in 1831, to the General Assembly, and to report to the next General Assembly. Accordingly the following year the "Terms of Agreement" with the Synod of Pittsburgh were submitted for adoption. This action met strong resistance on the part of the New School party which favored the American Board, and a resolution was introduced declaring it inexpedient "that the Assembly should form a separate Foreign Missionary Institution." A long debate now ensued and when the vote was finally taken the New School was found to have carried its point by 111 to 106.[19] This victory of the New School party, instead of settling the matter, simply stirred the Old School party to greater exertions and throughout the year the great matter of contest between the parties was the missionary question.

Causing even more concern to the Old School leaders than loose discipline and missionary rivalry was the creeping into the church of heretical opinions largely from New England and Congregational sources. In fact this phase of the controversy has been given far more attention by Presbyterian historians than any of the others, though the other phases were no doubt of equal importance, and in some localities of even greater significance. The major emphasis placed upon the doctrinal phase of the controversy by Presbyterian writers is doubtless due to the doctrinal-mindedness of the Presbyterian body, as well as to the voluminousness of the documents relating to it. This phase of the controversy has been adequately set forth by nu-

[18] *Minutes of the General Assembly*, 1835, p. 33.
[19] *Minutes of the General Assembly*, 1836. Each party set forth their views which were printed in the Minutes for 1836.

merous writers, and will therefore be but briefly sketched here.[20]

During the years in which the great Congregational stream was flowing westward into Presbyterianism, New England Calvinism was undergoing what seemed to the stiff-backed Presbyterian, a radical and dangerous modification. Indeed this modification had been in process for many years and what was known as Hopkinsianism, the school of thought farthest removed from strict Calvinism, was widely accepted. Timothy Dwight, the President of Yale College from 1795 to 1817, was a New Divinity man, and the numerous young Yale graduates coming into the West during those years were thoroughly imbued with his system of Divinity.

The bitter controversy with Unitarianism in the early part of the nineteenth century had served to emphasize New England orthodoxy, and gave country-wide distinction to such defenders as Lyman Beecher, more or less obscuring the fact that many of the so-called defenders of orthodoxy were themselves far from traditional Calvinism. The new revivalism which swept through New England and New York in the early years of the nineteenth century was the result of the New Divinity teaching, with its larger emphasis upon human responsibility. There was also much opposition to the "New Measures" fathered by Charles G. Finney and his associates, in the New York revivals. Thus there came to be a feeling among the full-fledged Presbyterians that the New England stream was tainted with heresy.[21]

[20] See accounts by Gillett *op. cit.*, II, Chap. XL, XLI, and XLII; Thompson, R. E., *A History of the Presbyterian Church in the United States* (New York, 1895), Chap. X and XI; Croker, Z., *The Catastrophe of the Presbyterian Church in 1837* (New Haven, 1838); Brown, I. V., *A Historical Vindication of the Abrogation of the Plan of Union* (Philadelphia, 1855); Baird, S. J., *A History of the New School* (Philadelphia, 1868); Woods, H., *The History of Presbyterian Controversy* (Louisville, 1843); Stansbury, A. J., *Trial of the Rev. Albert Barnes before the Synod of Philadelphia* in Session at York, October, 1835, etc. (New York, 1836); Junkin, George, *The Vindication, Containing A History of the Trial of the Rev. Albert Barnes,* etc. (Philadelphia, 1836). [21] Gillett, *op. cit.*, II, pp. 457-459.

This general feeling of suspicion was crystallized between 1828 and 1830; first by a sermon preached in New Haven in 1828 by Nathaniel W. Taylor, professor of didactic theology in the Theological Seminary, giving expression to views that even Hopkinsians repudiated, and second, by the open acceptance of these views by Albert Barnes, a graduate of Princeton and at the time the pastor of the strong Presbyterian Church at Morristown, New Jersey. The calling of Barnes to the mother church of the denomination in Philadelphia, 1831, gave a national significance[22] to the charges of heresy which were lodged against him, by conservative members of the Presbytery of Philadelphia, led by Ashbel Green. From this time on for six years Barnes was the storm center in the Presbyterian church. Year by year his case, in one form or another, was brought before the General Assembly, and in 1835 a new charge of heresy was lodged against him by Dr. George Junkin, president of Lafayette College and a rigid Calvinist. Eventually Barnes was vindicated by the General Assembly of 1836, and his protest and appeal was sustained.[23]

The Barnes case was the signal for other heresy charges in other parts of the church. In 1833 two of the young professors of Illinois College, and the president, Edward Beecher, the son of Lyman Beecher, were arraigned before the Presbytery of Illinois for preaching the New Haven doctrines. A trial resulted in their acquittal by a large majority, and though their accuser appealed to the Synod, the case was not pushed further.[24] Of larger interest, from

[22] Thompson, R. E., *A History of the Presbyterian Churches in the United States*, p. 107.

[23] The General Assemblies from 1831 to 1835 inclusive had New School majorities; the Assembly of 1835 had an Old School majority; but again in 1836 the New School was in control.

[24] Rammelkamp, Charles H., *Illinois College: A Centennial History, 1829-1929* (Yale University Press, 1928), Chap. VI, "Fundamentalism and Modernism in the Early Days." The charges were brought by William J. Frazer, who proved to be a very unscrupulous man and had a checkered career in the ministry. The other men accused beside Beecher were William Kirby and J. M. Sturtevant.

the standpoint of the West, were the heresy-hunting activities of Joshua L. Wilson of Cincinnati. In 1831 Wilson
had started a paper called *The Standard* in Cincinnati, as
an Old School organ, and although he was not its editor
he controlled its editorial policy, as a member of its editorial board. The paper received the approval of numerous neighboring ministers of Old School leanings, one of
whom stated in a letter to Wilson: "I thank God that
you have the moral firmness to raise a *Standard* of truth,"
for "with the exception of the *Standard*, it would appear
that the tongues and pens of the Old School are para-
lyzed."[25] It was through the columns of this paper that
Wilson now began to defend the faith by calling attention
to any heretical tendencies on the part of his fellow ministers.

The first instance of this sort was in relation to Rev.
Asa Mahan,[26] who had come from the Presbytery of Rochester to the pastorate of the sixth Presbyterian Church of
Cincinnati, in 1831. Wilson accused Mahan of stating
that he had never adopted the Confession of Faith. A
committee of the Presbytery was appointed to conduct an
investigation of the charges, and meanwhile *The Standard*
continued to publish further evidence against Mahan.
Charges were now brought against Wilson by two of Mahan's lay supporters for "unchristian conduct," and in September, 1832 there were three cases against Wilson before
the Presbytery.[27] His appeal to the Synod led to such a
parliamentary tangle that all parties were willing to accept
the "advice and injunction" issued by the Synod.

Of much greater significance, however, were the heresy
charges lodged by Joshua L. Wilson against Lyman
Beecher. Beecher had come to the presidency of Lane

[25] Wilson Papers in the Durrett Collection. J. L. Montgomery to Joshua
L. Wilson, October 25, 1832.
[26] Mahan, Asa, *Autobiography, Intellectual, Moral and Spiritual* (London,
1882). See article on Asa Mahan, *Dictionary of American Biography*, by E.
D. Eaton, XII, pp. 208-209. Mahan sympathized with the Lane students in
their revolt and eventually became the first President of Oberlin.
[27] Hightower, *op. cit.*, pp. 177-181.

Theological Seminary through the influence of Arthur Tappan, who had agreed to give a substantial endowment to the new institution on condition that Beecher accept the presidency. Wilson, as a trustee and a member of the committee to select a faculty, urged Beecher's acceptance.[28] But between the election of Beecher and his arrival in Cincinnati to take up his duties, Wilson had become convinced that Beecher was not theologically sound, and when Beecher arrived in November, 1832 the controversy began.[29]

Wilson was undoubtedly sincere in feeling that upon his shoulders largely rested the responsibility of freeing Presbyterianism from the devastations of "error." At the first meeting of the Cincinnati Presbytery after Beecher's arrival (in January, 1833), Wilson introduced a resolution calling for a committee to investigate reports of Beecher's unsoundness. This the Presbytery refused to do, later voting down another motion requesting that the Presbytery appoint a committee to investigate Beecher's printed sermons. These expedients having failed, Wilson entered formal charges against Beecher in 1834. The trial before the Presbytery which followed resulted in Beecher's acquittal, whereupon Wilson appealed to the Synod. This appeal resulted in the Synod's admonishing Beecher "to be more guarded in the future." But this mild treatment did not accord with Wilson's stern idea as to how "heresy" was to be dealt with, and he appealed to the General Assembly. When the General Assembly of 1836 convened, however, it was found that there was a New School majority and Wilson was persuaded to withdraw his appeal.[30]

[28] For the whole story of the relationship of Wilson and Beecher see Hightower, op. cit., pp. 181-195.

[29] As has been noticed, Wilson had at first urged the union of the missionary work in the West, and the coöperation of the Old and New School parties in the establishment of Lane. By 1832 he had changed his views and resigned from the Lane Board of Trustees. Hightower, R. L., "Joshua L. Wilson, Frontier Controversialist," in *Church History* (December, 1934), pp. 300-316. This is a summary of Mr. Hightower's Ph.D. Thesis already noted under the same title.

[30] Gillett, op. cit., II, p. 465, note, thus explains Wilson's willingness to

It has generally been the contention of Presbyterian writers on this period that slavery had little part in the controversy which finally divided the church. That slavery did not appear in the debates in the General Assemblies of 1837 and 1838 as a primary issue is undoubtedly true, but that in the minds of many it was a determining factor, I think can now be established.[31]

There was widespread anti-slavery sentiment throughout the United States from the beginning of the Revolution to about 1830, which was even more manifest in certain sections of the South than in the North. In 1826 there were 101 anti-slavery societies in the United States, and of these less than one-fourth were in the Northern states: there were forty-one in North Carolina, twenty-three in Tennessee, six in Kentucky, and numerous others scattered through the South.[32] In Tennessee Quakers and Presbyterians were the most active. This first anti-slavery movement was due to several factors, among them the influence of the Revolutionary philosophy which declared that among the inalienable rights of man is that to life, liberty and the pursuit of happiness. All the great Revolutionary leaders in the new nation were anti-slavery in sentiment, among them Washington, Adams, Jefferson, Franklin, Madison, Henry and Mason. During this period in which anti-slavery opinion was commonly held throughout the nation the American churches were likewise anti-slavery, and the Baptists, Meth-

---

withdraw his appeal: "The real fact was, some rogue on the boat in the Ohio River stole the doctor's coat, money, and papers in the case of Dr. Beecher; and he was glad of any excuse for dropping the matter." Wilson's explanation was that on arriving at the Assembly he was besought by his own friends to drop the prosecution. "They considered it inexpedient to incur the odium of attacking Dr. Beecher, and they flattered themselves, from things he had said and done, that he would come out right at last."

[31] The recent publication of the *Letters of Theodore Dwight Weld, Angelina Grimké Weld and Sara Grimké, 1822-1844,* edited by Gilbert H. Barnes and Dwight L. Dumond, 2 Vols. (New York, 1934), throws new light on the slavery question as an issue in the Presbyterian church in the thirties. See also Barnes, Gilbert H., *The Anti-Slavery Impulse* (New York, 1933).

[32] Gillett, *op. cit.,* II, p. 523; Martin, A. E., "Anti-slavery Societies in Tennessee," *Tennessee Historical Magazine* (December, 1915), pp. 261-280.

odists and Presbyterians all passed strong anti-slavery legislation.

The resolutions on slavery passed by the General Assembly of 1818 take the strongest anti-slavery position of any Presbyterian declaration. They state:

We consider the voluntary enslaving of one part of the human race by another, as a gross violation of the most sacred rights of human nature; as utterly inconsistent with the law of God, which requires us to love our neighbors as ourselves; and as totally irreconcilable with the spirit and principles of the Gospel of Christ. . . . It is manifestly the duty of all Christians who enjoy the light of the present day, when the inconsistency of slavery both with the dictates of humanity and religion, has been demonstrated, and is generally seen and acknowledged, to use their honest, earnest, and unwearied endeavors to correct the errors of former times, and as speedily as possible to efface this blot on our holy religion, and to obtain the complete abolition of slavery throughout christendom, and if possible throughout the world.[33]

Following these resolutions the General Assembly recommended support of the American Colonization Society;[34] urged all their people to facilitate and encourage the instruction of their negroes in religious principles; and enjoined all church sessions and presbyteries to discountenance and prevent all forms of cruelty, the separation of families, and the buying and selling of slaves. This action becomes all the more significant when it is realized that it was adopted unanimously by the General Assembly.[35]

By about 1830 the first phase of anti-slavery agitation in the United States came to an end, and a new and more

---

[33] *Minutes of the General Assembly,* 1818, p. 28.

[34] "The American Society for the Colonization of the Free People of Color of the United States" was formed in 1816 for the purpose of carrying free negroes out of the country and of colonizing them in Africa. It was generally thought at this time that the influence of colonization would be in the direction of the ultimate abolition of the institution of slavery. The American churches supported it with almost complete unanimity to about 1830. This Society eventually absorbed most of the public interest in the negro, which was one of the causes for the dying out of the early anti-slavery societies. Barnes, *Anti-Slavery Impulse,* pp. 27-28.

[35] *Minutes of the General Assembly,* 1818, p. 29.

aggressive movement was about to begin. Gradually the anti-slavery sentiment in the churches became quiescent and their united voice was no longer heard in protest. The first anti-slavery movement had been largely negative. To most of its leaders the question of the abolition of slavery was a theory to be held rather than a fact to be accomplished. Thus anti-slavery societies could flourish in the South and slave owners themselves could and did belong to these organizations, and slave-owning church members were found willing to vote for resolutions calling for the eventual abolition of slavery.[36]

The disappearance of this phase of the anti-slavery movement came about as the result of two principal factors: the first was the agricultural revolution which took place in the South between 1790 and 1830; the second, the rise of a new and aggressive anti-slavery movement, especially in New England and in those sections farther west which had been settled by New England people. The invention of new spinning and weaving machinery created an increased demand for cotton, and the invention of the cotton gin in 1792 made it possible for the South to supply this increased demand. Thus cotton culture grew to be the greatest single economic factor in the South, and the export of cotton the most important factor in the trade of the nation. This made slave labor increasingly important and widely extended the area of cotton production.

The new anti-slavery propaganda which arose after 1830 demanded the immediate and uncompensated emancipation of the slaves. This new gospel of abolitionism was very different from the old negative anti-slavery doctrine. Its early leaders, William Lloyd Garrison and Wendell Phillips and others of their type, carried on their propaganda most ruthlessly, at least as far as the feelings of the slave holders were concerned, which soon aroused their resentment and eventually their bitter hostility. Thus at the very time the institution of slavery was becoming increasingly

[36] For a fuller discussion of this position see Sweet, W. W., *Story of Religions in America* (New York, 1930), pp. 412-427.

important to the economic life of the South this bold and aggressive abolition movement began in the North. Such is the background for the conflict over slavery which soon arose in every one of the great democratic churches, whose members were to be found in both North and South. Let us now consider how this situation affected the great Presbyterian church.

Among the most important of the leaders in the inauguration of the new anti-slavery movement were certain Presbyterian laymen, chief among them being Lewis and Arthur Tappan, wealthy merchants of New York. The Tappans and those associated with them, conceived of the American Anti-Slavery Movement as a part of the great benevolent system, which they had helped to inaugurate, consisting of Sunday-School, Education, Mission, Temperance, Tract, Bible and other societies, whose work was to be carried on in the interest of inter-denominational benevolence, but "was actually controlled through a series of interlocking directorates" made up of a small number of Presbyterian and Congregational ministers and laymen. At first they were associated with William Lloyd Garrison and his cohorts in the formation of the American Anti-Slavery Society in 1833, but they soon found themselves out of harmony with Garrisonian methods, which had aroused bitter opposition, because of his "rancorous denunciations and brawling ferocious abuse." The Society itself was unpopular and its agents met with resistance and indignation. Throughout the East there was indifference to the demands of immediate emancipation while in the South anti-slavery propaganda was barred from the mails by the postal authorities. In the West, however, "there was in preparation" a new agency for agitation which was to give new hope to the cause of abolition. This new anti-slavery tool was to arise out of Lane Theological Seminary, and was to prove itself eventually the most powerful of all the anti-slavery agencies.[37]

[37] These facts in regard to the New York philanthropists, the formation of the American Anti-Slavery Society and its early years of activity are set

When Lane Theological Seminary was opened in 1832, a large proportion of its students were recruited from central and western New York, many of whom were the converts of Charles G. Finney. Among these students was Theodore Dwight Weld, a graduate of Oneida Institute, later Hamilton College, a remarkable personality, and a man of extraordinary ability. Weld was a convert of Finney's, and soon gained such leadership among the Lane students that as Lyman Beecher, the president of the Seminary, stated, "he took the lead of the whole institution." In fact, "they thought he was a God."[38] Weld had promised Lewis Tappan to discuss the abolition of slavery among the students. Most of the students regarded abolition "as the climax of absurdity, fanaticism and blood," and there were at first no abolitionists among them except Weld and one or two others whom Weld had quietly converted to the cause. Little by little this group of converts was enlarged by the quiet work of Weld and by those whom he had influenced, and finally, they asked and received permission from President Beecher to hold a public debate on the question. The actual outcome was a protracted meeting which lasted for eighteen nights and which resulted eventually in bringing practically the entire student body of nearly a hundred, to the acceptance of abolition views.[39]

Nor were the new abolition converts content merely to accept abolition as a theory, but immediately they began to work at it, and set out to elevate the blacks in Cincinnati by establishing reading rooms, libraries and schools for them. As a result there was much mingling of the students with the Cincinnati colored population. Meanwhile the

forth in the light of newly discovered documents noted above, in Barnes, *Anti-Slavery Impulse*, Chap. I to V. See also the Introduction to the *Weld Grimké Letter*, I, pp. 5-9.

[38] *Autobiography and Correspondence of Lyman Beecher*, Edited by Charles Beecher, 2 Vols. (New York, 1865), II, pp. 326, 321. Weld to Angelina Grimké, *Weld Grimké Letters*, II, pp. 592-293: "They strangely and stupidly idolized me and it used to distress me to see how blind they were to my defects and how implicitly they yielded themselves to my sway in all confidence and love."

[39] Barnes, *Anti-Slavery Impulse*, Chap. VI, "The Lane Debate," pp. 64-72.

Lane debate and the results from it reverberated throughout the nation. The conversion of some of the southern students[40] to the cause aroused hopes among the eastern abolitionists that the conversion of the South to abolitionism had actually begun. The action of the students aroused bitter antagonism in Cincinnati, for the growing negro population of the city had already caused alarm, and there was little disposition to love the negro, and ugly rumors were afloat that social amalgamation between negroes and Lane students was under way.

Such was the situation when the summer of 1834 arrived and President Beecher went east to attend the annual meetings of the Benevolent Societies. He found that the Lane debates had stirred the entire student world, and similar discussions were under way in all the colleges. His absence from Cincinnati soon brought things to a crisis at the Seminary, for the Trustees now took a hand in the situation. Resolutions were passed abolishing the student's antislavery society and all future discussions were to be conducted under censorship of the board, which asserted their power of dismissal. As might have been expected, a storm now broke which soon caused the withdrawal of a large share of the Lane students, nor was Beecher, on his return, able to cajole them into submission and return. Eventually a majority of the Lane rebels gathered at Oberlin[41] for the spring term of 1835, bringing with them Asa Mahan, the only Lane Trustee who had stood with the students, and who now became the first president of the new college.[42] Such was the new abolition tool which was being forged in

[40] Among the southern students who became abolitionists as a result of the Lane debate were Augustus Wattles, Marius Robinson and James Thome.

[41] *Weld Grimké Letters,* I, *op. cit.,* Introduction, pp. IX-X, XVII.

[42] This extraordinary story has been well told in Barnes, *Anti-Slavery Impulse,* pp. 72-77. The revolt left Lane in the following situation as far as the student body was concerned: of the forty students in the theological department the year previous but two remained; in the literary department, of the sixty students but five remained and as a result this department was discontinued. Of the sixteen new students who arrived during the course of the rebellion half of them left the Seminary after talking with the rebels. Barnes, *Anti-Slavery Impulse,* p. 230, note 19.

the West, made up, as Lyman Beecher described it, of "He-Goat men who think they do God a service by butting everything in the line of their march which does not fall or get out of their way."[43]

And this tool was soon to be used in the most effective anti-slavery propaganda yet attempted. Most of these young men were soon engaged in zealous anti-slavery activity, using the Finney revival methods in winning converts to the cause of immediatism, though the immediatism they preached was "an immediatism of repentance from sin," and making "the sin of slavery the standard to which the abolitionist is to rally." In their widely extended propaganda throughout central and western New York, western Pennsylvania and Ohio, they made the "anti-slavery cause identical with religion" and called upon men and women to join in the pious task of purging the land of the sin of slavery.[44]

To get the significance of these facts as far as Presbyterianism is concerned it must be remembered that this movement was largely carried on within Presbyterianism itself. Many of the meetings had been held in Presbyterian churches, and the New School Presbyterians gave to the cause its principal support. In June, 1835, Weld was in Pittsburgh during the session of the General Assembly. His purpose in attending, as stated in a letter to Elizur Wright, was "to ascertain by intercourse with ministers, elders and others, assembled here from every state in the Union, the exact position of the slavery question, recent shifts of position, progress of abolitionism, etc." He also wished to organize two or three abolition meetings and to secure the open advocacy of some of the men of standing in the church. After two weeks of active mingling with the delegates during which he had personal conferences with commissioners from every state represented in the As-

---

[43] *Autobiography and Correspondence of Lyman Beecher*, II, p. 345.
[44] *Weld Grimké Letters*, I, Introduction, p. 10; the work of Weld and the other Lane "rebel" agents is fully described in Barnes, *Anti-Slavery Impulse*, pp. 79-87.

sembly he reported that forty-eight commissioners were "with us in sentiment on the subject of slavery, of whom twenty-seven are ministers and six of these are from the slave states."[45]

A letter of the Presbytery of Chillicothe to the Presbytery of Cincinnati, dated December 24, 1835, condemns the "buying and selling of or holding slaves for the sake of gain" as a "heinous sin," and declares the reason for the lack of success of the church in recent years is because slavery has been permitted to exist within it.[46] It is also of interest to note that each of the four synods which in 1837 were exscinded, had within two years passed strong resolutions condemning slavery and were well known in the church as anti-slavery centers.[47]

In the General Assembly of 1836 twelve different memorials were presented asking that body to take action against slavery.[48] After a prolonged debate it was decided that due to the shortness of the time and the urgency of the business of the Assembly it was "impossible to deliberate and decide judiciously on the subject of slavery in its relation to the Church"; therefore it was resolved to postpone the whole subject indefinitely.

The response to the anti-slavery agitation was immediate. An article in the *Biblical Repository* for April, 1836, thus describes what had taken place:

How altered is the present state of our country! Instead of lamentations and acknowledgements, we hear from the South the strongest language of justification. . . . What has produced this lamentable change? No doubt, many circumstances have combined in its production. We think, however, that all impartial observers must acknowledge that by far the most prominent cause is the conduct of the abolitionists.

[45] *Weld Grimké Letters,* I, p. 224.
[46] Wilson Papers in the Durrett Collection.
[47] The Synod of Genesee adopted such resolutions in October, 1835; similar resolutions were adopted by the Synods of Utica, Geneva and Western Reserve. See Croker, *op. cit.,* pp. 65-66.
[48] *Minutes of the General Assembly,* 1836, p. 273.

Joshua L. Wilson thus tersely puts the situation:

Hint at the absurdity of a republican and more particularly of a Christian holding his fellow-men in bondage and up steps the Presbyterian preacher with the Declaration of Independence in one hand, and the Bible in the other to prove that negroes cannot take care of themselves and must have masters.[49]

Thus by 1836 there had come to be distinct anti-slavery and pro-slavery wings in the Presbyterian church, though there was also a large body of moderates in both North and South, many of whom were anti-slavery in theory and supporters of the American Colonization Society. Joshua L. Wilson of Cincinnati and R. J. Breckenridge[49a] of Kentucky were western representatives of this type of opinion. Both men were opposed to "New Schoolism" and both were anxious to rid the church of those influences which made for looseness in doctrine and polity.

With all of these exciting controversial matters before the church which have been described: the creeping in of loose discipline and the tearing down of strict Presbyterial polity, as the result of the working of the Plan of Union; the growing missionary rivalry between societies controlled by the Presbyterian church and the great voluntary societies; the doctrinal controversies and the numerous exciting heresy trials; and last of all the cleavage arising as a result of the rabid anti-slavery propaganda largely fostered by the New School Presbyterians; in the light of these facts, the bisecting of the church by the General Assembly of 1837 becomes fully understandable.

Throughout the Presbyterian church, as the thirties wore on, there came to be more and more talk of the possibility of division. Some felt that the only solution was for the church to divide. "But a little while ago," wrote the editor of *The Western Presbyterian Herald*, in June, 1836,

[49] Letter to John Burtt. Published in *The Standard*, Cincinnati, Ohio, May 23, 1834.

[49a] For the position of R. J. Breckenridge on the slavery question see Moore, E. A., *Robert J. Breckenridge and the Slavery Aspect of the Presbyterian Schism of 1837*. ["Church History," Vol. IV, No. 4, Dec., 1935, pp. 282-294.]

"we would have heard of division almost with horror; now it is the subject of conversation in almost every circle."[50] "Slavery is a vast evil, and a tremendous sin," wrote a correspondent to Joshua L. Wilson in 1835, "and is not God preparing to visit it [the church] with His judgments? Look! The Northern Abolitionists and the Southern Spirits of Violence! Are they not together hastening on a crisis, the most tremendous? . . . Separation! Separation!! This fearful note is already being sounded by the *Northern Section of the Church*."[51] In April, 1836, the Charleston Union Presbytery instructed their commissioners to the General Assembly that in case any attempt be made to discuss the question of slavery they were expected to meet it at the threshold, and should they fail of accomplishing their object in forestalling such discussion, they would be expected to withdraw from the Assembly "with becoming dignity . . . not willing to be associated with a body of men who denounce the ministers and members of southern churches as pirates and man stealers, or coöperate with those that thus denounce them."[52]

The victory of the New School party in defeating the transfer of the Western Missionary Society of Pittsburgh to the General Assembly in 1836 was the signal for immediate action on the part of the Old School party,[53] and they began at once to take steps for the division of the church. Their first move was to win over the moderates to their side. In the East the heart and center of this party was the Princeton Theological Seminary faculty. The bringing of Princeton to the Old School side was greatly furthered by the establishment of Union Theological Seminary in New York by the New School party in 1836. Their next step was the calling of an Old School convention to meet in

[50] *Western Presbyterian Herald* (Louisville, Ky.), June 16, 1836.
[51] Wilson Papers in the Durrett Collection. Joseph E. Harrison to Joshua L. Wilson, Boone, Kentucky, November 4, 1835.
[52] *Western Presbyterian Herald* (Louisville, Ky.), October 13, 1836.
[53] The leaders of the Old School party had evidently decided upon division in some form before the members of the Assembly of 1836 dispersed. Gillett, *op. cit.*, II, p. 496, Note.

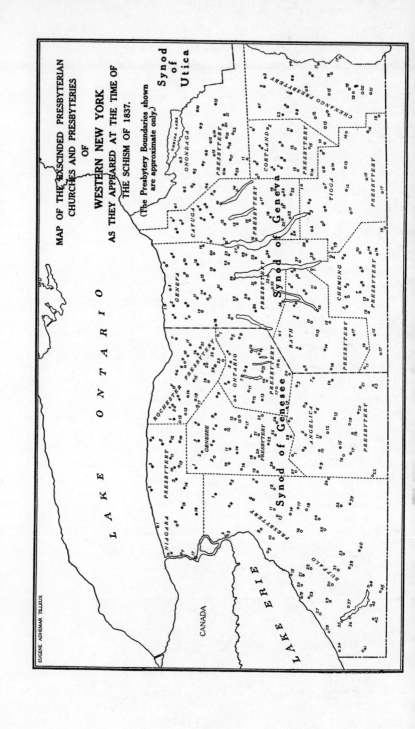

MAP OF THE EXSCINDED PRESBYTERIAN
CHURCHES AND PRESBYTERIES
OF
WESTERN NEW YORK
AS THEY APPEARED AT THE TIME OF
THE SCHISM OF 1837.

(The Presbytery Boundaries shown
are approximate only.)

Synod
of
Utica

Synod of Geneva

Synod of Genesee

EUGENE ADHEMAR TILLEUX

Philadelphia a week preceding the opening of the General Assembly, while throughout the year there had been continuous propaganda urging the presbyteries to send Old School commissioners to the General Assembly.[54]

The purpose of the Old School convention was to enable them to formulate "effectual measures for putting an end to the contentions which for years had agitated the church."[55] It was finally decided to prepare a memorial to the Assembly setting forth the complaints of their party, and demanding the abrogation of the Plan of Union; the discountenancing of the several voluntary societies; and the dissolution or exclusion of every church, presbytery, or synod nominally connected with the Assembly which was not organized on strict Presbyterian principles.

When the General Assembly of 1837 convened in the Central Presbyterian Church of Philadelphia on May 18, it was soon found that the Old School party was in the majority, and their candidate for moderator was elected by 137 votes to 106. The vital questions of the Old School memorial came up on May 22, and after an exceedingly able debate the first step was taken in the abrogation of the Plan of Union. Next came a declaration exscinding the Synod of the Western Reserve from the church, to be followed immediately by similar resolutions exscinding the Synods of Utica, Geneva and Genesee. Five other synods

[54] "The Commissioners of a General Assembly are usually elected by the Presbyteries in rotation" and "not on account of views held." It is therefore only quasi-representative. "From this method of selection it also results that the personnel is almost entirely changed from year to year." This helps explain the changing complexion of the General Assemblies throughout the thirties. See the review of Vander Velde, *The Presbyterian Churches and the Federal Union, 1861-1869,* by A. A. Hays, *Church History,* II, No. I (March, 1933), p. 63. See documents, Chap. XIX.

[55] No means had been spared to promote the objects of the convention. A confidential committee of correspondence had been appointed to get in touch with ministers and elders known to be in sympathy with them, to secure their help in seeing that the right kind of commissioners were appointed to the General Assembly. A "secret circular" had been sent out to those supposed to have been dissatisfied with the proceedings of the General Assembly of 1836. When the convention met there was much difference of opinion as to what was to be done, as it was not yet known which party would have the majority. Gillett, *op. cit.,* II, pp. 495-499.

were directed "to take order" of certain of their presbyteries which were charged with disorder in doctrine and practice, while provision was made for ministers and churches within the bounds of these several synods which were simon-pure Presbyterian in every respect, to seek membership in those presbyteries most convenient.[56] This having been accomplished, the Assembly then proceeded to separate the Church from the voluntary and interdenominational societies and adopted the Western Missionary Society as the Assembly's Foreign Mission Board, while it declared their own Boards of Education and Domestic Missions to be their only agents in those respective fields of endeavor.

In the debates over the issues before the General Assembly of 1837, the question of slavery did not enter. What were the reasons for its exclusion? In the Old School convention which had preceded the General Assembly it had occupied considerable attention. In that convention Robert J. Breckenridge, evidently replying to a suggestion that he and his followers aid in repudiating the Presbyterian stand against slavery said:

I stand on the decisions of the General Assembly while it was yet the synod of New York and Philadelphia,—and the decision of the same body reiterated again and again from 1785 to 1818. I cannot unsay what our fathers said. We must not be asked to do it. We cannot eat those words. Let not our brethren come to us in time of trouble and offer to assist us, only on the condition of our changing. We are discussing the great principles which concern salvation and the integrity of the Presbyterian Church and must not be asked to change old Presbyterian principles on the subject of slavery. It is ruinous to the souls of men and hazarding the truth to make such demands, as the price of laboring together with us.[57]

When Joshua L. Wilson was asked if he were not going to bring up the slavery issue in the convention, he replied, "I believe that I shall let the Southern brethren manage their

---

[56] Thompson, *op. cit.*, p. 117.

[57] Speech delivered by Robert J. Breckenridge before the convention in Philadelphia, May 11, 1837. *Western Presbyterian Herald* (June 1, 1837).

own concerns in their own way, they will probably take care of them the best.''[58]   In a speech before the convention Wilson also had stated:

I can hardly believe that anybody in the Convention has struggled more than I have . . . or that anybody desires to be separated from those who are unsound more than I do.[59]

If there had been an attempt to introduce into the memorial the slavery views of such Old School men as Breckenridge, Wilson and David Rice it would have split the Assembly apart and might very probably have led to the withdrawal of a majority of the Southern commissioners and the formation of a Southern Assembly.   In that case the Northern Old School party would have been left in a hopeless minority and would have been compelled to withdraw and organize by themselves.   To secure coöperation among Old School men, North and South, it was necessary to leave the slavery issue entirely alone.   Because slavery did not appear as an issue on the floor of the Assembly of 1837 it has generally been maintained from that day till this that the question of slavery had nothing to do with the division of the church.   An interesting example of the determination to keep out slavery as an issue is the following resolution adopted by the Synod of North Carolina in September, 1837:

. . . Resolved, that this Synod regards the attempt to give Abolition a principal influence in bringing about that result [exscinding of the synods] as making a false issue; & as it was not alluded to in the debate, they believe it had little or no influence in bringing about the decision, but they believe the question was honestly debated & decided on its merits.[60]

[58] Foote, W. H., *Sketches of Virginia,* Second Series (Philadelphia, 1855), p. 520.   Also quoted in Gillett, *op. cit.,* II, p. 526.
[59] *Western Presbyterian Herald* (Louisville, Ky.), June 1, 1837.
[60] Chap. XIX, Extracts from the *Minutes of the Synod of North Carolina* (September, 1837).   See Gillett, *op. cit.,* II, pp. 526-527.   A speech of Rev. W. S. Plumer before the Convention contained the following:
"As to the General Assembly legislating on the subject of the morality of slavery as an institution the gentleman from South Carolina [Mr. Smith] has expressed views which so far as I am informed are acceptable to the South, when he said that he wished the subject of slavery to remain un-

This precipitate action took the New School party completely by surprise, while many among the Old School were indignant at the high-handed manner in which the church had been divided. In August, 1837, the New School body held a convention at Auburn, New York, where it was determined to stand by the Plan of Union, and to make an attempt, at the next General Assembly, to regain their place in the church. They also drew up a document maintaining their doctrinal soundness and declared the exscinding acts unconstitutional. The very violence of the majority party tended to keep the New School party together, and strengthened their determination to regain their place in the church.

Their plan to regain their standing in the church however was completely unsuccessful. When the General Assembly of 1838 assembled in the Seventh Presbyterian Church of Philadelphia, commissioners were present from all the presbyteries of the exscinded synods, but all attempts to gain recognition were in vain. The moderator refused to "know" anyone from the exscinded synods and declared their every attempt to gain the floor as out of order. Nothing was now left for the New School commissioners to do but to withdraw, which they proceeded to do, after having elected a moderator and clerks, while standing in the aisles of the church, it being announced in a loud voice at the doors and in the body of the Assembly that the Assembly had adjourned to the First Presbyterian Church.[61]

The great Presbyterian church, after prolonged and bitter controversies, controversies which found their cause primarily in the exigencies and problems which arose as the church expanded westward, was now split in twain. After the organization of the New School body into a church, other synods and presbyteries outside the exscinded synods

touched. All we ask is that the Supreme Judicatory do nothing in the way of legislation on this subject. We wish them not to touch it in any way of legislation."

Ibid., June 1, 1837.

[61] A most interesting account o. these happenings may be found in Gillett, *op. cit.*, II, pp. 528-531; see also Chap. XXXV, Baird, *History of the New School*.

joined them, so that eventually the New School represented about four-ninths of the ministry and membership of the old church.   In many instances synods, presbyteries and churches were divided.   All over the country, in every synod and presbytery and in many church sessions, resolutions were adopted either supporting or condemning the action of the General Assembly.   The last chapter of this volume furnishes numerous examples of such action.

PART II

DOCUMENTS

ILLUSTRATING THE WORK OF PRESBYTERIANS
ON THE FRONTIER

CHAPTER VI

EXTRACTS FROM THE MINUTES OF THE
TRANSYLVANIA PRESBYTERY, 1786-1837

INTRODUCTION

[The Minutes of the Transylvania Presbytery constitute the most important single document for the history of early western Presbyterianism. At its organization in 1786 it embraced the whole of Kentucky and the settlements on the Cumberland, and was one of the original sixteen presbyteries when the General Assembly was formed in 1789. It was within the bounds of this presbytery that the Great Revival in the West had its most conspicuous manifestations and it was here also that the principal western schisms occurred. The document also serves to illustrate the methods by which the Presbyterians followed moving populations, as well as the process by which ministerial standards, moral, educational and doctrinal, were maintained.

The original manuscript of the Minutes of the Transylvania Presbytery is in the possession of Dr. J. Q. S. McDowell, Danville, Kentucky, the stated clerk of the Synod of Kentucky. The first seven manuscript volumes contain the Minutes to 1842. The typed manuscript copy from which the extracts here printed was taken was made by Miss Elizabeth Rutledge of Louisville from a certified longhand copy of the Minutes in the possession of the Louisville Theological Seminary. The full typed manuscript contains more than 750 pages.

In making the extracts here printed routine matters have been omitted, as far as possible, and only those parts have been selected for publication which seemed to have the greatest historical significance.]

Tuesday, Oct. 17th, 1786.

The Rev. David Rice, Adam Rankin, Andrew McClure, & James Crawford, met in the Court House at Danville, on the day & year above written, by an appointment of the Synod of New York & Philadelphia, which appointment Mr. Rice read from an extract of the proceedings of the

Synod, dated May 17th, 1786, the substance of which is as follows.   The Synod divided Abingdon Presbytery into two presbyteries,[1] the one by the name of the presbytery of Abingdon, the other by the name of the presbytery of Transylvania, comprehending the district of Kentucky & the settlements upon Cumberland River, consisting of the Rev. David Rice, Thomas Craighead, Adam Rankin, Andrew McClure, James Crawford & appointed the presbytery of Transylvania to meet at Danville in the district of Kentucke on the third Tuesday of October, 1786.

Ubi post preces sederunt qui supra except the Rev. Thos. Craighead.   Ruling Elders present, Messrs. Richard Steel, David Gray, John Bovel, Joseph Reid.   MR. ANDREW McCLURE, clerk.

Mr. Terah Tamplin, lately ordained agreeable to an appointment of Hanover Presby., & residing in the district of Kentucky prior to the appointment of Synod for forming the presb. of Transylvania, is received as a member & takes his seat.   Mr. Joseph Reid, a ruling Elder, takes his seat.

Presb. agree to receive verbal supplications, as the churches under their care are not acquainted with the manner of presenting them.

A verbal supplication from the inhabitants of Toner is presented by Mr. Rankin.

Adjourned till ten o'clock tomorrow morning.   Concluded with prayer.

Wednesday morning, ten o'clock, met according to adjournment.   Ubi post preces sederunt qui supra Jeremiah Frame, a ruling Elder, takes his seat.

Ordered, That the proceedings of the Synod of New York & Philadelphia dated May 17th, 1786, be read.

Presb. took under consideration the Synod's plan for constituting a General Assembly[2] & arranging four Synods

[1] For the functions of a presbytery see *The Form of Government and Forms of Process of the Presbyterian Church in the United States of America as Amended and ratified by the General Assembly in 1797.*   Book I, "Of Government," Chap. X, "Of the Presbytery" (see numerous later editions).

[2] In 1786 the Synod of New York and Philadelphia took into serious consideration a plan for the erection of several new presbyteries, the division

under it; and as far as their information enables them to judge, do in the main approve of said plan.

The Synod having earnestly recommended to all the vacant congregations under their care to meet together every Lord's day at one or more places for the purpose of prayer & praises & the reading the holy Scriptures together with the works of such approved divines as they may be able to procure; & that the Elders[3] be the persons who shall pray & select the portions of Scripture & other books to be read by any proper persons whom they may appoint; the Presb. does approve and recommend the same to all the vacant churches under their care.

The Presb. having taken under consideration the Synod's resolution with respect to catechising vacant congregations do agree to comply with it as far as may be competent with their circumstances. And that the design of this resolution may be more fully answered it is agreed that catechists shall be appointed for the purpose of instructing the young & ignorant, but that no person shall be appointed to this office till he is first nominated by a pastor or minister of the gospel, examined & approved of by Presby; & that he shall not by virtue of this appointment attempt to expound the Scriptures, preach the gospel or dispense the sealing ordinances thereof.

Whereas the Synod declare that in consequence of their viewing with serious concern the decay of vital religion & the prevalence of immorality they appoint in the present year the third Thursday of August to be observed as a day of solemn fasting, humiliation & prayer by all the churches

of the old synod into four synods, and the government of the whole by a general assembly. The plan was not finally carried out until May, 1789.

The Synod of Virginia embraced the Presbytery of Redstone in western Pennsylvania, the Presbytery of Hanover in eastern Virginia, the Presbytery of Lexington in the Valley and west of Virginia, and the Presbytery of Transylvania including the district of Kentucky and the settlements along the Cumberland River.

[3] "Ruling elders are properly the representatives of the people chosen by them for the purpose of exercising government and discipline, in conjunction with pastors or ministers." *Constitution of the Presbyterian Church,* 1822.

under their care; & as the ministers of this district had not
notice of the appointment till the day was past, the Presb.
for the same reason appoint the fourth Thursday of March
next to be observed by all the churches under their care.

Adjourned till tomorrow morning, eight o'clock, to meet
at the Rev. David Rice's. Concluded with prayer.

Tuesday morning, eight o'clock, Presb. met according to
adjournment. Ubi post preces sederunt qui supra.

[Hereafter the routine record of the opening and closing of sessions will be omitted.]

Mr. Thomas Meek having offered as a candidate for the
gospel ministry & being examined as to the operation of
religion on his own heart, & the motives that influence him
to seek the sacred office, agree to postpone the consideration
of it until the next session; & assign him as part of trial this
question, What is the nature of a sound conversion & its
natural order; & also a lecture on the 15th Psalm.

The Presb. resolve to seek after & give proper encouragement to the members of our society scattered up & down
in small settlements; to assist in organizing & supplying
them as far as our circumstances will allow, & each member, before the next session shall supply four Sabbaths &
shall give account of his attention to this resolution.[4]

Mr. Tamplin is to supply the vacant churches in Jefferson & Nelson counties. Mr. Rice is to supply at New
Providence, Harbison's & Whitley's. Mr. McClure is to
supply one Sabbath on the Hanging Fork, one at Paint
Lick, one at Ewing's & one at Stoner. Mr. Crawford one
at Paint Lick, one on Kingston & one on the north fork
of Elkhorn.

Mr. Rankin is to supply Glen's Creek, Licking & the
north fork of Elkhorn.

Pres[b]. recommended that a competent number of Deacons be chosen in each church, whose office shall be to take

[4] This resolution to supply scattered congregations with preaching and
to assist them in organizing churches indicates the Presbyterian method of
expansion on the frontier where there were few bodies of members of that
church strong enough to call a regular pastor.

care of & see to the right arrangement of the temporalities of the church, such as collecting money for building and re-pairing churches; providing linens, cups, &c for the Lord's table; & directing the collection & payment of the minister's salary; & it is farther recommended that in the choice of Deacons a proper attention be paid to their Scripture character.

Ordered, That a particular account be taken annually of the state of each church & report made by persons appointed by their respective sessions; that any disorders taking place may be rectified before they become incurable.

Ordered, That the Moderator inform the Synod in writing that the presbytery approve the plan for a General Assembly & arranging four Synods under it.

Adjourned till the fourth Tuesday of April, to meet at Lexington church. . . .

DAVID RICE, Moderator.

Lexington Church, Tuesday, April 24th, 1787.

Presbytery met according to adjournment & was opened by a sermon delivered by the Rev. Andrew McClure from I John, 3, 13th. Ubi post preces sederunt the Rev. David Rice, Adam Rankin, Andrew McClure, Jas. Crawford & Terah Tamplin, Elders, James Camper, David Logan, John Frame, John McGee. Absent, Rev. Thos. Craighead. Mr. Rankin is chosen Moderator & Mr. McClure, Clerk.

Ordered, That supplications be presented.

A supplication from Paint Lick Church.

A supplication from Hopewell church.

A verbal supplication from the south fork of Licking by Nathan Sellers.

Mr. Tamplin fullfilled his appointments.

Mr. Crawford fulfilled his appointments in part and his reasons for not fulfilling the rest sustained.

Mr. McClure fulfilled his appointments.

Mr. Rankin fulfilled his appointments in part and his reasons for not fulfilling the rest sustained.

Mr. Rice fulfilled his appointments.

Mr. Rice fulfilled his appointment—that he should inform the Synod of this presbytery's approbation of the plan for constituting a General Assembly & for arranging four Synods under it.

Presb. Adjourned till ten o'clock tomorrow morning. . . .

Wednesday morning, ten o'clock, met according to adjournment. . . .

Ordered, That the minutes of yesterday be read.

Mr. Bryant Farguson, an Elder not before present, takes his seat. Mr. Rice is appointed to supply at Paint Lick, New Providence & Harbison's. Mr. Rankin is to supply two Sabbaths in Hopewell Church & Mr. Tamplin one. Mr. McClure is to supply one Sabbath at Paint Lick & one on Licking. Mr. Crawford is to supply two Sabbaths on the South fork of Licking.

Mr. Thomas Meek having read his answer to the question 'What is the nature of sound conversion & its natural order?' & a lecture on the 15th Psalm, Presb. sustains both as parts of trial, & appoint him as a subject of farther trial, to be delivered at the next session, a sermon on Luke 24th, 32d.

Mr. James Camper, being nominated by the Rev. David Rice for a catechist, was examined on divinity & approved of, & upon his declaring that he would not by virtue of this appointment attempt to explain the sacred Scriptures, preach the gospel or dispense the sealing ordinances thereof, is hereby appointed to the office of a catechist.

The consideration of Mr. Thomas Meek's first examination is deferred till the next session.

Adjourned till ten o'clock tomorrow morning. . . .

Thursday morning, ten o'clock. . . .

Resolved, That a convention meet at the Rev. David Rice's meetinghouse in the Fork of Dick's river on the last Tuesday of July next composed of Presbyterian ministers & one member from each church under their care; to which we invite as members of said convention the ministers of other denominations together with one member from each church under their care, for the purpose of consulting whether any effectual measures can be adopted which may tend to suppress open vice in the district.

Adjourned till the first Tuesday in October next to meet at the Fork meeting house. . . .

JAMES CRAWFORD, Stated Cl'k.

[Cane Run, Oct. 6, 1789.]

Mr. William Scott, an Elder, enters an appeal from Mount Pisgah session on account of being suspended from the communion of the church for inviting the Baptists frequently & permitting a Methodist to preach in his house.

[Cane Run, Oct. 7, 1789.]

Presbytery taking into serious consideration the reasons for Mr. William Scott's suspension from communion in sealing ordinances, judge them to be insufficient & agree that said William Scott be free from such suspension.

Mr. Rankin saw cause to appeal from the judgement of Pby., but Pby. is of opinion that an appeal in any such case would be irregular.

Mr. Camper's popular discourse being considered is sustained as a part of trial. Mr. James Camper is permitted as a probationer for the gospel ministry to preach under the direction of Mr. Rice while he continues in the study of divinity on trial.

Mr. Rankin & mr. Logan enter their dissent against the licensure of Mr. James Camper.

Pby. adjourned until 6 o'clock this evening, to Mr. Hagan's. . . .

Mr. Hagan's. Wednesday evening, October 7th. . . .

Ordered that Mr. Rice supply one Sabbath at Salem. That Mr. McClure & Mr. McConnel supply each one Sabbath at Salem. That Mr. Crawford supply one Sabbath at Ash Ridge.

Sundry papers being presented to Pby. containing various charges against Mr. Adam Rankin,[5] but things not being suitably prepared for trial,

[5] Rev. Adam Rankin, from Augusta County in Virginia, arrived in Lexing-

Resolved, that Mr. James McConnel, Samuel Shannon, & James Crawford be a committee appointed to meet at Mount Zion church the third Monday in November 1789 ensuing, to prepare the way for trial at the next session of pby.

Adjourned to Mount Zion to sit the fourth Tuesday of April next. . . .

JAMES CRAWFORD, Stated Clerk.

[Walnut Hill Church, Oct. 6, 1790.]

Mr. Crawford's, 6 o'clock.

Resolved that a circular letter be sent to certain gentlemen hereafter appointed, requesting them to use their influence to raise collections for the support of missionaries to be employed in the bounds of the Synod of Virginia[6] agreeable to an order of said Synod. . . .

[Collectors Appointed.]

Adjourned to meet at the church in the fork of Dick's river on the fourth Tuesday of April next. . . .

JAMES CRAWFORD, Stated Clk.

[Dick's River Church, April 27, 1791.]

A petition of a number of Pisgah congregation was presented to Pby. praying a dismission from the pastoral care of the Rev. Adam Rankin, & Pby. not being so fully acquainted with the circumstances of that congregation as to take said petition under consideration at present, do appoint the Pby. to meet at Pisgah church the third Tuesday in

---

ton, Ky., October 1, 1784, and immediately found himself surrounded by a large congregation. At times 500 communicants attended the sacramental services. He objected to the use of Watt's psalms in the churches, and carried his objections to the first General Assembly in Philadelphia, May, 1789. The Assembly listened to him and endeavored to conciliate him but in vain. No sooner had he returned home than he vented the most censorious invectives against the Presbyterian clergy as deists, blasphemers, rejectors of the revelation, and revilers of God's word. He debarred from the sacramental table all admirers of Watts in his congregation. Davidson: *Presbyterians in Kentucky,* pp. 88, 89.

[6] The Transylvania Presbytery was within the bounds of the Synod of Virginia until the Synod of Kentucky was formed in 1802.

May to consider said petition & for any other business that may come before it; & Mr. McConnell is appointed at said Pisgah two Sabbaths before the meeting of Pby. to preach & give notice to the congregation to attend the meeting of Pby.

[Mt. Pisgah Church, May 10, 1791.]

May 10th.

. . . Pby. resumed the consideration of the petition of a number of members of Pisgah congregation relating to a dissolution of the pastoral relation between the people of Pisgah & Mr. Rankin.

The Pby. having as maturely considered said petition as circumstances would allow came to the following resolution, viz: that it is their opinion, (as Mr. Rankin has absented himself without order from his charge upwards of twelve months) the people of Pisgah are at liberty to apply to Pby. for supplies for the present, & do recommend to them to study & promote unity & peace among themselves & earnestly to plead with the great head of the church that he would direct them in all things to act for his glory & the advancement of true religion amongst themselves. [Supplies ordered.]

JAMES CRAWFORD, Stated Clk.

[Stonermouth Church, April 25, 1792.]

Pby. met according to adjournment. . . .

Ordered that the minutes of the intermediate pby. be read.

A supplication from the north bend of the Miami purchase.

Mr. Crawford executed the order of the last Pby. to cite Mr. Rankin & the parties concerned in his trial.

The Pby. proceeded to the trial of the Rev. Adam Rankin, all persons concerned being present except James McDowell, Alexander Maxwell, & William Walker, all witness[es] the latter of whom is dead. The witnesses were examined, the depositions recorded, & subscribed by them.

Pby. adjourned to meet tomorrow at 8 o'clock. . . .

Thursday, April 26th.

Mr. Crawford is called on as an evidence in Mr. Rankin's trial & his deposition recorded & subscribed by him.

Whereas it has been proved before this Pby. that the Rev. Adam Rankin has declared & said that he is the subject of extraordinary Divine revelation, that he has taken the same as a director in part in discharge of his ministerial function & in all matters of importance, & has been the means of prevent[ing] him joining in communion with those who were in the use of Dr. Watt's psalms, & that he calls Dr. Watt's psalms the rivals of the word of God, & says himself that he does not join with some of the members of this Pby. in communion so long as they continue to countenance Dr. Watt's errors; with other declarations & things proved, of the like nature, as appears from the depositions taken; therefore, the Pby. judge said Mr. Rankin answerable.

The Pby. having judged as above called in Mr. Rankin to bring him to acknowledge these things proved against him. He refused & said, I appeal to God, angels & men that I protest against the proceedings of pby. & will be no longer a member of Transylvania Pby. Mr. Rankin then withdrew & Mr. Logan, an elder.

Pby. then proceeded & suspended Mr. Rankin from the whole exercise of the ministerial office until the next stated Pby.

Pby. adjourned. . . .

[Col. Caldwell's, Oct. 4, 1792.]

Oct. 4th.

Pby. met according to adjournment. . . .

Whereas Mr. Adam Rankin was suspended the last stated session of Pby. & the present session unanimously approved of said judgement, & Mr. Rankin, since his suspension, has not been subject to his brethren in the Lord, but has preached as frequently since as before his suspension,[7] has been forming a number of congregations & administered the sealing ordinances of the gospel repeatedly, & having sufficient reason to believe he is fully determined to go on in the same course; this Pby. do unanimously declare that said Adam Rankin has no right to exercise the ministerial function at any time nor in any place & that, as he was set apart to the office of a gospel minister & the discharge of the duties of the same by the officers of the Presbyterian church, so by the same authority, (being until now a minister & member of this Pby. under suspension,) the said office is taken from him & he forbid to discharge any of the duties of the same, & it is hereby done, & declared to be done, by that authority which Christ, the head, has given his church; & his congregations, or pastoral charge, is declared vacant.

[Cartwright's Creek Church, Oct. 6, 1792.]

Saturday, Octo^r. 6th.

Whereas the General Assembly has proposed three years for the study of divinity previous to the licensure of candidates for the gospel ministry, we are of opinion that would by no means suit the state of our country & of our churches in the remote parts of the United States.[8]

[7] Mr. Rankin, being summoned to hear the opinion of the court, refused to acknowledge fault or to make any concessions. "I appeal," he cried "to God, angels and men. I protest against the proceedings of this Presbytery." The Presbytery immediately declared him suspended.

He had not resolved upon this step without first calculating his strength. No sooner had he pronounced his declinature, than a hundred of the spectators stepped forward, and giving him the right hand of fellowship, pledged themselves to stand by him. He and his party were admitted into the Associate Reformed Church in May, 1793. After he left them the churches he had gathered struggled along for a while until they perished. An example of how Presbyterians followed Rankin is given by Robert McAfee, Clerk of the New Providence Church. Draper MSS. 14cc102. (See p. 40 of McAfee's *New Providence Church.*)

[8] In addition to the urgent need of ministers on the frontier, it is likely that the example set by the Methodists and Baptists in supplying their churches and circuits with preachers who were trained while in service, or in "Brush College" influenced this opinion.

Ordered that Mr. Rice transmit a copy of said minute to the next General Assembly.

Whereas christianity strongly & directly leads us to mutual love & good will & to consult the true interests of one another as individuals, or as societies; looking every one, not on his own things, but on the things of his neighbor, we are afraid this is not attended to in all cases in the formation of new congregations, or erection of houses for the public worship of God, therefore it is ordered, That every congregation send one member to the next stated Pby. which will sit at Walnut Hill, the fourth Tuesday of April, to consult on such measures & establish such rules as may prevent the weakening or destroying congregations already formed by the erection of new ones.

Adjourned to Walnut Hill, to meet the fourth Tuesday of next April. . . .

JAMES CRAWFORD, Stated Clk.

INTERMEDIATE SESSION

Cincinnati, Oct. 21st, 1792.

Mr. Rice, Mod. & Mr. Tamplin Clk.

Pby. adjourned until tomorrow to meet at 12 o'clock.

Monday, Oct. 22^d.

Pby. met according to adjournment et p p s q s. Mr. James Kemper delivered a sermon on 2 Tim. 2, 3. as a specimen of trial previous to his ordination, & was examined on the constitution, discipline & government of the church & the qualifications necessary in the subject entitled/ to christian communion, which examination together with his popular discourse are sustained.

Ordered that Mr. James Kemper be ordained tomorrow.

Pby. adjourned until tomorrow, to meet at 10 o'clock. . . .

Tuesday, Oct. 23.

Pby. met according to adjournment. . . .

The Rev. Terah Tamplin preached the ordination sermon.

The Rev. David Rice, the presiding minister, having proceeded in the preparatory work of the present solemnity agreeable to the form of government; & the candidate, Mr. James Kemper, & the people of the churches of Cincinnati & Columbia, (whose pastor he is now constituted,) having respectively answered the questions in the affirmative, as directed in the government of our church, then the presiding bishop, by prayer & with the laying on of the hands of the presbytery, according to the apostolic example, solemnly ordained the said James Kemper to the holy office of the gospel ministry, & was constituted the pastor of the Cincinnati & Columbia churches. The presiding minister then gave the charge to the newly ordained bishop[9] & the people of his charge. . . .

JAMES CRAWFORD, Stated Clk.

[Walnut Hill Church, April 24, 1793.]

On motion it was agreed that the Pby. take up the order of the last session, viz: to consult upon such measures, & establish such rules as may prevent the weakening & destroying congregations already formed by the erection of new ones.

Ordered that no congregation be formed where the house of public worship belonging to such congregation shall be within the distance of ten miles of an older congregation, unless express leave is first obtained from the Pby. & this order shall be considered affecting & comprehending those congregations that come within its view who have not built their houses for public worship.

[Woodford Church, April 24, 1794.]

The committee report progress, which is as follows:

Whereas human literature is confessed by every judicious & wise observer as a matter of this life of great consequence & the more encouragement it meets with, & the more its influence prevails the farther are mankind removed from the brutal creation & the nearer the ap-

[9] The title of *bishop* is here used in the early New Testament sense.

proach to superior spirits in knowledge. The Pby. of Transylvania, therefore, taking into consideration this important matter, & wishing to promote learning, came to the following resolutions.

Resolved, that Pby. appoint one grammar school within their bounds, & that David Rice, James Crawford, James Blythe, Robert Patterson & John Caldwell, or any three of them be commissioners to fix on a suitable seat for the same & that it be earnestly recommended by the pby. to those under their care that they encourage learning as much as possible by sending their children to said school or by promoting others elsewhere. 2. That the Grammar School be under the particular care of a minister, a member of the pby. of Transylvania,[9a] & shall be visited by them / or their committee, at least once in every year, & that the most effectual measures be taken & means used to fill said school with students, such as from genius & disposition may promise usefulness in life, & to promote industry & application in study, moral virtue & practical religion. 3. That serious youth shall be sought for of promising abilities, & put to school to obtain a liberal education, & if they or their parents are not able to defray the expenses of the same they shall be supported by collections, & that provision for this purpose may be made it is earnestly recommended by this pby. to all the people under their care, that is to say, at least all heads of families, to contribute annually to this laudable & charitable design for four, two shillings & three pence; & record shall be made of the names of all persons who contribute in every congregation, with the sums respectively thereto annexed. 4. That proper persons shall be appointed in each congregation, . . . [here follows a list of collectors for the forty-

---

[9a] The Presbyterians saw that Transylvania seminary, founded in the home of David Rice, 1785, was passing from their control. They prepared themselves by establishing Kentucky Academy which later became Centre College. Mr. James Moore, a Presbyterian, was ejected as teacher of the Transylvania Seminary by the Board of Trustees, and the Reverend Harry Toulmin, a Liberal, was placed at its head. The Presbyterian members of the board objected but were over-ruled.

six congregations now composing the Presbytery] And the said collectors shall pay the monies which they may receive into the hands of James Crawford, Stated Clerk of presbytery, who shall dispose of the same for the purposes herein mentioned, as the Presbytery shall from time to time direct; & also a copy of the names of the contributors with the several sums respectively thereto annexed shall be transmitted to said clerk to [be] filed & preserved by him.   5. That Pby shall from time to time, as may be found necessary, appoint a person or persons, properly qualified, to teach the youth in said school; & in case of the death or resignation of said teacher, or teachers, in recess of the pby. the minister who superintends said school may fill such vacancy, or vacancies, with another fit person or persons, who shall continue till the end of the next session of pby.   6. As soon as may be thought convenient a place, which is judged/ the most proper, shall be fixed upon as a permanent seat for a public seminary.   7. Subscriptions for erecting public buildings, procuring a library, & for such other purposes as may be thought conducive to the interests of said seminary, shall be immediately set on foot.   And that more effectual provision may be made for defraying the expenses of this institution one or more ministers shall be sent, commissioned by pby. to solicit donations in the Atlantic States. 8. A library with such philosophical apparatus as may be judged necessary shall be procured as soon as sufficient collections are made for that purpose.   9. When the public seminary is erected & opened it shall be under the care of a minister of the gospel, who shall be president of the same, of the most approved abilities in literature & acquaintance with mankind that may be obtained, & zealously engaged to promote the interests of real & practical religion.   10. The number of trustees of said seminary shall not exceed twenty one, of which the ministers of the Pby. of Transylvania, (or if divided into two or more presbyteries, the ministers composing them) shall always make one half.   11. Two thirds of the whole number of trustees in service shall constitute a board to do business, & the voice of a majority of the whole number present shall decide on any question, motion, resolution or appointment, except in the appropriation of the funds, forming the constitution, fixing & establishing the permanent seat of the Seminary, electing the president & other officers & fixing their salaries, in all which cases the same number of trustees shall concur as is required to constitute a board, & where such concurrence is wanting the decision of the board, shall be of no avail. 12. No endeavor shall be used by the president or other teachers to influence the mind of any student to change his religious tenets or embrace those of a different denomination any further than is consistent with the general belief of the gospel system & the practice of vital piety. 13. The same persons who are appointed in the several congregations as collectors or receivers of donations for serious youth shall be collectors of money subscribed for the use of the public seminary & shall pay the same into the hands of the stated clerk of presbytery. Lands, money or property that may be subscribed for & given for the use of the public seminary shall be under the direction of the Pby. until trustees be regularly appointed. 14. No donation given or received for the use of the public seminary shall be appropriated to the use of any Grammar School whatever.

The above resolution & plan of education, being maturely considered, was agreed to by Pby. . . .

Adjourned to meet at Mr. Shannon's tomorrow morning at 8 o'clock. . . .

April 25th, 1794, Samuel Shannon's

On motion agreed that on the third Wednesday in May the members/ of Pby. & others meet at Clear Creek church, to inquire into the general causes of the prevailing declension of religion, & what may be the best methods of removing those causes, & to implore the divine aid in this important case.

On motion ordered that the committee report.

The committee report that they have formed the preamble of a subscription to raise funds for the public seminary, which, after the blanks were filled up, is as follows:

We, the subscribers, for the purpose of promoting learning & useful knowledge, do subscribe the following sums annexed to our names for the use of a public seminary as agreed on by the Pby. of Transylvania, one third of which shall be paid in cash, & the other two thirds in the following specific articles, viz: live cattle, pork, flour & hemp; the cash to be paid on or before the first day of November next to collectors appointed for that purpose, & the property shall be payable on demand at any time after the first day of Decem. next, to be delivered at some convenient place & to some proper persons who shall be appointed in each country respectively, for the due & faithful performance of the above, we, the subscribers, (each for himself,) do bind ourselves, our heirs, executors & administrators, (unto Col. John Caldwell, Col. Robert Patterson, Col. James Smith, Col. Joseph Crockett, & Mr. James Thompson, surveyor, in trust for said seminary until trustees are appointed thereto,) in the penal sum of one hundred pounds cash, as witness our hands & seals this ———— day of May, one thousand seven hundred & ninety four.[10]

The committee further report that they have prepared an address to the people at large on the subject of education, which, being read, it was ordered that Mr. Rice revise & bring it forward before the Pby. rise.

[Woodford Church, April 29, 1794.]

Tuition money at said school shall be four pounds per scholar per annum, payable at the end of every half year if required.

Mr. Rice brought forward the address as revised which was read & approved.

Mr. Crawford & Mr. Blythe are appointed to superintend the printing of the address & the proposals for a Grammar School & public seminary.

[10] See subscription list of the Walnut Hill Church, MS Shane Collection, Presbyterian Historical Society, Philadelphia.

[Paint Lick Church.]

Octo^r. 10, 1794.

Ordered, that no congregation, or church, under the care of this pby. shall make any proposals to any minister or ministers—preacher, or preachers, of the gospel from another pby., or from foreign parts, to settle amongst them as their minister, nor take in subscriptions for that purpose, until he is approved of by this pby.[11] or their committee, nor shall any congregation invite or allow such minister or ministers to preach more than once until he has obtained said approbation; &, (for the convenience of such minister & people,)—that the Rev. Thomas Craighead, Mr. Thomas Donald, Mr. Robert King & such other persons as they may appoint, or any three of them, be a committee for the settlements of Cumberland; The Rev. David Rice, Mr. Cary H. Allen, Mr. James Thompson & Mr. George Marquis, or any three of them, be a committee for the south side of Kentucky; Messrs Robert Finley, James Crawford, Robert Marshall & Malcolm Worldly, or any three of them, be a committee for the north side of Kentucky; & the Rev. James Kemper, Col. Oliver Spencer, Mr. Moses Miller & Mr. Reeder, or any three of them, be a committee for the settlements of the Miami; & said committees within their respective bounds are hereby authorized to examine into the testimonials of any minister or preacher, coming as above expressed, & make such other inquiries as may be necessary for their satisfaction, & approve or disapprove as the case may be, & they shall annually report to this pby.　Ordered that a copy of the preceding order be taken by each minister of pby. & duly published throughout their bounds.

Pby. adjourned to meet at Paint Lick Meeting House at eleven o'clock ante meridian. . . .

---

[11] The frontier regions were visited by many imposters who traveled under the guise of ministers of the various denominations or with a new brand of religion.

[Paint Lick Meeting House, Oct. 13, 1794.]

Ordered that all persons under the care of Pby. holding *slaves* shall teach every slave not above the age of fifteen years to read the word of God & give them such good education as may prepare them for the enjoyment of freedom, & shall instruct such slaves of the above description, and all others under their care, as far as they can find it practicable in the principles & precepts of the christian religion & that the masters of such slaves shall by every rational means in their power urge their attendance on public & family worship, & shall make a return of all their slaves under the above age to the church session under whose care such masters may be.

[Paint Lick Meeting House.] Oct. 14th, 1794.

Ordered that the stated Clerk in transcribing the minutes of pby. be allowed the liberty of making choice of words & correcting inaccuracies in form & grammar, yet retaining the sense of pby.; & also that a book be prepared by Mr. Marshall against the next meeting of pby. in which the clerk pro tempore shall record the minutes of pby. & have them ready for the Moderator to sign at the end of the session.

Resolved, that any Grammar school of the number of fifteen scholars shall be under the care of this pby. provided the managers or trustees of said school request it.

Resolved that proper commissions & recommendations be prepared & given to the solicitors of donations for the public seminary to enable them to enter on that business.

Ordered that the commissions of the commissioners to the General Assembly be signed by the Moderator & Clerk.

Ordered that Mr. Crawford & Mr. Marshall be a committee to draw a petition soliciting the General Assembly of Kentucky at their next session to enact a law establishing the public seminary founded by this pby., to which shall be annexed a bill to be enacted into a law, prepared by said Crawford & Marshall, agreeable to the resolutions of this pby. in that case, including the following nominations of trustees to be incorporated as trustees of said seminary, viz: David Rice, Caleb Wallace, Jacob Froman, Samuel Shannon, Terah Tamplin, John Miller, James Crawford, Robert Finley, Andrew McCalla, William Ward, Robert Marshall, Notly Conn, James Blythe, & Cary H. Allen; & that petition be signed by as many names as can be obtained between this & the 8th of next November, & be lodged at Col. Patterson's by the above date. Ordered that the Rev. David Rice wait on the Assembly & lay the said petition & bill before them.

Pby. adjourned to meet the 2ᵈ Tuesday in April at Cane Ridge Church. . . .

[Ash Ridge Church, Feb. 17, 1795.]

Resolved, that the following list of books be recommended to the Grammar School, under the care of Presby.

On the Latin

Ruddiman's Grammar with prosody
Cordery with an English translation
Aesop's Fables ——Do——
Erasmus ——Do——
Selectae e veturi testamento without
Selectae e profanis   Do
Cornelius Nepos Translation
Caesars Commentaries without
Ovid's Metamorphosis with or without
Virgil ⎫
Horace ⎭ Pantheon
Cicero's Orations. Ainsworths or Youngs Latin Dictionary
Patoun's Navigation
Sanderson's Algebra
Guthrie's Geography
Ferguson's Lectures on Natural Philosophy & Astronomy

Greek Authors

Wittenhalls Grammar,— Screvellius Lexicon
Greek Testament with Latin translation
Lucian's Dialogues with Murphy's notes.
Xenophon's Cyropaedia
Homer's Iliad, 1st volume
Longinus upon the Sublime
Kennet's Roman Antiquities
Potter's Greek   Do
Holmes' Rhetoric
Dilworth's Arithmetic
Watts' Logic
Stone's Euclid
Blair's Lectures on Eloquence
Lowth's English Grammar
Witherspoon's, Hutchinsons or Smith's Moral Phil.

or any other school or schools which may hereafter be under its care.

Mr. Hannah is now present. His reasons for absence are sustained.

A paper containing certain queries upon the subject of *slavery* being presented to pby. was read. On motion resolved to consider the purport of said queries. On motion resolved to refer the consideration of said queries to the next Genl. Assembly by the hands of the commissioners. On motion ordered that Mr. Rice & Mr. Crawford be a committee to state, in as clear a manner as possible, the aforesaid queries to be laid before the Genl. Assembly.

[Ash Ridge Church, Feb. 18, 1795.]

Whereas there are certain reports of the sin of drunkenness alleged against the Rev. Robert Finley come to the ears of this presby., & certain papers requesting them to take up & examine into the truth or falsehood of said reports,—on motion for that purpose, resolved to take notice of these reports & devise some plan for examining into the truth or falsehood of them.

Mr. Finley petitions presby. in the following words:

'I petition [that a] minister, with a session collected from the neighboring churches sit at Cane Ridge to inquire into reports relative to Mr. Finley; & try an action of scandal, exhibited by Mr. Finley, against Jno. Huston, Peter Huston & Richard McNamara.' This petition being given in as a motion was seconded & the votes taken, which are as follows:

Yeas—Moses Mitchell, Wm. McConnell

Nays,—Jas. Crawford, Jas. Kemper, Wm. Calhoun, Robt. Marshall, Jas. Hannah, Jno. McCabe.

On motion Resolved that Presby. inquire into these reports at next session.

After having proceeded thus far in Mr. Finley's case he read & handed in the following protest: Gentlemen, I perceive that the proceeding of presby. is without a warrant from the word of God & without a precedent from any form of government in the church of Christ, therefore am bound to protest against it as arbitrary & unwarrantable. Therefore I throw up my presbyterial seat & consider myself no longer a member of your body nor under your government; & request that my reasons may be entered upon your minutes. . . . My reasons for not appealing to Synod are the immense distance & the exceeding frailty of body, or want of health. Signed, Rob't. W. Finley (directed) To ye Mod. of the Presby. of Transylvania. . . .

Adjourned to meet tomorrow morning at 8 o'clock.

Thursday morning, Feby. 19th.

Resolved to resume the business respecting Mr. Finley.

From the preceding petition it appears that Mr. Finley's desire was, (as he expressed it in his petition before it was amended,) that a minister or two, with elders from the neighboring churches, should meet at Cane Ridge & be a session to inquire into reports relative to Mr. Finley & to try three men specified by name in said petition, who, he said, had raised & spread certain reports of scandal against him. This petition was rejected by a large majority, as appears from the yeas & nays upon that subject. Upon which account Mr. Finley has entered his protest & declared himself no longer a member of this presby. nor under its government.

For rejecting Mr. Finley's petition Presby. have the following reasons.

1st. The matters appear too complicated & weighty for a session to determine.

2. The trial of these three men is so clearly connected with reports circulating against Mr. Finley, & with the papers which have come to hand praying us to take up & enquire into matters, the Pby. do not think it can be committed to a session.

3. As these reports are circulating against Mr. Finley

himself & are of a public & flagrant nature they cannot be inquired into nor judged by a session, because no judicature lower than a presby. has any authority to take up, examine into any reports, or charges, in which a minister of the gospel is concerned, or becomes a party.

4. Reports of this nature respecting Mr. Finley have circulated in this country for some years past & appear now to have become recently flagrant; the Presby. therefore think the honor of religion requires that they should inquire into the truth or falsehood of these reports.

5. The Presby. by previous appointment are, within a few weeks, to sit at the place.

Whereas Mr. Robt. Finley has read, signed, directed & delivered to this presby. his protest declaring that he is not to be considered any longer a member of our body nor under our government, therefore, Resolved, as our unanimous opinion, that for his contumacy & disobedience he has not now any right or authority derived from the presbyterian church in/ these United States, to preach the gospel of Christ or administer any of its ordinances so·long as he continues in this his contumacy & disobedience. And Presby. do hereby declare the congregations of Ash Ridge & Concord, the late charge of Mr. Finley, vacant, as he himself in open presbytery did also acknowledge.

Ordered, that a copy of the preceding minute respecting Mr. Finley be read & published throughout the bounds of this Presby. & especially within the bounds of his late charge. . . .

Adjourned to meet this evening at 7 o'clock. Concluded with prayer.

[Ash Ridge Church, Feb. 19, 1795.]

Thursday evening.

Mr. Shannon resumes & takes his seat as Mod.

The following charges were exhibited against Mr. Stephen Bovel, a licentiate under the care of this Presby., by the Rev. James Kemper, a member of the same,—'I charge Stephen Bovel with treachery, lying & deception, in which he has been engaged for a course of years immediately preceding his licensure, in a manner & also in a matter, particularly with respect to marriage, in which his conduct directly tends to the ruin of individuals, the great injury of society & the establishment of irreligion. These charges are supported by the accused's own letters & confessions; by the Rev. James Crawford, Mr. Aaron Tullis, Mr. Wm. Barbee, Mr. Claburne Rice, Mr. Malcolm Worley, Mrs. Sarah Graham & Miss Betsey Rice.[']

    Intermediate Session ⎫ Exhibited by me
    Feb, 1795   ⎬   James Kamper.

    Adjourned to meet tomorrow morning at 7 o'clock. . . .

                   Friday morning, Feby. 20th.
    Resumed the charges against Mr. Bovell.

    Mr. Bovel was inquired at whether he acknowledged the charges. Mr. Bovel acknowledged them in the following terms,—'I acknowledge the justice of the above charges according to their plain, literal & grammatical sense, with this reserve, that I never made a protestation in the affair referred to without feeling an intention to comply with it.[']

                 Signed, Stephen Bovell.

    In consequence of the above acknowledgement the accuser voluntarily rests the final issue of the accusation referred to with this Presby. (These terms are in the accuser's own words.)

    Mr. Bovel, being asked what, in his opinion, he ought to do with regard to preaching from this time till his trial issue, answered that he would rather choose to be silent. And having asked the Presby. what their opinion was in this case, they answered they were of the same opinion.

Resolved that Mr. Bovell's trial lie over for farther consideration till the next session of Pby. . . .

Ordered that James Crawford & Robt. Marshall draw up commissions for the solicitors of donations & that they be signed by the Mod. & Clerk. . . .

SAM'L SHANNON, Mod^r.

[Cane Ridge Church, April 16, 1795.]

Whereas it is evident from Mr. Robert Finley's protest, as well as the proceedings of pby. that he is not now a member of this pby. nor under its government, & as he proposes to become a member & be under its government & says he misunderstood the pby. as the reason why he protested, this Pby. think it necessary that Mr. Robert Finley make the following acknowledgements & promises, —I acknowledge I misunderstood the Pby. when I protested, which was the cause of my protesting, in doing which I was wrong & acted rashly & did not go according to the rules of government in the Presbyterian church because I did not appeal to the Synod, or take some other regular step, instead of withdrawing from the Presbyterian church & from under its government; & I also promise, (in case I am received to my former standing in the church at the time before I protested,) that I will submit to the judgment of this presbytery in case of any trials which may respect me & will never attempt to take any irregular steps without first appealing to the higher judicatories of this church.

Pby. unanimously agree that the above acknowledgements & promises are reasonable & necessary to be made by Mr. Robert Finley before he is received as a member of this pby. The same was judged necessary by the unanimous voice of all the elders present of Cane Ridge & Concord, . . .

Mr. Finley was then called in & agreed that said acknowledgements & promises were reasonable, & rose from his seat & went to sign them, when a member of Pby. observed that Mr. Finley might be under a mistake in supposing Pby. had agreed to proceed in any trials that might concern him agreeable to certain proposals he had read & handed to the members of Pby. out of doors. It being then said that these proposals were not agreed to Mr. Finley refused to sign said acknowledgements & promises but took it under consideration until the next morning.

[Examining Committee appointed.]

[Cane Ridge Church, April 17, 1795.]

The Pby. took under further consideration the trial of Mr. Stephen Bovell. It appears that there was a solemn promise of marriage between him & ——————— & the fullest repeated assurances on the part of Mr. Bovell that this promise would be fulfilled; that he was very rash & criminal in marrying so hastily before proper measures were taken to dissolve the above obligation. In these things Mr. Bovell was very guilty & his crime highly aggravated as there appears not the least cause in ——————— why he should treat her as he has done, she being, from first to last, a person of unblemished character, & both from character & promise entitled to his warmest affection & fidelity; but having been censured & suspended from preaching since the last Pby.; having acknowledged his crime fully & his guilt, as also his sorrow & repentance; & being fully satisfied that he is sincere in these his professions & acknowledgements, we agree to restore him, & he is hereby restored to his former standing in the church & as a licentiate of this Pby. . . .

Cane Ridge, April 20th, 1795.

Mr. John Howe read a sermon which is sustained as a part of trial & is assigned a lecture on Romans, 12, 1,2,3, to be read at the next session, & a popular sermon on Rom. 5,1, to be delivered at the next stated session. . . .

An intermediate Pby. is appointed [for the purpose of ordination].

Supplies [appointed for eighteen vacant congregations].

[Table of Appointments of Supplies]

Sab.	Cane Run	F. Dick's River	Clear Creek	Pisgah	
2			Calhoun		
3				Cameron	
4					
5	Bovel				
1		Templin		Marshall	
2		Templin & Crawford			Sacrament
3	Templin				
4	Templin		Crawford		
1	Robinson			Calhoun	
2		Bovell			
3			Shannon		
4				Crawford	
1					
2	Shannon	Calhoun	Howe		
3	Shannon & Calhoun			Howe	Sacrament
4			J. Finley		
5		Marshall		J. Finley	
1	Cameron	Howe	Shannon		
2		Howe		Marshall	
3					
4			Crawford & Marshall		Sacrament
1				J. Finley	

Adjourned to meet tomorrow morning at 9 o'clock. . . .

April 21st, 1795.

Mr. Cameron & Mr. Bovell are appointed to supply in Cumberland as many sabbaths as they may find convenient & particularly in Shiloh congregation if the dangers of the road admit of their going there.

PREAMBLE Whereas Mr. Robert Finley having acknowledged he misunderstood Pby. & acted wrong when he entered his protest & declared himself no longer a member of this Pby. nor under its government, is now again, by signing his acknowledgements & promising regular submission in case of any trials which may respect him, become a member & has taken his seat accordingly; & whereas the same reports of the sin of drinking spirituous liquor to excess by Mr. Finley still exists unexamined & untried & are generally known throughout the bounds of this Pby. to the injury of religion & the wounding of the godly; & as Pby. have been & still are requested to inquire into these reports & have now in their hands a large list of witnesses' names, therefore

Resolved, as our unanimous opinion that on Thursday after the fourth Tuesday in July next Pby. sit at Cane Ridge church, then & there to examine into & try the validity of said reports & censure or acquit Mr. Finley accordingly; & the said witnesses are hereby required to reappear at time & place of meeting of said Pby., & all other persons concerned or having knowledge of said reports are also required to come or send forward to Mr. James Crawford, stated Clerk of Pby., so that the defendant Mr. Finley may have them at least ten days previous to the said meeting of Pby., a list of names of other witnesses, if any there are, to make good said reports or ever after be silent & held as unworthy slanderers of the brethren. And Mr. Finley, or any other proper person or persons on his behalf, are at full liberty to produce witnesses, if any they have, to extenuate the crime, if such there be, or invalidate the force of said reports, or show just cause or reason why these witnesses or any of them, or any others, should not be admitted as witnesses in his trial.

Pby. have now given to Mr. Robert Finley a copy of the above preamble & resolution, specifying the crime alleged against Mr. Finley, etc., & a copy of the names of the witnesses, with the times & places, as far as they could be ascertained, when & where Mr Finley should have been seen by them intoxicated with spirituous liquor. And Mr Finley is cited to attend his trial at the above specified time & place.

Witnesses Cited [in trial of Robert Finley].

Adjourned to meet at Pisgah Church on the first Tuesday of next October.

TERAH TAMPLIN. Mod^r.

[Little Mountain church, July 28th, 1795.]

At Cane Ridge the 1st day of August, 1795, the Presbytery of Transylvania having received sufficient testimonials in favor of Mr. Samuel Finley, of his having gone through a regular course of literature, of his good moral character & of his being in the communion of the church, proceeded to take the usual parts of trial for his licensure; & he having given satisfaction as to his accomplishments in literature, as to his experimental acquaintance with religion & as to his proficiency in Divinity & other studies; the Presbytery did & hereby do express their approbation of all the parts of trial; & he having adopted the Confession of Faith of this church & satisfactorily answered the questions appointed to be put candidates to be licensed, the Presbytery did & hereby do license him, the said Samuel Finley to preach the gospel of Christ as a probationer for the holy ministry, within the bounds of this presbytery or wherever he shall be orderly called.

Adjourned to meet on Monday morning at 8 o'clock. Concluded with prayer.

[Cane Ridge, Aug. 3, 1795.]

Augt. 3^d. Presby. met according to adj. . . .

Whereas the Rev. Robt. W. Finley has signed, directed & delivered by the hands of a certain John Lockridge to this presbytery his declinature & declaration, holding forth that he is no longer to be considered as a member of our body nor under our government, when, notwithstanding, he had at last pby. himself given under his own hand absolutely & unconditionally to submit to the judgment of presby. in case of any trials that might respect him & never to take any irregular steps without first appealing to the higher judicatures of the church, And whereas, further, instead of coming forward in a Christian & regular manner after being three times duly cited to appear at the time & place appointed to stand his trial, he has obstinately refused to appear & has moreover loaded this pby. with many very grievous charges of lying, deception & heterodoxy,

Therefore, resolved, unanimously, as our opinion, that he has acted contrary to all order and regularity in the church of Christ, & he is hereby suspended from the whole exercise of the ministerial office till the next stated session of Pby. & the congregations of Cane Ridge & Concord, the late charge of Mr. Finley, are again declared vacant.

Aug. 4th, 1795.

Whereas a charge of scandal was brought by Mr Finley against Richard McNemar, John Huston & Peter Huston & said Finley has refused to prosecute said charge because Pby. would not commit the trial of said charge to the judicature of a church session; & the Pby. after enquiry knows of no evidence to support the above charge, therefore said charge against Richard McNemar, John Huston & Peter Huston ceases in the same manner as if it had not been brought against them.

Mr. Richard McNemar having applied to this Pby. as a candidate for the gospel ministry, & having received sufficient testimonials in favor of his moral & religious character, of his being in the communion of the church & being satisfied that he has gone through a regular course of literature, having examined him on his repentance towards God & faith in our Lord Jesus Christ & the motives that influence him to seek the office of the holy ministry, are satisfied with said examination & agree to receive him on trial as a candidate for the gospel ministry. Mr. McNemar read a discourse on Rom. 5,1, as a specimen of trial & it is sustained & he is assigned for farther trial a lecture on Jude from 6th to the 13th.

Supplies [appointed].

Ordered, that Mr Robert Finley be cited to attend the Pby. to sit at Pisgah the 1st Tuesday of October to answer to his conduct relative to his trial, & Mr. William Maxwell is ordered to cite said Mr Finley. . . .

SAMUEL SHANNON, Mod^r.

[Pisgah Church, Oct. 6, 1795.]

[Petitions for supplies.]
Messrs Crawford, Shannon, Tamplin, Marshall, Howe & Caldwell, or any three of them are appointed a committee to meet this evening for the examination of such of the candidates upon the languages as have not been before examined.   Mr. McConnel is now present.

Adjourned to meet tomorrow morning at 9 o'clock. . . .

[Wednesday morning, Oct. 7, 1795.]

Ordered to read the minutes of last stated session. . . .

A letter directed to him was read by Mr. Crawford, stated clerk, from Miss Frances Kemper, requesting him to return her the original letters now in his hands which passed between Mr Bovell & her: Upon which resolved, that Miss Kemper, or any other person authorized by her, are at full liberty to take authentic copies of said letters, either which, or the original she may carry off & preserve at pleasure.   Ordered, that Mr. Crawford send to Miss Kemper a copy of the above resolve.

[Reports of Supplies.]
Mr Jno. Bowman, a licentiate from the Pby. of Orange, having come into the bounds of this Pby. desires leave to itinerate here for some time.   Pby. having received sufficient testimonials in favor of Mr. Bowman's being a regular preacher of the gospel, do hereby give him leave to itinerate at discretion & he is hereby recommended to the vacancies under our care.

[Reports of Supplies.]
A supplication for supplies from New Providence & for the administration of the Lord's supper.

REPORTS [of Supplies].
A call from Lexing. congregation & another from Georgetown, each for the one half of Mr. Welch's labors

were received by Pby. & presented to Mr Welch which he takes under consideration.

The committee appointed to examine the candidates upon the languages report that they examined Andrew Steel, Arch^d. Steel, Jno. Dunlavy & Rich^d. McNamar upon the latin & greek languages & are satisfied. Pby. agree to sustain the report.

On motion ordered, that no person in the Presbyterian church shall take the liberty to exhort publicly unless he is first appointed by the Pby. or has express liberty from the Pby. for that purpose. The above order was brought forward as a motion & being seconded was debated at some length & the decision of it is deferred till tomorrow.

Adjourned to meet this evening at Mr Dunlap's at half past 6 o'clock. . . .

[Oct. 8, 1795.]

The order of yesterday upon the subject of public exhortation has passed in the affirmative as it there stands.

A supplication from the inhabitants of Fleming Creek in Mason county for supplies & a petition for liberty to erect a house for public worship. Pby. think, at present they cannot grant liberty to build, but will endeavor to appoint them such supplies as they can afford.

Pisgah, Friday morning Oct. 9th.

Pby. met according to adjournment, ubi post preces sederunt qui supra.

Supplies [appointed].

Messrs Robt. Marshall, Jno. Howe, Thos. Dinwiddie & James Poag are appointed a committee to settle a dispute between the session of Cane Ridge & Mrs Ann Richey, widow, who stands suspended from church privileges; to meet at Cane Ridge church on Monday after the 2^d sabb. in next December, & they shall make report to next Pby.

Mr. Templin & Mr. Blythe, ministers, Gen. Jno. Caldwell & Andw. McCalla, ruling elders, are appointed commissioners to attend the next meeting of the Gen'l. Assy. of the Presbyterian church, to be held at Philadᵃ. on the third Thursday of May next: & Mr. Shannon is appointed alternately in the room of Mr. Blythe, Mr. Marshall in the room of Mr. Templin, William Scott is appointed in the room of Gen. Caldwell & Jacob Fishback in the room of Andw. McCalla.

Ordered, that the Moderator & Clerk sign their commissions.

Mr. Welch now comes forward & informs the Mod. that he accepts of the calls from the congregation of Lex. & the congregation of Georgetown, & upon application for his ordination, the Pby. appoints to meet at the First Presbyterian meeting house in the town of Lexington on the third Wednesday in Feby. next in order for Mr. Welch's ordination. And Mr. Welch is appointed to preach a sermon as a specimen of trial on John 6,37, previous to his ordination. Mr. Crawford is appointed to preach Mr. Welch's ordination sermon, & Mr. Marshall to preside & give the charge.

[Pisgah, Oct. 9, 1795.]

Whereas Mr. Robt. Finley has been three times duly cited to attend for his trial at the last meeting of Pby. but did not attend & was suspended, & has been duly cited a fourth time (as appears by certain information recd. in writing from Wm. Maxwell, who served the citation) to attend this meeting of Pby. & still absents himself. And notwithstanding his suspension it appears he still continues to preach, Therefore, by the authority which Christ has given his church for edification, said Robt. Finley is deposed & he is hereby deposed from the whole exercise of the ministerial office. Ordered that the clerk transmit to Mr Finley a copy of the above resolution.

[Pisgah, Oct. 9, 1795.]

Richᵈ. McNamar, Jno. Dunlavy[12] & Andʷ. Steel have lib-

---

[12] McNemar and Dunlavy followed Barton W. Stone in the New Light schism in 1803. They left him to join the Shakers in 1805; see chap. IV.

erty to exhort publicly under the following limitations: that
they do not exhort oftener than once in two weeks, & not
without first carefully digesting the matter of their exhortations; & they are directed not to exceed forty five minutes in
the length of their exhortations.

[Feb. 18, 1796.]

Adjourned to meet at Col. Patterson's this evening. . . .

Met according to adjournment. Mr. Blythe & Mr. Scott,
his elder are present, reasons for absence sustained.

A supplication for supplies from Point Pleasant. Mr.
Bovell is appointed to supply one sabbath at Point Pleasant.

Mr Tull has hereby leave to preach in our vacancies &
is hereby recommended to the people.

Messrs Blythe & Welch are added to the committee on
the north side of the Kentucky river, for the purpose of
examining into the credentials & character of itinerating
ministers.

Presby. recommend to the trustees, deacons, & other persons appointed, or that may hereafter be appointed, to
manage the church temporalities, in the several churches
under their care, to give to every member removing out of
their bounds a full discharge against the calls that may have
been given to their ministers & in which they may have been
bound during the time of their residence within the bounds
of said congregations.

Ordered that Mr Crawford, Mr Shannon, Mr Marshall,
Mr Blythe, Mr Calhoun & Mr. Welch, or any three of
them, be a committee to seek for a proper person to teach
the grammar school under the care of Pby., who shall succeed Mr Steel, should he relinquish the business; also to
attend the 8th day of March, at 10 o'clock, upon said
school, for the purpose of examining the students & enquiring into the state of the school.

Adjourned to meet at Col. Patterson's tomorrow morning
at 9 o'clock. . . .

[Lexington, First Presbyterian Church.] Feb. 19, 1796.

Pby. met according to adjournment, . . .

Ordered that the minutes of the last stated session be read. . . .

A petition being presented to Presby. praying them to take up & as far as in their power to redress some grievances arising from the practice of slavery, therefore, ordered, that the different ministers belonging to this Presby. request all persons within their several bounds, (who may be desirous to come forward, either by their representatives or by sending forward their sentiments in writing to our next stated Presby., in order that they may state the grievances under which they may labor, respecting the subject of slavery & that they be invited to propose any remedy they may think proper for that evil, so that Presby. may fully investigate this important subject. . . .

Rob't. Marshall, Mod. pro temp.

[April 13, 1796.]

[Supplies' Reports.]

Mr. Crawford informed Pby. that the committee appointed at the intermediate Pby. for procuring a teacher to succeed Mr Steele as teacher of the Grammar school, provided he resigned, had fulfilled their appointment, & report that Mr James Moore is employed to take charge of said school.

Petitions [for administration of Lord's Supper and supplies].

[Supplies Ordered.]

Adjourned to meet tomorrow morning at 9 o'clock.

[Cane Run Church, April 14, 1796.]

A remonstrance against slavery with proposals for emancipating of slaves, &c, was presented & read, also a letter from Bourbon county signed James Smith to the same effect.

Ordered, that the consideration of the same be postponed till tomorrow.

[Paris, Oct. 4, 1796.]

The Rev. William McGee,[13] from Orange Presby. North Carolina, appearing in Presby. & expressing a wish to become a member, Presby. conceiving Mr McGee's testimonials satisfactory, admitted him a member & invited him to take a seat.

[Paris, Oct. 4, 1796.]

A call from Shiloh congregation was brought forward by their commissioner Dr. Donald, to be presented to Mr McGee, & upon consideration Presby. agreed to present said call to Mr McGee for his acceptance. Mr McGee, upon receiving the above call informed Pby. that he accepted it.

Paris, October 6, 1796.

Presby. met . . .

Mr And^w. Steele being examined on divinity, Presby. judged his knowledge of theoretic & practical theology satisfactory & unanimously agreed to license him to preach the gospel.

The committee appointed on yesterday to converse with Mr Arch^d. Steele reported that they had conversed with Mr Steele on the subject of difficulties under which Presby. labored concerning his continuance on their minutes in order to licensure & that Mr Steele left it wholly to Presby. to determine whether now to dismiss him or continue him for farther trials, as he could cheerfully acquiesce in their decision either way. After serious conversation on the subject of the above report, Presby., that they might take every step which would tend to relieve their difficulties & promote Mr Steele's interests, directed their Moderator to give Mr Steele a candid statement of what had passed in Presby.

---

[13] William McGee and his brother John McGee, a Methodist preacher, were present at Red River in July, 1799 when the bodily exercises originated as a phenomena of the Great Revival.

concerning him on this & the preceding day, leaving it to Mr Steele's choice whether he would desire now to be discontinued on their minutes or whether he wished Presby. to determine as to the propriety of his farther continuance.

Mr. Steele being before Presby. the Moderator gave him a plain representation of what had passed in conversation respecting him, as to the defects of his lectures & composition in general, as to the volatility of his temper & want of the gravity & prudence which should characterize a candidate for the ministry & as to some jealousies which existed in the mind of Presby. concerning his present sincerity & his future usefulness, & then directed Mr Steele to inform Presby. whether he now wished to decline the farther prosecution of his trials, or whether he still wished Presby. to decide as to his continuance or dismission.

Mr. Steele candidly acknowledged the defects alleged by Presby. but complained that some earlier intimation of them had not been given him by Presby. & expressed a wish that if it were consistent with the views of Presby. that they wd. still continue him on their minutes & assign him farther parts of trial. Upon inquiry it appeared that Presby. at their last stated session had some private conversation of a similar kind, of which they chose to make no record, & had particularly appointed some members to mention to Mr Steele what appeared to them defects in his conduct. Mr Steele recollected that a member had mentioned to him a certain act of imprudence since that meeting of Presby. which was committed prior to that period.

Mr. Steele now retired. Upon mature deliberation Presby., as their difficulties were not yet removed, being unwilling to precipitate a final judgment in such a case & hoping that time might correct Mr Steele's imprudences, or at least make things assume a less dubious appearance, concluded still to continue him another term & assigned him as presbyterial exercises the subject of his last lecture, & Titus 2:6-8, to be delivered at the next stated session of Presby.

A memorial from the session of Woodford congregation containing a reference in the case of J. Meek, who had been admitted to the ordinance of baptism for his child in that church after a profession of repentance & public acknowledgement for past misconduct, was laid before Presby. for their judgement, by the Rev. S. Shannon.

On considering the case of Mr Meek & the conduct of that judicature from the contents of the memorial, Presby. were of opinion that the session had acted in that affair with prudence & propriety.

At Paris, the 6th day of October, 1796, the Presbytery of Transylvania having received sufficient testimonials in favor of Mr Andrew Steele; of having gone through a regular course of literature, of his good moral character & of his being in the communion of the church; proceeded to take the usual parts of trial for his licensure; & he having given satisfaction as to his accomplishments in literature, as to his experimental acquaintance with religion & as to his proficiency in divinity & other studies, the Presby. did & hereby do express their approbation of all these parts of trial; & he having adopted the confession of faith of this church & satisfactorily answered the questions appointed to be put to candidates to be licensed, the Presby. did & hereby do license him, the said Mr And^w. Steele to preach the gospel of Christ as a probationer for the holy ministry, within the bounds of this Presby. or wherever he shall be orderly called.

Resolved that supplies be now appointed, . . .

Wednesday, January 4th, 1797.
. . . Pby. proceeded to examine Messrs McNamar & Dunlavy on divinity which examination was sustained as part of trial & agree to license them to preach the gospel.

At Paris the fourth day of January, 1797, the Pby. of Transylvania having received sufficient testimonials in favor of Messrs John Dunlavy & Richard McNamar, of their having gone through a regular course of literature, of their good moral character & of their being in the communion of the church, proceeded to take the usual parts of trial for their licensure; & they having given satisfaction as to their accomplishments in literature, as to their experimental acquaintance with religion & as to their proficiency in divinity & other studies; the Pby. did & hereby do express their approbation of al these parts of trial; & they having adopted the Confession of Faith of this church & satisfactorily answered the questions appointed to be put to candidates to be licensed, the Pby. did & hereby do license them, the said John Dunlavy & Richard McNamar to preach the gospel of Christ as probationers for the holy ministry within the bounds of this Pby. or wherever they shall be orderly called.

Whereas Mr Barton Stone & Mr John Anderson, probationers from the Orange Pby. of North Carolina, making application for liberty to preach within the bounds of this Pby. the Pby. examined their credentials & likewise their acquaintance with doctrinal & experimental religion, & having received satisfaction on these points, agreed to permit them to preach in our bounds, & do hereby recommend them to our vacancies.

Salem Church, Logan County, March 7th, 1797.

The want of notice to the people prevented our opening as usual with a sermon. . . .

Mr. Tamplin was chosen Modr & Mr Craighead Clk.

Mr McGrady[14] having proposed to become a member of this Pby. & having produced a satisfactory dismission & recommendation from the Pby. of Orange, was received as a member & took his seat.

The Pby. adjourned till tomorrow at ten o'clock. . . .

Wednesday, March 8th.

On motion resolved that Messrs Craighead & McGrady be a committee to draught a letter to be addressed to the Transylvania Pby. at their next stated session on the subject of dividing the Pby.

[14] McGready was later to become the leader of the revivalistic preachers among the Presbyterians.

[Stanford, April 17, 1797.]

The Rev. David Rice having made application for a dismission from his congregations Pby. granted his request.[15]

[April 14, 1797.]

Ordered that Mr Houston be now ordained.

The Rev. William Mahon preached a sermon on the occasion & previous thereto from Gal. 1 & 9. after which Mr Houston having answered to the Rev. Terah Tamplin, (the presiding bishop) in the affirmative the questions required by our directory to be proposed to candidates, & likewise the people of Paint Lick & Silver Creek churches having answered in the affirmative the questions directed to be proposed to them, Pby. proceeded, & by prayer & the laying on of the hands of the pby. did ordain him, the said Matthew Houston to the holy work of the gospel ministry; & after a solemn charge given by the aforesaid presiding bishop to the newly ordained one & also to the people of his charge the whole was concluded with prayer. Mr Matthew Houston, at the invitation of the Modr. takes his seat in presbytery.

[Pisgah, Sep. 14, 1797.]

A resolution was brought in by Mr Crawford as follows, viz: Resolved that this presbytery give & they hereby do give up their care of Pisgah grammar school, as also their right to the house in which said school is taught & any & all lands given for its use, to the Trustees of the Kentucky Academy to dispose of the same for use of said Academy as

---

[15] David Rice, at the age of sixty-five, was troubled with an affection of the head which incapacitated him for close attention to any subject, and subjected him to habitual melancholy. Pecuniary difficulties also oppressed him. He had purchased land on faith of his congregation guaranteeing the payment, but this was deferred until the sons had forgotten the promises of their fathers, and the sheriff held up before his eyes the terror of imprisonment. While in this state he refused to administer the Sacrament in Danville on the ground that it was not right to admit to the holy table persons who were unfaithful to their engagements. A great sensation followed. This was probably the immediate reason for his withdrawal. (Davidson: *Presbyterian Church in Kentucky*, p. 69.)

they may think proper, so soon [as] said Academy shall be opened.

Presbytery adjourned to meet tomorrow at 8 o'clock. . . .

Thursday morning, Septr. ye 15, 1797. . . .

This presbytery being informed that there are certain books in the hands of the Rev. David Rice which were given for the use of students of Theology in this state & to be under the care of this Presbytery, Resolved, that the Pby. think it will best answer the design of the donors to invest the trustees of the Kentucky Academy with the said books for the use of students in theology & therefore order that the Moderator write Mr Rice requesting him to deliver the books to the said trustees.

Pby. adjourned. . . .

WILLIAM MAHON, Mod^r.   James Welsh, Clk.

[Bethel Church, Oct. 4, 1797.]

Verbal supplications from Clear Creek, W. of the Ohio, from the Big Prairie & from Turtle Creek for supplies.

A letter was laid before presbytery requesting their opinion relative to the marriage of Elihu Sanders & Mary Beedle & the following resolution was adopted: Resolved, as our opinion, that the marriage of Elihu Sanders & Mary Beedle is unlawful because said Mary has not obtained a divorce, neither does she appear to have taken any orderly steps to obtain it & it is doubtful whether the reasons for a divorce in her case as stated in her letter be sufficient.

The question was put whether pby. should take under consideration the subject of slavery agreeably to a petition presented for that purpose; the question was carried in the affirmative.   Presbytery resolved to postpone the consideration of the above business until tomorrow.

[Bethel Church.]

October 5th, 1797. . . .

Upon motion the question was taken up, "Is slavery a moral evil?" it was determined in the affirmative.   The question was likewise considered, "Are all persons who hold

slaves guilty of a moral evil?" & it was voted in the negative. A 3d question was proposed as follows, "Who are not
guilty of moral evil in holding slaves?" Resolved that the
question now before presbytery is of so much importance
that the consideration of it be put off till a future day.

Bethel church, October 6th. . . .

The committee for the Pisgah grammar school report
that they have appointed John Thompson to teach said
school until January next.

The Rev. Peter Wilson, member of the presbytery of
New Brunswick, being recommended by said presbytery as a
minister of full standing, sound in the faith, of good moral
character, & recommended to the Christian care & attention
of any pby. of the presbyterian church in the United States
of America, where Providence may direct his lot, & said
Wilson having received a dismission from the said presbytery, this pby. do agree to receive him & he is hereby received a member of the presbytery of Transylvania.

The committee appointed to examine Mr Steele on the
sciences, examined him on geography, Natural Philosophy
& astronomy & agree to sustain his performance. The same
committee also in compliance with their appointment examined Mr George Sutherland on the Latin & Natural Philosophy & have also agreed to sustain his performance so far.
Also Presby. have accepted of & agreed to the reports as
above.

Mr Steele delivered a popular discourse from Isaiah
55th, 7th, as a part of trial which was sustained. Mr Steele
was examined upon criticism, upon Moral Philosophy & /
Divinity, & his examination was sustained. Resolved that
Mr Steele be now licensed.

At Bethel church, October 6th, 1797, the presbytery of
Transylvania having received sufficient testimonials in favor
of Mr Archibald Steele, of his having gone through a regular course of literature, of his good moral character & of
his being in the communion of the church, proceeded to take
the usual parts of trial for his licensure; & he having given

satisfaction as to his accomplishments in literature, as to his experimental religion & as to his proficiency in divinity & other studies, the presbytery did & hereby do express their approbation of all these parts of trial; & he having adopted the Confession of Faith of this church & satisfactorily answered the questions appointed to be put to candidates to be licensed, the pby. did & hereby do license him, the said Archibald Steele to preach the gospel of Christ as a probationer for the holy ministry within the bounds of this presbytery or wherever he shall be orderly called.

The following arrangement was adopted in appointing supplies. . . .

[Nov. 7, 1797.]

Wednesday morning. . . .

Mr Dunlavy being present Pby. proceeded to examine him on Church Government, which examination they sustained & then unanimously agreed to ordain him.

Therefore it is ordered that Mr Dunlavy be ordained, & therefor, agreeably thereto Mr Rannels preached a sermon from 1 Tim. 4,16; after which Mr Robinson, the presiding bishop, after having recited in audience of the people the proceedings of pby. preparatory to the important ordinance of ordination, & having spoken a little on the divine authority of that ordinance, & he, the said Mr John Dunlavy, having answered in the affirmative those questions appointed to be put to candidates previous to their being set apart to the work of the holy ministry; & also the people, who laid in their calls for Mr Dunlavy, having answered in the affirmative the questions appointed to be put to them on such occasions; proceeded by prayer & the laying on of hands to set him apart to the holy work of the gospel ministry. And a solemn charge in the name of God being given to the newly ordained bishop & to the people to persevere in the mutual discharge of their obligations by the presiding bishop, the whole was concluded with prayer.

Mr Dunlavy was invited to take a seat in pby. & he com-

plied with the invitation / & then Pby. concluded with
prayer.

WILLIAM ROBINSON, Modr.

[New Providence Church, April 10, 1798.]

Mr Barton Stone, a probationer from the Orange Pby.,
on making application to this presbytery to be received under their care & producing his regular dismission & recommendation from S^d. presby. of Orange, he was & is hereby
received under the care of this presby. . . .

Calls from the united congregations of Cane Ridge &
Concord for Mr Barton Stone were by consent of pby.
presented to him for his acceptance, which he accordingly
accepted. A call from Cabin Creek for Mr Richard Mc-
Namar for the two thirds of his ministerial labors, & by
consent of pby. it was presented to Mr McNamar for his
acceptance, which he accordingly accepted.

[April 11, 1798.]

The business of dividing pby. was taken up. After considerable deliberation the question was put, Shall pby. be
divided? & it was carried in ye affirmative. The question
was then put, Shall pby. be divided into two or more parts?
It was carried into more than two. The business was then
submitted to a committee (namely, Messrs Rice, Tamplin,
Blythe, Speer & Robinson,) appointed to prescribe the limits
of each & report tomorrow morning.

Messrs Tull, Cameron & Huston are appointed a committee to examine Mr Sutherland upon geography, astronomy, moral philosophy & criticism & report tomorrow
morning.

Adjourned to meet tomorrow morning at 9 o'clock.

[New Providence Church.] Thursday, April 12th. . . .

The committee for maturing the business respecting the
division of presby. reported. Resolved that it is the mind
of your committee that this pby. should be divided into
three pbys., the division to be as follows: that all the breth-

ren on the east side of main Licking & those on the north west side of the Ohio be a presby. consisting of the Revd. Messrs Wilson, Camper, Campbell, Speer & Dunlavy, to be known by the name of Union presby. The brethren on the west side of main Licking & on the north side of the Kentucky be one presby. consisting of the Revd. Messrs Crawford, Shannon, Tull, Marshall, Blythe, Howe, Welsh, Robinson & Rannels, to be known by the name of Providence Presby. The brethren on the south side of Kentucky, together with the brethren in Cumberland, to be one pby. consisting of the Revd. Messrs Tamplin, Mahon, McGrady, Cameron, Finley, Houston & McGee, to be known by the name of Transylvania Presby.

Presby. approved & accepted the report of the committee.

Resolved that Messrs James Crawford, Robert Marshall, James Blythe & James Welch be a committee to draft a petition addressed to the Synod of Virginia praying a division of the pby. agreeably to the plan now adopted & forward the same to Synod.

[New Providence Church, April 12, 1798.]

Several charges stated against the Revd. Wm. Mahon,[16] by some of the members of his congregation were laid before presby. By consent of all parties, on motion resolved that this business be now entered upon.

The 1st charge was stated by Mr Sam. Dickey who saith that about the 12th of Feby. 1797, Mr Mahon whipped his negro woman unmercifully, can prove it by James Buchanan & Geo. McAfee. Mr. Buchanan being duly sworn, saith that he did not see Mr Mahon whip the negro woman but that he heard an unusual crying at intervals about the space of half an hour which he understood from Mr Mahon was occasioned by his whipping her; also that he seen the negro woman the day following but did not discover any

[16] Mr. Mahon's drinking and cruelty are well described by Robt. McAfee in his account of the Salt River Settlement, pp. 19, 23-24.

marks of whipping on her, but that he did not examine her. James Buchanan.

Mr. Geo. McAfee, being duly sworn, saith that James Buchanan, Jno. Mothershead & Sam'l Dickey told me that they expected that Mr Mahon had whipped his negro woman too much & desired me to go & talk with him. I thought it prudent first to go to Mr Armstrong & take his advice respecting the business. I did so, he advised me to go. I did so & when I came to Mr Mahon I asked him to walk with me. We went to the woods together & when alone I told Mr Mahon I had something to say to him. He asked me what it was. I told him I had been informed by James Buchanan, Jno. Mothershead & Saml. Dickey that he had whipped his negro woman too much; upon which Mr Mahon called up his negro woman & had her stripped in order that I might see if she was abused & when she was stripped he requested me to take a whip & whip her well which I refused tho he handed me the hickory. Upon examining the woman I found her skin cut in two places upon her left arm & a hole in her right side; otherwise her skin was not broken. The hole appeared to have been made at the time the wounds on her arm was made. Mr Mahon then gave her a few cuts himself. He also deposeth that the right shoulder appeared to be bruised with some kind of a big weapon, her shoulder appearing of a yellow & green color. Mr McAfee farther deposeth that when we sat down on the log, when he repeated what the men before alluded to had said he rose off the log & appeared to me to be very angry, & he walked about two steps from me & turning round said, Mr McAfee, if you were not the man you are I would give you an answer that you are not expecting. Geo. McAfee.

Mr. Mahon produced the following witnesses. Mr Saml Gray, being duly sworn, saith that on the 21st of April, that at a public meeting of the congregation at the meeting house Mr Geo. McAfee said he had seen Mr Mahon's negro woman & that she had two cuts on her arm about an inch & ½ long, likewise that she had a hole under her right breast, that he had picked the hole & found it to be thro the skin & that he was informed his woman had struck her with the pot-hooks which occasioned the hole; likewise that she had a large bruised place upon her right shoulder, he examined it & found a black & bruised place as big as the palm of his hand.   Mr Mahon then asked him whether it was the black of the skin or the black of the pot.   Mr McAfee said it was black bruised blood.

Samuel Gray.

Mr John Bunton, being duly sworn, deposeth that he heard Mr Geo. McAfee/ say that he understood that what made the hole in the negro woman's side was made by a stroke with the pothooks given her by Mr Mahon's woman.

John Bunton.

Mr Saml. Graham deposeth that Mr Geo. McAfee said that he understood the hole in her side might be made by a stroke of the pothooks given her by Misses Mahon.

Samuel Graham.

Mr. Wm. Shields, duly sworn, saith that Mr Geo. McAfee said upon examining the negro woman after she was stripped he observed two marks upon her left arm which appeared about an inch & an half long, likewise a mark upon her little finger nail, next also a hole under her right breast through the skin & likewise a bruised mark upon her right shoulder.   Mr McAfee said respecting ye hole I was informed that your woman struck her with the pot-hooks which occasioned the hole; the shoulder was bruised black.

Wm. Shields.

2d charge, Saml. Dickey also complains of the Revd. Mr Mahon with saying he might as well taken the meat out of his meat-house, or one of his horses, or the watch out of his pocket, as did what he did; can prove it by Geo. Buchanan

& Geo. McAfee, & wish the Presby. to inquire what I have done that is so criminal

Mr Mahon acknowledged the charge as true.

3d. After what had happened Wm. Armstrong, Geo. McAfee & Saml. McAfee made an appointment to have a few to meet at the meetinghouse. Mr Armstrong was to give Mr Mahon notice of it, to make up the difference if possible. Mr Mahon did not attend; can be proven by any two of the three above. Mr Mahon acknowledged this as true.

4th. We appointed a second meeting at James Buchanan's & Wm Armstrong was to give Mr Mahon notice of it. Mr Armstrong requested Geo. Buchanan as a neighboring elder to meet with us & Mr Mahon did not attend. The design of this meeting was to make up the difference as neighbors & in a friendly manner, proven by Wm. Armstrong & Geo. Buchanan. Mr Mahon acknowledged he did not meet.

5th. Sometime after this Geo. Buchanan came past us & said we had better call a neighboring minister & some elders & submit our differences to them & that he had a letter from Mr Rice to Mr Mahon advising us & him to that method. We agreed to the proposal. Mr Buchanan went to Mr Mahon, gave him Mr Rice's letter & requested him to meet us & agree on what time & place, minister & elders we should call on. Mr Mahon did not comply with the proposal.

6th. We complain that Mr Mahon never met us any day that we appointed nor never made any appointment himself that we know of, or believe that we could have an opportunity to settle our difference. Known to all the congregation. Mr Mahon acknowledged this as true.

7th. We complain of Mr Mahon for having an election for elders at a time when this difference was in the congregation & ordained them when there was but nineteen members voted out of eighty one; known to the congregation. Mr Mahon acknowledged this as true.

8th. We complain of Mr Mahon for sending a new subscription paper through the congregation to continue him

as their minister, unbeknown to a number of the congregation & before the disturbance was settled. Proven by Wm.
Armstrong, Jas./ McAfee, Sam'l. Adams.

9. Geo. McAfee complains that Mr Mahon first gave
him orders to go round the subscribers to see who wished to
continue their subscriptions & who not, & afterwards denied
it. Proven by Wm. Armstrong, Jas. McAfee & John Bunton. The above withdrawn by the complainant.

10. Saml. McAfee complains on Mr Mahon for preaching a sermon on the 1st verse of the 133 psalm & in his
preaching said that any member that stayed away from public worship to they first gave their reasons ought to be
censured for it. Proven by Robt. McCarney & James
McAfee.

11th. That before that we had made two appointments
to get Mr Mahon & the people that stayed away together
that the people might have a chance to give their reasons &
Mr Mahon stayed away himself. Proved by Geo. Buchanan & Wm. Armstrong. Mr Mahon acknowledged this
as true.

12. About the 20th of March 1798 Saml. McAfee went
to Mr Mahon & gave him Mr Shannon's letter, & after Mr
Mahon read it I asked him if he would state our facts or if
he would let pby. take up the matter & enquire into it; Mr
Mahon said he did not care a pin which way or whether
ever pby. took it up or not. I asked him if he thought it
best to let it drop after so much being said. Mr Mahon
said he did not know what had been said. I told Mr Mahon
I thought he could not be ignorant of it, he knew more about
it nor any one man in the congregation. Proved by Joseph
Lapsley, Joshua L. Wilson. Mr Mahon acknowledged this
as true.

[April 13, 1798.]

Presby. proceeded to appoint the supplies. . . .

On motion resolved that Mr Stone be ordained at our
next stated meeting of pby. to sit at Cane Run, provided the
remaining parts of his trials be sustained. The pby. as-

signed Mr Stone as a subject of trial Rom. 8,15. Mr Welch was appointed to preach the ordination sermon. Mr Marshall to preside & give the charge.

On motion resolved that an intermediate pby. do meet on the first Wednesday of August, at Calvin Creek, in order to ordain Mr McNamar in case his trials be sustained & to do whatever else may appear proper. Mr McNamar was appointed to prepare a sermon on Gen. 3,6. Mr Robinson was appointed to preach the ordination sermon & that Mr Campbell preside & give the charge.

[New Providence Church, April 13, 1798.]

Mr Mahon produced Mary Wilson, a witness, who being duly sworn saith that she heard Mr Mahon's negro woman tell her negro woman that she had her master in a good way now, that if he did whip her she would make all the no[i]se she could, would holler & they would have him up about it.

her
Mary X Wilson
mark

The Presby. after mature deliberation, came to the following conclusion respecting the charges exhibited against Mr Mahon, that whereas with respect to some of the things alleged against Mr Mahon the pby. have not sufficient evidence to form a judgment, it also appearing to this pby. that the charge relative to his treatment of his slave is not sufficiently established & whereas Mr Mahon has acknowledged that he did conduct in the manner mentioned in the charges respecting the various meetings of the congregation, Resolved therefore as the mind of this pby. that Mr Mahon should receive a friendly admonition from the chair for his neglecting to use the means in his power to compromise the difference between him & his people; for his imprudent measures in the affair of appointing an addition to the session considering the then pending state of the congregation; & that he also be advised to be very careful in guarding his temper in his intercourse with all men & particularly with his slaves.

It is further resolved as the mind of Presby. that since Mr Dickey was offended with Mr Mahon & did not agreeably to the requirements of the Word of God go first & converse with Mr Mahon, resolved that Mr Dickey receive a rebuke in brotherly love & be admonished to be more careful in future & also as Mr Dickey failed fully to establish the charge alleged against Mr [Mahon. . . .]

[Aug. 2, 1798.]

Mr Robertson, according to previous appointment preached a sermon from Heb. 13,7. Afterwards Mr Campbell, the presiding minister, did briefly recite from the pulpit in the audience of the people the proceedings of the pby. preparatory to this transaction; he also pointed out the nature & importance of the ordinance, endeavoring to impress the audience with a proper sense of the solemnity of the transaction. Afterwards Mr Campbell addressed himself to Mr McNamar & proposed those questions which are appointed to be put to candidates previous to their ordination, which questions he answered in the affirmative. The people also gave their assent to the questions proposed to them, as is usual on such occasions.

Pby. did then by prayer & laying on of their hands, according to the apostolic example, solemnly ordained him to the holy office of the gospel ministry; after which Mr Campbell & the other members of pby. did give to the newly ordained bishop the right hand of fellowship.

Mr. Campbell then proceeded to give a charge to the newly ordained bishop & an address to the people as suitable to the occasion.

On motion resolved that the pby. do now proceed to the licensure of Mr Geo. Sutherland.

At Cabin Creek, 2d August 1798, the Pby. of Transylvania having received sufficient testimonials in favor of Mr Geo. Sutherland, of his having gone through a regular course of literature, of his good moral character & of his being in the communion of the church proceeded to take the usual parts of trial for his licensure, & he having given satisfaction as to his accomplishments in literature, as to his experimental acquaintance with religion, as to his proficiency in divinity & other studies, the pby. did & hereby do express their approbation of all these parts of trial, & he having adopted the Confession of Faith of this church & satisfactorily answered the questions appointed to be put to candidates to be licensed, the pby. did & hereby do license him, the said George Sutherland, to preach the gospel of Christ as a probationer for the holy ministry within the bounds of this pby. or wherever he shall be orderely called.

[Cane Ridge, Oct. 2, 1798.]

The pby. took into consideration the sermon delivered by Mr Barton Stone with reference to his ordination & agreed to sustain it as part of trial. The Revd Messrs Mahon, Rannels & McNamar were appointed a committee to examine Mr Stone upon the languages, the sciences, church history & church government.

Pby. adjourned to meet tomorrow morning at 9 o'clock. Concluded with prayer.

Wednesday morning, October 3d, . . .

Ordered that the minutes of yesterday be read.

The committee appointed for the purpose of examining Mr Stone reported that they have attended to that business & were fully satisfied with his examination. The Presby. agreed to accept the report. Resolved that it is the mind of pby. that they will on tomorrow proceed to the ordination of Mr Stone. Mr Welsh being appointed at the last stated session of pby. to preach the sermon previous to Mr Stone's ordination, but he being absent Mr Blythe was appointed to that business.

[Cane Ridge, Oct. 4, 1798.]

Pby. proceeded to the ordination of Mr Barton Stone. Mr Blythe preached a sermon suitable to the occasion from Acts 20,24. Afterwards Mr Marshall, who had been previously appointed to preside in the business recited from the pulpit the several steps that had been previously taken agreeably to the directory of this church.   He then proposed to Mr Stone those questions appointed to be put to candidates previous to their ordination & Mr Stone having answered those questions in the affirmative [17]; & the congregations having answered those questions appointed to be proposed to them in the affirmative by holding up their right hands, the presiding bishop did then by prayer & with the laying on of the hands of the pby. according to the apostolic example, solemnly ordain & set apart the said Mr Barton Stone to the sacred office of the gospel ministry.   After which the presiding minister & the several members of pby. gave to the newly ordained bishop the right hand of fellowship.   The presiding minister did then give a solemn charge, in the name of God, to the newly ordained bishop, & to the people suitable to the occasion, & did by prayer recommend them both to the grace of God & his holy keeping. The moderator did then invite Mr Stone to take a seat in pby. which he accordingly did.

[Cane Ridge, Oct. 4, 1798.]

The committee appointed to meet at Pleasant Point made their report to pby. which was received & accepted.   The report was as follows, viz: "Pleasant Point, August 14th, 1798.   The committee of pby. met according to appointment, . . . Mr Blythe was chosen / chairman, Mr. Welsh clerk.   The committee then proceeded to consider the business for which it was appointed, viz: An inquiry into the

---

[17] In his account of the ordination Stone says that he had some difficulty in assenting to the confession, and on telling James Blythe and Robert Marshall, they labored in vain to remove his difficulties and objections. "They asked me how far I was willing to receive the confession. I told them as far as I saw it consistent with the word of God. They concluded that was sufficient.   I went into the Presbytery, and when the question was proposed, 'Do you receive and adopt the Confession of Faith as containing the system of doctrine taught in the Bible?' I answered aloud, so that the whole congregation might hear, 'I do as far as I see it consistent with the word of God.' No objection being made, I was ordained." (Rogers, J., *Biography of Barton W. Stone,* pp. 29, 30.)

nature of some reports relative to some disturbances in Mr Tull's domestic affairs. The committee having inquired of Mrs. Tull respecting her opinion of Mr Tull's holding an improper intimacy with his negro woman she declared she had no charge to exhibit against him on that subject & that she never had any real suspicion of him respecting such kind of intimacy. Mrs Tull further confessed the great impropriety of her conduct in alleging such a thing & that she was sorry for her improper conduct in that case. The committee then having called in the congregation, the chairman after having briefly called to the recollection of the people the great frailty of human nature & its liability to go astray from God, as also the great necessity of mutual forbearance with one another, he then in the first place published to the congregation Mr Tull's acknowledgement respecting certain things in his conduct & expressions by which they had been aggrieved & which had in a private way been settled according to the gospel direction; viz: that at different times he had been improperly passionate towards Mrs Tull. The chairman also published to the congregation Mrs Tull's exoneration of Mr Tull respecting his negro girl, her confession of impropriety of conduct & sorrow. The committee then concluded with prayer & adjourned to meet tomorrow morning at 7 o'clock at Mr. Tull's. Wednesday morning August the 15th, 98 the committee met according to adjournment, members present as above. The committee having constituted by prayer proceeded further to consider the business of their meeting & having as fully considered as they could the nature of the case on both sides by inquiries at each party & conversation with both & having received the acknowledgements of both & promises of future amendment from both, the committee agreed by the chairman in a friendly & Christian way to admonish each of the parties to exercise a greater degree of vigilance & circumspection in their future conduct & that they should earnestly endeavor to walk together thro life in the uniform exercise of mutual love & as becomes those who are expectants of being finally the happy heirs of the grace of life. The chairman then, agreeably to the desire of the committee discharged his trust of admonishing each of the parties. The committee then concluded with prayer.

JAMES BLYTHE, Chairman.

[Cane Ridge, Oct. 5, 1798.]

In consequence of some difference which took place between the Rev^d Wm Mahon & some of his people some time ago, they did by mutual consent proceed to destroy the call they had given to Mr Mahon by erasing the names of the persons from it who had signed it. The business / appeared before pby. in this situation. The pby. considered this proceeding as illegal, but notwithstanding, pby. did, for prudential reasons, declare the union between Mr Mahon & the congregations of New Providence & Benson dissolved & said congregations are hereby declared vacant.

Mr Tull applied to pby. for leave to resign his pastoral charge of the united congregations of Green Creek & Pleasant Point & informing pby. that he had previously published to both congregations this his intention, which was also confirmed by their ruling elder representing said congregations in pby., & no objections being made by said elder to his resignation Mr Tull's resignation was accepted & the said congregations of Green Creek & Pleasant Point were hereby declared vacant.

[Lexington, March 27, 1799.]

The Pby. received a copy of the minutes of the Synod of Virginia, whereby the prayer of the petition of Transylvania pby. relative to a division of pby. appears to have been granted. This copy is as follows, viz:

A petition was presented to the Synod through the committee of overtures from the Transylvania pby. praying for a division of said pby. into three presbyteries to be known by the names of the Transylvania, bounded on the north east by the Kentucky river, on the north & north west by the Ohio, as also on the south comprehending all the settlements of Cumberland and its waters, consisting of the Rev.

David Rice, Thos. Craighead, Terah Tamplin, Wm Mahon, James McGrady, Arch^d Cameron, Samuel Finley, Matthew Houston, Wm. McGee, & Jno. Howe. Another pby. to be known by the name of the Western Lexington presbytery, bounded by the Kentucky on the south & south west, by the Ohio on the north & north west & by main Licking on the north & north east; consisting of the Revd James Crawford, Samuel Shannon, Isaac Tull, Robert Marshall, James Blythe, Jos. Howe, James Welsh, Samuel Rannells, & Wm Robinson. Another to be known by the name of the Washington pby. comprehending the remaining part of the state of Kentucky lying north east of Main Licking, & the settlements on the north west side of the Ohio, consisting of the Revd Peter Wilson, James Kemper, Jno. Campbell, Jno. Finley, Wm. Speer, Jno. Dunlavy, Rich'd McNamar.

The Synod proceeded to consider the petition of the presbytery of Transylvania & agreed to grant their prayer. They appointed the pby. of Transylvania to hold their 1st meeting at Cane Run on the second Tuesday of April next, at 11 o'clock A.M. where the Rev. David Rice or in case of his absence the sen^r member present shall open pby. with a sermon & preside until a new Mod^r be chosen. Synod appointed the Western Lexington pby. to hold their 1st meeting at Lexington on the third Tuesday of April next at 11 o'clock A.M. when the Revd James Crawford, or in his absence, the sen^r member present shall open pby. with a sermon & preside until a new Mod^r be chosen. Also that Washington pby. hold their 1st meeting at Johnson's Fork meeting house on the second Tuesday of April next at 11 o'clock A.M. when the Revd Peter Wilson, or in case of his absence, the senior member present shall open pby. with a sermon & preside until a new Mod^r be chosen.

A true copy. — WM HILL, Stated Clerk.

Ordered that a copy of the minutes of the Synod relative to the division of the pby. be transmitted to the several moderators.

On motion resolved that all the business now on the records of pby. & yet unfinished be referred to the different pbys. within whose bounds it may fall.

Presbytery impressed with the sense of convenience & importance of a Synod in this district of country & considering the difficulty of taking measures relative to such a business in the different presbyteries at their first meetings, do, previous to their separation express their approbation of such a measure & agree to recommend & they do hereby recommend/ to the separate presbyteries to instruct their member or members attending the next May session of the General Assembly to make application for an order authorizing the presbyteries of Transylvania, Western Lexington & Washington to constitute a synod.

Signed WM. ROBINSON. Mod.

[Oct. 2, 1799.]

Supplies [appointed].

[Muddy River Church, April 9, 1800.]

Ordered that the request of this presby. be preferred to the General Assembly for the appointment of a Synod in the Western country composed of the presybteries of Transylvania, West Lexington & Washington & that Mr Rice be appointed to transmit a copy of this minute to the presbyteries of West Lexington & Washington, & in case of their concurrence (it) be forwarded to the General Assembly. Presby. adjourned to meet at New Providence on the first Tuesday of October next. . . .

THOMAS B. CRAIGHEAD, Mod.

[Oct. 8, 1800.]

Supplies [appointed].

The congregation of New Providence, in their petition for supplies, further requests of pby. that upon account of the prevalence of sickness in that & other parts in the bounds of this pby. a day of fasting, humiliation & prayer to Almighty God be appointed. Upon motion resolved, That for this cause & also upon the account of the prevalence of vice

& infidelity, the great apparent declension of true vital religion in too many places, the second Saturday of next month be observed for this purpose by the different congregations under the care of this presbytery, whether they may have an opportunity of attending preaching or even convening for public worship or not.

[April 16, 1801.]

Supplies [appointed].

Joshua L. Wilson offered him self a candidate for the gospel ministry. Having received of him sufficient testimonials of his good moral character, Presbytery proceeded to examine him on his acquaintance with experimental religion & of the motives which influenced him to desire the sacred office of the gospel ministry, have agreed unanimously to take him under their care. On motion being made Mr Wilson is permitted to exhort occasionally under the discretion of one or other of the members of presbytery. Mr Wilson is appointed to prepare a sermon on Gal. III, 29th, as a specimen of trials to be read at the next presbytery.

[Muddy River, Oct. 7, 1801.]

A motion was made by a member of this pby. for liberty to baptize by immersion some scrupulous persons in his charge; & it was resolved that such persons as could not in conscience receive baptism by affusion might be baptized by immersion.

Mr Joshua L. Wilson read a sermon from Gal. 3d, 29th, which was assigned him as a specimen of trials, & the performance was unanimously sustained.

[Oct. 9, 1801.]

October the 9th. . . .

Whereas Messrs Finas Ewing, Alexander Anderson, Saml. King, & Ephraim McClain offered themselves to presbytery for the service of the church Pby. have appointe s^d men to the business of exhortation & catechising & have directed them to prepare discourses upon the following subjects. Subjects to be read at the next spring session of presbytery. Mr Anderson on John 1st 16th; Mr Ewen on 1st Peter, 2d, 1st clause of the 7th verse; Mr King on Ezekiel 33d, 11th; Mr McClean on Hosea 13th, 9th.

Mr McGready was appointed to supply one sabbath in the neighborhood of Clarkesville & one at discretion. Mr Rankin was appointed to supply two sabbaths at Sharon. Mr Howe was appointed to supply one sabbath at Cook's Knob and one at discretion. Mr Craighead was appointed to supply one sabbath at West Harper & one at discretion. Mr Donnell was appointed to supply one sabbath at Big Spring & one at discretion. Each of the absent members was directed to supply two sabbaths at discretion.

[Beaver Creek Church, April 16, 1802.]

In order to free any regular presbyterian minister from the effect of an order passed last session, declaring it disorderly for any member to come within the bounds of any other now settled Mr Wm Hodge freely invites & solicits any brother of regular standing, belonging to this synod, to come & preach in his pulpit or any part of his charge occasionally,[18] & Messrs Sam'l Wilson & Zaccheus Wilson as the representatives of some members of Shiloh congregation engage that the doors of that house shall be open to every regular member of good standing in the presbyterian church.

[Spring Hill Church, Oct. 6, 1802.]

Pby. took into consideration the petitions for licensing certain men, namely, Finis Ewing, Ephraim McLain, Samuel King & Alexander Anderson to preach the gospel & it was agreed, after giving pby. sufficient satisfaction, they should be licensed to preach the gospel. Pby. adjourned to meet tomorrow morning at 9 o'clock. . . .

[18] This move is in favor of the evangelistic preachers holding revivals throughout the country. See McDonnold, *Cumberland Presbyterians*, p. 39; Davidson, *op. cit.*, p. 131.

Thursday, Oct. 7. . . .

Pby. proceeded to examine Mr Anderson, Ewing, McLain & King on experimental religion with their motives & views to the ministry, which was sustained as a part of trial for licensure. Pby. called upon Mr Anderson, Ewing, McLain & King to deliver each one a discourse as part of trial, which they accordingly did.

Pby. adjourned to meet tomorrow morning at 9 o'clock. . . .

Friday, Oct. 8. . . .

Pby. proceeded to examine the discourses delivered by Mr Anderson, Ewing, McLain & King, which discourses were sustained.

Pby. proceed to hear & judge of the discourses assigned Mr Wm. Dicky & Joshua Wilson at their last fall meeting, which discourses were sustained. Pby. proceeded to examine Mr Dicky, Wilson, Anderson, Ewing & King on divinity.

Pby. adjourned to meet with candle light. . . .

Pby. proceeded to judge of the examinations of Mr Dicky, Wilson, Anderson, Ewing & King, which were sustained as the last pieces of trial for licensure.

At Spring Hill, October the 8th, 1802, the Pby. of Transylvania having received sufficient testimonials in favor of Wm Dicky & Joshua L. Wilson having gone through a regular course of literature, of their good moral character & of their being in the communion of the church, proceeded to take the usual parts of trial for their licensure; & they having given satisfaction as to their accomplishments in literature, as to their experimental acquaintance with religion & as to their proficiency in divinity & other studies, the Pby. did & hereby do express their approbation of all those parts of trial; & they having adopted the confession of faith of this church & satisfactorily answered the questions appointed to be put to candidates to be licensed, the Pby. did & hereby do license them, the sd. Wm. Dicky & Joshua L. Wilson to preach the gospel of Christ, as probationers for the ministry, within the bounds of this pby. or wherever they may be orderly called.

Messrs Alexander Anderson, Finis Ewing & Sam'l King[19] being taken under the care of pby. at our last Fall meeting as catechists & then licensed to exhort & catechise in our vacancies, & as their labors were attended with a divine blessing as pby. have reason to believe, & being universally acceptable to our vacancies, several petitions having come forward from many of our vacancies earnestly & importunately praying pby. to license them to preach the gospel,— pby. after mature deliberation considered this matter as coming under the view of that extraordinary excepted in the book of discipline, examined them on their experimental acquaintance with religion, the evidences of their call to the ministry & examined them upon their knowledge in divinity; in which trials pby. received satisfaction & licensed them to preach the gospel.

We, whose names are under written, dissent from the judgement of pby. in / licensing Messrs Ewing & King, because, though they were rejected at the last session of pby. as persons unfit to be continued as candidates, & were now received by petitions from the people, which we think ought not to have been received as they had a tendency to influence the minds of the members who were bound by solemn vows to judge impartially of their qualifications, & because their trials on this occasion consisted only in one short sermon & an examination on experimental religion & divinity, being destitute of classical learning, & they discovered no such extraordinary talents as to justify such measures. Thos. B. Craighead, Sam'l Rannel, Jas. Balch; ministers. Dan'l McGoodwin, John Hannah, elders.

[19] These young men were later ordained by the Cumberland Presbytery at the insistence of churches who wanted them as ministers. The Commission sent to the Presbytery by the Synod of Kentucky declared them unqualified to minister the ordinances. This was a prominent factor in the Cumberland schism. See *Minutes of Cumberland Presbytery,* October 7, 1803, April 4, 1804, and October 7, 1806; Davidson, *op. cit.,* pp. 224, 227, 229; McDonnold, *op. cit.,* p. 53.

[Spring Hill Church, Oct. 8, 1802.]

Ordered that each member of pby. supply at discretion. Pby. sensible of gratitude of the supreme Being for the present refreshing season & sending out laborers into the vineyard, do appoint Saturday, the 30th of this inst. as a day of public thanksgiving throughout the churches in our bounds.

[Danville, April 14, 1803.]

The committee reported to pby. that they examined Messrs Cleland, Lapsley & Wood on Natural Philosophy, Geography & Astronomy & were satisfied. Messrs Finley & Houston were appointed to examine Messrs Lapsley & Wood on the languages & reported that they were satisfied. Pby agreed to receive both the above reports. Pby. proceeded to examine Messrs Vance & Cleland on Theology & were agreed to sustain their examinations.

[April 3, 1803.]

Whereas the Rev. Wm Mahon has failed to comply with a formal citation to attend & answer to a charge, upon a fama clamosa, of the intemperate use of spirituous liquors, —on motion, Resolved, that Mr Wm. Mahon be again cited to appear at the next stated session of pby., & on the 2d day of the same, to be held at Hardin's creek church the 1st Tuesday of October next, & the clerk is hereby ordered to forward a copy of this order to Mr Wm. Mahon in due time together with the names of the following additional witnesses, viz: Andrew Cunningham, Sally S. Cunningham, Sam'l Ewing, — — — Mussin, Samuel McDaniel, Joseph McDaniel, — — — Sanders, Robt. B. McAfee, & John Irvine.

Supplies [ordered.]

Adjourned to meet at Harden's Creek church on the 1st Tuesday of October next. . . .

[Oct. 5, 1803.]

Whereas the Rev. Wm. Mahon has failed to comply with former citations to attend & answer to a charge upon a fama clamosa of the intemperate use of spirituous liquors; on motion, Resolved by pby. that the Rev. Wm. Mahon be again cited to appear at our intermediate pby. to be held at the brick meeting house in Mr Finley's charge, in Lincoln county, on Saturday the 15th of this month, between the hours of eight & eleven o'clock, to answer to said charge. The clerk was directed to forward the above citement to Mr Mahon in due time. Pby. adjourned to meet at Mr McElroy's tomorrow morning at 9 o'clock. . . .

[Oct. 10, 1803.]

Pby. took into consideration the case of the Rev. Wm. Mahon charged with the crime of intoxication. After mature deliberation it appeared to pby. that from Mr Mahon's non-attendance on former meetings of pby. as well as the present he ought to be suspended; & pby. do hereby suspend him, the sd. Wm. Mahon, from the office of the gospel ministry until the next stated session. Whereas Mr Wm Mahon has failed to comply / with former citations to attend & answer to a charge on fama clamosa of the intemperate use of spirituous liquors, on motion, Resolved by pby. that the Rev. Wm. Mahon be again cited to appear at our next stated session to be held at Cane Run meeting house, the second Tuesday of April next. Ordered also that the clerk be directed to forward in due time a copy of the suspension together with a citation to Mr Mahon; & moreover the clerk is ordered to cite the above witnesses to appear at the next stated meeting of pby. . . . Pby. adjourned to meet the second Tuesday in April at Cane Run. . . .

MATH. HOUSTON, Mod.

[April 11, 1804.]

Whereas Mr Mahon has failed to attend at this pby., &

it appearing to pby. that he was providentially prevented from coming, on motion resolved that Mr Mahon's suspension from the gospel ministry be continued, & that he be again cited to appear on the first Tuesday of October next: & that Mr Robinson be appointed to cite Mr Mahon & all the witnesses formerly mentioned to attend.

[April 12, 1804.]

A call was presented from Bairdstown for Mr Wilson to be ordained to the work of the gospel ministry which was presented to him & accepted. Ordered that the pby. appointed to meet at Union church for the further trials & ordination of Mr Cleland be appointed to attend to the further trials & ordination of Mr Wilson also; & that Mr Wilson produce as a specimen of trial a sermon from Rom. 6, 14.

[April 12, 1804.]

Pby. being in doubt concerning the propriety of giving to persons permission to exhort publicly, without a view to the gospel ministry, have agreed to refer the matter to the General Assembly by letter, requesting their advice & counsel by letter again, as soon as may be convenient; & that Mr Rice be appointed to draft & forward said letter.

Ordered that the stated clerk procure a book of convenient size, for which he shall be paid by pby. & that he without fail transcribe the minutes of this pby. from the time of our division into several presbyteries into s^d book & forward it to the next meeting of Synod for their revision./

Supplies [appointed].

MATTHEW HOUSTON, Mod^r.

The pby. after having examined Mr Wilson & Mr Cleland upon different subjects & having obtained all proper satisfaction in their examination resolved to proceed to their ordination.

Mr Cameron then preached a sermon accomodated to

the occasion from Ezekiel, 33d, 7-8th, & Mr Wilson & Mr Cleland & the representatives of the congregations who called them having answered in the affirmative the questions directed by the book of discipline to be proposed in such cases, the probationers were solemnly ordained to the holy office of the gospel ministry by the imposition of the hands of the pby. & with prayer.

[New Providence Church, Oct. 2, 1804.]

Ordered that the Rev. Arch^d. Cameron do collect & transmit to the Rev. Ashbel Green & Mr Ebenezer Hazard of Phila. a true statement of the rise & progress of the church under our care. It is ordered that each minister do furnish Mr Cameron with materials from their respective charges at or before our next stated session.

Pby. proceeded to the trial of Mr Wm Mahon, he being present, & being inquired at by the Moderator whether he acknowledged the crime charged upon him, he answered in the negative.[20] Pby. then proceeded to take depositions, which are as follows.

Mrs Jane Gray, being duly sworn, deposeth & saith, That sometime in the fall of the year 1798 Mr Mahon came to her house & the conversation turned on the drinking of spirituous liquors, that Mr Mahon then observed that it would soon be time for him to quit drinking spirits, & went on further to state that he had a brother who had drank until a certain age & then quit. — I then observed that I thought it would be time for him to quit as old age was coming upon him & it might increase. — Afterward in the month of October, as well as this deponent recollects, in the year 1799, Mr Mahon came to my house on Sunday morning & informed me that he had come from Mr John Meaux's; I asked him if he would eat breakfast, he answered No, that he was unwell. After some other

[20] "Before Presbytery W. Mahon plead that he drank only what was for the benefit of his health. He filled his liquor into a teapot out of a closet. He sometimes took it down into a study. It was called, taking his tea." Robt. McAfee, New Prov. Church, Draper MSS. (Draper MSS. No. 1466, p. 146.)

conversation we began to talk about a child that he had
lost by death, & that Mr Mahon could not tell until after
some considerable time which of his two children, Archibald
or James, was the eldest, & after I had corrected him
several times. Mr Mahon smelled very strong of whiskey
& from every appearance of his conversation I thought that
his recollection at that time was impaired by drinking
whiskey or some kind of spirituous liquor. Afterward, on
the last evening of 1800, Mr Mahon came to my house
about nine or ten o'clock at night & as soon as he came into
the house he smelled very strong of whiskey. I asked him
how far he had come since dark; he answered that he had
come from Maj. Lillards. From his conversation & conduct I verily believed that he had drank very freely of
whiskey. Mr Mahon appeared to be very sick & puked
which I then thought was occasioned by drinking whiskey
as he smelled very strong of it. — Query by Mr Mahon.
Did you ever discover in me anywhere else where there
were spirituous liquors any symptoms of intoxication? Ans.
No. And further this deponent saith not. Jane Gray, her
✕ mark.

The deposition of Samuel Gray taken by consent of
Mr Mahon. — This deponent being first sworn & of lawful
age, deposeth & saith that some time in the fall of the year
1798 I rode down with Mr Mahon to Benson meeting & in
the evening we started together home, it was on Sunday
& we rode together as far as Mr Robertson's & asked for
water which when brought he complained it was not good
& said that he had better ride to Mr Jett's tavern on the
road which we did. He, Mr Mahon, there called for water
& on Mr Jett's asking him if he would take some whiskey
he said yes, & a half pint was brought. Mr Mahon first
drank a grog & I drank a moderate grog out of it & Mr
Mahon drank the balance & when we started away Mr
Mahon's conversation on the road I really thought unbecoming & scandalous for a minister to make use of, & I
then conceived that it originated from his having drank
too much whiskey which he got at Jetts; & a sickness that

he complained of before he got the whiskey was not complained of any more. Farther, Mr Gray saith that at a log rolling at his own house some time before the above circumstance took place Mr Mahon appeared to be in liquor from his conversation. He was required to ask a blessing twice before he performed. Farther this deponent saith not. Saml. Gray.

Saml. McDowell, Jr., being first sworn deposeth & saith, that some time in November 1799, he was in company with Mr Mahon in Danville & from his conduct, the smell of his breath, & foolish conversation he thought he (the sd Wm. Mahon) was drunk by drinking too much spirituous liquor. Query by Mr Mahon. Did you not bring forward this testimony because you are prejudiced / against me? Ans. No & further this deponent saith not. Saml. McDowell.

John Ervin being duly sworn deposeth & saith that on the evening before Christmas day in the year 1800, as he thinks, Mr Mahon came to his house, he being from home, & the children informed him Mr Mahon asked for some spirituous liquors saying his blood was stagnated by riding in the cold, after he came home, the bottle being on the table, he asked Mr. Mahon to take a dram & he took a dram or two; before they went to bed Mr Ervin asked Mr Mahon to take the books & while they were engaged in singing Mr Mahon went to sleep once or twice & once slept a minute or two with the book in his hand, afterward went to prayer & nodded once or twice during prayer. From these circumstances he concluded that Mr Mahon had taken too much spirituous liquor. 1st Question by Mr Mahon, Whether supper did not intervene between the time of taking the spirituous liquor & family worship? Answer, Yes. 2d Question, Whether before, at or after supper he seen anything irregular or unusual in his conduct or conversation previous to family worship? Answer, No, except drowsiness. 3d Question. Did he discover anything irregular after worship till bedtime? Answer, not remembered; & further this deponent saith not. John Irvin.

John Armstrong being duly sworn deposeth & saith that while Mr Mahon lived in the bounds of this congregation he went to his house, he informed him he had a quantity of excellent wheat whiskey whereof he asked him to drink, he said he took a dram, that he stayed about half an hour, during which time Mr Mahon took four drams himself & that after an hour's absence he returned, the bottle still standing on the table; while he detained them, which was a short time, Mr Mahon took two grogs, that he felt alarmed & really thought from his looks, conduct & conversation he was intoxicated. Some time after the above he met Mr Mahon on the great road near to Mr Meaux's & thought Mr Mahon was so much intoxicated that he could not sit with usual steadiness on horse back, that likewise his conversation led him to the same conclusion. That he discovered a short time after, viz: about two weeks, Mr Mahon remembered nothing of the previous conversation. He saith further that about the 1st of January, 1801, Mr Mahon came to his house in the evening in company with a man who was intoxicated, that he thought Mr Mahon was intoxicated from his conduct & conversation, particularly as Mr Mahon said it was about 2 o'clock whereas it was near sunset. Quest 1st by Mr Mahon, Whether Mr Armstrong was not at that time very much attached to him & he to Mr Armstrong? Answer, that Mr Mahon showed him every mark of respect, that he respected Mr Mahon, that on account of his office he was grieved to find him in that situation. Ques. 2d, Whether Mr Armstrong upon any occasion after those alarming fears took place, ever in a private friendly manner intimated it to me? Answer, No. Ques. 3d. Whether Mr Armstrong since that time has been brought under any prejudice by the influence of party spirit against me? Answer, No. Ques. 4. Was that the only time you, Mr. Armstrong, suspected the intemperate use of spirits in my own home? Answer, Yes. Ques. 5th, Was not the day cloudy & snowing? Yes. Further this deponent saith not.

John Armstrong.

Pby. adjourned to meet at Jas. McAfee's this evening at 7 o'clock. . . .

Pby. met according to adjournment. . . .

Pby. after mature deliberation upon the case of Mr Mahon did unanimously agree that the charge of intoxication exhibited against him has been sufficiently supported tho but a few of the witnesses attended who had attended at former meetings of pby. to give their testimony, & those absent are generally such as could give information / more recent than those who did attend, but they live more remote & we believe their patience in waiting upon us was exhausted. We did not restrict our testimony of the knowledge of facts to one year previous to the commencement of the prosecution because the scandal had become recently flagrant & instances both new & old were forced upon our ears from every quarter of Kentucky which had witnessed Mr Mahon's conduct. It was further agreed that Mr Mahon's ill-natured messages to our pby. & his contumacious conduct towards it had merited a just censure & go to prove an unchristian disposition. Upon the whole we viewed the crime of drunkenness in the present circumstances of Mr Mahon's case attended with very high aggravations & deserving the highest censure of our church. Wherefore this pby. did agree to depose the said Wm Mahon & he is hereby deposed from all the functions of the gospel ministry until his deepest sorrow for his sin & sufficient time of eminent & exemplary humble & edifying conversation have healed the wound & given full satisfaction to the church. Ordered that Mr Cleland forward an attested copy of the above judgement of pby. to Mr Mahon as soon as possible.

Pby. adjourned to meet at Mr Dayhoff's house in Danville the third Wednesday in this month at 3 o'clock, P.M. Concluded by prayer. SAML. B. ROBERTSON, Modʳ.

[Green Town, Siloam Church, April 10, 1805.]

A letter was forwarded to this pby. from Matthew Houston[21] giving us information that he had relinquished

[21] On the 10th of April Mr. Houston had forwarded to the Transylvania

the faith of our church & declined the authority of our judicatories. Resolved, upon mature deliberation that pby. have sufficient evidence of Mr Houstons declinature & schism from his own letter, & as we do not consider our discipline embracing the idea of a man's stepping into our society and obtaining ministerial authority & stepping out of the society & from under its jurisdiction again for the purpose of propagating his private & schismatic views,— Therefore this pby. do suspend Mr Matthew Houston from all the functions of the gospel ministry, & he is hereby suspended until he shall have returned to order & satisfied the church as to his reformation & submission to its rules & authority.

[April 10, 1804.]

Mr Cleland was appointed to supply in the Ind^a. Territory as much of his time as he can with conveniency. Messrs Howe & Abel to administer the ordinance of the Lord's supper at Beaver Creek church. Messrs Robertson, Abell & Finley to administer the ordinance of the Lord's supper at Concord church. Mr Cameron to supply at discretion.

[Beardstown]

Wednesday morning, six o'clock, Oct. 2d 1805. . . .
Reports [of supplies].
The Rev. Thomas Cleland fulfilled his appointments in the Indiana, Territory. . . . Messrs Cleland & Wilson complied with the order of last stated session respecting the preparation of materials for the history of the church. Pby. considering the importance of faithful church history do again most earnestly enjoin it upon all members that have not yet forwarded historical information to take the earliest opportunity in their power of transmitting to the

Presbytery a letter informing them that he had relinquished the faith of the church and declined the authority of her judicatories. He followed Barton W. Stone in the New Light schism, and was one of that group who went over to the Shakers.

Rev. Archibald Cameron a true statement of the situation of the churches under their immediate knowledge.

Reports [of appointments filled].

Pby. proceeded to take under consideration the case of Mr Houston & upon mature deliberation are of opinion that he ought to be deposed & he is hereby solemnly deposed from the exercise of all the functions of the gospel ministry, & it is hereby ordered that the Rev. Saml. Finley or the John P. Campbell attend at Silver Creek church & there make known to the people who were formerly under Mr Houston's care the determination of pby. relative to him & that the stated clerk immediately forward to Mr Finley an attested copy of this order.

The Rev. Joshua L. Wilson desired leave to resign his pastoral charge of Bardstown congregation. Ordered therefore that said congregation be cited & they are hereby cited to attend by their commissioner at our next stated session to show cause if any they have why he should not make s^d resignation.

[April 8, 1806.]

Reports [of appointments filled].

[Bethel, April 9, 1806.]

Mr Jno. Forbes produced a written discourse on John III, 36, the subject of which was assigned him at the last stated session as a part of trial, which pby. found so defective[22] they would not sustain it. Pby. having in their judgment made sufficient trial of the qualifications of Mr Jno. Forbes for the gospel ministry, & believing that he does not possess that aptness to teach which the nature of that office requires & having no prospects of his ever obtaining the degree of literary knowledge & distinctness of expression which would make him an edifying minister of the word, determined no longer to continue his trials for the said important office.

Jonathan A. Rice produced a written discourse on a subject assigned him at the last spring session of pby. as a part of trial, which discourse was considered defective[22] in point of composition & that he did not give the most natural exposition of his subject, but upon the whole pby. thought it deserved some commendation as an introductory part of trial & under that view they did sustain it. Tho pby. could not see their way clear in fully encouraging Johathan A. Rice in aiming at the gospel ministry they thought it not proper to dismiss[22] him from trial for the present, but to appoint him another subject on which he may produce a discourse at our next stated session; he was accordingly directed to prepare a discourse on second Timothy II, 15. Pby. adjourned to meet tomorrow morning at 6 o'clock at Mr Andrew Cunningham's. . . .

Tuesday morning, 6 o'clock. April 10.

Pby. Met according to adj't. . . . Pby. having heard an exegesis written by Mr Wm. Gray as a part of trial, the subject of which was assigned him at the last fall session, after due deliberation were of opinion that as his performance was defective[22] for not embracing the main points contained in the subject, & in other respects, they could not sustain it as a part of trial. Mr Gray was directed to prepare an exegesis on the same subject to be read at the next stated session of pby. Pby. then proceeded to examine Mr Gray on the Latin & Greek languages, which examination was not sustained & he was again directed to prepare for an examination on those languages at the next stated session.

The stated clerk was directed to use his exertions to procure certain books for this pby. from Phila. which were allotted by the General Assembly to be distributed gratis amongst the poor in the churches under their care.

A verbal supplication was made from Stockdon's Valley for supplies. A supplication from Upper & Lower Benson

---

[22] A stiffening of the educational requirements followed upon the defection of the Cumberland Presbytery. That body having been dissolved, candidates for the ministry who lacked educational qualifications found the doors closed to them in the "Old Presbyterian Church."

praying for one third of the Rev. Mr Shannon's ministerial labors in each congregation, presented & read. . . .

Wednesday, Oct. 15. . . .

A verbal supplication was made in behalf of Paint Lick for supplies. A verbal supplication from the Illinois grant for supplies. The Rev. Joshua L. Wilson appeared in pby. & his reasons for absence were sustained. Ordered that the minutes of the last session of pby. be read.

Reports [of appointments filled].

Mr Nathan H. Hall exhibited an exegesis on a subject assigned him at our last stated session which pby. found so defective that they could not sustain it as a part of trial & accordingly directed Mr Hall to prepare a discourse on the same subject to be read at our next stated session.

Messrs Irvin & Armstrong obtained leave of absence until tomorrow morning.

[Oct. 15, 1806.]

Mr Jonathan A. Rice produced a written discourse on 2 Tim. II, 15, the subject assigned him at our last stated session as a part of trial which was not sustained, & as pby. had not a sufficient prospect of his future improvement in literary knowledge & being apprehensive that his bodily infirmities will render him incapable of performing the duties of the gospel ministry, determined no longer to continue his trials for the sacred office. . . .

A letter from Rev. James McGready, addressed to the stated clerk was presented & read setting forth that bodily indisposition & the inclemency of the season prevented his attendance. Resolved that the Rev. Messrs John Andrews, John Howe, Saml. B. Robertson, Thomas Cleland, & Joshua L. Wilson, with Mr Clayborne Rice, ruling elder, or any two of them, be a committee to attend at Russellville on the second Tuesday in February next to inquire into the conduct of the Rev. James McGready relative to those things alleged against him by the late Cumberland pby. as stated on their minutes respecting a house & lot in the town of Russellville & make report to this pby. at their next stated

session.   The Rev. Archibald Cameron informed pby. that
200 copies of the Shorter Catechism had been transmitted
to him from Philadelphia to be distributed gratis, together
with seventy extracts from the minutes of the General Assembly for the year 1806; & that the amount of the carriage
was 240 cts.   Ordered that pby. defrayed expense at their
next stated session & that the stated clerk as early as possible distribute sd books among the members of pby. according to due proportion.   The Rev. Thos. Cleland received
10 catechisms for himself, & ten extracts for himself,
Messrs Rice, Finley, Howe, Abell & the vacant congregations of Paint Lick & Silver Creek.   The Rev. Saml. B.
Robertson received 10 catechisms for himself, & four extracts for himself, the Rev. John P. Campbell & the sessions
adjacent to them.   The Rev. Archibald Cameron retained
40 catechisms, & 7 extracts for himself, Messrs Vance &
Shannon & the vacancies near them.   The Rev. Joshua L.
Wilson retained 10 catechisms & three extracts for himself
& Bardstown session.   Ordered that the committee appointed to meet at Russellville inquire particularly into the
state of the congregations in the bounds of the late Cumberland pby. with a view to furnishing matter for church
history & report to this pby. at their next stated session. . . .

SAML. B. ROBERTSON, Modr.

JOSHUA L. WILSON, Clerk.

[Bardstown.]   Friday morning, April 17, A.D. 1807.
The committee appointed to attend at Russellville for the
purpose of examining into the Rev. James McGready's
conduct relative to a house & lot in sd town, reported as
follows, viz: "Agreeably to a resolution of the pby. of Transylvania, held at Bardstown, Dec. 17, 1806, appointing the
Rev Messrs John Andrews, John Howe, Saml. B. Robertson, Thos. Cleland & Joshua L. Wilson with Mr Claiborne
Rice, ruling elder, to attend at Russelville on the 2d Tuesday in Feb. 1807, & inquire into the conduct of the Rev.

James McGready relative to the things alleged against him by the late Cumberland pby. as stated on their minutes respecting a house & lot in the town of Russellville. On the day appointed for the purpose aforsd the Rev. Messrs Samuel B. Robertson & Thos. Cleland with Mr Claiborne Rice, ruling elder, were the only members who appeared, but being a quorum, proceeded to do business. Mr. Robertson in the chair & Mr Cleland clerk. The committee then took the case into which they were appointed to inquire under their deliberate consideration & report that they have with circumspection & attention examined the various evidence brought before them, which is as follows.—George McLean of Logan county, being duly sworn, deposeth & saith—I was sheriff of Logan county & Israel McGready was a deputy in good credit & gave eight or ten securities of good fame during which time the sd Israel had a spell of sickness at his brother's, the Rev. James McGready, at which time he was in as high credit perhaps as any man in the county, could have gotten trust or security for any sum almost. Sometime after he, the sd Israel, began to depriciate in property & credit, occasioned by intemperance. I began to be a little alarmed, & being immediately concerned it became necessary for me to make inquiry concerning his affairs. At length the time of sheriffry expired & I was moved against in several instances for the conduct of sd Israel. In conversation with Mr James McGready on the subject he informed me of a house & lot that Israel had given him in trust for his third daughter agreeably to a declaration made by him at a sacrament near the double Licks in 1805 which was afterwards. I further state that the sd. Rev. James McGready mentioned a tract of land that Israel had assigned to him but that he wished it sold for its value & that he intended to apply every penny to the payment of Israel's debts, that he would not keep one cent of the price back. At the time of the sd Israel's sickness as aforesd he was thought to be in a prosperous way as to this world's good. All this information I came to the knowledge of before the sacrament before mentioned & as to the house & lot, (altho I was so materially interested,) I was perfectly satisfied that there were no fraudulent designs & I believe the house & lot ought to have remained & I expect will remain a bona fide sale or gift which I informed the jury when trying the right of property. But it was my impression that the jury intended to give judg^t vs. Mr McGready at all events.

Geo. McLean. Feb. 11. 1807.

Ephraim McLean & Benj. Johnson, being first sworn, depose & say that they were present at the meeting near the Double Licks when the Rev. James McGready made a statement or declaration respecting the property of Israel McGready which was said to be in his hands & held by him in order to defraud the lawful creditors of the sd Israel which charges or reports were conceived by James McGready to be injurious to his character & thought it necessary on that occasion to make a proper statement which was nearly after the following manner as well / as these deponents recollect.—James McGready declared that there was no property of Israel McGready's in his possession except three species, viz: one piece of land near Russellville, a house & lot in the same town & a five hundred dollar bond on John Washington. The first he declared he had an assignment on & had offered for sale & did intend to sell to the best advantage & that the money should be applied for the relief of Israel McGready's creditors. The second, namely the house & lot, he said he had a legal title to, not as his own property but held it in trust as a guardian for his third daughter. The bond he said he had traded for with his brother & declared he had obtained possession of all this property at a time when he conceived his brother Israel to be in good standing in the county both as to property & credit. Given under our hands this tenth day of Feb. 1807.

Ephraim McLean.   Benj. Johnson.

The deposition of Winifred Ewing, a member of the West Fork congregation.—This deponent saith that on a sacramental occasion near the double Licks she heard the Rev. James McGready make a public declaration respecting the affairs of Israel McGready. So far as related to the insinuations dropped by I suppose malicious persons against him the sd Rev. James McGready. I recollect hearing him say that Israel McGready had lain sick at his house likely to die at a time when his affairs as to the world were prosperous. He put into this the sd James' possession a bond or deed for a lot in Russellville in trust for his third daughter. After some time the said Israel recovered & the sd James proposed & offered the sd instrument of writing to him the sd Israel again, but that he refused, stating that he always allowed it for the sd third daughter & he wished him to keep it for her, stating that the sd girl always seemed particularly fond of him the sd Israel & he of her; stating also that the sd Israel had said he intended to give her all his property if he died without an heir. Sworn to before me Goring Ewing, a justice of the peace for Christian county this 9th day of Feb. 1807.

Goring Ewing, J.P.

Samuel McLean of Christian county, being duly sworn, states that Mr James McGready declared in a congregation at the Double Licks that he had but three species of property in his hands of Israel McGready's, viz: one bond upon John Washington which he the sd James McGready traded for, but this deponent does not recollect the amount of sd bond; one piece of land assigned to Mr James McGready which sd McGready declared should be sold for the discharge of Israel McGready's debts & that every cent of it should be paid out for that purpose; & a deed made to Mr James McGready of a piece of property which sd James was to keep in trust or as a guardian for his third daughter. Samuel McLean.

I do certify that on a sacramental occasion in the fall of the year 1805, near the Double Licks, I heard the Rev. James McGready say publicly from the stand that some time previous to that time Israel McGready had been sick at his house & during his illness made a deed or some other instrument of writing, to a house & lot in Russellville in trust for his third daughter. But after the sd Israel recovered he offered the writing to him & he refused to receive it stating that he intended it for his daughter as stated.   Elizabeth Ewing, her ✕ mark.

The deposition of Urben Ewing of Logan county deposeth & saith that some time in the fall of the year 1805, to the best of his knowledge at a sacrament near the Double Licks that he heard the Rev. James McGready publicly state that there was a report in circulation injurious to his character respecting a house & lot in the town of Russellville & that his brother Israel McGready had given the house & lot aforesd to the sd James' third daughter & that he the sd James did not intend to appropriate the lot aforesaid to his own use. I do further state that I was so well satisfied previous to the declaration aforesd that the lot was for the child, it being universally believed, that I paid very little attention to the declaration, being perfectly satisfied in my own mind.

                    Urben Ewing, 11th of Feb. 1807.

I, Joseph Ficklin, of Russellville, being duly sworn, do make the following representation of / statement relative to a house & lot purchased by the sd Ficklin of the Rev. James McGready, that is to say in March 1806. I the sd Joseph Ficklin understood the house herein named to have been sold as the property of Israel McGready & I then observed to sundry persons that I would buy the Rev. James McGready's title believing it to be the best & at the same time knowing the unwillingness that the Rev. James McGready must have to a law suit. I accordingly purchased the title aforesaid in company with Judah McGready. This purchase I made without hearing of the Rev. McGready the particulars of the purchase, or how the debts between him & Israel McGready stood. My knowledge of the Rev. James McGready induced me to believe he was guilty of no improper conduct to invalidate the purchase of sd lot & after the purchase made by myself & Judah McGready we commenced suit against the purchasers at sheriff's sale & after the commencement of sd suit James Hunter the acting purchaser at the sheriff's sale agreed to pay to the sd Joseph Ficklin the rent for sd house for ten months which amounted to 40 dollars & to give up his claim & has actually directed the sheriff to make a deed to the sd J. F. on the condition that the sd Joseph Ficklin would pay the cost of suit & 40 dollars, the purchase money at the sheriff's sale, to which the sd Joseph Ficklin agreed, not from a fear that anything would be established to injure his title but from a wish to have a clear title to enable him to sell. I further state that from the inquiries I have made myself of sundry persons & from the accounts I have had from those persons immediately interested & opposed to me in the suit I can hear of nothing fraudulent on the part of the sd James McGready to injure the sd Ficklin's title, for about the time the deed was made by Israel McGready to his brother it appeared from the current report that the sd Israel was in a very easy situation & in no danger of being insolvent.

Joseph Ficklin.

In the case of the charge exhibited against the Rev. James McGready, John P. Oldham being duly sworn, deposeth & saith that he appeared as counsel on a trial respecting a house & lot in Russellville claimed by sd McGready in which a verdict was rendered against him. In which trial he well recollects that there was no legal evidence that a deed which was produced executed by Israel McGready to sd James was fraudulent. This deponent also recollects that it was proven on sd trial that the debt which was the subject of sd trial was contracted by sd Israel subsequent to the date of sd deed & as he believes subsequent to the recording of the same. This deponent is further of opinion that the aforesaid verdict was contrary to evidence & unsupported by legal principles & conceives that the jury must have been misled or they could never have found the same.

Jno. P. Oldham.

The deposition of Solomon P. Sharp, taken by commissioners of the Transylvania Pby., who being first sworn, deposeth & saith that some time in the year 1806 the Rev. James McGready applied to this deponent to attend for him at a certain inquest to be held to try the right of property in his house & lot in the town of Russellville which was then taken in execution to satisfy a judgement obtained against Israel McGready. This deponent attended at the time & place & when the jury were impanelled & sworn he stated to them their duty & produced the deed of conveyance from Israel to James McGready which was dated some time in the year 1803 as near as this deponent recollects, & as this deponent then was & still is of the opinion, was conclusive evidence of James McGready's title. The deed expressed a valuable consideration in the face of it & from the date appeared to have been made before this deponent, & he believes or any other person, had an idea of Israel McGready's insolvency. But it being before the sheriff, & there being no court or any person to direct the jury what was legal evidence, the attorney on the opposite side called in parole testimony to prove to the jury that the debt originated for work that was done to the house on sd lot & it ought to pay it. This deponent further states that being personally acquainted/ with some of the jury & knowing their prejudices he conceived, altho he was satisfied he had both law & justice on his side, that he had very little chance to get a verdict of the jury in his favor, & as near as this deponent recollects, he mentioned at the time to Col. Caldwell, or some other person standing by, that he would have to forbid the sale for the jury would find against him. This deponent further states that after the jury had retired by themselves they sent word there was evidence they wished to hear & this deponent being dissatisfied with the conduct of some of the jury & expecting them to find against him agreed not to go up but to let the jury hear the evidence & decide on it themselves. The evidence that the jury heard in private, as this deponent was informed afterwards by several of the jury themselves, was respecting certain declarations that James McGready should have made at a sacrament stating that the lot belonged to his daughter & not to himself, which declaration this deponent knows nothing of his knowledge, which declarations some of the jury stated to be the principal grounds for their finding as they did, & which this deponent only conceived to be an apology for their finding so palpably contrary both to law & evidence. This deponent further recollects of mentioning to the attorney on the opposite side after the sale of the sd lot that he could not certainly be serious in what he contended before the jury, & inasmuch as the verdict of that jury did not in the least finally decide the right of property, that the person who purchased at the sale would eventually lose it, or words to that effect. He replied that he knew the purchaser had no chance for the land & he would not give anything for his title, but that he was employed to make the money on the execution by getting the lot sold, & so he effected that he did not care what went with the title, or to that purport. This deponent further states that he was informed that James McGready afterwards sold the house & lot for less than its value rather than contend for it, whereas if this deponent could have had his title to the lot under the same circumstances he would not have taken a cent less than he thought was its value on account of the verdict of the inquest.

Solomon P. Sharp.

Logan Circuit. To wit. I, Armistead Morehead, clerk of sd. court, do certify that on the 2d day of Sept. in the year of our Lord one thousand eight hundred & 3 Israel McGready appeared before me & acknowledged a deed of conveyance to a certain house & lot of ground in Russellville to James McGready. At that time there were no suits pending, nor executions against sd Israel McGready, except one in the name of Kelly & Brent for about twenty dollars; & two in the name of William Stewart, one of which was for about the sum of forty dollars, & the other for about 20; & having been sworn to give my opinion before the committee on the trial of sd James McGready as to the solvency of sd Israel McGready at the time of the conveyance above mentioned, I have no hesitation in declaring it as my opinion at that time that the sd Israel McGready was in good credit & had considerable visible property, nor do I believe that a fraud was intended by the conveyance. Given under my hand this 11th day of Feb. 1807.

Armistead Morehead.

James Hunter, being duly sworn, deposeth & saith that he sometime past bought a certain house & lot in the town of Russellville, or at least, Israel McGready's right & title to sd house, for the sum of forty dollars & further saith that the reason of sd house selling so low was on account of Mr James McGready having deed for sd lot which was generally supposed might probably be the best claim, & further saith that he understood Mr James McGready had said the deed was made to him for the benefit of one of his daughters.

James Hunter.

As well as I can charge my memory I was called to attend Mr Israel McGready in a severe spell of bilious remittent fever in the fall of 1803 & was uncertain how his case would terminate, in fact I did suppose that it would not be favorable. Nevertheless after a tedious length of time he regained his health, at which time I believed him to be in good circumstances & never knew to the contrary till about two years ago. Given under my hand this 10th day of Feb. 1807.

Walter Jones.

Testimony of John Latham.—I do hereby certify that in the year 1802, some time in Sept. Israel McGready came to my father's to board & continued about a year; that sd Israel was at that time in good circumstances, shewed me certificates for tracts of land which I conceived to be valuable; that he did sell in the year 1804 one tract of land to Mr Washington for near or about $1000. I farther certify that I frequently heard Israel McGready say he intended to leave something handsome to Peggy A. R. McGready, a favorite niece of his if he should die without heirs; & further, some time after said Israel had a severe illness he informed me that he had made a deed to his brother James McGready for a house & lot in Russellville. Which was to be the property of the above mentioned Peggy A. R. McGready when she should come of age or marry. Given under my hand this 10th day of Feb. 1807.

John Latham.

Henderson County Sc. I do by these presents certify that in the month of Sep. 1803 I was living at the house of James McGready. At that time Israel McGready lay sick to appearance dangerously ill at the house of the said James McGready. At that time he made a deed to his house & lot in the town of Russellville to the sd James McGready. I myself was a witness to sd deed & I can certify that the intention of Israel McGready, as he expressed it then & always afterwards in my hearing, was that the sd James McGready should hold the whole right title & property of the sd house & lot according to law but in trust for his daughter Peggy A. R. McGready, so that the sd Peggy A. R. McGready should possess it as her lawful right & property when she should be of age. I further certify that at this time when the said Israel McGready made this deed to the said James McGready he the sd Israel was generally believed to be in independent circumstances, in good credit in the county & no person expressed any apprehension of his breaking or becoming insolvent. Furthermore I certify

I know that sd Israel McGready possessed several tracts of land at the time he made the said deed to the sd James which he sold after his recovery, which I have every reason to believe he never assigned to any person till he actually sold them. And I do further certify when the sd James Mc-Gready sold the house & lot to myself & Joseph Ficklin from the conversation between the said James & myself I have every reason to believe he intended the money arising from the sale of sd house & lot for his daughter Peggy A. R. McGready when she arrived at age. Given under my hand this 26 day of January 1807.

Juda McGready.

Henderson Sct. This day Juda McGready personally appeared before me Phillip Barbour one of the commonwealth's justices of the peace for sd county & made oath to the truth of the above certificate. Given under my hand this 26 of Jan. 1807.

Philip Barbour, J.P.

Henderson County. Sct. I do hereby certify that I was witness to the deed that Israel McGready made to James McGready of his house & lot in Russellville, which was in the month of Sept. 1803 or thereabout. I likewise certify that at the time sd Israel made the deed to James Mc-Gready I did believe him the sd Israel McGready to be in prosperous circumstances & that his credit was good throughout the county of Logan for near two years afterwards. I myself took him for 80 dollars which was due me by one of the most wealthy citizens of that county.

H. Knox.

Henderson County, Sct. This day Hugh Knox personally appeared before me Philip Barbour one of the justices of the peace for said county & made oath to the above certificate. Given under my hand this 21st Jan. 1807.

Philip Barbour, J.P.

Samuel Caldwell of Logan county & town of Russellville, being sworn, states that as well as / he recollects, in the year 1803, the Rev. James McGready asked this deponent that if a deed made to an infant for land would be good & binding, this deponent answered that it would. Mr McGready then observed that his brother Israel McGready had, for some time, taken a particular fancy to one of his little daughters & had given her a certain house & lot in the aforesaid town, but that they, to wit, the Mr McGreadies, had concluded that a deed made to the little girl would not be legal, she being an infant, & that Israel McGready had made the deed for sd house & lot to him James McGready in trust for sd infant, & that sd James might make the deed for sd house & lot to her when she should come of age; & as well as this deponent recollects, the sd James McGready mentioned to this deponent that he had that day delivered the aforesaid deed into the clerk's office for recording. This deponent further states that at that time he considered sd Israel in a prosperous way & making money insomuch that he lent sd Israel sums of money long after that period.

S. Caldwell.

As far as I can I will without any introductory remarks state such information as appears to be relative to the inquiries made of me. In the year 1803 I suppose that the property of Israel McGready must have been of much more value than his debts could have amounted to. Being aware of the difficulty of perfect correctness as to dates I feel the necessity of caution & wish to observe it particularly in any statements I may give. My mind, however, is well satisfied that Israel McGready after 1803 did sell to John Washington land to the amount of $950; he also possessed a tract called the Allen spring which was sold for $400 in trade. Another tract, called Story's claim, which I think worth $400; & he had a claim upon another tract in the name of Buxton which I believe was sold for $400 in trade. I also understood he had a tolerable valuable tract of land in the Georgia settlement of this county. He had another claim in the neighborhood of Russellville which has sold for $300 in trade, & I am satisfied could not be got for less than $600 or $800 at this time. He also had a considerable amount of fees due him which accrued by virtue of his office as he stated to me & which I believe to be correct, & altho I have practiced much as a lawyer & presided as a judge in this county & consequently ought to know something of the demands against sd Israel there is nothing which occurred in 1803, or since then, that I can possibly recollect, which would show that his debts were equal to one half of the value of the property I have stated, & I should be unwilling to assert that they bore that proportion in 1803. It is difficult to penetrate the intention of any person, & it can only be discovered by external circumstances. I will not then say there was not a fraudulent combination between James & Israel McGready, but will state such circumstances as have come under my observation that may elucidate the inquiry & enable any other person to deduce as certain & correct an opinion as I could give. This I think the most correct, as no man's opinion ought to be relied on unless the grounds of it would warrant the deduction. As well as I recollect, the lot which Israel is said to have deeded to the sd James was of but little value. I would not now give $150 for it with only the improvements it then had on it. I think I have heard Israel, about the time spoken of, or in the succeeding year, say he had given the lot to one of his brother's daughters; & I thought & still think that the treatment, the friendship & the services he had received from his brother & his family might very well have justified the gift as a token of his gratitude, & it probably ought not to be considered even as an ill-timed liberality. From a knowledge I have had of James McGready since the year 1799, having since that period lived within about two miles of him, & for some years of the time adjoining him, being his nearest neighbor as I believe, I have been clearly of opinion that he was one of the most honest men & possessed & practiced the most exemplary piety of any man I ever saw or was acquainted with. He appeared to

me more abstracted from the things of the world & more
devoted to religion uniformly than any / man whose conduct I had as particularly observed & I cannot forbear the
repetition of an observation I have often made, tho it might
appear improper, or indiscreet, or ill-timed or irrelavant,
except as far as it goes to show the uniformity of my
opinion & corroborate the statement I now make,—his conduct has made such an impression on my mind that I have
frequently & as sincerely declared I would rather have his
chance of future happiness than any man's I ever saw. I
have only one more observation to make & I shall finish this
incoherent deposition, written in great haste & in a very
short time. If Israel & James McGready had colluded to
defraud the creditors of the former it appears somewhat
strange that Israel should have conveyed so small a portion
of his property only. The facts above related, as well as
my memory serves me, are correct & true.

Ninian Edwards.[23] 12th Feb. 1807.

The following Indenture is truly copied from the original
which James McGready made to Peggy A. R. McGready
his daughter, which instrument was written & acknowledged
at the same time that Israel McGready deeded the house
& lot in question to his brother James, & was signed by
the same witnesses who attested sd Israel's deed to Mr
James McGready. The original deed from which the following copy was taken was laid before the committee at
the time of their sitting. — This indenture, made this 2d
day of Sept. 1803, between James McGready of Logan
county & state of Kentucky of the one part & Peggy Alexander Ramsey McGready, daughter of the said James
McGready of the other part, Witnesseth, that the sd James

[23] Ninian Edwards, a native of Maryland and educated at Dickinson College, came to Kentucky in 1795. In 1803 he was appointed to the bench and
four years later became chief justice of the Kentucky court of appeals. From
1808 to 1818 he was the governor of Illinois Territory. On Illinois' rise to
statehood Edwards was chosen to represent Illinois in the United States
Senate, which post he held until his appointment as minister to Mexico. In
1826 he was elected governor of Illinois.

McGready, for, & in consideration of one hundred dollars
to him in hand paid by Israel McGready, in the name &
upon the consent of the sd Peggy Alexander Ramsey Mc-
Gready, hath granted, bargained & sold & by these presents
do grant bargain & sell to the sd Peggy Alexander Ramsey
McGready a certain house & lot in the town of Russellville
containing half an acre of land, on the north side of the
north street designated in the plat of sd town No 10, together with all & singular the advantages & appurtenances
thereto belonging, or in any wise appertaining, to have & to
hold the said lot in sd town of Russellville, together with
all & singular the advantages & benefits thereunto belonging or anywise appertaining, to the sd Peggy Alexander
Ramsey McGready, her heirs & assigns forever. The sd
James McGready covenant with the sd Peggy Alexander
Ramsey, her heirs & assigns, that he will warrant & forever
defend the sd lot of land in the sd town of Russellville
against himself & successors & against all persons claiming
under him. In witness whereof the said James McGready
hath hereunto set his hand & seal the day & year above
written.   James McGready (SEAL)

Signed, sealed & delivered in   Henderson county Sct.
presence of H. Knox   Hugh Knox & Judah Mc-
          Judah. McGready   Gready formally ap-
                                     peared before me.

[Russellville, Feb. 11, 1807.]

Whereupon your committee do not hesitate to declare or
give it as their opinion that the statement made to Synod
by way of reference to them on the minutes of the late Cumberland pby. respecting the conduct of the Rev. James
McGready is PARTIAL & INCORRECT. That the
declaration of the sd James McGready at the meeting near
the Double Licks appears to have been more full & explicit
than the sd pby. have stated in the charge; that the deed
for a house & lot in the town of Russellville was lawfully
executed to James McGready by his brother Israel Mc-

Gready while he the sd Israel was in solvent circumstances & in good standing both as to property & credit; that the said house & lot was to be held by James McGready in trust as a guardian for/ & to be applied to the sole benefit & behoof of Peggy A. R. McGready his third daughter, but he omitting to execute a deed from himself to her the title to sd house & lot did not reach to Peggy A. R. McGready but was properly vested in her father James McGready & was improperly wrested from him by a jury either uninformed or misled when trying the right of property.   Your committee farther report that upon the whole there does not appear to have been any fraudulent design or malintention in James McGready to defraud the creditors of Israel McGready in the case of the house & lot in question or in any circumstance appertaining thereunto; but he appears to have acted with lawful upright & honest intention.   Your committee farther report that owing to the inclemency of the season, their short stay, fewness in number, together with various other circumstances, they did not acquire such a competency of knowledge as would be satisfactory respecting the state of the church, or aid in furnishing materials for its history.

   Saml. B. Robertson.   Thos. Cleland.
   Russellville, Feb. 11th, 1807. Claiborne Rice.

Which report[23a] was agreed to & the pby. having obtained by their committee full & circumstantial evidence from men of respectability, legal knowledge, & particular knowledge of all the facts necessary to be known in the investigation of this case, are fully satisfied that the late Cumberland pby. in their reference to the Synod of Kentucky gave a false, iniquitous & malicious representation of the conduct of the Rev. James McGready relative to a house & lot in the town of Russellville.   But this pby. do not pretend to say how far the late pby. of Cumberland were misguided by the false statements of their informers.   Neither do we think that

[23a] Further lengthy testimony regarding Mr. McGready is omitted.

the ill intended official conduct of incorporate bodies does necessarily imply a malicious intention in each member of such bodies, & there is nothing more distant from our minds than to suppose it of each member of the aforesaid Cumberland pby., but we are sure that inquity, falsehood & malice have given existence to the charges which were referred to the Synod of Kentucky against the Rev. James McGready & when we find that the pby. were inattentive to the rules of discipline & that the testimony of those who were the proper persons to give information upon this subject & who ought to have been applied to is in pointed contradiction to the charges preferred by the late Cumberland pby. we cannot avoid thinking that the pby. involved themselves in the slander which they were so officious as to realize in their record. Ordered by this pby. that a correct copy of this record upon the presiding subject together with the report of the committee be transmitted to our next Synod, including the documents.

Ordered that the Rev. Archibald Cameron be appointed to supply ¾ of his time in the united congregations of Fox Run, Shelbyville & Tick Creek till next stated session. Ordered that the rest of the members of this pby. supply in those vacancies which are nearest them as many sabbaths as convenient. Ordered that the Rev. Samuel B. Robertson be appointed to attend in Knox County, Indiana Territory, in order to answer the prayer of a petition from that place.

Mr. Michael Wrench obtained leave of absence for the remainder of this evening. Whereas a petition has come forward from a number of people who attend worship at Big Spring meeting house praying that a division line between the congregation of Bardstown & that of Big Spring be as follows, viz: the line of division between sd congregations shall be along the road that leads from Ferguson's Mill to James Allen's, & thence to Cartmels on the road leading from Bardstown to Louisville, where the road crosses Cox's Creek. Resolved, therefore by this pby. that the above prescribed line be the boundry between the con-

gregation of Bardstown & that of Big Spring.   Resolved
that the resolution respecting contributions in order to meet
the expenses of this pby. shall have a special reference to
the expenses that should be incurred by attendance of the
present commissioner at the next Gen. Assembly.

[New Providence Church, Oct. 7, 1808.]

Thursday morning, Oct. 7th. . . .

Pby. being solicitous to reduce their presbyterial business
to a more orderly condition & desirous to obtain the attendance of all their members for that purpose, agreed to adjourn to meet at Glasgow, in the county of Barren, on
Wednesday the 22d day of March next, & the stated clerk
was directed to notify all the absent members of pby. of the
time & place of meeting, & likewise the other ministers of
our society who have settled within our bounds; & moreover urge the necessity of their punctual attention to the
annual reports of their congregations & collections of money
for the pby. & other purposes; & further that a letter be
written by this pby. to Messrs Hodge, McGready, McGee,
McAdow & Rankin, requesting them to come forward to
that pby. that they might have a friendly interview with
them respecting the subjects of difficulty existing in their
case, & that they might inform any of those whom the late
pby. of Cumberland had formerly recognised as ministers
of the gospel, to come forward likewise & be sharers in this
friendly interview.   Pby. then draughted & adopted the following letter for the purpose above mentioned.   "Dear
Brethren.   We are anxious to see you & have a friendly interview with you respecting the difficulties which exist in
your case.   The Synod of Kentucky have directed us to
endeavor to settle the business which lay before them respecting you.   We hope you will meet with us at Glasgow,
in Barren county, on Wednesday the 22d day of March
next, & bring with you as many of those men who were
declared by the commission of Synod to be destitute of authority to preach the gospel as may to you seem proper that

they may be sharers in the friendly interview. May the Lord direct us & heal every disorder. Farewell.

To Messrs Hodge, McGready, McGee, McAdow
        & Rankin.   THOS. CLELAND, Clk.
                JOSHUA L. WILSON, Modr.

Mr Archd. Cameron handed in annual reports from the congregations of Tick Creek, Shelbyville & Fox Run. Mr Arch. Cameron collected three dollars for the use of pby. from Tick Creek congregation.

Ordered that the treasurer pay the proportion of money which may be proper for the members of our pby. when demanded, for the purpose of defraying the expenses of the stated clerk of Synod.

Pby. adjourned to meet at Glasgow, in Barren county, on Wednesday the 22d of March next.

                JOSHUA L. WILSON, Modr.

Examined by committee of Synod thus far & approved.

STATED SPRING SESSION

        Glasgow Church.   March 22d, 1809.

ROLL . . .

Thursday. Mar. 23d. . . . The letter written by pby. at the last session requesting Mr William Hodge & others to come forward to the present session for the purpose of a free & friendly conference on the subject of existing differences not having reached Mr Hodge, but he having heard that such a letter was written, appeared in pby. in order to meet their wishes as expressed in their letter; whereupon pby. resolved to engage in the conference. After several hours spent in conference with Mr Hodge in a friendly & familiar way without coming to any certain determination relative to his case & those with whom he is connected, & wishing further time to deliberate on this matter pby. agreed to postpone any further proceeding in the case till tomorrow. Mr Howe obtained leave of absence until tomorrow morning, 9 o'clock. Mr Cleland was chosen to officiate as clerk in his absence.   Whereas it appears that Mr David Wood, a licentiate of this pby. has for several years been absent, & he having neglected to attend or give any information respecting his situation, they thought proper to cite Mr Wood & he is hereby cited to attend the next stated session to show cause of his long absence; & the stated clerk was directed to transmit a copy of this minute to Mr Wood as soon as possible & also to notify him of the time & place of the next stated session.

Whereas common fame loudly proclaims the disorderly conduct of the Rev. John Bowman in propagating & encouraging heresy & schism contrary to the peace & harmony of our church as well as against our Confession of Faith & discipline, & pby. having a desire to redress as speedily as possible all such disorders & irregularities, agreed to cite the said John Bowman, & he is hereby cited to attend our next stated session to answer to the above charge & the clerk pro tempore is directed to forward a copy of this minute to Mr Bowman with as much certainty & dispatch as possible.

Pby. taking into consideration the loud & urgent call in Providence to a day of fasting & humiliation on account of the great declension in religion, the abounding of error & infidelity, the great inattention manifested toward the means of grace & ordinances of the gospel, together with the precarious situation of our national affairs in respect to foreign nations; & Synod having appointed the fourth Tuesday in May next to be set apart as a day of humiliation & thanksgiving, pby. do cordially acquiesce in that appointment, & solemnly enjoin it on all the members to pay a particular attention thereunto, & the members present are requested to give as early information as convenient to the absent members & vacant congregations contiguous to them of the time & object of this appointment. . . .

Friday, March 24th, . . .
Pby. deeply regretted the absence of so large a majority of the members, likewise of the minutes of last pby. by reason of which they are unable to make out a full & just report

to the Synod & General Assembly. Sensible of the importance of this business & of their obligations of the General Assembly, Resolved, therefore that the Rev. David Rice write a letter to all the absent members of pby. earnestly requesting them to attend our next stated meeting for the purpose of furnishing congregational reports & for other necessary & important business. Pby. being sufficiently satisfied respecting the scandalous conduct of Mr John Rankin in continuing to propagate & encourage heresy & schism & manifesting no disposition to return to the faith & discipline of our church, they thought proper for the welfare & purity of the church to depose the said Mr John Rankin & he is hereby solemnly deposed from all the functions of the gospel ministry until his repentance & submission to the authority of the church be manifested. Pby. resumed the unfinished business of yesterday relative to Mr Hodge & others. In conformity to a particular & final request of Mr Hodge expressed in the course of the conference held with him, viz: that pby. should write him & his brethren in connection a letter stating on what terms a reconciliation could be effected, & after considerable deliberation upon the case pby. resolved that the Rev. Thomas Cleland & John Howe be a committee to answer the request of Mr Hodge & make report tomorrow morning. . . .

March 25th, 1809. . . . Messrs. Cleland & Howe reported that they had complied with the resolution of pby. relative to the request of Mr Hodge. The letter being read was approved. On motion resolved that the letter be inserted in the minutes & a copy be transmitted to Mr Hodge by the clerk pro tem. "Glasgow, March 25th, 1809. Dr Sir. Agreeably to your request pby. have thought proper to address you by letter, & through you all those likewise who are interested with you. We again renew our declaration of an earnest solicitude & unfeigned anxiety that the unhappy breach which has taken place between us may be healed & the present existing differences removed; & as you have requested a direct & formal statement from us of the terms on which that desirable & important object may be effected, we with the same friendly spirit that was manifested in our late conference, & we hope with that honesty & integrity of heart which ought to actuate the servants of our divine Lord & Master, do proceed to state those terms & requisitions which, to descend to the lowest stage of accomodation, we think are necessary. And in the first place, as to yourself, we think the ground of your suspension by Synod just, & consequently the reasons for that procedure right & proper. With this impression we conceive your restoration can only be effected by a proper acknowledgement of the faith & submission to the authority of our church as contained in our book of discipline to which you are referred. The same will be required of those brethren who are yet under citation for not submitting to the authority of Synod as exercised by their commission. Anything less than this would subject us to the censure of that body, a part of which we compose, & of whose adjudications in the case of the late Cumberland pby. we approve. In the next place, with regard to the young men licensed & ordained by the aforesaid pby., we do humbly conceive that a formal examination of them respecting doctrine & discipline is indispensable as the only way under present circumstances for us as a pby. to be satisfied respecting their sentiments & consequently whether we are agreed in point of doctrine, without which a union would be inconsistent & afford no security for future peace & harmony in the church. From hence it may be easily inferred that an unequivocal adoption of our Confession of Faith is also indispensable.

This would only be placing them on the same ground on which we ourselves stand, & any other could not be advisable or desirable to either those young men or ourselves. For them to adopt the Confession only *in part* & we in *the whole* would by no means, in our opinion, effect a union according to truth & reality, & we conceive a mere nominal union would not prove a sufficient security against future difficulties. And whatever inferences may be drawn by others respecting what is called fatality from our views as expressed in the Confession respecting the Divine sovereignty in the decree of predestination & election, we conceive that no such conclusion can follow from the promises as there laid down.   After our desire that the great Head of the church may interpose & direct you & us to that which is right & proper, with every sentiment of conciliation & esteem, you have our best wishes for your welfare here & happiness in a change of existence."

Whereas the Rev. William McGee & Samuel McAdow have hitherto not complied with the citation of Synod, & the business respecting their case having been transferred to this pby., therefore, Resolved, that the aforesaid William McGee & Samuel McAdow be, & they are hereby again, cited to attend our next stated session to show cause why they have not submitted to the authority of Synod as exercised by their commission.   Ordered that the clerk pro tempore forward a copy of this minute to each of the above mentioned members as soon as possible.

The Rev. James McGready not having made a formal submission to the authority of Synod as exercised by their commission & pby. thinking it necessary that such submission ought to be made, however they may be satisfied as individuals of Mr. McGready's disposition to make that submission, yet it was thought proper to cite him again, & he is hereby cited to attend our next stated session to meet the object of pby. in that case.   Ordered that the clerk pro tem. transmit an extract of the above minute to Mr McCready as soon as convenient.

[Oct. 5, 1809.]

A letter was received from Mr McGready in which he has expressed due submission to the discipline of our church in every point of view in which the citation of pby. affected him, which was satisfactory for the present. Pby. however look forward with expectation that he will appear at our next stated session & make the requested submission in person.

Friday, Oct. 6th. . . . The Rev. Joshua L. Wilson applied to this pby. by letter for a dismission in order to join the pby. of Washington, whereupon it was agreed that Mr Wilson be & is hereby dismissed & affectionately recommended to the attention of that pby.

[Springfield, Oct. 6, 1809.]

Pby. thought proper to attend to the important subject of the education of poor & pious young men for the gospel ministry agreeably to the recommendation of the General Assembly, & more effectually to embrace this desirable object thought it most expedient to appoint a special committee who were to use their exertions to find out such young men as are contemplated by the Assembly & make such other arrangements as may appear to them almost eligible & likely to effect the object in view. Resolved that the Rev. Messrs Howe, Cleland, Robertson & Vance, or any three of them, be & they are hereby appointed a committee for this purpose & report to each stated session of pby.

Mr William Hodge, in conformity to a letter addressed to him by the last pby., appeared in this pby. & after some time spent in conference with him relative to his case, & without doing anything decisive on the subject, agreed at the request of Mr Hodge to refer his case to Synod. Messrs McGee & McAdow not having appeared agreeably to former citations, the stated clerk was directed to cite them again to appear at the next stated pby.. Messrs. Finley & Pemberton obtained leave of absence the remainder of the session.

The General Assembly having authorized this pby. to appoint a missionary for four months in the country of the Natchez, but upon inquiry no person being found to fulfill such an appointment, the pby. considered themselves unable to meet the objects of the Assembly & the clerk pro tem. was directed to give this information to the committee of missions in due time. Mr Balch obtained leave for the remainder of session. Messrs Andrews, Templin & Cleland have leave of absence until 9 o'clock tomorrow. Mr Shannon was appointed to officiate as temporary Moderator & Mr Vance temporary clerk. Pby. adjourned to meet this evening at Gen. M. Waltons, at 7 o'clock. . . .

[Greentown, Siloam Church, Dec. 6, 1809.]

Mr Wm. Hodge appeared before pby. & informed them that he came forward as an individual, & he made such statements, acknowledgements, professions of sorrow for past irregularities, together with a determination to submit to the authority & discipline of our church, & that he fully & unequivocally adopted & adhered to the Confession of the Faith of this church, all which were considered as satisfactory reasons for the re-instatement of Mr Hodge into the pastoral office; whereupon pby. proceeded to restore Mr Hodge & he is hereby restored to the full exercise of all the functions of the gospel ministry, & was invited to take a seat as a member of pby. which he did accordingly. The Rev. Jer. Abell appeared in pby. & his reasons for absence were sustained. . . .

Thursday morning, Dec. 7th. . . . Messrs Thos. Nelson & Saml. Hodge,[24] two of the young men formerly licensed & ordained by the late Cumberland pby. & prohibited by the commission of Synod, came forward & expressed their desire to submit themselves to the wisdom & determination of this pby. whereupon pby. proceeded to consider their cases, & having lengthily & particularly examined them so far as was thought expedient, & on account of the difference of their situation from that of ordinary candidates pby. thought it unnecessary to record the parts of trial in detail & being satisfied with Messrs Nelson & Hodge in reference to their doctrinal qualifications for the gospel ministry, their aptness to teach, & after their accepting the Confession of Faith & discipline of our church & promising in a solemn

[24] These two men complied with the demands of the commission which declared many of the ministers licensed and ordained by Cumberland Presbytery destitute of authority to administer the sealing ordinances. (See *Minutes of Cumberland Presbytery*, April 3, 1805 and October 7, 1806.)

manner conformity to the rules & regulations of the church & submission to the brethren in the Lord, their licensure & ordination were recognized & confirmed unanimously & they authorized to exercise all the functions of the gospel ministry agreeably to the rules of our church. They were consequently recognized as members of this pby. & invited to take their seats which they did accordingly.

Whereas it appears that several ministers of other presbyteries are residing & preaching within / our bounds & have continued so to do for a considerable time without attaching themselves to this pby. or informing us of the reasons of this failure, therefore ordered that the clerk pro tempore affectionately address these brethren & inform them that this pby. feel it their duty to express their disapprobation of such irregularities & earnestly solicit them to attend our next spring session at Bardstown on the 1st Tuesday in April. . . .

JOHN HOWE, Moderator.   THOS. CLELAND, Clk. pro tem.
JAS. VANCE. S.C.T.P.

[Bardstown.]

Thursday, April 5th 1810. . . . The Rev. John Bowman & Saml. McAdow having been duly & repeatedly cited to appear before this pby. to answer to certain charges preferred against them & they having failed to appear & pby. being sufficiently advised of their schism & declinature in having renounced the jurisdiction of the pres. church & of their having connected themselves with disorganizing parties contrary to all order & good fidelity, & pby. viewing them as enemies of the faith & discipline of this church, thought it their duty for the glory of God & the interests of religion to suspend the said John Bowman & Saml. McAdow & they are hereby suspended from the exercise of the pastoral office until their repentance & return to the faith & discipline of our church. Ordered that the stated clerk transmit a copy of the above minute to Messrs Bowman & McAdow as soon as convenient. Pby. being informed of the peculiar & distressed condition of the mind of the Rev. Wm. McGee[25] thought it expedient & most advisable to appoint a member to write an affectionate letter to him, requesting him to come forward to our next stated session that a friendly conference may be had with him respecting his case; whereupon Mr Cameron was appointed to write to Mr McGee embracing the object of pby.

[Bardstown, April 5, 1810.]

The pby. with grief recognized the contumacious & disorderly conduct of the Rev. Thos. B. Craighead in the case of his late publication consisting of a *Sermon on Regeneration & an address to the Synod of Kentucky together with an appendix*, as laying them under the the necessity of taking special notice of him for the pernicious errors & many misrepresentations of facts & characters which are found in said publication; therefore they specify the following charges against the said { Rev. Thos. B. Craighead, viz;

2nd we charge him with denying, vilifying & misrepresenting the doctrines of divine foreordination, divine sovereignty & election. 1st,

We charge him with denying & vilifying } N.B. Error in copying

the real agency of the Spirit in regeneration, in the production of saving faith, in sanctification in general.   3rd. We charge him with denying & vilifying the doctrine of love of God & His law from a principle of virtue in the heart & teaching that the selfish principle of interest produces christian obedience which is acceptable to God.   4th, We charge him with perverting the doctrine of faith in destroying the difference between an evangelical faith & that faith which devils & wicked men may have of divine realities.   5th, We charge him with perverting, abusing & misstating the definitions, descriptions & real sentiments of the preachers &

[25] Mr. McGee joined the Cumberland Presbyterian Church in the fall and was suspended shortly thereafter. Samuel McAdow also joined the Cumberland body. McDonnald, *op. cit.*, pp. 90-91.

writers of our connection upon the subjects of faith & regeneration.   6th, We charge him with false coloring of
facts which transpired in Synod & the commission of Synod.
Wherefore the pby. resolved that the Rev. Thos. B. Craighead be cited & he is hereby cited to appear at the intermediate pby. at Springfield church on the second Monday in
June next to answer to the above charges which are to be
proven from his own publication in conjunction with the
members of Synod & commission of Synod.   Ordered that
the stated clerk forward a copy of the above minute to the
Rev. Thos. B. Craighead by the Rev. Mr Stephenson.

Pby. adj'd. to meet at Mr. Woodcock's tomorrow morning 6 o'clock.   Concluded with prayer.

Thursday, Oct. 4th, 1810. . . . Pby not having received any answer to the letter addressed to the Rev. Wm.
McGee, thought it expedient to defer any discussion in his
case & ordered that Mr Cleland be appointed to write a
friendly letter still requesting an interview with him & an
explicit declaration of his disposition towards the pres.
church, & that the letter be forwarded by Mr Brown who
is directed to confer personally with Mr McGee on the
above subject & report to the next session of pby. Messrs
Finley appeared in pby. & their reasons for absence were
sustained.

Resolved that Messrs McGready, Finley, Brown & Robertson be a committee to draft a petition to the Synod praying a division of this pby. into two or more pbys., designate
the boundaries & report as soon as possible before the adj't
of pby.   Mr Cloyd obtained leave of absence for the remainder of the session.

[Bardstown, Oct. 5, 1810.]

Resolved, the business of yesterday relative to Mr Craighead be resumed.   The committee appd. to examine Mr
Craighead's book reported & the report was read & each
charge separately considered & voted upon by the pby.
The committee presuming that a complete & perfect enu-

meration of all the objectionable parts of said book is not
expected have called the attention of the pby. only to the
following particulars which they conceive to be contrary to
the Confession of the Faith of the pres. church & go to establish the charges against Mr Craighead on account of his
late publication. Charge 1st, We charge him with denying &
vilifying the real agency of the Spirit in regeneration & in
the production of faith & sanctification in general. See
page[s] 4,6,7,8,11,17,21,46,53,72,88. Charge 2d. We
charge him with denying, vilifying & misrepresenting the
doctrines of divine foreordination, sovereignty & election.
See pages 13,28,45,62,86,87,89. Charge 3d. We charge
him with denying & vilifying the doctrine of love of God &
His law from a principle of virtue in the heart & teaching
that the selfish principle of interest produces christian obedience which is acceptable to God. See page[s] 17,20,50,
69,73. * Charge 5th. (* 4th Below) We charge him
with perverting, abusing & mistating the definitions, descriptions & real sentiments of the preachers & writers of our
connection upon the subjects of faith & regeneration. See
page[s] 15,20,24,37,39,46,51,54,57,58,60,63,68,69,70,74.
Charge 6th. We charge him with the false coloring of
facts which transpired in Synod & the commission of Synod.
See page[s] 56,61,62. Charge 4th. We charge him with
perverting the doctrines of faith, in destroying / the difference between an evangelical faith & that which devils &
wicked men may have of divine realities. See page[s] 12,
26,69. Pby. having maturely deliberated on the case of
Mr Craighead & having particularly attended to each
charge with the references supposed to establish them, together with statements given by several members of this
pby. relative to the last charge, were of opinion that all the
charges are sufficiently established & it is the judgment of
this pby. that Mr Craighead ought to be suspended, but as
it is required that a Synod be consulted in such cases it was
agreed that this matter be laid before the ensuing Synod[26] &

[26] Evidently the Synod upheld the decision of the Presbytery for Mr.
Craighead's name fails to appear on the succeeding rolls of the sessions.

request them to adjudicate on his case or do whatever in their wisdom they may think proper.

STATED SPRING SESSION

Bardstown church, 9th April, 1811.

Members present, the Rev. Thos. Cleland, Saml. B. Robertson & Joseph B. Lapsley, with Rob't. Johnson & Rob't. Armstrong, elders. Absent, the Rev. David Rice, Benj. Irvine, Sam'l Shannon, Arch^d. Cameron, Jas. Vance, Jer. Abell, Saml. Finley, John Todd & Saml. K. Nelson.

Mr Robertson was chosen Moderator & Mr Lapsley clerk pro tem.

Pby. took into consideration the recommendation of the Gen. Assy. respecting the method of obtaining contributions for the Theological Seminary & after mature deliberation were of opinion that they could not at present adopt any prompt or decisive measure on that subject with hope of success, but recommended to each member of pby. to pay such attention to the recommendation of the Assy. on that subject as he may think most advisable.

Pby. proceeded to make out supplies. Mr Robertson to supply the congregations of Shiloh, Ebenezer, & South Bethel as much of his time as he may think proper. Mr Lapsley 2 sabs. at Shepherdsville. Messrs Cleland, Shannon, & Nelson one sab. each at N. Providence & Cane Run. Mr Finley at Pt. Lick & Silver Creek one sab. each, & direct these churches to pay attention to pby. in sending a representative to our meetings & also to forward their sessional records & congregational reports. Pby. then adj'd to meet at Harden's Creek church the 2d Tuesday in April next. Concluded with prayer. SAML. SHANNON, Modr. THOS. CLELAND, Clk. pro tem.

A true record. Atteste. THOS. CLELAND, S.C.T.P.

(See *Minutes*, April 9, 1811, and succeeding minutes.) In 1812, April 17, charges similar to those against Craighead were preferred against Jno. Todd. He was deemed worthy of suspension but was admonished to change his ways. April 5, 1813 he was suspended. An appeal to the General Assembly resulted in his restoration to the Presbytery, Oct. 10, 1817.

Mr McElroy's, 6 o'clock. . . . A resolution of Synod, Oct. 16, 1810, in conformity to the directions of the Gen'l Assembly respecting the catechizing of youth &c, was laid before pby., whereupon after due deliberation, Resolved. 1, That each member of pby. be, & they are hereby, directed to pay a particular attention to the catechizing of youth in their respective charges & particularly enjoin it on parents to attend to their duty on that subject. 2, That each member of pby. in connection with the several sessions pursue such a course as may appear to them most advisable to secure the proper exercise of discipline over our baptized youth & also that they take such order as shall seem prudent to secure the religious instruction of slaves together with a humane & christian treatment.

Mr Wm. Mahon appeared before pby. & expressed a wish that they wd take under consideration his case & if possible remove the sentence of deposition which had so long existed & restore him to his former standing. Whereupon pby. agreed to attend to Mr Mahon's request & desired him to make such communications as might enable them to act in that matter. Pby. having heard Mr Mahon's statements, after due deliberation were of opinion that no satisfactory evidence appeared to afford any ground to authorize them to restore him to his former standing in our church.

Mr Tate obtained leave of absence for the remainder of the session. Adj'd to meet at Wm. McElroy's tomorrow morning, 6 o'clock. Concluded with prayer.

Friday morning, 6 o'clock. At Mr McElroy's Pby. met according to adj't. . . .

It is with grief & reluctance that pby. find themselves under the necessity of noticing & inquiring into the conduct of the Rev. John Todd, who, according to the loud & frequent reports of common fame is industriously engaged in propagating heretical sentiments & manifesting a schismatical spirit/ all which are highly inimical to the doctrines & discipline of our church & the interests of the Redeemer's kingdom in general. Therefore pby. deem it their indispensible & bounden duty to enter process against Mr Todd & have prepared the following charges against him, viz: 1st. We charge him with disseminating & defending the Pelagian & Arminian sentiments contained in the writings of Thos. B. Craighead, which sentiments have been condemned by this pby. & the higher judicatures of our church. 2. We charge him with setting himself in opposition to the proceedings of the judicatures of our church against the said Thos. B. Craighead, which conduct is calculated to bring into contempt & thereby defeat the object of discipline as exercised by them in the case of sd Craighead. In order to support the above charges pby. names the following persons as witnesses, viz; Col. G. J. Johnson, Jas. Gilkison, Jas. Vance, N. H. Hall, John R. Moreland, Sam'l McElroy, Stoughton Edwards, Arch'd Cameron, Greenby Gaither & John Reaugh. Ordered that the stated clerk forward a copy of the above charges with the names of the witnesses to Mr Todd, & that he also cite the witnesses in due time. Resolved that there be an intermediate pby. app^d for the above purpose to meet at Brunerstown the second Thursday in August next.

Adj'd. to meet at New Providence on the first Wednesday in Oct. next. . . .

JOS. B. LAPSLEY, Mod^r. SAML. B. ROBERTSON,
Clk. pro tem.

Atteste. THOS. CLELAND, S.C.T.P.

14th Aug. . . . Pby. proceeded to consider the case of Mr Todd & the charges being read the following named persons were procured & deposed as followeth, to wit. G. J. Johnson being sworn deposeth & saith that shortly after the publication of Thos. B. Craighead's sermon on Regeneration he was passing by the door of the Rev. John Todd in Louisville when Mr Todd came to the door & invited him in, the deponent went in & after a little while Mr Todd inquired of the depon^t whether he had seen Mr Craighead's sermon on regeneration, the deponent replied that he had not. Mr Todd then produced it & declared it to be in his opinion one of the best that he had ever read; he spoke of it in such high terms of commendation that the depon[t] was induced to ask the loan of it for a few days, this was granted & the depon[t] in the perusal of the sermon found several objectionable parts containing doctrines hostile to what he believed & still believes to be the truth, & noted some of them in ye margin altho the book was not his own, & perhaps he may have indulged himself too far in so doing. The book was returned to Mr. Todd with whatever marks or notes the depon[t] had made. Before the depon[t] had left the house of Mr Todd on ye evening af[d] he introduced a conversation with this depon[t] upon the subject of regeneration & inquired of him what his thoughts were; the depon[t] stated his view & ascribed the conversion & sanctification of a blind sinner to the will & power of the Divine mind operating upon the creature by *immediate* influence & bringing him / from darkness to light ordinarily with the word. Mr Todd alleged that the Spirit was in the word & that there was sufficient energy in the word to convert a sinner & that being rec'd into ye mind as the truth by its inherent & appropriate powers lead to correct & virtuous conduct & it would sanctify the soul. The depon[t] does not pretend to state the identical words used by Mr Todd, he is positive however as to the sentiments expressed. He denied the *immediate* agency of the Divine Spirit in the conversion of a sinner, that the Spirit was in & accompanied the word, that man of himself could believe the truths of the gospel to the saving of his soul, that this gospel was received by faith & acted under, & that in his view of the subject there was no necessity for the *immediate* agency of the Spirit of God. The depon[t] farther states that he once heard Mr Todd deliver similar sentiments from the *pulpit*. Shortly after this the depon[t] declined hearing Mr Todd as a minister of the gospel, not owing *entirely* to the opinions entertained by Mr Todd being different from those of the depon[t] in this respect, but to other causes which need not here be noticed. Question by Mr Todd. Do you recollect whether I said the Spirit was in the word or accompanied the word?

Ans. I am not positive, the idea which I took up from the conversation was that the Spirit accompanied the word or that there was a sufficient energy in the word abstract from the *immediate* operation of the Spirit of God. Q by same. Did you consider that my idea was that there was any independence of the creature upon the Creator in any mental act, or that there was no concern or agency of Deity in support of his establishment of instructing & governing his creatures thro the medium of words & ideas? A. I am unable to answer the questions. It seems to me to have no point. I never heard you say that the creature was independent of the Creator. I suppose the mind as well as all other things are dependent on the will of God & perhaps this may have been your idea. Q by same. Did you ever understand me to communicate the idea that the word in any influence produced by it on the human mind could be considered abstractly from the will & appointments of God to use it as a means of communication? A. I understood you to say in substance that the word was when received into the mind by faith capable of converting the sinner in exclusion of the immediate operation of the Spirit, that the influence wrought in the mind was by virtue of the word, that this word was given by the will & app^t of God, was the efficient mean of salvation, & God had done all that was *necessary* for the establishment of his church on earth, that the word was the effective cause of regeneration. Q. I hope you did not understand me to mean that God was not concerned in the effecting all His ends by His word as a mean, did you? A. I have, I think, fully answered this question already. I understood you to say that the Spirit accompanied the word & that there was such energy in the word as to produce, (when received by faith in the mind,) conversion, &c. Q. Did you not understand me to teach that God was the agent & his word a mean necessary to communicate ideas? A. I understood you to exclude the *immediate* agency of God. Q. Did you not understand me as pointing out the danger of trusting to the being taught by the Spirit without the word? A. You spoke of delusions, fancies, imaginations, &c, & I do not remember that the danger you speak of was mentioned. Q. Did you understand me at any time to deny any agency of God, or did you not understand me as teaching the necessary presence & agency of God in some sense in order to the effecting all things? I have answered this question generally & particularly. I have stated & now state that you denied the immediate agency of God in regeneration, ascribing it to the energetic influence of the word rec'd by faith & acted on. I do not know how God who is omnipresent could or can in any sense be considered as not present or absent. Q. Does Col. Johnson remember that I used the expression that man of himself could believe the truth of the gospel to the saving of the soul? A. I understood as I have already stated in various parts of this deposition that Mr Todd said & meant, as I thought, that the gospel was the effective mean of salvation & that man could by faith receive it as the truth. As to the expression "to the saving of the soul" I am not positive, the idea is a clear one & clearly expressed, the saving of the soul & salvation in my mind being synonymous; & further this deponent saith not. Ga. J. Johnson.

The Rev. James Vance being duly sworn deposeth & saith that he has heard the Rev. John Todd in conversation speak not only favorably of Mr Craikhead's book which contains a sermon on regeneration &c, but maintain/ & defend with zeal the doctrines contained in s^d book. He hath heard him say to Mr Cameron in company with Mr Lapsley & himself that he, (Mr Todd) did not believe any man could lay his finger on a sentence in Mr Craighead's book that is contrary to our Confession of Faith or the Scriptures. This depon^t hath heard Mr Todd preach frequently & has no doubt but his sentiments in several of his sermons were the very same as contained in Mr Craighead's book. Mr Todd in his preaching which his depon^t hath heard never, as he observed, spoke of the Spirit's accompanying the Scriptures, but as in ye Scriptures. Mr Todd has appeared to this depon^t guardedly to avoid any such expressions as the operations of the Spirit, the influence of ye

Spirit, the energy of the Spirit or the light of ye Spirit in his speaking of the conversion of a sinner or in the great work of regeneration [in] the sinner's heart. This depon^t hath heard Mr Todd use frequently the expression "the grace of God", but on asking Mr Todd what he meant by the grace of God he said he meant by it the manifestations which God has made of Himself in His word addressed to the mind, promising life to all who w^d accept of it. This deponent hath heard Mr Todd deny the positive direct influence of the Holy Ghost in regenerating the sinner's heart. This depon^t hath heard Mr Todd say that saving faith in Jesus Christ must be prior to regeneration. He hath heard Mr Todd deny that there is any light, any energy, any influence or operation of the Holy Spirit necessary more than what is in the word to dispose a sinner to choose life & salvation as offered in the gospel; that the *Will* is from the constitution of man possessed of a self determining power to choose life & salvation as offered in the gospel without any positive direct aid of the Holy Spirit determining him to that choice. This depon^t is confident these ideas Mr Todd has again & again declared to him & in his hearing with some little variation only in his mode of expression Mr Todd has said that this depon^t don't understand him, but whatever difficulty there may be in understanding Mr Todd's idea from his mode of expressing them this depon^t must think he does not mistake his meaning. This depon^t hath heard Mr Todd censure the pby. for attempting to call Mr Craighead to an account for what they supposed to be his error. He hath heard him censure the Rev. John P. Campbell for writing against Mr Craighead & he hath heard him speak in terms of the greatest disapprobation of Mr. Campbell's first reply to Mr Craighead, & also of Mr Campbell's second reply called the "Pelagian detected". He hath also heard Mr Todd say that he did think Mr Campbell to be *dishonest*. This it is thought was said by Mr Todd with reference to Mr Campbell's controversy with Mr Craighead. Question by Mr. Todd. Does Mr Vance distinctly remember to have heard me use the express

term that the Spirit is in the word? Ans[r]. I heard you use
the expression "in the Scriptures" both in preaching & in
private conversation. Q. In answer to the question what I
meant by the grace of God does Mr Vance distinctly remember that I only included the manifestations made of Himself
in His word & left out of view all agency of God in restraining lusts, passions, ordering of circumstances & a concurring in many ways providentially to secure the blessings
of the new covenant to mankind, & overruling invisible malicious spirits & even suggesting to the mind good thoughts,
yet understanding that all knowledge is communicated by
the Scriptures? Ans. I remember no such additions or explanations. Q. In denying the positive direct influence of
the Holy Ghost did not Mr Vance understand me as not
agreeing with what he considered physical agency? A. I
do not remember using the term physical when in conversation with Mr Todd on the subject of regeneration. Q. In
denying that there is any light & energy, any influence or
operation of the Holy Spirit more than what is in the word,
&c, see the 2[d] question. A. See my answer to question
2[d]. Q. Did not Mr Vance understand me to say he saw no
need to admit a necessary determination of the will by
physical power? A. I do not recollect that you used the
expression "a necessary determination of the will by physical power". I understood you as expressing yourself as
stated in the body of my deposition. Q. Did I not distinctly say that I could scarcely believe J. P. Campbell to
be altogether honest in that publication the Pelagian detected, specifying particularly his candor in his writing on
that subject? A. The expressions as used in my deposition
I believe to be identical expressions used by you in speaking
of Mr Campbell; what you might have said in a way of
explanation I am not able to state for I was put to confusion in hearing you express yourself in so improper a manner. And farther this deponent saith not. James Vance.

Archibald Cameron, being sworn, witnesseth & saith that
he has not been in conversation with Mr Todd much upon
any subject, that he has heard of Mr Todd's having

frequent conversations with others about Mr Thos B. Craighead's objectionable doctrines upon the subject of regeneration & the operations of the spirit & of his highly approving those objectionable sentiments for which Mr Craighead was censured; that some time, he thinks in June, 1810,
he fell in with Mr Todd between Bardstown & Springfield,
being in company with Messrs Vance & Lapsley, Mr Todd
introduced a conversation with the depon^t about Mr Craighead's printed sermon on Regeneration & the charges preferred against s^d Craighead by pby.   In that conversation
Mr Todd said he would not for all Kentucky have any hand
in preferring such charges against Mr Craighead as those
brought against him by the pby., that the respectability of
the presbyterian church in the western country fell or stood
with Mr. Craighead's sermon, & some other things to that
effect.   The depon^t. wishing to know whether Mr Todd approved of Mr Craighead's views on regeneration & the operations of the Spirit, or had misunderstood him, asked Mr
Todd his opinion respecting the operations of the Spirit in
regeneration, to which inquiry Mr Todd answered in a de-
sultory & unsatisfactory manner.   Then the depon^t inquired
of Mr Todd whether the Spirit did not work in the heart to
quicken & dispose it for complying with the word, & whether
it is not by an operation of the Divine Spirit internally working that the mind of a blind sinner is brought to proper conceptions of the word, or did he think those effects were
produced only by the arguments, instruction & motives of
the word laid before the mind.   To which, after a little
pause, Mr Todd replied with apparent displeasure "Your
distinctions consist in words only, I do not understand you.
I wish you w^d be more explicit".   Though the depon^t was
inclinable to think that Mr. Todd could not avoid understanding him & that his unwillingness to give direct answers
was the reason or cause of his saying so, in order to remove
all pretensions to this want of understanding & inexplicit-
ness of language the depon^t stated that the Scriptures represent man as dead, blind & disposed to evil by nature.   In
effecting a change from this deadness, blindness & evil

disposition of heart the Scriptures further speak of the quickening, renewing & opening of the heart; the question proposed is whether these effects are produced by the instructions of the word alone or does God, by the same Spirit which dictated the word, operate on the heart beside & beyond what the word can do in quickening, renewing & disposing it for realizing what the word teaches. Mr. Todd still alleged that these distinctions were unintelligible & spoke of the Spirit of God as always present with the word. From Mr Todd's whole conversation no doubt remained on the mind of the depon^t of Mr Todd's holding that the mere word is the only effective cause of regeneration. This depon^t further saith that he then indulged himself in some little reasoning & questions, upon predestination & election & efficacious grace in general, to all which Mr Todd gave such evasive, equivocal & negative answers as induced him to conclude that Mr Todd was unacquainted with the doctrines of his own church or chose not to acknowledge them; the depon^t was the more confirmed in this opinion at the pby. which was held at Danville in October following, where Mr Todd offered the authority of Drs. Beattie & Read, Arminian philosophers, to justify Mr Craighead's views of necessity & free-agency. Question by Mr Todd. In the conversation with respect to the agency of the Divine Spirit on the heart did I not refer to the notion of physical agency as a ground of difference in our conceptions? Ans. Not at all. So far as I understood you or now recollect; the greatest of difference most apparent to me was that you did not admit of many agency of God upon the heart or mind of man, but the word or something of which the mind could have a conscious idea, & of course you rejected the secret influence of Deity in regeneration & providence which secret influence upon the/ mind I professed to believe in all things without pretending to ascertain God's mode of acting under the distinction of physical & moral agency. And farther this depont. saith not. Archibald Cameron.

Nathan H. Hall, being sworn, deposeth & saith, that he hath at different times & places heard the Rev John Todd espouse & defend the sentiments contained in a book written by T. B. Craighead on Regeneration &c., & in behalf of which he expressed the strongest predilection without excepting any part thereof. This depon^t says that he has heard Mr Todd deny that there was any immediate or direct agency of the Holy Spirit in the work of regeneration; that the Spirit did not accompany the word by any direct agency, but was in the word itself, & that man by his natural powers with the assistance of the Scriptures could work himself into the belief of the truth & in that way become a Christian, & yet the whole would be of grace, or by the Spirit. This depon^t farther states that he has heard Mr Todd repeatedly speak in the most severe manner against the judicatures of our church for their conduct in proceeding against Mr Craighead, saying that the members acted with duplicity, & that it was his opinion Mr Craighead did not deserve such treatment. These & similar remarks of Mr Todd did appear to this depon^t to be calculated to throw contempt upon our judicatures in the exercise of discipline in the case of Craighead. Question by Mr Todd. I hope Mr Hall, (for a long time has elapsed since any conversation on these subjects between us,) does not design to say the expressions used in the deposition were all what I used but that he would only communicate what he understood me to mean, does he? A. The language is in part Mr. Todd's, in part not, but the substance on the whole is the same. Q. by same. When you heard me at different times & places as stated before defend the sentiments taught in Mr Craighead's book was not the conversation directed to yourself & not in company at least of one or two. How often have I mentioned the subject to you? A. Sometimes in the company of a few, sometimes when by ourselves; the number of times I do not recollect. The sentiments stated above & those which I conceive to be contained in Craighead's piece depon^t hath heard Mr Todd preach. Q. Did Mr. Hall ever hear me say that the members acted with duplicity or use any term with equal or like import? A. I did, or if not that term Mr Todd used the term *under-*

handedly. And farther this depon[t] saith not.   Nathan H. Hall.

John Reaugh, being duly sworn, deposeth & saith that being invited by the Rev. John Todd to spend the evening at his home a conversation took place respecting Mr Craighead's book on "Regeneration, &c". Mr Todd spoke of s[d] book in terms of approbation, & in the course of the conversation the subject of the decrees of God was mentioned. Mr Todd saith that if God had fore-ordained whatsoever comes to pass there could be no sin in the world. Q. by Mr Todd. Perhaps Mr Reaugh recollects that I mentioned the doctrine of necessity as opposed to liberty & observed that admitting necessity it appears to me that man could not be a moral agent & that all the disorder & sin in the world must be properly reckoned to the account of him who laid him under that necessity; that this was the am't of what was said rather than the expression used in the deposition, does he not? Ans. Mr. Todd talked of the doctrine of necessity, that it had been taught & that it was hurtful; but Mr Todd then turned his discourse to the doctrine of the decrees & expressed himself, I believe, as stated in my deposition. And farther this depon[t] saith not. John Reaugh.

Pby. having then considered the nature of the charges preferred against Mr Todd at the last session & deliberately weighed the evidence which was produced relative to those charges, & having heard Mr Todd in his own defense, they were unanimously agreed that the said charges were fully established. On motion pby. then proceeded to determine what kind & degree of censure should be employed in the case of Mr Todd & agreed that suspension is fully incurred by him & especially because he professes justification of his conduct & errors; but pby. feeling a lenity on the occasion & willing to give Mr Todd time to review the impropriety of his conduct & thinking it proper to take the advice of the Synod before they proceed to pronounce the sentence of suspension, which they think a proper one, Resolved, for the present that Mr. Todd be solemnly admonished from the chair; which was done accordingly.

Pby. having finished the business before them concluded with prayer. . . .

JOS. B. LAPSLEY, Mod[r].

Pby. proceeded to the consideration of Mr Todd's case, he being present. Several hours were spent in a free & friendly conversation with him relative to those erroneous sentiments of which he was judged guilty by a former decision of this pby., & from all that the pby. heard from him on these subjects were further convinced of his errors, & labored patiently & in the most friendly manner to bring him to repentance, but have to regret that all their efforts proved unavailing as he showed no disposition to recant those objectionable sentiments or manifest such a repentance as is required by the word of God & our Discipline. Therefore the pby., with the directions of the Book of Discipline in view in such cases, as also the advice of the last Synod, were of opinion that the former judgment of this pby. ought to be confirmed & that Mr Todd be, & he is hereby, suspended from the exercise of the functions of the gospel ministry until a suitable manifestation of his repentance.

Adj'd to meet at this place tomorrow morning, 7 o'clock. Concluded with prayer.

Mr Todd prayed an appeal to the Synod from the judgment of this pby. relative to his case which was granted. Ordered that the stated clerk have all the records & documents relative to the case before Synod when called for.

[Supplies appointed.]

Pby. adj'd to meet at Springfield church the first Wednesday in October next. . . .

SAML. SHANNON, Mod[r].
THOS. CLELAND, Clerk, pro tem.

Sept. 1. . . . On motion resolved that the stated clerk be directed to write a friendly letter to Mr Abell & request him to be more punctual in attending pby. or forward his reasons for absence.

Pby. received a lengthy & friendly letter from the Rev.

John Todd praying a removal of his suspension, which letter was carefully read & attentively considered, & after mature deliberation it was the opinion of this pby. that there was nothing in Mr Todd's letter expressive of any recantation of those sentiments which were considered erroneous & for the maintaining & propagating which he was formerly suspended by this pby. Therefore resolved unanimously that pby. cannot legally or conscientiously grant the request of Mr Todd, & that the stated clerk be & is hereby directed to forward a copy of this minute to him as soon as convenient. Pby. recognized a recommendation of the Gen. Assembly to all the presbyteries under their care to adopt speedy measures to induce the societies within their respective limits to petition Congress to pass a law against the transportation & opening the mail on the Sabbath day, in which recommendation this pby. does most heartily concur, & although from the moral sentiment of the public on this subject as well as from disappointments in former attempts of this kind they have little hopes of success, nevertheless do sincerely recommend to each member of this pby. to take such measures on this important subject as he may deem most advisable & most likely to meet the design of the Assembly's recommendation.

This pby. record with heartfelt emotions of sorrow the departure of our venerable aged & beloved father in the ministry the Rev. DAVID RICE. He was the first Moderator of this pby. which met in this place on the 17th day of Octr 1786 and of which he has since been a constant & faithful member until his entrance into rest, which was on the 18th day of June, 1816.

Friday morning, 4th Apr. . . . On inquiry it appeared that the order of pby. relative to members unconnected with any particular church had been partially complied with. Re-

solved that this order be & it is hereby renewed.   On motion
resolved that the Stated clerk be & he is hereby directed to
forward to the Gen. Assembly, in obedience to the order of
Synod, all the documents on which this pby. have heretofore
acted in the case of Mr. John Todd.

[1817]

Wednesday, Oct. 8th. . . .
On motion resolved that this pby. highly commend the
design of the G. Assembly in raising funds for the support
of domestic missions & to aid in effecting this object do
earnestly recommend to each church under their care to
form a missionary society within their bounds.

On motion resolved that the stated clerk of this pby. correspond with the stated clerk of the G. Assembly, (as directed by a resolution) respecting our situation in respect of
poor & pious youth educating for the gospel ministry, &
solicit the application of a part of certain funds raised for
this object by several presbyteries to the relief of Mr Jas. C.
Barnes & Mr David Phillips, who are candidates for the
ministry & at this time students of theology at Princeton.

[Oct. 10, 1817.]

On motion resolved that pby. do now take up the case of
Mr John Todd, aggreeably to directions of the G. Assembly. .After some deliberation had on the case of Mr Todd
pby. adjourned to meet in the Court house this evening at 6
o'clock.   Concluded with prayer.

Pby. met at the Court house according to adjournment.
. . . Pby. heard Mr Todd at considerable length on those
points of doctrine which were the cause of his suspension, in
which conversation Mr Todd denied the charges alleged
against him & gave to the pby. satisfaction on those subjects so far as to induce them to restore him to his former
standing: therefore resolved that his suspension be & it is
hereby removed & he is restored to all the functions of the
gospel ministry.

Adjourned to meet at this place tomorrow 2 o'clock. P.M. . . .

Saturday Oct. 11th. . . . Mr Todd applied for a dismission from this pby. with a view of joining the pby. of Louisville & he was dismissed accordingly & the clk. pro tem was directed to furnish Mr Todd with a copy of the above dismission.

Adjourned to meet at this place Monday morning, 7 o'clock. . . .

[Greentown, April 3, 1818.]

This pby. highly approving the plan & cordially reciprocating the recommendations of the Gen. Assembly on the subject of Domestic Missions & considering the great importance & utility of such a measure in promoting the interests of our church; therefore, Resolved that this pby. form themselves into a Domestic Missionary Society & that Messrs Cleland & Hall be a committee to form a constitution & report tomorrow.

Adjourned to meet at this place tomorrow morning, 9 o'clock. . . .

Saturday Apr. 4th. . . . The committee appointed to draft a constitution for the purpose of forming a missionary society reported one, which being read & the blanks filled was unanimously received & adopted & being signed by the members of pby. together with other individuals, proceeded to the choice of officers & made the necessary arrangements to carry the designs of the society into operation. Messrs Hall, Abell & Rose obtained leave of absence during the remainder of the sessions of pby. On motion resolved that the Stated Clerk be & he is hereby allowed the sum of $10 out of the funds of pby. for past services. Ordered that the members respectively supply one sabbath each in the vacancies they may deem most convenient. Pby. adjourned to meet at New Providence church the first Wednesday in Oct. next. . . .

SAML. B. ROBERTSON, Mod[r].
THOS. CLELAND, Clk. pro tem.

With the most tender & affectionate recollections this pby. record the death of the Rev. Terah Tamplin, which took place on the 6th day of Oct. 1818. He was admitted a member of this pby. at its first meeting in Ky. on the 17th day of Oct. 1786, to all the duties of which while he continued with us he was a faithful & punctual attendant until his death. During the whole course of his religious profession he daily appeared to walk with God. In his deportment before the world he exhibited an undissembled pattern of piety & in all his intercourse with mankind was "an Israelite indeed in whom was no guile."

Messrs Abell, Findley, Howe, Robertson, Cleland, Hall, Barnes & Hynes contributed $2 each in support of the commissioner's fund agreeably to a standing rule of this pby. Ordered that the above sum be transmitted by the Treasurer to the Commissioners' Fund.

On motion, Resolved that it be & hereby is recommended to & enjoined upon the church sessions within our bounds to use proper exertions to raise a fund for defraying the expenses of our commissioners to the Gen. Assembly, & other contingent expenses of the pby. which fund shall remain in the hands of the pby. for their disposal: & it is further required that those congregations which are vacant send up their contributions by their representatives to each spring pby.

Pby. received a communication from the Synod of Tennessee requesting their cooperation in the establishment of a Theological Seminary. On motion Resolved that this pby. do not think it expedient at this time to agree to the proposed cooperation with the Synod of Tennessee in their attempts to found a Theological Seminary. . . . Adjourned to meet at Big Spring church the Friday before the second Wednesday in Oct. next. . . .

SAML. FINDLEY, Mod'.

JAS. C. BARNES, Clk. pro tem.

Saturday. Oct. 7th. . . .

An appeal from a judgment of the United sessions of Springfield & Hardin's Creek churches on case of Adultery charged by public rumor against James Gilkison, a member of Springfield church, was regularly brought up & laid before pby., who having read all the papers & carefully examined all the testimony relative to the afores^d case: whereupon, after due deliberation, Resolved as the mind of pby. that the judgment of the aforesaid sessions of Springfield & Hardin's Creek churches be, & the same is hereby affirmed. Mr Hall obtained leave of absence until Monday morning.

A letter was received from the Rev. Saml. Findley setting forth a difficulty that had arisen in the Buffalo Spring church relative to the case of a man's marrying his former wife's sister, praying the decision of pby. on that case, or otherwise to refer the same to the Synod. After some time spent in deliberation on the above case it was on motion Resolved that this matter together with the letter of Mr Findley be & they are hereby referred to the Synod, with an earnest request of that body that they would form an explicit decision on the subject, that our churches may thereby be enabled to act uniformly & correctly in such cases.

Adjourned to meet at this place on Monday morning 9 o'clock. . . .

Saturday morning, April. 7th. [1821]. . . .

Whereas James Gilkison did appeal from the decision of this pby. against him at their last stated sessions on charge of Adultery to the Synod of Kentucky, which decision of the pby. was reversed by the Synod, from which judgment & reversal the pby. hath appeal to the Gen. Assembly, & whereas since the appeal of pby. aforesaid new & important testimony has been discovered which goes to establish indecent & criminal familiarities with the girl alluded to in the charge, identifying the place where sd Gilkison had illicit commerce with her as stated in the testimony of sd girl, this pby. therefore in order to support their former judgment & maintain the honor & welfare of the church do petition the G.Assy. to remand the aforesaid case back to the united sessions of Springfield & Hardin's Creek churches that a new trial may be had thereon. Ordered that the Stated Clerk forward an attested copy of the above resolution to the G.A. in due time.

Adjourned to meet at Harrodsburg church on the Friday preceding the 2d Wednesday in Oct. next. . . .

SAML. B. ROBERTSON, Mod^r.
JOHN HOWE, Clk. pro tem.

[Harrodsburg, Oct. 6, 1821.]

On motion resolved that a missionary sermon be preached & a collection taken up at each stated meeting of pby. for aiding the funds of our missionary society. Mr. Barnes was appointed to preach the missionary sermon at our next meeting & Mr Scott his alternate.

[Bardstown, Oct. 12, 1822.]

The missionary sermon was preached by the Rev. Jas. C. Barnes & a collection of twenty four dollars taken up. Resolved that the Rev. John Howe preach the next missionary sermon & the Rev. Thos. Cleland be his alternate. Adjourned to meet at Bardstown the first Thursday in April next. . . .

THOS. CLELAND, Mod^r.
JAS. C. BARNES, Clerk, P.T.

[Paint Lick Church, April 2, 1824.]

Mr Robert Holeman was introduced to pby. as a young man of good moral character & in full communion in our church who expressed a desire to become a candidate for the gospel ministry. Pby. proceeded to the examination of Mr Holeman as to his acquaintance with experimental religion & his views to the gospel ministry which was unanimously sustained. Mr Hamilton obtained leave of absence until tomorrow morning. Pby. then proceeded to examine Mr Holeman on the Greek & Latin languages, which was unanimously sustained. Adjourned to meet at this place tomorrow morning 8 o'clock. . . .

Dr. Reid's, Saturday morning, 8 o'clock. . . . Pby. further proceeded to the examination of Mr Holeman as to his knowledge of Rhetoric, Logic, Natural Philosophy, Philosophy of Mind, Geography & Astronomy, all which were sustained unanimously as parts of trial. Pby. then assigned Mr Holeman as further subject of trial a Latin exegesis on the following words. An sit Christus vere Deus & a critical exercise on Heb. VI.4-8, inclusive, to be read at the next stated sessions of pby.[27] Adjourned to meet at the church at 11 o'clock.

[Danville, Oct. 11, 1824.]

Monday morning, 8 o'clock. Oct. 11th. . . . Pby. having learned with deep regret that *common fame* proclaims the conduct of the Rev. Jer. Abell to be imprudent, immodest & unchristian, relating to improper familiarities with certain females; & as the honor of religion, the character of the gospel ministry, as well as the special request of Mr Abel by letter, require investigation as soon as possible. Therefore, with a view to this investigation, Pby. proceeded to state the charges brought to their knowledge by *common fame*, which are as follows, viz: I. That he, the said Jer. Abell, took indelicate liberties with Mrs Annas Buchanan at the home of Sam'l. Caldwell in the county of Green, Ky. Witness, Annas Buchanan. II. That he also used similar indelicate familiarities with Mrs Sally Johnston at the house of her husband, Robt. Johnston, in Adair county, Ky. Witness, Sally Johnston. III. That he used similar liberties with Mrs. Jane Prayburn at the house of Melton Prayburn her husband in Adair county, Ky. Witness, Jane Prayburn. Resolved that a meeting of pby. be held at Ebenezer church on the Friday before the third sabbath in next month to attend to this business. Ordered that the Stated Clerk forward citations in due time to all concerned in this case.

[27] The standards of admission into the ministry had been raised since the beginning of the century.

ADJOURNED MEETING
Ebenezer church, Nov. 19, 1824.

The Rev. Saml. Findley was chosen Moderator & David C. Proctor, clerk pro tem. Adjourned to meet at Mr Moore's 5 o'clock. Concluded with prayer.

At Mr Moore's, 5 o'clock. Pby. met. Constituted with prayer. Present as above. Minutes of the last sessions were read.

Pby. inquired of the Rev. Jer. Abell whether he had received the citation of pby. to which was given an affirmative answer. Pby. resolved to enter on the investigation of the charges preferred against the Rev. Jer. Abell. Proceeded to the examination of witnesses.

Mrs. Annas Buchanan was introduced & being duly qualified deposed & said, That sometime in the month of June or July 1823 she was at her brother's, Saml Cauldwell, that she slept in the room with her brother & his wife & children, that Mr Abell lodged in the same room, that in the night Mr Abell came to her bed & awaked her by inviting her in a whisper to go to the kitchen to smoke. She refused audibly: that he then made some forcible essays to excite her passions by thrusting his hand into her bosom & by approaching parts peculiarly feminine, that after passing an hour at least in these indecencies he retired. That in the morning between / break of day & sunrise she was awaked by the pressure of his hands in her bosom; that he continued for sometime making his attempts as before until as she supposed he saw or heard her brother coming into the room; that before he left the house in the morning he told her that his conduct if related would appear censurable, but expressed his confidence that she would not divulge it. The witness further states that she could not account for his conduct but by supposing him to be deranged & she thinks she discovered slight evidence of insanity in him before the family retired to rest in his light, jocose & unclerical manner. Further this deponent said not.

Isaac Tate being qualified deposed & said,—Question by

the accused, When you & I were at Mrs. Buchanan's did she not say we in the night talked aloud & that for some time, so that she expected her brother & sister would hear & that she inquired of them in the morning if they heard them talking? Answer, I do not recollect. Question by the same, Have you ever known Mrs Buchanan's veracity to be impeached? Answer, No. Further this witness said not.

Mr Samuel Cauldwell being qualified deposed & said, Question by the pby. At the time referred to in Mrs Buchanan's testimony did you discover any appearance of derangement in Mr Abell? Answer, No. Question by the same, Did you observe any unusual levity in his conversation or manner. Ans. I do not recollect that I did. Question by the accused. Do you recollect Mrs Buchanan's answer when I asked her whether I talked like a courtier? Ans. I have a confused recollection that she said no. Question by the same. Did she say we talked aloud. Ans. I do not recollect. Ques. by the same. What was Mrs Buchanan's reply when I asked her if I did not talk like an old pious christian? Ans. I do not recollect. Ques. by the pby. Has Mrs Buchanan been generally considered a woman of truth? Ans. So far as I know she has.

Messrs John Tate & Daniel Brown being qualified deposed & said. Ques. by the pby. Has Mrs Buchanan sustained a reputation for truth? Ans. by each, She has.

Miss Betsey Shields being qualified was interrogated. The questions proposed by the accused were judged by the pby. inadmissible & the witness had leave to withdraw.

Rev. Elijah King being qualified deposed & said. That during the latter part of the summer of 1823 he thought he discovered appearances of derangement in Mr Abell. Pby. adjourned to meet tomorrow morning, 7 o'clock. . . .

Saturday morning, 7 o'clock. . . . Mr. Wm. Dickson a licentiate of this pby. requested pby. to designate the places in which he should labor until next spring. Pby. authorized Mr Dickson to supply two sabbaths at least at Perryville, one at Round Top, & one at Bethel in Madison county, & at such other places as his judgment may direct. Mr Dick-

son's request to be ordained as an evangelist was granted &
pby. resolved to attend to his ordination at the next spring
sessions.   Matt. XXII, 45 was assigned to Mr Dickson as
a text, on which to prepare a sermon for the occasion.   Mr
Howe was appointed to preach the ordination sermon & Dr
Cleland to preside & give the charge.   Pby. adjourned to
meet at Mr Martin Scott's in Adair county at 3 o'clock
this afternoon. . . .

Mr Scott's, 3 o'clock. . . . Pby. proceeded to the examination of witnesses in Mr Abell's case.   Mrs Jane Ray-
burn being qualified, deposed & said, That on or about the
22nd of November 1823, Mr Abell called at the house of
her husband, that after the usual civilities he inquired if she
was alone, she said she was, but expected her mother in
soon, that she invited him to sit down which he refused to
do unless she would sit upon his knee, that she objected to
sitting on his lap & said she would sit on / a chair, that he
still insisted & drew her to him, that during the time she
was sitting in this position, (which was, she believed, ten or
fifteen minutes) he hugged & kissed her, that his conversation during the time was that of strong affection, saying he
loved her as a child, had the same anxiety for her temporal
& spiritual welfare as for that of his own children, that he
cautioned her against letting the world know his conduct
saying it would not do to let the world know how intimate
he was with his sisters, that she often attempted to rise &
that Mr Abell urged her to sit still, slightly holding her, saying it was more pleasant to be with her than to ride the lonesome road to Marrowbone, that at length she heard a noise
& told him his horse was breaking loose, he then went out,
on his return his conduct was respectful so far as recollected.
The witness further states that in all this she did not suspect him of criminal intentions but considered it rather the
result of fondness & freedom of affection.   Further this deponent testified not.

Mrs Sally Johnston being qualified deposed & said.
That in Dec. 1823 Mr Abell came home from preaching
after her husband who had invited him, that the next morn-

ing early he wished his horse to start home, that while her husband went for his horse Mr Abell came to her bed & put his hand into her bosom, that she expelled his hand by drawing the bed clothing more closely over her, that he left her bed supposing, as the witness thinks, he heard footsteps, that he again returned & was there until footsteps were heard or supposed to be heard again; that upon her husband entering the house he took a chair & sat by the bed & played with her children. The witness on interrogation as to the subject of conversation at her bed, testified that it was principally on his starting home.

Pby. having heard all the testimony in the case proceeded to consider & adjudicate on the conduct of Mr Abell from the evidence before them & after mature deliberation came to the following resolution, viz: Resolved that it is the unanimous opinion of this pby. that the Rev. Jer. Abell ought to be & he hereby is suspended from the exercise of the office of the gospel ministry until restored by an act of pby. Adjourned to meet at Hardin's Creek church on the first Wednesday in April next. . . .

SAM'L FINDLEY, Moderator.
DAVID C. PROCTOR, Clerk pro tem.

A true record, JAMES C. BARNES, S.C.T.P.

[Danville, April 29, 1825.]

At Mr Chamberlain's, half past 2 o'clock. . . . Mr Abell appeared before pby. & prayed the removal of the censure of suspension under which he was laid by a decision of pby. last Nov. Pby. having heard at length his acknowledgements & concessions on the subject of the charges brought against him, on which he was suspended & having carefully attended to & duly weighed his expressions of unfeigned sorrow for his imprudent conduct & unclerical deportment in reference to the occasions of complaint against him & having maturely deliberated on the subject, came to the following resolution, viz: Resolved that the sentence of suspension passed on Mr Abell be & it is hereby removed & he is *restored* to the full exercise of the office of the gospel ministry.[28]

[Danville, April 20, 1825.]

It is a subject of sincere regret that not only the people at large within our bounds, but also the people of our several charges are greatly ignorant of the peculiar, essential & valuable features of presbyterianism, of the business to be transacted at every meeting of pby.; of the reciprocal duties existing between pastor & people; of the duties of church sessions & of the importance & application of the collection to be taken up in our congregations; therefore, Resolved, that Dr Cleland & Mr Barnes be a committee to draft a letter intended for publication to furnish the necessary information upon the above-mentioned subjects to our churches, to be submitted to pby. at the next stated meetings. And further resolved that at each stated meeting of pby. an appropriate sermon be / delivered by previous appointment, embracing as far as practicable the above subjects, for the information & edification of our churches where the pby. may meet, which sermon shall be considered as embracing the objects specified by the former appointments of missionary & pastoral sermons & that a collection be taken up for the purpose of aiding the pby. in defraying their incidental expenses & answering the various demands of education, commissioners, missionary & other religious purposes, which collection shall be subject to the order of pby. respecting their objects as they may deem most expedient & desirable; & it is also most earnestly recommended that each church under our care take what course they may deem most advisable & efficient to raise collections annually to aid the pby. in meeting the above desirable purposes; & the pby. recommend at least the following apportionment in specie among the churches, viz: Siloam, five dollars; Bethel, five dollars; Shiloh five, Ebenezer, five,

[28] The early restoration of Mr. Abell to the full exercise of the privileges of the gospel ministry, after he had been suspended for immorality, is a commentary on the liberal attitude of the frontier on matters of sexual morality.

New Providence ten, Harrodsburg ten, Danville ten, Lancaster six, Paint Lick nine, Hanging Fork nine, Buffalo Spring nine, Springfield ten; Hardin's Creek ten, Silver Creek five, Union five, Harmony five. Mr Barnes was appointed to preach the above-mentioned *periodical sermon* at the next stated meeting of pby. with privilege to appoint his alternate if practicable & necessary.

[Danville, The College, Oct. 10, 1826.]

Dear Brethren. With a heart full of love I address you for the last time & rejoice in all your joys & sorrow in all your sorrows. I need not say much, for under your view of things it will not be probable you would do otherwise than condemn my present purpose were I to write a volume. I have put it off, to make it a matter of prayer & serious reflection, to the last hour, till started on a journey, & probably may not have the means of conveying a letter after my return, I hastily drop this scrap. Strange document! you say. Yes, but not stranger than my fate. Altho from my infancy rash & eccentric, I was the family favorite for affection & integrity. Thro all the stages of youth was viewed in the same light by the church & the world. Before I joined pby. I was living in peace with all the people of God, & seeking to advance no party, I was happy then as I have been ever since. I wish to return to that peaceful region because I have tried it. I was rejoiced in a season of relaxation from rule. I was not informed what was immediately afterwards made a sine qua non. Like a fish left by the tide, I saw my situation & panted to get away, but having embraced in full the sentiments of that church I durst not leave it for a matter of mere feeling. Some years afterward I got to believe some things contrary to the (spirit) of the Confession of Faith. This was known to some & they watched me from that day & afterwards. Made worse by mending, I am now as near to halting with the mode of church government & discipline of any *other* church (of Trinitarians) as with our *own*. I am no longer bound by *conscience* to be an incumbent; I resign. I intend to join no other while I live; but with such of every society as may be convinced, (if I live long enough,) that I have not followed Christ for loaves & fishes, or tried to walk orderly for fear of church censure alone. My soul is above making friends clandestinely at the expense of the church that confided in me as her steward. I have mentioned my difference of sentiment to a few persons who, I considered, were well established, & have not tried to confuse the ignorant. When people are satisfied in a society that holds the great essentials I know it is dangerous to confuse them; I never will try. When once they swarm we cannot tell where they will settle. Abram parted with Lot not because he did not love him. I think the presbyterian church one of the purest branches of the Reformation & that there is not more piety or honesty in any other society, But notwithstanding the privations this step will cost me, when I think of ceasing from man & casting myself on God alone, & loving all God's people for his sake & pursuing my former course of disinterestedness, an atmosphere of peace & joy surround my heart. If you be tempted to despise me recollect the reply of Solon to Croesus & wait 'till death'. You have nothing to fear from me. This letter will quench the friendship of the last friends I have out of my own family. The world now censure & suspect me. My principles have kept me poor. My labors have destroyed the melody of my voice & age my pronunciation. All I possess is an affectionate family, who, I trust, will all get to heaven, & inward peace with God thro our Lord Jesus Christ. I am yours in love in Christ Jesus. Farewell, Jeremiah Abell. N.B. I would attend pby but cannot leave home. Just blot me off in any way you think right. If cited or censured for not coming on if required to give satisfaction for this departure from rule, I say, I joined peaceably as a free man, I depart peaceably as a free man & shall say no more." Therefore resolved that Mr Abell is no longer authorized to preach the gospel, or administer or receive the ordinances in our church, until he furnish us with satisfactory evidence of reformation & repentance.

[Buffalo Spring, April 8, 1827.]

Dr. Cleland & Mr Wilson were appointed a committee to draft a presbyterial report & report before the rising of pby. Congregational reports were received & read from the churches of New Providence, Harrodsburg, Lancaster, Buffalo Spring, Hanging Fork, Springfield, Lebanon, Bethel, Siloam, Harmony, Paint Lick, Silver Creek, Richmond & Columbia. The two last-named churches having been organized since our last presbyterial report. Resolved that the churches of Richmond & Columbia be now received under the care of this pby. & that the church of Columbia be & it is hereby united with the church of Shiloh under the pastoral charge of the Rev. Saml. Wilson. Whereas it appears that the church of Union which has been for a number of years under our care is at present without a session, nor is there any prospect at present of obtaining one for the want of male members & the remaining members being widely scattered therefore, Resolved that the name of said church be discontinued & the members belonging thereunto recommended to unite with some one of our churches to which they may be convenient.

[Richmond, April 4, 1828.]

Pby received a letter from the Rev Gideon Blackburn, D.D.[28a] enclosing his dismission from the Louisville pby. & requesting to be received as a member of this pby. Resolved unanimously that the request of Dr Blackburn be granted & he is hereby affectionately recognised as a member of this pby. Dr Blackburn reported to pby that he constituted & organized a church at Perryville on the 3d day of Feb. last consisting of 23 members, named the presbyterian church of Perryville, & another on the 10th of Feb. in Casey County, named Piedmont, consisting of 16 members. Resolved unanimously that the churches of Piedmont & Perryville be now taken under the care of this pby.

[28a] For career of Gideon Blackburn, see *Dictionary of Am. Biography*, Vol. II, pp. 314-315.

ADJOURNED MEETING

Danville church, July 15th, 1828. . . . Resolved that Messrs Sneed & Dickson, Moderator & clerk of last stated sessions of Pby. be continued during the present sessions. The minutes of the last stated sessions of pby. were read. . . . The Rev. Jas. K. Burch, a member of the pby. of West Lexington was invited to a seat as a corresponding member & he took his seat accordingly. . . . Mr Barnes informed pby. that on the 28th of June a church was constituted by Dr Blackburn in Mount Vernon, consisting of 35 members, named the presbyterian church of Mount Vernon. Resolved that sd church be now taken under the care of this pby. A petition was presented to pby. signed by a number of persons, members of our church in the neighborhood of Bethel meeting house in Washington county, praying that measures may be taken to have them organized into a church, which petition was granted, & the Rev Messrs Cleland & Sneed were appointed a committee to attend to that duty & administer the sacrament of the Supper to that people on the first sabbath in August next.

[Harrodsburg, Oct. 3, 1828.]

Dr Cleland & Mr Sneed reported that on the 2d day of Aug. last they organized a church at Bethel meeting house in Washington county to be known by the name of Bethel Union church, consisting of 29 members, whereupon it was resolved that this church be taken under the care of pby. The Rev John Howe appeared in pby. & assigned satisfactory reasons for tardiness & absence from the last two meetings of pby.

[Centre College, Oct. 11, 1828.]

Mr Howe introduced Mr Archy B. Lawrence to the notice of pby as a member in full communion & in good standing in our church, who expressed a desire to enter in to the gospel ministry, whereupon Pby agreed to take under consideration the case of Mr Lawrence which appeared to be involved in some difficulty & in substance is as follows: it appeared to the satisfaction of pby from documents both official & private that Mr Lawrence is a graduate of middlebury College, that he was regularly licensed several years ago by the pby of Rochester & afterwards transferred to the care of the pby. of Ontario, that owing as they state in their official records to some improprieties arising from constitutional impetuosity of temper, &c, he was suspended from preaching the gospel as a licentiate, that subsequently his license was renewed for a limited time, at the expiration of which time the pby refused for the same as above mentioned to renew his license. Notwithstanding the questionable regularity of these proceedings, & aside from this consideration Mr Lawrence expressed his full acquiescence in the justice of their proceedings & the rectitude of their intentions & now professes sorrow & regret for the improprieties that required the censure of that pby & hopes from the subsequent dealings of Providence with him that all occasion for a similar procedure is now removed. Whereupon, pby after maturely considering this case are unanimously of opinion that they may, without any violation of order & discipline reinstate Mr Lawrence as a licentiate after requiring of him the adoption of our Confession of Faith & satisfactory answers to the questions usually put to candidates in such cases. Pby then proceeded to license Mr Archy B. Lawrence, who having solemnly adopted the Confession of faith of our church & having answered in the affirmative the questions required to be put to candidates in such cases, he was licensed to preach the gospel in the bounds of this pby or wherever else he may be orderly called. Adjourned to meet in Richmond the Thursday before the first sabbath in Feb. next. Concluded with prayer.

JAMES C. BARNES, Mod.
THOS. CLELAND, clerk pro tem.
A true record, JAMES C. BARNES, Clerk of Trana. pby.

STATED FALL MEETING

Lancaster church, October 8th, 1829.
The minutes of the last sessions of pby were read. . . .
The Rev. Jas. K. Burch forwarded a dismission from the
pby of West Lexington, whereupon, Resolved that he be
affectionately recognized as a member of this pby.   Bro
Cleland reported that he had attended the sessions of the
last Gen. Assembly, agreeably to appointment.   On motion
resolved that the stated clerk of this pby. write to the Home
Missionary Society for the labors of a missionary for one
year in the towns of Manchester, Barbourville & London,
& that this pby bind themselves for one half the expense.[29]

[Lancaster, Oct. 9, 1829.]

Court house, half past 8 o'clock.   Oct. 9th. . . . Pby.
having received sufficient evidence that two churches have
been regularly organized within our bounds since our last
meeting, viz: one at Elizabethtown in Hardin county by
the name of Elizabethtown church & the other in Munfordsville, Hart County, by the name of Munfordsville
church, resolved to take these churches under their care,
& said churches having petitioned pby for the labors of Mr
Wm Rannells, as a stated supply some portion of his time,
not being able at present to procure the whole therefore
resolved that their petition be granted; & in order further
to promote the interests of our church in that section of
this pby., Resolved, that it is expedient as soon as possible
to ordain Mr Rannells to the office of the gospel ministry
as an Evangelist.   Resolved also that Mr Robt. L. McAfee
be ordained as an Evangelist at the same time & place.   Pby
assigned the following trials to the candidates, viz: to Mr

[29] The letter making this request is in the American Home Missionary
Society Collection at The Chicago Theological Seminary.   "The Presbytery
in their late session passed the following resolution, 'Resolved that the stated
clerk of this Presbytery be directed to write to the Home Missionary Society
for the labors of a Missionary for one year for the towns of Manchester,
London, and Barboursville, and the Presbytery will bind themselves for
one half of the expenses'."   (Letter from Rev. James C. Barnes, Clerk of
Transylvania Presbytery, Paint Lick, Ky., Nov. 12, 1829.)

Rannells II Tim. III, 16, & to Mr McAfee Acts XIII 38.
Resolved that on the final adjournment of this pby. it
adjourn to meet in Elizabethtown on the Friday before
the first sabbath in December next. Pby took up the unfinished business of last evening & proceeded to the further
examination of the candidates before them, on Rhetoric &
Logic which examination was unanimously sustained. Proceeded to assign the following trials to the candidates, viz:
to Mr Shaw a Latin exegesis on Quid est Deus, & a critical
exercise on I Pet. III, 18-22 inclusive; to Mr Jones a Latin
exegesis on (Rom. IX.1-5 inclusive) Qui unus Deus diatur
& a critical exercise (above); & to Mr Cocke a Latin
exegesis on Cur Christum verum hominum use oportuit, &
a critical exercise on I Cor. XI.17-22 inclusive; all to be
read at the spring sessions of pby. On motion resolved
that the members of this pby be directed to read from
their respective pulpits the following paragraphs in the
Assembly's Digest on the subject of slavery, viz: Part 4th,
Chap. II, Sec. 4,5 & 6th, also Part 13th, Chap. 1, Secs.
2,3,&4: & that they exhort their respective charges in the
spirit of love on the subject; & be it further resolved that
the sessions under the care of this pby be directed to take
immediate measures to carry into effect the spirit of the
above sections.

[Lancaster, Oct. 10, 1829.]

On motion Resolved that this pby highly approve the
resolutions of the Gen. Assembly on the subject of *intemperance* at their last sessions, pages 375 & 376 of their
minutes & believing the traffic in ardent spirits, & the use
of them to be utterly unchristian they solemnly exhort the
churches under their care to fly from this deadly plague.
They moreover direct the members belonging to this pby
to read this resolution with the resolutions of the Gen.
Assembly to their people & affectionately warn them of the
danger arising from the use of this "liquid fire". On motion, Resolved that this pby apply to the Am. Sab. School
Union for the labors of Mr Joseph Huber as an agent

within our bounds for the purpose of promoting the interests of sabbath schools & Bible classes. The pby believe also that the agent might obtain a considerable portion of his support by taking up collections in the churches. The committee appointed to draft a presbyterial report reported which was received & approved & ordered to be signed by the stated clerk & forwarded to Synod.

[New Providence, Oct. 9, 1830.]

Inasmuch as several sessional records have been examined & it appears that they have transacted business without prayer, (tho this has in some instances been an omission of the clerk), whereupon, Resolved that it be & it is hereby recommended to the sessions of the churches under our care when practicable, to constitute & adjourn with prayer & that the clerks of sessions be particular to record the fact.

[Harrodsburg, Dec. 23, 1830.]

Pby being advised that the Rev. Gideon Blackburn, D.D. requested a dismission in order to attach himself to the West Lexington pby. resolved that said request be granted & that he be & he hereby is dismissed as a minister in good standing & affectionately recommended to the attention & christian kindness of that pby.[30]

[30] Rev. Gideon Blackburn had been president of the Centre College until 1830 when he resigned at the insistence of the Synod. Two views are presented:

Letter from J. C. Barnes, Lancaster, Ky., Nov. 9, 1830, to A.H.M.S., "For some time (right or wrong) the synod have not had confidence in the litterary attainment of the faculty of that institution, especially of the president. So much was said at the late meeting of the Synod on the subject that Dr. Blackburn has since resigned, and the Rev. John C. Young of Lexington has been elected. . . . I may judge improperly but I think our college is more likely to prosper under the present arrangement than it has ever been."

Letter from Rev. Dr. Gideon Blackburn, Versailles, Ky., December 9, 1830, "I presume before this reaches you the news of my resignation and the facts leading to it have been seen in the Cincinnati Journal. You have also seen no doubt the summary containing some false and slanderous remarks dictated by the party who are afraid lest my influence may check their schemes in making the institution pass under Princeton influence."

Mr David Todd was introduced to pby as a young man of good moral character & in full communion in the church, who expresses a desire to become a candidate for the gospel ministry, whereupon pby proceeded to examine him with respect to his experimental acquaintance with religion & his views to the gospel ministry, which examination was unanimously sustained. He was then examined on Logic, English Grammar, Rhetoric, Natural Philosophy & Astronomy. The examination was discontinued to hear Mr Jones' popular sermon, which sermon was sustained as part of trials.

[Buffalo Springs Church, Oct. 8, 1831.]

Pby took under consideration the subject of Missions to the heathen & after an interchange of views the following resolutions were adopted: 1st. Resolved that we ought as a pby to do something in aid of the great work of sending the gospel to the pagan world; 2d. That we will endeavor to raise if possible annually as much as will support one missionary among the heathen; 3d. That the Rev. Wm. P. Alexander now about to sail for the Sandwich Islands under the patronage of the A.B.C.F.M. be the one selected for the present; 4th. Resolved that the Rev. Jas. K. Burch, John D. Paxton, John C. Young, with Messrs John Green & Michael C. Youse be a standing committee to superintend this concern, to adopt ways / & means for raising the proposed funds & to report semi-annually to pby. Adjourned to meet in this place on Monday morning, 9 o'clock. Concluded with prayer.

[Danville, Oct. 15, 1831.]

On motion, Resolved that the following preamble & resolutions recently adopted by the Synod of Ky. now in session in this place be & they are hereby adopted by this pby as the instruction given to our delegates to the Cincinnati convention, which are as follows, viz: The Gen. Assembly of

Dr. Blackburn refused a commission to Alabama and Tennessee on account of his anti-slavery views, but accepted one to Illinois in 1833. He organized Blackburn College at Carlinville, Ill. See A.H.M.S. Cor. Blackburn, G. to Peters, A., III, 1836.

the Pres. Church at its last meeting recommended to the Synods & presbyteries of the church in the west to agree on some plan for conducting missions in the valley of the Mississippi. In consequence of this recommendation it becomes the duty of this Synod to express its opinions on this important subject. The power to send missions to any part, to plant churches or to supply vacancies is one of great importance. The peace & prosperity of our church depend on the proper exercise of this power. Those who wield it can give to the church almost any character they please & the question to be decided is where can this power be deposited to do the most good with the least danger of abuse. The tendency of all power is to accumulation & abuse & it has been a matter of great difficulty in church & state to select proper agents to execute important trusts & to secure their accountability. The powers of government have usually been vested in one man, or a few men, & the result has been the abuse of their authority & the oppression /& misery of the great body of the community. Power, once obtained, has been held with a firm hand & the only remedy in most cases has been revolution. The statesmen who formed the civil government of our country adopted the principle that the people are the source of all power & provided for their chosing & removing the officers of government should those in office abuse the trust reposed in them; the people upon whom their acts operate will soon see & feel it & apply the remedy. The same principles are recognized in the government of our church & we believe they are "agreeable to Scripture". All our churches in the United States constitute one church in which the majority governs. Those who exercise authority in the church are elected by, & are responsible to, the people. The General Assembly, which is elected annually is the highest judicature in the church & represents in one body all the peculiar churches of one denomination. It "constitutes the bond of union & peace, correspondence & mutual confidence among all the churches." "To it belongs the power of superintending the concerns of the whole church", & of "sending missions to any part, to plant churches or to supply vacancies." Shall we now change the constitution of our church? which all our ministers, elders & deacons have publicly & solemnly approved & take from the whole church, through their representatives, the power of conducting our missions? & vest the power in a part of the church or in any other body of men? Who would most faithfully perform this high & important trust? And if it be abused where can the remedy be most easily & certainly applied? The members of the Gen. Assembly are elected annually, & if they do not faithfully represent the churches they will not be re-elected, but others will be chosen who will represent them. If our missionary concerns were all under the control of the Gen. Assembly efficient & useful missionaries would be employed & our union cemented. For should the Gen. Assembly, or their agents, so far forget their duty as to become the organs of a *party* the days of their power would be numbered. But if independent missionary societies have power to send missions into all our churches they will be formed by parties & conducted to promote party purposes. Where is the remedy? The church will be afflicted with continual ecclesiastical warfare, its union & peace destroyed, & it will have no power to prevent it. In favor of the union of our church we would adopt the language of Washington concerning the union of this Republic: "We should watch for its preservation with zealous anxiety, discountenancing whatever may suggest even a suspicion that it can in any event be abandoned & indignantly frowning upon the first dawning of every attempt to alienate any portion of our (church) from the rest or to enfeeble the sacred ties which now link together the various parts." The rulers in our church have been careful to prevent collisions between its various parts & to secure them from foreign interference. In our Directory for Worship, Chap. VI, it is provided that it is expedient that no person be introduced to preach in any of the churches under our care without the consent of the pastor or church session. The Form of Government provides that when any pby shall send any of their ministers or probationers to distant vacancies the missionary shall be ready to produce his credentials to the pby or presbyteries through the bounds of which he may pass, or at least to a committee thereof & obtain their approbation. And to the Gen. Assembly alone is given the power "to send missionaries to any part, to plant churches or to supply vacancies." Recent events have demonstrated the wisdom of these regulations. It has been objected that the Gen. Assembly is not a safe depository of power & that there is no security in its annual election because the whole church may become corrupt, & that this is possible the history of the church in past ages affords sufficient proof, & then the Gen. Assembly itself would be a most terrible engine of evil. If the whole church be not a safe depository of power of conducting its own missions it is not of any other power. But there is safety in the annual election of the Gen. Assembly until / the church does become corrupt; & is it more liable to become corrupt than a missionary society composed of all who will pay their money? The history of the world in past ages affords sufficient proof that Republics have become corrupt & then the people were not safe depositories of power. Shall we therefore abandon our republican Institution & bestow the powers of government on a few—a society or a king? or have no government? The time may come when all men under the influence of the gospel will do right & then there will be no necessity for any government. But melancholy experience tells us that this time has not yet come & so long as it is necessary to vest power somewhere we subscribe to the doctrine that a majority of the whole shall govern. Entertaining the foregoing opinions we have come to the following resolutions, viz: 1st. Resolved that we still approve of the Form of our Church Government on the subject of missions, & that we will not agree to any plan for conducting missions in the valley of the Mississippi which shall take that important power from the control of

the representatives of the whole church in the General
Assembly.[31]   2d. Resolved that it be recommended to all

[31] This resolution is directed against the American Home Missionary
Society in favor of the Board of Missions of the General Assembly. It
resulted from a call upon Western synods to decide upon a unified missionary
program. See Baird, *History of the New School*, pp. 376ff.

The above resolution sets forth the Old School position on the subject of
missions. A letter from Rev. Gideon Blackburn, Versailles, Ky., Dec. 9, 1830
to A.H.M.S., reads: "The world should be appraised that under the sanction
of the Board of Missions the party in Kentucky are resolved to take high
handed weapons, and the advantages to have been received from Centre College must be sought at Oxford and Cincinnati, where already about 30 of
the Senoir class and the beneficiaries are located, all of whom are looking
forward to the ministry. I think Danville will be crippled in their struggle
for power. They will be determined to promote the Assembly Board to the
utmost in Kentucky, and have Old School men put in every corner. I will
however make a stand in West Lexington Presbytery and have an organization for your board."

Feeling against the American Home Missionary Society grew during the
succeeding years. A letter from George G. McAfee, Henderson, Ky., Jan.
23, 1835, reads: "The first Sabbath in November 1834 begins my labors
in Henderson. I had been expected and was received with open arms by
the old Presbyterians, which I presume they would not have done if they
had known that I had been commissioned by your society. This I thought
it prudent not to mention until we got a little acquainted."

In 1836 the Synod of Kentucky asked the Home Missionary Society to stay
out of its bounds. They resented its New School leadership. A letter from
Rev. Jas. Lane, Lexington, Ky., July 15, 1836, reads: "Some of our delegates from Kentucky have returned from the General Assembly panick
stricken in view of the fearful ravages of New Schoolism, and are saying
that 'Dr. Peters and Dr. Skinner threw dust into the eyes of the Assembly
and then led them just where they pleased!!!' The Western Presbyterian
Herald is holding up the 'Home Missionary Society' in connection with
'Albert Barnes the heretick and schismatick,' and thus attempting to cast
out the dust from the eyes of good Presbyterians of Kentucky."

A report of the excluding resolutions follows in a letter from Rev. R.
Davidson, Lexington, Kentucky, Oct. 28, 1836,

"Resolved 3, that this Synod do hereby solemnly and deliberately declare
that the further operation of the American Home Missionary, and the
American Education Societies within our bounds is contrary to our wishes
and against our consent.

"Resolved 4, that we do earnestly desire and hereby request that those
societies will without delay retire from our bounds and attempt to make no
further collections in our churches, nor in any way attempt to continue to
operate within the geographical limits of the Synod of Kentucky."

A friend of the Society writes. Letter from Rev. Harvey Woods Glasgow,
Ky., Jan. 4, 1837, "You have heard how that the Synod of Kentucky desires none of your aid. I was not at the meeting but I am told that even
friends of the A.H.M.S. voted for the resolutions for the sake of trying to

the presbyteries connected with this Synod to send delegates to the proposed convention on the subject of Missions,[32] which is to be held in the city of Cincinnati on the 23rd of November 1831.

William W. Robertson was then introduced as a person wishing to be taken under care of pby as a candidate for the gospel ministry. Pby proceeded to examine Bro. Robertson upon his acquaintance with experimental religion & his views in seeking the sacred office, together with the Latin & Greek languages.

[Rock Spring, April 4, 1833.]

Resolved that the Missionary committee of pby be instructed to use efforts for procuring two missionaries to be stationed within the bounds of this pby. one at Monticello & another at Barboursville.[33]   Brn Howe & Barrett

arrive at peace. But is it not strange that when we have whole countries lying together, and thousands of people with no Pres. ministers that our Synod should request you to keep your men and your money to yourself. But all of this grows out of our being too ecclesiastical and too orthodox. We are like the old negroes tree, so straight we lean over."

[32] A letter of Rev. E. N. Sawtell, Louisville, Ky., April 21, 1831, gives the Resolutions of the Louisville Presbytery vs the A.H.M.S.:

"1 Resolved, That the transaction of missionary business as pertaining to the church in her distinctive character, is too sacred to be safely confided to any irresponsible and self-created body.

"2 Resolved that we consider the present organization of the Board of Missions of the General Assembly as most consistent with the order and most conducive to the peace and purity of our church.

"3 Resolved That we consider it more proper for the Presbytery of Louisville to be auxiliary to the Board of Missions of the General Assembly than to any other missionary association or body.

"4 Resolution against any amalgamation of G.A. Board & A.H.M.S."
A minority report was made.

West Lexington Presbytery passed a resolution requesting A.H.M.S. and A.E.S. to withdraw from its bounds in favor of the Assembly Board on account of conflicts.

For an account of the Cincinnati Convention of 1831, see Chap. V; also Gillett, op. cit., II, p. 451.

[33] The Presbyterians were permanently weakened in Southern Kentucky at that time as a result of the Cumberland schism. A letter from Rev. Harvey Woods, Glasgow, Ky., June 29, 1836, reads: "I am in that part of Kentucky called 'The Green River Country.' This is like many portions of the West destitute of Presbyterian preaching except here and there a spot. The Green River country embraces about one third of the

obtained leave of absence from the remaining sessions of
pby. Bro. Yantis was placed on the committee to draft

state, but at least ¾ of the counties have no Presbyterian minister. There
have been in Ken. and especially in these parts for the last 30 or 40 years
peculiar difficulties in the way of Presbyterianism. This was the ground
embraced in that great excitement of 1800 which sorely wounded the Presbyterian Church. Cumberland Pres. tho upon the whole a good people,
have had the ascendency, also Methodists and Baptists, until since Mr.
Campbell has figured so extensively, now the Campbellites in many places
have the ascendency."

Letter from J. C. Barnes, Lancaster, Ky., Nov. 9, 1830, "The Presbytery
of Transylvania has appointed a committee to correspond with the Board
of the General Assembly and with A.H.M.S. with reference to missionaries to labor in the field.

"We have still funds in the hands of our treasurer and would be glad
to have a missionary to labor in the above named places, which in a great
measure are a moral wilderness."

The following letter from the Muhlenberg Presbytery, which was formed
from the Presbytery of Transylvania, would lead one to believe that the
country was entirely destitute (May, 1827): "The bounds of this Presbytery are extensive being about 200 miles in length by nearly a 100 in
breadth, part of which may truly be called a frontier country. Though
settled a number of years since it has not been favored with preaching
till of late. The number of preachers who labor in these bounds is few;
and being settled ministers their labors are principally confined to a few
congregations. A large portion of country is still unoccupied, and there
are many parishes which either have no preaching or perhaps a sermon
once in six months. The number of vacancies is sixteen."

Undoubtedly the number of vacancies in the Presbyterian churches was
great, but the frontier communities were by no means without preaching
as a young missionary discovered after having yielded to such propaganda.
A letter from Rev. Saml. R. Alexander, Russelville, Ky., Feb. 12, 1828, reads:
"As to the situation of this section of country, that is this Green river
country as it is called, I had by no means a correct idea when I agreed
to come here. I thought that it was almost entirely destitute of the privileges of the gospel; but this is by no means the case. I am credibly informed by several ministers of the different evangelical denominations that
in this section of the country there are at the lowest calculation 60 Methodists ministers 50 of whom are local preachers: 40 Cumberland and 25 or
30 Baptist ministers, in all 125 or 130. And the country is so cut up between the denominations that a Presbyterian can scarcely if at all make
a lodgement among them.

"In Russellville, the place where I reside and preach half my time, there
are four congregations, viz., one of the Methodists, one of the Baptists, one
of the Cumberlands and one poor little starved despised child of the Presbyterians.

"For seven or eight years past there have been attempts made by different
Presbyterian ministers to effect a lodgement here and, I may say, they have

the narrative of the state of religion, in the place of Bro. Howe. Pby then had a free conversation on the state of religion within our bounds, after which the committee appointed to draft the narrative made a report which was received & adopted & is as follows: With respect to the state of religion within their bounds during the past year the pby of Transylvania make the following report. With the exception of the New Providence congregation, to which near fifty have been added, they are not able to report any special outpourings of the Spirit of God. It has been more barren of additions to our churches than several years past. There has been much activity among some of the more prevalent errorists[33a] & other evils are to be deplored. On the other hand there has on the whole we think been rather an improvement with respect to some if not all the charitable institutions of the day. This is more especially the case with respect to the cause of Temperance & Colonization; & when the Mission cause, domestic or foreign, has been brought before our churches more interest & liberality, we think, than formerly have been excited. Centre College, located within our bounds is we think in an improving condition & we are especially gratified to learn that the spirit of active benevolence & of Foreign Missions is on the increase among the pious youth connected with it. The financial committee made a report of the assessment of the sum necessary to defray the expenses of the commissioners to the Gen. Assembly which was received & approved & is as follows: "Ebenezer $3; Richmond $10; Harrodsburg $12; Springfield $12; Danville $12; Lebanon $12; Pisgah $3; Paint Lick $8; Rock Spring $2; Munfordsville $6;

utterly failed. And I doubt now exceedingly the propriety or expediency of my making the attempt; for in the first place the people are well supplied with preaching and secondly they are prejudiced against the Presbyterians for it was just in this neighborhood the Cumberlands broke off from the Presbyterians, and the old Presbyterians as they are called received their death blow or nearly so. And so it is throughout this Green river country so far as I can learn."

[33a] By "errorists" is meant the Cumberland Presbyterians, Methodists, New Lights, Baptists and Campbellites.

Buffalo Spring $8; New Providence $8; Hanging Fork $8; Greensburg $8; Silver Creek $5; Glasgow $5; Tompkinsville $2; Piedmont $1; Lancaster $5;

[Harmony Church, Oct. 4, 1833.]

Pby fully believing that it is the duty of every church to aid in the support of those who preach the gospel to them[34] & believing that the neglect of this duty is a sin against which they should warn all the churches under care, would recommend that each vacant church give some compensation to those ministers of the gospel who may occasionally by order of pby supply them with preaching. Ordered that the stated clerk send to each of our vacant churches a copy of the above minute. Brethren Smith & Young obtained leave of absence during the remaining sessions of pby. Henry G. Comings read a lecture on Rom. VIII. 1-6, which was sustained as part of trial. Pby then appointed Bro. Comings for a popular sermon Acts V.41-42. The reference from Hanging Fork was taken up & the papers in the case were read in part when pby adjourned to meet tomorrow morning at 8 o'clock. Concluded with prayer.

[Glasgow, Oct. 4, 1834.]

Resolved that this pby rejoice in the prospect of a visit from an agent of the Assembly's Board of Missions & recommend that Board to the patronage of our churches. Ordered that the stated clerk communicate this resolution to the Secretary of the Assembly's Board. A communication having been received from the session of the Munfordsville church on the subject of the duty of christian parents to present their children to God in baptism & the duty also of instructing the children of the church in the

---

[34] A letter of Rev. J. T. Hamilton, Louisville, Ky., March 31, 1829, reads: "There are many of the clergy engaged in teaching schools for a subsistence who under your patronage would be efficient ministers of the gospel. There are now not five clergymen in the state who receive a competent support from their congregations."

Shorter Catechism, Resolved, as the opinion of this pby. that both these duties are solemnly obligatory on all christian parents. Members of pby were called upon to state the manner in which they had fulfilled their appointments to supply vacancies within our bounds to which they were appointed by the last pby; when it appeared that all the ministers present had complied with their appointments with the exception of Bro. Howe whose reasons for failure were sustained.

[Danville, Oct. 7, 1834.]

On motion Resolved that Bro Barnes would serve the cause of Christ more efficiently by devoting half his time to missionary labors. Resolved that it be recommended to Bro. Barnes to relinquish his connexion with Paint Lick church after the first of January next & take an appointment for performing missionary service during that period which he has heretofore devoted to the service of that church. Further Resolved that the presbyterial committee on missions be instructed to procure for Bro. Barnes an appointment to act as a missionary for half his time from the Assembly's Board of Missions, or (in case of a failure in the application to the Assembly's Board of Missions) from the American Home Missionary Society.

[Oct. 9, 1834.]

Brother Harvey Woods requested by letter dismission to join the pby. of Cincinnati which was granted & he is hereby dismissed from this pby in good & regular standing & affectionately recommended to the pby of Cincinnati. Adjourned to meet tomorrow evening at 6 o'clock. Concluded with prayer.

[Springfield, April 3, 1835.]

A letter was received from Bro. Harvey Woods, to whom a dismission had been forwarded to join the pby of Cincinnati, stating that he had received that dismission &

having now fixed his residence in Arkansas Territory[35] which request was granted & the stated clerk directed to forward his dismission.

Certain papers relating to the Lebanon church having been present to pby by the stated clerk, it was ordered that those papers together with the records of Lebanon church session be referred to a select committee consisting of Brn. Young, Barnes & Brown. Pby. then took a recess until this committee examine the papers & prepare a report. After recess the committee reported as the order of proceedings. 1st that the sentence of the session of Lebanon church suspending Samuel E. McElroy, ruling elder, from the privileges of the church should be read.   2nd, the appeal/ of said McElroy & the complaint of a minority of session & certain members of the Lebanon church respecting the decision of the session of said church against Saml. E. McElroy: & that the case be then proceeded in according to the form prescribed in our book of discipline, Chap. 7th, Section 3d, Division 8th.   The report of the committee was adopted & the proceedings in the case were commenced. Pby. Before the case was concluded adjourned to meet at the house of Mr Davidson at half past 7 o'clock; closed with prayer.

Pby met at half past seven according to adjournment; constituted with prayer. Took up the case of appeal from Lebanon church. The Moderator gave the members of pby. the usual charge in view of the solemn duty now devolving upon them as judges in a court of Jesus Christ. After proceeding in the case to the point at which the original parties were to be heard the appelant, Saml. E. McElroy, requested that the further consideration of the

---

[35] Rev. Harvey Woods returned from Arkansas to teach at Bowling Green, 1836, and in 1840 became a New School missionary in southern Kentucky.

H. Woods, Cane Hill, Ark., March 14, 1836, to A. Peters—returning to Kentucky. A.H.M.S. Correspondence.

H. Woods, Glasgow, Ky., Jan. 4, 1837, to A. Peters.

Rev. A. C. Dickson, Bowling Green, Ky., June 15, 1840, to cor. secy. Desires aid for Mr. H. Woods. Field open to New School. A.H.M.S. Correspondence.

cause should be postponed until tomorrow morning, which was accordingly done.

The regular business before pby was then / resumed, viz: the appeal of Saml. E. McElroy from the decision of Lebanon session suspending him from the privileges of the church.   Mr McElroy stated his wish to be heard through his counsel, whereupon Bro. Thomason a corresponding member addressed pby in support of the appeal.   Mr Hughes, the original prosecutor, was then heard in support of the decision of session.   The members of the inferior court were then reminded that it was their privilege to be heard in explanation of the grounds of their decision. After all the parties had been fully heard the members of the inferior court withdrew.   The roll was called & the members of pby had the opportunity of expressing their views, when the final vote was taken & is as follows, viz: While the pby believe that session of the Lebanon church acted in the case of Saml. E. McElroy according to the best of their judgment & with good intentions & that the session therefore incur no censure from the reversal of their judgment.   Still, believing that the session erred in the decision precluding Saml. E. McElroy from adducing evidence justifying his views when that evidence related to conduct which had taken place more than a year previous to the utterance of his language, & believing that the charges in the 2d & 3d specifications, considering the extenuating testimony in relation to them, would not justify a sentence so severe as that of suspension; therefore, Resolved that the session of the Lebanon church be instructed to proceed to a new trial in the case of Saml. E. McElroy & that until such trial take place Mr McElroy continue to enjoy his privileges as a member & ruling elder of Lebanon church

The session of Lebanon church referred the case of Saml. E. McElroy & prayed the pby to give a decision in the case from the testimony presented on the record.   Brn. Young, Barnes & Barnett were appointed a committee to confer with the parties in the case of this reference & to ascertain whether it be possible to settle the business without the intervention of a decision of pby.   Adjourned till tomorrow morning 9 o'clock.   Closed with prayer.

The committee appointed to confer with the parties in the case of the reference from the Lebanon church session beg leave to submit the following report.   The committee having conferred with all the parties implicated in the reference have effected an amicable adjustment of all the difficulties on the following terms.   1st, Brethren Saml E. McElroy & Joseph Maxwell do voluntarily agree to cease from the exercise of their functions as ruling elders in the church of Lebanon & to have this fact entered on the records of said church.   2d, Brother Samuel B. Robertson agrees to cease his ministrations within the bounds of the Lebanon church & congregation with the exception of New Market & Liberty.   3d, Brethren Saml. E. McElroy & Edward Hughes do agree to abide by such decision in relation to their personal difficulties as the committee shall form after a perusal of the testimony taken in their case. This decision has been formed & it is as follows, viz: The committee are of opinion that while the conduct of Edward Hughes appears from the record to have been in some respects blameworthy & inconsistent with christian propriety still that the facts as proved in the record do not justify the language used by Br. McElroy in reference to the character of Br. Hughes.   They do therefore decide that Br. McElroy owes it to himself as well as to Br. Hughes to express his sorrow that he has used such language as to the character of this brother.   Resolved that Brethren Cleland, Barnes, Breckinridge, Young & Lynn supply Lebanon church one sabbath each previous to the next meeting of pby.   Resolved that pby enjoin upon its members to remember their engagements & obligations to collect funds in aid of the support of Brother Wm. P. Alexander now laboring amongst the heathen in the Sandwich Islands & report progress at each stated meeting of this pby.   Adjourned to meet in the Harrodsburg church at 7 o'clock P.M. on Thursday subsequent to the last Monday in March. . . .

THOS. CLELAND, Moderator.

JOHN C. YOUNG, Clerk, P. T.

[Harrodsburg, April 1, 1836.]

In the course of a free conversation on the state of religion it was incidentally mentioned that one of the brethren in the Danville church had sold a colored brother in good standing as a member of the same church; whereupon the pby resolved that the session of the Danville church take up & issue this case agreeably to the principles in our book of discipline & the act of the Gen. Assembly on slavery passed in 1818. Adjourned to meet in this place tomorrow morning 9 o'clock. . . .

9 o'clock, Apr. 2d. Pby. met according to ádjournment. Constituted with prayer. The committee on supplies reported that it shall be the duty of each minister to supply the vacancies within his reach as frequently as he can consistently with his stated ministrations until the next stated meeting of pby. which report was received & adopted. Brethren Terrill & Venable obtained leave of absence from the remaining sessions of pby. The committee on the apportionment of the commissioners' fund, &c, reported that there ought to be one hundred dollars raised to pay our commissioners to the next Gen. Assembly for their travelling expenses & the further sum of twelve dollars for the Contingent Fund. The committee recommended that the aggregate amount aforesaid be raised by the congregations represented in the present pby. in the following portions, viz: Richmond church $5; Paint Lick $7.12; Lancaster $16.25; Harmony $4.12; Buffalo Spring $5; Hanging Fork $5.25; Pisgah $5; Danville $20; Harrodsburg $12; Providence $15; Perryville $4.25; Bethel Union $3; Springfield $5; Beech Fork $1.25; Lebanon $10.75; Greensburg $2.50; Piedmont $1.25; Rock Spring $2.50; This report was received & adopted.

[Harrodsburg, April 2, 1836.]

The committee of Synod on the subject of slavery laid before pby the following plan for the moral & religious instruction & future emancipation of slaves, viz: "1st we would recommend that all slaves now under 20 years of age & all those yet to be born in our possession be emancipated as they shall reach their 25th year./ 2d We recommend that deeds of emancipation be now drawn up and recorded in our respective county courts specifying the slaves whom we are about to emancipate & the age at which each is to become free. This measure is highly necessary as it will furnish to our own minds, to the world, & to our slaves satisfactory proof of our sincerity in this work & it will also secure the liberty of the slaves against all contingences. 3. We recommend that our slaves be instructed in the common elementary branches of education. 4. We recommend that strenuous & persevering efforts be made to induce them to attend regularly upon the ordinary services of religion both domestic & public. 5. We recommend that great pains be taken to teach them the holy scriptures & that, to effect this, the instrumentality of sabbath schools, wherever they can be enjoyed, be united with that of domestic instruction. A resolution was then offered that pby recommend to the churches under their care to adopt the plan presented by the committee of Synod. On this question the yeas & nays being called for the vote was taken & stood as follows. Yeas, Howe, Robertson, Barnes, Young, Lynn, Root, (Brown,) Green, Landram, Hoagland, 10. Nays, Thompson, Penick, Wade, 3, Non liquit, Cleland, Rose, Ray, Holtsclaw, Hays, Cabell, 6. Resolved that each minister of this pby. in the congregation to which he preaches, & each session of the vacant congregations, be *required* to read before the church the report of the Synodical Committee of 1834, containing the plan of instruction & emancipation of slaves recommended by this pby. at least once a year.

Adjourned to meet in Richmond church on the last Friday of September next at 11 o'clock A.M. . . .

JAMES C. BARNES, Moderator.

TIMOTHY ROOT, clerk, pro tem.

Pby took up the consideration of the letter on the subject of slavery which had been received from the Chilicothe pby. The following resolutions were then offered & adopted. 1st. Resolved that while we receive the communication from the brethren of the Chilicothe pby. on the subject of slavery in the same spirit of kindness in which it was doubtless made we would inform our brethren that we deem the mode of action which they suggest inexpedient & hurtful & that we have ourselves recommended to our churches the adoption of a plan which appears to us better calculated to remove the evils of slavery. 2d, Resolved that the stated clerk of this pby transmit to the pby of Chilicothe a copy of the preaching resolution together with a copy of the plan of action on the subject of slavery which this pby have recommended to the churches under their care. Attest. JAS. C. BARNES, Stated Clerk. The committee appointed to examine the records of the Transylvania Pby. report that they find those minutes well kept Bardstown, Oct. 16, 1836. S. LYNN, Mod. of Synod.

CALLED MEETING

Danville, June 23d, 1836. Agreeable to a call of the Moderator pby met at 7½ o'clock P.M. June 23d, in the pres. church in Danville & was opened with a sermon by the Moderator,—Ps. 32,10th. Members present, ministers, Barnes, Young, & Root; elders, M. G. Youse & Hugh Hays. The Moderator stated the object of the called meeting to be to dissolve the pastoral relation between Bro. Barnes & the congregation of Lancaster & to grant to Br. Barnes a dismission from this to join the pby of Miami. The Moderator, Br. Barnes having called Br. Young to the chair, presented his application for the dissolution of the pastoral relation between himself & the

Lancaster church & for a dismission from this to join the pby. of Miami.[36]   Pby. having heard the reasons of Br. Barnes & having heard read a communication from the session of / the Lancaster church expressing their concurrence in those reasons, Resolved that his request for the dissolution of his pastoral relation as well as that for his dismission be granted.   Br. Root was appointed to preach in the church in Lancaster on the 2d sabbath of July & declare the church vacant.   Br. Young was appointed stated clerk in room of Br. Barnes resigned.   Pby. adjourned.

JNO. C. YOUNG.

[Hanging Fork Church, April 7, 1837.]

The elder from the Danville church reported that the session had enquired into the case of the member, (mentioned page 46 Minutes) who had sold a colored brother, a member of the same church, & that, on examination they find nothing censurable in his case.[37]

[36] Mr. Barnes was one of the anti-slavery men who found it expedient to move to a free state.   A letter from Rev. Harvey Woods, Glasgow, Ky., June 29, 1836, reads: "Many of our ministers and people have gone and continue to go to free states.   Rev. Hugh Bass until recently stated clerk of the Synod of West Tennessee has gone to Illinois.   Rev. Jas. C. Barnes stated clerk of this (Transylvania) Presbytery is going to Ohio.   I see the best of men flying from the South."

[37] Slavery was probably a strong factor in making a majority of Kentucky Presbyterians Old School.   They were happy to have services for slaves but trod warily upon the grounds of emancipation.   The Church forbad selling slaves who were church members but offenders were exonerated. A letter from Rev. Henry Little, New Market, Ky., July 21, 1825, reads: "They are exceedingly sensitive on the subject of slavery.   Even true Christians are by no means prepared or ready to do their duty, and of course unrepentant worldly men are not.   But to my own mind those things which are inducing many of the best ministers to flee are just the reasons why we should make extra effort to bring in and sustain an efficient ministry here."   A.H.M.S. Correspondence.

An example of the attitude of the Presbyterian ministry to slaves is given in the letter of Rev. George G. McAfee, Henderson, Ky., Jan. 23, 1835. "The blacks are numerous in this town and county, and their masters are entirely willing that they should hear preaching.   It has generally been supposed that they would not go to hear a white preacher, but I feel confident that this opinion is without foundation.   In the sermon one Sabbath morning I told the white congregation that I would preach to the blacks at three o'clock on the first command.   I requested them to inform their servants. At the appointed hour the house was filled, and I never preached to a more attentive and interesting congregation. Having long felt a deep interest for this portion of our community I assure you that I rejoice to find that they are more than willing to hear the gospel. That a white preacher should care for their salvation removes their prejudices and enlists their feelings. I have almost been ready to weep when one of them has taken me by the hand and with tears in his eyes uttered, 'My dear young master may the Lord help.'

"They still continue to come and my expectations are more than realized. I feel greatly encouraged to go on in my labors with them. It is true they are very ignorant, but a plain and affectionate exhibition of truth goes right to their hearts. And as for myself, I had rather preach to them than to any white congregation I have ever seen. I look upon them as the most hopeful part of my charges, and thru them I think the whites may be reached. . . . My black congregation amounts to 150." A.H.M.S. Correspondence [Kentucky]

CHAPTER VII

THE MINUTES OF THE CUMBERLAND PRESBYTERY,
1803-1806

INTRODUCTION

[This document is a record of events within pioneer Presbyterianism in Kentucky and Tennessee which led to schism and the rise of the Cumberland Presbyterian Church.

In 1785, the Synod of New York and Philadelphia divided Abingdon Presbytery to form Transylvania Presbytery with jurisdiction in the district of Kentucky and the Cumberland settlements. By 1802, the work had grown into the Synod of Kentucky with three presbyteries, West Lexington, Washington and Transylvania. In the same year the new Synod formed the Cumberland Presbytery from the southern portion of Transylvania.

The Cumberland presbyterial house was divided against itself from the beginning. The four major issues involved were: Revivals; Ministerial education; Doctrine; and Constitutional rights.[1] However, the frontier setting of this schism should not be forgotten. The story would not have been the same in a more settled community. The revivals were highly emotional in comparison to those of the more Eastern sections. The need for a vital ministry seemed to approach a famine. There was little equipment or leisure in such a society for theological refinement, and resourcefulness meant far more than any Constitution.

At the first meeting, the ten ministers of the Presbytery were equally divided on the revival issue which had disturbed many minds since the first revival in the community in 1797. The coming of Rev. James Haw gave the revival group a balance of power which was increased by further ordinations. Licensure and ordination continued over a conservative minority protest.

In 1805, the Synod of Kentucky appointed a commission to investigate affairs of the Presbytery. This commission met at the Gasper meeting house December 3, 1805. "Mr. Lyle preached the opening sermon, on the call and qualifications necessary to the Gospel min-

[1] B. W. McDonnold, *History of the Cumberland Presbyterian Church* (Nashville, Tenn., 1888), pp. 20-81.

istry from the text, 'And no man taketh this honor unto himself, but he that is called of God, as was Aaron.'—Hebr.v.4.   The sermon was three hours long, but the audience were very attentive."[2]   The commission declared twenty-seven licensures and ordinations irregular on the ground that the men were illiterate and held erroneous doctrines.   They were prohibited from preaching or administrating the ordinances.   Three of the older ministers, William Hodge, William McGee and John Rankin, were cited to appear before the Synod to answer charges of erroneous doctrines.   They refused on the ground that the Presbytery was competent to try its own members.   The point at issue was constitutional, and involved the right of the Synod to go into the presbytery and discipline its members. When the commission dissolved the revival members formed themselves into a Council consisting of ministers, elders and representatives from the vacant churches.   They absented themselves from the succeeding meetings of the Presbytery.

The Synod of Kentucky in session at Lexington, October, 1806, dissolved the Cumberland Presbytery, re-annexing it to the Presbytery of Transylvania.   The insurgent members formed themselves into a Council and continued the work.   Moves toward reconciliation were made, but without success.   McAdow, Ewing and King organized an Independent Cumberland Presbytery February 4, 1810, and ordained Ephraim McLean.   By 1820, the Cumberland Presbyterian Church numbered approximately 1,000 members in Kentucky.[3]]

MINUTES OF THE CUMBERLAND PRESBYTERY

Ridge Meeting House, April 5, 1803.

Presbytery met agreeably to an order of the Synod of Kentucky which specified the boundary line between said Presbytery and that of Transylvania, the names of the members and time of their first meeting.   Presbytery was opened by a sermon preached by the Rev. Thomas Craighead who was appointed by Synod to preside on that occasion.   Presbytery constituted with prayer.

Members present: The Rev. Thomas Craighead, Terah

[2] Davidson, Robert, *History of the Presbyterian Church in the State of Kentucky* (New York, 1847), p. 234.

[3] W. W. Sweet, *The Story of Religions in America* (New York, 1930), p. 312.

Templin, James McGready, William Hodge, William McGee and Samuel McAdow, Ministers; Robert King, John Ewing, Joseph Brown, Benjamin Hudson and Samuel Hodge, Elders.

Col. Henry Clark produced a certificate of his appointment as a representative from the united congregations of Spring Creek, McAdow and Clarksville, Charles Eades from the congregations of Little Muddy Creek, John Williamson from the united congregations of Sand Spring and Poplar Meetinghouse, Ephraim McLean, Sr., from the united congregations of West Fork, Hebron and Finley's settlement, Samuel Harris from united congregations of Smith Fork and Big Spring, and Matthew Hall from Gaspar River, all of which took their seats as members of Presbytery. Mr. James Haw, formerly a regular minister in the Republican Methodist Church, having been received as a member at the last session of the Transylvania Presbytery came forward and took his seat. Members absent: James Balch, Samuel Donnell, John Rankin and John Bowman. Mr. Templin was chosen moderator and Mr. McGready clerk. Adjourned to meet here tomorrow at nine o'clock. Concluded with prayer.

Wednesday Morning, April 6th.

Presbytery met according to adjournment, constituted with prayer, members present as above.

A petition for supplies from the united congregation of Spring Creek, McAdow and Clarksville, praying also the administration of the Lord's Supper. A verbal supplication from the congregation of Fountainhead. A verbal supplication from Smith's Fork and Big Spring, praying the administration of baptism and the Lord's Supper. A verbal supplication from Sand Spring and the Poplar Meetinghouse praying the administration of baptism and the Lord's Supper. A verbal supplication from West Fork, Hebron and Finley's settlement praying the administration of the Lord's Supper. A verbal supplication from Stewart's Creek. Ordered that the minutes of the last Transylvania

Presbytery be read. They were read accordingly. Messrs. Hugh Kirkpatrick and Ephraim McLean having subjects assigned them for popular discourses at the last session of the Transylvania Presbytery which were to have been delivered at the next session at Mt. Pisgah, but as that meeting was disappointed through want of members sufficient present to constitute, Presbytery ordered their trial to be continued. Messrs. Alexander Anderson, Finis Ewing and Samuel King being regularly licensed to preach the gospel by the last meeting of Transylvania Presbytery and as their local situation is within the bounds of the Cumberland Presbytery, resolved that they be continued as licentiates under the care of this presbytery. Resolved likewise that Messrs. John Hodge and William Dickey formerly licensed to preach the gospel by the Presbytery of Transylvania be continued as regular licentiates under the care of Cumberland Presbytery agreeable to their local situation. Messrs. Lawrence Rolleson, Robert Bell and James Farr being licensed to exercise their gifts as public exhorters by the last meeting of the Transylvania Presbytery are continued as regular exhorters under the instruction of the Presbytery of Cumberland. . . . [The arrangements for the trial of Rev. James Balch vs. Mr. Thomas Sharp are here omitted] . . . ordered that the supplies to the vacancies be discretionary.

Presbytery considering Robert Guthrie, Robert Houston, Matthew Hall and Samuel Hodge as persons of good standing in the church whose abilities also promise usefulness to the souls of their fellowmen, do authorize and license them to make public appointments and exercise their gifts in exhortation in any congregation or settlement within the bounds of this presbytery.

Resolved that an intermediate presbytery be appointed to meet at Shiloh upon the first Friday in May for the purpose of ordaining Mr. Alexander Anderson provided his trials be sustained. Mr. Anderson is appointed to prepare a sermon upon I John 2:3. Mr. McGready is appointed to preach the ordination sermon or in his absence

Mr. McGee. Mr. Hodge to preside and give the charge. Adjourned to meet at Salem meeting house on the first Tuesday in October next. Concluded with prayer.

TERAH TEMPLIN, Moderator.

Salem Meeting House, Tuesday, October 4, 1803.

The presbytery met according to adjournment and was opened by a sermon delivered by Mr. Hugh Kirkpatrick, a candidate under the care of presbytery. Constituted with prayer.

Members present: Rev. James Balch, James McGready, Wm. Hodge, William McGee, John Rankin, James Haw and Alexander Anderson, Ministers; John Dickey, Robert Paisley, Patrick Barr, Hugh Kirkpatrick and Robert Bell, Elders. Absent the Rev. Thos. Craighead, Terah Templin, Samuel Donnell, Samuel McAdow and John Bowman. Adjourned to meet tomorrow at 9 o'clock. Concluded with prayer.

Wednesday Morning, October 5.

The presbytery met according to adjournment and was constituted with prayer. Members present as above with Mr. Craighead and Mr. Bowman who are now come. Robert Wilson produced a certificate as commissioner from Harpath Lick and Franklin two vacancies able to support a settled minister. Mr. James Berry commissioner from Spring Creek, McAdow and Clarksville produced a certificate stating their ability to maintain a settled minister, John Boin elder from Stones River, Mr. Eades commissioner from Little Muddy Creek, Ephraim McLean, Sr. commissioner from Hebron and West Fork of Red River, able to support a minister, John Hancock commissioner from Sharon able to support a settled minister, all which took their seats as members of presbytery.

Mr. Rankin was chosen moderator and Mr. Bowman clerk. Mr. Rankin, Mr. Balch, and Mr. Bowman's reasons for not attending the last spring session of presbytery were sustained. Ephraim McLean delivered a sermon assigned at the last meeting of the Transylvania Presbytery, before its separation.   Presbytery proceeded to consider the discourses of Messrs. Kirkpatrick and McLean as parts of popular trial and they were sustained as such.   Adjourned to meet at Mr. Boyd's 9 o'clock this evening.   Concluded with prayer.

Presbytery met according to adjournment and was constituted with prayer.   Mr. John Hodge applied for dismission from our presbytery with a view of settling in Georgia and though it appears that he was considered as a licentiate under the direction of the Transylvania Presbytery, presuming it be a mistake as his local situation casts him in the bounds of this presbytery, he was dismissed accordingly.

Messrs. Kirkpatrick and McLean were examined on divinity and their examinations sustained.   Mr. James Porter offered himself as a candidate for the gospel ministry, was examined upon experimental religion[4] and his motives to the ministry which examinations were sustained. Messrs. Crawford and Dooly applied for license to exhort. Presbytery proceeded to examine them on experimental religion and motives inducing them to such exercise.   After giving satisfactory answers they were licensed to exhort within the bounds of this presbytery or wherever God in his providence may call them.

Adjourned to meet at the meeting house at 9 o'clock tomorrow morning.   Concluded with prayer.

Presbytery met according to adjournment pursuant as above.   Constituted with prayer.

Robert Wilson, James Druggan, Michael Findley and David Foster came forward expressing their desire to exercise their gifts in exhortation.

Presbytery proceeded to examine them on experimental religion also the motives inducing them to exhort publicly. Presbytery after receiving sufficient satisfaction licensed them accordingly.

[4] Note the absence of an examination on educational qualifications.   Compare with the minutes of the Transylvania Presbytery for April 14, 1803.

Ordered that the Moderators James McGready, William McGee and Wm. Hodge form a committee to examine James Porter and make appointments.

Adjourned to meet here at 9 o'clock tomorrow morning. Concluded with prayer.

Friday Morning, October 7th.

Presbytery met according to adjournment pursuant as above, except Messrs. Craighead, Balch and Bowman. Constituted with prayer.

A written petition[5] from the congregations of Spring Creek, McAdow and Clarksville praying the ordination of Finis Ewing, in whose circuit these congregations are included. Considering the petition of those congregations and particularly because of the large circuit[6] and many young societies earnestly desiring and really needing the administrations of the sealing ordinances amongst them presbytery agrees that Mr. Ewing be ordained on the Friday before the third Sabbath in November next. Ordered that Messrs. McGready, McGee, Haw and McAdow, attend as members of that presbytery. Mr. McGee to preach the ordination sermon, Mr. McGready to preside and give the charge, Mr. Ewing to prepare a sermon upon John 15:7. Ordered likewise that Mr. Porter attend said presbytery to deliver a discourse upon the subject assigned him at the present session, to be examined upon the sciences and receive further trials.

The moderator finding it his duty to go home Mr. McGee was nominated in his place.

The committee of the last evening came forward and made the following report: Ordered that each licentiate exhort and exercise himself in composition on any subject he chooses and that he shows as many pieces of such com-

[5] The licensures and ordinations, which the Commission declared irregular, were in answer to the demands of the churches for ministers. Ordinations often followed direct petitions from congregations as in the case of Ewing.

[6] Note the use of terms common to the Methodists, such as "circuit" and "exhorter."

position to the nearest minister as he can conveniently between each stated session of presbytery.

Ordered that Robert Wilson, David Foster, Robert Bell, Samuel Hodge be appointed each a text to prepare a discourse upon by the next stated session. Mr. Porter's examination on the languages was sustained. Ordered that each settled minister supply two Sabbaths at discretion.

Ordered that Mr. McLean supply two Sabbaths at Mt. Carmel, two at Little Muddy and two at Sharon. Mr. Kirkpatrick two Sabbaths on the head of Marrowbone. Mr. Ewing and McLean supply each one Sabbath in Ohio county in the neighborhood of Hartford.

[The trial of Balch vs. Sharpe is omitted. Balch found not guilty. Reconciliation followed.]

Ordered that Mr. James Porter prepare a discourse upon 2 Cor. 7:1.

Adjourned to meet at Shiloh church on the first Friday of April, 1804.

Concluded with prayer.

WILLIAM McGEE, Moderator.

Shiloh Meeting House, April 3, 1804.

Presbytery met at Shiloh agreeably to adjournment. Opened with a sermon by James Porter from Romans 8:9. Constituted with prayer.

Members present Messrs. Creaghead, Hodge, Balch, McGready, Rankin, McAdow, McGee, Donnell, Bowman, Haw and Ewing, ministers. Absent, Mr. Templin.

Elders present, Dr. Donnell, Jno. Boyd, Thos. Sharp, Robert Bell, Samuel Hodge, Henry Brun. Charles Eads, John Adams and Robert Wilson representatives.

Proceeded to the choice of moderator and clerk, Samuel M'Adow was chosen moderator and Samuel Donnell clerk.

A petition for supplies through the medium of Finis Ewing from the congregations of Hartford and Mt. Carmel. Another through the medium of Mr. McGready

from the congregations of old and new Sharon. Another
by Hugh Tedford for Sugg's Creek, Fall Creek, Stewart's
Creek and Rock Spring congregations. Adjourned until
tomorrow 9 o'clock concluded with prayer.

Wednesday morning, presbytery met according to adjournment with members present as above. Constituted
with prayer.

Ordered that the minutes of the last session be read,
they were read accordingly. Some of the members having
some difficulty respecting the legality of Mr. Ewing taking
a seat as a member, presbytery took the matter into consideration, the decision of which was that he was invited
to a seat by a large majority.[7]   Robert Wilson, David
Foster, Robert Bell and Samuel Hodge having been appointed each a discourse on subjects assigned them at our
last session, upon inquiry it was found that Robert Wilson
was not prepared. Foster, Bell and Hodge delivered the
discourses appointed, Bell's and Hodge's being popular
discourses, all of which were sustained as parts of trial.

James Farr expressing his desire to join presbytery as a
candidate for the holy ministry, delivered a discourse as
a specimen of his abilities. The presbytery judging thereof
received him as a candidate and appointed him to prepare
a discourse on Mark 8:34 to be delivered at the intermediate presbytery.

Adjourned to meet at Dr. Donnell's 8 o'clock this evening. Concluded with prayer. Wednesday night, 8 o'clock,
presbytery met according to adjournment, members present
as above except Messrs. Balch and Craighead. Mr. Porter's examination on divinity was sustained as the last of
his trial for licensure as well as his sermon at the opening
of presbytery.

At Shiloh, April 4, 1804, the presbytery of Cumberland
having received sufficient testimonials of his having gone
through a regular course of literature; of his good moral

---

[7] The efforts of the anti-revivalistic minority to uphold the presbyterial
regulations as to education and time of study are here overruled by the
revivalistic majority.

character; and of his being in the communion of the church; proceeded to take the usual parts of trial for his licensure. He having given satisfaction as to his accomplishments in literature, his experimental acquaintance with religion, his proficiency in divinity, and other studies, the presbytery did and hereby do express their approbation of all these parts of trial; he having adopted the confession of faith of this church, and satisfactorily answered the questions appointed to be put to candidates to be licensed, presbytery did and hereby do license him, the said James Porter, to preach the gospel of Christ as a probationer for the holy ministry within the bounds of this presbytery or wherever he shall be orderly called.

Thomas Nelson from N. Carolina expressing a desire to join this presbytery, produced a certificate, was examined on his experimental acquaintance with religion, and was accordingly received as a candidate. He delivered a discourse on Matt. 11:28 as part of trial, which was sustained.

John Hodge and Thomas Colhoun expressing desires to exercise their talents in exhortation, were examined on experimental religion, the motives inducing them to public exhortation, which examinations were sustained and they were licensed accordingly.

Reuben Dooly was appointed to prepare a discourse on Acts 16:31, James Crawford on Romans 5:1, to be delivered at our next session of presbytery.

Four supplications from the frontier societies for the ordination of Mr. King. Ordered that an intermediate presbytery meet at Red River on the Friday before the 2nd Sabbath in June for that purpose. Mr. King was appointed to prepare a sermon for ordination on 2 Cor. 5:20; Mr. Rankins to preach the ordination sermon, and Mr. Hodge to preside. Robert Wilson was appointed to prepare a discourse on Romans 3:31; Samuel Hodge to prepare a discourse on 2 Cor. 5:11 first part, and Robert Bell a discourse on Isaiah 45:22, both to be popular discourses. Mr. Nelson to prepare a discourse on Isaiah 3:10 and to be examined on the language and sciences.

Adjourned to the meeting house at 9 o'clock tomorrow morning. Concluded with prayer.

Thursday morning. Presbytery met according to adjournment. Constituted with prayer. Members present as above except Mr. Balch who is absent through indisposition. Messrs. Rankin, Ewing, McLean were appointed to administer the Lord's Supper at Hartford any time before our next stated session. Messrs. McGready, Ewing and McLean to administer the Lord's supper at Mount Carmel at discretion. Mr. McLean was appointed to supply at Red Banks and New Sharon one Sabbath each place. Messrs. King and Porter to supply in the vacancies at discretion. Mr. Kirkpatrick to supply at the head of Big Barren two Sabbaths and the rest of his time discretionary. Ordered that all the other members supply two Sabbaths at discretion. Mr. Dickey to supply two Sabbaths at discretion. Ordered that Messrs. Hodge, McGee and Dr. Donnell form a committee to draw up a circular letter to the vacancies recommending them to be careful to contribute to the support of those preachers and exhorters who labor among them, which letter the committee will forward in whatever manner they judge proper. Whereas the body of people formerly a part of Shiloh congregation having separated themselves from said congregation prepared a petition to presbytery praying themselves to be known by the name of the Shiloh Presbyterian congregation, presbytery considering that this people having separated from the communion of Shiloh church as they inform us in their petition, because their brethren held communion with those holding Armenian[8] principles and likewise because presbytery had sufficient ground to believe

[8] This renunciation of a portion of a congregation because they refused to have fellowship with their brothers of Arminian sympathies shows how far the majority of the members of the Cumberland Presbytery had swung away from the orthodoxy of Presbyterianism while under the spell of the great revival. The portion of the Shiloh congregation here referred to was recognized by the Synod of Kentucky, and received by the Cumberland Presbytery on April 1, 1806, as "the orderly part of Shiloh congregation." See Minutes below.

they uniformly opposed and condemned the present blessed revival in our country and lastly because their representatives at a former presbytery at Muddy River, October 8, 1804, declared that they were no longer in communion with our body, presbytery considering them a people not under their jurisdiction refuse to attend to their petition. Said petitioners not being satisfied with the judgment of presbytery appealed to Synod. David Foster was appointed to prepare a discourse on Rev. 22:11 to be delivered at our fall session. Adjournment to meet at Mt. Pisgah on the first Tuesday of October, 1804. Concluded with prayer.

SAMUEL MCADOW, Moderator.

SAMUEL DONNELL, Clerk.

Mt. Pisgah Meeting House, October 2, 1804.

Presbytery met according to adjournment. Opened by a discourse upon Mark 10:49 by James Farr a candidate for the ministry. Constituted with prayer.

Members present: Messrs. McAdow, Hodge, McGready, McGee, Haw, Ewing and King, ministers; Patrick Barr, James Hambleston, Wm. Clark and John Billingsley, elders.

Eneas McAllister, of Sharon congregation, Robt. Wilson from Franklin, Big and West Harpath, Hugh Tedford from Stewart's Creek, Suggs Creek, Fall Creek and Rock Springs, Job Bass from Big Spring, and Smith's Fork, Stephen Clinton from Spring Creek, McAdow and Clarksville, Michael Findley from Little Muddy commissioners. Members absent Messrs. Craighead, Templin, Balch, Bowman, Donnel[l] and Rankin. Proceeded to the choice of moderator and clerk, Mr. McGready was chosen moderator and Mr. Ewing clerk. Presbytery proceeded to consider Mr. Farr's discourse which was sustained as part of trial. Mr. Wilson delivered a discourse on the subject assigned him at our last session, which was sustained as part of trial. Adjourned to Mr. Ewing's at 8 o'clock this evening. Concluded with prayer.

At Mr. Ewings Presbytery met according to adjournment. Members present as above except Mr. Rankin who is now come. Constituted with prayer.

Messrs. Wm. McClure, Stephen Clinton, Samuel Blythe, William Moore and Samuel Donnell, came forward begging to be taken under the care of presbytery and be permitted to exercise their gifts in public exhortation. Presbytery proceeded to inquire into their experimental acquaintance with religion and motives inducing them to warn their fellow creatures to flee from the wrath to come. During the time of this examination the influences of the eternal spirit as a refreshing shower from the everlasting hills were poured out so copiously that the members, candidates and almost all present were made to rejoice with a joy that is indeed unspeakable and full of glory.[9] Presbytery having received sufficient satisfaction in the examination, do license them to exercise their gifts as public exhorters in our bounds.

Ordered that Monday the fifteenth of this month be observed as a day of fasting and prayer to God in all our charges that he may defend his cause, graciously pour out his Spirit, revive and carry on His blessed work among us and through the world. Adjourned to the meeting house tomorrow morning at 10 o'clock. Concluded with prayer.

Wednesday morning.

Presbytery met according to adjournment, members present as above except Mr. Craighead who is now come. Constituted with prayer. John Boyd a representative from Mt. Tabor and Salem congregations now takes his seat. A call from Sharon congregation was presented to Mr. Samuel Hodge which he took under consideration until our next stated session of presbytery. A petition from Bethany congregation for supplies and the administration of the Lord's Supper was received.

[9] Note that the spirit of the camp-meeting pervades the business session of the Presbytery.

A draught of a letter was brought in and read to be addressed to the General Assembly with respect to the remarks upon the exercises attending the revival which was unanimously adopted except by Mr. Craighead who disputed and Mr. Boyd who refused to vote. Ordered that Mr. Haw attend the session of Union Congregation to moderate in a matter of debate in said session. His attendance to be as soon as convenient. Mr. Robert Wilson and Mr. Foster each delivered a discourse on subjects assigned them at our last stated session which were sustained as parts of trial.

Mr. McLean came forward and confessed to presbytery that he had been guilty of intoxication, hoping to be restored upon his confession as he had voluntarily ceased from his public ministration since the crime was committed. Presbytery in order to obtain all possible information on the aggravations attending the same, ordered that John Tate, Robert Houston, William Lee and George M'Lean be cited to attend our next stated session as witnesses in this case. Adjournment to meet at Mr. Bryan's at 8 o'clock. Concluded with prayer.

Mr. Bryan's at 8 o'clock.

Presbytery met according to adjournment, members present as above. Constituted with prayer. The amendments proposed by the General Assembly in the Book of Discipline were taken into consideration and adopted. Ordered that Mr. Haw administer the sacrament of the supper at Bethany and that Mr. Porter assist in preaching on the occasion. Ordered that Mr. Samuel Hodge supply two Sabbaths at Mt. Carmel, Mr. Bell two Sabbaths at Yellow Creek, Mr. McGready one Sabbath at Mt. Carmel and one at Muddy Creek. Ordered that Mr. Wilson prepare a popular sermon on 2 Cor. 5:17 to be delivered at our spring session, Mr. Foster prepare a popular sermon on John 1:12 to be delivered at our next stated session, Mr. Blythe prepare a discourse upon John 10:9, Mr. Samuel

Donnell a sermon on Romans 8:1, Mr. Rolleson a sermon upon Isaiah 45:22, Mr. Calhoun a sermon upon Romans 5:1, Mr. John Hodge a sermon upon Isaiah 3:10,11, which discourses are all to be delivered at our spring session. Ordered that Alexander Chapman exercise his gifts as a public exhorter.

Presbytery proceeded to examine Mr. Farr upon experimental religion, also his motives to the ministry, which were sustained, also Mr. Farr and Mr. Nelson on divinity, which examinations were sustained as parts of trial.

Presbytery having received sufficient testimonials of the good standing of Thomas Nelson, his having gone through a regular course of literature, of his good moral character and of his being in the communion of the church, proceeded to take the usual parts of trial for his licensure. After having received satisfaction on all those parts of trial, also having adopted the Confessions of Faith, and answered such questions as are appointed to be put to candidates, presbytery did and hereby do license said Thomas Nelson to preach the gospel of Christ as a probationer within the bounds of this presbytery or wherever he may be orderly called.

Presbytery having likewise received full satisfaction of the good moral character of Mr. James Farr, his experimental acquaintance with religion, his knowledge of divinity, having also given good specimens of his abilities and usefulness in the church as a public exhorter under the care of presbytery, having purchased to himself a good degree among the churches where he has exercised his gifts, having also adopted the Confession of Faith and answered the questions appointed to be put to candidates, presbytery did therefore license him to preach the gospel of Christ within their bounds or wherever God in his providence may call him.

Adjourned to meet on the first Tuesday in April at the Ridge meeting house. Concluded with prayer.

JAMES McGREADY, Moderator.

Ridge Meeting House, April 2, 1805.

Presbytery met according to adjournment.

Present the Rev. Thomas Craighead, James Balch, James McGready, William Hodge, Wm. McGee, Samuel McAdow, Samuel Donnell, John Bowman, James Haw, Finis Ewing, and Samuel King, Ministers.

Absent Rev. Terah Templin and John Rankin.

Present Daniel McGoodwin, Joseph McDowell, Robert Anderson, Robert Guthrie, John Bone and Young Ewing, elders.

Samuel Henry representative from the united congregations of Bethany and Salem in Livingston County, James Hutchison from Spring Creek and McAdow, Josiah Wilson from Franklin and Harpath Lick, Robert Smith from Stewart's Creek, Falling Creek, Suggs Creek and Rock Springs, David H. Stephens from Carmel and Mt. Zion and Michael Findley from Little Muddy Creek, produced their certificates as representatives and took their seats.

Presbytery was opened by a sermon upon Eph. 6:23 by the Rev. Archibald Cameron, a member of the Transylvania Presbytery.   Constituted with prayer.

Proceeded to the choice of moderator and clerk.   Mr. McGee was chosen moderator and Mr. Hodge clerk.   Mr. Cameron from Transylvania Presbytery being present was invited to take his seat as a corresponding member but for certain reasons he declined.   (He had been appointed on a Committee of Inquiry, by Synod and was the only member present.)   Adjourned to meet here tomorrow morning at 9 o'clock.   Concluded with prayer.

Wednesday morning.

Presbytery met according to adjournment.

Present as above.   Constituted with prayer.   A call from the united congregations of Bethany and Salem to Mr. Dickey, which being presented he took into consideration, promising either to receive or return it before the close of the meeting.

A call from the united congregation of Mt. Zion and

Carmel was presented to Mr. Nelson which he accepted. A written petition for supplies and the administration of the Lord's Supper from a newly formed society known by the name of Bethany on the waters of Barton's creek, and a petition for supplies from the inhabitants of Rays Branch and Cooks Knob north of Big Barren, were received.

Ordered that the pastoral letters from the General Assembly and the Synod of Kentucky be read and they were read accordingly.

A petition for supplies was received from the united societies of Little River. The call presented to Samuel Hodge from Sharon congregation at our last stated session, he now receives.

Samuel Blythe delivered a discourse assigned him at our last term. The vote being put whether he shall be received as a candidate was carried by a majority. Robert Wilson was called upon to deliver a discourse, on a text appointed him at our last session as a popular sermon, but upon his declaring he was not prepared, his whole popular trials were deferred until some future time.

David Foster having a popular subject appointed at our last session, being called upon plead not prepared. The public trials also were deferred until some future period. Samuel Donnell, Thomas Calhoun, Jno. Hodge, each having a text appointed at our last session being called upon informed presbytery that they were not prepared.[10] Mr. Dickey being asked whether he were ready to accept the call answered he was and received it accordingly.

Ordered that an intermediate presbytery be appointed for the ordination of Mr. Dickey at Bethany Meeting House at Crooked Creek on the Friday before the third Sabbath of June next, Mr. Donnel[l] to preach the ordination sermon and Mr. Templin to preside and give the charge. Mr. Dickey to prepare a sermon on the middle clause of 13th verse of Rom. chapter 8. Ordered that an intermediate presbytery be appointed for the ordination of

[10] Cameron representing the Synod of Kentucky was present and was considered a spy from the Commission; hence, the excuses.

Samuel Hodge and Thomas Nelson at Red River on the Friday before the second Sabbath in June next. Mr. McGee to preach the ordination sermon, Mr. McGready to preside and give the charge, Mr. Hodge to prepare a sermon on Psa. 55:5. Mr. Nelson to prepare on Rom. 5:1. Ordered that Mr. Rankin and Mr. Bell administer the Lord's Supper in Muddy Creek congregation at any time convenient between this and the Fall session.

Samuel Blythe appointed to prepare a sermon on Isa. 45:22 to be delivered at our next term. Ordered that Mr. McLean be cited to appear at our Fall term to answer a charge for which he remains suspended and the same witnesses be cited which were formerly, namely John Tate, Robert Houston, Wm. Lee, and George McLean.

Ordered that Messrs. Ewing and Nelson administer the sacraments at Mr. Scotts on Little River, at discretion. Mr. King to administer the sacraments at Bethany and Mr. Porter to assist in preaching. Mr. McGready to administer the ordinance at Griders Meeting House and Mr. Kirkpatrick to assist in preaching. Adjourned to meet at Red River Meeting House on the first Tuesday in October next. Concluded with prayer.

WM. McGEE, Moderator.

Red River Meeting House, October 1, 1805.
Presbytery met according to adjournment. Present the Rev. James Balch, James McGready, William McGee, James Haw, Finis Ewing, Samuel King, Thos. Nelson, Samuel Hodge, and William Dickey. Absent the Rev. Thos. Craighead, Terah Templin, William Hodge, John Rankin, Samuel McAdow, John Bowman and Samuel Donnell. Elders Michael Henderson, William Clark, John Whitside, and Ephraim McLean, Sr. Stephen Clinton appeared as representative from the congregations of Spring Creek and McAdow, Joseph Motherall from Shiloh, George Calhoun from Franklin and Harpath Licks, Michael Findley from Little Muddy Creek, Reuben Bed-

well from Sugg's Creek, Stewart's Creek, Fall Creek and
Rock Springs, having produced their credentials, took their
seats. Presbytery was opened by a sermon on 2 Cor. 5:17
by Mr. Robert Wilson which text was assigned him at a
former session as the subject of a popular discourse, likewise by a sermon on John 1:12 by Daniel Foster which text
had been appointed him as a subject of his popular trial.
Constituted with prayer. Presbytery proceeded to the
choice of a moderator and a clerk, accordingly Mr. Haw
was chosen moderator and Mr. McGready clerk. Mr.
Ewing requested leave of absence during the session which
was granted. Ordered that the minutes of the last stated
meeting be read and they were read accordingly. Adjourned to meet at 8 o'clock tonight. Concluded with
prayer.

Eight o'clock p. m.

Presbytery met according to adjournment and constituted
with prayer. Present as above except Mr. Ewing who had
obtained leave of absence, and Messrs. Whitside and Mc-
Lean who have not come.

Proceeded to consider Mr. Wilson's discourse which was
sustained. Adjourned to meet tomorrow morning at 9
o'clock. Concluded with prayer.

Wednesday Morning, 9 o'clock.

Presbytery met according to adjournment, present as
above and constituted with prayer. Mr. Samuel Blythe
delivered a discourse assigned him at our last session which
was sustained. Mr. Thos. Calhoun delivered a discourse
assigned to him at a former session, which was sustained.

Proceeded to examine Messrs. Wilson and Foster upon
divinity which examinations were sustained.

Mr. Craighead appeared and his reasons for tardiness
were sustained.

[Note: At this time the charges against Rev. Mr. Mc-
Lean were taken up and after a full hearing he was restored

to the full office of the ministry.   The evidence in the case is
here omitted.]

Mr. Donnell appeared and his reasons for not coming
sooner were sustained.   Ordered that the calls and supplications be read and they were read accordingly.   A call from
Little Muddy Creek was presented to Mr. Bell.   The call
being defective in some things was not received.   Several
petitions from different vacancies for Mr. Porter's ordination were brought in and read.   Presbytery considering
these petitions improper, rejected them.   A supplication
from Yellow Creek for supplies was read.   A verbal supplication was received from Drakes Creek for the administration of the sacrament and other supplies.

Presbytery having received satisfaction of the good moral
character of Robert Wilson and David Foster, their experimental acquaintance with religion, and their knowledge of
divinity, and they having given good specimens of their
abilities and usefulness in the church as public exhorters
under the care of presbytery and having purchased to themselves a good degree where they have exercised their gifts,
having adopted the Confession of Faith and answered the
questions appointed to be put to candidates, presbytery did
license them to preach the gospel of Christ within the
bounds of this presbytery or wherever God may call them.

Ordered that Mr. Rankin administer the sacrament at
Drake's Creek the first Sabbath in December and Messrs.
Bell and Farr to assist in preaching and Mr. Farr to preach
there two Sabbaths besides.   Ordered that Mr. Ewing
preach one Sabbath and Mr. Bell two Sabbaths at Yellow
Creek.   Ordered every member of presbytery to supply two
Sabbaths at discretion before the next stated session.   Or-
dered that Mr. S. Blythe prepare a sermon Rev. 3:20, Mr.
Chapman to prepare a discourse on Matt. 11:28 and Mr.
Clinton a discourse on Romans 8:14 against the next stated
session of presbytery.

Ordered that the presbyterial book be delivered to Mr.
Donnell and that he be directed to lay it before Synod.

Adjourned to meet at Red River the first Tuesday in April. Concluded with prayer.

                                    JAMES HAW, Moderator.

JAMES MCGREADY, Clerk pro tem.

N. B. Time would not permit to transcribe the minutes of the two intermediate Presbyteries I have therefore laid them up for the Stated Clerk.—J. McC.

Mt. Pisgah Church, Apr. 1st, 1806.

The Presbytery of Cumberland met according to adjournment. Constituted with prayer. Members present, the Rev. James Balch, William Dickey and Samuel Donnell. Absent, the Rev. Thomas B. Craighead, Terah Templin, John Bowman, James McGready, William Hodge, William McGee, John Rankin and Samuel McAdow.[11] There were also present the following elders: James Graham, Joseph Reed, William Donnell and William Baird, who was regularly chosen and sent forward by a congregation which had liberty granted them by the orderly part of Shiloh congregation. Presbytery proceeded to choose a moderator and clerk. Rev. J. Balch was chosen moderator and Rev. S. Donnell, Clerk. Ordered that the minutes of the last session of Presbytery be read but upon inquiry it was found that they were not present. Ordered that supplications for supplies be presented. A written petition for supplies was presented from Smyrna congregation and a verbal one from a congregation styling themselves the regular part of Shiloh congregation, formed agreeably to a resolve of Synod, for supplies and the administration of the Lord's Supper amongst them. Ordered that Mr. Dickey supply at Smyrna

[11] The revivalistic members absented themselves from the meeting of the Presbytery following the convocation of the Commission of Synod in December, 1805. All those absent except Templin and Craighead were revivalists. The names of the following new ministers, which had appeared on the roll October 1, 1805, were omitted upon the orders of the Commission: James Haw, Finis Ewing, Samuel King, Thomas Nelson, and Samuel Hodge. They, with the older men, had formed themselves into a Council. Thomas Nelson and Samuel Hodge submitted to the requirements and were admitted to the Transylvania Presbytery in 1809.

on the first Sabbath in April and Mr. Balch to supply at Smyrna the first and the fourth Sabbath in April and the others at discretion. Mr. Craighead and Mr. Bowman each to supply one Sabbath in that congregation styling themselves the orderly part of Shiloh congregation and Mr. Donnell one Sabbath. Mr. Craighead and Mr. Donnell ordered to administer the sacrament of the Lord's Supper amongst them. Mr. Craighead appeared in Synod and his reasons for absence were sustained.

A verbal supplication for supplies at Franklin and its vicinity through the medium of Mr. Craighead likewise one from Suggs Creek were presented. Mr. Craighead and Mr. Donnell apopinted each to supply one Sabbath at or near Franklin and Mr. Bowman to supply one Sabbath at Suggs Creek. The Presbytery recommended to Rev. Mr. Templin to supply at discretion on account of his age and infirmity. Presbytery adjourned to meet at Spring Hill Church on the first Tuesday of October next. Concluded with prayer.

JAMES BALCH, Moderator.

SAMUEL DONNELL, Clerk.

Spring Hill Church, Oct. 7th, 1806.

Presbytery met according to adjournment and was opened with a sermon by the Rev. James Balch from I Cor. 12:27. Constituted with prayer. Members present: The Rev. Thomas B. Craighead, Terah Templin, James Balch, John Bowman, Samuel Donnell and William Dickey.[12] Absent: The Rev. James McGready, William Hodge, William McGee, John Rankin and Samuel McAdow. Elders Mr. Hugh Cathey, John Robinson and Samuel Stewart, present. Rev. Terah Templin was chosen moderator and Rev. William Dickey clerk. Ordered that the minutes of the last stated session of Presbytery be read. A petition for supplies was presented to Presbytery by Mr. Stewart, from the orderly part of the Shiloh congregation. A petition for supplies at

---

[12] These men represent the anti-revivalistic minority of the Presbytery. The members of the majority have absented themselves.

Franklin through the medium of Mr. Craighead was presented and one for supplies at Bayes Fork through the medium of Mr. Balch. Mr. Templin's reasons for not attending the last sessions of Presbytery were sustained and also Mr. Bowmans. Ordered that our Presbytery Book be inquired after. Mr. Balch and Mr. Dickey reported that they had fulfilled their appointments at Smyrna.

Mr. Craighead and Mr. Donnell reported that they had fulfilled their appointments at Shiloh and their reasons for not fulfilling their appointments at Franklin and its vicinity were sustained. Mr. Bowman's reasons for not fulfilling his appointment amongst the regular part of Shiloh congregation were sustained, and he reported fulfilling his appointment at Suggs Creek. Mr. Templin complied with the request of Presbytery in supplying at descretion. Presbytery adjourned to meet tomorrow at 9 o'clock. Concluded with prayer.

Spring Hill Church, Oct. 8, 1806.

Presbytery met according to adjournment at 9 o'clock. Constituted with prayer. Mr. Craighead and Mr. Donnel[1] were appointed (qui supra) to supply two Sabbaths each at Shiloh one Sabbath each at Suggs Creek and one Sabbath at discretion. Mr. Bowman was appointed to supply two Sabbaths in the vicinity of Franklin, one Sabbath at Suggs Creek and another Sabbath at Discretion. Mr. Balch was appointed to supply two Sabbaths at Bayes Fork, one Sabbath at Concord and another at discretion. Mr. Templin and Mr. Dickey were appointed to supply one Sabbath each in the Presbyterian congregation in Muhlenburg and three Sabbaths each at discretion.

[A matter concerning Rev. Jas. McGready and a house and lot in Russellville, Ky., was referred to the Synod of Kentucky, and is omitted here.]

Whereas we are credibly informed that the Rev. James McGready, William Hodge, William McGee and John Rankin persist in encouraging and in holding Christian and ministerial communion with those young men declared by

the Commission of Synod[13] to be destitute of any authority
to administer sealing ordinances, preach or exhort in the
Presbyterian Church, notwithstanding the fact that said
young men neglect said declaration. Therefore be it Resolved, That it is the duty of this Presbytery to report the
same to the Synod. Resolved that Mr. Donnell write to
Rev. Jacob Lake informing him when and where the next
stated session of Presbytery will meet and that they expect
his attendance.

Presbytery adjourned to meet at Smyrna on the first
Tuesday of April next, 1807. Concluded with prayer.

TERAH TEMPLIN, Moderator.

[13] The report of the Commission of Synod in December, 1805, declared
the proceedings of Cumberland Presbytery irregular. They called upon
young preachers who had been licensed and ordained to come forward to
be examined. On the advice of their elders the young men refused to comply. The Commission thereupon declared said ministers without authority
to preach the gospel and prohibited them doing so. William Hodge, William
McGee and John Rankin were cited to appear before the Synod for proga-
gating doctrines contrary to the Confession of Faith. See *Minutes of the
Synod of Kentucky,* I, pp. 92, 95. Also Davidson, *op. cit.,* pp. 239-240.

CHAPTER VIII

MINUTES OF THE SYNOD OF KENTUCKY, 1802-1811

INTRODUCTION

[According to the Presbyterian "Form of Government" the Church is governed by four judicatories: the Session, the Presbytery, the Synod and the General Assembly. A synod is composed of not less than three presbyteries. Seven ministers and any number of lay elders, convening at the officially designated time and place, constitute a quorum, provided not more than three of the ministers belong to one presbytery. The synod convenes annually and reports its proceedings to the General Assembly. The chief functions of the synod are: to adjudicate all cases referred to it by the constitutive presbyteries; to review the records of presbyteries with a view to approval, censure or redress of whatever has been done contrary to the constitution of the church; to erect, unite or divide presbyteries; to promote unity, purity of doctrine and in all matters, the spiritual uplift of the presbyteries, sessions and people under its care; and to propose to the General Assembly such measures as may promote the general edification of the church.

The proceedings of the Synod of Kentucky, 1802-1811, given below, illustrate these various functions of a synod during a most critical period in the history of the Presbyterian church in the new West. An acquaintance with this document is vital to a correct understanding of two significant divisive movements in frontier Presbyterianism, namely, the secession of the Cumberland Presbytery and the forming of the Cumberland Presbyterian Church, and the "New Light" or "Stoneite" schism.]

A copy of the minutes of the Synod of Kentucky from the year one thousand eight hundred & two to the year one thousand eight hundred & ten being contained in the first volume of the Records —

A copy of Rules or bye Laws for regulating and governing the Synod in all it deliberations.

1.   The moderator or in his absence the senior Minister present shall on the day to which the Synod Staies [Stands]

adjourned open synod with a sermon; and immediately after shall call the members to order.

2nd   When the Mode^r shall call to order each member shall take his seat, & give due attention to business avoiding all unnecessary walking talking, whispering and every thing else that is inconsistent with good order and becoming gravity.

3^d   The Members shall be particular in attending at the stated hours and no member shall absent himself during the session without leave from the Moderator

4   After a record of the Meeting the names of the members present and absent is made, the members present shall proceed to elect a new moderator and Clerk or Clerks

5——   The synod early in every session shall appoint a committee of Overtures whose duty it shall be to prepare and arrange business for the consideration of Synod

6——   Petitions References Appeals and all questions or propositions tending to permanent regulations shall be laid before the Committee of Overtures before they are offered to Synod.

7——   The Moderator may speak to points of Order in preference to other ministers — rising from his seat for that purpose — shall decide Questions of Order subject however to an appeal to Synod; but he shall not take a share in the usual debates.

8——   An motion made must be seconded and afterwards repeated by the Moderator or read aloud before it is debated & every Motion be reduced to writing; if the moderator or any member require it.

9——   Any person having made a Motion shall have liberty to withdraw before any debate is had thereon but not afterwards without leave from the Synod.

10   On questions of Order Adjournment Postponement Commitment, on the previous question, no member shall speak more than once —   On all other questions no member shall speak more than three times; without leave from the Moderator.

11   When a question is under debate no motion shall be

received, unless to amend it to committ it for the previous question — or to adjourn.

12   The previous question shall be in this form "Shall the main question be now put?" and until it is decided shall preclude all amendments and further debate on the main question.

13   An Amendment may be moved on any motion, and shall be decided before the Original motion.

14   If any question under debate contains several parts, any member may have it divided, and a question taken on each part.

15   Every member when speaking shall address himself to the Chair, and shall treat his fellow members with decency and respect; in no case casting personal reflections. — And if a member acts disorderly, it shall be the duty of the Moderator, and the privilege of the other members, to call him to order. — If two members rise at the same time to speak the Moderator shall determine who shall proceed.

16   A question shall not be called up, or reconsidered at the same Session of Synod at which it has been decided, unless by a Majority of two thirds.

17   Any member who may think himself aggrieved by any decision of Synod, shall if he chooses, have his dissent, or protest, with his reasons, entered on the records, or filed among the papers of Synod if given in before its rising.

18   A fair copy of these Rules shall lie on the table, during the Sessions of Synod, for the perusal of the Members, and the Stated Clerk shall furnish the said copy which shall be read aloud at the beginning of each Session

19   The Clerk pro tem under the Superintendence of the Stated Clerk shall record as Minutes of Synod, all business which comes regularly before Synod, and all final decisions on such business which minutes as soon as draughted shall be read before Synod, in order that they may be considered and corrected, and at the close of the Session he shall read the whole Minutes, that they may be reviewed in connexion and corrected by the Synod prior to its adjournment

20   The Stated Clerk shall transcribe the Minutes of

Synod into a book kept for that purpose; which book he shall produce at the beginning of each Session, with all the minutes already transcribed therein in a fair and legible hand — for such service he shall receive such compensation as the Synod shall judge sufficient.

21   If any member acts contrary to these rules, the Moderator shall reprove, or otherwise censure him, as the Synod shall think proper—   And if any member shall think himself denied of any right, or unjustly blamed by the Moderator, he shall not speak disrespectfully to him, but modestly require the decision of the Synod in the case.

22   Seven Ministers,& as many elders as may be present shall be a quorum to do business; provided there be three members from at least each of two of the Presbyteries. — But any number less than a quorum may adjourn from day to day, for two days — and if a quorum does not then appear, they may adjourn to the same place for the next annual Meeting Rescinded Oct. 10 1811.

Presbyterian Meeting house Lexington Thursday October 14th 1802

The Synod of Kentucky met agreeably to the appointment of the General Assembly and was opened with a sermon from Isaih. 8 chapter 20th verse by the Rev David Rice constituted with prayer.

Members present from the Presbytery of Transylvania — The Rev Messrs David Rice, Saml Finley, Matt Houston, & Samuel Robinson, Ministers with Andrew Wallace, James Bigham, and Court Vous, Elders —

From the Presbytery of West Lexington, the Rev. James Crawford, Saml Shannon, Isacc Tull, Robt Marshall, James Blythe, James Welch, Joseph P. Howe, Samuel Rannels, & John Lyle, Ministers; with James Bell, Robert Maffat, Malcom Worldly, Wm Scott, Joseph Walker, Wm McConnel, Saml Hayden, and Wm Henry, Elders —

From the Presbytery of Washington — the Revd Messrs James Kemper, John P. Campbell, Richard McNemar, & John Thompson, Ministers — with Robert Gill, and Jno

Campbell, Elders —— Absent, in the Presb^y of Transylvania The Rev Messrs Thomas Craighead, Terah Tamplin, James Balch, James McGready, Wm Hodge, John Bowman, W^m McGee, John Rankin, Saml—— Donald, Wm Mahon, Samuel Macadow, Jno Howe, James Vance, Archibald Carmeon, and Gorem Abel. ——

Fm West Lexington The Revd Messrs Barton W. Stone, and Wm Robinson.

Fm the Presbytery of Washington the Revd Messrs Jno. E. Finley John Dunlavey & Matt. G. Wallace[1];

The Rev. Robert Wilson, from the Presbytery of Lexington was present, and being invited took his seat as a corresponding member.

On motion to choose a Moderator and Clerk Mr Rice was chosen Moderator and Mr Marshall Clerk. Messrs Crawford, Kamper, Lyle, Houston and Campbell were appointed a Committee to frame Rules for the regulation and government of Synod—to report tomorrow morning—. Adjourned to meet tomorrow morning at 8 O-clock. Concluded with prayer.[2]

Friday Morning October 15th Synod met according to adjournment —— Constituted with prayer Members present as above[2]

Upon application to divide the Presbytery of Transylvania into two Presbyteries, it was voted in the affirmative —— The Division is as follows —— The Members lying on the South side of a line drawn along Bigbarren river to the Mouth, and from thence to the mouth of Salt River shall constitute one Presbytery which shall be known by the name of the Presbytery of Cumberland[3] consisting of the Revd Messrs Thos Craighead Terah Templin, James Balch, James McGready, Wm Hodge, Jno Bowman, W^m McGee, Jno Rankin, Saml Donald Saml Macadow, and shall hold

[1] Archibald Cameron and William Robinson appeared later. Hereafter the roll of members present and absent, and references to members arriving during the session will be omitted.

[2] Routine phrases, used in opening and closing sessions, will hereafter be omitted.

[3] See Minutes of the Cumberland Presbytery in this volume, Chap. VII.

its first meeting at the Ridge Church on the first Tuesday of next April; and the Rev Thomas Craighead or in case of his absence the next senior minister present shall open and preside at said meeting— And those members not expresed in the Presbytery of Cumberland, belonging to the Presbytery of Transylvania, shall continue the Members of said Presbytery — and in addition to its former bounds, it shall extend on the North West side of the Ohio River, to include the settlements contagious, & any other which may be made, and shall choose to attach themselves to said presbytery — and it shall hold its first meeting at Danville on the second Tuesday of April & the Rev. David Rice, or in case of his absence, the next Senior Minister present, shall open and preside at said Meeting.

The Committee, appointed to form rules for the regulation and government of Synod made report, which after some amendment was agreed to and is as follows — viz

A System of Rules for regulating and governing the Synod in its deliberations.[4]

Committee of Overtures

Resolved, That Messrs James Crawford, Jno. P. Campbell Matt Houston, Jno. Campbell, Andrew Wallace, & James Bell be a committee of Overtures.

Messrs. Houston and Finley laid before Synod the following Petition — We your petitioners, taking into consideration our remote situation from any central Meeting of the Transylvania Presbytery to which we now belong, do pray your Reverent Body to strike us off from said Presbytery and annex us to Western Lexington, to which we lie much more contagious, and we your Petitioners do ever pray &c.

Signed { Matt Houston
         Sam¹ Finley

Synod took into consideration said petition, and heard

---

[4] The rules were written on the blank leaves at the beginning of the Record Book, and are therefore placed first in this document.

the reasons upon which it was founded — and the question being put, it was voted in the Negative.

The Committee of Overtures upon the Subject of Psalmody beg leave to make the following report

Psalmody

Whereas it is of material importance, that there should be an uniformity in the Psalmody in use throughout the Churches, under the care of this Synod — your Committee, on application to that subject, are of opinion, that the Synod, during the present Sessions, should take the matter under consideration, and give such advice, as to them shall appear best.

On motion Ordered that the Ministers of this Synod read to the people of their respective charges the extracts of the Minutes of the General Assembly respecting the Psalmody they have allowed, and that it be recommended to them to procure the Same

Monday, Oct. 18.

Resolved that the Stated Clerk forward to the next Session of the General Assembly an extract of the proceedings of this Synod respecting the division of Transylvania Presbytery into two Presbyteries.

Resolved that the Synod proceed to make out a report of all the ministers, & licentiates within its bounds, to be forwarded by the Stated Clerk to the next General Assembly.

Licentiates, In the Presbytery of Transylvania Jno Hodge, John W. Lexington, And^w Steele, & Robt Stuart.

Ordered that the Stated Clerk Inform the General Assembly that the Synod were not able to make a return of the Ministers charges & the vacancies within its bounds for want of the Records of the Several Presbyteries — the absence of distant members, and other circumstances.

Resolved that the annual meeting of this Synod shall be on the first Tuesday of Septr until otherwise appointed by the Synod.

Resolved, that when this Synod adjourns, it shall adjourn

to meet at Lexington, on the first Tuesday of Septr. In the year of our Lord 1802

Whereas the vast extended frontiers of this Synod render it necessary that Missionaries be kept among them for the propagation of the Gospel — and as they find their numbers greatly inadequate to the demand, and as the General Assembly is the proper Channel, through which Missionaries can be sent, therefore —

Resolved that Synod request the attention of the General Assembly to this subject within our bounds; and that the Stated Clerk (be) do forward a copy of this resolution to that Body at their next Session.

Synod adjourned to meet at the time and place above mentioned. Concluded with prayer.

DAVID RICE Mod^r

A true copy Teste   ⎫
  ROB^T MARSHALL C.K. ⎬
                       ⎭

First Presbyterian meetinghouse in Lexington Sept^n 6th 1803. Synod met according to adjournment, and was opened with a sermon from Isaih 21st 11th & 12th by the Rev. David Rice. Constituted with prayer. Members present from the Presbytery of Transylvania — David Rice, Saml Findley, Samuel Robinson, and Archibald Cameron, Ministers

From the Presbytery of West Lexington, Samuel Shannon, Isacc Tull, Robert Marshall, Jas Blythe, James Welch, Joseph P. Howe, John Lyle, and Barton W. Stone, Ministers; with John Henderson, David Purviance, James Wardlaw, J. McDowell, and Charles McPheeters Elders.

From the Presbytery of Washington, James Kemper, John P. Campbell, Richard McNemar, John Thompson, John Dunlavey, & Mathew G. Wallace, Ministers, with Daniel Redder, Aaron Tullis, Moses Miller, James Ewing, Thomas Bennington; and Andrew Henderson, Elders —

From the Presbytery of Cumberland none

Absent from Transylvania Presbytery. The Revd Messrs

Wm Mahan, Mathew Houston, John Howe, James Vance, and Jeremiah Mill. —

From West Lexington — Saml Rannells, Wm Robinson, and Robert Stewart. —

From Washington Presbytery John P. Campbell and John E. Findley, Synod proceeded to the choice of Moderator & Clerk. — The Rev. Samuel Shannon, was chosen Moderator, and the Rev Samuel Findly Clerk — The Rev Robt Wilson from East Lexington Presbytery was present, and invited to take a seat as a corresponding member

Messrs Stone and Wallaces reasons for absence from the last Session sustained . . . — Ordered that Messrs Kemper, Cameron, Campbell, Welsh, and Blythe, Ministers; with Messrs John McDonald & Moses Miller Elders be a committee of Overtures.[5]

Wednesday Septr 7th 1803. . . . The Committee on Overtures report that certain petitions with sundry other papers came before the committee relative to the Revd Messrs McNemar and Thompson as to doctrines delivered by them — Which Petitions and papers the Committee think it their duty to Overture & lay before Synod — These being read, were ordered to lie on the table for the Consideration of Synod. —

Resolved that the Synod enter upon the consideration of the report of the Committee of Synod relative to Messrs McNemar and Thompson —

Resolved that the Revd Messrs John P. Campbell and Mathew G. Wallace, be a committee to present, the thanks of Synod to the Revd David Rice for his sermon delivered at the opening of Synod; and to request of him a copy thereof for publication.

Resolved that the Synod recommends & they do hereby recommend to the people under their care to procure as early and general as possible the confession of Faith of this church —

On the Subject Stated in the report of the Committee of Overtures relative to Messrs. McNemar and Thompson;

[5] Hereafter the personnel of the committee on overtures will be omitted.

Synod were of the opinion that the business contained in the papers lying before them, will regularly come forward, through the report of their Committee who are appointed to examine the book of Washington Presbytery Ordered that Said Committee be prepared to report tomorrow morning, early. . . .

Thursday, Septr 8th 1803.

The Committee appointed to examine the Presbytery book of Cumberland, report that the book of Said Presbytery was not brought forward — The Committee appointed to examine Transylvania Presbytery Book report that said book was not forwarded.

The Committee appointed to examine Washington Presbytery book report as followeth (viz) We your committee report that we have gone through the examination of the minutes of the Washington Presbytery — We found nothing worthy of remark except one omission page 48, till we came to the Session of April 6″ 1803 at springfield pages 78 & 81 — We your committee think the Washington Presbytery acted contrary to the constitution of our church, and the interests of religion in casting the petition of Lamme and others under the table and taking no further notice of it seeing the said petition implicated a charge of a most serious and important nature. — If the charge were false Presbytery ought to have investigated and found it so, and have dealt with the complainants according to the Calumny or imprudence of their conduct. — This appears to have been necessary in order to have complied with the book of discipline, and also necessary to clear Messrs. McNemar & Thompson from the *odeum* cast on their characters — But on the other hand as it appears from a previous orderly examination of Mr. McNemar that he held Armenian tenets, the Presbytery ought as guardians of the Churches under their care, to have entered on an enquiry into those important matters laid before them. Your Committee also report that we think it was improper and irregular in Said Presbytery to present a call to Mr McNemar whose religious opinions stood condemned on their minutes — It being a mat-

ter of question whether two out of three Presbyteries
present in case of the reprehension of one of them can form
a quorum to do business and the question being put it was
determined in the affirmative. . . .

Resolved that Synod now proceed to take up the report
of the Committee — Upon motion made and seconded the
question was put "Shall Synod approbate the proceedings of
the Presbytery of Washington in that part of their minutes
which respects the examination of Mr. McNemar?

The Yeas and Nays being taken were as follows: Ayes
Sam¹ Findley, Archᵈ Cameron, Mat Houston, James Hen-
derson, Joseph Moore, William Nourse, Isacc Tull, James
Blythe, Joseph Howe, Jno Lyle, Robert Stewart, Samuel
Rannells, John Henderson, James Wardlaw, John Mc-
Dowell Charles McPheeters, William McConnell (17)

Nays Robert Marshall, James Welsh, Bartom W. Stone,
William Robertson, David Purivance, Malcom Worley, (6)

Non Liquits, Sam¹ Robertson (1)

On Motion resolved that the Synod now take up and determine this question (viz) whether the Presbytery of
Washington were in order in publishing to the churches
under their care; that the doctrines Mr. McNemar held
were of dangerous tendency, and contrary to the constitution of our church, — which question being Called for was
carried in the affirmative

Friday Sept. 9 1803.

On motion Resolved that Synod take up and determine
this question (viz) "Were the Presbytery of Washington in
order in making appointment for Mr. McNemar at the
Same Session at which they had taken a vote of censure on
some of his Tenets?"

The yeas and nays being called for yere as follows (viz)
Ayes — 7 — Nays — 10 — Non Liquits — 11 — Synod
went on farther to consider the report of the Committee
relative to the conduct of Washington Presbytery and it was
moved and seconded whether that Presbytery were in order
when they rejected the petition of Lamme & others? —
After mature deliberation the question was determined in

the negative — Nays — 18 — Ayes 5 — Non Liquits — 1
— It was then enquired whether that Presbytery were orderly in presenting a call to Mr McNemar, while he lay
under a vote of censure by a preceding Session & was determined in the negative

The Committee appointed to examine the West Lexington Presbytery Book report that their Minutes in many
places appear defective in phraseology and the recording
some facts which must necessarily have been transacted;
and Synod having attended to the report of their Committee recommend to that Presbytery to be more attentive
in future to the formation, connexion and preservation of
their Minutes, and also when certain deficiencies appear
they endeavor to supply them[6] — The Committee appointed to return thanks to Mr. Rice for his sermon delivered at the opening of Synod and request a copy for publication report that they have waited on Mr. Rice and
obtained his leave for its publication

Saturday, Sept. 10.

WHEREAS this Synod have taken into consideration
certain petitions and papers respecting the conduct of Washington Presbytery at Springfield and which conduct this
Synod have said was out of order and, On Motion Resolved
that the Synod now enter on the trial or examination of
Messrs. McNemar and Thompson according to the prayer
of the Petitioners; and the charges therein stated, and also
that this Synod resolve the questions of doctrine seriously,
and reasonably prepared in those Petitions — While Synod
were deliberating on the propriety of adopting the above
resolution Messrs. Marshall, Stone, McNemar, Thompson,
and Dunlavy appeared in Synod and having given their reasons for not attending earlier, they presented a paper
through Mr. Marshall which that gentleman stated to be a
protest against the proceedings of Synod in the affair of

[6] The examination of presbyterial records was one of the principal functions of the synod. Due to the routine character of the reports, subsequent
references to examination of records will be omitted except when some
unusual interest attaches thereto.

Washington Presbytery, and a declaration that they withdrew themselves from under the jurisdiction of Synod —
The paper was read and is as follows (viz)
"To the Moderator of the Kentucky Synod,
   Revd Sir
      We the undersigned members of Washington and
West Lexington Presbyteries do hereby enter our protest
against the proceedings of Synod in approbating that Minute of Washington Presbytery, which condemned the sentiments of Mr. McNemar, as dangerous to the Souls of men
and hostile to the interests of all true religion, and the proceedings therewith connected; and for reasons which we
now offer, we declare ourselves no longer members of your
Rev^nd Body, or under your jurisdiction, or that of your
Presbyteries. —
   1st We conscientiously believe that the above Minute
which you have Sanctioned, gives a distorted and false representations of McNemars Sentiments, and that the measure was calculated to prevent the influence of truth of the
most interesting nature.
   2^ndly We claim the privilege of interpreting the Scriptures by itself according to Section 9 Chapter 1st of the
confession of faith, and we believe that the Supreme Judge
by whom all controversies of religion are to be determined;
and all decrees of Counsels, opinions of ancient writers,
doctrines of Men, and private Spirits are to be examined,
and in whose sentence we are to rest—, can be no other but
the Holy Spirit speaking in the Scriptures. — But from the
disposition which the Synod manifests it appears to us that
we cannot enjoy this privilege, but must be found up to such
explanations of the Word of God as preclude all farther
advances after truth.
   3dly We remain inviolably attached to the doctrines of
grace which through God have been mighty in every revival
of true religion since the Reformation. These doctrines
however we believe are in a measure darkened by some expression in the confession of Faith which are used as the
means of strengthening sinners in their unbelief and sub-

jecting many of the pious to a spirit of bondage.— When we attempt to obviate these difficulties we are charged with departing from our Standards, viewed as disturbers of the peace of the Church, and threatened to be called to account. The proceedings of Presbytery have furnished the world with ample encouragement to proceed in this mode of opposition and the Sanction those proceedings have now received from your Rev^nd Body cuts off every hope of relief from that quarter, from which we have at least faintly expected it. We therefore feel ourselves shut up to the necessity of relieving you from the disagreeable task of receiving Petitions from the public, and ourselves from being prosecuted before a Judge*, whose authority to decide we cannot in Conscience acknowledge.

Reverend, Sir our affection for you as brethren in the Lord, is and we hope shall be ever the same, nor do we desire to separate from your Communion, or exclude you from ours; we ever wish to bear, and forbear, in matters of human order or opinion, and unite our Joint Supplications with yours for the increasing effusions of that divine Spirit which is the bond of peace.

With this disposition of Mind we bid you adieu until through the providence of God it seem good to your Revd Body to adopt a more liberal plan respecting human Creeds & Confessions
Done in Lexington, Ky—
Septr 10th 1803—"

ROB^T MARSHALL
JOHN DUNLAVEY
RICHARD McNEMAR
BARTON W. STONE.
JOHN THOMPSON[7]

* Confession of Faith.
[7] This group formed the temporary Presbytery of Springfield. See *An Apology for Renouncing the Jurisdiction of the Synod of Kentucky* (Lexington, 1804). Also, *The Last Will and Testament of the Springfield Presbytery.* For secondary accounts: Sweet, W. W., *The Story of Religions in America,* pp. 337ff.; Moore, W. F., *Disciples of Christ,* pp. 232ff.; Garrison, W. E., *Religion Follows the Frontier,* pp. 150ff.

By the secession of Mr. Marshall the office of Stated Clerk was now vacated; and a ballot being taken the Rev James Welsh was duly elected to that office.

On motion. Resolved that Messrs. Archibald Cameron John P. Campbell, and Joseph P. Howe be a committee to draft a letter to Lamme and other petitioners within the bounds of Washington Presbytery assuring them that Synod do strictly adhere to the doctrines of our confession of Faith; and that said letter embrace such other subjects and circumstances, as to your committee may appear necessary and report to Synod before it rises.

On Motion Resolved that Messrs David Rice, Mathew Houston, and James Welsh be a committee seriously and affectionately to converse with Messrs. Marshall, Stone Mc-Nemar Thompson and Dunlavy, to labour to bring them back to the Standard and doctrines of our Church and report on Monday morning.

WHEREAS the General Assembly of our Church have by an act at their last sitting prohibited us from publishing or encouraging any other edition of the Confession of Faith of our church than that published by Robt Aitken in 1797: On Motion Resolved that Messrs. James Blythe, John Lyle, and Robert Stewart be a committee to write to the committee of the General Assembly appointed to revise said Confession, praying leave to print one thousand (1000) Copies from the above named Edition for the use of this State. —

On Motion Resolved that, the Synod order the Presbyteries of which it is composed, to take measures that the annual Collections for Missionaries purposes be made within their bounds and forwarded as early as possible to the Treasurer of the General Assembly —

On Motion Resolved that Mr. Joseph P. Howe be added as a member to the committee appointed to converse with Messrs. Marshall, McNemar, Dunlavey, Stone, and Thompson. — The Committee appointed to converse with Messrs. Marshall Dunlavey, & others report as follows (viz) "That the aforesaid gentlemen agree that as a body they will confer with Synod on points of Doctrine in the following manner, that is to say: they will answer any questions proposed to them by Synod which may be stated in writing; . . . and that they are ready to enter upon the business as soon as they may receive notice for that purpose — The whole of the questions shall be given in at once

JAMES WELSH ⎫
JOSEPH P. HOWE ⎬ Committee
MATHEW HOUSTON ⎭

On Motion Resolved that Synod do accede to the proposal of Messrs. Marshall, Stone, Dunlavey & others in examining them on their tenets — This Resolution was negatived — The yeas and nays being called for were as follows

Yeas Mathew Houston, James Henderson, Jas Welsh Joseph P. Howe, Wliliam Robinson, James Wardlaw, Charles McPheeters, — Nays Archibald Cameron, Joseph Moore, Isacc Tull, James Blythe, John Lyle, Robert Stewart, Saml Rannells, John Henderson, James Kamper, Thomas Bennington, John Campbell, Samuel Findley.

On Motion Resolved that Messrs. Rannells, Kamper and Houston be a Committee to wait upon Messrs. Marshall, Dunlavey, Thompson, Stone, and McNemar to enquire of them what objection they have to our Confession of Faith, or, to any part of it, which they have in their remonstrance declared they cannot in Conscience submit to be judged by; and that they transmit such objections to us in writing; by our Committee on tomorrow morning or before Synod rises — On Motion Resolved that Synod enter upon the consideration of Mr. Archibald Steeles Petition, which Petition was read and the further consideration thereof deferred until tomorrow morning; . . .

Tuesday Septr 13 . . .

On Motion Resolved that the Annual Meeting of Synod be held on the third Tuesday of October until otherwise appointed by Synod.

On Motion Resolved, that the next Annual Meeting of Synod be held at Danville; . . .

On Motion Resolved, that in Mr. Steeles case the Presbytery of Washington be and is hereby recommended to them, to return his licensure to him provided the circumstances which then influence them to decide as they did be now removed which motion was carried in the affirmative. —

The Committee appointed to wait upon Messrs. Marshall Stone, &ᶜ reported that they have put the resolution of Synod in the hands of those gentlemen but they have as yet received no answer.

On Motion the following resolution was introduced and on a vote being taken was carried in the affirmative.

Whereas Messrs. Robert Marshall, John Dunlavey, Richard McNemar, Barton W. Stone, & John Thompson, have declared themselves no longer Members of our body or under our jurisdiction, or that of our Presbyteries and whereas it appears from their remonstrance laid before this Synod, that they have seceded from the Confession of Faith of the Presbyterian Church, and no more wish to be united with us, until we adopt a more liberal plan respecting human creeds and confessions; and whereas a Committee has been appointed seriously and affectionately to converse with the above members, in order if possible to reclaim them to the doctrines and Standards of our Church, which Committee has proved entirely unsuccessful: And Moreover whereas said gentleman came into Synod and informed us, that they have constituted themselves into a separate Presbytery and have refused to comply with every solicitation to return to their duty but persist in their Schismatic Disposition There-fore Resolved that Synod do and they hereby do solemnly suspend Messrs Marshall, Dunlavey, McNemar, Stone and Thompson from the exercise of the function of the Gospel Ministry until sorrow and repentance for the above Schism be manifested, leaving it however with the Several Presbyteries to which they above Members may have belonged, to restore them as soon as they give satisfactory evidence of repentance; and their congregations are hereby declared vacant. —

On Motion resolved, that the Revd Messrs. Blythe, Lyle, Welsh and Stewart be a Committee to draft a circular letter to our churches relative to the unhappy division now existing; to state the principles upon which Messrs. Marshall, Stone, Dunlavey, McNemar, and Thompson have separated from us; and embrace such other objects in the address, as the peace and unity of the Church may require. — The voice of the Synod being taken on this resolution it was carried in the affirmative.[8]

On Motion resolved that Commissioners go to the Several congregations where Messrs. Marshall Stone, McNemar Dunlavey and Thompson have Statedly preached, to declare those congregations not before vacated, now vacant — To State the conduct of Synod respecting those gentlemen and to exhort the people to unity and peace, and the Commissioners be as follows (viz), Shannon & Lyle to Bethel and Blue Spring; Messrs. Howe and Rannels to Cane Ridge and Concord Mr. Blythe to Eagle Creek Mr. Wm Robinson to Springfield and Turtle Creek

The following case having been laid before the Comittee of Overtures (viz) "Should not the Synod require their members to attend with punctuality to the business of Catechizing their people and so be particularly careful that the Black people in their congregations participate in those instructions.

On Motion resolved that Synod require their members to perform the aforementioned duties Which was carried in the affirmative. — A question was referred to Synod (viz) "Is true and Saving faith a grace; and can a person unaided by the Holy Spirit act it? which was postponed to the next Stated Session of Synod. — The Committee appointed to draft a letter to Lambe and others; reported one which was read and adopted —

On Motion Resolved that the Revd Messrs. Blythe Lyle

---

[8] This *Circular Letter* was drawn up by John Lyle and published the following year, 1804. See Davidson, *op. cit.* p. 196.

& Stewart, be a committee to write to Scott and others, who petitioned Synod yesterday relative to Messrs. Marshall and Stone; to inform them that they seem to have mistaken the ground upon which the Synod have proceeded with these men; and the latter may embrace such other objects as may tend to satisfy their minds of said petitioners. . . .

A letter was then received from the Suspended Members, and being read was ordered to be filed among the papers of Synod.

Adjourned to meet at Danville on the third Tuesday of October, 1804 at 12 oclock.   Concluded with prayer.

SAMUEL SHANNON, Mod^r

Test   SAM^L FINDLEY, C.P.T.

Presbyterian Meeting House Danville Tuesday Oct 16" 1804.

Synod met according to adjournment and was opened with a Sermon from Psalm 97,1, by the Reverend Mr. Shannon the former Moderator:

The Rev. James Camper [Kemper] was elected Moderator and the Rev John P. Campbell, Clerk pro tempore. —

Wednesday Morning 9 Oclock October 17, 1804

It was with pleasure the Synod recognized the presence of the Rev Doc^t James Hall, the Rev Thomas Marquis, and the Rev Nash LeGrand, who appeared as a committee from the General Assembly to meet with this Synod with a view to heal the disorders which have recently taken place within our bounds; and the Committee having proposed a plan by which to accomplish the object of their mission, Wherefore on Motion resolved that Synod do accede to the plan proposed by the said Committee for introducing the business for which they were delegated by the General Assembly.

Synod were happy to be informed by the Assemblys Committee that our protesting brethren four of whom being present, (viz) Mr. Robert Marshall, Mr. John Dunlavey, Mr Barton W. Stone, and Mr. John Thompson had also concurred in the plan of said Committee.

As the divine blessing alone can ensure success in any undertaking, and as the Smiles of heaven in the business contemplated by the Committee, were most earnestly desired by Synod it was unanimously resolved to spend some time in solemn prayer to Almighty God for his gracious Countenance and aid upon all to be engaged in transactions so important as those before Synod and in conformity to their resolution Synod acted accordingly and Messrs Marquis and Marshall were called upon to lead the devotions of Synod

On Motion Resolved that the afternoon of next friday be set apart by this Synod to be spent by this Synod in Solemn fasting and prayer to Almighty God, for the out pouring of his divine Spirit and the Spread of the Gospel not only within their bounds but generally throughout the World and that the Revd Messrs Blythe and Welsh be a committee to select the Persons who shall conduct the Worship.

The Petition from the united Presbyterian Societies on Big Barren was considered and the prayer of the said Petition granted and that tract of country given the Presbytery of Cumberland and shall be known by the following lines of demarcation (viz) beginning on the North side of Big Barren at the Mouth of Beaver Creek from thence to Squire Wallaces at the Pilot Knob; thence to the dripping spring: thence to Green River at the Mouth of Nolin, thence to the Mouth of Big Barren.

Thursday morning IX O.C. Oct. 18th 1804

On Motion resolved that the Copies of the Confession of Faith transmitted to this Synod by the General Assembly be received, that the Said Books be disposed of at one Dollar each; and that each Member be required to apply for as many Copies as he may wish to dispose of in the bounds of his ministry. . . .

In order better to promote the Sale of the Copies of the Confession of Faith forwarded by the General Assembly, On Motion, Resolved that each of the Members of Synod be directed to open Subscription for the Copies of the Confession of faith now sent on by the General Assembly at the price fixed on by the Synod. . .

Mr. Joshua L. Wilson, is chosen Clerk protempore instead of Mr John P. Campbell who is absent with leave.

On Motion Resolved that Messrs. David Rice Sam[l] Findley, James Blythe, John Campbell, and James Allen, be a committee to confer with the Committee of the General Assembly relative to the object of their Mission and to report as early as possible.

Whereas at our last Meeting of Synod, a case was brought up to Synod through the Committee of Overtures including these two questions (viz) "Is true and saving faith a grace? and can a person unaided by the Holy Spirit act it?" which questions were postponed as to their decision until their present Session of Synod; therefore on motion Resolved that those questions are explicitly and fully answered in our confession of Faith Chapter XIV. The above resolutions were unanimously adopted.

On enquiry it appeared that the Presbyteries had not attended to the Order of Synod respecting the annual Collections for Missionary purposes; they are therefore enjoined to pay particular attention to that object.

On enquiry at the Washington Presbytery it was found that nothing had been done in the case of Mr Archibald Steele's through a want of the Minute of Synod on that Subject, the Presbytery of Washington are therefore directed to pay as early an attention to the order of Synod at its last Session as may be practible . . .

On enquiry that the Committee appointed to write a circular Letter to the Churches under the care of Synod had duly attended to the duties of that appointment therefore, Resolved that Synod enquire of said Committee how they disposed of the Circular Letter What expenses have been incurred by the publication and what monies they have received by the Sale of Said letter.

Enquiry being made upon the above resolution the Committee reported to Synod that they have as far as possible circulated the Letter, and sufficient Monies have received to defray the expenses incurred by the publication.

Friday, Oct. 19, 1804.

On enquiry whether members appointed to visit the Churches over whom the suspended members had formerly presided and to declare such churches vacant, exhorting them to unity and brotherly love, had discharged that duty; it was found that said members had discharged that duty except the Revd James Blythe whose reasons for not fulfilling the appointment of Synod were sustained

The Members having been interrogated whether they had complied with the order of synod respecting the Catechising of the people under their care it was found that they had partially complied with the recommendation of Synod on that Subject, and Synod still continue to urge the observance of this important branch of Ministerial duty on all its members.

It was then enquired whether Messrs. Blythe, Lyle, and Stuart had complied with the object of their appointment as a committee to write and forward a letter to Scott and others at the last meeting of Synod and it appears that those gentlemen had written and forwarded said Letter according to order.

On Motion Ordered that Synod have a recess at half after IV O.C. this evening. — During the recess from Synodical business the attention of the Members together with a large congregation was called to engage in solemn prayer to Almighty God agreeably to an order of Synod made on Wednesday last.

Social Worship being ended Synod was called to order . . .

Whereas the Synod have been favoured with a Letter from the Rev Doc^{tr} Ashbel Green, relative to the widows Fund together with an exhibit of the principles upon which that Fund is grounded —

On Motion Resolved that the Stated Clerk be directed and he is hereby directed to write to Doc^{tr} Green acknowledging the receipt of the Letter and exhibit and returning him the thanks of Synod for his attention. . . .

Saturday October 20th 1804

The Rev M. G. Wallace from the Committee appointed to examine the Transylvania Presbytery Book Made report that the Committee had gone through the examination and discovered certain defects which report was received for consideration. . . .

On Motion ordered that Synod have an interlocutery and the doors were accordingly Closed.

On Motion ordered that the report under consideration be put upon the Docket and that the doors be now opened.

The Joint Committee of the General Assembly and Synod of Kentucky appeared in Synod and reported as follows (viz) On Motion ordered that the report of Said Committee be taken into consideration — On Motion resolved that the report of the Joint Committee now under consideration of Synod be and the same is hereby unanimously approbated — On Motion ordered that certain observations communicated in writing by the Committee of the General Assembly on certain points of Ecclesiastical government be filed with the papers of Synod which was done. The Revd Thomas Marquis and Nash LeGrand having finished the business of their appointment as Committee of the General Assembly were invited by Synod to sit with them as Corresponding Members and took their seats accordingly.

On Motion Resolved that Rev Messrs Rice, Marquis, LeGrand and Major John Campbell elder be a Committee to draft an address to the Churches under the Care of this Synod relative to the unhappy division which has taken place in the Synod of Kentucky to State in what point of view the dissenting Brethren are to be considered and to publish such parts of the proceedings of the Joint Committee of the General Assembly and the Synod as to them may appear necessary, and to embrace such other objects as the peace and prosperity of the church may seem to require.[9]

Monday, Oct. 22nd, 1804.

On Motion ordered that the doors be closed and that

[9] To the *Serious Address* were appended the Report of the Committee of Conference, An Extract from the Assembly's Narrative on the State of Religion, A Letter from the Assembly to David Rice and a Pastoral Letter from the Assembly. The Synod ordered 750 copies to be printed and distributed. (See below, p. 330.)

the letter from the Rev Thos. B. Craighead and others be read a second time.

Whereas a Letter having been addressed to Synod containing certain charges &c and referring to a protest from The Rev. Thomas B. Craighead and others having been taken under consideration and Synod having found it impractible regularly to investigate and issue the business at their present Session Ordered therefore that the parties both, the complained of and being cited to appear at the next Stated Session of Synod with all the light and testimony on the Subject that can be afforded; and further that the Rev Messrs David Rice, James Blythe, John Lyle, Archibald Cameron and Samuel Rannels or any two of them be a committee in the meantime to attend the earliest meeting of the Cumberland Presbytery to enquire into the Case and report at the next meeting of Synod.

Synod having now resumed the business of the Petition of Shiloh Congregation — On Motion Resolved that the Committee appointed to visit Cumberland Presbytery be also directed and they are hereby directed to attend to the business of Said Petitioners and report at the next Session of Synod.

On Motion Resolved (upon reconsideration two thirds of the Members concurring) that the bounds of the Transylvania Presbytery and those of Cumberland Presbytery be the Same that they were before the meeting of Synod.

Whereas Doctʳ James Hall of North Carolina has not accepted the appointment of a Mission Assigned him by the General Assembly in the bounds of Washington, On Motion resolved that Messrs. Kemper, Blythe and Welsh be a committee to write to the Committee of Missions praying them to appoint (if it be in their power) the Rev David Rice to itenerate instead of Doctor Hall, and that the money appropriated to that Mission be paid to Mr Rice.

On Motion resolved that Synod now take under consideration the ground upon which the dissent in the licensure of Ewing and King (referred to in the report of the Committee to examine Transylvania Presbytery Book) took place.

Synod having taken into Consideration the conduct of Transylvania Presbytery in Licensing certain men to preach the Gospel whose names are stated in the dissent of Craighead and others and Synod finding this matter evidently included in the Complaint of Said protestors deferred in a previous minute until the next annual Minute; therefore Synod are of the opinion that they cannot with propriety determine this case at present but enjoin it on each of the Presbyteries comprising this Synod that they pay a particular attention to the rules laid down in the Constitution of our church and the Letter of the General Assembly on that Subject.

On Motion resolved that the next annual Session be held at Danville on the third Tuesday of October 1805 at, XII, O.C.

Tuesday Morning October 23, 1804

The Committee appointed to prepare an address to the Churches under the care of Synod appeared and read an address prepared by them. — On Motion ordered that said address be now taken into consideration On Motion resolved that said address is hereby unanimously approved.

On Motion Resolved that Messrs. Findly and J. P. Campbell be and they are hereby appointed a committee to Superintend the printing and distributing address of Synod to the churches under their care; together with such extracts as are referred to in the address and they are hereby directed to have seven hundred and fifty copies printed and circulated as soon as possible.

The Synod fully impressed with the necessity of giving as general circulation as possible to the address and extracts about to be published ordered that every Member of this Synod read the address and extracts when published, in their several charges and accompany them with such other remarks as may be thought proper and also that the Rev James Welsh go as early as possible to the Congregation where Messrs. McNemar, and Thompson, preached, the

Rev James Blythe to Bethel and Blue Spring; the Rev Sam[l] Rannels to Cane Ridge; The Rev Joseph How to Concord; and the Rev Robert Wilson to Eagle Creek and Red Oak to perform the Same Services.

Synod then adjourned to meet at Danville on the third Tuesday of October 1805 at XII O.C.

JAMES KAMPER Moderator

Danville Church Tuesday Oct 15, 1805

This being the day to which the Synod of Kentucky stood adjourned the Rev Messrs James Kampor, Isacc Tull, Joseph P. Howe and Samuel Findley met but not being a quorum adjourned till tomorrow 11 O.C.

Wednesday Morning Oct 16th 11 O.C.

Synod met according to adjournment and was opened by the Rev James Kamper the Moderator at the Last Sessions, with a Sermon from I Peter II 5 "Ye also as lively stones are built up a Spiritual House an holy Priesthood to offer up Spiritual Sacrifices acceptable to God by Jesus Christ."

The Rev James Blythe was chosen Moderator and the Rev Messrs Robert Stuart and Joshua L. Wilson temporary Clerks

Thursday Morning at 9 O.C. Oct 17th

The Committee appointed to examine the Cumberland Presbytery Book reported — On Motion resolved that the Synod now take under consideration said report.

After mature deliberation upon the said report resolved that Synod do concur with the report of their Committee. Ordered that said report be recorded as follows (viz) "We your committee appointed for the examination of the Cumberland Presbytery Book have attended to that business and report as follows (viz) — The Minutes of two intermediate Presbyteries appointed last spring have not been sent forward. The records of this Presbytery are extremely defective many important words are omitted doubtful ones are frequently used, — The history in some places is obscure and the mode of transacting business frequently violates our rules of discipline — is various and discordant. In page

2nd James Haw is Style[d] a regular Minister of the Methodist Republican Church and takes a seat in Presbytery — We have recognized no such regular Church, and never heard of Mr Haws recanting those sentiments which he once public espoused though they be inimical to the faith of our Church.[10] — We find in different places that persons were examined upon experimental religion and licensed to exort in Some instances in the bounds of that Presbytery only, and in other instances that they were allowed to appoint Meetings and exhort wherever God in his providence called them — Which proceedings we are of opinion are disorderly — These are generally called regular exhorters sometimes licentiates. The number of these exhorters is about Seventeen some of whom are now ordained to preach: see pages 4, 5, 8, 9, 17, 19, 26, 27. Messrs. Crawford and Dooly who reside in the bounds of Transylvania Presbytery, were contrary to our Book of Discipline taken under the care of the Cumberland Presbytery, licensed to exhort and afterwards appointed subjects for trial, See pages 8 and 19, Page 10 we find this phrase, "Finis Ewing's Circuit". In the case of Balch's trial no charges or depositions recorded page 12 Page 21 A Presbyterial act forming a committee to write a Circular Letter recommending to the people to contribute for the support exhorters which we deem illegal. Resolve of Presbytery respecting Shiloh Congregation pages 21 & 22 Farr an illiterate man licensed with approbation page 31 . . .

Synod agreed to have a recess of one half hour, The Recess being over the Mod^r resumed the chair . . .

On Motion Resolved the Synod post pone the farther consideration of the business relative to the Cumberland Presbytery untill to morrow morning

Resolved that Synod proceed to enquire of their Several Members whether they have complied with the order of Synod respecting the Sale of those confessions sent by the General Assembly and it appeared that most of the members had complied with said order, and likewise the reasons

[10] Davidson, *op. cit.*, p. 228.

of those who had not were sustained, . . . Resolved that the Confessions of Faith now on hand be distributed among the poor at the low rate of 50^{cts} per copy, . . . Synod proceeded to examine the Several Presbyteries whether they have complied with the order of Synod respecting the Collection of Monies for Missionary purposes and it was found that none had complied except the Presbytery of Washington which have collected the sum of $38.75^{cts} and it is most earnestly enjoined upon all the Presbyteries belonging to this Synod that they pay particular attention to that important business in future.

Upon enquiry it appeard that the Presbytery of Washington had complied with the order of Synod respecting Archibald Steele. . . .

Upon enquiry it was found that none of the Members appointed as a committee to attend the last Spring session of Cumberland Presbytery had attended except the Revd Archibald Cameron, the reasons of the other members being heard were sustained . . .

Upon enquiry it appeared that Messrs Campbell and Findley had complied with the order of Synod in superintending the printing of the Circular letter, Enquiry was made whether the Members had complied with the order of Synod, respecting the reading of the Circular letter in their respective charges, and it was found that the members had substantially complied except Mrs Vance and Clelland. Mr Vance was excused and Mr Clellands reasons for non compliance were sustained

Friday Morning 9 OClock October 18th

. . . The Committee appointed to examine the Transylvania Presbytery Book made report — thereupon Resolved that the Synod disapprove of the conduct of that Presbytery in licensing Mr John Forbis to exhort and catechize when they could not receive him as a candidate for the Gospel Ministry. Synod also disapproves of the method of that Presbytery in appointing one of their Members to supply at discretion without reference to time or place.

The following plan was brought in by the Committee of

Overtures and adopted (viz) "The Synod taking into consideration the great want of men properly qualified to preach the everlasting Gospel, and believing that some of the most useful men have been found in the abodes of obscurity and poverty and have been brought to usefulness by the pious and benevolent exertions of individuals have adopted the following plan a compliance with which is enjoined upon the Several Presbytery composing this Synod (viz) The Presbytery of Transylvania, West Lexington Cumberland and Washington shall each of them immediately seek a poor and pious youth in their bounds and take measures to have him educated for the Gospel Ministry. In the choice of young men to be educated on the foregoing plan great care is to be taken not only that they may be pious but also that they be young men of talents; great care also is to be taken that they be not hastily introduced into public life but be thoroughly prepared.

Resolved that the Stated Clerk of Synod be appointed treasurer for the purpose of receiving all monies which may be collected by the Presbyteries under the care of Synod for the Support of Missionaries.

At every meeting of Synod a Missionary Sermon shall be preached, the person who is to deliver the sermon shall be appointed at the previous meeting, a collection shall always be raised immediately after the delivery of the Sermon, and the Money forwarded to the Committee of Missions by the Moderator of Synod together with the Monies which may be in the hands of the Treasurer for Missionary purposes.

It was and is hereby recommended to the Several Presbyteries composing the Synod that they make annual collections among the churches under their care in order to meet the expenses arising from our Synodical Meetings and that the money so collected be deposited with the Clerk of the Synod.

The Rev David Rice was appointed to preach a Missionary Sermon on the first Saturday after the Commencement of the next Session of Synod and in case of his failure that duty shall devolve upon the Rev⁴ John P. Campbell, ...

On Motion the business respecting Cumberland Presbytery was again taken up; After considerable deliberation it was Resolved that the Rev⁴ Messrs. John Lyle, J. P. Campbell, Archibald Cameron, Joseph P. Howe, Samuel Rannals, Robert Stuart, Joshia L. Wilson, Robert Wilson, Thos Clelland, and Isacc Tull, together with Messrs. Wᵐ McDonald, Robert Brank, James Allen, James Henderson, Richard Gaines, and Andrew Wallace, elder[s] or any seven Ministers of them with as many of the above Elders as may be present be a Commission vested with full Synodical powers to confer with the Members of Cumberland Presbytery and to adjudicate upon their Presbyterial proceedings which appear upon the Minutes of said Presbytery for the purpose aforesaid and taken notice of by the Committee appointed by Synod to examine said Minutes — that the said Commission meet on the first Tuesday of December next at Gasper meeting house Logan County in the bounds of Said Presbytery, for the purpose aforesaid — that notice be given to the members of said Presbytery by the Stated Clerk of Synod to attend on that day and at the place aforesaid so that a full, fair and friendly investigation may take place — that the Said Commission take into consideration and decide upon a letter from The Rev⁴ Thomas B. Craighead, and other and an appeal from the Judgement of Said Presbytery by certain members of Shiloh congregation and that the Stated Clerk of Synod furnish the Commission aforesaid with the papers and documents relative to the whole of the aforesaid proceedings.

The Stated Clerk of Synod together with Messrs Lyle, Donald and Dickey, were individually directed to use all necessary exertions inciting the Members of Cumberland Presbytery to attend the above mentioned Meeting of the Commission of Synod and especially the written citation to be sent by the Stated Clerk of Synod to the Moderator of Said Presbytery and to the Rev James McGreadey. . . .

Saturday Morning, 9 Oclock October 19ᵗʰ 1805 . . .

Inquiry being made of the Several Presbyteries whether they had appointed Commissioner to the General Assembly it appeared that the Presbytery of West Lexington and Washington had appointed Commissioners but that the Presbyteries of Transylvania and Cumberland had failed to perform that duty and their reasons for non compliance were not sustained. Resolved that the Rev. John Lyle or in his absence the next named Minister in the Commission be moderator of the Commission heretofore appointed until they constitute and that he open the Commission with a sermon.

On Motion unanimously resolved that the first Wednesday in December next be a day of Solemn fasting, humiliation and prayer to Almighty God for his special presence and blessing upon the efforts of Synod, by their Commission which will then be sitting for the important purpose of regulating the disorders which have taken place in Cumberland Presbytery and that Solemn prayer and Supplication be made by all the Churches under the care of Synod to whom this resolution may be made known for the out pouring of the divine Spirit within our bounds and throughout the *World*.

Synod then adjourned to meet at Lexington in the Presbyterian Meeting House on the third Tuesday of October next 12 Oclock

Concluded with prayer.

ROBERT S[T]UART

        } Clerks

JOSHUA L. WILSON

            JAMES BLYTHE Mod^r

Gasper Meeting House Logan County Tuesday Dec. 3, 1805

The Commission of the Synod of Kentucky met according to appointment and was opened with a sermon from Hebrews 5,4, "And no man taketh his honor unto himself but he that is called of God as was Aaron" by the Rev John Lyle, Constituted with prayer.

Members present the Revd Messrs. John Lyle, Archibald Cameron, Joseph P. Howe, Samuel Rannell, Isacc Tull, Robert Stuart, Thomas Clelland and Joshua L. Wilson with Messrs William McDowell, James Allen, Richd Gaines Robert Brank and Andrew Wallace, Elders, —

Absent The Rev Messrs John P. Campbell, and Robert Wilson, with Mr. James Henderson, Elder, — The Rev Joseph P. Howe was chosen Moderator and Messrs James Allen and Joshua L. Wilson Clerks, — Upon enquiry it appeared that the Moderator and Members of Cumberland Presbytery had been cited to meet the Commission according to the order of the Synod of Kentucky. . . .

Gasper Meeting House Logan County Wednesday Dec 24th 1805

. . . The papers and documents respecting the appointment of the Commission and the objects of Said appointment were read and laid on the table.

On motion resolved that Mr William Anderson a witness in the case of an appeal from Shiloh Congregation be admitted to give his testimony immediately as he is under the necessity of returning home. After taking Mr. Andersons deposition. The Commission had a recess from business, during which they and the members of the Cumberland Presbytery, Joined with a large Assembly of people in Solemn prayer to Almighty God for his presence and blessing on the present meeting and for the outpouring of the Holy Spirit throughout the World

After recess the Moderator resumed the chair and the Commission took under consideration the case of Mr James Haw as stated in the report of the Committee appointed to examine the Cumberland Presbytery Book; and were unanimously of the opinion that the Cumberland Presbytery had acted illegally in receiving Mr James Haw as a regular minister of the Methodist Republican Church without examining him on divinity, or requiring him to adopt the Confession of Faith of the Presbyterian Church. — On Motion resolved that the Commission of Synod enquire into the Sentiments of Mr James Haw relative to the Doctrines of the Gospel. . . .

Gasper Meeting House Thursday December 5th 1805 . . . An address from the Rev James McGready and other to the Commission of Synod was read by the Clerk and ordered to be laid upon the table— On Motion resolved that the Commission of Synod now take into consideration the conduct of Cumberland Presbytery relative to licensing and ordaining men to preach the Gospel.— The Commission of Synod agreeable to the above resolution proceeded to hear and receive testimony from the Records of the Cumberland Presbytery — and confer with them relative to the Said business; but not having time to finish, it was postponed until to morrow. . . .

Gasper Meeting House Friday December 6th 1805. . . . The Commission of Synod resumed the Conference with the Cumberland Presbytery and proceeded to receive the balance of the testimony concerning the charge of licensing and ordaining men to preach the Gospel contrary to the rules and discipline of the Presbyterian Church. And it appearing to the Commission that among other irregularities they had required only a partial adoption of the Confession of Faith by persons licensed to preach. The Commission then requested in a friendly manner the majority of the Cumberland Presbytery to give their reasons why in licensing and ordaining persons to preach the Gospel, they required them to adopt the Confession of Faith, so far only as they in reason, think it corresponds with the Scriptures — The Said Majority of the Cumberland Presbytery through the Rev James McGready then offered their reasons as follows (viz) That the Confession of Faith was Human composition and fallible, and they could not in conscience feel themselves bound any farther than they believed it to correspond with the Scriptures. — Whereas as it appears to the Commission of Synod from the records of the Cumberland Presbytery from the dissent of the Minority of said Presbytery, and from the open confession of those who were, at the time of the dissent, a majority, that they did license a considerable number of young men to preach the gospel; and some of them they ordained to preach the Gospel and administer ordinances in the Church contrary to the rules and regulations of the Presbyterian Church in such case made and provided. And whereas these men have been required by Said Presbytery to adopt the Said confession of Faith and Discipline of the Said church, no farther than they believe it to be the word of God. by which no man can know what they believe in matters of Doctrine and whereas it is alledged by Cumberland Presbytery acknowledging that those men possess extraordinary talents by which they have been induced to license and ordain them without attending to the book of discipline.

Wherefore on motion resolved that the Commission of Synod do proceed to examine those persons irregularly licensed [and] irregularly ordained by Cumberland Presbytery and judge of their qualifications for the Gospel Ministry

The Majority of Cumberland Presbytery through the Rev Mr. Hodge refused to Submit to the foregoing resolution for the following reason (viz) That they had the exclusive privilidge of examining and licensing their own candidates and that Synod had no right to take the business out of their hands Several of the members of that Presbytery individually refused also to submit to said resolution; wherefore they were warmly, seriously and Solemnly addressed by several members of the Commission — on such hasty and disorganizing conduct and earnestly entreated with many persuasive arguments to Submit to the authority with which the Commission was vested. . . .

Gasper Meeting House Logan County Saturday Dec 7th 1805 . . .

On Motion Resolved that the Majority of the Cumberland Presbytery be adjured through the Medium of our Moderator to submit to the authority which God has established in his church, and with which this Commission of Synod is clothed and that by the same authority those men who were licensed and those who were ordained in a dis-

orderly manner be adjured to come forward and submit to
an examination by the Commission of Synod. The said Majority of the Cumberland Presbytery requested leave to
retire for consultation which was granted.

The persons also who had been licensed and the persons
who had been ordained irregularly by the Said Presbytery
requested leave to retire that they might converse together,
upon this important matter which was granted.

The Commission then with the assembly present united
in Solemn Prayer to God for his protection and blessing. —
The above named Majority of Cumberland Presbytery returned and the Moderator of the Commission according to
the foregoing resolution solemnly adjured them to submit to
the authority which God had established in his Church, and
with which this Commission of Synod is now clothed The
Members were individually called up and the question proposed to each "Do you submit? or not submit? And the
Said Majority (viz) The Rev⁰ James McGrady, Wᵐ
Hodge, Mr McGee, John Rankin, and Samˡ McAdow refused to submit — The Moderator of the Commission
then proceeded to adjure the persons irregularly licensed
and those irregularly ordained by the Cumberland Presbytery to submit themselves to the Authority which God has
established in his church and with which this Commission is
now clothed, Standing an examination according to the
resolution of Said Commission They were then individually called and the question proposed to each Do you submit? or not Submit? those who would not submit were Mr
Robert Guthrie Samuel Hodge, James Porter, David Foster, Finis Ewing Hugh Kirkpatrick, Thomˢ Nelson, Samˡ
King and Samuel Donald Junior.

Messieurs Robert Bell and Samˡ Blythe requested leave
to consider upon the subject untill Monday next which was
granted

Persons absent Messieurs Lawrence Rollison James Farr,
Robᵗ Houston, James Crawford Reuben Dooly, Robert
Wilson, James Duggins, Michael Finley, Ephraim McClain,
John Hodge, Wᵐ McClure Stephen Clinton, and Wᵐ Moor.

According to a resolution entered into on Wednesday last the Commission called upon Mr James Haw, to submit to an examination and he refused, . . .

Gasper Meeting House, Monday 9 December 1805 . . .

Mess Samuel Blythe and Robert Bell who requested leave until this day to consider upon the subject of Submission or non-Submission agreeable to a former resolution of the Commission, were called upon who said they did not submit.

Whereas the Commission of Synod have in a friendly manner, conferred with the Cumberland Presbytery and have examined into the proceedings of Said Presbytery in licensing men to exhort and to preach the Gospel and in ordaining some to administer ordinances and have found that those proceedings were very irregular and whereas, when those men irregularly licensed &c were called upon to come forward to be examined by the Commission, Mess Wm Hodge, James McGrady W^m McGee, John Rankin, and Samuel McAdow interposed to prevent the examination, — And also that the Moderator called upon the following persons (viz) Robert Guthrie, Saml Hodge, James Porter, David Foster, Finis Ewing, Hugh Kirkpatrick, Thomas Nelson, Thomas Calhoun, Samuel Donald Junior, Samuel King, Saml Blythe, and Robert Bell to come forward and stand an examination as to their qualifications for the Gospel Ministry they refused to comply, thereby virtually renouncing the jurisdiction of the Presbyterian Church, and it being proclaimed by common fame that the majority of these men are not only illiterate but erroneous in Sentiment Resolved that as the above named persons never had regular Authority from the Presbytery of Cumberland to preach the Gospel &c the Commission of Synod prohibit and they are hereby solemnly prohibit the said persons from exhorting, preaching and administering ordinances in consequence of any authority which they have obtained from the Cumberland Presbytery, until they submit to our jurisdiction, and undergo the requisite examination   And it is farther resolved that the following persons (viz) James Fan, Lawrence Rollison, Robert Houston, James Crawford James Duggins, Michael Findley, Ephraim McCain, John Hodge, Alexander Chapman, W^m McClure, Stephen Clinton and Wm Moore, who are now absent together with James Haw be laid under the same prohibition.

Although we conceive the Commission have Synodical power to adjudicate upon the conduct of the Rev James McGready, William Hodge, William McGee, John Rankin, and Samuel McAdow in not submitting to the examination of those men, who had been irregularly licensed and ordained when solemnly adjured by the Moderator agreeable to the resolution of the Commission; yet we decline pronouncing sentence, and remand said persons to the Synod of Kentucky and they are hereby cited to appear at our next annual Session to be held in the Presbyterian Church in Lexington on the third Tuesday of October next to account for said conducts. And whereas common fame loudly proclaims that the Revd Messrs Wm Hodge, W^m McGee, and John Rankin, hold and propagate doctrines contrary to those contained in the Confession of Faith of the Presbyterian Church. Resolved that they be and they are hereby cited to appear before the Synod of Kentucky at their next Session there to answer to the above Charges. And the Cumberland Presbytery are hereby most Solemnly charged to perform their Presbyterial business in an orderly manner and they be more accurate in keeping their records in future.

Whereas it appears to the Commission that Thomas Nelson, has been irregularly ordained as the Pastor of Mount Sion and Carmel and whereas the said Nelson, is now prohibited from preaching under any Authority derived from the Presbyterian Church: On Motion Resolved that the said congregation be and are hereby declared vacant and that Messrs Cameron & Joshua Wilson \ preach at Mount Carmel and Mount Sion, as early as possible after the rising of this Commission and read to them this resolution.

Whereas Common Fame loudly proclaims that the Revd Thomas B Craighead[11] propagates doctrines contrary to the System of doctrines contained in our Confession of Faith, (viz) that he in effect denies the doctrine of election and that the special or supernatural operations of the Holy Spirit are necessary in order to believing conversion and sanctification; Resolved that at the request of Mr Craighead, the Commission of Synod examine him on these doctrines —

Gasper Meeting house Tuesday 10th December 1805

The Commission of Synod resumed the business of the Shiloh Appeal. Whereas it appears that it is a case so far as it relates to the property of the Meeting house of Shiloh Congregation cognizible in a civil Court only, and therefore does not properly come under the notice of this commission but so far as relates to the decision of the Cumberland Presbytery in declaring the Appelants were not under the jurisdiction of the said Presbytery is void, Therefore resolved accordingly, that the said decision be void and that the appellants have the liberty of congregating themselves to be known by any name except that of Shiloh.[12]

Whereas Mess Wm Hodge, John Rankin, and William McGee have refused by written address to obey the citation of the Commission of Synod, alledging that the Commission have not acted constitutionally, Resolved that the business be reconsidered according to a rule of the Synod of Kentucky for that purpose — Whereas a majority of the Cumberland Presbytery are involved in charges which appeared before the Commission of Synod and whereas it appears to the Commission that there is not a sufficient number of members who are disinterested to adjudicate upon some matters of Common Fame; Resolved therefore as Common Fame loudly proclaims that the Rev Wm Hodge, William McGee, and John Rankin hold doctrines contrary

[11] For a discussion of the views and activity of Thomas B. Craighead, see Davidson, *op. cit.*, pp. 264-276. Also, see Transylvania Records in this volume, Chap. VI.

[12] See Minutes of the Cumberland Presbytery in this volume, Chap. VII.

to those contained in our confession of Faith, (viz) that they in effect deny Election; and hold that there is a certain sufficiency of Grace given to every man which if he will improve he shall obtain more, and continue till he arrive at true conversion. This Grace has sometimes been expressed by the following Phrases or Phrases of similar import with the following, (viz) A power to accept the offer of Salvation — a Spark of light given to every man in his natural State Talent &c &c — Resolved that the above named men be cited and they are hereby cited to appear at our next annual Session of Synod to be held in the Presbyterian Church in Lexington on the third Tuesday in October next to answer the above charges.

On Motion Resolved that although the Cumberland Presbytery have acted disorderly in some respect, in the trial of the Rev James Balch, yet upon the fuller view of the case, the Commission see no cause worthy of censure in said Presbytery in transacting said business — Resolved also that the Revd Thos B Craighead and, Samuel Donald and John Bowman, have acted irregularly in taking up the case upon fama clamora and not by dissent.

Agreeable to a former Resolution the Commission of Synod proceeded to the examination of the Revd Thomas B. Craighead, and having asked him a number of questions it is the opinion of said Commission that the questions proposed to said Craighead, were by him answered agreeable to the Confession of Faith; except a few questions which were not entirely satisfactorily which were as follows, (viz)

1st Question. Did God decree all things which came to pass?

Answer. As to the good actions of men, the decree is positive, but as to the criminal actions permissive only.

2nd Question. Is there not an influence distinct from and superior to the word in illuminating the mind? Answer No.

3^d Is there any difference between the foreknowledge of God and his decree? Answer yes. . . .

Wednesday Morning 7 oclock. . . . On motion resolved that the questions proposed to the Rev Thomas B

Craighead together with his Answers be committed to record which are as follows viz

1 Question   Did God decree all things which come to pass?

Answer. As to the good actions of men the decree is positive but as to the Criminal actions of Men permissive only.

2nd   Do you believe god unconditionally foreordained whatsoever comes to pass? Answer Yes.

3rd What is a permissive decree? Answer. That which the Divine Majesty will not obstruct or hinder.

4th Is the foreknowledge of God founded on his decree? Answer. The condemnation of Sin is founded upon the foreknowledge of Sin.

5th Is there any difference between the foreknowledge of God as to the good actions of men, and the foreknowledge of God as to the wicked actions of men? Ans There is a difference

6th Is there any difference between the foreknowledge of God and his decree? Answer Yes.

7 Do you believe that God loved his people before the foundation of the world with a peculiar love with which he did not love the rest of mankind? I do.

8th Do you believe that God loved them independent of any good quality in them or done by them? Answer, I do.

9 Do you believe that God has chosen or ordained man also? An. I do.

10th Are those chosen in Christ from eternity effectually called in time? Yes.

11th Are those effectually called Justified, adopted, and Sanctified kept by the power of God through faith unto Salvation? Ans. Yes.

12th Do you believe that God chose his own people according to the ceresel [probably "counsel" with "n" omitted] of his own will, independent of any other thing in them or done by them? Answer. Yes.

13. Do you believe that God of his mere free grace and love chose his people without any foresight of Faith or

good works or perseverance in either of them or any other thing as conditions in them or causes moving him thereto? Ans. Yes.

14th Is there any difference between effectual calling and the common call mentioned in the Gospel Yes.

15th Did God pass by and ordain to distruction and wrath those of Mankind for their sins to the praise of his glorious justice? Yes.

16th Is this doctrine of Predestination a high mystery which should be handled with special prudence and care? Ans. Yes.

17th What is Faith? A. It is a belief of the Testimony of God.

18th What do you mean by the Spirit? A. The Spirit is the third person of the Adorable Trinity, promised to the Ministers of the Gospel to be with them and the people of God to the end of the world

19th Does the word of God only produce saving faith without operation of the Spirit of God? Answer, No.

20th Do you believe the Spirit of God attends his word so that faith is wrought thereby? Answer, Yes.

21st Is this operation supernatural? A. Yes.

22 Does the Spirit operate independently of the Word? Ans. No, but by and with the word.

23rd Does this expression "Believe and thou shalt be saved"; Imply any power in the creature to act faith or comply with the Command? Answer, No.

24th Has God exerted all his power in his word that he does by his spirit? A. No the word is ineficatious without the Spirit

25th Who produces the fruits of Righteousness in believers Answer He, the present Spirit work by the word to produce the fruits of Righteousness,

26th Is the faith of Gods elect a grace? Answer, Yes.

27th Is the act of faith produced by the power of God or is it a physical act of the creature neither more nor less? A. It is produced by the power of God upon the mind.

28th Is the mind of a fallen creature enlightened before the act of faith? As Yes

29 Is there not an influence distinct from and superior to the word in illuminating the Mind? A. Yes.

30th Does God act equally on all who hear the word? A. No.

31st Cannot God operate upon the mind of the Creature without the word? Yes.

On Motion Resolved that the Revd Messrs Archib^d Cameron, John Lyle, and Robert Stuart or any two of them be a committee to superintend the printing of the minutes of the commission of Synod and make such remarks as to them may appear necessary. The Commission dissolved

JAS ALLEN
JOSHUA L. WILSON } Clerks   JOS. P. HOWE Mod^r

Oct 21st 1806. The Synod of Kentucky met in Lexington agreeable to adjournment and was opened with a sermon by the Revd James Blythe the Moderator of our last annual Session of Synod from Rom 9.5, and constituted with prayer.

On Motion Synod proceeded to the choice of a Moderator and Clerks, when it appeared that the Revd Jas Wealsh was chosen Moderator and the Revd Rob Stewart and Robert Wilson, Clerks.

Wednesday Oct 22nd 1806.

On enquiry whether the Presbyteries have raised contributions for Missionary purposes agreeably to the order of last Session of Synod it appeared that the Presbyteries of Transylvania, West Lexington, and Washington had not complied with the requisition of Synod in a Presbyterial capacity, but individuals of those Presbyteries have collected the following sums, Viz from the Congregation of Cane Run and Providence $20.50 by Mr Robinson from Union and Hardins Creek $23 25 by Mr Clelland; from Bairdstown $20; from big Spring $10 — and from Springfield $1 with a donation from Mrs Peggy Lewis of Bairds of $8 — by Mr Joshua L. Wilson. From Duck Creek and

Hopewell $6 — from Clear Creek $6 — from Dicks Creek $5, from 7 Miles Creek $2,50; From Beulah $6.50. From Springfield (on Mad River) $5.05; from Dayton $10 48 1/2 ; from Springfield (Mill Creek) $6. — by Mr Kemper, And from Danville $18 — amounting in all to $150.58 1/2 — The Cumberland Presbyteries are excused for not attending to the requisition of Synod, not being in General acquainted with it; but they are hereby required to pay attention to it in future. had complied with their order in seeking out poor and pious young men, of promising abilities for the purpose of educating them for the Gospel Ministry. It appeared that the Presbyteries in General had attended to it in a measure. On Motion the Minutes of the Commission of Synod appointed to meet at Gaspar Meeting House on the third day of December last were read.

Thursday, Oct. 23, 1806
On motion the Committee of Overtures laid before Synod the following resolution which was adopted (viz) Resolved that all Representatives from vacant congregations wishing to obtain a seat in Presbytery or Synod shall for the future produce with their testimonials of a regular appointment a written Statement of the number of regular members in the Congregation or congregations from which they may have come and also a subscription or other written document exhibiting the Sum each congregation is able and willing to contribute in supporting a Minister — And that the exhibition of such documents to the Presbyteries or Synod shall be the only sufficient evidence of those Representatives being entitled to a seat.

Synod now proceeded to enquire whether the several members of Synod had complied with the order respecting the keeping of the first wednesday of December 1805 as a day of fasting humiliation and prayer, and on enquiry it appeared that the members in general had complied with the order.

On Motion Resolved that Synod now attend to the subject of the citation of Messrs James McGrady, John

Rankin, Wm Hodge Saml McAdo and Will McGee, for refusing to submit to the discipline of the Presbyterian Church. — And after due deliberation it was voted that the Revd Messrs David Rice, Jas Blythe, Jas Kamper John Andrews, and William Williamson be a committe to converse with the Revd Messrs William Hodge and Jno Rankin respecting the subject of their citation before Synod and make their report tomorrow morning.

Upon enquiry it appeared that Mr Joshua L. Wilson, had complied with the order of the Commission of Synod in declaring the Congregations of Mt Carmel & Mt Zion vacant

On motion resolved that Synod now take under consideration the report of the Committee to examine the Presbytery Book — on motion Resolved that the Presbytery of Cumberland acted improperly in the case of Mr McGrady in taking it up so hastily —

Friday, Oct. 24, 1806.

On Motion Dct^r Andrew McCalla was chosen Treasurer of Synod and a Surplus of $2.50 of the contribution was deposited with him.

The Committee appointed to examine the accounts of Doct^r Andrew McCalla, respecting the copies of the confession of Faith forwarded to him by Mr Isacc Snowder Treasurer of the General Assembly, reported as follows (viz) That they had examined the accounts of Mr Andrew McCall and found them to be accurate and that a balance of $72,65 in cash is in the hands of Mr McCalla for Synod.

On motion resolved that all the Copies of the Confession of faith disposed of subsequent to the Meeting of Synod in October 1805, be accounted for with the Treasurer at fifty cents per copy.

The vote being taken, Shall the report of the Committee to examine the Cumberland Presbytery Book be received as amended? It was carried in the affirmative; and is as follows (viz) "On the first page at the bottom an elder was admitted to a seat in Presbytery as the representative of a people newly congregated who Style themselves, "the orderly part of Shiloh Congregation" The same people appear upon record in the second & fifth and sixth pages. We think it disorderly to admit an Elder to a seat in Presb^{rs} from a mere fragment of a congregation, and the name which these people assume shows that they are but a part. (See form of Church Government Chapter 9th Section 3rd. The name which these people have assumed and their ostensible object in our opinion violates the order of the Commission of Synod who adjudicated upon the case of that people last fall.

The Committee appointed to examine the Washington Presbytery Book reported as follows (VIZ) "It is the opinion of your Committee that the Presbytery of Washington deserve credit for their attention to business, regularity of their proceedings and the accuracy of their records in general.

Saturday Oct 25th 1806.

The Committee appointed to converse with the Revd Messrs. Wm Hodge and John Rankin, Reported which is as follows that they had entered into a free and friendly conversation with Messrs Hodge and Rankin, and have laboured to bring them to a sense of duty on that Subject which gives rise to their citation before this Synod. Your Committee are sorry to say their efforts have been in a great measure Abortive. — It appears Messrs William Hodge and John Rankin are willing to be examined by synod on points of Doctrine but they do positively refuse to submit to their authority exercised by their Commission particularly in silencing certain young men licensed by Cumberland Presbytery. Your Committee beg leave to suggest that it is their opinion that no valuable purpose can be answered by examining Messrs. Hodge and Rankin on points of doctrine seeing they refused to submit to the Authority of Synod.

On request it was granted that the Revd Messrs Craighead, Donald and Dickey should be excused from voting on the above report.

Messrs. Wm Hodge and John Rankin were called upon and enquired at whither they do now Submit to the

Authority of Synod as exercised by their Commission in Silencing certain young men named in the Minutes of Said Commission? and the question being put to them individually by the Moderator "Do you now submit or not submit?" they answered "we do not submit". Resolved that the Synod go into a free conversation upon the case of Messrs Hodge and Rankin, and determine what degree of censure shall be inflicted upon those men for refusing to submit to the authority of Synod. And after due deliberation had thereon the following was moved and adopted (viz) That the Revd Messrs Saml Shannon John P. Campbell, and Rob Wilson be a committee to inform the Revd Messrs Will Hodge and John Rankin of the mind of Synod upon their case and seriously and solemnly advise them to reconsider what they have done and recant before the rising of Synod and that they report on Monday.

Monday 27 October 1806.

Resolved that the Revd Messrs Jas Kamper, Will Williamson, and Rob Wilson or any two of them be a Committee to write to the Synod of Pittsburg informing them that it is the desire of this Synod that the boundary between this Synod and the Synod of Pittsburgh be ascertained and to take other measures on the subject as they may think proper.

Enquiry was made of the several Presbyteries whether they were ready to report to Synod respecting the State of the different Churches under their care And it appeared that the Presbyteries were yet unprepared to report. It was therefore enjoined upon them to be more attentive to this business in future

Enquiry being made of the Several Presbyteries whether they had appointed Commissioners to the General Assembly for the year 1806 it appeared that they had not attended to this business

The Committee appointed to converse with Messrs. Hodge and Rankin reported as follows (viz) That they have conversed with these Gentlemen at some length and find them adhering to their former determination not to submit to the authority of Synod exercised by their Commission in Silencing certain young men licensed by the Cumberland Presbytery

Synod having maturely deliberated upon the case of Messrs Hodge and Rankin and having taken without effect every cautionary measure to reclaim them to a due sense of the authority of Synod and submission to the order and discipline of the Church proceeded to suspend them and they do hereby suspend them the said Will Hodge and John Rankin from the exercise of all the functions of the Gospel Ministry and from the Sacraments of the Church until they manifest repentance and Submission.

The question was then put to Messrs Hodge & Rankin Do you appeal from the judgment of this Synod? They answered that they had not thought of appealing to any Earthly Tribunal

Ordered that the Stated Clerk again cite the Revd Messrs James McGrady, W^{ill} McGee, & Saml McAdo to appear at our next annual meeting of Synod

Agreeable to an order of last Synod a Missionary sermon was delivered on Saturday by the Revd David Rice from Proverbs 3rd and 9th. After which a collection was made of eighty eight dollars, twenty nine cents ($88 29^{ct}) and deposited with Doctor Andrew McCalla the Treasurer. . . .

The following question was brought before Synod by the Committee of Overtures. Did not the Sermon preached on yesterday by the Revd Thomas B. Craighead contradict the doctrines of our Church? and the answers given by himself to the Commission of Synod as recorded on their minutes particularly on the influence of the Divine Spirit and the doctrine of Predestination.

Synod agreed to take under consideration the above questions and deliberate on them and the Members were then called upon individually to express their opinion, and Mr Craighead was permitted in the progress of the business to offer any explanations which occurred to him as necessary to his Justification — Whereupon it appeared that it was the opinion of Synod that the Sentiments of Mr Craighead as expressed in his sermon were inconsistent with the Doctrines of our confession of Faith upon the Subject of divine Influence. . . .

Tuesday October 28ᵗʰ 1806 . . .

Synod resumed the business of yesterday and the following was moved and adopted, That Messrs Kamper, Campbell, Williamson and Cameron be a committee to form a minute expression of the opinion of Synod, respecting Mr Craighead's views of the operations of the Divine Spirit in the work of regeneration as expressed in his sermon.

On Motion Resolved that Synod now take into consideration, the following subject brought forward through the Committee of Overtures. Whereas it appears that difficulties of a particular nature exist in Cumberland Presbytery so as in a great measure to incapacitate them for doing business, the Synod having taken this matter under consideration came to the following Resolution. — Resolved that the Presbytery of Cumberland be and it is hereby dissolved and the Members which composed it are hereby annexed to the Transylvania Presbytery

Resolved that the reference of the Cumberland Presbytery respecting the Revᵈ James McGrady be and it is hereby disposed of in the following way. The Presbytery of Transylvania to which Mr McGrady now belongs are ordered to take cognizance of this affair and use means to have it issued as soon as possible.

Resolved that the judgment of Synod respecting the reference of Cumberland Presbᵉʳ in the affair of the Revᵈ James McGrady be reconsidered. After some deliberation had thereon — on motion resolved that the Presbytery of Cumberland have acted improperly in the case of Mr McGrady in taking it up so hastily without seeing and conversing with Mr McGrady in a brotherly way before they took it up in pronouncing the report credible without confronting witnesses in referring it at so early a stage and especially in not giving Mr McGrady due notice of their proceeding.

The Revd Messrs Thos Craighead and Sam Donald, entered their protest against the proceedings of Synod relative to the business of Shiloh Congregation and Mr Mc-Grady which protest was filed among the papers of Synod.

The following question was overtured to Synod from the congregation of Lexington, What are the qualifications of Electors in choosing a minister?

In answer to the congregation of Lexington respecting the qualifications of Electors in voting for a minister the following was moved and seconded (viz)

Synod do express it as their opinion, and think the Constitution of the Church clearly authorizes it — that none but persons entitled to all the privileges of the Church shall have the Right of Suffrage And after some deliberation had thereon it was referred to the General Assembly of the Presbyterian Church to meet in Philadelphia on the third Thursday of May next . . .

Wednesday October 29th 1806. . . . A letter was received from the Revd James McGrady assigning reasons why he did not obey the citation of Synod which reasons were abundantly satisfactory to Synod.

On Motion Resolved that the Revd John P. Campbell be appointed and he is hereby appointed to deliver a Missionary Sermon at the next annual session of Synod, or in case of his failure then the Revd Jas Blythe.

The Committee appointed to form a minute expressive of the opinion of Synod respecting Mr Craighead's views of the operation of the Divine Spirit in the work of regeneration as expressed in his sermon reported as follows which report was received, agreed to and committed to record.

It is the opinion of Synod that Mr Craighead in his sermon on last Sabbath, and his explanations before Synod clearly communicated the following ideas in reference to the operation of the divine spirit in the work of regeneration (viz) — That there were two distinct operations or administrations of the Holy Spirit at the time of the Apostles. The one respecting the working of Miracles, the other the communication of truth to the mind in order to regeneration. The first was given after believing was individually possessed by all believers and was soon withdrawn. The last was designed to supply the defects of the revelation already written and make display of the truth to the minds in order to regeneration and holiness, and was superceded by the written word, when the cannon of revelation was complete; which word was of higher Authority and more infallible certainly than this indwelling of the Spirit for revealing truth, because said he, the subjects of it were directed to try the Spirits by the word and quoted 1st John 4-8 to that effect in reference to their preparation of the heart, in the parable of the Sower. Mr Craighead asserted that no more was meant than a careful examining heart. — He disavowed any thing done in the heart to change its moral state and disposition merely by means of the Gospel, its Solicitous attention is engaged that the truth or matter of the revealed word as applied to the Mind in preaching the Gospel is the only energy of the Spirit, which is employed in regeneration, that God does not employ any operation or influence in or upon the Mind to dispose it to rectify it or excite it to a compliance with the call and direction of the Gospel.

That the Word of God presented to the mind in the name of God, has all the force that can be employed on intellectual beings, and that — the word of God thus presented to the mind is all that God does in the production of Faith and regeneration. — Mr Craighead in our opinion rejected every idea of the operation and influence or energy of the spirit as employed in the heart to dispose and lead it out to meet the word of God in acts of compliance. But that the action of the word upon the mind is the only operative principle *by which* the regeneration of a sinner is effected. He alledged that the Soul is passive in the same sense in which the eye is passive to the rays of light. Nothing was necessary but the opening of the eye to admit the light and in the same manner nothing is necessary but the attention of the Mind to the word, by which attention the Mind becomes as susceptible of regeneration and faith as the eye is susceptible of the images of objects when the light is let in upon it; . . .

At the request of Mr Craighead the following explanation was entered upon the minutes

I am unhappy to have to communicate to Synod I did not design waving metaphysical distinctions about the moral power of man. I want only to exhibit him as actuated upon by the Spirit of God through his truth beginning with the belief that Jesus is the Christ, and that his instructions were of course of infinite importance; that his understanding and heart were of course in the reach of divine power by the truth of his Gospel provided the intellectual eye was not closed against it in the act of rejecting the counsel of God against his own Soul; I described the several branches of this truth with the necessary affections arising from them with mind and practice

Without designing to go through every part of the necessary truth — In both cases I meant to follow as a clue the practical use of having knowledge in the Confession of Faith I did waive representations of antecedent — operations before the knowledge and belief of the truth entered into the heart which would have been the subject of disquisition had not it have been a Sacramental Sabbath. I did Say that an indwelling Spirit to supply the wants of written words was a common Gift of the young converts of the Apostolic age who manifested his divinity by miracles and that there were also delusive Spirits and that therefore they had to try the spirits by the word which had its Authority or Authenticity settled on all the Miracles and all the prophecies on record, that in this state of things the means of mediate indwelling were not in existence and of course the indwelling was immediate, when the means were given the indwelling becomes mediate.

I did mean that when God acted upon the understanding by his word and when it is received in the understanding as it is in truth not the word of man but of God it did necessarily produce faith as necessarily as light in the eye produced vision. If there were in the sermon other doctrines I give them up freely to your censure, according to my present recollections

Synod had an interlocutory and after some deliberation came to the following resolution (viz)

It is with deep regret that Synod observed that any difference of Opinion exists between Mr Craighead and themselves or that they should be compelled to take any measure relative to that difference, but circumstances, as they are, a sense of duty makes it necessary for them to adopt the following resolution,

On Motion Resolved that the Revd Thos B. Craighead be entreated and he is hereby entreated earnestly to be cautious in future as to the matter of his sermons and careful not to offend against the doctrines of the Confession of Faith and the feelings of his Christian brethren and that the Moderator be directed to read this minute to Mr Craighead Synod taking into consideration the low estate of religion within their bounds with the many and increasing errors of the present day think public, solemn, fasting and prayer a duty which God in his provi [sic] is loudly calling for, Synod do therefore appoint the first Tuesday in January, and it is hereby appointed for the above purpose of solemn fasting and prayer to Almighty God for the outpouring of his spirit, the revival of true religion, and arresting & counteracting all error and delusion throughout the world — And Ministers and Churches under the care of Synod are solemnly enjoined to regard the day accordingly.

Synod adjourned to meet at Lexington on the third Tuesday of October next Concluded with prayer

Thus far examined and approved a few inaccuracies and obscurities excepted, and also some proceedings relative to the Cumberland Presbytery of at least questionable regularity

In General Assembly at Philadelphia May 1807

ARCHIBALD ALEXANDER
Moderator

October 20th 1807

Synod met according to adjournment in the first Presbyterian Meeting house in Lexington and was opened with a sermon from I John 1 and 3 by the Rev Joshua L. Wilson

After sermon the Moderator being absent Mr Tamplin the Senior Member present called the members to order and constituted Synod with prayer. —

Synod proceeded to the election of a moderator and temporary Clerks, and upon taking the vote it appeared that the Revd Archibald Cameron was duly elected Moderator and the Revd Messrs. Robt G. Wilson and Joshua L. Wilson were elected Clerks

Oct 21st—On motion ordered that inquiry be made at the Presbytery of Transylvania respecting their procedures in the case of Mr McGrady

To this enquiry Presbytery Answered by reading their decision from which it appeared that Mr McGrady's character stood good and fair

Oct 22nd Ordered that the Reports of the Presbyteries be filed with the papers of Synod and that the Stated Clerk make out and forward to the General Assembly a Synodical Report.

Through the Committee of Overtures the following regulation was proposed and being amended was adopted (viz) "That —it be one of the Rules of this Synod that the Moderator Preach the action Sermon, at the Synodical Communion and appoint the members who are to preach during the Sessions as early as possible provided always that if convenient the Minister of the place shall be consulted in such cases."

On Motion Ordered that the several Presbytery pay to the Treasurer of Synod the sums they have collected for the support of Missionaries, and the Treasurer report before the Rising of Synod . . .

The Stated Clerk reported that agreeable to order he had by letter cited the Revd Messrs James McGrady, Wm McGee, and Saml McAdow to appear before Synod at the present meeting who have not yet appeared. Whereupon resolved that as the case of these men is intimately connected with the case of the late Cumberland Presbytery it be deferred until the whole be taken up together

On enquiry it appeared that the injunction of Synod on

its members to observe as a day of fasting and prayer the first Tuesday of January Last was not as generally attended to as could have been wished, the injunction being forgotten by some and unknown to others

A letter was received written by the General Assembly to this Synod advising a review of the case of Cumberland Presbytery and the business connected with it

On Motion resolved that this letter be taken up by paragraphs. — The first paragraph of the Assembly's letter is in these words: "that your proceedings in demanding the young men regularly licensed and ordained, be given up to your Body for examination is of questionable regularity."

After spending considerable time in deliberating on these proceedings without coming to any issue a motion of adjournment was moved and seconded . . .

October 23. . . . A Motion was made and seconded to read the minutes of the commission of Synod relative to the proceedings under consideration — They were read accordingly and a lengthy discussion ensued. The question was then put on the first paragraph of the Assembly's Letter. "Were the proceedings of Synod in requiring the young men irregularly licensed and ordained to be given up to their body for examination regular?" and determined in the affirmative and then yeas and nays being called for were as follows

YEAS Samuel Shannon, S. Findley, S. Donald, John Howe, J.L.Wilson, T.Cleland, William Dickey, J. Blythe, Isacc Tull, Joseph P. Howe, John Lyle, R. Stuart, Saml.T. Scott, Court Vhooris, David Dickey, Charles Philips, Francis Allen, John Henderson, Wm Henry, John Adams, Robert P. Allen, Robert Robb — 22

NAYS Robert G. Wilson, James Welsh, Mathew G. Wallace, and Andrew McCalla, — 4 . . .

October 24th . . . The minutes of yesterday were read and the Synod proceeded to the consideration of the second paragraph of the Assembly's Letter (viz) "that your proceedings in suspending the irregularly ordained ministers without processes in their case is at least of questionable regularity," it was then moved and seconded that the question for discussion be "Did the Synod by its commission suspend any men irregularly licensed or ordained without process in their case? . . ."

After deliberation upon the question aforestated the vote was taken upon the distinct parts of it — 1st   Did the Synod suspend those men irregularly licensed or ordained.   Ans^d, No.   2nd Did the Commission declare them irregularly licensed and ordained and prohibit them from preaching &c without prces [sic]?   Answered, No.

The yeas and nays being called for on the first question were

NAYS   Shannon, Donald, I Howe, J L. Wilson, Will Dickey, Blythe, Tull, J.P. Howe, Lyle, Stuart, Scott, Vhooris, D. Dickey Frances Allen, Henderson, Henry and Adams, — 17

YEAS   R.G.Wilson, Welsh, Wallace, McCalla, Robb, — 5

The Yeas and Nays on the Second question were as above except R.G.Wilson and Robert Robb who voted in the negative —

The Synod then proceeded to the third paragraph of the Assembly letter, (viz) "That your proceedings in suspending Messrs Hodge and Rankin for not submitting to the examination of the Young Men are of questionable regularity."   The follownig question was then moved and seconded for discussion were the proceedings of Synod regular in suspending Messrs Hodge and Rankin for not submitting to the Jurisdiction of Synod? . . .

After due deliberation had on the above question it was determined in the affirmative the Yeas and Nays being called for stood as follows,

YEAS   Shannon, Donald, J. Howe, I.L.Wilson, Wm Dickey, I.P.Campbell, Tull, I.P.Howe, Lyle, Scott, Vhooris, D.Dickey, F.Allen, Henderson, Henry and Adams, — 16

NAYS   Blythe, R.G.Wilson, Welsh, Wallace, McCalla & Robb. — 6

Monday 26th October

The Synod having reviewed their proceeding according to the recommendation of the Assembly Resolved

That Messrs Hodge and Rankin be committed to the Presbytery of Transylvania within whose bounds they are now placed which is competent to restore them when that can be done consistently with the discipline of the Church.

Resolved that the Revd Messrs. James Blythe, John Lyle, Joshua L. Wilson, and Robert G. Wilson, be a committee to draft a Letter to the General Assembly respecting the proceedings of this Synod toward Cumberland Presbytery and report tomorrow morning.

On Motion Resolved that the Revd Messrs. J. P. Campbell, and John Howe, be a committee to draft a letter in answer to the Letter from Shiloh Congregation on the Subject of the restoration of Mr Hodge, and that they report before the rising of Synod.

On Motion Resolved that the Revd Messrs James McGrady Wm McGee, and Saml McAdow, who are now under citation to appear before the Synod of Kentucky, be committed to the Presbytery of Transylvania who are hereby directed to take such measures in their case as they may think proper according to the discipline of the Church.

The Committee appointed to examine the Records of the West Lexington Presbytery Reported that they found them well kept and that particular attention had been paid to the rules of our discipline, a few omissions and inaccuracies excepted.

The Committee appointed to review the records of Washington Presbytery Reported that they found them kept in an orderly manner with the exception of some obscure and inaccurate phrases . . .

The Committee appointed to draft a letter to Shiloh Congregation relative to the restoration of Mr Hodge, Reported one, which being read and amended was adopted and is as follows

Dear Brethren — We no less than yourselves deprecate your separation from the Presbyterian Church such an event should it ultimately happen will be to us a matter of Serious and lasting regret, You may rest assured you have our Sympathy on that Subject — and were it consistent with our views of duty and a due regard to the order and discipline of the Church we would at once remove the Suspension and restore Mr Hodge to his former standing among us, But as Synod are not possessed of any assurances on the part of Mr. Hodge of his return to order and of his submission to the constituted Authorities and discipline of the Presbyterian Church, it is not yet possible for them to release him from that censure which was inflicted at the last Session of Synod. We still However invite him to the Bosom of the Church and affectionately pray for his restoration on the footing of order & amendment And that the way be open for his return at any time, Synod have adopted the following measure with reference to such an event. "The Synod having reviewed their proceeding according to the recommendation of the General Assembly Resolved that Messrs Hodge and Rankin be committed to the Presbytery of Transylvania within whose bounds they are now placed which is competent to restore them when that can be done consistently with the Discipline of the Churchs." That a Merciful God may visit you with the blessings of his Rich Grace is the prayer of yours in the Gospel of our common Lord

Ordered that the Stated Clerk Sign and forward this letter to Shiloh Congregation —

The advice of Synod was requested by the Presbytery of Washington in the case of John Paul and his sister in the bounds of Honey Creek Congregation who formerly lived in *incest* but now profess repentance and desire admission to the Communion of the Church. — Whereupon Resolved that the Session of Honey Creek be advised to admit John Paul and his sister to the Communion of the church upon condition they separate and give satisfactory evidence of their repentance and Reformation . . .

October 27 . . .

The Minutes of Yesterday were read. The Synodical Treasurer agreeable to order reported as follows

6ʺ of October 1807 Recᵈ of Mr Scroggin of Cherry Run
    Congregation by his son as per Recᵗ Given $16.03
22ⁿ October Recᵈ of Robert Robb, from Washington   15.12½
    Do of Rev Joshua L. Wilson   20.00
    Do of Rev. Joshua L. Wilson   2.00
    Do P. Samuel Findley   3.25
    Joseph P. Howe $10.37
      "   "   3.88
      "   "   2.62
      "   "   3.50

           20.37   20.37
    " Samuel Donald   14.80
    " Samuel T. Scott   10.50
25 Oct of Revᵈ Samuel Rannells Paris $23.76
      "   "   24.75   48.51
  "   John P. Campbell Danville   16.25
  "   James Blythe Pisgah   10.00
      Collection of Lexington   58.75
      Revᵈ Robert Stuart   13.05

      Amounting to   254.64
      Of Major Parker & Sister   2.00

    The following accompt was rendered by our Treasurer and ordered to be entered of Record

                 Lexington Oct 26 1807
The Synod of Kentucky to Andrew McCalla, Treaˢ Dʳ
For amount paid Mr. Essex for binding the Minute Book $2.00
For amount paid Mr Hudson for bringing the printed
    Minutes from Philadelphia   .50

Supra   Cr $2.50
    by cash left in his hands last year   2.50

    The Committee appointed to examine the Records of the Presbytery of Transylvania made their Report — which being amended was adopted and is as follows VIZ "The Presbytery of Transylvania appear to have bestowed some care on their minutes which are in general correctly kept, But upon examination the Committee find that the Presbytery acted irregularly in receiving Mr Nathan Hall on trials before he had gone through a regular course of Literature, Page 226, and also that the Presbytery of Transylvania did in their minutes use expressions too harsh and severe respecting the late Cumberland Presbytery in the affair of Mr Jas McGrady Page 131 and 132 —

The Committee appointed to draft a letter to the General Assembly reported one which being read and amended was adopted.

Adjourned to meet at Doc^{tr} Andrew McCalla at VI O.C. this evening. . . .

Doct^r McCalla's, VI O.C. . . .

Through the Committee of Overtures an amendment was proposed to the Rule regulating the admission of lay members, to a seat in Presbyterys or Synod so that instead of *"all vacant congregations"* it shall read all *congregations* not *Statedly Supplied* which Amendment was adopted . . .

On Motion Resolved that Synod will apply to the next General Assembly to define the North Eastern boundary of this Synod and that the Revd Robt G. Wilson be appointed to write to the Presbytery of Ohio informing them of this Resolution; and that the Revd Messrs. James Kamper, Wm Williamson Robert Wilson and Robert G. Wilson be a Committee to lay this matter before the General Assembly.

Agreeably to an order of the last Synod a Missionary Sermon was preached on Saturday by the Rev John P. Campbell from Isaiah 42.4 (last Clause). After which a Collection was made of Sixty dollars seventy five cents ($60.75^{cts}) and deposited with Doct^r Andrew McCalla Treasurer, —

. . . The Rev James Blythe was appointed to preach a Missionary sermon at next Meeting of Synod, and in case of his failure the Rev Robert G. Wilson was directed to perform that duty.

On Motion Resolved that the first Tuesday of January next be observed as a day of humiliation and prayer, for the revival of true religion among us and throughout the world and all the members of this Synod are enjoined to pay particular regard to the appointment. . . .

Synod adjourned to meet in the first Presbyterian Meeting House in Lexington. on the second Wednesday of October next

Concluded with prayer

ARCHIBALD CAMERON

Moderator

Teste ROBERT G. WILSON Clerk protempore

A letter to the General Assembly which is directed to be made matter of record with reference to Page 147 —
Rev^d and Dear Fathers

The Synod of Kentucky return their thanks for that paternal care which the General Assembly have always manifested for the welfare of this distant branch of the Church. The Synod assure the General Assembly that they have carefully reviewed their proceedings which were by you deemed of questionable regularity and beg leave to lay before you the result of their proceedings with a summary of the reasons on which they founded their decisions. — The attention of the Synod was first directed to the following question arising from the Assemblys Letter   Were the proceedings of the Synod, in requiring the young men irregularly licensed & ordained to be given up regular? — The Synod determined by a large majority that their proceedings were regular

In Support of this decision the Synod offer the following reasons — We find that a very extensive power is conceded to Synod by the Book of Discipline in these words "The Synod have power to redress whatever hath been done by Presbyteries contrary to order." The Synod do not suppose they have the power of licensing and ordaining candidates. This they think is the duty and prerogative of Presbyteries. But Synod do conceive that when a Presbytery has introduced insufficient men in the Ministry and there is evidence to believe that the majority of the Presbytery are so disposed as to leave no rational probability that the evil will be redressed by them it becomes the duty of Synod to enquire into the qualifications of the persons in question and Confirm or disannul their licensure; and inasmuch as the Book of Discipline has prescribed no form in which Synod should proceed in redressing disorders of this kind we thought ourselves to exercise a sound discression and choose that mode which appeared to us best, provided we did nothing contrary to our Directory or the decisions of the General Assembly

The Synod farther observe that they were called upon by letter containing complaints and a Petition in 1804 to issue a matter in dispute between the Majority and Minority of the late Cumberland Presbytery. The Minority namely five members complained that incompetent men and men unsound in the faith were introduced into the Gospel Ministry

The Majority being six members asserted that these men professed extraordinary talents and were competents to the work of the ministry — The only alternative therefore was either to disregard the dissent and complaint of the Minority, or examine the men whose qualification were in question for the Synod conceived the manifestation of their qualification was the only evidence on which the controversy could be decided — Farther Synod thought that among so many young men there might at least be found a few who shortly would be qualified for the office of the Gospel Ministry could they be induced to use the proper means. The Synod are of opinion that they did not suspend the young men irregularly licensed and ordained as intimated in the Assemblys Letter. They think no person can be suspended from the exercise of the Ministry who has never been regularly introduced into that sacred office. The Synod think that the persons in question never had any regular standing as Ministers; therefore did simply prohibit them from exhorting, preaching or administering ordinances in consequence of any authority derived from the Cumberland Presbytery as appears from their Record Page 93.

Another point which the Assembly Letter brought under the review of Synod was the conduct of the Commission in forbidding the young men irregularly licensed and ordained to preach &c without process had in their case: In Justification of their conduct in this particular Synod take the liberty to remind you that the irregularity of the licensure of those men has been a subject of dispute between the Majority and Minority of Cumberland Presbytery for more than two years.   The Presbytery had been cited to appear before Synod to render an account of these licensures.   They did not appear — The Commission was appointed the records of Presbytery were produced, the open confession of the Majority was made that the Sacred office had been conferred without regard to the requirements of our discipline and the young men refused to give any evidence of their qualifications for the Minstry   Synod therefore supposed it a sacred duty which they owed to the Church of Jesus Christ to declare solemnly that these young men were introduced to the important work of preaching the Gospel contrary to our Constitution, — and in a manner which imperiously demanded their prohibition from every part of the Minsitry with us   Therefore all the process was had which the nature of the case admitted

The third part of the Assemblys letter to which the attention of Synod was turned gave rise to the following question: "Were the proceedings of Synod in Suspending Messrs Hodge and Rankin for not submitting to the Jurisdiction of Synod regular?" which was answered in the affirmative by a large Majority.   As the Synod believe it has always been taken for granted that when any member declined the jurisdiction of a church judicatory or would not submit to its authority such persons ought to be suspended or deposed it is presumed that a review of our records is all that will be necessary to justify this decision.   Synod do not admit that Mr Hodge and Rankin were suspended merely for differing from them in an unimportant question nor for a single act of rebellion against the Government of our Church.   If their error had existed in speculation only, Synod trust that fervent charity would have covered their fault.   But as early as October 1803 they introduced the practice of li-

censing illiterate and unqualified men to preach the Gospel
and notwithstanding the minority of Presbytery entered a
dissent against their proceedings and sent a letter to Synod
in 1804 containing a petition and complaint as to this matter, these men obstinately persisted in their pernicious practices; in so much that in October 1805 they had licensed
about 27 persons to preach and exhort and but few of them,
according to the information we had, believe the doctrines
of our confession; — As Synod thought it their duty to
spend and to be spent to vindicate the doctrines of the Gospel and the discipline of the church, as contained in our
confession of Faith they would have acted a very inconsistent part had they suffered those suspended brethren to
persist in the practice of licensing men who were calculated
to diffuse enthusiasm and error through the world; Synod
therefore instituted the process mentioned in a preceding
part of this letter against the Cumberland Presbytery &
cited them to appear at our next stated Session (see minutes
of Synod page 79)   They did not appear at the Session
of 1805

They were therefore again cited to appear before the
Commission of Synod (page 82) to answer to the complaints of the Minority and so on.

They appeared and confessed that they had irregularly
licensed and ordained men to the work of the ministry, and
that they had done this without requiring them to adopt our
Confession, — Some of the reasons those Brethren offered
in justification of this latter part of their conduct were so
far from being satisfactory that Synod deemed them an ag-
gression of their guilt   The principal reason they offered
was (see page 86 & onward) that they could not in conscience demand that the young men should receive the Confession except so far as they believed to be true, for they
themselves did not believe all contained in said Confession —

This, Synod thought extraordinary seeing these men had
at their licensure adopted the Confession   They also declined the Jurisdiction of Synod by refusing to give up the

men, they had licensed and ordained when Synod requested
them to appear before them as evidence in order to issue
the above mentioned important controversy between the
Majority and Minority of Cumberland Presbytery Synod
thought as these young men were members in Communion in
our church, the Judicatory had power to call them in as evidence. If so it was an act of rebellion in those Brethren
(see page 89-92) to interpose and hinder them from coming forward Synod did not at that time suspend those
Brethren, but cited them to appear at our next stated Session (October 1806) to answer for their misconduct and
for errors in doctrine (see page 94-97) ——

Messrs William Hodge and John Rankin appeared (see
page 111 and onward) and notwithstanding it must be
granted, they had time for consideration and the exercise
of repentance, it was found that they had still persisted in
encouraging the young men to preach and so on, on whom
the Synod had laid a solemn prohibition: and notwithstanding everything as we supposed was done to reclaim them,
they declined our jurisdiction. Synod then Solemnly suspended them not for a speculative opinion but for persisting
in a practice very injurious to the cause of truth, and for renouncing the jurisdiction of the Church, which conduct has
always been considered a crime worthy of suspension or excommunication. Our Saviour says "let him that will not
hear the church be as an heathen man and a Publican ———

That the Great Head of the Church may be with you and
direct you in all your deliberations is the prayer of yours,
Dear Fathers, in one Common Lord.

Lexington First Presbyterian Church Oct. 12, 1808.

The Synod of Kentucky met according to adjournment.
The meeting was opened with a sermon from Mat 8,13, by
Mr Cameron the moderator of the former meeting and was
constituted with prayer.

— Mr Williamson was chosen Moderator of the meeting and Messrs. Robert Wilson and Hoge Clerks pro tempore, — Messrs. Samuel Rannels, Joshua L. Wilson Arch[d]

Cameron, John Campbell, Robt Robb & Jos Alexander were appointed a committee of Overtures. . . .

Friday, Oct 13. . . .

On enquiry it appeared that the Stated Clerk had failed to make a Synodical Report from the filed Reports of the Several Presbyteries and forward it to the General Assembly and his reasons for failure were sustained

On Motion Resolved that Messrs Gilleland Vance be a committee to make out a Synodical report which shall pass the review of Synod before it rises —

The Committee appointed to ascertain the North Eastern boundary of this Synod Reported that the boundary line was fixed by the General Assembly as appeared by the following extract from their Minutes

"Resolved" "That the Southern boundary of the Synod of Pittsburg be from the Mouth of Sciota up the Ohio up to the Mouth of the Great Kenhawa; thence by a line due East to the top of the Alleghany Mountains. And that the Western boundary of said Synod begin at the Mouth of Sciota River and thence up said River to its Source."

Synod on enquiry found that the letter to the General Assembly drafted by their Committee, amended and adopted at their last Sessions has not been recorded or forwarded; and the Synod did judge the reasons of the Stated Clerk for not recording and forwarding said Letter sufficient to Justify him, Nevertheless, Synod do direct that this letter be inserted on the records with reference to page 147 [of Records]

On Motion Resolved that Messrs. Campbell, Stuart, and Joshua L. Wilson, be a committee to write to the General Assembly informing them what Synod has done relating to the Cumberland business, and that they report before the rising of Synod . . .

On Motion Resolved that the fourth Tuesday of May next be observed as a day of fasting and Prayer and that Messrs Cunningham, R. Wilson and Tull be a committee to State the objects to be Particularly remembered on that day and to report on to morrow morning

On Motion resolved that the synod farther instruct and they hereby do instruct the Committee appointed to draft a letter to the General Assembly to embrace in their letter the main objects of their letter prepared for the General Assembly last year

Friday, Oct. 14.

The following question thro the Committee of Overtures was laid before Synod Is it orderly in a Presbytery to dismiss an ordained uninstalled minister and recommend him to another Presbytery when no call has been presented from any Church Within its bounds

On motion Synod proceeded to the Consideration of this question and after mature deliberation determined that it is orderly . . .

Through the Committee of Overtures this Question was Proposed to Synod Viz ought not Barton W. Stone, Robert Marshall, John Thompson, Richard McNemar, John Dunlevy who have been suspended now be disposed

On motion Synod Proceeded to Consider this Question after some deliberation Messrs Gilleland, Rannells and Cameron were appointed a Committee to draft a Minute Expressive of the sense of Synod on this subject & report on tomorrow

Saturday 15th October

. . . The following Question this the Committee of overtures was laid before Synod VIZ is it orderly for a Presbytery to examine a Candidate for the Gospel ministry on any parts of trial by a Committee

On Motion Synod Proceeded to Consider this Question and after mature deliberation decided that it is not Orderly . . .

The Committee appointed to draft a Minute expressive of the sense of Synod with case of Barton W. Stone and these Reported . . . their report being read and amended was adopted and is as follows

Whereas Robert Marshall, Barton W. Stone Richard

McNemar John Dunlevy and John Thompson were suspended by this Synod for declining the Judisdiction and seceding from the confession of faith of our Church and have Continued ever since to enlarge their schism to multiply their erroneous opinions to Scandalize the Presbyterian Church to oppose, a, number of essential doctrines of our holy religion, and Whereas the Church have already used every effort in their Power to reclaim them and our form of Government directs that ministers acting in such a manner be deposed and cut off from the Church, Resolved therefore that the above named Robert Marshall, Barton W. Stone, Richard McNemar, John Dunlevy, and John Thompson be deposed and in the name of Christ and by the Authority Committed to us as a Judicatory of the Church of Christ they are hereby deposed from all the functions of the Gospel Ministry and Cut off from our Communion

the Rev James Blythe agreeably to appointment of the last Meeting of Synod delivered a missionary sermon Collected $70.50cts.

The Committee appointed to lay before Synod the objects to be particularly remembered on the appointed fast Reported the report being read and amended was adopted and is as follows the Committee to lay before Synod the objects to be particularly remembered on the appointed fast Recommended that every friend of Zion Should Confess with Sorrow the sins of age in Neglecting the ordinance of God's House and the religious education of Youth, in increasing fondness for intemperance, balls, horse-Races and theatrical Amusements and therefore we recommend that Christians implore God for Christs Sake to arrest the Calamities with which we are threatened in civil and religious Society and that he could be pleased to restore peace to the Contending nations of the earth, Pressure this professing people from the spirit of the World pour out his Spirit abundantly on the Churches bless the labourers of Missionaries the Gospel and fill the earth with his Glory. . . .

The Committee appointed to draft a letter to the General Assembly Reported, their report was taken up on motion Synod proceeded to Consider it by Paragraph after some deliberation on the report Synod adjourned to Meet at Mr McCallas, at 5 oclock P M . . .

Mr McCallas 5 o'clock P M

. . . Synod resumed the report of the Committee appointed to draft a letter to the General Assembly and having maturely Considered & amended it the letter which they Reported was approved & adopted and is follows.

Rev^d and Dear Brethren

The Synod of Kentucky regret that the General Assembly have heard nothing officially concerning their proceedings in october 1807 At that time a letter was Received from the general Assembly to which particular Attention was paid especially in Revising the proceeding therein stated to be of questionable Regularity After a Revision of the Several parts of their proceedings pointed to in the Assembly's Letter the Synod drafted a Communication Stating the Result of their Revisal giving their Reasons in detail which it appears has never been transmitted

The Synod lament that anything like a difference of opinion should exist between them and the General Assembly with regard to the Government of our Church and in order to give a Just view of the Ground traced and Retraced by the Synod upon those point deemed of questionable Regularity the Assembly are Requested to attend to the following Statement

the Synod thought their proceeding Regular in adjuring the Cumberland Presbytery to Deliver up the young men irregularly licensed and ordained, to them for examination in as much as they are vested with power by our book of Discipline to redress whatever is done by presbytery, Contrary to order When a part of the presbytery of Cumberland Complained that the Majority had violated Discipline of our Church by licensing and ordainary insufficient men to preach the Gospel administer its ordinance and when the majority expressed a determination to persevere the same course it became the duty of Synod to Rectify the disorder, in doing which they conceived themselves at liberty to exercise a discretion as to the mode, The Synod do not think that they Did Suspend those young men because they are of the opinion that no one Could be Suspended from an office with which he was never legally invested but they declared them destitute of any Ministerial Authority Derived from our Church until they Should be inducted according to its discipline

as to the Suspension of Messrs Hodges & Rankin Synod take the liberty to state that not a mere difference of opinion on a point of discipline but a formal and Repeated declination of Jurisdiction of the Church was the Principal ground on which they acted in Suspending them as will be evinced by a Careful Review of their Record but we wish it also to be observed that our Decisions in either Case, have not been founded on a Solitary insulated [isolated] fact but upon a train of facts commencing several years prior to their entry on our Journal & terminating in 1806. From a connected Survey of the whole business it will be seen that a small Majority of the presbytery in defiance of order, in defiance of the solemn opposition of a respectable minority, and of the interposition of Synod to prevent their disorder; went on to violate the plainest law of our constitution, the Constituted Authority of the Church send forth into the World a number of Preachers and exorters most of whom were as it appeared to us no less remarkable for their want of information than for unsoundness in faith it was for this defiance of order as well as for individual act, it was for a series of disorderly Conduct operating to produce and aggravating (?) positive acts of Rebellion against Ecclesiastic Authority that we were led to decide as we have done. The Same Spirit of Antipathy and Revolt which had influenced those men prior to the Measures of Synod in 1806 has ever since Continued to Produce a Similar course of Conduct instead of Approaching the General Assembly in the Constitutional way of appeal from our judgment they Call upon them to redress their Supposed grievances. by letter or petition and that too after Solemnly declaring in the face of Synod that they wished no appeal to any tribunal   It was to be expected that persons who were sincere in their approaches to your venerable body and wished to pursue an honorable and correct Course without Artifice or management would have before this, acted upon the instruction of the General Assembly and make some Communication to the Synod of Kentucky but this has not been done, for two years we have heard nothing from them, so that to the disregard of Authority which they have uniformly discovered toward us they have Superadded Contempt for the advice of the Highest Judicatory of the Church   We Submit these reflections to the Consideration of the General Assembly and hope that upon taking a Review of our whole Conduct in an affair of Great Difficulty and delicacy it Will be found substantially Correct With unshaken attachment to the doctrine and discipline of our Church, with sincere Respect for the Supreme Judicature with united Prayers for the prosperity of Zion we are dear brethren yours in the Gospel our blessed Lord

Ordained that the Stated Clerk Copy this Letter and forward it to next General Assembly . . .

Synod adjourned to meet at the first Presbyterian Church in Lexington on Monday next at 9 Oclock . . .

Monday October 17ᵗʰ 1808 . . .   Committee appointed to draft a Synodical Report to the General Assembly Reported which was approved and the Stated Clerk is directed to forward a copy to next General Assembly

. . . Synod appointed the Rev R. G. Wilson to preach the Missionary Sermon at the next meeting of Synod   Mr Gilleland was appointed his Alternate   Resolved that Synod in future shall not return thanks to any member for preaching a Missionary Sermon as the member who preaches the Sermon does no more than his duty and if the Sermon be good thanks are immediately due to Almighty God   Ordered that the Stated Clerk forward the name B W Stone Robert Marshall Richard McNemar John Dunlevy John Thompson for publication in the Assembly Magazine as deposed from the ministry, ex Communicated

The Committee of Overtures brought before Synod the following Resolution which was adopted viz whereas the Committee appointed by the Synod of Pittsburg and Kentucky to ascertain the boundary line between this and that Synod have Recommended a Reciprocal intercourse between those bodies   Resolved that Messrs R.G.Wilson and Hoge be a Committee to write to the Synod of Pittsburg and invite them to a brotherly interchange of Correspondence and inform them of the time and place of our next meeting and that owing to a want of information of the time and place of the meeting of that body it is Deemed not expedient to appoint any member to meet with them until information be Received thro an official channel of their willingness for the interchange and suitableness of the time and place of these committee meeting   On Motion ordered that several persons who have money in their hands for Missionary purposes pay it to the Treasurer and that the treasurer Report before the Rising of Synod Ordered that the Treasurer of Synod make a communication to the treasurer of the General Assembly Stating the several sums paid into his hands for the missionary fund giving him information as far as he has documents of the places and persons from whom such sums have been by whom collected and requesting that said person places and sums be published next year in the Assembly Extracts   On Motion Resolved that each member present Contribute 50cts as his proportion of the Compensation of Stated Clerk for past Services this contribution was made and amounted to $9.50cts which was deposited with the treasurer to be by him paid to Stated Clerk   On Motion Resolved that it be a Standing order of this Synod that each presbytery be prepared to pay its proportion of Synodical Expenses   The Treasurer Reported as follows viz

Received from Rev Thomas Cleland   } $6 75cts
Harden Creek and Springfield Congregation }

—from Revd Samuel Robertson from Cane Run $6 11
—from Rev Samuel Rennells from Paris $2.45cts
    do   do   Mouth of Stone   11.25   23.68
—at Lexington at a Missionary Sermon   70.50
  from Rev Joseph Howe from Pleasant Point $ 1.50
    do   do   Mount Stirling $ 3.33⅓   4.83⅓
  from Rev R.G.Wilson Treasurer }
  of the Washington presbytery by }   19.83
  the hand of Rev James Hoge   }
—of the Rev Issac Tull from Irwan spring &
  Sugar Ridge   2.93
  of the Rev John Lyle by Mr Terence from
  Cherry Springs $10.80
  of do by Andrew Robinson from Concord   10.93
                         —————
                    $21.73   2103$

Synod adjourned to meet at the first Presbyterian Meeting House in Lexington on the Second Wednesday of October next at 12 Oclock   Concluded with prayer

ROBERT WILSON }   { May 20 1809
            } Ck   {   WILLIAM WILLIAMSON
          } pro ten {   Modr
JAMES HOGE }   { approveth thus far by the
                        General Assembly.
     a few inaccuracies excepted

Lexington First Presbyterian church october 11th 1809
The Synod of Ky met agreeably to adjournment and was opened by the Moderator the Rev William Williamson with a sermon from 2 Corinth. 2 16 Ranells was chosen [Moderator] and Mr Hoge and Mr Stewart temporary Clerk

October 12 9 Oclock A.M.
The committee of overture laid before Synod a Communication from the presbytery of union to the presbytery of Transylvania together with a Resolution on the Subject of ascertaining the boundary line between the synod of

the Synod Carolinas and Kentucky which was amended and adopted is as follows viz   Resolved that the Stated Clerk of Synod be and is hereby ordered to make application to the General Assembly requesting them to take measures that the boundary line between the Synod of the Carolinas and Kentucky be ascertained and that the Presbytery of Transylvania give notice of this application to Union presbytery   On Motion Resolved that Messrs Lyle and Stewart and Tull be a committee to lay before Synod such extracts from the minutes of General Assembly as Require our attention

By the Committee of Overtures an application from the presbytery of Washington for division of said presbytery was laid before Synod.

On Motion Resolved that Synod do not think the presbytery of Washington Ripe for a Division at present . . .

An Answer to the letter sent by the Synod to the last General Assembly was Received and Read and ordered to be filed among the papers of Synod

Messrs Lyle, Cunningham and Cameron and Stewart were appointed a Committee to consider the Expedience of Establishing Religious tract societies and to devise a plan for carrying into effect the Recommendation of the General Assembly on the Subject and to Report before the Rising of Synod.

On Motion Resolved that on tomorrow 3 Oclock P M the Synod will take into Consideration the state of our Congregations and attempt to devise a plan for putting them in a more favorable Situation

Through the Committee of Overtures an appeal by Session of Concord came before Synod from the Judgment of West Lexington presbytery by which a judgment of said Session suspending from the privilege of the Church John Moore for exposing to sale by public Auction a Negro boy at Nicholas Court house was reversed and Said Moore was by Presbytery restored to the Communion of the church

after maturely considering the case Synod determined that the Judgment of the presbytery ought to be Reversed and it is hereby Reversed and the decision of the Session of Concord is Confirmed . . .

Oct. 13, 1809 . . . On Motion Resolved unanimously that Synod reconsider their decision of the appeal in the case of John Moore after spending some time on this subject it was postponed and the order of the day agreeably to the resolution of yesterday was taken up The Revd Benjamin Quinn of the Synod of Virginia on invitation took his seat as a Corresponding Member

On motion resolved that Synod enter into a free Conversation on the State of the Churches under their care Messrs Robert G. Wilson Joshua L. Wilson and Robert Stewart were appointed a committee to take notes of the Conversation after progressing some length Synod adjourned to meet on tomorrow at this place 9 o clock A M . . .

October 14 1809 — 9 o clock A M a Missionary sermon was delivered by the Revd Robert G Wilson after sermon $60 was Collected for missionary purposes Mr Hodge together with Thomas H Nelson and Samuel Hodge presented to Synod their petition praying the appointment of a Commission of Synod for the purpose of considering their case Synod took the Petition under consideration and agreed that it ought to be granted Synod adjourned to meet at this place on Monday morning at 9, O.Clock A.M.

Synod met agreeably to adjournment Constituted with Prayer Members present as on Saturday Synod resumed the consideration of the case of Hodge & others On motion resolved that Messrs Rice, Shannon, Tamplin, Andrews, Stuart, Joshua L. Wilson, Cleland, Robert Wilson, and Hoge ministers, and James Allen John Cowan and Claiborne Rice Elders, seven of these ministers, and of the Elders as many as may attend be and they are hereby appointed a Commission to meet at Greensburg on the first Wednesday of December next at 12 O.C. and that the Rev David Rice open the meeting with a sermon and preside until a moderator be chosen On motion Synod resolved to reconsider the propriety of appointing a commission of

Synod according to the Petition of Mr, Hodge After considering this question Synod resumed their former proceedings on the subject and determined that this request of Mr, Hodge and others ought not to be granted, Synod adjourned to meet at this place on tomorrow 9 O clock A,M.

Synod met agreeable to adjournment Constituted with Prayer. Members present as on yesterday Mr Hodge came forward this morning and Proposed that he in consequence of a fuller deliberation on the Subject of his petition and reference wished the Synod to remand his case and all the other business which was before the Commission of Synod respecting the late Cumberland Presbytery to The Presbytery of Transylvania To which request the Synod agreed and that the business may have speedy termination the Presbytery of Transylvania is directed to meet for this and other purposes at Greenstown on the first Wednesday of december next 12 OClock Messrs Blythe & Cunningham and Andrews were appointed a Committee to draft a Letter to the persons mentioned in the above minute inviting them to attend at the time and place above mentioned. On Motion resolved that five dollars be allowed the Stated Clerk for his services for the past year and that each Presbytery pay one third of this sum

The consideration of the appeal from the judgment of the West Lexington Presbytery in the case of John Moore by the Session of Concord was resumed.

On Motion resolved that this case be remanded to the Session of Concord, that they reconsider their proceedings that they be careful to act agreeably to the Book of Discipline, and that they particularly inquire whether John Moore did take due pains to sell his negro boy at private sale before he [was] exposed to public sale On Motion Resolved that it be enjoined on all the Churches under our Care Require of all persons pretending to preach whom they do not know to be orderly members of The Presbyterian church to produce the proper credentials of their authority to preach the Gospel before they encourage them as preachers. The Committee appointed to take notes of the free

Conversation on the State of the Churches under our care &
to devise some measures for the advancement of the Cause
of Christ Recommended the adoption of the Following —
the free Conversation on the State of our Churches has
brought fully to view the Low and the Languishing state
of true religion within our bounds   Many who were once
united with us in professing the faith of Jesus Christ and
in the practice of Christian duties have departed from that
faith and walk no more with us many who not long since
discovered a zeal becoming the Christian name have now
fallen in a state of stupid formality the precious ordinance
of God's house are not generally valued   Sought after and
Delighted in as means Communion with a God we love
but are Considered as Common things that may be negelcted
with impunity or attended to only under circumstances unfavourable to Religion and moral improvement Spiritual
deadness and the spirit of the world reign around them
which appear in the ardency with which men pursue earthly
object[s] and in their taste for the Gaeities and fashions
which prevail in the land but above all neglect of parents in
maintaining the worship of God in their houses and instructing their Children in the principles of Religion and morality
have an unhappy influence on the mind of our youth it is
much to be lamented that parents should neglect the best
interest of their Rising offspring for the vanities of this
perishing World and that the ministers of Christ should be
Constrained to neglect the great duty of instructing the
youth growing up under their ministry by the imperious call
of temporal or domestic concerns   the few exceptions to
the general deadness which has been mentioned will, we
hope, excite our warmest gratitude to the Head of the
Church who Remembers his promise that Gates of Hell
shall not prevail against it   the small appearance of Renewed attention to the Gospel message which has been adduced animate our dying hopes and encourage most vigorous and persevering effort
    Wherefore Resolved
    1st That the several presbyteries composing this Synod be

ordered in Conformity to the direction of the Assembly to pay the strictest Attention to the conduct of their Members and see that catechizing of the youth and the due exercise of discipline over them be not Neglected

2nd That the presbyteries in the State of Kentucky and Tennessee When Slavery is admitted by law, take such order as to them may seem prudent to secure the Religious instruction of Slaves held by those in our Connection and also to secure for them a human and Christian treatment

Ordered that the Stated Clerk of synod forward to each presbytery an attested copy of this Minute

The Synod having at considerable length heard Mr Rice as to plans prepared for putting our churches into a better state are of opinion that however highly they may think of these plans they have not at this late hour time to digest them sufficiently the Consideration of them is therefore deferred until the next annual meeting and the different Presbyteries are Requested to Collect such farther information on these subjects as may be in their power the Committee appointed to draft a letter to Mr Hodge and others Reported their Report was adopted and the Temporary Clerk is ordered to forward an attested copy of the Letter by Mr Zacchius Wilson Mr Gilleland was appointed to preach the missionary sermon at our next meeting and Mr Hoge was appointed his alternate The Committee on the Expedience of Religious tract Societies was discharged from Consideration of this Subject and each presbytery was formed into a Religious tract Society

Lexington 18 October 1809

Am^t Rec^d since the meeting of Synod on the 11th instant for Missionary Fund	$227.81¼
Am^t Rec^d from the member from their Stated Clerk including 50^{cts} over what paid the last year	$5.32¾

ANDREW MCCALLA Treasurer

Synod adjourned to meet at Lexington on the second

Wensday of October next at 12 o'clock   Concluded with
prayer

JAMES HOGE   } temporary
ROBERT STUART   }   Clerk
SAMUEL RANNELS
Moderator

First Presbyterian Meeting House in Lexington Ky October 11th 1810

The Synod of Kentucky met according to adjournment
and was opened with a sermon from John 1.14 and the
word [was] made flesh and dwelt among us and we beheld
his glory the glory of the only begotten of the father full of
grace and truth by Moderator   The Revd Samuel Rannells
Constituted with prayer . . .

Synod proceeded to choose a moderator, and Clerks.

Mr Robert G. Wilson was chosen Moderator and Joshua
L. Wilson and Robert Stuart Clerks.

The Minutes of the last session were read.

On inquiry it appeared that the Stated Clerk had not
complied with the order of Synod, which directed him to
transmit a copy of a minute of Synod to the several Presbyteries on the subject of catechising and disciplining the
members in our connexion, and the instruction of Slaves in
those parts where slavery is tolerated by law, and his reasons for non-compliance were sustained.

Thursday Morning October 12

By Laws of Synod

On inquiry it appeared that the Stated Clerk had not
Complied with the order of Synod respecting the boundary
line between this Synod and the Synod of Carolinas and his
reasons for non compliance were sustained . . .

On motion it was agreed that the following orders of
Synod be and they are hereby renewed Viz

1st that the Several Presbyteries composing this synod be
ordered in conformity to the direction of the General Assembly to pay the Strictest Attention to the conduct of their

members and see that the Catechising of youth and the due
exercise of discipline over them be not neglected

2ⁿᵈ That the Presbyteries in those parts of our bounds
where Slavery is admitted by Law take such order as to
them may seem prudent to secure the religious instruction
of Slaves and also to secure for them a humane and Christian treatment,

3 that the Stated Clerk to forward to each Presbytery an
attested copy of these orders

ordered that the Missionary Sermon be Preached on next
Saturday at XII O Clock.

On enquiry it appeared that the Presbyteries had done
nothing with capacity of Religious tract Societies and the
order upon that Subject was renewed. . . .

A Petition was received thro the Committee of Overtures
from the Transylvania Presbytery Praying that they may
be divided into three Presbyteries.

Synod Proceeded to take Said petition under Consideration and it was moved and seconded that the prayer of said
Petition be granted but before any decision was had therein
a motion for Postponement prevailed. ———

Through the Committee of overtures the following reference was brought before Synod from the Transylvania
Presbytery VIZ the Committee appointed to examine Mr
Craigheads Book, relative to the Charges specified against
him by the Presbytery reported, and the report was read
and each Charge Separately considered the reference read
and being proposed was voted upon — by the Presbytery
The Committee Presuming that a complete and perfect
enumeration of All the objectionable parts of said book is
not expected have called the attention of the Presbytery
only to the following Particulars which they conceive to be
contrary to the confession of faith of the Presbyterian
Church and go to establish the Charge against Mr Craighead on account of his late Publication

Charge 1ˢᵗ We charge him with denying, & vilifying
the real agency of the Spirit in Regeneration and in produc-

tion of faith and Sanctification in general   see Page 4,6,7,
8,11,17,21,26,46,53,72,88.

Charge 2   We Charge him with denying and vilifying
and misrepresenting the doctrine of divine foreordination
and Sovereignty and election   See Page 13,28,45,46, 62,
86,87,89

Charge 3ʳᵈ We charge him with denying and vilifying the
doctrine of Love to God and his law from a principle of
virtue and Teaching that the Selfish Principle of interest
Produces christian Obedience which [is] acceptable to God
See 17,20,50,69,73

Charge 4ᵗʰ We Charge him with perverting the doctrine
of Faith in Destroying the difference between an evangelical
faith and that which devils and Wicked Men may have of
divine realities See 12,26,69.

Charge 5ᵗʰ We Charge him with perverting, abusing and
mistaking the definition description and real Sentiments of
the preachers and Writers of our Connexion upon the Subject of faith and regeneration   Page 15,20,24,37,39,45,
51, 54,57,58,59,60,63,68,69,70,74

Charge 6ᵗʰ We Charge him with false Coloring of facts
which Transpired in Synod and the Commission of Synod
Page 56,61,62.   Presbytery having maturely deliberated
with [the] Case Mr Craighead . . . and having Particularly Attended to each Charge with the Reference, supposed
to establish them, together with Statement Given by Several
Members of this Presbytery relative to the last charge were
of opinion that all the charges are Sufficiently established
and it is the Judgment of this Presbytery that mr Craighead ought to be Suspended but as it [is] required that a
Synod be consulted in such cases it was agreed that this
matter be laid before the ensuing Synod and request them
to adjudicate upon his case or do whatever in their Wisdom,
they may think proper

Through the Committee of Overtures the following
queries was laid before Synod

1ˢᵗ is the doctrine of an equal provision being made for

the Elect and non-elect in redemption agreeable to our Confession of faith . . .

2nd Does the idea of the infinitely Sufficient nature of the Atonement Justify the members of our Church in opposing the doctrine of Particular redemption

3   Is it not the duty of Presbyteries to test trial sermons by the confession of faith of the Presbyterian Church

Friday Morning, Oct. 13, 1810

The Synod took under Consideration the reference from the Transylvania Presbytery Concerning the Rev Thomas B Craighead and on Motion the following was adopted Viz it is with Regret the Synod have noticed the disorderly and Contumacious Conduct of the Rev Thomas B Craighead in Publishing a sermon on regeneration. Stated to be in Substance The Same he Preached before this Synod at a former Meeting and for which he was Solemnly Censured and Cautioned to be more careful in future . . . not to propagate such pernicious Sentiments and he having notwithstanding the most tender and affectionate treatment of the Synod and Contrary to their advice and Expectations, gone on more openly and extensively to diffuse his error the Synod were of opinion that his offence was greatly exaggerated and merited the Highest Censure   Synod then Proceeded to enquire into the proceedings of the Transylvania Presbytery relative to mr Craigheads case and were of opinion that that Presbytery had acted with becoming zeal and Promptness and in Preparing the business for a Speedy issue and the Presbytery having given it as their Judgment, that the Said Thomas B Craighead ought to be Suspended yet thinking it most advisable and agreeable to discipline to Consult the Synod and having requested their adjudication on the case therefore resolved that this Synod do accord with the Judgment of Transylvania Presbytery VIZ that the Said Thomas B Craighead ought to be Suspended as we do hereby Pronounce him Suspended from the exercise of the office of the Gospel Ministry and he is farther cited to appear before Presbytery of which he may be a member at their next Session and there make a Solemn recantation of those errors with which he is Charged otherwise, it is the instruction and direction of this Synod to that Presbytery that he ought to be deposed without delay

Synod proceeded to Consider the queries laid before them by the Committee of Overtures on yesterday and after deliberation they Answered the first in the negative refused to answer the second and Answered the third in the Affirmative

The Synod resumed the Consideration of the Petition from Transylvania Presbytery, Praying to be divided into three Presbyteries and the Prayer of said Petition Granted as follows VIZ that one Presbytery be known by the name of West Tennessee lying South of a line beginning at the mouth of Tennessee River, thence up, and with Said river to the place where the State line Crosses it thence with Said Line to the Place where it Crosses the Cumberland River thence up and with Said river to the Place where line again Crosses it . . . thence with said line to the Place it meets with the Western boundary of Union Presbytery and thence Southerly With Said boundary and that the members within said bounds VIZ Mess- James W Stevenson, Duncan, Brown, Samuel Donald, and Samuel Hodge, hold their first Meeting on the third Wensday in November Next Bethesda [sic], x x x x x x x And that the Revd James W. Stevenson, or in case of his absence the Senior member Present open the Presbytery with a sermon and Preside until a new Moderator be Chosen and afterward to meet on their own adjournment

2nd that the Second Presbytery be known by the name of Muhlenburg lying north of the first mentioned line and south of a line beginning at the mouth of Salt River thence to the mouth of Big Baum River, thence up with the east fork of little Barren thence up With Green River to the mouth of little Barren River thence a direct line to the Western boundary of Pulaski thence with said boundary to the Cumberland River thence south to the State Line and that the members within Said boundaries VIZ Messrs Terah Tamplin, James McGready, James Balch, Thomas

B. Craighead, William Hodge, John Howe William McGee, William Dicky, and Thomas Nelson, hold their first meeting at Mount Carmel Church on the first Tuesday in april next which meeting Shall be opened With a Sermon by the Rev Terah Tamplin or in his case of Absence Senior member Present who Shall Preside till a new moderator be chosen and afterwards meet on their own adjournments that the third Presbytery be known by the name of Transylvania including all that tract of Country lying between the last mentioned line and the Kentucky River and that Said Presbytery meet on their own adjournment already made . . .

The Committee of Overtures laid before Synod a petition from the Washington Presbytery Praying a division of Said Presbytery by a line which bounds the Virginia Military reserve Westward and from the mouth of the little miami by the ohio River to the Mouth of Licking and that the members of east of said line Continue to be the Washington Presbytery and meet on their own adjournment Already made and that the Revd Robert G Wilson be the moderator until a new moderator be Chosen Also that the members west of said line be a Presbytery known by the name of Miame whose first Meeting shall be held at Dicks — Creek Meeting house on the friday before the third Sabbath in November next which meeting shall be opened with a sermon by the Revd Joshua L. Wilson or in case of his absence the Senior member present who shall preside until a new moderator be Chosen and afterwards the Presbytery aforesaid are to meet on their own adjournment

The Committee of Overtures laid before Synod a petition from the Session of Flemingsburg and Johnstone fork Congregation Praying that they may be Placed under the care of the Presbytery of West Lexington which was granted

The Committee of Overtures also laid before Synod a Paper Containing a Plan for the diffusion of Religious instruction and the formation of Societies in Places where the Gospel is not Statedly Preached

Saturday Oct. 14, 1810.

Messrs Lyle and Finly were appointed a Committee to take under Consideration the Plan relative to missions and to Report on Monday next whereas it appears that the reference Respecting baptized Persons from the Presbytery of West Lexington to this Synod at their last Session and by synod referred to the General Assembly has not been entered upon the Records and forwarded to the General Assembly therefore ordered that the said reference be entered upon the records and forwarded to the next General Assembly which is as follows xxxxx The following Ecclesiastic case from the Session of the Parris church was laid before Presbytery being deeply Affected with the Progress of vice and immorality in our country and viewing with concern its ensnaring influence upon our rising youth, having resolved upon all occasions to lay before our baptized members not in communion but arrived at the years of maturity their duty to use means to impress their minds with the Claim the Church has upon them but having some difficulty what steps we should take with disorderly and Contumacious members, desirous that the church should profess uniformity of sentiment and practice in this case do earnestly request opinion of Presbytery on this Point Whereas Presbytery upon deliberating on said case viewed it as one of great concern and general interest to the church therefore agreed and they do hereby agree to refer it to the decision of the Synod at their next annual meeting

Resolved that this afternoon be spent in a free Conversation on the state of Religion in our bounds

Mr Gilleland delivered a missionary Sermon on Psalm 41.1st (first clause) blessed is he that Considereth the Poor —— $82.62cts, were collected for missionary Purposes

Monday, Oct. 16, 1810.

The Committee appointed to report upon the Plan Overtured respecting missions laid their report before Synod which was recommitted for Amendment and that the Committee might have instructions, it was agreed that Synod Consider and express their mind upon each question Contained in said Plan After Considering each question the Committee was discharged from further Consideration of this Plan and each Presbytery was directed to take such order as they may think Proper respecting vacancies & destitute settlements Within their bound

The Treasurer laid his report before Synod from which it appeared that since the last meeting he had received the sum of $225 14cent for Missionary Purposes

The Synod resumed the Consideration of the Plan for a Stated Missionary and after deliberation agreed to strike out the whole of Said Plan except that Part contained in the following Question which was respectfully Submitted to the Attention of the General Assembly would it not be Proper for a Stated missionary to be Settled Somewhere in the Western Country (Say on the Wabash) and for him to be constantly Employed in the Missionary service

Resolved that the unfinished business of Transylvania Presbytery which respects Persons now within bounds of Muhlenburg Presbytery in Particular that the case of Mr Thomas B Craighead, and the case of Mr William McGee, be transmitted to said Presbytery, and they are authorized to take up and determine said business according to our Book of discipline and that the Clerk be appointed to give an attested copy of this resolution to some member of Muhlenburg Presbytery now Present

Ordered that the Stated Clerk of Transylvania Presbytery furnish the Moderator of Muhlenberg Presbytery with an Authentic copy of All the documents relative to the unfinished business, falling in the hands of that Presbytery xxx

Synod Met at Mount hope according to adjournment and Constituted with Prayer

The Committee appointed to Condense the narrative obtained in the free Conversation made their report which being Amended was adopted as follows VIZ the Synod having heard from its members a Circumstantial account of the State of religion within their bounds are of opinion that through the Course of the last year the cause of God and religion have in General been Progressive In those portions of our Country which have regular administration of the Gospel ordinances and in those vacant Congregations Visited by the Missionaries and Supplied from our Presbyteries there appears a Gradual advancement in knowledge and in increased Attention and respect to divine instructions in various Parts of our bounds to which the Synod extended their enquiries new Churches are forming and those Already formed, are receiving additional members. It is with great pleasure we state that even from the partial reports made, more than 250 members have been taken into the church under our care. Tho' we cannot note anything like a general revival of religion, yet in some parts there have been visible evidences of the Divine Power in leading both the aged and the young to a sense of their duty, and in reclaiming some from the fatal influences of infidelity. It was with great pleasure the Synod received information that the influence of the Schismatics in several parts of our bounds had considerably diminished, and that many who had united with them had returned to order. For these great blessings let God be praised. Yet notwithstanding these displays of the divine love and mercy, we have too many instances of human weakness, depravity and vice. The sincere worshipers of God, compared with the irreligious, are but few. The important duties of religion in many parts are neglected, and in others but partially attended to. The Synod have also to deplore a disposition still existing in some to depart from the truth and to countenance schism. They also lament the profanation of the sacred name of Jehovah, the violation of the sabbath debasing intemperance in the use of ardent spirits, and in inordinate attachment to the things of this world. they farther lament that where the Situation of many affords opportunity for religious instruction they are disposed to neglect that blessing But above all we deplore the prevalence of unbelief that the state of mind which is enmity against God and reproaches redeeming Love

On Motion resolved that the committee appointed to

make out a Synodical report be Discharged and that the Stated Clerk transmit to the General Assembly as Perfect a report as the documents in his hands will enable him to make

Resolved that the Stated Clerk be allowed $10.00 for his services in the past year

The Synod then adjourned to meet in the first Presbyterian Meeting House in Lexington Kentucky on the Second Wensday of October next XII OClock

Concluded with Prayer

ROBERT G WILSON. Moderator

JOSHUA L. WILSON ⎫
and   ⎬ Clerk
ROBERT STUART   ⎭ pro Tempore

May 21ˢᵗ 1811

Approved thus far by the General Assembly
ELIPH. NOTT Moderator

CHAPTER IX

SESSION RECORDS OF SOME FRONTIER PRESBYTERIAN CHURCHES

1. United Congregation of Cincinnati and Columbia, in the Miami Purchase, 1790-1795.
2. Duck Creek Church, Ohio, 1815-1847.
3. Sessional Record of the First Presbyterian Church of Murfreesboro, Tennessee, 1812-1829.
4. Sessional Records of New Providence Church, Kentucky, 1822-1823.

INTRODUCTION

[The church session consists of the pastor (or pastors) and the ruling elders of a particular congregation. The pastor always acts as moderator at meetings. The church session is responsible for the spiritual government of the congregation. To this end, it has power to inquire concerning the Christian conduct of the members of the church; to summon and examine the accused and witnesses; to admonish, suspend or exclude from the sacraments offenders deserving such censure; to receive members into the church; to inaugurate measures for promoting the spiritual welfare of the congregation; and to appoint delegates to the higher judicatories of the church. The session is expected to keep an accurate record of its proceedings, of baptisms, marriages, new members, deaths, persons admitted to the Lord's table and of names removed from the church roll by dismissal or otherwise.[1]

The extracts from session records here given are illustrative of the normal functioning of the local judicatory in Presbyterian churches on the frontier. They are taken from the session records of the following churches: (1) The United Congregations of Cincinnati and Columbia, organized in 1790, this being the first Presbyterian church north of the Ohio; (2) Duck Creek Presbyterian Church, organized in 1796 as the continuation of a part of the former United Congregations of Cincinnati and Columbia; (3) First Presbyterian Church of Murfreesboro, Tennessee, organized in 1812

[1] See the *Presbyterian Confession of Faith*, 1821, pp. 354-357.

by Rev. Robert Henderson; and (4) New Providence Church, Kentucky, organized in 1785 by Rev. David Rice.]

I. REGISTER FOR THE UNITED CONGREGATIONS OF CINCINNATI AND COLUMBIA, IN THE MIAMI PURCHASE, 1790-1795

Congregations: when and how formed

In October, 1790, the Rev. David Rice, of Transylvania Presbytery, Kentucky, visited Cincinnati and Columbia, and before his return, constituted a church composed of the following members, viz.,[2]

Cincinnati— Daniel Ketchel—   Dec. 6—1790 decd.
          Jacob Reeder—   Elder and deacon.

          Joseph Reeder.
          Annie Reeder.
          Samuel Serin.
Columbia— Sarah Serin.
          Jonathan Tichenor.
          Isaac Morris.

We, the subscribers, inhabitants of the Miami country, earnestly

[2] In his *Historical Discourse* delivered on the fiftieth anniversary of the Presbytery of Cincinnati Rev. J. G. Montfort makes the following statement:

Tradition says that David Rice organized the first church of Cincinnati in October, 1790. He seems to have been here soon after Mr. Kemper's first visit. The organization, however, was not properly so called. Mr. Kemper, in a letter to the Rev. Dr. Romeyn, of New York, says he formed "an organized church composed of six males and two females, in Columbia and Cincinnati. The Church was one for the two places." He states he was ordained, in 1792, its pastor, though still unorganized, because they thought the number of male members too small to select a promising session. The church lying in the seat of war, and being every way circumscribed in circumstances, progressed slowly, and there were only nineteen adult male members on the 5th of September, 1793, when, they all being present, "unanimously elected out of their number five ruling elders and two deacons." In the same letter Mr. Kemper says of the formation of the church: "I had a few objections, from the beginning, though I passed them over. The chief of these was, they were formed on a written agreement, only expressing the name of the church and church government, in a compendious way, without any reference made in it to the confession of faith, and I think without the members having a sufficient knowledge of that book."

(The foregoing is found in *Presbyterian Pamphlets*, Durrett Collection, III, No. 44.)

imploring the divine presence and blessing, do this 16th day of October 1790, voluntarily asociate ourselves together in a religious society or church, for the purpose of worshipping God, and mutually promoting our own and others spiritual edification, on the following principles. viz.

1. A church is a society of Christians, voluntarily asociated together, for the worship of God, and spiritual improvement & usefulness.

2. A visible church consists of visible or apparent christians.

3. The children of visible christians are members of the visible church, though in a state of minority.

4. A visible christian is one, who understands the doctrines of the Christian religion, is acquainted with a work of God's Spirit in effectual calling, professes repentance from dead works, and faith in our Lord Jesus Christ, and subjection to him as a king; and whose life and conversation corresponds with his profession.

5. Sealing ordinances ought not to be administered to such as are not visible christians.

6. A charitable allowance ought to be made for such, whose natural abilities are weak, or who have not enjoyed good opportunities of religious instruction, when they appear to be humble and sincere.

7. Children and youth, descended from church members, though not admitted to all the privileges of the church, are entitled to the instructions of the church, and subjected to its discipline.

. . .

In June, 1791, Mr. James Kemper,[3] probationer under

[3] James Kemper was born on November 23, 1754, at Cedar Grove, Warrenton, Fauquier (then Prince William) County, Virginia. He was reared in the Episcopal church, the church of his parents. Beginning married life in 1772 as a farmer, he soon added the duties of a school-teacher. His reading led him into the Presbyterian church. In it his fifteen children were baptized. He studied engineering and became a surveyor, but in April, 1785, he went to Kentucky to "read divinity" under David Rice. Kemper became the teacher in Rice's log-cabin grammar school the next month after his arrival in Kentucky. On April 24, 1787, he was chosen Ruling Elder of Rice's church at the Forks of Dicks River, and the Transylvania Presbytery made him a catechist. In this latter capacity he visited Cincinnati in December, 1790, and again the following June. In the meantime he had been licensed (April 27, 1791) and appointed "supply in the churches of the Miami at discretion." He helped restore morale in that region after St. Clair's defeat by the Indians. On Monday and Tuesday, October 22 and 23, 1792, James Kemper was ordained and installed pastor of the Church of Cincinnati and Columbia. He resigned in October, 1796,

the care of the Transylvania Presbytery, visited this church, and before his return, engaged to labor among them for one year, from the ensuing fall. At the close of the year, a call was presented to Kemper, through Presbytery, for his taking the pastoral charge of the church, for the space of three years. This call being accepted, the church proceeded on the following plan:

1. No person shall be received as a member, whether formerly and elsewhere a member or not, but by being examined and approved, as to their knowledge and piety.

2. This examination shall be made by the male members, in conjunction with the pastor, till their member shall be so increased, as to render that inconvenient, and to make it convenient to elect a session out of their body.

3. The person or persons applying for admission, shall ordinarily be examined at two different times at least, especially where it is the 1st. application, either in this church, or elsewhere. . . .[4]

Sept: 5-1793. Male heads of families having before this increased to a number proper, in the judgment of the church, for the election of Elders and Deacons, this 5th. September was appointed for that purpose. Accordingly, the whole of the male members being met, and now consisting of 19 heads of families, proceeded by joint vote, and elected to the office of Ruling Elder, the following persons. viz.

Moses Miller
Joseph Reeder

but continued for a time to preach at the two churches formed from Columbia: Duck Creek and Round Bottom. He was installed pastor of Hopewell and Duck Creek on April 4, 1805. In 1808 the Washington Presbytery granted him leave to travel out of its bounds for a year. The following year he accepted a call to the churches of Fleming and Johnson, in Kentucky. In 1814 he returned to Cincinnati where he was instrumental in beginning the Second Church from a dissenting party within the First. Besides being a pastor Kemper was a missionary and a teacher. He lived until August 20, 1834. See Kemper, Andrew Carr, *A Memorial of the Rev. James Kemper* (1899), Pamphlet.

[4] The lists of members have been omitted throughout this document. At this point the names of twenty-nine new members: twenty-three at Columbia and six at Cincinnati, admitted between December 6, 1792 and September 5, 1793 are listed.

Capt. Daniel Reeder   Elders.
David Reeder
Jonathan Tichenor.
and to the office of Deacon — Col. Oliver Spencer.

           Jacob Reeder.   Deacons.

On the same day, at said meeting was added to the above members of session, the above deacons, by their being elected to the office of Ruling Elder also. The above members of session being publicly set apart, as also the deacons, to their several offices. . . .

Jan: 24; 1794. The session being convened for the purpose of (fixing and) establishing a register of the congregation, and concerting such measures as may be most conducive to the spiritual interests of the church, the members present, viz. Rev: James Kamper, Moderator, Oliver Spencer, Daniel Reeder, Moses Miller, David Reeder, Jacob Reeder, proceeded, after choosing Daniel Reeder as their stated clerk, as follows. Ordered, that all births, baptisms, marriages, additions to the church, deaths, and other removals, be registered. . . .

JAMES KAMPER, Modr.   DANL. REEDER, Clerk

Jan: 31. . . . Ordered, that all baptized minors be immediately inrolled; and that the lists of such minors be given in by the parents, masters, or guardians, under whose care and direction they are, as being included in, and making a part of their family. . . .

Resolved, that whereas the baptized youth in our churches are solemnly acknowledged to be members, and as by that act, they are intitled to the privilege of the discipline of Christ's house, in the same manner as adults, according to their age, capacity, and other circumstances; That therefore all the youth in this church shall not only be intitled to the watch, pious instructions, and encouragement, of the adults, the admonition and rebuke of the church, and shall not only be subject to that natural suspension from the Lord's table under which they are by reason of incapacity, but, shall be subject to actual suspension, and even to excommunication itself after . . .

arrived at the years of discretion and maturity. And that when in the judgment of session, sufficient pains has been taken for a proper length of time, which shall in no case be less than their child's state of dependence, and they still neglect to confirm their covenant engagements, entered into for them by their parents, masters, or guardians, in their baptism, and give evidence of their being void of special grace, that then these censures shall be actually practised upon them.

Ordered that for the better accomplishing the end of the two immediately preceding minutes, and for the more regular instruction and government of the church, the session immediately assign to their individual members their several bounds, within which they shall have the oversight of the members, and more especially exercise the duties of their office. Resolved that it be earnestly recommended to all heads of families, members of this church, not to violate their covenant obligations entered into for their power to comply with them, but putting them from under their own immediate direction, under the tuition and direction of non church members. . . .

JAS: KAMPER, Modr.   DANL. REEDER, Clerk.

Monday, 3d. Feb: 1794. . . .

Resolved, that whereas there are in every society a number of persons who are not members in the communion of the church, who yet merit the particular regard and attention of the church, That therefore all such persons as are willing to subject themselves to the public catechetical instructions, and to the private family visitations and examinations of the church, shall be equally intitled to them, with the real members. And whenever such persons, having been sufficiently instructed, shall express a desire to be admitted to sealing ordinances, and shall appear, after examination, according to the rules of the church, to be qualified for a sight attendance upon them, shall than be received and admitted to the communion of the church.

Resolved, that public catechising, and private family visitation and examination, be immediately set up in the church by the pastor, whose proper business it is.

Resolved — that the session shall henceforward, besides occasional meetings, meet statedly on the 1st. Tuesdays in April and September successively, for the purpose of inspecting into the state of the congregations, and particularly for enquiring into the manner in which the several members of session, and all the officers of the church discharge their (respective) duties. And farther, that as soon as may be, after every such meeting, the whole church be required to meet at a convenient place or places, and that at the first of these meetings, the whole of our preceding records be read to the church; and at every succeeding meeting, the minutes of the preceding session at least, with such explanations and observations on the whole, as may be necessary for the full information of the church, as to the business and state of the congregations, which exercises shall be followed with preaching, singing psalms, social prayer, or christian conferences, as the prudence of the eldership may direct. . . .

Tuesday, April 1-1794. . . . Resolved, that whereas the many interruptions from various circumstances, to the regular compliance with several parts of ministerial duty, and also with the contents of the last minute of the session of 3rd. February last have been great, that therefore, for the satisfaction of those concerned, the above minute, with the whole of our church records, be read to the congregation after public worship at Cincinnati on the 1st. or 2d. occasion of worship there. . . .

JAMES KAMPER, Mod:

.   .   .

Sept. 1-1795. . . . Whereas the session, on account of various obstructions, failed meeting last spring, it appears that in consequence thereof, catechizing has been entirely omitted, and but half the congregations visited during the spring & summer. And whereas in consequence of a mutual agreement between the congregations and their pastor, the connection between them might be dissolved at the option of either party in the fall 1795, and also the connection by which the congregations are united with each other, Therefore resolved, that the minds of the people and pastor be taken on this subject, and communicated to each other

at a general meeting of session at Columbia, on Thursday
the 17th. inst. . . .

JAMES KAMPER — Modr.[5]

.   .   .

Dec: 22-1827. To the memory of the first session of
the United churches of Cincinnati and Columbia, all now
deceased, with the exception of Joseph Reeder, and Francis
Bedle, (the latter of whom has long since joined the society
of Shakers,) I must say, they formed the most pious, and I
may add the ablest first court in the Presbyterian church I
have ever seen. The weakest, and also the least informed
member, was probably Francis Bedle. The remains of a
sound, & I may say penetrating judgment, are yet quite
evident in Joseph Reeder, now about I think in his 85 or
86 year. The two last meetings of the session mentioned,
were broken, and much interrupted by the effects of the
indian war.

I now spent sometime without a charge, untill the formation of Hopewell and Duck Creek, now Pleasant Ridge,
in union, and retired from them after 7 or 8 years, chiefly
for want of a support, as I had done from Cincinnati and
Columbia. But I should be very thenkful that I never left
a congregation without the warm attachment of the principal persons in it.

In advanced life, I have taken the charge of the 1st.
church on Walnut Hills, chiefly that I might have some
oversight, and some occasional hand, in the ministrations

[5] After the resignation of Kemper no appointment was made at Cincinnati
for a year. William Arthur and Peter Wilson filled the pulpit during a
period of dissension. The question of the latter's settlement was not decided at the time of his death on July 29, 1799. Soon afterwards Matthew
Green Wallace came to Cincinnati from the New Castle Presbytery. He
served as pastor for two years from 1800, and as stated supply until April,
1804. Montfort says, "The church in Cincinnati from April, 1804 to April,
1805, was not a little tainted with New Lightism; so that presbytery refused
to allow a ruling elder to sit as a member of presbytery. The church allowed the suspended New Lights to preach in its pulpit, and the people were
much distracted for nearly two year." See Montfort, *A Historical Discourse,
etc.* (Cincinnati, 1872), Pamphlet.

there, the various branches of my own family generally composing the congregations.

1828. Sabbath, June 22d. Preached at Columbia, in their stone school-house, from Exodus 18;7. And they asked each other of their welfare. I then introduced the discourse by observing that near forty years ago, I had preached for several years once in two weeks at Columbia — generally in the baptist meeting house, sometimes in a large framed bark-house belonging to a tanner, sometimes in private houses, and sometimes under the shady beech trees, on the bank of the Ohio River. Our text was appropriate and applicable. I then observed the propriety of making the inquiry at several elapses of society in church and state.

. . .

2. DUCK CREEK CHURCH, OHIO, 1815-1847

Duck Creek Meeting House, August 25th, 1814.

Session met at the call of the Moderator, constituted with Prayer. Members present, Daniel Hayden Moderator, James Baxter, William Wilson, Enos Hurin and William McIntire. Elder Enos Hurin was chosen clerk of Session in the room Daniel Reeder Deceased.

Application for admission to Communion was made by John Agnew and his wife Rebecca, Jesse Coalman and his wife Metildah, Isabella Williams and Margaret Agnew who were received on examination.

An application was made by Mr. William Williams for admission to Communion, who states that he had belonged to the Communion of the church under the pastoral care of the Reverend Mr. Gilliland, but had brought no Certificate and as no other satisfactory evidence was obtained

A charge was preferred to Session by Mr. Thomas Russel against Sally Reeder, a member of Duck Creek Church, for falsehood and slander. Session having considered the nature of P. charge and finding it to be of a private and personal nature and not finding that P. Russel had attended to the means of reconciliation required in the Book of Discipline and Word of God Mat.18th- 15-16 and because the time, etc. of P. offences are not stated, are of opinion that they as a Session cannot constitutionally take it up until those things are attended to, and the Clerk of Session was direced to send an attested copy of the above Minutes to Mr. Russel.

— Concluded with Prayer.

August 26, 1814.

A Charge was preferred to Session by Mrs. Katherine Russell against Sally Reeder for abuse and scandal. Session being convened and conceiving that some difficulties attended the admission of the charge, agreed to defer any proceedings until an opportunity should offer of consulting some of the Reverend Brethren on the subject.

August 29th, 1814.

At Sacrament Collection received $10.25, five of which went for the expense of the elements three for cleaning the house and two twenty-five cents to Mr. Hayden.

Monday 24th October 1814.

. . .

Session proceeded to consider the Charges and hear the witnesses on the following specifications viz. 1st Sally Reeder hath asserted that I am an unlawful woman, 2nd that I live with and have children by a man to whom I was never married, 3rd that none of my children can ever go to heaven, 4th that I am contentious and have quarreled with all my neighbors — 5th that I am a whore and that is my common character.

7th. After asserting that a number of professors had no religion she positively denied having made any such assertion.

Session decided that the testimony of Mr. and Mrs. Russel cannot be received inasmuch as their characters are implicated in the Charges and that they are evidently a party.

Mrs. Reeder being asked what defense she could make to

these Charges answered that she was not guilty as charged in the above specifications. Session then called upon Mrs. Burrows to give in her testimony who refused to be quallified but declared her willingness to relate to the best of her recollection what she knew in the case. Being interrogated on the above charges declared that she had heard Mrs. Reeder speak of Mrs. Russels not being lawfully married but did not recollect whether she gave it as a matter of common fame or private opinion, also that she had frequently tried to aswage the animosities between the parties, whereupon the Session are of the opinion that the Charges are not supported. They therefore acquited Mrs. Reeder from the Charges. Mrs. Reeder requested a dismission, being about to remove to a distance, which was granted.

1815 March 26.

A collection for defraying the expense of a Commissioner to the General Assembly raised $8.25 Jesse Coalman's Child Baptised. . . .

. . .

June 2nd.

Catherine Harper made application to join the church and passed the examination of Session and was propounded and on the sixteenth had her children Baptized.

August 31, 1816.

Duck Creek Congregation met after due notice and proceeded to the election of 2 elders and the votes being counted it appeared that James Lyon had 16, John Clark 14, Daniel Schenk 6, Nathaniel Bryant 2, Joseph Reeder 1, Samuel Peirson 1, Samuel Cosby 1, and it was urged before voting that if either of the two highest will not stand then the next shall be considered elected.

D. HAYDEN.

. . .

Duck Creek Meeting House September 7, 1816.

. . . Samuel McKee having been in Communion here and having fallen into the practice of intoxication he has stood back from Communion for some time but appeared before Session this day and gave full satisfaction of his repentance and resolution to amend.

Also John A. Wandorin was received on examination also Mrs. Simonson was received on Certificate for occasional Communion.

Concluded with Prayer.

.   .   .

1818 April 19.

A collection for defraying the expense of a Commissioner to the General Assembly raised $6.00.

Duck Creek Meeting House August 8th, 1818.

Session met agreeable to appointment, constituted with prayer. Members present Daniel Hayden, Moderator William Wilson, James Lyon, James Baxter, William McIntire, John Clark and Enos Hurin, Elders. Application made Anna Drake, David Wilson and Ann his wife and passed examination likewise Mrs. Noah Harvis produced a Certificate in the words following it is hereby certified that Noah Harvis and Hannah and Betsey his daughters are members in good standing in the Church of Bridgetown and are recommended as such to the Communion of any Church where God and his providence shall cast their lot.

By order of the Session.

JONATHAN FREEMAN, Modr.

It will be remembered that Noah Harvis only was received here the two daughters not being in this country. . . .

Duck Creek Meeting House August 20, 1818.

.   .   .

I do hereby certify that Mr. Hugh Scofield and his wife

are members in full Communion in this Church and they are hereby recommended to the attention of any Church where God in his providence may cast their lot.   Given under my hand this 2 day of September in the year of our Lord 1817.

> Methuselah Baldwin Pastor
> of the Presbyterian Church in
> Scokhtown Orange County, State of
> New York[5a]

.   .   .

August 24th collection raised at Sacrament $10.37½. Six dollars eighteen and a fourth cents were given to the Reverend James Kemper and the remainder to defray the expense of the elements.

March 7th, 1819 Collection raised for Missionary fund fourteen dollars.

.   .   .

Pleasant Ridge Meeting House June 10th, 1819.

Session met members present Joshua L. Wilson, Moderator, James Lyon, James Baxter, William Wilson, John Clark and Enos Hurin, Elders. . . .

> Thos. Grier Md.

Pleasant Ridge Meeting House June 12th 1819.

Session met agreeable to appointment constituted with prayer.   Members present David Monfort Moderator, James Lyon, James Baxter, Wm. Wilson, Wm. Meintier, John Clark and Enos Hurin, Elders.   Application made David Terril presented a Certificate in the words following viz., this is to certify that David Terril the bearer hereof and his wife are members of the Congregational Church of Christ in this place in regular standing and as such they are recommended to the Communion fellowship watch and love of any church of Christ in Communion with us wherever God in his providence may cast their lot and when received

---

[5a] Jonathan Freeman was from New Jersey and Methuselah Baldwin from New York. Gillett, I, pp. 379, 381.

by such church we shall consider their relation as ceasing with us.

By vote of the Church

CHARLES A. BOARDMAN, Pastor.

New Prerton Parish
Washington
Litchfield County
Connecticut
August 18th, 1818.

.   .   .

Sabbath morning October 3rd. . . .
Collection raised $10.62½ of which four dollars fifty cents went to pay for the elements and three dollars to pay for sweeping the house and the remainder $3.12½ was agreed should be given to the Reverend Mr. Slack for his assistance.

October 28 Mr. Baxter put $2.00 into the treasury as Mr. Slack would not receive it.

.   .   .

Pleasant Ridge Meeting House Friday September 2nd 1820. Session was presented with a Certificate by Mrs. Catherine Scobey in the following words, viz., This may certify that the bearer, Mrs. Scobey has for many years been a member of the Presbyterian Church in Chester in good and regular standing and is hereby recommended to the Christian Communion and fellowship of that Presbyterian Church in the town where God in his providence may fix her residence and when she shall have been received by that Church she will be considered as dismissed from this.

JOHN E. MILLER, Pastor
of the Presbyterian Church at
Chester Presbytery of Jersey.

April 22nd, 1820.

.   .   .

May 21, 1821. . . . Session Proceeded to examine their

records of members to know whether some names aught not to be expunged and it was agreed that each member of Session should make inquiry on that subject and report at some future meeting.

August 27th 1821. . . . Session proceeded to inquire into the state of this church. Upon inquiry it appeared that Ann Conklin and Nancy Stars had joined the Methodist Episcopal Church. Their names were ordered to be striken from our list also that John Laymans and wife Lydia had joined Hopewell Church and they were dismissed from us also that Mary Harlin had joined the Reformed Dissenting Presbytery and she was dismissed. Mr. Stephen Conklin through Mr. James Lyon requested a dismission from this Church which was granted.

Messrs. Wilson and Lyon were appointed a Committee to wait on Mr. James Wood Senr. and John Clark and William Login a Committee to wait on Mr. Samuel McKee and converse with them upon the subject of their intemperance.

Messrs. Clark and Hurin were appointed a Committee to wait on Mr. Andrew Baxter and confer with him on the subject of some reports respecting his conduct agreeable to Chapter 8, Sec. 2nd form of Government and each Committee to report to Session at its next meeting. Session then adjourned to meet at this place on Thursday the 6th of September at 9 o'clock A.M. Concluded with prayer.

Thursday September 6th, 1821. . . . Mr. Wilson reported that he and Mr. Lyon has attended to the duty assigned them at the last meeting that Mr. Wood did not deny his intemperance even since a former conversation with him: but — stated that he had laterly refrained measurable hoping that by the help of the Lord he would gain an entire victory that he requested them to pray with and for him: and agreed if health permitted to hold a Conference with Session this day. . . .

· · ·

Saturday morning 10 o'clock. . . .

After sermon Session met and it being late, resolved that the Moderator prepare a report to be read in the congregation tomorrow morning before divine service exhibiting the substance of the above minutes respecting Messrs. Wood, McKee, and Baxter and present the same to the members of Session tomorrow morning for their inspection which report passed the inspection of the members of Session on Sabbath morning and was read in the congregation and is as follows, viz., Session of Pleasant Ridge deem it their duty to report to the church that they have by a committee waited on Mr. Samuel McKee, that he confessed his having been intemperate in the use of ardant spirits but that latterly he had refrained and hoped by the help of God to do so no more. He gave such evidence of repentance that Session deem him worthy of brotherly love that they also by a committee waited on Mr. James Wood, Senr. He confessed his intemperance even since a former committee waited on him but stated that for some time he had been more abstemious and hoped for an entire victory and promised to wait on Session on Thursday last if health permitted. Session have a pledge from Mr. Wood that he will not ask for privileges whilst his difficulty remains which they deem an equivalent to a suspension and on Mr. Wood's part, more honorable.

Also having heard Sunday reports respecting Mr. Andrew Baxter Session agreeably to discipline instituted a judicial inquiry and report to the church that after tracing up reports they have not found any ground of charge but discover that some of the reports are evidently palpable falsehoods: and others gross misrepresentations of his conduct. Session feel it their duty to bear testimony against the practice of handing about unfavorable reports and specially in church members who are bound by laws of church to a different course and enjoin it upon the members of this church in such cases to observe the rules laid down in our book of discipline.

November 18, 1821 a Collection for the education of poor and pious youth raised $4.25 and by the hand of Elder J. Clark to the treasurer.

.   .   .

January 15, 1822, reported by D. Hayden that he had sold 24 Bible belonging to the Sabbath School. Society agreeably to the resolution of the congregation and received $8.37½ in favor of the Education Society.

.   .   .

Pleasant Ridge June 9, 1822. Edward Y. Kemper made application for a dismission from our Church and his name not being on our records it was ascertained by Joseph Reeder a former Elder, that he had been a member formerly and he not being within the boundary of our congregation at the commencement of these records, he was unknown by the present Session as one of our members but from the information of Mr. Reeder the Session ordered the Clerk to give him a Certificate.

Pleasant Ridge Meeting House, Friday August 9, 1822. . . . Proceeded to business and took up a certain report in circulation that our Church had come to a resolution not to exercise Church discipline in case of offences but to let the tares grow among the wheat. Resolved to do or say nothing farther but that Mr. Hayden preach a sermon on the subject of church discipline — and Session being informed that some reports were in circulation unfavorable to the Christian conduct of Isaac McColister a member of this church. Resolved agreeably to book of discipline Chapter Section   to send a committee of two to converse with him on that subject and report to Session at its next meeting and Messrs. Wm. Wilson and James Lyon were appointed that Committee. Messrs. Hurin and Clark were requested to give notice of the above appointment to the members of P. Committee. Concluded with prayer.

                    Signed
                    D. HAYDEN (Mod.
                    ENOS HURIN (Clerk.

Thus far examined and the Session advised to keep the records more accurately.
Oct. 16, 1822.

J. WELSH, Modr.
of
The Cincinnati Presbytery

John Clark, Elder to Presbytery on the 8 April 1823. Collection for Commissioners fund 13 April 1823, raised $5.00.

.   .   .

N.B. It will be remembered that the reason that the above[6] was not put on record before the sitting of the Presbytery was their other business connected with it and it being a query with the Session whether it ought to be on record or not, therefore, it was referred to the Presbytery and it was there decided it should not.

Be it remembered that on Monday, 2nd September 1822, an Auxiliary Missionary Society to the Foreign Missionary Society formed in Pleasant Ridge Church.

.   .   .

Thursday August 21st, 1823. . . .
Mr. Hurin informed Session that he had cited Mr. James Wood, Senr. to appear before Session on this day to answer to the charge of intemperance on common fame and that the notice had been given at least ten days previous and Mr. Wood not attending nor giving any reason for his absence by letter or otherwise, Session ordered the Clerk to issue a second citation to be served according to the Book of Discipline in such case requiring Mr. Wood to attend on Saturday next at the hour of 10 o'clock A.M. to answer to said charge. Session then adjourned to meet at this place on Saturday morning next at 10 o'clock. . . .

Saturday morning Session met pursuant to adjournment, constituted with prayer. . . . On enquiry it appeared that

[6] This refers to several routine matters dated August 20, 1822 and August 31, 1822, which had been entered following the entry of October 16, 1822.

the 2nd citation had been duly served on Mr. Wood and he not attending Session resolved to take up his case and prosecute the trial. Mr. Wm. Wilson was appointed to manage the defence of Mr. Wood and Messrs. William Baxter, James Lyon and William Logan being duly qualified declare etc. paper No. 1 the testimony being closed Session were unanimously of opinion that the charge of intemperance was fully proved and were also unianimously of opinion that he ought to be and hereby is suspended from the Sacraments of the Church until he repent., and further that this sentence be announced from the pulpit immediately after sermon in the church today. Session deem it necessary to add for the sake of understanding the course that they have dealt with. Mr. Wood for some years on the subject of his intemperance in use of ardent spirits that they have sent committees to wait on him and have individually expostulated with him on this subject and that they have frequently entertained good hopes that their mild measures under the blessing of God would be attended with his reformation. They also deem it expedient to state that at the time their first committee waited on Mr. Wood he appeared deeply impressed with a sense of his sin and agreed to stand back from communion until he should give the church satisfactory evidence of repentence and this voluntary agreement was published in the church but recently all their hopes of his amendment appear to be taken away and the honor of the church and their duty as a judicatory they conceive fully justify them in bringing the matter to a judicial issue and further that they directed Mr. Hayden to cite Mr. Wood as above.

Signed
DANIEL HAYDEN, Modr.
ENOS HURIN, Clerk.

On Saturday immediately after sermon the above decision was published from the pulpit. . . .

.   .   .

These records approved with a few exceptions noted by the examining Committee.
Hamilton Oct. 9th, 1823.

FRANCIS MONFORT, Modr.

. . .

August 27th 1824. . . . Jeremiah McKee had previously requested his name to be stricken from off our records as he did not consider himself any longer a member of our church which Session resolved to do. They then found on examination that Margaret Agnew had withdrawn from their Society and joined herself to Mr. Warwick's church. They therefore dismissed her from this Church. They likewise found on examination that John A. Wandoren had removed a considerable distance out of the bounds of their Society and had been absent for about six years without applying for a dismissal and his present standing in society is not known to them, they therefore resolved to dismiss him from their records. No other business being before Session they concluded by prayer.

. . . [7]

Pleasant Ridge Sept. 23rd, 1826. . . . Session proceeded to correct their minutes in order to making out a Presbyterian report, and found on their records the name of Easter Lyon who it appears from satisfactory evidence, had some years since obtained a dismission from our church which dismission was not recorded. Session had also satisfactory information that Mrs. Rebecca Able, Rosalinda Ross, Hannah McKee and Margaret Rodgers had regularly joined other Christian denominations and decided that their names ought not to be continued on our records. It appeared on settlement with E. Huron, Treasurer for Session, there remained in his hands fifteen dollars 62½ cts. Session then received a copy of the minutes of the Synod of Ohio on the subject of a Memorial sent to the Presbytery

[7] The records here omitted, deal entirely with routine matters.

of Cincinnati at its last fall meeting on the subject of Domestic Missions, from the Presbytery of Cincinnati which was read, and the consideration of it was postponed until copies of the original papers can be obtained.   No other business before Session, concluded with prayer.

Sept. 23rd, 1826.   Five dollars sixty two and a half cents was sent to Presbytery to sit in Harrison the 3rd of Oct. next, for Missionary purposed by the hands of Wm. McIntire, Elder.

Approved thus far

N. S. BISHOP, Mdr. Prby.

. . .

August 25, 1827.   Session met persuant to adjournment. Members present as on yesterday.   No business being before them, they concluded with prayer.

On the same day Mary Elizabeth Hayden, infant daughter of the Rev. Daniel Hayden and wife, was baptized.

August 26, [1827] Raised a collection of sixteen dollars and twenty five cents and sent by the hands of the Rev. Mr. Byington to the Missionary board at Cincinnati for the purpose of aiding in the work of translating the Scriptures into the Indian tongue.

Session ordered the treasurer to pay James Lyon one dollar and twenty five cents for wine which he provided for a sacramental occasion.

On the sixteenth day of September, Elizabeth and Rebecca Pierson, infant daughters of Jessee & Martha Pierson, were baptized.

Sept. 2nd, raised a collection of four dollars for the domestic Missionary Society and conveyed by hands of Wm. Logan, Elder, to Presbytery, to sit in Oxford Oct. 2, 1827. Examined and approved thus far,

DAVID ROOT, Moderator.

October 14th Session ordered Enos Hurin, Treasurer to pay James Lyon five dollars seventy cents out of the funds belonging to the congregation for a Bible which he purchased for the use of Sd. Cogn.

. . .

[April] 26th. [1828]   Session met on adjournment, constituted with prayer.   Members present Daniel Layden, Mdr., Wm. Wilson, Wm. Baxter, Francis Kennedy, John Clark, Wm. Logan, James Lyon, and James Clark.   Absent Wm. McIntire and Enos Huron.   Proceeded to the examination of Eunise Swift, Katharine Stickle, Jane Long and Susann McClain and admitted them to church membership. No other business being before Session, they concluded with prayer.

April 27th, . . .   One dollar was taken out of the treasury to purchase candlesticks for the meeting house.

Same day baptized John Schenck, infant sone of Daniel and Margaret Schenck, also Hester Mariah McColister, infant daughter of Isaac and Eleanor McColister.

August 10, 1828.   Session met at the call of the Modr. and after being constituted by prayer, the following persons were received to the Communion of the church on examination, viz.,[8] Wm. Quigly, Rachel Steward, Mary Bayly, Mary B. Parmeter, Rebecca Rodgers, Horace Noble, Sarah Ann Noble, Thomas H. Hayden, Nancy B. Hayden, Hannah Buxton, Allis Mount, Mary Ann Wood, Mary Ann Goudy, Margaret Wilson, Mary Long, Robert Alcorn, Julian Logan, Rebecca Pierson, Walter Mount, John Riker, Wm. Johnson, Elizabeth Williams, Jane Rodgers, Eliza Ann C. Clark, Samuel Pierson, Phebe Gresmore, Charlotte Thomson, Lewis Pierson, Hannah Pierson, Rebecca Kennedy, Sophia E. Williams, Rebecca Reeder, Herman B. Terrel, Lydia Marsh, Jared M. Stone, Phebe Brisbin, Ru-

[8] The summer of 1828 was marked as a period of revival of religion in the Presbyterian churches of Kentucky and Ohio.   As the result of a protracted meeting in the First Presbyterian Church of Cincinnati, 248 new communicants were added to its membership in the month of July.   This increase necessitated the organization of the Third Presbyterian Church of Cincinnati.   See Hightower, Raymond L., *Joshua L. Wilson, Frontier Controversialist.*   Typed Ph.D. Thesis, University of Chicago, 1933, p. 152.

mina Will, James W. Robison, Jane Brown and on the Sab-
bath following which was the 17th of the same month, those
whose names are inserted below were united to the church
— Fanny Stone, John M. Cox, Ann Wilson, Elizabeth
Reeder, Gilbert Scofield, Caleb Will, Samuel Gresmere,
Mary Gresmere, Lydia Quigley, Mary Robison, Rachel
Davis, Robert Brisben, Mary Cosner, Sarah Cosner, Jane
Baxter, Almira Noble, Lewis M. Wood.

.   .   .

Sept. 28th, 1828. Raised a collection of three dollars &
forty cents for the purpose of aiding in the support of a
Missioner to the Penitentiary of this State and was conveyed together with the funds for the Domestic Mission to
the Presby. to sit in Montgomery on Friday next, by the
hands of Wm. Logan Elder to Presbytery.

Examined & approved thus far,   N. H. BISHOP
Oct.4th, 1828.   Modr. of Pby.

.   .   .

April 3rd Collected on a subscription thirty dollars and
forwarded by the Reverend Daniel Hayden to Presbytery
in order to promote domestic Missions within the State of
Ohio. The above money was collected through the instrumentality of the Rev. Mr. Bare, seven dollars and seventy
five cents was received by him. The whole amount of the
subscription was $44.75 cents leaving a balance of $6.75
unpaid.

.   .   .

Sabbath Dec. 14th, 1829. Isaac & Mary Ann Wood had
their children baptized, viz. Ann Mariah and Sylvester C.
Wood.

Feby. 25, 1830. Session met at the call of the Modr.
Members present Daniel Hayden, Modr., Enos Huron,
Wm. Logan, Francis Kennedy, Wm. Baxter, & James Clark,
Elders. Absent James Lyon, Constituted with prayer. Ses-
sion after consulting on various matters relating to the wel-

fare of the church resolved unanimously that this church adopt the Apostolic rule recorded 1 Cor. 16:1-2 now etc. On the first day of the week let everyone of you lay by him in store as God has prospered him that there be no gathering when I cam and for the more convenient management of these charitable donations they appointed Wm. Baxter, Treas. & Francis Kennedy, Clerk, who under the superintendence of the Session shall receive and pay over to the proper officers of such associations as may be supported by this church all monies or articles that may be given by individuals and keeping a fair record of the same for the inspection of the church every year. Session recommend to the charities of the church the U.F.M.S., the General Ass. B. Miss. Home Miss., S. Trsut. Society, Educational S. & that of our State Prison. Also, that on a Sabbath previous to a collection the specific object shall be stated from the pulpit.

Session also resolved to strike Susan D. Frazie's name from off these records by her own request stating that she designed to unite herself to the Methodist Society.

Concluded by prayer.

March 28th, 1830. Elder James Lyon was appointed a representative to Presbytery to sit at Pleasant Ridge on Friday next.

.   .   .

On Monday the 16th of August 1830 ten dollars were given as a present to the Rev. Mr. Morison, a missionary, five of which was taken out of the treasury and the balance was made up by the Session.

At the camp meeting at Mt.Gomery on the 29th of August the following persons were admitted to privileges as members of Pleasant Ridge church, viz., William Logan, John Logan, Patience Parmeter, Elmira Smith, Matilda McKee, Mary Pierson.

.   .   .

Oct. 30th, 1830. Session was of the opinion that it was

their duty to visit the congregation believing that it would
be attended with a blessing to the church. Therefore resolved that the Elders go two and two and visit every family
in which there is a member of this church, holding free conversation on religious subjects, exhorting and praying with
them, and as far as possible to remove any difficulties that
may exist on the minds of individuals, and to report at their
next meeting.

Nov. 26th.

Session met constituted with prayer. Members present
Daniel Hayden, Modr., James Lyon, Enos Huron, Wm.
Logan, Francis Kennedy, Wm. Baxter and James Clark,
Elders. J. Lyon and E. Huron reported that they had
visited that part of the congregation assigned to them, that
they were received with much friendship and met with no
serious difficulties. Wm. Baxter and J. Clark reported the
same in substance. Wm. Logan and F. Kennedy reported
that in their visit John Riker stated to them that he did
not wish to be considered a member of the Presbyterian
church any longer that he was dissatisfied with her rules,
and that if he joined any church hereafter it would not be
the Presbyterian. J. Riker had for a considerable length of
time absented himself from the privileges of the church.
After the Session had deliberately considered his case, they
resolved to strike his name from off these records.

.   .   .

Nov. 27th, Session being all present they were constituted with prayer. Elexander McClintic and Louisa, his
wife, were received to the privileges of the church on Certificate. Tunis Vandmidlesworth and Ellen his wife, having
come into the bounds of our church and wishing to be attached to it, were admitted from satisfactory information of
their good standing in the Presbyterian Church in Montgomery. Betsy Clark and Athelia Drake, were admitted
on examination & were baptized. Wm. Goldtrap also desired to be received into this church as a member. Session
being acquainted with the circumstance of his joining the

Presbyterians at their late Camp Meeting at Montgomery, and being satisfied that he had not united himself to any other branch of this church, his name was enrolled with us. No other business before the Session, they concluded with prayer.

Dec. 26th.   James Clark, Elder was appointed to attend Presbytery at their next meeting in Cincinnati Third Church, to meet the first Friday in January next.

David Lee, Elder attended Presbytery at New Richmond April 1831.   Israel Brown, Elder attended Presby. at Hamilton August 1831.

John Wilson, Elder attended Presby. in Pisgah Church Oct. 1831.

Israel Brown, Elder attended Synod in Dayton 1831.

. . . .

Friday August 10th, 1832 . . .   Satisfactory information was received by Session that Martha Alcorn, a member of this church, had joined a Church known to us by the name of Cambelites therefore it was resolved that her name should be stricken off these records which was accordingly done.   No other business being before Session, concluded by prayer.

Sabbath Sept. 2nd, 1832 . . .

Session being acquainted with the circumstance of Eunis Swift joining the Cambelite Baptist, ordered that her name should be stricken off these records.

Oct. 2nd, 1832.

Francis Kennedy, Elder, was appointed to represent the church at the next Presbytery, to meet in Cincinnati the present month.   Also David Lee, Elder, was appointed to attend Synod at Chillicothe next month as a representative from this Church.

. . . .

Thus far examined in Presbytery and approved with the exception of erasing names of persons who leave the communion of this church and join the Campbellites.   April 5, 1833.

THOS. J. BIGGS,
Modr. of Pby.

.   .   .

Pleasant Ridge, August 16th, 1833.   Session met at the call of the Mdr.   Constituted with prayer.   Members present Daniel Hayden, Mdr., Wm. Logan, Wm. Baxter, David Lee, Francis Kenedy, John Wilson & James Clark, Elders, Absent Enos Huron & Israel Brown.

Mrs. Morison, a member of this Church voluntarily came before the Session and confessed that she had been guilty of the crime of fornication and professed repentance, but the Session being informed that the crime was generally known to the church and that the minds of many of the members were dissatisfied with her conduct, were unanimously of the opinion that she should be suspended from the privileges of the Church until she gives evidence of her repentance, to which decision she gave her ascent and was, accordingly suspended.

The Session was informed by John Wilson, one of its members that Mary Dill, a member of this Church, had joined the Cambelite Society in Carthage and after a deliberate consideration of the case, the Session were unanimously of the opinion that her name should be stricken from off these records.   There being no other business, concluded with prayer.

.   .   .

Examined and approved by Presbytery thus far, April 2, 1834. A. MAHAN, Moderator.

Pleasant Ridge, April 12th, 1834. . . .   The following persons were received to church membership on certificate, viz., John Mahard and Mary his wife, Edward Fergason, Jenny Cameron, also on Examination James Cadwell, and Lydia Ann Vanmidlesworth.   The Session, upon reviewing their records find that several members of this church have removed without our bounds, and been absent for a considerable time without taking letters of dismission and recommendation as required by the discipline of the Pbr. Church, and others who altho they still reside within our bounds neglect the ordinances of Christ.

Resolved that the Mdr. of Session read from the pulpit after sermon on next Lord's Day, so much of the book of discipline Ch. 11, as relates to the removal of members of one church to another and in connection therewith so much of the minutes of the Gen. As. of the Pby. Church of 1835 as relates to this subject, that our members may be fully apprised of our rules of order in case of removal, & not ignorantly subjecting themselves to discipline. Session also directed that the following names be read on two successive Sabbaths after sermon, as persons who by their own neglect have laid themselves liable to suspension from our Ch., in as much as Session wish to gain all information they can before they proceed to the ultimate decision in their case.

Resolved that Session feel bound to call to account those members of our Ch. who still reside within our bounds, but who neglect, or contemn the Ordinances of God's House, and the Session express a hope that members will not oblige them to exercise that discipline which is designed to edify the body of Christ and not to destroy it.

.   .   .

July 26th, 1834. . . .
Session . . . took into consideration the act and testimony drawn up and signed by James McGraw, Robt. Breckenridge and others at Philadelphia, dated May 27th, 1834, and on mature deliberation resolved,

1st. This Session do hereby declare their hearty approbation of said act and testimony.

2nd. We do hereby solemnly adopt that act & testimony as our own & hereby avow our determination to adhere to the principles therein expressed, believing that our ordination vows, according to the formularies of our church, solemnly bind us to sustain and carry out the principles, expressed and recommended in the act and testimony, at all hazards, to whatever spiritual results may be necessary for that purpose.

3rd. The Clerk of Session is hereby instructed to forward a Certified copy of the foregoing resolutions to the publisher of the Presbyterian, No. 9 George Street, Philadelphia, another to the editors of the Standard and retain the Original on the files of Session.

. . .

August 28, 1835. The Church was called to mourn over the loss of their beloved Pastor who departed this life the 27th instant.

. . .

Friday, Nov. 6th, 1835. The Rev. Dr. Wilson baptized the following children, viz., Andrew P. Mahard, infant son of John and Mary Mahard, who was born August 2nd, 1835.

Also Daniel J. Hayden, infant son of Thos. & Amanda Hayden, who was born April 13th, 1835.

Also Margaret S. Sampson, infant daughter of James & Eleanor Sampson, who was born Sept. 3rd, 1835.

. . .

March 11th, 1836.

The Congregation met pursuant to notice previously given, for the purpose of electing a pastor. The Rev. J.L. Wilson, D.D. who had been invited was present and delivered a discourse from Jeremiah 3-15th — And I will give you pastors according to my own heart, which shall feed you with knowledge and understanding. After sermon the congregation preceeded to elect a pastor. The Rev. S.H. Crane was unanimously elected. A call was then made out for the Ministerial labors of the Rev. Simeon H. Crane, two thirds of his time as pastor of Pleasant Ridge Church, promising him for his temporal support three hundred and thirty five dollars per annum, payable half yearly. The Rev. J.L. Wilson, D.D. Moderated the call. The call was signed by a select committee chosen by the congregation, viz., John Mahard, Jn. James Clark, John C. Wood, David Lee, John Wilson.

. . .

August 7th, 1836.

Session met constituted with prayer. Members present Rev. John Burt, Modr., Francis Kenedy, Wm. Baxter, John Wilson, Israel Brown, David Lee, & James Clark. Absent Wm. Logan & Enos Huron.

. . .

Sabbath August 8th, 1836.

After Sermon Rev. John Burt baptized Sarah Ann, infant daughter of John and Sarah Clark, who was born the 25th of Nov. 1835.

. . .

Pleasant Ridge, Dec. 17, 1836.

Session met at the call of the Modr. Constituted with prayer. Members present Rev. A.J. Miller, Modr., Israel Brown, John Wilson, David Lee, Francis Kenedy, Wm. Baxter, & James Clark, Elders. Absent, Enor Huron & Wm. Logan.

William McIntire, William Brown & Margaret Brown his wife, were received to the membership of this Church on Certificate. Mrs. Juliann Walker made application and was received on examination.

Session having finished their business, adjourned by prayer.

JAMES CLARK, C.S.

. . .

Pleasant Ridge Church, Feb. 4th, 1837.

. . .

David Lee & Francis Kenedy were appointed to visit Mr.

William Cosby and hold a free conversation with him on the subject of intemperance, a crime of which it is reported he is guilty.

Wm. Baxter was appointed to visit Mr. Charles Wood who was charged by common fame with attending balls and dancing parties.

It being reported that James Caldwell, a member of this church had been seen intoxicated, and he having been visited and admonished by a committee of Session on a former occasion for the same crime, the Clerk was ordered to issue a citation for him to appear before Session on Wednesday the 22nd of Feb. instant at the hour of 11 o'clock A.M. to answer to the charge of intemperance.

. . .

Pleasant Ridge Feb. 22nd, 1837.

. . .

A written communication was received from Mr. James Caldwell in which he plead guilty of the charge of intemperance and expressed a determination to persevere in that course, stating that he would resign back to the church all the privileges that they gave him and withdraw if required. After due deliberation, Session resolved to suspend James Caldwell from the privileges of the church until he gave satisfactory evidence of his repentance and that the Mr. S.J. Miller read the decision of this Session in the above case from the pulpit on next Sabbath.

Mr. Lee one of the committee appointed to visit Mr. Samuel Grismore and wife, reported that he had discharged his duty in the case and that they stated there were some difficulties which prevented them from attending the means of Grace and wished the Session to indulge them with a few weeks, with a view of having those difficulties removed. Session resolved that one month be allowed them for that purpose.

Messrs. Kenedy & Lee reported that they had visited Mr. Wm. Cosby and after conversing with some time he partly acknowledged the truth of the charge (intemperance) but did not render that satisfaction which they desired. James Clark was requested to visit Mr. Cosby and inform him that if he did not refrain from intemperance, and attend more punctually to the means of Grace, he would be dealt with according to the discipline of the church.

Wm. Baxter reported that he had visited Charles Wood and that he did not deny the charge, viz. attending balls and dancing parties, but made no profession of repentance. The Clerk was therefore ordered to issue a citation for Charles Wood to appear before the Session of this church on Wednesday the 22nd of March next, to answer to the above charge.

.   .   .

Pleasant Ridge, March 30th, 1837. . . . Mr. Charles Wood who had been cited the second time appeared before the Session and acknowledged the truth of the charge preferred against him by *common fame*, viz., that he had attended balls and dancing parties, that he was not sorry he had done so. He further stated that he had never considered himself regularly admitted to the privileges of the church, being received at a time of considerable excitement, that a short time after he was admitted he discovered he never experienced a change of heart, that with this view of himself he requested his name be erased from the list of members, and thought his request had been granted, and therefore, in attending the places above alluded to, he went with the impression that he was not a member of the church. The Session after mature deliberation resolved to suspend Mr. Charles Wood from the Communion of the church until he repent. The suspension was announced in his hearing with a suitable admonition, by the modr.

.   .   .

March 30th, 1837.
The Congregation of Pleasant Ridge met agreeable to a previous notice, for the purpose of choosing a pastor. The

Rev. John Burt, having been invited, was present, and delivered a discourse, with other appropriate exercises. After Sermon the congregation went into the election of a pastor, and the votes being taken, it was found the Rev. Samuel J. Miller was unanimously elected pastor of this church. A call was then prepared in due form by the Rev. John Burt. The congregation promising the Rev. S.J. Miller four hundred dollars per annum, to be paid in half yearly payments, for his temporal support. . . .

Pleasant Ridge Church, April 14th, 1837.

The Rev. Samuel J. Miller was regularly installed the Pastor of this church, the Rev. John Burt preached the sermon, the Rev. J.L. Wilson, D.D. presided and gave the charge to the Minister, the Rev. Adrion Aton gave the charge to the people after the religious exercises were over the congregation was dismissed.

.   .   .

Pleasant Ridge, June 10th, 1837. . . .

Samuel Grisemore, a member of this church, having been requested to attend, was present; and after a free conversation on the subject of his living in the neglect of the means of Grace, it was ascertained to the satisfaction of the Session that this neglect arose from some neighborhood difficulties of a private nature which the Session deemed inexpedient to investigate and at his own request he was dismissed and recommended to the Christian care and fellowship of the Church of Reading.

.   .   .

Saturday, June 17th, 1837.

Session met pursuant to adjournment. Constituted with prayer. Members present, Rev. S.J. Miller, Modr., Enor Huron, William Baxter, John Wilson and James Clark, Elders. Absent, Francis Kenedy, Wm. Logan, & David Lee.

Mr. William Cosby, who had been cited a second time to attend and answer to the charge of intemperance did not appear. Jacob Castner & John T. Johnston who had been cited as witnesses were present. The session after appointing Enos Huron, Elder, to manage the case for Wm. Cosby, proceeded to trial. Jacob Castner being duly sworn, states that he was called on to attend to Wm. Cosbey who was said to be intoxicated. He did so and found him at the side of the road near Mount Carmel Meetinghouse in a fence corner and was so intoxicated as to be helpless or not able to help himself. He left him for the space of about two hours when he returned but did not find him. He supposed this to be in the month of March last. Has seen said Cosbey intoxicated before and since that time but not so as to be helpless.

John G. Johnston being duly sworn, states that he was called in company with the above witness and saw Mr. Wm. Cosbey in the condition as above described. He believe this to be in the month of March last. The testimony being closed, the Session after duly considering the case, resolved to suspend Wm. Cosbey from the privileges of the Church until he repented. It was then resolved that the Modr. publish the above decision after Sermon, Session then adjourned. Concluded with prayer.

JAMES CLARK, C.S.

Pleasant Ridge, Nov. 24, 1837.
Session met at the call of the Modr. Constituted with prayer; members present, Rev. S.J. Miller, Modr., James Clark, John Mahard, Wm. Baxter, Albert Cortleyou; Elders absent, Francis Kenedy, David Lee, John Wilson, Wm. Logan and Enos Huron. At a previous meeting Session was informed that a report was in circulation stating that Hannah Buxton, a member of this church, had joined the Camelites. James Clark, Elder, was appointed to visit Mrs. Buxton and ascertain the truth of the report. Mr. Clark was called on to report, which report was accepted, and is as follows, viz., "I waited on Mrs. Buxton agreeable to the request of session. She acknowledged that she had

left our church and had joined the Campbelites, that in so doing she had acted conscienciously, that she believed in immersion, that she did not leave our church through any disrespect, as she believe there were many good Christians in it, and that she was sorry that she had put the Session to any trouble that she did not know that it was her duty to apply for a dismission or certainly she would have done so." Whereupon it is the opinion of this Session that as there is no probability of reclaiming her at present, the greatest amount of good will be done to the church in this case by disowning her as a member. Therefore, resolved that Mrs. Hannah Buxton be declared no longer a member of this church.

Mr. Hiram Kellog and his wife Thankful, were admitted to the membership of this church on Certificate from the church of Bethany, New York, and Mrs. Elizabeth Street was received on certificate from the Church of Reading, Ohio.

It was ascertained by Session that Miss Athelia Drake, a member of this Church, was charged by common fame of attending balls and dancing parties. Mr. John Mahard, Elder, was appointed a committee to confer with her on the subject and report at our next meeting. The business for which the Session had convened being finished, adjourned to meet in this place on Friday, the 15th of Dec. next after sermon. Concluded with prayer.

JAMES CLARK, C.S.

Pleasant Ridge Church, Dec. 15, 1837. . . .

Mr. John Mahard reported by letter that he had discharged the duty assigned him at our last meeting which report was accepted and is as follows, viz. "I visited Miss Drake on the evening of my appointment, and had a free conversation with her on the subject of attending balls and dancing parties. As preferred against her in the charge by common fame, she acknowledged the crime, but professed no sorrow or repentance, and intimated a determination to pursue that course and at the same time expressed a desire that she should no longer be considered a member of this church. After conversing with her for some time endeavoring to convince her of her error but found no likelihood of succeeding, I left her." The Session after hearing the report resolved to cite Miss Drake to appear before them at this place on the first Monday of Jan. next at 10 o'clock A.M. . . .

Jan. 1st, 1838. . . .

Miss Athelia Drake, who had been cited to meet the Session today to answer to the charge of attending balls and dancing parties, did not appear. It was stated by one of the members of Session that she had attended a dancing party since the citation was served. The Clerk gave notice that he had received a written communication from her which was read and is as follows:

January 1, 1838.

Sir. I will just drop a few lines to inform you that I shall not attend the meeting and that is agreeably to my wishes to be set aside from the church and as to any further satisfaction, I shall not give no more at present.

Athelia Drake.

James Clark.

Whereupon, after mature deliberation on the whole matter, it was unanimously resolved that she should be and that she hereby is, suspended from the privileges of this church until she gives satisfactory evidence of her repentance and that the Modr. announce the above decision from the pulpit on some future occasion.

· · ·

Pleasant Ridge, April 19th, 1839. . . .

Session then proceeded to take up the cases of Lewis Pierson and Hanna his wife, & Samuel Grismore and Mary his wife, who had taken letters of dismission and recommendation to join other churches more than two years ago and had during that time neglected the means of Grace and the Ordinances of God's house in this place. A committee having been previously appointed to visit them, reported that they expressed their unwillingness to join any other church or to come back to this. The Session the Session [*sic.*] then ordered the clerk to cite them to appear before the Session of this church on Monday the 6th of May next at the hour of one o'clock P. M. to answer to the sin of neglecting the means of Grace.

The Session having closed their business, concluded with prayer.

JAMES CLARK, C.S.

. . .

May 20th, 1839. . . .

The Session being informed that a Second Citation had been duly served on Samuel Grismore and Mary his wife, Lewis Pierson and Hannah his wife, and as they did not appear the Session proceeded to consider their case and after due deliberation, resolved that the afforesaid Samuel Grismore and wife Mary, Lewis Pierson & wife Hannah, be suspended from the privileges of this church for their contumacy until they repent.

Session then adjourned. Concluded with prayer.

JAMES CLARK, C.S.

. . .

Pleasant Ridge, Feb. 2nd, 1840. . . .

The case of Sabia Moore, formerly Sabia Wood, who had absented herself from the means of Grace and Ordinances of the church in this place for more than one year, was taken up. Whereupon it was resolved the Clerk be ordered to cite Mrs. Sabia Moore to appear before the Session of this church on Saturday the 14th of March next at the hour of 1 o'clock P.M. and assign her reasons for this neglect of church privileges.

. . .

Pleasant Ridge, March 21st, 9 o'clock.

Session met agreeable to adjournment. Constituted with prayer. Members present, Rev. S.J. Miller, Modr., Fran-

cis Kenedy, James Clark, John Mahard, John Wilson &
Albert Cortleyou, Elders; absent Wm. Baxter, Enos Huron,
Wm. Logan. The Clerk reported that a second citation
had been given to Mrs. Sabia Moore, she not being present
after due deliberation, Session resolved that Mrs. Sabia
Moore be and she is hereby excluded from the communion
of this church for the *sin of contumacy* until she repent.

Pleasant Ridge, August 16th, 1840. . . .
Session having received satisfactory information that
Hiram Kellog and Thankful his wife had removed out of
the bounds of this church in a disorderly manner, not applying for dismissions, and having been absent for more than
one year and not hearing from them or knowning where they
were, Session resolved unanimously that the above named
persons should be and they are hereby suspended from the
privileges of this church until they repent.

Session having finished the business for which they are
convened, concluded with prayer.

JAMES CLARK, C.S.

Pleasant Ridge Church, Dec. 31st, 1840. . . . Mr.
Daniel Huey presented a request through Mr. Miller for
a letter of dismission and recommendation for himself and
wife, stating as his reason that he was about to remove the
ensuing spring from the place he now lived and wished to
join a Presbyterian church where God in his providence
would cast his lot. The following resolution was offered,
and voted in the negative, viz., Whereas Mr. Huey has not
named any church to which he wishes to be recommended,
and whereas he does not expect to leave the bounds of this
congregation until next spring, and perhaps not until next
fall, and possibly not even then, therefore, resolved, that in
the judgment of this Session it is not necessary but unex-
pedient to grant the request of Mr. Huey at present. The

vote was then taken on Mr. Huey's request, which was granted.

The Session then adjourned, concluded with prayer.

JAMES CLARK, C.S.

.   .   .

March 18th, 1841.

The following overture was sent to the Presbytery of Cincinnati by the Session of this church, viz., What is the duty of a church Session in the case of a member of the church, the head of a family, who for years has neglected to present his children to the Lord in the Ordinance of Baptism, and who when conversed with on the subject, stated that after a careful examination of the Word of God, he cannot be convinced that the doctrine of infant Baptism is taught therein, but is of the opinion that the Baptists have more scripture for their views and practice in relation to infant baptism than Presbyterians have, and who, moreover, informed his brethren that he does not wish to hear anything more on the subject because when discussed it perplexes his mind and renders him uncomfortable.

Pleasant Ridge, May 14th, 1841. . . .

The following answer was received from the Cincinnati Presbytery to the overture recorded on the previous page, viz.,

Cincinnati, 7 April, 1841. Presbytery Cinc. in Session. The Committee on the Overture from Pleasant Ridge church respectfully report the following reply viz., That although they consider it unadvisable for Session to receive into the church persons whose views on important points are at varience with our church standards, yet when such persons, after having stated their scruples are nevertheless received, and continue open to instruction and admonition, they should be treated with forbearance. If on the contrary they refuse to listen to the kind and Christian teaching and admonition of the pastor and Session, they violate their engagements as members of the church, (see questions addressed to congregations, Form of Government, Chap. xlll,

Sec. 4, and Chap.xv, Sect.13) and the Session should take such order on the subject as they think may be for edification, and in accordance with our ecclesiastical standards.

A true abstract from the minutes.

JOHN BURT, Stated Clerk.

The above answer of the Presbytery to the overture from this Session on the subject of infant baptism, was read by the Moderator, and after some deliberation it was resolved that the overture together with the reply of Presbytery, be entered on the records of Session and that the Clerk be directed to furnish the person referred to with a true copy of both. Resolved further that said person be informed by the Clerk, that Session deeply regret that he has for so long a time absented himself from the means of Grace in this church and they earnestly desire that he would carefully and prayerfully review and consider his course, comparing it with the Word of God, and the references in the answer of Presbytery to the overture, and endeavor to discover and forsake his error, and return to the means of Grace, and engage in the discharge of Christian duty.

.   .   .

Pleasant Ridge, Nov.12th, 1841. . . .

The committee that had been previously appointed to wait on Samuel Pierson and inquire into the truth or falsehood of some reports which had been in circulation respecting him, reported that they had waited on Mr. Pierson and by conversing with him, were led to conclude that the reports in circulation were in a great measure false. The committee further stated that Mr. Pierson was anxious to come before Session accordingly and have the matter investigated. Session accordingly adjourned to meet in the church of Pleasant Ridge on the 19th instant, to afford Mr. Pierson an opportunity of introducing his case, and attend to any other business which might come regularly before them.

Concluded with prayer.

Pleasant Ridge, Nove. 19th, 1841.

Session met agreeably to adjournment, constituted with prayer, Members present, Rev. S.J. Miller, Modr., Albert Cortleyou, John Wilson, Francis Kenedy, & James Clark; absent, John Mahard, & Enos Huron. Mr. Pierson appeared before the Session and was heard at length in relation to the reports above referred to. He stated that he had been unexpectedly led into circumstances in which he was unavoidably engaged in an affray. He acknowledged that during the disturbance he used *one word* which is generally used in a bad sense and regarded as profane language but stated that he did not use the word in that sense nor attach that meaning to it. But merely meant to convey the idea that his answer had so far departed from the truth that without repentance, condemnation would be the result. Mr. Pierson further stated that in conversing with his assailant, he became angry. This he acknowledged was wrong and regretted that he had suffered his passion to rise. From all the information received from Mr. Pierson and from other sources in which confidence can be placed, Session are of the opinion that Mr. Pierson was unexpectedly led into the affray in which he was unfortunately engaged and that he acted only in his own defence. In the judgment of the Session, no censure ought to be inflicted on Mr. Pierson, but that he be, and he hereby is advised to be specially on his guard in future, and that he exercise a spirit of kindness and forgiveness toward those who have proved themselves his enemies. Session would further state, that in their judgment when professing Christians are assailed by ruffians, it is better for them in most cases to see redress from the civil law than to defend themselves by muscular force.

.   .   .

The following letter was received from Mr. Clark, February 27th, 1843. To the Session of Pleasant Ridge Church. Dear Brethren; I now offer you my resignation as Clerk of Session. I have served you in that capacity for nearly twenty years, I wish to resign and hope you will grant my request and appoint a more suitable person to fill my place. I also respectfully ask of you a letter of dismission and recommendation for myself and wife, to join the Presbyterian Church of Reading. Dear Brethren, I have not come to this conclusion hastely I have made it a subject of earnest meditation and prayer that I might be directed in this matter by the Great head of the church, and now under present circumstances I am fully persuaded that it is my duty to make the above request. Ever since I have been a member of the church, my great object has been to promote her interest, and I have no doubt but under present circumstances, I can be more useful in the church of Reading than I can to remain with you. I cherish no unkind feeling toward any member of the church, and although I may have erred in judgment in some respects, I feel conscious I have discharged my duty in others. I hope, dear Brethren, you will embrace the earliest opportunity to consider this matter, and grant the above request, and may the God of Peace be with you. Yours feelings of respect,

James Clark.

This letter had been before the Session a few weeks previous to this meeting, and it was objected to granting the request of Mr. Clark until Session would learn from him what he meant by the phrase, present circumstances, which occurred twice in his letter and upon which different constructions might be put. A member of Session stated that Mr. Clark authorized him to give the following explanation, viz., by present circumstances I mean this "my Mother now lives with me and she is connected with the church of Reading and wishes to remain in that church, the distance to Reading being less than to Pleasant Ridge. She can attend there with less fatigue than to go to the latter place, but if, I and my family come to the Ridge, she cannot get to Reading, thus under these circumstances I consider it my duty to go to Reading." This explanation was deemed satisfactory and his resignation was accepted and John Wilson appointed Clerk of Session in his place. His request was also granted and the Clerk directed him to furnish him and wife with the requisite testimonials.

Session had recess until tomorrow after public worship. Saturday afternoon, April 15th, Session met. Members present as on yesterday, Wm. W. Wood, Jeremiah M. Clark and Samantha his wife, were received to the communion of the church on examination.

Session adjourned, concluded with prayer.

JOHN WILSON, Clr. of S.

*   *   *

Pleasant Ridge, Sept. 15th, 1844.

Session met at the call of the Modr. and was opened with prayer. Rev. Edward Wright, Modr., Francis Kennedy and John Wilson, Ruling Elders.

On motion, Mr. Francis Kennedy was appointed to represent this church at the next meeting of Synod, to be held in Cincinnati on the 3rd Thursday of Sept. inst. and John Wilson to represent this church at the next stated meeting of Pres. to be held at Mount Carmel, first Tuesday of Oct. 1844.

On motion, adjourned. Closed with prayer.

J. WILSON, Ck.

Session met at the house of Rev. E. Wright, December 9th, 1845. Opened with prayer. Revd. E. Wright, Modr., Francis Kennedy and John Wilson Ruling Elders. . . .

Resolved that the names of the following persons be erased from our list of members, having removed from our bounds and been absent more than two years: Catharine Irwin, Joseph Chambers, Robert Wilson and C. I. Huey.

On motion, Session adjourned. Closed with prayer.

J. WILSON, Clk.

Session met at the church March 26/44, opened with

prayer. Revd. E. Wright, Modr., Francis Kennedy, Columbus Williams and John Wilson, Ruling Elders.

Minutes of last meeting were read and approved. Session ordered the following record to be made.

A Call was made out on the 27th day of Feby. 1844 by this congregation for the Ministreal services of Revd. Edward Wright, one half of his time, and he having accepted the same, was Installed by Presbytery on 13th day of December, 1844. . . .

Session resolved to prepare a narrative of the state of religion in the congregation to send to Presbytery which is as follows:

We regret to be compelled to report to Presbytery that religion in our church and congregation is in a low condition. At times we have thought that we discerned indications of good which encouraged us and then again we have felt that the time to favor us had not come. The attendance on the means of Grace for the past winter has been as good as for the last three years and the prospect of the congn. are at least as favorable as could well be expected under a peculiar circumstances. The church & congregation seem to be in a state of transition & the result is yet to be determined. Pastoral visitation & Catechetical instruction have for the past winter been faithfully attended to by the minister & eldership & we cannot but hope that in time with the blessing of God, some good may result. The monthly concert of prayer has not been regularly attended during the past year. The cause of temperance is stationary. No Sabbath School has been kept up during the past year but an effort will be made to revive one this spring.

By order of Session,

Edw. W[right] Modr.

Resolved that the following objects of benevolence be attended to in the order mentioned —

Assembly Bd. of Education during April & May.

Bible cause during Jun & July

Assembly Bd. of Dom. Missn. August & September,
Do.   ”   For. Missn. October & November
Do.   ”   Tract Pub. December & January
Commiss. & Contig. fund of Assy. February & March

.   .   .

The subject of loaning the church edifice for other than sacred purposes was taken up for consideration & discussed, whereupon it was resolved that the Moderator be requested to prepare a communication to the Board of Trustees, expressive of the views of Session & report at the next meeting.

Adjourned and closed with prayer.

J. WILSON, Clerk.

Examined in Presbytery and approved.

EDWARD WRIGHT, Modr.

Goshen, O.
April 2nd, 1845.

Session met at the church

April 18th, 1845.

Present, Rev. Edward Wright, Modr. . . . The moderator who had been requested to prepare a minute in regard to the use of the church edifice, reported the following; viz., Whereas the church of Christ is represented in the Scriptures as the pillar & ground of the truth & whereas the church edifice used by this congn. has been solemnly dedicated to the worship & honor of the Triune God, i.e. to the proclaiming of his glory & the maintenance of his truth,

Therefore Resolved that in the judgment of this Session the church edifice should be loaned only for such sacred purposes as may be comprehended in this general design — that is, — for purposes either strictly sacred, viz., Divine Worship & proclaiming what is commonly called the

Evangelical system of faith, or embracing plans of reform which have a bearing upon the eternal destiny of man.

And whereas in the promotion of the great & good cause of temperance some measures have at times been adopted not in harmony with this sacred design of the Sanctuary, *Therefore, Resolved* that whilst we recognize the cause of Temperance as coming within the aim of the Christian Church, yet in the judgment of this Session it is inconsistent with the sacred uses of the Sanctuary to tolerate any of those varied measures which excite associations inimical to religious worship.

Resolved that a copy of these resolutions be sent to the board of Trustees & they be urgently requested to co-operate with the Session in carrying out the views as above expressed.

Resolved that the aforesaid resolutions be read from the pulpit & the people be requested to aid in forming a correct public sentiment on this subject.

The above report of the minute was accepted & adopted.

.   .   .

Session met at the house of Mr. John Wood, March 16, 1846. . . .
Session entered into conversation on the state of religion & prepared a narrative for Presby. which is as follows:

The Session of Pleasant Ridge Church in making their report to Presbytery this spring, do it with feelings of peculiar solemnity. We have few favorable fact to report but much that is discouraging. We have looked for good and at times rejoiced in the prospects before us & then again our hopes have been repressed. After our report last spring, we were much encouraged. It appeared as tho the blessing of God was with us. It seemed as the old difficulties were healed but it was only in appearance. A Sabbath School was opened under quite favorable circumstances & averaged thro the summer from 20 to 60 scholars. The attendance on the Sabbath was good, & the attention encouraging. Irregularities & disorder into which some of the youth had fallen & which disturbed on evening meetings especially, have been gradually rectified & the deportment of our youth has much improved.   The eldership has attended with the pastor to family visitation & Catechetical instruction.   The visitation meeting appointed by Presbytery so far as the adaptation of means can go, was every thing that could have been desired; but we have the sad evidence that its peculiarly solemn influence was unheeded. In view of the good congregations that we usually have, & had at that time, we the more deplore the existence of formidable difficulties among us which, to a dreadful extent, hinder the Gospel of Christ.   As however, the state of the church will come before Presbytery in another form, we will add nothing to this general statement.

By order of Session,

J. W. Clerk.

Session adjourned and closed with prayer.

for JOHN WILSON, Clerk.

Session met the house of the Modr., March 27th, 1846. Present — Rev. Edward Wright, Modr.,

John Wilson,
Columbus Williams, } Elders.
Francis Kennedy

.   .   .

Mr. John Wilson stated to Session that as he had been charged with haste partiality & indiscretion in the continuance of the relation & as some in the congregation had at a late meeting thrown their influence with those who made this charge, he is compelled to conclude that he is unacceptable in his official character & that if he can obtain no relief he deems it his duty to leave the church. Mr. W. farther stated that he did not wish to influence others that his course will be the same whether the present pastoral relation be continued or dissolved — he regarding the charge made and his duty respecting it as entirely independent of that question. Wherefore, it was unanimously resolved;

 1. That Session regrets exceedingly the grievance of which Mr. Wilson complains & acknowledges that he has just cause of grief & complaint. As however the charge is so manifestly unfounded, Session expresses it as its most solemn belief that the people could not have intended by their action to sustain it & that therefore, Mr. Wilson be requested to exercise a longer forbearance.

 2. Resolved that the other members of Session entertain the strongest confidence in Mr. Wilson & highly estimate his disinterested & efficient services for the good of the church & would deplore his loss as a great affliction.

 3. Resolved that we regard ourselves as identified with Mr. Wilson in the settlement & continuance of the present pastor — that the charge as circulated is one which bears not only against him but the whole Session & that we cheerfully sustain with him the responsibilities of the case. We moreover regard this charge as one which under ordinary circumstances would require judicial process against its author or authors, but under the peculiar & distressing state of our affairs, we judge that a longer forbearance is our duty & trust that Mr. Wilson will acquiesce in this view of the case.

 Resolved that these resolutions be read from the pulpit two Sabbaths preparatory to what farther action may be requisite in the case.

 Mr. Wright having given public notice to this congregation last February that he intended to ask leave of Presbytery at its next meeting for the dissolution of the relation between himself & this people, & Session being informed of the reasons which influence Mr. W. in taking this step, thinks proper now to take some action in the case. Wherefore, it was unanimously resolved —

 1. That Session regarded & do still regard the settlement of Mr. Wright as pastor of this church under the peculiar circumstances as highly favorable, & that it indi-

cated a season of returning prosperity. The unanimous expression of the congregation requesting the Session to procure the settlement — the full & satisfactory trial for three months — the regular steps in making out the Call — the little opposition made to it in the divided state of the congn., only three or four voting unfavorably — the revived expectations of the people all conspired to show that he was earnestly called & desired to undertake the pastoral office & to give cheering evidence that the blessing of God attended it.

2. That the members of Session regret exceedingly & are confounded at the charge of haste, partiality & discretion that is now made against them in relation to the settlement inasmuch as the responsibility was in the usual way devolved on the congn. & every step that was taken was of course a congregational act, deliberately & regularly performed.

3. Inasmuch as these favorable indications have been so far blighted as to lead Mr. W. to ask for a dissolution of the relation, resolved that we deem it proper to declare that our confidence in him remains unabated — that we cherish the same regard for his ministrations in the gospel & the same affection for his person as we did in his settlement among us, & that we regard the difficulties in which we are involved as having their origin in cases which are entirely disconnected with him & which began to operate before his settlement.

4. Cherishing the same confidence in the ministerial character & personal worth of Mr. W. as we expressed in our call, & having found by farther experience that his ministrations in the gospel have been & are profitable to our spiritual interests, & as we hence desire the continuance of the relation, we think proper to say that in our final action we intend to oppose the disolution. As however, we are charged with partiality & a desire to make our convictions & preferences a rule for others — it is resolved farther that the members of this Session are not sensible of having ever manifested such a disposition nor are they

conscious of cherishing such a desire — on the contrary we regard the welfare of the church as supreme over private affection & partiality & that therefore should it appear that the majority of the people do desire the relation to be dissolved the members of session will acquiesce & yield their preference & regard as supreme the wish of the people.

Resolved that this action be read from the pulpit on two Sabbaths.

.   .   .

Session met at the Church June 9th, 1846. . . .

Session opened with prayer, entered into conversation with Reverend E. Wright to ascertain his views in regard to his resigning his pastoral charge, after the visitation meeting by Presbytery, and he having expressed himself decidedly, the following action was had in the case;

In as much as Mr. Wright before the final vote was taken in relation to the disolution of the relations stated that he had seen no reason to change his mind in regard to his application, and that he was decided and could not be induced to change his views, and in as much as he requested his friends to acquiesce and yield their preference for the sake of peace and a Christian example, therefore, resolved that we concur in his request.

Session adjourned; closed with prayer.

JOHN WILSON, Clr.

Session met at the church September 4th, 1846. . . . Mr. Samuel Pierson appeared before Session and renewed his application for his dismission, whereupon Session made inquiry in regard to the rumor in relation to his being engaged in a fight, to which Mr. Pierson acknowledged the charges but insisted he acted only in self defence. He then gave a full detail of all the circumstances in the case, after which Session resolved that the explanation be deemed satisfactory and the Clerk was directed to furnish him with the requisit testimonials.

Session had recess until tomorrow after public worship.

Session met at the church Sept. 19th, 1846. . . . Took into consideration the case of Mr. John F. Johnston who united himself with this church about fifteen years ago. Some five years since he commenced absenting himself entirely from the communion and by committees visited said Johnston several times, expostulated with him, & etc., He however, persevered in the same course, and has not been to our place of public worship for several years. Therefore, resolved that said Johnston be, and hereby is, cited to meet the Session at Pleasant Ridge Church Oct. 31st, inst. at 2 o'clock P.M. to answer to the above charge of unchristian neglect of duty, and Mr. Columbus Williams was appointed to serve the citation on said Johnston.

* * *

Pleasant Ridge, Oct. 31st, 1846. . . .

G. Williams reported that he had complied with the direction of Session — in delivering to J.F. Johnston a copy of the minute in his case — that he said Johnston appeared to be deeply affected in view of his neglect of duty — only excuse he offered was a fear that he is not a Christian. Stated he would not blame the Session if they now would exclude him from the Sacraments of the church in view of Mr. Johnston's distress and difficulties — and the uprightness of his moral conduct, Session concluded not to proceed to his suspension at this time or to issue a second citation — but to visit and to have some farther conversation with him.

J. Wilson reported he had served the citation on Mrs. J. Kennedy. She appeared to be much concerned about her present situation and stated some particular difficulties in her way. Session concluded not to proceed further in her case at present.

* * *

Pleasant Ridge, March 28th, 1847.
Session met.

Present — Rev. S.R. Burch, Modr.

    F. Kennedy, ⎫
    C. Williams ⎬   Elders
    J. Wilson ⎭

Mrs. Rachel Davis was received as a member of this church on certificate from the Presbyterian Church of Preariville, Indiana.

Also Mr. John W. Caldwell and Eleanor Caldwell from the Presbyterian Church of Franklin, Ohio.

Mr. Columbus Williams was appointed to attend the next stated meeting of Presbytery and F. Kennedy alternate.

JOHN WILSON, C.S.

Thus far examined and approved by Presbytery at Walnut Hills, April 8, 1847.

JAS. K. BURCH, Moderator.

3. SESSIONAL RECORD OF THE
FIRST PRESBYTERIAN CHURCH OF
MURFREESBORO, TENNESSEE, 1812-1829

[The original MS in the possession of the Historical Foundation of the Presbyterian and Reformed Churches, Montreat, North Carolina. Vol. I. 1812-1830]

April 1812

A number of persons living in the neighbourhood of Murfrees-Spring, in Rutherford County Tennessee, being desirous that a Church should be organized in that neighbourhood of the Presbyterian order, met, and were accordingly organized into a Church, denominated the Murfrees-Spring Church by the Rev. Robert Henderson[9]—
Composed of the following members — namely

[3] Robert Henderson (May 31, 1764-July, 1834) was born near Abingdon, Virginia and studied under Rev. Samuel Doak. After his ordination about 1788 he was for many years pastor of the churches of Westminster and Hopewell before he crossed over the Cumberland Mountains to accept a call from the churches of Pisgah and Murfrees Spring. He received the D.D. degree from Greenville College in 1818 and finally settled as a teacher at Franklin. Here Gideon Blackburn, distinguished Presbyterian orator, pursued his theological studies under Henderson. See Sprague, *Annals*, III, pp. 528-532; IV, p. 44.

Robert Wasson ⎫
John Smith   ⎬ Ruling Elders.
Wm D. Baird   ⎭

Joseph Dickson	1	Frances Henderson	6
Margaret Dickson	2	Mary Stewart	7
Mary Dickson	3	Abigail Baird	8
John Henry	4	Margaret Jetton	9
Susanna Henry	5	Mrs. Sameul Wilson	10

Grace Williams	11
Elizabeth Kelton	12
Margaret Wasson	13
Jane C. Smith	14
Isabella Smith	15

During the year 1813 this Church received half of the ministerial labours of the Rev. Robert Henderson in 1814 he removed and was succeeded by the Rev. Thomas J. Hall who ministered half his time in this Church. In 1815 it received the united labours of the Rev. James Bowman and Rev. George Newton each one fourth of his time. In 1816 the Rev. George Newton and Rev. Jessee Alexander each one fourth of his time. In 1817 the Rev. Jessee Alexander one third of his time. April 19th 1818 the Rev. Robert Henderson D.D. resumed the Pastoral charge of this Church.

June 1818 the Lords supper was administered and the following persons admitted to chuch [sic] membership (viz) Joseph Marlin & Elizabeth Marlin by certificate Elizabeth Purdy on Examination. On the same occasion 9 Infants were baptized.

WILLIAM D BAIRD S[tated] C[lerk].

August 6 Infants were baptized.[10] . . .

The name of this Church was changed to that of the first Presbyterian Church [of] Murfreesborough.[11]

[10] Similar statements relative to the administration of the sacraments, admission to church membership, and the baptism of infants occur repeatedly throughout the records and have usually been omitted here.

[11] The Murfreesborough Church was in the Presbytery of West Tennessee which was formed in 1810. Gillett, op. cit., II, pp. 211, 212.

April 1819. The Sacrament of the Lords supper was administered when 16 Infants were Baptized.

WM. D. BAIRD S.C.

April 1820 The sacrament of the Lords supper was administered. Two adults and 6 Infants were Baptized. A collection of $22.68¾ Cents was taken up, which was appropriated to meet the expenses of the Church for the last 2 years. Joseph Marlin and Samuel Trott formerly Elders of [sic] were added to the members of this Church Session.

WM D BAIRD S.C.

*   *   *[12]

October 1822. The sacrament of the Lords supper was administered. Added on examination 9. Six infants and one adult were Baptized. A meeting was held for the purpose of consulting the most suitable means for having our house of worship kept. It was resolved that each Pew holder pay annually one Dollar, to a Committee to be appointed for the purpose of keeping the house repaired. The following persons were appointed that Committee (viz) Benj McCulloch, Alexander Lacky & James Maney.

WM. D. BAIRD S.C.

*   *   *

June 1825. The sacrament of the Lords supper was administered. Three additional members of Session were elected (Viz) Benj.McCulloch, James C Mitchell and James Maney, who were solemnly set a part by prayer to the Office of Ruling Elders the following month.

WM.D.BAIRD S.C.

Semptember 10th, 1825. The Church Session convened at the request of Sameul Trott, who complained of grievances which had prevented him from worshiping with us,

[12] [Minutes of five meetings of the Session are omitted.] The five entries here omitted record the fact that the "Lord's supper was administered."

since June 1824.   Members of Session were all present.
The Rev Robert Henderson D. D. Moderator.

The Session after hearing the grievances of the complainant and his reasons for absence from public worship adjourned to meet on Satrudy [*sic*] 24th Instant at this place.   Concluded with prayer.

WM.D.BAIRD S.C.

[The spelling throughout this document is so irregular that hereafter misspellings will be indicated only in rare instances.]

1st Presbyterian Church, Murfreesboro.
September 24th 1825. . . .
Ordered that Samuel Killough attend before the Session on Saturdy 8th of October next, to answer a complaint of common fame against him for the sin of intoxication and that Wm D Baird give him notice thereof.

Ordered that Charles R. Abbot be and he is hereby required to attend the meeting of Session on the 8th of Oct. next, to give evidence in the case of said charge, tabled against the said Killough and that James Maney, give him notice of this order.

Ordered, that the Stated Clerk write to Mr.Charles Guyger and request him to attend the above meeting to give evidence in the said case.   Adjourned to meet at this place October 8th,1825.   Concluded with prayer.

WM D BAIRD S.C.

First Presbyterian Church Murfreesboro.   Octo.8.1825.
Session met according to adjournment.   Members present Rev Robert Henderson D.D. Moderator, Joseph Marlin, James Maney, James C. Mitchell & William D.Baird ruling Elders.   Constituted with prayer.   Mr.Saml.Killough appeared according to citation & acknowledged that he was sensible of being intoxicated as charged; yet not so as to destroy his reason, or prevent him from attending to his necessary business; but inasmuch as it appeared to be discovered to the wounding of the friends of Zion & to the

opening of the mouths of gainsayers against the cause of Christ, & to the injury of his own soul, he was truly sorry that he had not been more guarded in his conduct; & having promised that he would be more specially guarded against this sin in future he was restored in the spirit of love & meekness to the full communion & fellowship of the Church. Concluded with prayer.

Wm.D.Baird S.C.

Octo.10,1825.

.　　.　　.

Church Session addressed the Rev.J.W.Hall inviting him to supply this Church for twelve months, promising him as a compensation $400.

Wm.D.Baird S.C.

December 3rd,1825. The Rev.J.W.Hall[13] accepted our proposals and commenced his Ministerial labours amongst us.

.　　.　　.

Report of the first Presbyterian Church Murfreesboro. Sept.1st,1826.

Total in communion fr last report	70
Dismissed	6
Suspended	1
Diseased	3
Added on examination	21
Added by certificate	10
Total now in communion	91

[13] The period of John W. Hall's pastorate at Murfreesboro, 1825-1829, was a season of evangelistic fervor and ingathering, a part, seemingly, of the revivalistic wave which swept over the frontier during these years. One of his distinguished converts was S. M. Williamson, a graduate of Yale, who gave up the legal profession and rendered exceptional service as a missionary among the Indians and as a pastor at Memphis and other points. Hall continued his pastoral labors at Gallatin and Shiloh, Tennessee. See Gillett, *op. cit.,* II, pp. 328, 333.

Baptized Adults 2
     "   Infants 30
Collected domestic Missions $1.00
     "   Chickasaw Mission 21.00
     "   Presbyterial fund 1.00
     "   Theological Seminary 133.00
     "   Education Society 20.50

Wm D Baird S.C.

1st Presbyterian Church Mur[f]reesboro
September 1st, 1826. . . . Rev. John W. Hall Moderator. . . .

Resolved that this Session meet statedly on the first Mondy in each month.

Resolved, that this Session educate some poor and pious young man, of promising talents for the gospel Ministry and that the Rev.J.W.Hall be appointed to select one such, as soon as it can be done conveniently.

Mr. William Kelton a member of the Cumberland Presbyterian Church, filed a petition before this Session praying to be received as a member of this Church. Whereupon it was resolved that Messrs Wm D.Baird and Joseph Marlin be appointed a committee to enquire into the moral character and standing of said Kelton and also to confer with him in relation to his contemplated union with our Church and report to the next stated Session.

Resolved that Mr. Jonathan Currin Treasurer be requested to have the floore of our house of worship raised, and certain other repairs done to it. And that he be authorized to pay for the same out of any monies in the treasury not otherwise appropriated.

Resolved that we agree to pay Mr.J.J.Choat 25 Dollars and give him the use of the Pew No.51, for keeping our house of worship twelve months, commencing the fourth day of August. . . .

J.W.Hall,Moderator
Wm.D.Baird S.C,

1st Presbyterian Church Murfreesboro
1st Mondy October 1826.
Session met.
Present Rev.John W.Hall Moderator. . . .
It was made a question before the Session whether the lines of the Hymns and Psalms used in Divine worship be parceled out by the Clerk. Whereupon it was Resolved that this matter should be optional with the Clerk
It was also made a question before the Session whether the bodies of dead persons should be permitted to be brought into the Church, before interment; Whereupon it was Resolved that this matter should be left to the discretion of the friends of the disceased. . . .

Wm.D.Baird S.C.

1st Presbyterian Church Murfreesboro . . .[14]
On the reception of so many as we trust humble followers of the Saviour, the Session cannot but exclaim, "What hath God wrought! the Lord hath done great things for us whereof we are glad." The following Adults were baptized. John R. Wilson, Eliza P.Wilson, Susan R.Cockran, Susan Yandel, Susan Rucker, Martha Johns, Mary Stodart

1st Presbyterian Church Murfreesboro

On the Sabbath following the Sacrament of the Lord supper was administered. On mondy two Infants were baptized and John Wade was suspended for intemperance.

Wm D Baird S.C.

The second sabbath of December 1827. . . .
Miss Nancy Banks and Miss Mary Banks were dismissed by certificate, from this Church to join the Church of Christ wherever it may please Divine providence to cast their lots.

[14] The record here omitted states that thirty-two people were received by examination and six persons by certificate.

Baptized by the Rev. John W. Hall at the residence of William Wade the household of William Tenent. And Robert Bedford infant son of James C and Frances Mitchell.

On the 3rd Sabbath in April 1828 the sacrament of the Lords supper was administered — And the following persons, having been examined by the Church Session as to their experimental acquaintance with Religion were admitted as members of this Church (Viz) Elijah Staten, Eliza Reynolds, Adelaide Stokes McCulloch and Jane Car.

Elijah Staten and Jane Car were baptized on Sabbath morning.

.   .   .

The following is an exact copy of the Annual report of the 1st Presbyterian Church in Murfreesboro dated October 3rd 1828.

Total in communion for last report   138
Dismissed   3
Died   2
Suspended   1
Added on examination   5
Adults baptized   2
Infants Baptized 20
Total now in communion 137
                                      WM. D. BAIRD S. C.

The sacrament of the Lords supper was administered on the 3rd Sabbath of October by the Rev. Silas H. Morrisson[15] Obediah Jennings[16] and the Pastor of the Church.

[15] Pastor at Moulton, Tennessee. See Gillett, *op. cit.*, II, p. 393.

[16] Obadiah Jennings (December 13, 1778-January 12, 1832) was a descendant of one of the Pilgrim Fathers and was born in New Jersey. He was sent to the academy at Cannonsburg, Pa. Later he studied law and was admitted to the bar at Washington, Pa., in 1800. He practised in western Pennsylvania and Ohio, but after a religious experience he studied theology and was licensed to preach by the Presbytery of Ohio, in 1816; the following year he was ordained and installed pastor over the church at Steubenville, Ohio. In 1823 he accepted a call to Washington, Pa., where

The meeting was solemn interesting and we trust in some degree reviving to the members of the Church.

.   .   .

January 1829. James Patton a member of this Church being charged with having opened his house on the 8th of this Inst. for a ball or dancing party — Messrs Wasson & McCulloch were appointed a committee to confer with that Brother and report his views and feeling relative to said charge. Adjourned to the 2nd of February next

WM D BAIRD S.C.

.   .   .

Mr. Wasson reported that he had failed to comply with the order of Session. Whereupon the order was renewed — adjourned to meet on the 1st mondy of March next. Concluded with prayer.

WM D BAIRD S.C.

March 2nd.   Session met according to adjournment.
Present John W Hall Moderator. Messrs McCulloch, Maney, Mitchell & Baird.
Mr. McCulloch reported that he had failed to comply with the order of Session. And Messrs. McCulloch and Maney were appointed a committee for the above purpose. Rev. J.W.Hall was appointed to wait on Col.F.N.W.Burton and if possible to convince him of his error and breach of Church discipline in permitting his daughter to attend the above named party. . . .

March 14th. . . .
Messrs. Maney and McCulloch reported that they had obtained an interview with James Patton as ordered. But that in their opinion [sic]

he remained until 1828, when he became a pastor in Nashville, Tenn. Here he remained until his death. In 1830 he was drawn into a debate with Alexander Campbell. In 1831 the College of New Jersey awarded him the D.D. degree. See Sprague, *Annals*, IV, pp. 549-556; also Rule, L. V., *Forerunners of Lincoln in the Ohio Valley* (Louisville, 1927), pp. 121-124.

opinion he did not manifest that regret which becomes a follower of Christ, placed in his situation. Whereupon the Stated Clerk was ordered to cite Brother Patton to attend the next meeting of Session -. . .

WM D. BAIRD S.C.

April 11th. . . .
Resolved that the following communication be transmitted to Doc.J.R.Wilson.

Dear Brother.
Being appointed as the guardians of the spiritual interests of the Presbyterian Church in this place, of which you are a member, we have thought it advisable for your sake and for the sake of this Church to apprize you, that certain charges are rumored abroad concerning you, deeply injurious to you as a member of the Church and prejudicial to its interests: These are 1st that you have been guilty of intoxicating a Mr. Johns and when he was in that condition defrauding him out of a valuable tract of land.

2nly. That you have been guilty of oppressing Mrs Massy a woman whose husband had forsaken her.

3rdly. That you had disceived and attempted to defraud Mr.Robert McLin in a monied transaction. We specify these charges of public rumor to give you an opportunity of vindicating yourself and thereby wiping away the present reproach cast upon your character. And it is desirable this should be done at as early a period as possible. We therefore cite you, to meet the Church Session on tuesdy the 21st of this month at our Church at Nine Oclock A.M. We have delayed acting on these charges with a hope, they would die away, until public rumor has become so clamerous, that justice to you, to ourselves and to the Church loudly calls upon us, to adopt this course. Signed by order of Session. April 11th, 1829.

WM D BAIRD S.C.

April 21st. . . .
Docr.John R. Wilson appeared according to citation and

being call'd upon to answer to the charge, specified in the citation — Replied not guilty, and for his justification presented as to the first charge, the following certificate.

"I certify that the report of Doctor Wilson having made me drunk and defrauding me out of my land in the trade we made by exchanging the land for his house and lot, is false, malicious and unfounded, I also certify that the trade was made, honestly and farely [sic] and without any misrepresentations on the part of Docr.Wilson,   He acted a fare, open, and liberal part and we traded after having examined both pieces of property satisfactoraly—   That it was a trade of my own proposing and an agreement to a proposition made by myself"—

Given under my hand the day and date above written.
In presence of

      his
Wm Rullege   Signed 6th Sept.1828.   John H.Johns
   X
  mark

Ruben Bowls being duly sworn, deponeth and saith, I have reason to believe that persons unfriendly to Docr. Wilson have made impressions on Mr. Johns mind disrespectful of Doc.Wilson relative to the land transaction between them, and the same I told Doc. Wilson long ago.

Question by Session.   Did you ever have any conversation with Mr Johns himself on this subject?

Answer.   I did, he stated to me about the first of December 1828 that people had made themselves very busy about the trade, between him and Doc.Wilson and he wished they would mind their own business — That he made his own trades and intended to do so, and if it didnot please other people he didnot care — and further your witness saith not.

To the 2nd Charge Doc.Wilson presented the following certificate

"I certify that the report of Doc.Wilson having oppressed me when my husband left me, last winter is false and malicious, for his treatment to me was directly the reverse, he did every thing I could have asked of a humane man and friend.

He bought a bed and furnature among many other things and gave them to my sons — He gave me the pork — the cotton as much as I wanted to spin — the loom and many other articles, and took only such things as I didnot want or thought I could do without — he did this at a time when others had attachments and would have taken every thing I had on earth — I feel grateful for his kindness and shall always do so.

Given under my hand this 13th April 1829.

Attest

                           Signed   Sarah Massy.

  J.B.Henderson.

In answer to charge 3rd   Mr. S.P.Black being duly sworn saith, that of the monied trasaction alluded to in the charge, he new [sic] nothing until the time he was called on by C.T.Bowen to go his Security upon an appeal, from the Magistrates dècission upon a Note on Robert McLin which had been transferred to him by Doctor Wilson, I agreed to stand his security, but finding the trivial amount I undertook of my own accord to act as an agent in bringing about a compromise between them.   I saw Mr. McLin and bore a proposition from him to Doctr. Wilson which was acceeded to on the part of Doctr Wilson.   The proposition I bore from Mr. McLin was that he would give up the officers receipt to Doctr. Wilson; And provided the amount stil due Docr. Wilson which I understood to be about fourteen Dollars was not made out of the receipt by Christmas, that he would pay four Dollars, which was nearly one third — I having stated to him before such a trifling matter should go to Court and that by family connections that I would rather loan one third myself; And in this way I understood the matter settled between the parties and the appeal withdrawn — and further he saith not. — adjourned to meet on the 24th Inst. . . .

                                      WM.D.BAIRD S.C.

April 24th. . . .

Resolved that the case of common rumor against Doctr. Wilson, in the 3rd. Charge be laid over until the 1st Tuesdy in May next; and that Jonathan Currin, be cited to give evidence in the case, and that Wm. Ward, Enoch Jones, and Eli Allan, be requested to attend and give evidence on that occasion.

Mr. James Patton being present acknowleged he had opened his house for a party contrary to the rules of the Church and contrary to his own wishes in ordinary cases, but that he had no knowlege of it being intended as a dancing party until Tickets were distributed, nor agreed for his house to be used on the occasion, further than to sup, as first agreed until the day arrived. But the day being wet and the Streets muddy, he was under the necessity of either furnishing a room or loosing the expenses already incurred and exciting displeasure among his patrons and boarders. And Mr Patton having promised not to be taken in, in the same way in future — Whereupon Session taking all the circumstances into view particularly the indigent situation of this brother and his inexperience in accommodating the public, did again restore him to his former standing and fellowship in the Church . . .

Wм D Baird S.C.

1st Tuesday in May. Session met

Constituted with prayer

Present Rev. John W. Hall Moderator and Messrs. B. McCulloch, Wm D. Baird, and James C Mitchell. Mr. J. Currin attended according to citation and was duly sworn.

Question? Did you hear a conversation between Doc. Wilson and William Ward, respecting some money, which said Ward had to collect for Doc. Wilson.

Answer. I did. Doctor Wilson asked him if he had collected that money; Ward said he had not, but would have collected it, if he had not been stoped.

Question. Do you know whether the money here spoken

of was that alluded to in the transaction between R.McLin and Doctor Wilson.

Answer — I do not — but it was money to be collected from Eli Allan.

Question by Doctor Wilson. Do you know whether this conversation between Mr.Ward and myself took place before or after I had obtained McLins note for the money, he had borrow'd of me.

Answer — I do not.

The Session having heard all the testimony, appointed Messrs. McCulloch and Mitchell a committee to prepare a report on the above charges of rumor against Doctor Wilson.

The committee appointed to prepare a report in the case of common fame against J.R.Wilson a member of this Church, after patient and laborious examination of all the testimony procured, submit the following as their report.

1st. That the charge of said Wilson having intoxicated Mr J.H Johns and while in that situation defrauding him out of his tract of land, as appears from a certificate from under the said Johns own hand, to the contrary, and other credible testimony.

2nly. That the charge against him for having oppressed Mrs Massy is also entirely untrue, as appears from the certificate of Mrs Massy taken by a disinterested person, in which she states, that so far from Doctor Wilson's having oppressed her, that he had acted in such away towards her, as would ever excite her gratitude.

3rly. That as to the charge against him of having deceived and attempted to defraud R.McLin in a monied transaction — altho Mr McLin came before the Session and stated he could substanciate the charge by certain Witnesses and citations were issued and placed in the hands of Mr. McLin ten days previous to the day set apart for the investigation of the case, yet on the day of trial, no testimony came before the Session that was calculated to impress a belief on their minds that the charge was true. Wherefore the committee recommend the Session to withdraw each of these charges: The 1st & 2nd being proven to be entirely unfounded and the 3rd not being supported by any testimony that has come before them.

This report was adopted and ordered to be spread on the Minutes. Concluded with prayer.

WM.D.BAIRD S C

April 26th, 1829. . . .

Doctor John R. Wilson's name at his own request was erased from the list of members of this Church.

Sabbath 27th. the Lords supper was administered and collection of   Dollars was taken up, which after defraying the expenses of the occasion was put into the treasury of the Education Society. . . .

June 21st. S. D. Rowan a member of this Church, having met with insults from a neighbour too hard for the remaining corruption of his nature to bear, and having resented said insults after mature deliberation being convinced, that he had not copied the example of the Saviour, who when he was reviled, reviled not again and when he was persecuted he threatened not, Solicited an interview with the Session — explained the nature of his trials and acknowleged his error, in indulging his passions — and his sorrow for the same, to the full satisfaction of each member present. Whereupon said acknowlegements, and satisfaction were ordered to be announced to the congregation and entered on record.

Adjourned til the 1st Mondy of July next
Concluded with prayer.

WM.D.BAIRD,S C.

On the evening of the same day, the Session being convened by the Moderator at the request of two members and being informed that some of the members of this Church, had violated the rules of the Church, by permitting their daughters to attend a dancing party, proceeded to devise the most prudent measures, to correct and heal the disorder

Resolved that in as much as this is the first case of offence of this kind where the head of the family is a Church member, and as there is great want of information on this subject among our members, that Rev. J.W.Hall and Mr. B. McCulloch be an hereby are appointed a Committee to draft a report comprising the views of this Session on this subject. . . .

Wensdy 23rd, June . . .
J.W.Hall Moderator . . .
The committee presented the following as their report, which was adopted and ordered to be read in public at the close of the next forenoon Sermon.

The committee to whom was referred the question on the propriety of Members of the Church permitting their children, who are under their control to attend dancing assemblies: Beg leave to make the following report.

They are of opinion that the practice is contrary to the spirit of our discipline, that it is in direct opposition to the decision of our Synod on this subject, which declares that Parents who permit their children to attend dancing school and dancing parties, should be denied privilege in the Church and that it is plainly in opposition to the directions of the word of God, which teaches Parents to bring up their children in the fear, nurture and admonition of the Lord and to train up a child in the way it should go and when it is old it willnot depart from it. Wherefore your committee recommend to this Session the adoption of the following preamble and resolution on this subject.

Whereas the practice of Parents permitting their children to attend dancing parties is contrary to the spirit of our disciplin, contrary to the decisions of the highest Judicatures of our Church and contrary to the word of God, therefore Resolved that any Parents members of this Church, who shall hereafter permit their children with their consent to attend dancing parties while they are under their control, shall be dealt with according to the directions of our book of discipline in cases of public offence.

.   .   .   .   .

December 1829. Rev.John W.Hall resigned the Pastoral charge of this Church and in the same month Rev. William Eagleton[17] accepted an invitation to the Pastoral charge of said Church, with the promise of six hundred Dollars for the first year of his labours and five hundred for the subsequent year

Mrs. Catherine P. Hall, consort of the Rev. John W. Hall and Sarah J.Hall, his sister both members in good standing were dismissed and recommended to the fellowship of the Church of Christ at Gallatin.

4. SESSIONAL RECORDS OF

NEW PROVIDENCE CHURCH, KENTUCKY, 1822-1823

[The original MS Record is in possession of the Historical Foundation, Montreat, North Carolina. The New Providence Church had been organized by David Rice in 1785. See account of its organization as given by Robert McAfee in Chapter II.]

Oct. 6th, 1822. Session was convened by the requirement of the Moderator. Conversed with Roger Thompson and Martha his wife as candidates for Church membership; they were received and Mr. Thompson was baptized on the Same day after sermon — — —

Oct. 7th. Baptized four children of Mr. & Mrs. Thompson at their own house. Being about to remove they were upon their application dismissed from this church as members in regular standing —

March 4th. 1823 Session met at Mr. D.A. Burns, — examined and received John Cardwell as a member of this church.

March 9th. [1823] Mr. J. Cardwell received Baptism

[17] While at Kingston, Tennessee, in 1819, William Eagleton was a member of a presbyterial committee deputed to visit, examine and encourage the "Brainerd Mission" among the Choctaw, Cherokee and Creek Indians. See Gillett, *op. cit.*, II, p. 321; Walker, R. S., *Torchlights to the Cherokees* (New York, 1931), pp. 214-226.

after sermon being sabbath evening at Col. Robt. B.
M'Afee's; and likewise were Baptized his 4 children James
M., Floyd C., William E. and Evelina M'Coun. Baptized
also at the same time Lavisiana J., Sally C., William A. and
James C. M'Afee, Children of Col. R.B. M'Afee — — —
Also Mary Jane, Elizabeth Ann & Harvey Alexander —
children of Joseph Woods — — — Also Mary Ann & Har-
vey, children of Jenney, a woman of colour belonging to
Col. R. B. M'Afee — — — Also John Calvin, infant son
of John Covart.

March 15. Session received the resignation of John
M'Kanny as Clerke of session; and appointed Clerke
M'Afee to officiate in his place — —

Thus far received & approved by Presby. April 4th 1823
April 19th 1823 Session was convened by requirement of
the Moderator; proceeded to converse with Polly (a woman
of colour) on a report of her intemperate use of ardent
spirits, she readily and penitently acknowledged the crime
and gave full satisfaction of the sincerity of her repentance
as also promises of future vigelance, she was continued in
regular standing with suitable admonition and advice from
the Moderator.

Sabath April 20th the sacrament was administered previous to which Mrs. Sally Sharp was received into full communion on examination, and the session proceded to converse with Patsy Johnson on a report of her harsh &
imprudent conduct toward her husband Respecting which
report she made all proper and satisfactory acknowledgement with profession of repentance and future vigilance, she
was continued in regular standing.

Sabbath May the 18th A collection was made and eight
dollars sixteen cents was taken up. —

Friday July the 18th Agreeably to an appointment the Session met at the Church to consult on a rumor respecting
Samuel Gray's having invited Barton W. Stone to preach
the funeral of his wife in the bounds of this congregation;

which conduct was deemed by the session to be disorderly &
offencive in as much as Mr. Stone has long ago been deposed
for heresy, and it was the opinion of the session that the said
Sam'l Gray be debared from communion the ensuing sabbath
until the charge can be fully examined agreeably to Form
of Gov't Bk. 2 Chap. 4. sec. 18 and Daniel A. Brewer &
John M'Kenney were appointed a committee to inform him
of the decision of session, which they did accordingly
Sabath July 20th Communion; previous to which Mrs. Ann
Sharp & Elizabeth Storm were received into full communion
on examination. Sabath August 17th 1823 Being quarterly
collection $15.50 were taken up $10 of which was appropriated to the education fund.
1823   Saturday September the 6th the session met present
Daniel A. Brewer, John McKenney —— Armstrong &
Clark M'Afee with the Moderator, to converse with Capt.
Samuel Gray on a charge for inviting Barton W. Stone to
preach his wifes funeral. Capt. Gray informed the session
that it was in compliance with his promise to his wife who
just before her departure requested that Mr. Stone might
be invited to preach her funeral; that he did not when he
made the promise advert to the impropriety of doing so, or
the injurious tendency and ill consequences that might grow
out of the circumstance; that he had no wish or intention
to depreciate or injure the interest of the church with which
he was connected & for the doctrines & discipline of which
he professed the greatest attachment; and finally assured
the session, that were a similar circumstance to happen he
would be more cautious & act differently. Whereupon the
session expressed themselves satisfied; & from the peculiar
circumstance in which Capt. Gray is placed in regard of his
family in accordance with his wishes on the subject agreed
to make no further publicity of this matter. And after
suitable advices etc. by the Moderator concluded with
prayer
1823   September the 15th Isaac Smock and Rachel his wife
were dismissed from this church as members in good standing. September 20th Simon Convert and Polly his wife

were dismissed from this church as members in good standing

Annual Report of the Church of New Providence from
October the 1st. 1822 to Oct. 1st. 1823.

Total		20		Presbytery	C	
					D	
Baptized since the last report	Adults	2				
	Infants	18		Education	C	
Total in Communion		88			D	
Suspended				Theological Seminary	C 10, 4, 1	15
Dismissed		6			D	
Died		1				
Members since added	on Examination	6		Commissioners	C	
	on Certificate				D Miceoun...	
Total in communion per last Report		89	Data Oct. 1st 1823 (Signed) Thos. Cleland Pastor	Missionary	D C Maj. S. Miceoun... Mancy Boice...	

CHAPTER X

EXTRACTS FROM RECORDS SHOWING THE WORKING OF THE PLAN OF UNION

1. Records of the Presbytery of Cayuga (with an account of its relationship to the Middle Association).
2. Extract from a Record of the Proceedings of the Union Religious Society of Phelps, with Records of the First Presbyterian Church at Phelps, New York, 1813-1821.
3. Extracts from the Records of the Presbyterian Church of Franklin, Portage County, Ohio, 1819-1838.

INTRODUCTION

[The "accommodation plan" and the Plan of Union by which the Presbyterians and Congregationalists worked together on the frontier have been considered in Chapter Two of this volume. The following documents illustrate the working of the Plan of Union in a Presbytery and in two churches. The story of the transformation of the Middle Association of New York into the Presbytery of Cayuga is told in the extracts taken from the Records of the Presbytery of Cayuga. The second document tells how the Union Religious Society of Phelps, New York, became under the Plan of Union the First, or Oaks Corners, Presbyterian Church in Phelps. In the third document the interesting history of the First Presbyterian Church of Franklin, Ohio, is traced. Organized in 1819 as a "Presbyterian Church and Society," it was called the First Congregational Church in Franklin from 1831 to 1834, when it was organized as a Presbyterian Church. In 1839 it became again a Congregational Church.

Very few churches were organized under the Plan of Union in central and western New York, but rather under other plans of union "and preëminently by what is known as "The Accomodation Plan." Under this plan a Congregational church joined a presbytery, retaining Congregational internal government, but being in all other respects Presbyterian.[1]

---

[1] Hotchkin, *op. cit.*, pp. 85-87; see also Fowler, P. H., *Presbyterianism within the Bounds of the Synod of Central New York* (Utica, 1877), p. 59.

The Military Tract, in which the Middle Association of the Congregational Church was located, embraced the counties of Cayuga and Onondaga, New York. In 1803 it contained a population of about 30,000. The first settled Presbyterian minister in this region was David Higgins, who, in 1802, became the minister at Aurelius. Missionaries from the Connecticut Society had labored in this section for some years previous to this. Congregational churches had been organized at Genoa, Scipio, Locke, Aurelius, Camillus (Elbridge), Skaneateles, Pompey, Homer, and Nine-Mile Creek. An Association of these churches was formed in 1804. This was the Middle Association. In 1808, while retaining its name and Congregational form of government, it was received into the Synod of Albany. The Association grew so rapidly that in 1811 it was merged with the Presbytery of Geneva and divided into the Presbyteries of Cayuga and Onondaga. In 1812 the Synod of Geneva, embracing the Presbyteries of Cayuga, Onondaga, and Geneva, was constituted by the General Assembly. The course pursued by the Middle Association of the Military Tract exerted a decisive influence over the action of the other Associations of central and western New York.][2]

I. RECORDS OF THE

PRESBYTERY OF CAYUGA

[The original MS Records are in the possession of the Library of Auburn Theological Seminary, Auburn, New York.]

Origin of Middle Association

Although the Church of God rests upon a firm basis, being founded upon a rock; and although its continuance be certain, for the gates of hell shall not prevail against it; yet it has been attended with times of prosperity & seasons of decline. In many places where it formerly flourished it has now become totally extinct; & in other places where the true light never shone, till within a short time, there is now to be seen the lustre and beauty of Zion. In this part of the world we have a favorable testimony to this fact.

Within a few years the Kingdom of the Redeemer has

[2] Gillett, *op. cit.,* II, pp. 106-113.

been established and attended with considerable success in this region. Nearly all the Churches on the Military lands have been formed since the Commencement of the present Century. In the year 1803 so large a number of ministers and Churches were established on this territory as to give encouragement for forming a regular association connection among them. Accordingly, in January 1804 a Convention of the Ministers and delegates from the Churches was held at Marcellus, and a *Constitution* for an *Association* was adopted & signed by the greatest part of the members of that Convention for themselves & in behalf of the Churches which they represented. The name by which that body was designated was the *Middle Association* It was composed of the Ministers and Churches on the Military Tract & its vicinity.

In the Preamble of that Constitution it is stated, "The Ministers & Churches by their Delegates, whose names are hereunto subscribed, —considering it to be a matter of importance, that union and harmony should subsist among both Ministers & Churches of Christ; that, in their united capacity, they may be more helpful to each other; that discipline may be more uniformly & effectually administered; that there may be a permanent body to which individuals & Churches, in cases of doubt & difficulty, may have recourse for assistance & counsel — do propose forming themselves in an associate body."

The fifth article in said constitution is in the words following:

"Art. 5th.   The Ministers & Churches do consent & agree to hold themselves amenable to this association with regard both to sentiments & conduct; and that they will submit themselves to an examination & trial of the same, when requested by the association."

"Art. 7th.   Each Church belonging to this Association has a right to be represented by one Delegate & no more,. who shall hold his appointment during one year, unless the Church shall see fit to appoint another in his room."

"Art. 10th.   No Candidate shall be licensed, nor Minis-

ter ordained by this Association, unless there be the approbation of the majority of the Ministers present."

In the 6th Article of said Constitution it was agreed
"that nothing should be construed in opposition to the accomodating articles agreed upon between the General Assembly of the Presbyterian Churches in the United States of
America, & the General Association of the State of Connecticut."

In the Confession of Faith & Articles of practice it was
also agreed

"1st. That no person ought to be admitted into a Church
except those who give scripture evidence of real friendship
to Christ.

2ndly. That in order to obtain evidence of this, Churches
ought to examine into the doctrinal belief, religious experience & moral character of all those who manifest a desire
to unite with them.

3rdly. That believing parents & none others ought to present their children to Christ in the ordinance of baptism.

4thly. That in all matters of discipline each particular
Church, with a presiding Minister, shall be considered as
having full power to discipline its own members, according
to the rules of Christ. But in cases of peculiar difficulty it
is recommended that recourse be had to the Association, or
some sister Churches, for their advice & assistance."

Middle Association joined the Synod of Albany

It being a well known fact that the first constituted
Churches in this region were some of the Congregational &
others of the Presbyterian order; the first settled Ministers
viewing the difference to exist principally in the mode of
discipline, were deeply impressed with the importance of
a union. In order to extend the benefit of the common duties & ordinances of Religion; unite the influence of good
men in promoting the common cause; & form a barrier
against vice & infidelity, exertions were early made to effect
such a coalition. Daily experience more & more taught the
necessity & utility of such exertions.

To accomplish the aforesaid purpose the Association voted in June 1807 "to send a delegation to the Synod of Albany to meet at Cooperstown the first Tuesday of October next.   Mr. Leonard and Deacon Levi Jerome were appointed as that delegation." . . . In consequence of this measure a letter was received by the Association from the Synod of Albany, of which the following are extracts.

Cooperstown, Oct. 9th, 1807.

Rev. Brethren,

We received your communication by the Rev. Mr. Leonard with great pleasure, & were highly gratified with the object of his mission, which has occupied our serious deliberation.   Blended as our people are, in the same settlements, & holding the same Divine doctrines; it is certainly an object of importance that we should be connected in some intimate bond of union & correspondence.   Such an union would facilitate the establishment of the Gospel in many of the destitute settlements of our Country, by uniting our people in one common cause, & it would enable us to combine our exertions more effectually in suppressing error, licentiousness & vice; & promoting the great interest of pure morality & undefiled Religion.

Prompted by these considerations the Synod of Albany stand ready, with the approbation of the General Assembly, to form as intimate a connection with your Association as the Constitution of our Church will admit.   We most cordially invite you to become a constituent branch of our body, by assuming the characteristic & scriptural name of Presbytery; adopt our standard of doctrine & government, & sit & vote with us in all the great & interesting concerns of the Church.   Deeming the name, however, of less importance than the thing, although of consequence to uniformity in the same body; yet should you be solicitous to retain yours, it will not be considered on our part a bar to such an union. Nor do we confine our invitation to you as ministers, but we also extend it to delegates from your Churches, whom we are willing to receive as substantially the same with our ruling elders; to assist us in our public deliberations & decisions.   Knowing the influence of education & habit, should the Churches under your care prefer transacting their internal concerns in their present mode of Congregational government, we assure them of our utmost cheerfulness in leaving them undisturbed in the administration of that government; unless they shall choose to alter it themselves.

By order of Synod

SAML. F. SNOWDEN, Mod.

The Rev. Middle Association.

On the records of Association for June 1808 is the following minute:— "Mr. Leonard, of the delegation appointed at the last annual meeting of Association to the Synod of Albany then to meet at Cooperstown, made report.   On this business it was *voted unanimously*, that this body acceed to the plan of union with the Presbyterian Church in the United States, on the condition proposed by the Synod of Albany in their letter of Oct. 9th 1807, we retaining our present name and mode of Congregational government.   Also voted, that a delegation be appointed to attend the synod of Albany at Aurora, on the first Wednesday of Oct. next, to report the doings of this body on the subject of *Union*; and that the Rev. Mr. Wallace & Dea. Peter Hitchcock compose this delegation."

The Synod of Albany at Aurora in Oct. 1808 passed a resolution of which the following is an extract.   "Whereas it appears that the plan of union & correspondence, proposed by the Synod at their last meeting, between them & the Middle Association, has been transmitted to said Association; & whereas said Association have acceded to said plan of Union & Correspondence, as appears from the records of said Association, adduced by the Rev. Hugh Wallace & Dea. Peter Hitchcock, who were deputed to act on this subject; and whereas the General Assembly have permitted the Synod to form this plan of union & correspondence; *Wherefore Resolved*, that the Middle Association on the Military tract & its vicinity be received as a constituent branch of this Synod, retaining their own name & usages in the administration of the government of their Churches, according to the terms stated in the plan; and they are hereby received accordingly."

Division of Middle Association

In the records of the Association for June 1809, it is recorded; "Whereas this Association has become numerous & its limits extensive, & convenience calls for a division to take place at some future time, therefore resolved, that a committee of five members be appointed to investigate the expediency of the measure, & the manner in which a division may be effected to the greatest utility of the whole; & make report at the next annual meeting of the Association."

"In June 1810 the Committee appointed for that purpose made the following report."

"The Committee on the division of Association do report, that on account of the large territory over which the Association is at present extended, & the great number of members which constitute the body, a division is expedient & necessary; and therefore application be made to the Synod of Albany at their meeting in October next, to constitute & establish all the Ministers & Churches which now belong to the Middle Association & to the Presbytery of Geneva, within & eastward of the Counties of Onondaga & Courtland, excepting the Rev. Levi Parsons, & the Churches in Camillus & Skaneatales, into a Presbytery, which shall be known by the name of the Presbytery of ——. Also that they constitute all the Ministers & Churches which now belong to either of the aforesaid bodies, within the County of Cayuga, together with the Rev. Levi Parsons, & the Churches in Camillus & Skaneatales into a Presbytery which shall be known by the name of the Presbytery of ——. And that the Ministers & Churches belonging to the said bodies, & being westward of Cayuga Lake, in the State of New York, constitute the Presbytery of Geneva. And that all the Ministers & Churches & members of Churches which now belong to the Middle Association retain the privileges of Church discipline, agreeably to the articles of agreement for that purpose, between the general Association of Connecticut & the General Assembly of the Presbyterian Church."

In the minutes of the Association for June 1810 it is recorded. "The subject of the division of Association was resumed. Voted, to defer a further consideration of this subject till next annual meeting; & that the alteration of the name from Association to Presbytery be referred to the Churches for their consideration."

In the minutes for Sept. 1810 (*special meeting*) it is recorded. "The question for dividing the Association was taken up. On the general question, Association were unanimous in the opinion that a division was expedient. After some discussion respecting the name by which the two divisions shall be called, it was agreed (14 to 2) that we drop the name of Association, & assume that of Presbytery. That the western division be denominated the Presbytery of Cayuga. That we prefer that Mr. Osborne belong to the "Western division."

Presbytery of Cayuga formed

On a representation of the foregoing made to the Synod of Albany at their meeting in Troy Oct. 4th 1810, they passed the following. "*Resolved,* that all the Churches & Ministers, heretofore belonging to the Presbytery of Geneva & to the Middle Association, in the County of Cayuga, together with the Rev. Levi Parsons, the Churches of Skaneatales & Camillus in the County of Onondaga, & also the Rev. Jeremiah Osborne of the County of Tioga, be constituted as a distinct Presbytery, by the name of the Presbytery of Cayuga; That they hold their first meeting at the Village of Auburn on the second Tuesday of January next; & that afterwards they meet on their own adjournments."

Questions decided, & rules adopted

For the future regulation of the Presbytery of Cayuga it is necessary that the following rules & votes be preserved & regarded.

1st. Each Church within this Presbytery, in the important business of settling a Minister over them, shall refer the Candidate for settlement to an examination by the Presbytery or its Committee, previous to his giving his answer to their Call for settlement, unless he shall have been previously examined by this body.

2nd Question. Ought a Church to receive & act upon complaints brought against professors by persons who are not professors? Determined in the Negative.

3rd Quest. Whether those who deny the morality of the Christian Sabbath as founded on the authority of the fourth commandment, are to be admitted as members of the Christian Church? Decided in the Negative.

4th Quest. Is it expedient that a Church without a Pastor, should proceed to excommunicate a member, without the aid of a Minister?
Unanimously determined in the Negative.

5th Quest. Whether a uniform return of the number of the members of the particular Churches would not be desirable? *Voted* in the affirmative; & the Pastors, & representatives, where there are no Pastors, be directed to make an annual return of the number of deaths, dismissions, & additions; the number of baptised children, & the number of children baptised within the year.

6th Resolved, That, extraordinary instances excepted, we will neither encourage nor admit to examination before us any applicant for License to preach as a Candidate, unless he shall have received a Degree at some College, or produce evidence of having studied the Languages, Arts, & Sciences under some able teacher or teachers; & unless he be found on examination to possess a good degree of Knowledge of the Latin & Greek Languages, English Grammar, Mathematics, Logic, Rhetoric, Geography, & Natural Philosophy.

7th *Resolved,* That no complaint shall be brought in future before this body against any of its members but by some Minister, or Church, or religious professor, previously exhibiting undoubted credentials of belonging to some branch of the Kingdom of Christ, & acknowledged by us to be such. *Also resolved,* That gospel steps shall have been taken before the complaint is received & acted upon, — and that the offender shall have been served with the complaint at least ten days before the Meeting of Association.

The *accomodating Articles,* agreed upon between the General Assembly of the Presbyterian Church in the U. S. of America, & the general Association of the State of Connecticut, are adopted by this Presbytery as rules to regulate us in all cases therein mentioned; & the same are recommended to the Churches under our care for their observance & regulation.   Which Articles are as follows.

"Regulations adopted by the General Assembly of the Presbyterian Church in America, & by the general Association of the State of Connecticut with a view to prevent alienation, & promote union & harmony in those new settlements which are composed of inhabitants from these bodies.

1st.   It is strictly enjoined on all their Missionaries to the new settlements to endeavour, by all proper means, to promote mutual forebearance & accomodation between those inhabitants of the new settlements who hold the Presbyterian, & those who hold the Congregational form of Church government.

2nd.   If in the new settlements any Church of the Congregational order shall settle a Minister of the Presbyterian order, that Church may, if they choose, still conduct their discipline according to Congregational principles; settling their difficulties among themselves, or by a Council mutually agreed on for that purpose: But if any difficulty shall exist between the Minister & the Church, or any member of it, it shall be referred to the Presbytery to which he shall belong; provided both parties agree to it; if not, to a Council, consisting of an equal number of Presbyterians & Congregationalists, agreed upon by both parties.

3rd. If a Presbyterian Church shall settle a Minister of Congregational principles, that Church may still conduct their discipline according to Presbyterian principles; excepting, that if a difficulty arise between him & his Church, or any member of it, the cause shall be tried by the Association to which the said Minister shall belong, provided, both parties agree to it; otherwise by a Council, one half Congregationalists, & the other half Presbyterians, mutually agreed on by the parties.

4th. If any Congregation consist partly of those who hold the Congregational form of discipline, & partly of those who hold the Presbyterian form; we recommend to both parties, that this be no obstruction to their uniting in one Church, & settle a Minister; that in this case the Church choose a standing Committee from the Communicants of said Church, whose business it shall be, to call to account every member of the Church, who shall conduct himself inconsistently with the laws of Christianity, & to give judgment on such conduct; And if the person condemned by their judgment be a Presbyterian, he shall have liberty to appeal to the Presbytery; if a Congregationalist, he shall have liberty to appeal to the body of the male Communicants of the Church; In the former case the determination of the Presbytery shall be final, unless the Church consent to a further appeal to the Synod, or to the General Assembly; & in the latter case, if the party condemned shall wish for a trial by a mutual Council, the case shall be referred to such Council. And provided the said standing Committee of any Church shall depute one of themselves to attend Presbytery, he may have the same right to sit & act in the Presbytery as a ruling elder of the Presbyterian Church."

Passed in Association,
attest
NATHAN PERKINS, Scribe.

Litchfield, June 16th, 1801.

Rules of Presbytery

There shall be in future two Stated meetings of Presbytery; one on the third Tuesday in February, the other one on the third Tuesday in August, at two OClock in the afternoon. That a Moderator & Clerk be chosen at each Stated meeting. That a Treasurer, Register, & Committee of License & Certification be chosen annually in August; & that each of these Officers hold his election until another be chosen in his room. That the Treasurer be required to report annually in August. That the Moderator shall have power to convoke a Special meeting of Presbytery whenever he shall think it expedient; & it shall be his duty to call such meeting on application of one Chh. & one Minister; & no business of extensive importance shall be decided at any such special meeting but what was specified in his notification.

At each Stated meeting in February shall be instituted an inquiry into the manner in which the Ministers belonging to this body shall have discharged the duties of the Ministry the past year, in *Studying, preaching, administering ordinances, visiting & catechising* within the limits of their charges; & how their labors have been attended to, & themselves supported by their Churches & the Congregations under their care.

At each Stated meeting in August shall be instituted an inquiry into the state of Religion within our bounds, & in more distant regions. Each member in his place giving all the information on this subject which he may possess. This shall be done in order that a general & concise account of the state of Religion may be given publickly by the Moderator, or some one appointed by him, before the celebration of the Lords supper.

·   ·   ·

First Stated Meeting, at Auburn, Jan. 1811

The Presbytery of Cayuga convened at Auburn, January 8th, 1811 agreeably to the appointment of the Synod of Albany, & was opened with a sermon by the Rev. Hez. N. Woodruff, & constituted with prayer.

Present

Ministers	Delegates
Rev. Messrs. Hez. N. Woodruff	Roswell Franklin Scipio
David Higgins	Dn. Ebeneser Higgins Aurelius
Francis Pomeroy	Dn. Hez. Freeman
Royal Phelps	Dn. John Stoylles (Sempronius)
Levi Parsons	John Atwater
Seth Smith	Moses Fulton
Absent Jeremiah Osborne	James Leonard Mentz
Joshua Lane	

[Hereafter names of Ministers and delegates present and absent will be omitted.]

Mr. Woodruff was chosen Moderator, Messrs. Parsons & Smith Clerks. Rev. Messrs. Chadwick & Lansing members of the Presbytery of Onondaga, & the Rev. Mr. Sears of the Presbytery of Columbia being present, were invited to sit in Presbytery as corresponding members.

On request, Presbytery agreed to attend to the business of the Chh. in Aurelius tomorrow morning at half past ten O Clock.

Mr. Higgins was chosen Stated Clerk & Mr. Parsons Treasurer.

The second Church in Marcellus requested to be received as a Constituent member of this Presbytery. After hearing their Confession of Faith, Voted, that they be received. And Dn Josiah Frost took his seat as a delegate from said Church.

Presbytery having understood that there were certain difficulties existing in the Church in Locke which require their attention; the Rev. Messrs. Woodruff & Higgins were appointed a Committee to confer with said Church respecting said difficulties.

The Rev. Messrs. Higgins & Parsons were appointed a

Committee for the purpose of deducing from the records of the Middle Association, and from the doings of the Synod of Albany, a succinct account of the origin of this Presbytery; and for condensing rules for the proceedings of Presbytery.

The Treasurer was directed to Call on the Treasurer of the Middle Association for that proportion of money in his hands which belongs to this Presbytery.

Voted, That at each stated meeting of Presbytery there be a collection for the Contingent Fund.

Resolved, That all persons who shall be ordained or installed to the work of the Ministry by this Presbytery shall be considered as Constituent members of this body.

Voted, That this Presbytery be adjourned till half past ten O Clock tomorrow morning.   Closed with Prayer.

Wednesday morning Jan. 9th Presbytery met according to adjournment, & was opened with prayer.

According to the order of the day, Presbytery attended to the business of the Church in Aurelius.   The Church & Trustees of the Society presented certain papers to Presbytery stating their inability to afford the Rev. David Higgins[3] a competent support; and with the concurrence of Mr. Higgins agreed to refer the subject of his dismission to the decision of Presbytery.   Presbytery on attending carefully to the subject, Voted unanimously, That the Pastoral relation between the Rev. Mr. Higgins & the said Church & Society be, & hereby is dissolved.   The Rev. David Higgins being thus dismissed, the Presbytery cheerfully express the favourable opinion they have of his past fidelity in the ministry of reconciliation, and cordially recommend him to the Churches, wherever in Divine Providence he may be called

---

[3] Reverend David Higgins had begun his labors at Aurelius in 1802. Previous to this he had performed missionary service in the region of the Military Tract under a commission from the Connecticut Society.   He was the first settled pastor in this section of New York.   A graduate of Yale College (1785), pastor of the church in North Lyme, Conn., from 1787 to 1801, he accepted the call to the church at Aurelius and was installed in October, 1802, by a council of Congregational and Presbyterian ministers. Gillett, *op. cit.,* II, p. 106.

to labor, as an approved minister of Christ; praying that a door may be speedily opened for his resettlement, & that his usefulness may be more abundantly increased. Presbytery deeply regret that the Church & Society are under the necessity of parting with their worthy Pastor; They hope & pray, however, that the great Shepherd will not leave them comfortless, but that he will open an effectual door for their instruction & edification. While they commend them to the mercy & protection of Divine Providence, they recommend & exhort that they carefully study their duty; labor to preserve union; conscientiously maintain the worship of God, & the observance of the Christian Sabbath; diligently seek the resettlement of the Christian ministry; and steadfastly maintain the life of faith, looking forward & pressing toward the mark for the prise of the high calling of God in Christ Jesus our Lord.

Mr. Higgins was requested to preach to the Church & Society in Aurelius on the third Sabbath of the present month, and publish to them the doings of Presbytery on the subject of his dismission; & to declare said Church & society vacant.

The Churches were directed to hand in their annual reports at the next meeting of Presbytery. And those Churches which had not made Collections for the Commissioners fund were directed to attend to those Collections previous to the next meeting of Presbytery.

Resolved, That this Presbytery will observe the second Thursday in April as a Fast; & the second Thursday in November as a Thanksgiving annually.

The Rev. Mr. Parsons was appointed to attend the next meeting of the Presbytery of Onondaga, &, in union with a Committee from that body, draw up & publish an address to the Churches respecting the observance of the Fast & Thanksgiving the year ensuing.

The Rev. Mr. Bell of the Presbytery of Geneva being present was invited to sit in Presbytery as a corresponding member.

Agreed, that the next Stated meeting be at the house of

Deacon John Stoylles in Sempronius on the third Thursday of March next at 2 O Clock P. M.

Resolved, That the ordinance of the Lord's supper be administered at each Stated Meeting of Presbytery, & that a Preacher for the occasion be appointed at the preceeding Stated Meeting.   The Rev. Mr. Parsons was appointed preacher accordingly.

Voted to adjourn.   Closed with prayer.

HEZ. N. WOODRUFF, Moderator

LEVI PARSONS, Clerk.

Transcribed from the Minuets of Presbytery, Jan.1st 1812.[4]

DAVID HIGGINS, *Stated Clerk*

Second Stated Meeting, Sempronius, March 1811

Presbytery of Cayuga met at Sempronius on the 19th of March 1811 & was opened with a sermon by the Moderator, Rev. Hez. N. Woodruff & constituted with prayer.

[At this meeting there were present seven ministers, one elder and five delegates.]

Mr. Higgins was chosen *Moderator*, & Mr. Osborne & Mr. Smith Clerks. . . .

The report of the Committee appointed to confer with the Church in Locke respecting their difficulties was heard; & Presbytery were highly gratified with their success in happily removing the difficulties in said Church.

The Committee appointed for the purpose of deducing from the records of the Middle Association, & from the doings of the Synod of Albany, a succinct account of the origin of this Presbytery, & condensing rules for the proceedings of Presbytery, exhibited their report.   Deferred for a second reading till tomorrow morning.

Voted to adjourn till tomorrow morning, half past eight O Clock.   Closed with prayer.

Wednesday morning March 20th. . . .

The report of the Committee, made yesterday & deferred

---

[4] The notation, "Transcribed from the Minutes of Presbytery," dated and signed by the stated clerk appears at the end of the minutes of each stated meeting.   This will be omitted in the future.

till morning, was read a second time, and *Voted*, That it be accepted, & that it be recorded by the Stated Clerk at the beginning of the records of this Presbytery.   Collected for the Contingent Fund $2.93.

A letter was received from the Northern Associated Presbytery, communicated by the Moderator of this Presbytery, to which he was directed to return an answer.   The Committee appointed to draught addresses to the Churches on the subject of the Annual Fast, reported.

A statement was made to Presbytery respecting certain difficulties existing in the Church in Aurelius. *Voted*, That Messrs. Woodruff, Parsons & Pomeroy be a Committee to confer with said Church respecting their difficulties.   Mr. Woodruff was appointed a Commissioner to attend the General Assembly in May next: and Mr. Osborne his second.   Mr. Thaddeus Edwards a Delegate, & Dn. John Stoylles his second.

Voted, That the Churches be requested to exhibit their records for the inspection of Presbytery in August, annually.   At 2 O Clock P. M. attended public worship.   Mr. Parsons preached from I Cor. 10.16.   Attended the ordinance of the Lord's supper.   Mr. Pomeroy administered the bread, & Mr. Woodruff the cup.

Mr. John R. St. John was introduced to this Presbytery as a student in Divinity, & was taken under the care of Presbytery as a Candidate for License to preach the Gospel. Presbytery proceeded to examine him respecting his experimental acquaintance with religion.   Voted, That his communications on this subject are satisfactory.   Mr. St. John also read a part of a sermon.   Mr. St. John was directed to pursue his studies until the next Stated meeting of Presbytery, under the care of Mr. Woodruff, if convenient; & that he direct his attention more particularly to the Arts & Sciences.

Messrs. Higgins, Woodruff & Smith were appointed a Committee of License & Certification.   Agreed, that the next Stated meeting of Presbytery be at the house of Jacob Sheldon in Brutus.   Mr. Smith was appointed preacher at the next Stated meeting before the Communion.   *Voted*, that this Presbytery approve of the sermon delivered yesterday by Mr. Woodruff, & think it expedient that it be published.

Closed the Meeting with Prayer.

DAVID HIGGINS, *Moderator.*

JEREMIAH OSBORNE, *Clerk.*

Third Stated Meeting, Brutus, August 20th 1811

. . . Mr. Higgins was chosen Moderator, & Mr. Parsons Clerk. The minuets of the last meeting were read. On a request of the Chh. at Auburn to be received as a constituent member of this Presbytery, their Confession of Faith being approved, *Voted,* That said Church be received. Upon which Mr. Silas Hawley took his seat as a Delegate from said Church.

On a request of the Church at Western to be received as a constituent member of this Presbytery, & having heard their Confession of Faith, *Voted,* That said Church be received. Whereupon, Joseph Waldo took his seat as a Delegate from said Church. Adjourned to meet at this place tomorrow morning at 8 O Clock. Closed with prayer.

Wednesday Morning, Aug. 21st

Met according to adjournment, opened with prayer. Mr. St. John did not attend Presbytery, but by a communication received from him by Mr. Woodruff, it appeared that he had not been able to pursue his studies as had been contemplated.

The Committee appointed to examine the Treasurer's account reported, that on the Missionary & Commissioner's Fund the accounts are balanced; And that on the Contingent Fund there is a balance in the treasury of $2.93.

Mr. Woodruff, Commissioner to the General Assembly at their last meeting, reported that he had attended agreeably to his appointment; & exhibited at the same time a brief but interesting statement of the proceedings of the Assembly.

Mr. Higgins was reappointed Register, & Mr. Parsons Treasurer.   Messrs. Woodruff, Higgins & Smith were re-appointed Committee of License & Certification.

A Collection was made of the members of Presbytery for the Contingent Fund of $2.90.

The Church at Skaneatoles requested Presbytery to meet at that place on the second Tuesday of September next for the purpose of ordaining Mr. Nathaniel Swift & installing him Pastor of that Church & Congregation; whereupon it was voted, That when Presbytery adjourn they will adjourn to meet at Skaneatoles agreeably to the foregoing request. The report of the Committee appointed to examine the records of the Church in Locke was accepted. The Churches which have not exhibited their records at this meeting were directed to exhibit them at the Stated Meeting in February. . . .

Presbytery attended to the account of the Ministers & delegates respecting the state of Religion in this vicinity.

The Committee to visit the Church in Aurelius reported; on which report & on a Communication from said Church by their delegate, the following resolution was passed. *Resolved,* That the Church in Aurelius, and all the Churches belonging to this body of the Congregational order are entitled & have a right to all the privileges of a Congregational Church, as they were secured to them by the original Constitution of the Middle Association.

At 3 O Clock Presbytery attended public worship. Mr. Smith preached from *Luke 2.34.* Attended the ordinance of the Supper, in which Mr. Parsons administered the bread, & Mr. Woodruff the cup.

Voted, That the next Stated meeting of Presbytery be at Aurora; & that Mr. Pomeroy be the preacher before the Communion.

Mr. Smith was appointed preacher at the expected ordination at Skaneatoles in case of the failure of Rev. Dr. Nott.

Adjourned to meet at Skaneatoles at the house of Thaddeus Edwards on the second Tuesday of September next at eleven O Clock in the morning.

Closed with prayer.

DAVID HIGGINS, *Moderator*

LEVI PARSONS, *Clerk*

Special Meeting at Skaneatoles, Sept. 10th 1811

. . . Rev. Mr. Smith was chosen Clerk for the present meeting. Messrs. Daniel Adams & Nathaniel Swift Licentiates for the Ministry, being present, were invited to sit in Presbytery in that capacity.

Mr. Nathaniel Swift laid before Presbytery his Call from the Church & Society at Skaneatoles to be their Pastor, & his affirmative answer to said Call. He likewise presented sundry documents testifying his regular license to preach the gospel as a Candidate for settlement in the ministry, & his regular dismission from the Presbytery of Albany, which were received as satisfactory. He then offered himself to Presbytery for examination. And, having examined him relative to his knowledge in Divinity, & his acquaintance with experimental religion, approved him on these parts of trial, & agreed to proceed to the ordination of Mr. Swift tomorrow morning at eleven O Clock.

The Rev. Messrs. Chadwick & Lansing members of the Presbytery of Onondaga came in & were invited to sit in Presbytery as corresponding members.

In assigning the parts of the ordination exercise, Mr. Phelps was appointed to make the introductory prayer, Mr. Smith preach the sermon, Mr. Chadwick make the ordaining prayer, the Moderator preside & give the charge, Mr. Pomeroy give the right hand of fellowship, Mr. Lane make the Address to the Church & Congregation, and Mr. Lansing make the concluding prayer.

Mr. Pomeroy was appointed a Committee to confer with a Committee from the Presbytery of Onondaga, & prepare an adress to the Churches on the subject of the Annual Thanksgiving.

Adjourned to meet tomorrow morning at nine O Clock. Closed with prayer.

Wednesday Morning Sept. 11th. Met according to adjournment & opened with prayer.

In concurrence with an order from the General Assembly "that the Presbytery of Cayuga be authorised to employ a missionary for two months on Missionary ground within their bounds", *Voted*, That Messrs. Higgins, Pomeroy & Smith be a committee to employ a Missionary in the name of Presbytery.

At the hour appointed, Presbytery repaired to the house of public worship & attended to the ordination of the Rev. Nathaniel Swift. The several parts were performed according to appointment. Hands were imposed by Messrs. Higgins, Chadwick & Smith.

The Rev. Nathaniel Swift, being thus ordained to the work of the Gospel ministry, took his seat in Presbytery as a Constituent member.

The meeting was then Closed with prayer.

DAVID HIGGINS, Moderator

Fourth Stated Meeting, Aurora, Feb. 18th 1812

. . . On the request of the Rev. Daniel Loring, pastor of the Church in Candor to be received as a Constituent member of this Presbytery; & as several members of Presbytery were present at Mr. Loring's installation, & were satisfied as to his doctrinal knowledge & experimental religion; Therefore *Voted*, That Mr. Loring be received as a Constituent member of this body. He accordingly took his seat.

Rev. Mr. Walker member of the Presbytery of Onondaga being present was invited to sit as a corresponding member. Likewise Mr. Abel Cutter a Licentiate was invited to sit with Presbytery in that capacity.

Voted That the time of inquiring into the state of Religion within our bounds be altered from the Stated Meeting in August to the Stated Meeting in February. *Voted*, to attend to the state of Religion tomorrow morning, & that Messrs. Pomeroy & Walker be a Committee to digest the information received from the members, & to exhibit an account of the same.

Resolved, That the Churches be requested to appoint Delegates semiannually, viz. previous to each Stated Meeting of Presbytery.

The Committee appointed to employ a Missionary agreeably to the order of the General Assembly, reported, that they had not been able to procure one; therefore, *Resolved,* That said Committee be continued.

Messrs. Osborne & Parsons were appointed Commissioners to attend the General Assembly of the Presbyterian Church next May. And Mr. Loring was appointed alternate to Mr, Osborne. Likewise Deacon Josiah Frost & Mr. Stephen Webb were appointed Commissioners to attend the next meeting of the General Assembly.

Adjourned till tomorrow morning 9 O Clock. Closed with prayer.

Wednesday morning Feb. 19th. Met according to adjournment, opened with prayer; . . .

At 11 O Clock A. M. Presbytery attended public worship. Mr. Pomeroy preached from *Isaiah 40.1.* The ordinance of the Lord's supper was attended. Mr. Osborne administered the bread & Mr. Higgins the cup.

Presbytery, according to the order of the Day, having had a free conference on the state of Religion, the Committee appointed to digest the information received, reported; & their report was referred to the Commissioners to the General Assembly.

The Committee appointed to examine the records of the Chhs. in Sempronius, Scipio, Marcellus, & Genoa reported, that they found them generally kept correctly. . . .

Presbytery being informed that certain difficulties existed in the South Chh. in Genoa, appointed the Rev. Messrs. Woodruff, Higgins & Smith, & Deacon John Stoylles, Deacon Lyon, & Mr. Webb a Committee to attend to the state of said Church.

Mr. Parsons was appointed a Committee in union with a

Committee from the Presbytery of Onondaga to prepare an address to the Churches on the subject of the annual Fast.

A Collection was made from the members of Presbytery for the Contingent Fund of *two Dollars & seven Cents.*

Presbytery, agreeably to their rules, entered into an inquiry of the members present respecting the manner in which the word & ordinances have been administered; ministerial labors attended; & the Gospel supported in the year past.

Voted, That the next Stated meeting of Presbytery be held at the Church in Marcellus, & that Mr. Woodruff be the preacher on the Communion occasion.

Adjourned to meet at Marcellus on the third Tuesday in August at 2 O Clock P. M.   Closed with prayer.

DAVID HIGGINS, Moderator

Attest, LEVI PARSONS, Clerk

Special Meeting at Locke, May 13th 1812

Presbytery of Cayuga convened at Locke, agreeably to a special notification from the Moderator, for the purpose of attending to the request of Rev. Joshua Lane to be dismissed from his Pastoral Charge. . . . Opened with Prayer.   Rev. Mr. Smith was appointed Clerk.   Sundry communications were made to the Presbytery certifying that Rev. Joshua Lane had requested a dismission from his pastoral charge, & that the Church & Society had concurred with Mr. Lane in requesting Presbytery to convene to effect his dismission.   The Church & Society attended by their Committees, from whom communications were received. After seriously deliberating upon the subject, Presbytery came to the following result.   That we view it expedient, under existing circumstances, particularly as there are but few present, & that Mr. Lane's usefulness will probably be continued, that Mr. Lane should not be dismissed from his pastoral charge.   We hope & pray that after serious & prayerful consideration, Mr. Lane will be induced to continue his Ministerial labors with the people over whom God in his Providence has placed him; & that they will be excited to renew their exertions to relieve him of his burdens, & to encourage him in his pastoral work by a diligent attendance on his ministrations.   Adjourned tomorrow morning at 8 O Clock.   Closed with prayer.

Thursday morning, met according to adjournment, & opened with prayer.   On further consideration, we recommend to Mr. Lane, in consequence of his bodily infirmities, to abbreviate & condense his public exercises; & that the congregation be exhorted to exercise all due condescension. *Voted*, That Mr. Lane be requested to read the above doings of Presbytery in the congregation the next Lord's day. Closed with prayer.

DAVID HIGGINS, Mod.

SETH SMITH, Clerk.

Fifth Stated Meeting

Presbytery of Cayuga convened at Marcellus agreeably to adjournment on the 18th of August 1812. . . .

Mr. Higgins was appointed Moderator, & Messrs. Smith & Parsons Clerks.   Rev. Messrs, Chadwick & Lansing members of the Presbytery of Onondaga, being present were requested to sit as corresponding members.

A request was presented to Presbytery from the Church in Cato to become a Constituent member of this body. Having attended to their confession of Faith, it was *Voted*, That the Church in Cato be received as a Constituent member of this Presbytery.   David Brown then took his seat as a Delegate from that Church.

Presbytery then received & attended to an application from the Rev. Mr. Lansing, & J. Foreman Esq. in behalf of themselves & others in the town of Onondaga, "For approbation of a Theological Institution in Onondaga." *Voted*, To approve of the object contemplated; & that Messrs. Parsons, Smith & Hills be a Committee to endite a letter of Credence agreeably to the request of the above named gentlemen. . . .

Adjourned till tomorrow 8 O Clock.   Closed with prayer.

Wednesday morning, met according to adjournment, & opened with prayer.

The Committee appointed to employ a Missionary agreeably to the order of the General Assembly reported, that they had not been able to procure one : which report was accepted. In concurrence with an order of the General Assembly in their minuets of May last, authorizing the Presbytery of Cayuga to employ a Missionary or Missionaries for four Months within their limits & vicinity; Messrs. Higgins, Pomeroy & Smith were appointed a Committee to employ a Missionary accordingly.

Mr. Osborne, Commissioner to the General Assembly at their last Meeting, reported that he attended agreeably to his appointment : which report was accepted.

The Committee, appointed to prepare a letter of credence or recommendation, agreeably to the request of Messrs. Lansing & Foreman, reported the following.

Whereas information has been communicated to the Presbytery of Cayuga by the Rev. Dirck C. Lansing & Joshua Foreman, Esq. that an Academical Institution is about to be established in the town of Onondaga; & that it is contemplated to connect with said Institution a Theological School, in which young men may be prepared for the Gospel ministry: And whereas application has been made to this Presbytery by the above named gentlemen, in behalf of their Associates, for a letter of recommendation on the important nature & necessity of such a Theological Establishment on the principles & doctrines of the reformation; The Presbytery cheerfully state that they view such a Theological Institution as highly necessary to this portion of our Country, & calculated to be extensively useful to the establishment of Gospel truth, & building up the Kingdom of the Redeemer: and they do most cordially concur with the above named gentlemen & their associates in soliciting the aid of those who love the cause of the great King of Zion; in furthering an object of such deep importance to the Churches of Christ in this region; and (through the Divine blessing which we humbly implore) to generations yet unborn.

The above reported was accepted.

The Committee appointed to visit the South Church in Genoa reported; which report was accepted. Whereupon voted, That the Rev. Messrs. Higgins, Woodruff, Parsons & Smith, Dn. Lyon, Dn. Stoylles Mr. Sheldon, & Mr. Hills be a Committee to meet with the South Church in Genoa for the purpose of enquiring into their situation assisting them in the exercise of discipline, censuring those who are deserving of censure; recommending to the fellowship of other Churches those who appear to be worthy of such recommendation; & of dissolving said Church, if it should be thought expedient: which Committee are to meet the third Tuesday of October next at 1 O Clock in the afternoon, at such place as the Church shall appoint; & make report at the next Stated meeting of Presbytery.

Mr. Parsons was appointed *Treasurer*, & Mr. Higgins *Register*.

Voted, That Mr. Higgins be allowed one Dollar & nine Cents for Contingent expenses, & that the Treasurer pay him that sum.

The report of the Treasurer was made & accepted. *Voted,* That Messrs. Higgins, Woodruff, & Loring be a Committee of License & Certification for the ensuing year.

Collected for the Contingent Fund one Dollar & seventy one Cents.

The Stated Clerk reported that he had given Mr. John St. John a certificate of his regular standing in this Presbytery, in order that he might place himself under the care of the Presbytery of Geneva.

Mr. Benjamin Rice, a Licentiate from the Haverhill Association being present, was requested to sit with us in that capacity.

Had a recess till the time appointed for public worship. Then attended Divine service. Mr. Osborne preached from *Luke 1.78 & 79.* The sacrament of the Lord's supper was administered. The bread by Mr. Loring & the cup by Mr. Higgins.

The Committees appointed to examine the records of the Churches in Locke, Auburn & Marcellus, reported that they were kept with due care & correctness; which reports were accepted.

Voted, That the next Stated Meeting be at Genoa, first Church; & that Mr. Swift preach on the Communion occasion. Adjourned to meet at Genoa the third Tuesday in February. Closed with prayer.

DAVID HIGGINS Moderator

Attest, SETH SMITH Clerk.

These records have been thus far examined & approved by Synod.

DAVID HIGGINS, Moderator.

Geneva, Oct. 9th 1812.

Special Meeting at Skaneateles, Oct. 27th 1812

At a special meeting of the Presbytery of Cayuga convened by order of the Moderator at the Meeting-house in Skaneateles on Tuesday the 27th of October 1812, for the purpose of deciding upon the expediency of dismissing Rev. Nathaniel Swift from his pastoral charge. . . .
The meeting was opened with prayer. Mr. Smith was chosen Clerk. Business not being prepared, had a recess till 2 O Clock. . . . Mr. Benjamin Rice a Licentiate being present, was invited to sit with Presbytery in that capacity.

Communications were made to Presbytery by Rev. Mr. Swift, by the Committee of the Church, & by the Trustees of the Society relative to the object of the present meeting.

Rev. Joshua Lane & Mr. Daniel Bradley came in & took their seats. It appeared from documents exhibited, that Mr. Swift had requested the Church & Society to acquiesce with him in calling Presbytery together for the purpose stated above; & that the Church & Society did acquiesce. After full inquiry & investigation into the subject, Presby-

tery took the matter into serious consideration & came to
the following result, viz.

> That whereas it is the desire of Mr. Swift, & of the
> Church & Society with which he stands connected that
> the connection should be dissolved; & whereas it ap-
> pears that his usefulness is at an end; it is expedient
> that Mr. Swift should be dismissed; & he is hereby
> dismissed from his pastoral relation to this Church &
> people.
> Presbytery hope & pray that Mr. Swift may be relieved
> of his present bodily infirmity & that he may be made
> more extensively useful in the work of the ministry;
> & that the Church & Society in this place may be
> abundantly blessed & prospered, & that they may be
> speedily restored to the enjoyment of the Stated ad-
> ministration of the word & ordinances.

Voted, That Samuel Bellamy be requested to publish, or
cause to be published, this result the next Lord's-day.

Closed with prayer.

SETH SMITH, Clerk . . . DAVID HIGGINS, Moderator

Stated Meeting at Genoa: February 16th 1813

Presbytery of Cayuga convened at Genoa agreeably to
adjournment on the 16th of Feb. 1813, & was constituted
with prayer. . . .

Mr. Woodruff was appointed Moderator, & Messrs. Parsons & Dan Bradley Clerks.

Mr. Howell Bull, elder of the Church in Bath, being
present was invited to sit with us as a corresponding member.

Messrs. Higgins & Parsons were appointed Commissioners to attend the General Assembly next May: & Mr. Loring was appointed alternate to either. Likewise Dan
Bradley, delegate from the Eastern Chh. in Marcellus was
appointed a Commissioner; & Dn. John Stoylles his alternate

The Committee, appointed to attend to the case of the South Chh. in Genoa, reported, that they attended agreeably to appointment;— that they assisted the Chh. in excommunicating Silas Reeves;— that they recommended the several members of the Chh. to the Churches in Ithaca, Ulysses, & 2nd Chh in Genoa, and that they then dissolved said Church. Which report was accepted.

Mr. Higgins having removed out of the limits of this Presbytery, signified his desire to resign the office of Register; Whereupon Mr. Smith was appointed in his room.

Dn. Auther Smith & Mr. Silas Hawley were excused the remainder of the sessions.

Attended public worship in the evening; after which Presbytery adjourned till tomorrow morning at half past 8 O Clock. Closed with prayer.

Wednesday morning, met according to adjournment & opened with prayer. Collected for the Contingent fund $1.75. Collected for the Commissioners fund—

Church in Locke	$1.00	Church in Berkshire	$00.50
Church in Aurelius	00.50	Church in Sempronius	1.57
Church in Mentz	00.50	1st Church in Genoa	5.27
East Chh in Marcellus	4.65	Church in Auburn	3.10
Mr. Howell Bull	00.50		

Voted, That it be the duty of the Moderators of the several Churches belonging to this Presbytery to call upon their Chh's. annually for a collection for Commissioners Fund.

At eleven O Clock proceeded to the Meeting-house to attend public worship. Mr. Higgins preached the sermon from *Math. 15.26* after which attended to the Communion service, in which Mr. Woodruff administered the bread & Mr. Higgins the cup.

A Call from the Congregation in Bath to the Rev. Mr. Higgins, requesting him to take the pastoral charge of them was presented to this Presbytery by Mr. Howell Bull, elder of the Chh. in Bath. Whereupon *Voted,* That the Call be presented to Mr. Higgins requesting his answer to the same. The Call was then presented to Mr. Higgins, to which he gave an affirmative answer.   Whereupon it was *Voted*, to dismiss Mr. Higgins from this Presbytery & recommend him to the Presbytery of Geneva.

The Committee appointed to employ a Missionary four months agreeably to an order of General Assembly, *reported* that they have employed Mr. Loring & Mr. Osborne for the aforesaid term; which report was accepted.

Voted, That the Commissioners to General Assembly be instructed to solicit permission for this Presbytery to appoint a Missionary to be employed four months within the bounds of said Presbytery & its vicinity.

Mr. Pomeroy came in, & having rendered his reason for not attending, took his seat.

Presbytery proceeded to hear the statement of the several members respecting the state of religion within our limits; & Messrs. Osborne & Phelps were appointed a Committee to form a concise statement of the same.

Voted, to pay Mr. Higgins fifteen Dollars for his services as Register; of which sum Mr. Higgins generously gave in seven Dollars.   Whereupon *Voted,* that the thanks of Presbytery be presented to Mr. Higgins for the above gratuity.

> Presbytery having a sense of the arduous labors & extensive usefulness of Rev. David Higgins for many years past in this vicinity; & as he is now about leaving them, would hereby express their gratitude to him for his distinguished services among them; and while, as it respects themselves personally, they regret the circumstance of his removal, still they would cheerfully acquiesce in this disposal of Providence.   And at the same time they would pray the Father of mercies to render our worthy brother extensively useful in the region where he is now placed.

Respecting the collection for the education of poor & pious youth, this Presbytery have nothing to report, as they have made no Collections, owing to the Infant state of the Churches.

Voted, That a Committee of three be appointed to take

into consideration the sins of *Intemperance* & *Sabbath-breaking*, & to devise measures for supressing these vices; & to report to Presbytery at their next Stated meeting. Messrs. Woodruff, Dan Bradley & Parsons were appointed a Committee for that purpose.

The Committee appointed to exhibit a concise view of the state of religion within the limits of this Presbytery, reported as follows—

State of religion within the limits of the Presbytery of Cayuga.

"At a Stated Meeting of the Presbytery of Cayuga Feb. 16th 1813 enquiry being made of the members with regard to the State of religion within their respective Chhs. & Congregations, it appears, That although some of them are in a cold & formal state, yet generally they give heed to the word of truth which is preached, not only on the Sabbath, but occasionally at other times. They appear to walk in the order & harmony of the Gospel, & the Chhs. have generally had a few added to their numbers. In addition to this, with gratitude to the Author of all grace, we have the satisfaction to mention that a few of our Chhs. have been so increased in numbers as greatly to gladden the hearts of Zion's friends. The establishment of a number of praying female societies among us is another consideration which calls for our fervent gratitude & praise to him who rules as King in Zion. Finally, all things considered, we think we have abundant cause to rejoice; for the Lord hath greatly helped us." Which report was accepted.

Voted That a Committee be appointed to indite a concise plan for instructing & disciplining baptized children, & that they réport at the next Stated Meeting. Messrs. Woodruff, Pomeroy, S. Smith, & Dn. Bradley were appointed the Committee.

Voted, That when we adjourn, we adjourn to meet at the house of Maj. Lemi Bradley in Locke on Tuesday the 2nd day of March next at 2 O Clock·P. M.

Voted, That the next Stated Meeting of Presbytery in

August next, be holden at Berkshire; & that Mr. Pomeroy preach the sermon previous to Communion.

Voted, That the Ministers of this Presbytery be directed to preach as often as they shall deem expedient on the subject of the suppression of the vices of Intemperance & Sabbath-breaking.

Adjourned to meet at Locke the 2nd of March next. Closed with prayer.

HEZ. N. WOODRUFF, Moderator

Attest, LEVI PARSONS, Clerk. . . .

Special Meeting at Locke March 2nd 1813

Presbytery of Cayuga met at Locke agreeably to adjournment on Tuesday the 2nd day of March 1813 for the purpose of taking into consideration the subject of the Rev. Joshua Lane's dismission from his Pastoral relation to the Church in that place. . . .

Rev. Mr. Lane presented a written communication to Presbytery, certifying that, in consequence of his ill-health & his inability to discharge the ministerial duties, it is his request to be dismissed from his pastoral relation to this Chh. & people. It likewise appeared from the records of the Church, that, at a regular Church meeting, it was Voted unanimously to concur with Mr. Lane in his request to Presbytery for dismission. Mr. Lane, through bodily infirmity, having failed in the discharge of his Pastoral duties, does agree to relinquish his claims on the Trustees for one-half of his Salary, for the year ending the last day of April next. The doings of the Society relative to the subject were likewise laid before Presbytery; from which it appeared that they voted unanimously to concur with Mr. Lane in his request for a dismission.

After deliberating upon the subject, Presbytery *Voted*, That the request of Mr. Lane be granted for the reasons stated in the request.

Voted, That the Moderator make this result public this evening, & declare the Church & Society in this place vacant.

As nothing has appeared injurious to the Ministerial

character of Mr. Lane, we hereby recommend him, as a regular Minister of Christ, to the improvement of the Churches, should his health permit of his re-commencing the duties of the Pastoral office. *Voted*, That these be accepted as the doings of Presbytery at this session. Concluded with prayer.

N. WOODRUFF, Moderator.

Attest, SETH SMITH, Clerk.

Special Meeting at Auburn June 22nd 1813

At a special meeting of the Presbytery of Cayuga, convened at Auburn June 22nd 1813, by order of the Moderator, for the purpose of considering the expediency of dissolving the pastoral relation between the Rev. Hez N. Woodruff & the Church in Scipio; and of installing him Pastor over the Church in Auburn. . . .

Presbytery being opened with prayer, the Moderator on account of his being personally interested in the business to be submitted to Presbytery, requested that a Moderator might be appointed for the present meeting. Mr. Parsons was accordingly appointed Moderator for the time being, & Mr. Osborne Clerk.

Written communications were made to Presbytery, certifying that the Rev. Hez. N. Woodruff had requested the Chh. & Society in Scipio to concur with him in adopting such methods as would issue in the dissolution of their present connection; & that the Chh. & Society had concurred with him in this request. The expediency of dissolving the connection was accordingly submitted to Presbytery. After mature deliberation it was *Voted*, That said connection be, & is hereby dissolved. By a particular request from the Chh. in Scipio, *Voted*, to request Mr. Woodruff to assist that Chh. in administering ordinances, giving advice, & other things as he shall have opportunity. *Voted* also, that Mr. Woodruff be requested to preach to the Chh. & Congregation at Scipio at such time as shall be convenient, & declare the said Chh. & Congregation vacant.

A Call was presented to Presbytery for the Rev. Hez N.

Woodruff, from the first Congregational Chh. & Society in Auburn. By order of the Presbytery the Call was presented to the Rev. Mr. Woodruff; to which he returned an affirmative answer.

On motion, *Voted*, that, as Mr. Woodruff is a member of this Presbytery, & we have been long acquainted with him, the formality of an examination be dispensed with.

Voted, That the Rev. Mr. Woodruff be installed the Pastor of the Chh. & Congregation in this place; & that we proceed to the Installation tomorrow at 10 O Clock A. M. The parts to be performed were assigned as follows. Mr. Pomeroy to make the Introductory prayer; Mr. Woodruff preach the sermon; Mr. Parsons give the charge to Pastor & people; & Mr. Smith make the concluding prayer. Adjourned till tomorrow 9 O Clock. Closed with prayer.

Wednesday, met according to adjournment. Opened with prayer. At the hour appointed attended the public exercises agreeably to the previous arrangement. Closed with prayer.

LEVI PARSONS, Moderator.

JEREMIAH OSBORNE, Clerk.

Special Meeting, Skaneatoles, July 6th 1813.

Presbytery of Cayuga met at Skaneatoles, July 6th 1813, agreeably to notice given by the Moderator, to take into consideration the Call of the Chh. & Society in that place to Mr. Benjamin Rice, Licentiate from the Haverill Association, Massachusetts, to be ordained over them as their Pastor. . . .

Opened with prayer. Mr. Parsons was appointed Clerk. The Rev. Mr. Wilcox, member of the Presbytery of Onondaga, being present was invited to sit with us as a corresponding member.

The Call of the Church & Society of Skaneatoles for Mr. Rice, and Mr. Rice's answer to the same were laid before Presbytery. Likewise a remonstrance against the settlement of Mr. Rice, signed by a number of the members of the Society, was presented. Presbytery attended to said remonstrance, but did not come to a decision. Adjourned, to meet tomorrow morning at 8 O Clock. Concluded with prayer.

Wednesday Morning, met according to adjournment. Opened with prayer.

Rev. Ebenezer Lazell of the Oneida Association being present was invited to sit with us as a Corresponding member.

Application was made by the Church in Candor to be received as a Constituent member of Presbytery. The Articles of Faith & the Covenant were read & approved. Whereupon *Voted*, That said Church be received. Accordingly Mr. Timothy North took his seat as a Delegate from said Church.

The Presbytery then attended to the business for which they were convened; and further heard the parties for & against the ordination of Mr. Rice, and having heard the evidence on both sides with much deliberation, *Voted*, without a dissenting voice, that it was expedient to proceed to the examination of the Candidate with a view to his ordination.

The Presbytery, after a recess for dinner, attended to the examination of Mr. Rice as aforesaid, & finding, in the judgment of said Presbytery, that he is well instructed in the scriptures, sound in the Faith, & of good moral & religious character; *Voted*, that they will proceed to the ordination of the said Mr. Rice at 4 O Clock this afternoon, at the meeting-house at Skaneatoles. The parts were assigned as follows; Mr. Wilcox made the Introductory prayer; Mr. Woodruff preach the sermon, & deliver the charge to the people; Mr. Loring make the consecrating prayer; Mr. Parsons give the charge; Mr. Smith give the right hand of fellowship; & Mr. Lazell make the Concluding prayer.

At 4 O Clock Presbytery proceeded to the Meeting-house, & ordained Mr. Rice by prayer & laying on the hands of Presbytery; & installed him Pastor of the Church & congregation in this place. The parts were performed according to the assignment.

The General Assembly having authorized Presbytery to employ a Missionary four months, therefore *Voted*, that the Rev. Messrs. Woodruff, Parsons & Smith be a Committee to employ Missionaries accordingly.

Concluded with prayer.

HEZ. N. WOODRUFF, *Moderator*

Attest, LEVI PARSONS, *Clerk*.

Seventh Stated Meeting
At Berkshire, August 17th 1813

At a Stated meeting of the Presbytery of Cayuga held at Berkshire, August 17th 1813, . . .

Opened with prayer.   Mr. Woodruff was appointed Moderator & Mr. Smith, Clerk.

The Rev. Henry Ford, member of the Presbytery of Hudson, being present, was invited to sit with us as a corresponding member.   Mr. Artemus Dean, licentiate from the Northern Associated Presbytery, was invited to sit with us in that capacity.   Adjourned to meet tomorrow at Mr. Osborne's at 8 O Clock.   Closed with prayer.

Wednesday morning, met according to adjournment, & opened with prayer.   Mr. Pomeroy being absent, Mr. Rice was appointed to preach on the Communion occasion. The Moderator & Mr. Phelps were appointed to administer the ordinance of the Lord's supper.   Committees were appointed to examine the records of the Churches in Locke, Berkshire & Auburn.   Application was made from the Church in Lisle for a union with this body.   Having heard & approved of the Articles of Faith & Covenant used by that Chh. *Voted*, That said Church be received as a Constituent member.   Dn. William Osborne then took his seat as a Delegate from the Church in Lisle.

The report of the Committee appointed by the General Assembly to draught a plan for disciplining baptized children, & likewise the report of the Committee appointed by Presbytery for the same purpose, were read.   *Voted*, That these reports be committed to a Committee of three, to report at the next Stated meeting. The Moderator, Messrs. Parsons & Rice were appointed the Committee. Had a recess for dinner.

After dinner attended public worship. Mr. Rice preached the sermon from Psalm 78.6. In attending the Lord's supper Mr. Phelps administered the bread, & Mr. Woodruff the cup. The Committees appointed to examine the records of the Churches, reported that said records had been kept with care & accuracy; which reports were accepted.

The Church in Lisle having made out a Call to Rev. Henry Ford, member of the Presbytery of Hudson, to settle with them in the Gospel ministry, *Voted*, that a certificate be made out & forwarded to the Presbytery of Hudson, that said Church is a Constituent member of this body, & that they are in order in making out this Call.

Collected for the Contingent Fund $1.87.

The Committee appointed to take into consideration the sins of Intemperance & Sabbath-breaking & devise measures for the suppression of these vices, reported. This reported was recommitted to the same Committee for revision & publication.

Voted, That Mr. Vibus Osborne be furnished with a certificate that he has performed two weeks Missionary service in the name of this Presbytery.

The Commissioners to the last meeting of the General Assembly reported, that they attended agreeably to appointment; which report was accepted. *Voted*, that for every special meeting the Moderator shall give at least ten day's previous notice of sd. meeting.

Mr. Parsons was appointed *Treasurer*, & Mr. Smith *Register*. Messrs. Woodruff, Osborne, & Rice were appointed a Committee of License & Certification. The Treasurer made his report, which was accepted. The Committee on the subject of Intemperance & Sabbath-breaking were directed to publish 150 copies of their report, together with an address to the public on the subject; & to Call upon the Treasurer for monies to defray the expense of publication.

Voted, That the next Stated Meeting be held at Skaneatoles, & that Mr. Smith preach on the Communion occasion.

Voted, That the above minuets be accepted.

Adjourned, to meet at Skaneatoles, at Mr. Thaddeus Edwards in February.   Closed with prayer.

HEZ. N. WOODRUFF, *Moderator*

Attest, SETH SMITH, *Clerk.*

Special Meeting, at Lisle, Oct. 27th 1813

Presbytery of Cayuga Convened at Lisle on Wednesday the 27th of October 1813, by order of the Moderator, for the purpose of installing the Rev. Henry Ford Pastor of the Church & Congregation in that place. . . .

Opened with prayer.   The Moderator not being present, Mr. Osborne was appointed Moderator for the present meeting & Mr. Smith Clerk.

The Rev. Reuben Hurd, member of the Onondaga Presbytery, being present, was invited to sit with us as a corresponding member.

The Rev. Henry Ford presented a communication from the Presbytery of Hudson, certifying that he is a member of that Presbytery, & recommending him to this Presbytery. Mr. Ford was according received as a Constituent member of this body.   It appeared from the above that the Call from the Church in Lisle had been presented to Mr. Ford, & that he has accepted said Call.   Presbytery being satisfied as to the regularity of the Call, & the sufficiency of the support offered to Mr. Ford, proceeded to his examination. Having examined Mr. Ford respecting his acquaintance with Doctrinal & experimental religion, Presbytery cordially approve of his qualifications for a Gospel minister, & *Voted*, to proceed to the Installation this day at half past 1. O Clock.   The parts were assigned as follows, Mr. Rice make the Introductory prayer; Mr. Smith preach the sermon; the Moderator make the Consecrating prayer; & de-

liver the charge to the Pastor; Mr. Smith give the right-
hand; Mr. Hurd give the Charge to the people, & make
the Concluding prayer.

At the time appointed, proceeded to the Meeting-house
& Installed the Rev. Henry Ford, the Pastor of the Church
& Congregation in this place. The several parts were per-
formed according to the previous arrangement.

Read & approved.   Concluded with prayer.

JEREMIAH OSBORNE, *Mod. pro. tem.*
Attest, SETH SMITH, *Clerk*

Special Meeting at Mentz, Dec. 28th 1813

Presbytery of Cayuga convened at the house of Ira Hopkins Esq. in Mentz on the 28th of Dec. 1813 agreeably
to special notice by the Moderator for the purpose of dissolving the pastoral relation between the Rev. Francis Pomeroy & the Church & Congregation in Brutus. . . .

Opened with prayer by the Moderator.   Mr. Parsons
was appointed Clerk of the present meeting.

The request of Mr. Pomeroy to the Chh. & Society in
Brutus to be dismissed from his pastoral charge over them,
assigning his reasons for the same; together with the consent of the Chh. & Society to the said request, was laid
before Presbytery.   After making all necessary inquiries
of Mr. Pomeroy, & of the Chh. & Society respecting the
above request; and after taking the subject into serious
consideration, *Voted* unanimously, That the pastoral relation between the Rev. Francis Pomeroy & the Chh. & Society in Brutus be, & is hereby dissolved.   Presbytery deeply
regret that the dispensations of Providence have rendered
this measure expedient.   Still they would cheerfully acquiesce in the disposals of the great Head of the Chh.
They with pleasure bear testimony in favor of the Ministerial faithfulness of brother Pomeroy, & earnestly commend him to the grace of God; praying that he may be
extensively useful in some part of the Lord's vineyard.
They at the same time earnestly commend the said Chh. &

Society to the care of the great head of the Chh. that they may not be scattered as sheep without a shepherd. Presbytery at the same time earnestly impress upon them the duty of making all necessary exertions, speedily, to procure the preaching of the Gospel, & the reestablishment of the ministry among them.

Mr. Pomeroy being about to remove within the bounds of the Presbytery of Geneva, requested to be dismissed from the care of this Presbytery & recommended to the care of the Presbytery of Geneva. *Voted*, That his request be granted. *Voted*, That Mr. Pomeroy be requested to preach to the Chh. & Society in Brutus next Sabbath, & to declare them vacant.

Communications having been made to Presbytery by Solomon Jones, stating that difficulties exist between Eli Bacon, & the Rev. Daniel Loring, & requesting the attention of Presbytery to the same; therefore, *Voted,* that the Moderator be requested to notify Mr. Loring, & the parties concerned to appear with their witnesses before Presbytery at their stated meeting at Skaneatoles on the 3rd Tuesday of February next.

Hez. N. Woodruff, Moderator

Test. Levi Parsons, Clerk.

March 15th 1814. Transcribed from the minuets of Presbytery.

Seth Smith, *Stated Clerk.*

2. EXTRACT FROM A RECORD OF THE PROCEEDINGS OF THE UNION RELIGIOUS SOCIETY AND THE TRUSTEES THEREOF

[Oaks Corners Presbyterian Church in Phelps: Congregational Records.[5] The copy of the original Record from which this is taken is in Auburn Theological Seminary.]

[5] The town of Phelps, Ontario County, New York, lay within the bounds of the Ontario Association. In July, 1811, delegates from the various Associations in New York met in Clinton in order to discuss the desirability of forming a State Association. A diversity of opinion prevailed, and the influence of the Middle Association led to the conclusion that union with the Presbyterians was preferable. The Ontario Association was dissolved

At a meeting of Union Religious Society held in the Town of Phelps, at Stephen Holland's Inn on the ninth day of Jany. 1805 Agreeable to public Notice in order to elect two Trustees in the room of Jabez Swan & Joseph Hall & to transact such other business as the sd. electors shall deem expedient.   The following Resolutions were agreed to Viz 1st Philetus Swift Esqr. was chosen chairman & Joseph Hall Secty.

2nd. Willm. Burnet & Lemuel Banister were chosen inspectors of the elections.

3rd Joseph Hall & Jabez Swan were chosen Trustees.

4th That the Pews in the meeting house be finished upon an uniform plan.

5th That the pew ground Shall be sold.

6th That those who have subscribed & paid any certain Sum towards the building & finishing sd. meeting house, it shall be recd. in payment towards their bid on their pew ground.

7th That Lemuel Banister & Joseph Hall be appointed as a committee to bring forward a plan of the pew ground, at the next meeting.

8th That this meeting be adjourned to Wednesday the sixteenth instant, at four o'Clock P. M. on said day at Stephen Holland's Inn in Phelps Town.

Sign'd { PHILETUS SWIFT—Chairman
         JOSEPH HALL—Secty.

A true Copy of
the Original
    JOSEPH HALL Secty.

.   .   .

We the undersigned hereby certify that Jabez Swan &

and the ministers and churches united with the Presbytery of Geneva. The Union Religious Society of Phelps was first organized as a Congregational body, but in April, 1814 was constituted the First Presbyterian Church in Phelps within the bounds of the Presbytery of Geneva. Numerous churches in central and western New York took the name Union Religious Society at their organization.

Joseph Hall were duly elected Trustees the third class of Union Religious Society this ninth day of January 1805. Sign'd & sealed by

Attested $\left\{\begin{array}{ll} \text{DAVID BURNET} & \text{WILLM. BURNET} \\ \text{DAVID NORTHAM} & \text{LEMUEL BANISTER} \end{array}\right\}$ Inspectors of Election

The above a true copy of the original[6]
JOSEPH HALL Secty.

. . .

Agreable to Adjournment, Union Religious Society met at Mr. Stephen Holland's Inn, Phelps Town, on Wednesday 16 Jany. 1805 when the following resolutions were adopted Viz

1st That the Draft hereunto annexed shall be the plan after which the inner side of the meeting house shall be finished subject to the following amendment (to wit) that the two pews in the rear on either side of the broad alley on the lower floor shall be made into four seats.

2nd That the sale of the Pew-Ground shall commence on the ninth Day of February next at nine o'Clock in the morning at Stephen Holland's Inn.

3rd That every purchaser of a Pew shall immediately deposite in the hands of the Vendue Master two Dollars as part payment.

4th That the one third of the residue shall be paid by the first Day of May next.

5th That the residue shall be paid by the first day of January next.

6th That this meeting be dissolved & all farther business touching the sale entrusted to the Trustees.

PHILETUS SWIFT, Chairman

JOSEPH HALL, Secty.

[6] The notation, "The above a true Copy of the Original" will be omitted in subsequent records.

Conditions

The conditions of this Vendue is such. The highest bidder to be the purchaser. The purchaser shall on each pew he purchases pay into the hands of the Vendue master the Sum of two Dollars. One third of the residue to be paid to the trustees on or before the first day of May next, & the remaining two thirds to be paid on or before the first day of January next. Those who have Subscribed towards building the meeting house, The same shall be received in payment of their pews if any they purchase. Boards, Nails or any other materials necessary for finishing sd. house will be recd. in payment if delivered on or before the first day of May, & contracted for with the Trustees on or before the fifteenth day of March. Approved notes will be expected from each purchaser on the day of sale. Given under our hands at Phelps this ninth day of February 1805.

Signed { DAVID NORTHAM, PHILETUS SWIFT, THADEUS OAKS, JOSEPH HALL } Trustees

Phelps, July 19th 1805

At a meeting of the Board of Trustees of Union Religious Society for the purpose of appointing a Collector for the said society.

Resolved that Joseph Hall be appointed collector for this Board.

Resolved that the foregoing resolution be reconsider'd . . . and Resolved that David Northam be appointed Collector for this Board.

Signed, PHILETUS SWIFT, President

EXTRACTS FROM THE SESSION BOOK VOL. 1ST OF THE FIRST PRESBYTERIAN CHURCH IN PHELPS — IN THE COUNTY OF ONTARIO AND STATE OF NEW YORK

Constituted the first day of April 1813
At a Church meeting held at the dwelling house of Mr.

Thaddeus Collins on Thursday the first day of Apr. 1813 according to adjournment; opened with prayer.

1st. A motion was made seconded and carried by vote that this Church join the Presbytery of Geneva.

2nd. A motion was made seconded and carried by vote that this Church adopt the presbyterian form of government in full.

3rd. Dr. Peter Woodward was appointed as a delegate to attend the next association and Presbytery; and he was directed to inform the Association and Presbytery of the resolution of the Church. Adjourned to meet the first Thursday in June next at the same place for the purpose of chosing officers in this Church.

Concluded with prayer.

.   .   .

At a church meeting holden at the dwelling house of Mr. Thaddeus Collins on Thursday the third day of June 1813 according to adjournment opened with prayer.

1. Dr. Woodward who was chosed delegate to Presb'y. reported that the Presbytery ac'd this Church as a constituent member, and gave a certificate certifying the same.

Here follows a record of the certificate

> This may certify that at a meeting of the Presb'y of Geneva at Honeoye Apr. 22nd, 1813 the Presbyterian Church in the town of Phelps presented a request by Mr. Woodward their representative to be taken under the care of this Presbytery as a constituent member, and produced a certificate of their having adopted the confession of faith and form of Covenant of the Presbyterian Church; their request was granted.
>
> Attest CHARLES MOSHER, Clk

petition

2. Mr. Collins brought in a verbal request in behalf of Mr. Jonathan Melvin that he be dismissed from this Church and that a letter of recommendation be given him in order that he might join the church which was about to be constituted in Wolcot.

3. The Church agree that Mr. Melvin be dismissed and that Mr. Powel write him a letter of recommendation.

4. Adjourned to meet again at this same place the first Thursday in July next at 2 Oclock in the afternoon.

Concluded with prayer.

Attest JOHN BUCHAN Clerk

At a Church meeting holden at the dwelling house of Mr. Thaddeus Collins on Thursday the first day of July 1813 according to adjournment opened with prayer.

No business being done the Church adjourned to meet again at this same place the last Thursday in Aug. next at 2 P. M. concluded with prayer.

Attest JOHN BUCHAN Clk

.   .   .

At a church meeting holden at the dwelling house of Mr. Thaddeus Collins for the purpose of choosing ruling elders opened with prayer.

1. The Revd. Henry Axtell of Geneva was chosen to preside and preach a sermon after which the church proceeded as follows in which it was motioned and seconded that the Deacons and elders be chosen by uplifted hands.

2. The church voted that there be four ruling elders in the Church.

3. The Church proceeded to choose their Officers as follows: Dr. Lackey Morrow and Peter Woodward were chosen as Deacons and Elders and Messrs. Mathew Deniston and John Buchan were chosen as Elders in the Church and were ordained and set apart for that purpose by prayer.

4. Mr. Moses Young applied for dismission from the church and for a letter of recommendation to wherever the providences of God should cast his lot, and Mr. Axtel wrote him a letter, concluded with prayer.

Attest JOHN BUCHAN Clerk

.   .   .

At the first Session of this Church held at the dwelling

house of Joel Stern Esq on Tuesday the 25 day of Sept. 1813. Present

DR. LACKEY MORROW ⎫
PETER WOODWARD   ⎬ Elders
JOHN BUCHAN   ⎭

Opened with prayer

appoint

Proceeded to choose Dr. Peter Woodward a delegate to Presbytery. Concluded with prayer.

Attest JOHN BUCHAN Ck.

. . .

At a meeting of the first presbyterian congregation of Phelps commonly known by the name of the union religious society regularly convened at the union school-house at Phelps on Thursday the 14 day of Apr. 1814.

The Rev. Henry Axtel was chosen Moderator and John Buchan Clerk

1. On motion resolved that this congregation agree to unite and call Mr. Lyman Barrit to be the Pastor of this congregation.

2. Resolved that this meeting will adjourn to meet at this place on monday next at eleven Oclock A M — and that a committee of ten persons be appointed whose duty it shall be previous to monday next to circulate subscriptions throughout the congregation in order to ascertain the amount to be inserted in the call to Mr Barrit.

3. Resolved that John Buchan, Lackey Morrow, Moses Young, Joseph Griffiths Jr., Mathew Deniston, Thaddeus Collins, Caleb Cass, John Griffiths, Joseph Hall, and Thaddeus Oaks be appointed as members of this committee. Adjourned to meet at this place on monday next at eleven Oclock A M.

HENRY AXTELL Modr.

Attest JOHN BUCHAN Clerk

. . .

At an adjourned meeting of the first Presbyterian Congregation of Phelps known by the name of the "Union religious society" on monday the 18th Apr. 1814.

HENRY AXTELL Moderator
JOHN BUCHAN Clerk

Whereas it appears from the subscription papers which have been circulated since last meeting that the amount subscribed is not sufficient to warrant the congregation in offering an adequate support to a minister of the gospel, therefore

Resolved that it is inexpedient to proceed further in prosecuting a call for Mr. Lyman Barrit.

Adjourned sine die.

HENRY AXTELL Moderator

Attest JOHN BUCHAN Clerk

Phelps 23 March 1817

March 23, 1817.   Session met during intermission of Public worship and voted that Barkel Bortell, now Barkel Wilson have a letter of dismission to unite with the Church in Palmyra.

Attest C MOSHER Pastor

March 30.   Session voted a letter of dismission to Elizabeth McDowell to unite with the Church in Lyons.

Attest C MOSHER Pastor

April 13.   Session met (with the Church) during intermission, and voted letters of dismission and recommendation to Thomas Burnet, and Grace Burnet his wife to unite with the Church in Lyons.   They likewise received Laura Mosher from the Church in Geneva, by letter.

Attes CHARLES MOSHER Pastor

April 19, 1817.   The Session met (together with the Church) & opened with prayer.   Examined Eunice Lang as to her acquaintance with experimental religion, and knowledge of the gospel doctrine.   Voted that she be propounded[7] for admission to the healing ordinances of the Church.

Concluded with prayer.
Attest CHS MOSHER Pastor

Sabbath May 4. Session [met and received four persons into membership by profession of faith].[8]

Friday May 9. The Session (with the Church) met after Public worship at the Sacramental lecture, & examined Mary Hildrith and Elizabeth Patridge as to their experimental acquaintance with religion & knowledge of the gospel doctrines & voted that they be propounded for admission to the healing ordinances of the Church.

Attest CHARLES MOSHER Past

Sabbath May 11. Received to the communion the persons before propounded, and Eunice Lang and Mercy Humphrey were baptised.

Attest CHARLES MOSHER

Sabbath July 20. The Session met (with the Church). The following complaint was made (verbally) to the Church. Common report charges Ruhamah Hall (wife of Capt Wm Hall) with having been for a long time in the intemperate use of ardent spirits. And she having been labored with according to our Saviours directions Matth 18 Chapter, does not give christian satisfaction. The Church voted that she be cited to appear before them to answer to the above charges, at the meeting house on Thursday the 31 day of this month at 3 oClock in the afternoon and that

[7] The word *propound* has the ecclesiastic meaning, "to propose or name as a candidate for admission to communion with a church."

[8] In order to conserve space, in this and subsequent records of the church session, the formal notation used for recording the reception of members will be omitted. This notation is recorded in the following formula: ". . . *date* . . . Session met, . . . *time* . . . , and examined . . . *name* . . . as to . . . experimental acquaintance with religion and knowledge of gospel doctrines and voted that . . . be propounded for admission to the healing ordinance of the Church. Attest . . . Pastor."

Brethren M. Deniston, C. Cass & C. Philips give her this notice & labor further with her to bring her to repentance and confession.

Attest C. MOSHER Pastor

Thursday August 1, 1817. Session met (with the Church) according to adjournment. Opened with prayer. Brother Deniston in behalf of the committee appointed to Cite Ruhamah Hall & to labor further with her reported that they had performed the duties for which they were appointed, that she acknowledged the crime charged against her, said she was sorry, and promised reformation. That she said she would appear before the church at this meeting. The Church after waiting till near the close of the meeting & finding that she did not appear, made inquiry after her, & were informed by one of the Brethren that he heard her say that Morning that she would not come near the church. Whereupon voted to send her another citation by Brother Bell to appear before the Church the Sabbath after next during intermission to answer to the complaint preferred against her. During this meeting Abigail Winter was received on Certificate. And Eunice Cross wife of Robert Cross. Elizabeth Baker wife of Joseph Baker; Fanny Chase wife Seth Chase, & M. Bushnel, B Downs were examined as to their acquaintance with experimental religion and knowledge of gospel doctrines. Voted that they be propounded for admission to the healing ordinances of the Church.

Adjourned to meet during intermission the Sabbath after next

Concluded with prayer
Attest C MOSHER Pastor

Sabbath August 10th. Session met (with the Church during the intermission of Public Worship to attend to the case of Ruhamah Hall. She not appearing, voted that the Pastor send her another citation accompanied with an admonition, to appear at another Church meeting to be holden during the intermission of Public Worship on the Sabbath two weeks from this time to answer the charge preferred against her.

Attest CHARLES MOSHER Pastor

Wednesday August 13. During the Public Worship upon the Sacramental occasion the persons previously propounded were received upon their profession of faith & Fanny Chase was Baptised.

C MOSHER Pastor

Sabbath Augt 24 Session (with the Church) met during the intermission of Public Worship. Enoch Wing & Daniel Trobridge were received upon Certificate.

The case of Ruhamah Hall who had been three times cited to appear before the Church & answer to the charge of intemperance was taken up & considered, and full proof was given that she had been duly cited to appear & answer to the charge, & that she did not intend to appear. Whereupon voted that she is guilty of contumacy & hereby is suspended from the ordinances of the Church until she gives christian satisfaction & that the Pastor send her official notice of this act together with an admonition to repentance.

CHARLES MOSHER Pastor

Sabbath Novr. 9, 1817. Session (with the Church) met [and received two persons into membership. by profession of faith].

Sabbath Novr. 16, 1817. Session (with the Church) met during intermission & examined Reuben Bardwell & Sally his wife & Robert Griffith as to their experimental acquaintance with religion & soundness in the faith & voted that they be received to the communion of the Church. Likewise voted a letter of Dismission to Abigail Humphrey to unite with the Church in Galen. The persons previously examined and approved were this day received to the fellowship of the Church by profession of their faith & entering into covenant.

Attest CHARLES MOSHER Pastor

Friday January 16, 1818. Session met (with the Church). Opened with prayer. Deacon John Patridge from the Church in Dalton (Mass.) presented a letter of dismission and recommendation & was received. Letters of dismission and recommendation were given to John Brower, Cynthia Brower, Joseph Brower, Leah Brower, Aaron Post, Mary Post,   Sears, Mary Van Blaniom, Lucretia Brazer, Damaris Hall, & Sarah Thrum to unite with the newly constituted Church in the north west part of this town.

Concluded with prayer.

Attest CHARLES MOSHER Pastor

Jany. 31, 1818. Session met with the Church after Public Worship & received by letter Sally Trowbridge from the Church in Genoa & appointed Elder Mathew Deniston to attend the meeting of the Presbytery at Lyons next Tuesday at 2 P. M.

Attest C MOSHER Past

Thus far these records have been examined & approved by Presbytery at Lyons Febr. 5, 1818.

JESSE TOWNSEND Moderator

The following is a copy of the extract of the Records of Presbytery at Lyons Febr. 5, 1818

"The records of the Church in Phelps in the case of Ruhamah Hall, whom they have suspended for contumacy, were read approved & liberty given them to excommunicate her at their own discretion."

Attest CHARLES MOSHER Clerk

Sabbath April 26, 1818. Session with the Church met

during the intermission of Public Worship & voted that
Elizabeth Patridge have a letter of dismission and recommendation to unite with the Church in Hatfield (Mass.)
where she has removed, agreeably to her request.

Attest C MOSHER Pastor

Sabbath May 17.   Session met with the Church during intermission & examined James Shattuck & his wife Mary
Shattuck & Mrs Rogers as to their experimental acquaintance with religion & knowledge of gospel doctrines & voted
that they be propounded for admission to the healing ordinances of the Church.

C MOSHER Pastor

Sabbath May 24.   Session met [and received two persons
by letter and one by profession of faith].
Friday May 29.   The Session & Church met [and received
one person by profession of faith].
Sabbath May 31.   Session with the Church met during intermission & received James Armstead from the Church in
Camilus & during public worship received the persons before propounded & Elizabeth Griffiths & Freelove Beals
were baptised.

Attest C MOSHER Pastor

Sabbath July 12.   The Session with the Church met after
Public Worship & voted letters of dismission & recommendation to Reuben Bardwell & wife to unite with the
Church in Brighton, to Mary Hathway, Sophia Smith, &
Elizabeth Horton to unite with the Church in the North
west part of this town.   And received Electa Patridge by
letter from the Church in Hatfield Mass.

Attest C MOSHER Pastor

Sabbath Aug. 23.   Church & Session met during intermission.   Opened with prayer.   Voted a letter of dismission
& recommendation to Mathew Holliday & appointed Elder

Lackey Morrow to attend Presbytery at Woolcot next week.

Attest CHARLES MOSHER Pastor

Sabbath Sept. 13. Session met [and received one person into membership by profession of faith.]
Sabbath Sept. 20. Sarah Hawks united with the Church by making a profession of her faith & entering in covenant.
Sabbath Sept. 27. Session with the Church met after Public Worship & received by letter Thomas Eckley from the Church in Newark, N. Jersey.

Att C MOSHER Pastor

Phelps, Dec. 27, 1818. Session met [and received one person into membership by letter and one by profession of faith and baptism].
Sabbath Jany. 31, 1819. Session met during intermission of Public Worship & voted letters of dismission & recommendation to Lurinda Richard & Eunice Sagar & appointed Elder Mathew Deniston to attend Presbytery at Waterloo next Tuesday.

Attest C MOSHER Pastor

Thus far the foregoing records are approved by Presbytery. Waterloo, Febr. 3, 1819.

EVAN JOHNS
Moderator

Firday March 12. Session with the Church met according to appointment. Opened with prayer & examined Ann Carson as to her acquaintance with experimental religion & soundness in the faith & voted that she be propounded for admission to the Lord's Table.
    Concluded with prayer.

Attest CHARLES MOSHER Pastor

Sabbath May 2. Ann Carson was received to the communion by profession.
Sabbath July 25. Received Lucy Pullen by letter from the Church in Victor

Friday July 30, 1819. Church met at 2 P M & opened with prayer. Examined Theodore Patridge & Submit Brown the wife [of] William Brown as to their experimental acquaintance with religion & knowledge of the gospel. Voted that they be propounded for admission to the Lord's Table. Concluded with Public Worship.

Attest CHARLES MOSHER Pastor

Sabbath August 1, 1819. Received Theodore Patridge & Submit Brown by profession.

Phelps, Sept. 20, 1819. Session with the Church met according to appointment & opened with Prayer.

Voted a letter of dismission & recommendation to Louisa Baker to unite with the Church of Geneva.

Concluded with prayer.

Attest C MOSHER Pastor

Phelps, 20 September 1819

The Pastor of the Church having notified the members to meet this day at 2 O'Clock P. M. to see if they were willing that he should resign his Pastoral Charge; the meeting was accordingly held & opened with prayer.

Theodore Patridge was chosen clerk.

The Church taking into consideration the state of the society and the temporal support which the pastor receives are of opinion that he does not receive nor is likely to receive such a salary as that he can be useful to us in the Ministry. That however willing or desirous we should be to retain him as Pastor having nothing against his ministerial or Christian Character; Yet as the Church is small and many persons who were once members of this Society do not see fit to unite with us in his support, we can not object to his resigning his pastoral care over us. Voted by this Church that they are willing the Revd. Charles Mosher should resign his pastoral charge over them.

Attest THEODORE PARTRIDGE { Clerk of said Meeting.

Wednesday December 29th 1819

Samuel W. Brace was ordained and installed Pastor of the congregation in Phelps usually known by the name and style of "The Union Religious Society of Phelps," by a committee of presbytery.

Revd. Henry Axtell of Geneva Presided. Revd. William Clark of Woolcot offered the introductory prayer. Revd. Stephen Porter of Ovid Preached the Sermon from Romans. Revd. Jesse Townsend of Palmyra offered the Consecrating prayer. Revd. Francis Pomeroy of Lyons gave the charge to the Pastor. Revd. Joseph Merril gave the charge to the congregation, and Revd. William Bacon of Cayuga offered the concluding prayer.

Thursday Jany. 13, 1820. Session met [and received seven persons into membership by profession of faith].

EXTRACT FROM THE SESSION-BOOK OF THE FIRST
PRESBYTERIAN CHURCH IN PHELPS

Commenced 13th Feby 1820 & Ended Feb 7. 1832

(Pages 74-98.)

The Session met at the Rev. S. W. Brace's in the Village of Vienna on Monday the 17th day of September 1821.

Members Present—

Rev. S. W. Brace Moderator

Lackey Morrow ⎫
Daniel Trowbridge ⎬ Elders
Theodore Partridge ⎪
Charles Yale ⎭

Opened with prayer. A complaint was laid before the Session on the ground of common fame against John C. Gates a member of this Church in the words following—

"1st For breach of covenant in absenting himself from publick worship & gospel ordinances, & for neglecting the practical duties of religion for a long time,,

Witnesses   Henry Furbush, Osee Crittenden, Charles W. Glover, Joshua Merrill, Theodore Parsons, Daniel Mosher, & Seth M. Maltby.

"2nd   For heretical sentiments in raising objections against certain parts of the word of God & advocating the doctrine of universal salvation,,

Witnesses   Cephas Bridgeman, & Sophia Merrill.

"3rd   For profane swearing,,

Witnesses   Joshua Merrill, Cephas Bridgeman, Seth M. Maltby, & Daniel Mosher.

"4th   For aiding & abetting in horse racing,,

Witnesses   Daniel Mosher, Joshua Merrill, Benjamin Maltby, & Orin R. Famsworth.

Resolved that the Clerk be ordered to issue a citation in the name of the Session to the said J. C. Gates to appear before them at a meeting to be holden at the School house near Asahel Bannisters in Phelps on the second Monday in October next at 3 O'Clock P. M. to answer to the charges alledged against him.

2nd Elder Trowbridge Exhibited a complaint against Doctr Archelaus Gates a member of this Chh in the words following.

"To the Session of the Presbyterian Church in Phelps,,

"The Subscriber complains to you against Doctr Archelaus Gates a member of said Church,,

"1st   For breach of covenant in absenting himself from public worship & gospel ordinances & for neglecting the practical duties of religion for a long time past.,,

Witnesses, Rev Moses Young, Mather Marvin, Jacob Doremus, Stephen Allen, John Partridge, Caleb Phillips, Robert J Griffith, & Henry Hubbard.

"2nd   For heretical sentiments particularly in advocating the universal restoration of mankind & denying the doctrine of the future & eternal punishment of the wicked.,,

Witnesses, Rev. Moses Young, Mather Marvin, Jacob Doremus, Stephen Allen, and Mrs. George G King.

"Your complainant also certifies that the above named

brother has been laboured with once & again according to the directions of our Lord but to no good effect.,,

Signed   Daniel Trowbridge

Resolved that the Clerk be ordered to issue a citation in the name of the Session to the said Archelaus Gates to appear before them at a meeting to be holden at the School house near Asahel Bannister's in Phelps on the second Monday in October next at 3 O'Clock P. M. to answer to the charges alledged against him.

3rd Resolved that the Clerk be ordered to issue a second citation in the name of the Session to John Griffith a member of this Church to appear before them at a meeting to be holden at the school house near Asahel Bannisters in Phelps on the second Monday of October next at 3 O'Clock P. M. to answer to the charges alledged against him.

4th Elder Morrow Exhibited a complaint against Mrs. Mary Moffatt a member of this Church in the words following (viz)

"1st For breach of covenant in absenting herself from public worship with this Chh.,,

"2nd   Communion of this church & fellowship with the Brethren,,

"3rd   For uniting with the Methodist & in a disorderly manner withdrawing from this Chh.,,

Witnesses   Robert J Griffith Sally Moore Elizabeth Griffith Margaret Morrow George Vanauken

Signed   Lackey Morrow

Resolved that the clerk be ordered to issue a citation in the name of the Session to Mrs. M Moffatt to appear before them at a meeting to be holden at the School house near Asahel Bannisters in Phelps on the second Monday in October next at 3 O'Clock P. M. to answer to the charges alledged against her.

5th Elder Trowbridge Exhibited a complaint against Mrs. Jane Baggerly a member of this Church in the words following (viz)

"1st   For breach of covenant in absenting herself from public worship with this Chh.,,

"2nd   For absenting herself from the communion of this Church & fellowship with the Brethren.,,

"3rd   For leaving this Church in a disorderly manner & uniting with the Methodist.,,

Witnesses   Robert J Griffith, Elizabeth Griffith, Margaret Morrow John Ross George Van Auken

Signed   Daniel Trowbridge

Resolved that the Clerk be ordered to issue a citation in the name of the Session to the said Mrs. Jane Baggerly to appear before them at a meeting to be holden at the School house near Asahel Bannister's in Phelps on the Second Monday in October next at 3 O'Clock P. M. to answer to the charges alledged against her.

Closed with prayer

S W BRACE Moderator

Attest THEODORE PARTRIDGE Clerk

Session met at Samuel Howe's on tuesday the 25th day of September 1821

Members present . . .[9]

The occasion of the meeting was the following Benjamin F Hough, a young man apparently near the grave, had expressed an anxious desire publickly to profess his faith in the Redeemer receive the ordinance of Baptism & partake of the Lord's supper before he should leave the world. Sufficient evidence being given that he was a child of God through sanctification of the spirit & belief of the truth. The Session agreed that his request be granted.   Whereupon he was regularly admitted to the communion of the Church recd Baptism & with a considerable number of the Brethren partook of the sacrament of the supper; when a most solemn & interesting season was enjoyed by all present.

S W BRACE Moderator

Attest THEODORE PARTRIDGE Clerk

[9] In the record of this and subsequent meetings the list of the names of the members present will be omitted.

Note— The above named Brother departed this life, in a most joyful & triumphant state of Christian feeling a few hours after the profession of his faith

T Partridge

The Session met at the meeting House on Sabbath the 30th day of September 1821. . . .

Appointed Elder Yale to represent this Chh. in Presbytery at their meeting in Geneva on tuesday next at 10 O'Clock A. M.

Also appointed Elder Wing to represent this Church in Synod at their meeting in Geneva on tuesday next at 4 O'Clock P. M.

Voted a letter of dismission & recommendation to Sophronia Gould to unite with Christ's Church where ever God in his providence shall cast her lot

S W Brace *Moderator*
Attest Theodore Partridge *Clerk*

The Session met at the Meeting-house on Sabbath the Seventh day of Oct 1821 . . .

Opened with prayer

Resolved that Lucy Phillips a member of this Church who acknowledges herself guilty of the crime of fornication be suspended from our communion untill a further order be taken on the subject.

Resolved unanimously by the Church that we observe Wednesday the 17th Instant as a day of fasting humiliation & prayer for the out pouring of the Holy Spirit on the inhabitants of this town as recommended by Synod & that we invite other denominations to observe the day with us in their several places of Worship.

Closed with prayer

S W Brace *Moderator*
Attest Theodore Partridge *Clerk*

Session met at the School house near Asahel Bannisters on Monday the 8 day of Oct 1821 . . .

John C Gates having been cited to appear before the Session this day to answer to the charges alledged against him, not appearing,

Resolved that the Clerk be ordered to issue a second citation to the said J C Gates to appear before them at a meeting to be holden at Theodore Partridge's House in Vienna on Monday the 29th Instant at 3 O'Clock in the afternoon to answer to the Charges alledged against him. [This same minute was recorded in the cases of Dr. Archelaus Gates, Mrs. James Baggerly, and Mrs. Mary Moffatt, who also failed to appear.]

John Griffith having been once & again cited to appear before the session to answer to the charges alledged against him not appearing,

Resolved that he be & he hereby is suspended from the communion of this Church for contumacy untill a farther order shall be taken on the subject.

Closed with prayer

S W BRACE Moderator

Attest THEODORE PARTRIDGE *Clerk*

Wednesday the 17th Instant was observed by this Chh. as a day of fasting humiliation & prayer agreeably to the resolution taken on the 7 Instant.   The congregation was numerous & attentive & the season apparently interesting to those present.

THEODORE PARTRIDGE, Clerk

Sabbath 21 Oct 1821

Baptised Joel an Infant of Imley & Maria Prescott's

S W BRACE Pastor

Attest THEODORE PARTRIDGE *Clerk*

The Session met at Theodore Partridge's dwelling House in Vienna on Monday the 29 day of Oct 1821

John C Gates having been once & again cited to appear be-

fore the Session to answer to the charges alledged against
him, not appearing,

Resolved that he be & he hereby is suspended from the communion of this Church for contumacy untill a further order
shall be taken on the subject.

Mrs. Mary Moffatt having been once & again cited to appear before the Session to answer to the charges alledged
against her not appearing,

Resolved that she be & she hereby is suspended from the
communion of this Church for contumacy untill a further
order shall be taken on the subject.

Mrs. Jane Baggerly having been cited to appear before the
Session this day to answer to the charges alledged against
her, appeared & confessed to all the charges, which confession was received as satisfactory by the Session.   Adjourned to meet at the call of the Moderator.

Closed with prayer

S W Brace Moderator

Attest Theodore Partridge *Clerk*

The Session met at the House of Theodore Partridge in
Vienna on Monday the 29th day of Oct 1821 . . .

Resolved at the request of Mrs. Jane Baggerly that a letter
of dismission & recommendation be given her to unite with
the Methodist Chh in this place.   Closed with prayer

S W Brace Moderator

Attest Theodore Partridge *Clerk*

The Session met at the meeting-House on Sabbath the 4
day of November 1821 agreeably to adjournment. . . .

Doct Archelaus Gates having been once & again cited to appear before the Session to answer to certain charges preferred against him not appearing

Resolved that he be & he hereby is suspended from the
communion of this Church for contumacy untill a further
order be taken on the subject.

Resolved at the request of Miss Betsey Warner & Dolly

Trowbridge that they be taken under the care of this Church & that they be permitted to enjoy all the privileges of the Church while they remain among us.

Closed with prayer

S W BRACE *Moderator*

Attest THEODORE PARTRIDGE *Clerk*

The Session met at the meeting-House on Sabbath the 11 day of November 1821 . . .
Examined George W Glover & Rebecka Phillips (wife of John Phillips) with reference to their uniting with the Church. Evidence of their piety & belief of Gospel doctrins being obtained, Resolved that they be propounded. Closed with prayer

S W BRACE Moderator

Attest THEODORE PARTRIDGE Clerk

The Session met at the School House near Asahel Bannisters on Wednesday the 14th day of November 1821 . . .
Examined Robert Cross & Olive Burnet with reference to their uniting with the Church. Evidence of their piety & belief of Gospel doctrins being obtained,
Resolved that they be propounded for admission

Closed with prayer

S W BRACE Moderator

Attest THEODORE PARTRIDGE Clerk

Session met at the Meeting-House on Thursday the 15th day November 1821 . . .
Examined Elizabeth Humphrey (wife of Jeduthan Humphrey) & Mehitable Sumner with reference to their uniting with the Church. Evidence of their piety & belief of Gospel doctrins being obtained,
Resolved that they be propounded for admission.

S W BRACE Moderator

Attest THEODORE PARTRIDGE Clerk

At a meeting of the Church holden at the meeting-House on Thursday the 15th day of November 1821   opened with prayer

The summary Confession of Faith & form of Covenant adopted by the Presbytery of Geneva & recommended to the several Churches under their care, were unanimously approved & adopted as the confession & covenant hereafter to be used by this Church. Closed with prayer.

S W BRACE *Moderator*

THEODORE PARTRIDGE *Clerk*

Sabbath November 18th 1821

[Four persons were received into membership on profession of faith and three on baptism and profession of faith.] Session met at the School-house near Asahel Bannisters on Saturday the 22 day of Decbr. 1821

Examined Benoni Grover, Enoch Eddy, Miss Roana Nichols, Joanna Russell, and Harriet Hall with reference to their uniting with the Church. Evidence of their piety & belief of Gospel doctrines having been obtained, Resolved that they be propounded for admission.

S W BRACE *Moderator*

Attest THEODORE PARTRIDGE *Clerk*

3. EXTRACTS FROM THE RECORDS OF THE PRESBYTERIAN CHURCH OF FRANKLIN, PORTAGE COUNTY, OHIO, 1819-1838.

INTRODUCTION

[The Western Reserve was settled largely by immigrants from New England, Pennsylvania and Virginia, the New England group predominating.[10] Most of the professing Christians were Congregationalists and Presbyterians. Probably the first church to be organized was that at Youngstown by Rev. William Wick, who studied theology under John McMillan, was licensed to preach on August 28, 1799, and arrived on the Reserve a few days later. He was ordained and installed over the churches of Youngstown and

[10] See J. H. Fairchild, "The Story of Congregationalism on the Western Reserve," *Papers of the Ohio Church History Society*, V, pp. 1-2.

Hopewell on September 3, 1800.[11] The next church was organized by Rev. Joseph Badger at Austinburgh on Oct. 24, 1801.[12] He had arrived at Youngstown the previous December as a missionary of the Connecticut Missionary Society.[13] Badger and Wick were on friendly relations and probably welcomed the Plan of Union of 1801. In 1802 the Synod of Pittsburgh constituted itself the Western Missionary Society and began to commission men to serve on the Western Reserve. It coöperated with the Connecticut society; when the latter had fewer applicants among Congregational ministers than it was prepared to send to the field it granted commissions to Presbyterian missionaries supplied by the Synod of Pittsburgh. After 1812 the Congregationalists were able to send more men to the Western Reserve, and to remove possible difficulties it was agreed by the two denominations in 1814 to erect the Grand River Presbytery in the Reserve, under the Synod of Pittsburgh, the Congregational churches having the choice of local polity accorded them in the Plan of Union. As the population grew other Presbyteries were erected, and in 1825 the Synod of the Western Reserve was formed. While many stanch Presbyterians thought their Church was being "congregationalized," by the early thirties Congregationalists began to form associations in order to rescue their churches from the Presbyterian system.

The following extracts from the records of one church show how it was organized as a Congregational church in 1819, and changed from Congregational to Presbyterian in 1834. It reverted back to Congregationalism on September 17, 1839.[14]]

Franklin 18th June 1819.
Present: Messrs. C. Pitkin & S. Woodruff,[15] Missionaries.
After prayer for the guidance of the great Head of the

[11] Wm. S. Kennedy, *The Plan of Union*, p. 14. Gillett, *op. cit.*, II, p. 131. W. B. Sprague, *Annals of the American Pulpit*, IV, p. 443.

[12] Badger says this was the first church on the Reserve. *Memoir of Badger*, p. 32; cited by W. E. Barton, "Early Ecclesiastical History of the Western Reserve," *Papers of the Ohio Church History Society*, I, p. 25.

[13] Badger was dismissed from his church at Blandford, Mass., October 15, 1800. *Connecticut Evangelical Magazine*, I, p. 239.

[14] *Congregational Quarterly*, II (1860), p. 389.

[15] For brief accounts of Rev. Caleb Pitkin and Rev. Simeon Woodruff see William S. Kennedy, *The Plan of Union or a History of the Presbyterian and Congregational Churches of the Western Reserve* (Hudson, 1856), pp. 79-80, 66-72. Pitkin was born in New Hartford, Conn., in 1781. He graduated from Yale College in 1806 and was for several years at Mil-

church, the following persons presented themselves for examination, with a view of being organized into a distinct branch of Christ's visible church, viz. Samuel Andrews & Triphena his wife, Samuel L. Andrews & Myra Jones from the church in Tallmadge; Roxana Newbury wife of Wm. N. from the church in Rootstown, & Boadica Thayer, wife of Jared Thayer, from the church in Otisca, N. Y., & Patsy Loomis wife of Amos Loomis, & John Jones from the world.

The regulations of Portage Presbytery were read & approved. The confession of Faith & Covenant were also read, and with the insertion of a few words on the subject of vain amusements in the covenant, were aproved. After a careful examination of the above named persons, they were regarded as suitable persons to be united in a church. After a sermon on I Pet. 1.16 by the Rev. Simeon Woodruff, they gave their consent to the confession of Faith and the Covenant publicly, and were constituted a distinct church, and received a charge to walk worthy of their vocation. By a rule of Portage Presbytery, they were then placed under its care, subject to its rules & regulations.

CALEB PITKIN Missionary.

Confession of Faith, Covenant, and Articles of practice adopted May 1, 1822 by the Presbyteries of Grand River & Portage for the churches under their care —

Confession of Faith.

Art. 1. You believe their is one God, the Creator, Preserver, & Governor of the Universe; that he is selfexistent,

ford, Conn. He arrived on the Western Reserve in 1816, and was settled as pastor of the church at Charlestown on April 22, 1818. Here he labored until Jan. 7, 1826, when he resigned to enter upon an agency in behalf of the Western Reserve College. Woodruff was born in Litchfield, South Farms, Conn., July 26, 1782. He graduated from Yale College in 1809, then attended Andover Theological Seminary. At the request of the Missionary Society of Connecticut he was ordained as an evangelist on April 21, 1813, and in May set out for the Reserve. A year later he was installed pastor of the Congregational church at Talmadge, but spent part time as an itinerant preacher.

independent, unchangeable, infinite in mercy, wisdom, power, holiness, justice, goodness, and truth.

Art. 2.   You believe that the scriptures of the Old & New Testaments, were given by inspiration of God, that they contain a complete and harmonious system of divine truth; and are the only perfect rule of religious faith and practice.

Art. 3.   You believe that there are three persons in the God-head, the Father, the Son & the Holy Ghost, that these three are in essence one, & in all divine perfections equal.

Art. 4.   You believe that God governs all things according to his eternal and infinitely wise purpose, so as to render them conducive to his own glory, and the greatest good of the universe, and in perfect consistency with his hatred of sin, the liberty of man, and the importance of the use of means.[16]

Art. 5.   You believe that God at first created man in his own moral image, consisting in righteousness and true holiness, that he fell from that holy and hapy state by sinning against God, and that since the fall of Adam, all mankind came into the world with a disposition entirely sinful.

Art. 6.   You believe that in reference to the fall of man, God did from eternity appoint the Lord Jesus Christ, his only and well beloved son, mediator, who assumed our nature and made atonement for sin; that God can now consistently exercise mercy toward sinners, & that he will pardon all those who repent and believe the gospel. —

Art. 7.   You believe that as all men in their natural state reject Christ, God did from eternity choose some of the human race to salvation thro' sanctification of the spirit & belief of the truth, and that all those whom he had thus chosen, he will renew and sanctify in this life, and keep them by his power thro' faith unto salvation; and that all those whom he had not thus elected are left to pursue their own chosen way and suffer the punishment due to their sins.

Art. 8.   You believe that christians are justified freely by

---

[16] This article indicates a departure from the *particular election* of Old Calvinism.

grace thro' faith, & that altho' they are thus freely justified, still the law of God as a rule of duty remains in full force, and that all men are under obligation perfectly to obey it. —
Art. 9. You believe that personal **holiness** is the certain effect of the renewing operation of the Holy Spirit, and affords to believers the only scriptural evidence of their justification, and title to the heavenly inheritance; that you have been thus renewed, and that you exercise faith in Christ.
Art. 10. You believe that men are free and voluntary in all their conduct, that the requirements of God are perfectly reasonable, & that sinners are inexcusable for impenitence and unbelief. —
Art. 11. You believe that the visible church Christ, consists of visible saints, who publicly profess their faith in him, and that baptized children so belong to the church, as to be under its care and instruction.
Art. 12. You believe in the divine appointment of the christian Sabbath, & of the sacraments of the N. Testament, baptism and the Lords Supper, which all are under obligation in the exercise of faith to observe, & that it is the duty of parents to dedicate their children to God in baptism, and train them up in the nurture and admonition of the Lord.
Art. 13. You believe that the soul is immortal, & that at the last day Christ will raise the dead, & judge the world in righteousness, that all who die impenitent will go away into endless punishment, and the righteous be received to heaven to enjoy eternal felicity. — — — —

Covenant.

You, viewing yourselves subject of special divine grace, do now in the presence of God, angels, & men, renounce the service of sin, and choose the Lord Jehovah to be your God, and eternal portion; the Lord Jesus C. to be your only Saviour; and the Holy Ghost to be your sanctifier and comforter. You promise to take God's holy word for your directory, and by divine grace, to comply with all its injunctions. You solemnly engage duly to observe all the ordinances of the gospel. You promise to encourage family prayer and instruction, the seasonable dedication of children to God in baptism, and to govern and restrain from vicious practices and company all who may be under your care. You promise daily to maintain secret prayer, statedly to attend on the Lords Supper, and to remember the Sabbath day, & keep it holy. You promise to refrain from unnessarily associating with the vicious, & from vain conversation, & amusements[17]; & finally, to watch over the members of the church, and if necessary, to reprove them with christian meekness and brotherly love, to submit to the watch and discipline of this church, endeavoring in all things to promote its prosperity, & to walk worthy of the vocation wherewith you are called. Relying on divine good you thus covenant with God and this church.

We then, the members of this church, do cordially receive you into our communion and fellowship. We welcome you as members of the body of Christ, and as fellow travellers to his rest. We promise by the grace of God to watch over you with meekness and love, and by counsel & prayer, to help you forward in the way to heaven. And we pray God that we may live together as brethren, glorify him on earth, and finally join the church triumphant in heaven, there to unite in the praises of God and the Lamb.

Articles of Practice.

Art. 1. This church shall have a standing committee, chosen from among their number, consisting of not less than two, nor more than seven, whose duty it shall be to take cognizance of public offences and manage the prudential concerns of the church.

Art. 2. All persons applying for admission into this church, either by letter or otherwise, shall be examined in the presence of the church, and if they give satisfactory evidence of their christian character, they shall in ordinary

[17] See below, December 22, 1827.

cases, be publicly propounded at least two weeks before their admission.

Art. 3. This church deem it inconsistent with duty to admit members of distant churches, residing in this vicinity, to occasional communion, in ordinary cases, for a longer period than one year.

Art. 4. This church consider it the duty of male heads of families, and when circumstances do not render improper, for females daily to read the scriptures and pray in their families. They also recommend to heads of families, that singing praises to God, when it can be perf-[ormed] with propriety be considered a part of family worship.

Art. 5. This church consider it an important duty of heads of families to instruct and govern their children and all under their care, agreeably to the word of God, endeavoring to restrain them from evil practices, and from vicious company, and directing them by parental authority to attend, whenever circumstances will permit, catechetical lectures appointed by the Pastor or church.

Art. 6. This church consider it their duty to pay special attention to their baptized children, and agree that parents and others who are members of this church, having the more immediate care of such children, shall be accountable to the church for their religious instruction & government, so long as they continue members of their families, and for any evident neglect of these duties, shall be as liable to discipline as for any offence whatever.

Art. 7. This church consider the collecting of hay or grain on the Sabbath, attending to any part of the business of making sugar, the visiting of friends, and the prosetion of journeys on that day a violation of christian duty.

When the church was organized under the above regulations, Covenant & Confession of Faith, Amasa Hamblin Esqr & wife, of the Methodist ch. & the wife of David Lilly Jr. of the Baptist connexion, requested the privilege of being under the watch and care of this church, & of communing with it. After some conversation with them, their request was granted.

Dea. Samuel Andrews was appointed Clerk of the church, Attest Caleb Pitkin Missionary Sept. 2, 1819. At a legal meeting of the church Dea. Samuel Andrews was chosen Moderator & John Jones Clerk. —

Oct. 21. 1821. The above named members from the Methodist & Baptist churches, were, at their request dismissed from the care & watch of this church.

Attest. JOHN JONES Clerk.

At a legal meeting of the Presbyterian church and society of Franklin July 11th 1825, the following votes were passed—

Voted to give a minister, as a free donation, in land, produce, & materials for building, four hundred dollars. — — The above named settlement, the undersigned, consider ourselves holden to pay.

Dudley Williams
Joshua Woodward
Martin Burt　　　　Committee of the Church and Society.
Selah Clap
Barber Clark

Franklin July 12. 1825.

Sir, being satisfied as to your ministerial qualifications, we invite you to take the pastoral charge of the Presbyterian church and society in this town, As a pecuniary compensation, for one half of the time we agree to pay you annually two hundred dollars, $\frac{1}{4}$ in cash & the remainder in produce at the current cash price, and the settlement above specified. Samuel Andrews, Joshua Woodard, Dudley Williams, Committee of the church and society — to the Rev. George George Sheldon — 　　　　JOHN JONES, Clerk.

The above call was accepted and on the fourth of Oct. 1825, the installation was solemnized.—[18]

JOHN JONES, Clerk.

[18] George Sheldon was born in West Suffield, Conn., in 1797. He graduated from Yale in 1819 and continued his studies at Andover Theological Seminary. Soon after leaving Andover he settled in the Western Reserve at Painsville, Ohio, on December 17, 1823. During the period 1831-1835

Wednesday Dec. 6. 1826 the church having been legally notified, met, & was opened with prayer. The subject of having a standing rule in the church, in relation to public offences, was laid before the church, and after considerable disenssion, the following resolution was unanimously adopted. Resolved that it be a standing rule in this church, that nothing short of a sincere & public confession of its members, can satisfy the church for their public offences.

Dea. Samuel Andrews reported to the church sister Margaret Phelps, (formerly wife of Mr. Elisha Stephens deceased) as one who had been overtaken in a fault, & of whom he could not, by the first & second steps of Gospel discipline,[19] obtain satisfaction. The offence was, assenting to an illegal & unchristian marriage between her daughter Caroline Stephens and Mr. Wm. Brooks. The Dea. & the witnesses reported Sister Phelps to be sensible of her fault, but unwilling to confess it publicly; whereupon it was unanimously voted that nothing short of a sincere & public confession can satisfy the church; and that brethren Barber Clark & Wm. Stewart be a committee to wait on Sister Phelps, to inform her of the doings of the church & labor to bring her to see & feel in unison with the church.

Adjourned to such time and place as the above named

he was agent for the American Bible Society in Ohio and Michigan. See Kennedy, *op. cit.*, pp. 119-120. Sheldon wrote the secretary of the United Domestic Missionary Society, about January, 1826, as follows: "In Franklin there are about 120 families, most of them in debt for their lands, & many of them *pinched* with poverty. Some are altogether destitute of the bible & all religious books, & more which have but few tattered fragments of bibles testaments & sermons or tracts. A few heads of families cannot read at all, & many more, as to moral & religious principles are shrouded in the darkness of midnight, who do not attend meeting and are thus almost out of reach of the means of grace." On August 31, 1826, he wrote the corresponding secretary of the American Home Missionary Society that there were but five male members of his church, and "I believe but one of them has yet paid for his land. The people here give me nominally (for it is never realised,) $200, ¾ in produce, & your society $100, making a salary nominally of $300." MS *letters in the American Home Missionary Society Correspondence,* Chicago Theological Seminary, Chicago, Illinois.

[19] Matt. 18:15-17.

committee shall designate concluded with prayer. GEORGE SHELDON Moderator & Clerk.

Dec. 19 /26. The church met at the house of Sister Phelps for prayer and conversation. The committee appointed to labor with Sister Phelps reported no progress, whereupon it was voted unanimously, that Sister Phelp[s] be suspended till she satisfy the church. Closed with prayer. G. S. Clerk.

Sessions of Pres. Rootstown April 4. 1827, Thus far approved. CHARLES B. STORRS, Moderator.

July 6, 1827. The church was legally convened & opened for business. The case of Mrs. Phelps was taken up, and at the request of Sister Newbury defered, till Thursday of next week at 5 P. M. Mrs. Harmony Ann Sheldon, having communed with this church as long as its rules permit without uniting with the church or assigning special reasons for a further delay, She assigned reasons which were satisfactory and received permission to commune longer. Adjourned to meet at the Presbyterian schoolhouse on Thursday next at 5 P. M. Closed with prayer. G. S.

Thursday July 13th the church met, and the meeting was opened with prayer. After due consideration it was unanimously voted that Sister Magarett Phelps be excommunicated and the Lord's day Sept. 2, provided she does not previously satisfy the church. Adjourned without date. Concluded with prayer. — G. S.

Sept. 1st. the church met at my house, and the exercises were commenced with singing and prayer. — Sister Phelps came forward and agreed to satisfy the church by having a written confession read in public on the next Sabbath; which was accordingly done Sept. 2 and she was again welcomed to a seat among Christs friends

GEORGE SHELDON, Pastor.[20]

---

[20] Under date of October 6, 1827, Sheldon wrote Absalom Peters, Corresponding Secretary of the American Home Missionary Society, as follows: "It is with heartfelt satisfaction that I can announce to you the commencement of what *appears* to be a genuine work of the Holy Spirit. As to facts, I can only say, all our church difficulties are cordially adjusted — so that as far as I know, we are 'together with one accord.' A sister who

At a regularly convened & constituted meeting of the church Dec. 22, 1827, the printed confession faith was adopted, with the addition of the words, "and amusements,"[21] on page 6, after the words, "vain conversation."

At a meeting of the church regularly convened August 26. 1829, Martin Burt was chosen Moderator, & Wm. Russell Clerk pro. tem. The meeting having been opened with prayer, it was moved by Dea. Samuel Andrews & seconded by Barber Clark, that the church accept of the following settlement which had been made with the Rev. George Sheldon as the Pastor of this church, up to the 10th of this month. viz. for ministerial services performed two years & 6 Sabbaths the Said Sheldon has received on Subscription six hundred & ten Dollars & from the Home Missionary Society one Hundred ninety eight Dollars leaving A Balance now due Mr. Sheldon $12..50 Cash & 26..90 in produce together with what is now Due on the Subscriptions for 1827 & 1828. Resolved that we continue the Support of Mr. Sheldon.

Adjourned without day. Closed with prayer.

WILLIAM RUSSELL, Clerk, Protem.

At a Legal Meeting of the first Congregational Church in Franklin on the 9th day of Feb. 1831 & opened with prayer & proceed to business.

1[ly].   Made choice of John Andrews as Secretary Protem.

2[ly].   Motioned by Barber Clark & Seconded by Martin Burt that the Church unite with Rev. George Sheldon in Calling the Presbytery to dissolve the Connection between

had been suspended for some months, apparently under the influence of obstinacy, satisfied the church by a public confession, & was cordially received again to our communion, At the same time (which was last sabbath in Aug.) the whole church united in a confession before the world. Previous to that, I think that there were two hopeful converts, now there are between 20 & 30. Several seem to be still bowed down under a sense of sin. Of the above number 7 or 8 heads of families.— The work has thus far been characterized with stillness & great power. Convictions have been pungent & short, & remarkably free from animal feelings —."

[21] See Covenant, above.

Mr. Sheldon as the Pastor of the Church & the Church upon condition that Mr. Sheldon relinquish all pecuniary claims on this Church as A Church & sd Church on their part as A Church relinquish all Pecuniary Claims on Mr. Sheldon.   the Motion being put was passed in the affirmative.[22]

3[ly]. Motioned by Dea. Dudley Williams & Seconded by Martin Burt that the Presbytery be invited to convene in Franklin of Wednesday the 23 inst for the purpose of Dissolving the connection between Mr. Sheldon & this Church. The Motion being put was carried in the Affirmative.

4[ly]. Motioned by Martin Burt & Seconded by William Stevens that tuesday the 22d instant be spent by this Church in Fasting and prayer in view of the important Business to be transacted by the Presbytery & this Church & Minister.

Passed in the Affirmative.

5[ly]. Motiond that Dudley Williams be Appointed as A Committee to present the business of the Church before the Presbyterry at their Meeting in Franklin.

Passed in the Affirmative.

Adjourned to tuesday 22 instant & closed by prayer.

This record transcribed by Dudley Williams, Clerk.

Feb. 22d 1831   At a regular Church Meeting Clarrissa Bosworth now Clarrissa Wolcopp was dismissed from the watch of this Church & recommended to the Church in Farmington, Trumbull County, Ohio.

DUDLEY WILLIAMS, Clerk.

[22] On April 26, 1830, Sheldon wrote Absalom Peters, Corresponding Secretary of the American Home Missionary Society, as follows: "Previous to the close of the year ending August 8, 1829, by the influence of one man, (the last that was received into church,) our church and society was thrown into an unhappy state & has remained so. . . . I have repeatedly called the attention of the church to the subject and requested them to decide the question one way or the other, but it still remains undetermined whether the church will unanimously continue to *call* me their minister or not. I think however, that unless there should be soon a powerful revival of religion here again, that my continuance would not be profitable. . . . What disposal will be made of me in the providence of God I know not. I think for some months to come I shall act as an agent of the A. B. S." MS *letter in the American Home Missionary Society Correspondence.*

February 24th, 1831. The Presbytery of Portage County convened at Franklin According to the united request of Revd. George Sheldon & the Church of Franklin for the purpose of Dissolving the Pastoral relation between him & this Church. the Presbyterry opened the Meeting by prayr, & the business was presented to the Presbyterry by Revd. George Sheldon Pastor & Dudley Williams Committee. The Presbyterry requested us to Assign reasons why the relation between Mr. Sheldon & this Church should be Dissolved

               & were as Follows

Whereas circumstances have combined to diminish the pastoral influence of Mr. Sheldon so far that he cannot be extensively useful in the place & Also to render it impractible at present to raise an adequate Support for him & we do suppose that Mr. Sheldon & the Church have both Contributed to some extent by imprudence & neglect to produce this state of things, still the Church in view of the Gospel rules do not feel authorized to say that in their opinion Mr. Sheldon has done that for which his Christian or Ministerial Character ought to be impeacht & Mr. Sheldon in view of the Gospel Rules does not feel Authorized to say that the Church has done that for which its christian Character ought to be impeacht & that a wider door of usefulness is opened for him in an other sphere we are prepared still to move forward our Request that you should Dissolve the Pastoral relation between him & this Church & that we can as Church & Pasture Mutually Overlook & forgive what is past. But judging that a wider door is open for his usefulness in some other place or sphere therefore we still feel prepared to Continue our request that the Presbytery would Dissolve the Pastoral relation Between him & this Church.

      George Sheldon   Pastor
      Dudley Williams   Committee for the Church.

And the Presbyterry Accepted the reasons given & granted our Request & Declared the Pastoral relation Between Mr.

Sheldon & the Church Dissolve.   Attest, DUDLEY WIL-
LIAMS, Clerk.

At A Legal Meeting of the First Congregational Church in
Franklin on the 30 instant the Church Committee ——— in a
Complaint against Edithy Dewey A member of this Church
for the Church to Dispose of & the Church agreed that it
was a Disciplinable Case & by A vote of the Church ordered
the Moderator to Call a Meeting at some future day to
Attend to Case of Edithy Dewey the Moderator to request
her Attendance on sd day.
June 23 — 1832.   At 1 of the Clock P. M.   A Legal Meeting of the Church was held at their place of Public worship
to Attend the Case of Discipline against Edithy Dewey.
The Complaint against her was read in her presence &
Acknowledged by the defendant & the Church voted to receive Sister E. Dewey to their fellowship again if she would
Confess her error in departing from the Church as Stated
in the Complaint.
2^{ly} voted to Adjourn this Meeting untill Called by the
Moderator
DUDLEY WILLIAMS Clerk.

Nov. 22-1832 — At a Legal Meeting of the first Congregational Church in Franklin Convend for the purpose of Attending to the Case of E. Dewey.   Firstly read the 2d Admonition to Edithy Dewey & voted to Accept it.
2^{ly} Voted to Excommunicate Sister Editha Dewey from this
Church.
3^{ly} Voted that the Church Committee get an excommunication & see the business Accomplisht & it was done—
DUDLEY WILLIAMS Clerk.

Sept. 2d-1834 At a Legall Meeting of the first Congregational Church in Franklin Holden at their usual place of
Public Worship was opened by Prayr & proceeded to business as follows viz.
1st   Made Choice of three to Serve as Elders in this

Church After the Church becomes Organized as A Presbyterian Church.

Persons	Samuel Andrews	
Named	Dudley Williams	Appointed
	Martin Burt	Elders
& Adjourned —	Dudley Williams, Clerk.	

Sept 31 — 1834 At a Legall Meeting of the Church in Franklin at their usual place of Holding Meetings met for the purpose of being organized A Presbyterian Church.

& Samuel Andrews	Were ordained as
Dudley Williams	Elders
Martin Burt	Andrews & Williams Deacons

Ministerial Service performed by Revd. Mrss. Doolittle & Nash According to their Appointment by Presbyterry.

DUDLEY WILLIAMS Clerk

Oct. 20 — 1834   At a Legal Meeting of the Elders of the Presbyterian Church in Franklin Met at the House of Det. Simeon Bunger & Organized the Session of sd Church.[23]

	Martin Burt Moderator
Appointed	Dudley Williams Secretary
	Dudley Williams Clerk.

Nov. 6th 1834   The Session of the Presbyterian Church Met at the Dwelling House of Det. Simeon Bunger at one of the Clock P. M. for the purpose of examining Members for Admission to this Church & Nathaniel Dehaven was examined & Accepted by Letter.   Also Det.. Simeon Bung. & his wife by Letter.   Also Martin Burt jr. & his wife by letter & on Saturday following the wife of Nathaniel Dehaven & one of his Daughters were Examined & Accepted & the Above Rec'd. in full Communion.   Also Mrs. Lu-

[23] "The session is made up of ruling and preaching elders and is the governing body of the congregation. This body admits, disciplines, and dismisses members and also elects from itself delegates, or commissioners, to the higher bodies—the presbytery and the synod." W. W. Sweet, *Our American Churches*, pp. 49. ff.

cinda Heath was Examined & Recd by the Session into full Communion.

November 27 1835

The Session of the Presbyterian Church in Franklin Met at their usual place for Doing business upon or by the order of the Moderator of the Session & there Discust the Subject respecting Brother Barber Clarks Dealing with Sister Hannah Adams a member of this Church & others as report Says Dealing unjustly & the Session then agreed that the offence was against the Cause of godliness & injurious to the Cause of religion in this place & must Consider it A Disciplineable Case & that we ought to take the gospel rule to Effect a Settlement.[24]

Therefore the Session agreed to Call Brother Clark to appear before the Session as follows:

To Brother Barber Clark — Dear Brother, whereas Certain rumors are abroad accusing you of an offence against god & his Church are publicly Circulating to the injury of the Cause of Christ & the reproach of the Christian Character we the Session of the Church of which you are A Member feel it to be our Duty however painfull to take Cognizance of the offence the Crime of which you are Accused is for not Making just Measure in the Sale of Dryed fruit the report upon which we feel Authorized & required as the judicatory of the Church to proceed against you in a regular trial is that in Making Sale of Dryed fruit to Mrs. Hannah Adams A Sister in this Church Some time in the last of May or first of June 1834 at your house Defrauded her by giving her Scant Measure & we are Satisfyed that the report is not without some foundation & we Cite you to Appear before this judicatory on the Second Friday of December next at twelve of the Clock on sd Day at Brother Martin Burts to Answer to the Above Charge— the witnesses whereof we Cite to testify in the Case are Mrs. Hannah Adams, Martin Burt & his wife & Daughter.

By order of the Session

[24] See note 19, p. 524.

Franklin Nov. 28—1835

DUDLEY WILLIAMS Clerk

At a Regular Meeting of the Church & Society at their House of worship on the 5th day of Sept. 1836
Voted that Den.. Samuel Andrews present to the Presbyterry of Portage Co. at their next Session the Call of this Church & society to Revd. George Sheldon to become their pastor And Teacher Requesting them to meet with us on the 8th day Sept. to reinstall him.[25]   At a Regular Meeting of the Church Recd the report of the Committee Appointed to Select a note book & psalmody for the use of the Presbyterian Church & the Church Voted to Accept & Adopt the report of sd Committee which are as follows —

the Aforesd Committee recommend to this Church & Society a note book Entitled Handel & Haydon Collection & for Psalmody, A Book entitled Church Psalmody.

Meeting Closed with prayr,

DUDLEY WILLIAMS, Clerk.

---

[25] On March 31, 1838, Sheldon wrote to Milton Badger as follows: "It seems that you have not been notified as I supposed of course you had, by the Rev. P. P. Hoyt, of the history of my recent connection and disconnection with the people of Franklin Portage Co. O.—Before I had been settled the second time in Franklin 5 months, an application was made to me by the Trustees of the Western Reserve College to engage in a five year agancy for that institution. I resisted it for about three months, till finally it was got before the Portage Presbytery for advice. After hearing the arguments of the church & myself against it, and of the Trustees in favor of the measure, presbytery decided unanimously that it was my duty to accept said agency. It was & is—one of the greatest trials of my life to submit to the arrangement; but I did submit & on the 10th of April 1837 entered upon the duties of my new station. My residence is now in Hudson Portage Co. O. The reason I have not long ago stated all these matters to you with regular reports of labor has been, that I supposed the Rev. P. P. Hoyt was the organ for all the Home Missionaries on the Reserve to your Society. I reported quarterly to him. I hope you will therefore pardon this apparent neglect, & be assured it has not been the result of ingratitude or carelessness on my part.—During the five years of my absence from that dear flock, there had been no increase of numbers and apparently much declension in the discipline, spirituality and benevolent action of the church. During my short stay, there was a cheering indication of a speedy return to the good old ways again of truth & holy living. It was painful to me & apparently more so to them, to have the cord so soon cut again. But self-denial is what we preach and must not contradict it in practice." MS *letter in American Home Missionary Society Correspondence.*

On Thursday the 8th day of Sept. 1836 the Presbyterry met with the Church & Society in Franklin & reinstated Revd. George Sheldon as the Pastor of sd. Church. — Sept. 1836 Marvin Shemway & his wife presented A Letter of Recommendation from the Congregational Church in Constable Franklin County State of New York wishing to be Admitted into this Church After Satisfactory examination agreed to receive them as Members of this Church.

DUDLEY WILLIAMS, Clerk.

Sept. 11. The Above named persons were publicly received & the Sacrament of the Lord's Supper administered. G. S. Pastor.

1837. Jan. 5. The Church met according to previous notice at the Brick meeting house and was opened with prayer. On the complaint of common fame, it was resolved to cite Br. Alfred Adams, & his wife Hannah, & Sister Betsey Newton to appear at this place on Wednesday the 18th inst., and answer to certain charges.

The church went into the election of two more Elders, by ballot whereupon Brr. Calvin Williams & Joab Gillet were duly elected. — The church resolved themselves into a benevolent society Adjourned to meet at this place on Wed. next the 18th inst at 1 o'clock P. M. Closed with prayer.

GEO. SHELDON Pastor.

Wed. Jan. 18th. The church met according to adjournment. Constituted with prayer. Br. J. Gillet declining to serve as Elder, the church proceeded to ballot again and Br. James Holden was elected, & he and Br. C. Wms. signifying their acceptance, it was resolved that they be ordained at the close of public worship on Sab. the 22 inst. Br. A. Adams & the two Sisters above named not obeying the citations of the church, not making any communication to them it was resolved to forward to them soon a second citation. Adjourned to meet at this place on Frid. evening, Jan. 20, at 6 o'clock P. M. Closed with prayer.

GEORGE SHELDON, Moderator.

1837 March 30. The Session having met at the church by the call of the Pastor, & being constituted by prayer, it was unanimously resolved that, we will endeavor to effect a connection between this church & all presbyterian & congregational members residing within our bounds who adorn their profession, & that we will report all others back to the churches with which they hold an ecclesiastical standing. According to the above resolution Mr. John Gaylord & Joanna his wife and Nancy his daughter were reported back to the congregational church in Montgomery Mass. Adjourned to meet at this place on Mond. next. April 3d.

    Closed with prayer   GEORGE SHELDON Pastor —

Mond. April 3d. The Session met according to adjournment & was opened with prayer. Made arrangements for an other meeting on Mond. the 10. Adjourned. Closed with prayer. G. S.

    Examined and aproved thus far
    the Portage Presbytery   April 4 1837.
                by. E PIERCE
                      Moderator

Mond. April 10th. The Session Met according to adjournment. Had a season of prayer. Voted Mr. Shumway & wife a letter to the orthodox congregational church in Akron.

After a sufficient previous agitation of the subject, Rev. G. G. Pierce & Rev. Caleb Pitkin on the 26th March *1837* presented to the Pastor, church & congregation a request in behalf of the Trustees of the W. R. College that the Pastor of this church might be dismissed to engage in the duties of soliciting Agent for Said College. After a full presentation & discussion of the subject, it was resolved that the case be refered to Portage Presbytery for advice and decisive action in the case, at its then next session at Twinsburg April 4. 1837. Accordingly the case was refered, and the pastoral relation between Rev. George Sheldon & the Presbyterian church & congregation in Franklin Portage Co. O.

was dissolved. The church & congregation therefore this
day unanimously resolved to invite the Rev. Stephen W.
Burritt to labor with them a few Sabbaths on trial with a
view to Settlement. Adjourned to meet at the Brick Church
on Thurs. the 20th inst. at 3 o'clock P.M.

G. Sheldon Moderator &
Clerk.—

Franklin Mills. June 7th, 1837.
Session met at the Presbyterian Church on their own adjournment. Opened with prayer.

Present. S. W. Burritt, Moderator.

Elders—Martin Burt, James Holden, Calvin Williams, — Samuel Andrews. —

Absent. Dudley Williams —

Br. H. C. Hart appeared
voluntarily before Session & made a verbal statement respecting certain [rumors] in circulation about himself &
Mrs. Julia Norman. Session after some investigation of the
subject appointed Samuel Andrews & Calvin Williams, with
the Moderator a Committee to visit the parties & make further investigation of the subject. Adjourned to June 9th
1837 Closed with Prayer.

Franklin   June 9th 1837—

Session met according to
adjournment.. Opened with prayer.

Present..

Elders — Martin Burt. . .   Dudley Williams.

Absent.. Calvin Williams — James Holden.

The case of Mr. Hart was resumed. Committee reported
that they had visited the parties & heard their statements
separately & face to face. They agreed that Mr. Harts
Statement was in the main correct, tho they dissented from
him in personal particulars in relation to some of the circumstances not very essential to the case. After consider-

able deliberation Session agreed to receive the written statement & confession of Mr. Hart & that it be read next Sabbath at the close of morning service.   Closed with prayer by the Moderator.

Statement & Confession of Br. H. C. Hart was read according to agreement at the time appointed.

See file No. 5..   1837.

August 11th 1837

Session met at the chh— at the call of the Moderr. Opened with prayer.

Present Elders.— Burt. Holden, & C. Williams.

Absent D. Williams — Sm. Andrews.

1st   Resolved to make application to the Do. Miss^y Soc. of Western Reserve for aid to sustain the Gospel in this place.[26]

2d.   Resolved that a meeting be called on the 24 inst at ½ pas 5 PM. to consider the subject in relation to giving Rev. S. W. Burritt a call to settle with us in the Gospel ministry as Our Pastor & that it be published from the desk the two sabbaths preceeding.   Closed with prayer.

S. W. BURRITT.

Feby, 27, 1838.

Session met at the house of S. W. Burritt.

Opened with prayer.

Present, Martin Burt, Saml. Andrews Calvin Williams.

Absent D. Williams James Holden,.   Session took the case of several members, whose children have attended Dancing schools & balls.   Reported that they had conversed with them & were unanimous in the opinion that they ought to give the church satisfaction for their Apparent neglect of duty.   Session voted that the Moderator be requested to draw up a writing expression of their views on the subject & present it to them on friday.

[26] The Western Reserve Domestic Missionary Society was auxiliary to the American Home Missionary Society.

April 11th, 1838, Session met at the Brick church at the call of the Moderator. Opened with prayer.

Present. Saml. Andrews, Martin Burt James Holden, Dudley Williams, Calvin Williams.

Mr. Lewis Hall & his wife Caroline M. Henry Broad Book & his wife & Mrs. Lydia S. Richards present letters & were examined & approved.

After which the case of those members, whose children have attended balls & dancing schools was taken up. T[he] Pastor S. W. Burritt made a report that he had conversed with Mrs. Rachael Eddy, & that she declared that she could not restrain her daughter from attending those places of amusement refered to, tho she earnestly desired they would not attend, that her husband, not being a professor of religion, did not feel it to be his duty to restrain them but was willing that they should attend those places of amusement & that she did not think it her duty to command her children in opposition to the authority of her husband & felt that she had done all that she could do consistently with the peace of her family to restrain her daughters & they still continued to go.

Whereupon Session voted that her reasons were satisfactory & that there is no further cause of action in her case—

The case of Elder Holden was also taken up. He made a statement of the circumstances under which his children had attended balls & the dancing school. His daughter being of age claimed the right to do as she pleased & he stated that he did not consider that he had anything further to answer for in her case.

His son Lewis had attended two Evenings to see them dance without joining the ball, contrary to his knowledge & approbation at the time, that he did not wish to have his children attend those places of vain amusement, as they are carried on here especially & that he was determined to do all he could to restrain them from those places in what he considered a proper way. Did not consider it his duty to forbid them absolutely — that it would make them worse &

considered that he had used all proper means to restrain them hitherto. Said he did not understand the covenant as requiring him to compel his children absolutely or to force them to stay away or to tell them that they never should enter a ball room under any circumstances & that if they did he would disinherit they & if this was the meaning of the covenant he did not hold to it. He refused to sign the writing that Session had prepared for such as had been involved in the above amusements. But said he would make a confession on Next Friday 13th (being day of fasting) or that he had a hundred confessions to make & he considered this thing about his children attending the ball as the least of all, said he knew he was faulty in many respects & had many things to confess & he hoped that others would feel that they had too. Session were not satisfied with his explanations & the subject was postponed —

Adjourned to meet at the house of the Pastor on Friday 13th immediately after the publick exercises for the purpose of examining Mrs. Cockran (not able to attend at chh. on account of ill health) & any others that might be present and transact such other business as might come legally before them.

Closed with Prayr— —

S. W. BURRITT.

Decbr. 20th 1838. Met at the school room & ajourned to the house of the Moderator opened with prayer. Present Martin Burt Dudley Williams. Absent Elisha Beach, James Holden. Session took up the subject of raising a support for the comeing year & agreed to make an effort to have the seats sold for the support of the Gospel annually, if the owners wud. give them up.

Voted unanimously that Dudley Williams, Elisha Beach, James Holden & David McBride be a Committee to attend to the business & have it tried in the comeing January.

Elisha Beach was appointed on the Sabbath 10th to attend the meeting of Presbytery called at Hudson the 24

Decbr. at 10 Am. to ordain Rev. Mr. Benham as a Missionary to China.   A Thanksgiving Sermon was preached on the 19th to attentv audience from Ps. 74.9 "We see not our signs—"

Session closed with prayt

S W BURRITT Modtr.

CHAPTER XI

PRESBYTERIAL AND SESSION RECORDS ILLUSTRATING THE ADMINISTRATION OF DISCIPLINE

1. Minutes of Proceedings of the Session of the Church of Lebanon, Pennsylvania, 1822.
2. Records of Bellevue Presbyterian Church, Washington County, Caledonia, Missouri, 1833.
3. Records of the First Presbyterian Church of East Baton Rouge, Louisiana, 1838.
4. Apple Creek Presbyterian Church, Cape Girardeau County, Missouri, 1839.
5. Trial of a Minister before the Presbytery of Tombeebee, Starkville, Mississippi, April, 1839.
6. Extracts from the Records of the Missouri Presbytery, 1817-1820.
7. Excerpts from the Records of the Kentucky Presbytery, Associate Reformed Presbyterian Church, touching the case of Mr. John Snodgrass, 1801-1802.

INTRODUCTION

[Discipline in the Presbyterian Church is administered by four separate judicial bodies. The Session is the judicatory of the local church and is made up of the minister and at least two lay or ruling elders. It has power to inquire into the conduct of church members, to summon the alleged offender to trial, to admonish, to rebuke, to suspend or exclude from the Sacraments. The Presbytery is the judicatory made up of the ministers of a group of churches, its functions being the examining, licensing, ordaining and disciplining of ministers. It also reviews the records of church session. The Synod reviews the actions of presbyteries, examines their records, receives and issues complaints, and recommends policies to the General Assembly. The General Assembly is a delegated body made up of an equal number of ministers and ruling elders, representing presbyteries. It is the law-making body of the church and is the highest judicatory, reviewing the records of the lower courts, receiving appeals and deciding all doctrinal and theological controversies.[1]

[1] For the rules governing the conduct of the several courts and the admin-

The following documents are illustrations of the process of the administering of discipline to lay members by local sessions of frontier churches, and of the trial of a minister by a presbytery.]

I. MINUTES OF PROCEEDINGS OF THE SESSION OF THE CHURCH OF LEBANON, PENNSYLVANIA, 1822[2]

Feb. 26, 1822 — Session met by appointment   Constituted by prayer, Members present F. D. Baird, Moderator William Weightman, Thomas Hamilton, Johnson Glass, Robert Wallace Mr. Robert Wallace & Mr. Jacob Aber being duly sworn depose & say that there is a common report prevailing in their neighborhood that William Allison is subject to the habitual intemperate use of ardent spirits. Whereupon Resolved that a charge be exhibited against Mr. William Allison on account of this above report.   The following charge was accordingly exhibited with the witnesses annexed — viz — The Session of the Church of Lebanon having been informed that there is a common report of you William Allison being in the habit of using ardent spirits intemperately, do therefore charge you with the intemperate use of ardent spirits according to said report especially some time last fall when assisting John Large in loading a still-trough on the wagon carriage & on the 6th of this month at the house of Jacob Flander[s] and at other times — Witnesses — Jacob Aber, John McEllienney, Jacob Siekman, Lucius Finney, Isaac Large, Henry Large, Henderson Weightman Jacob Flanders, Jane & Thomas Patterson.

By order of Session

F. D. BAIRD Moderator

istration of discipline see *The Forms of Government and Forms of Process of the Presbyterian Church in the United States of America* as amended and ratified by the General Assembly in May, 1821. Book II, "Of Discipline," pp. 391-421, in *The Constitution of the Presbyterian Church in the United States of America*, etc. (Philadelphia, 1827). See also Bairs, Samuel J., *A Collection of the Acts, Deliverances, and Testamonies of the Supreme Judicatory of the Presbyterian Church etc.,* . . . *with Notes and Documents* (Philadelphia, 1856), pp. 91-151.

[2] Original MS in the Spence Library, Union Theological Seminary, Richmond, Va.

The following citation was then ordered viz.

Sir the Session of this Church being met this day according to appointment it was stated to them that you have been in the habit of intemperance & that you have on different occasions used too much ardent spirits; The Session therefore taking into consideration the dishonor done to religion & the violation of the law of God do cite you to appear before this Session on Monday the 11th day of March next at 2 o'clock to answer to the said charge.

By order of the Session

F. D. BAIRD Moderator

Mr. William Allison
Mr. Weightman was appointed to serve the aforesaid charge & citation.

Adjourned to meet at this place on the 11th of March at 11 o'clock.   Concluded with prayer.

March 11th 1822   Session met according to adjournment.   4 members present.

Allison did not appear & it was decided to send a second citation to appear before the Session on the 21st.

Thursday the 21st March 1822. 6 present — "Mr. William Allison having appeared before session according to the citation served by Mr. Hamilton; confessed his having been overtaken sometimes particularly twice within 18 months in using ardent spirits too freely requested the council & prayers of the people of God — expressed his sorrow for past transgressions & his resolutions in divine strength to be more watchful & exemplery in future. Whereupon the session resolved that although the confession of Mr. Allison is not as full in some particulars as would be agreeable to session yet 'considering ourselves lest we also be tempted' it is our opinion that Mr. Allison ought to be rebuked & admonished by the Moderator that his profession of penetance & resolutions of amendment be made known to the Congregation & he restored to his former standing in the church."

[Allison, on learning the decision of Session, refused to

submit to the decision, especially its publication in the Congregation. The Session then resolved to cite Allison to appear to answer specific charges. This he refused to do, but the Session resolved to proceed as if he were present.]

April 4th, 1822 Session met — seven members present — and proceeded to examine witnesses as follows:

"Henderson Weightman being duly sworn doth depose & say that on the 6th day of february last he was returning from evening sermon at the house of Mr. Williamson & having called at the house of Jacob Flanders to warm himself he observed Mr. William Allison setting by the fire & from his appearance but chiefly from his conversation was fully satisfied that he had drank to much ardent spirits.

Quest. by Mr. Hamilton. Have you seen Mr. Allison in a similar situation at any other time.

Ans. Not before the time already mentioned but I have since.

Qest. Have you been at any meeting of the neighbours at which Mr. Allison conducted in an orderly & temperate manner?

Ans. Have never seen him at any such places."

As other witnesses did not appear Session adjourned to meet April 12 & Allison was again cited to appear.

Session convened April 12, 1822 — six members present — and examination of witnesses resumed.

"Jacob Aber having been duly sworn doth depose & say: That last fall when removing a Sill-trough from the field of this deponent to John Larges Mr Allison was in company & appeared from his manner of sitting his horse & from his conversation (& from his conversation) to have been drinking too much.

Quest. Was your impression of his having drank too much very strong?

Ans. It was. It was my firm belief that drink was the cause of his acting in the manner he did.

Quest. Did you see him off his horse at all?

Ans. I did not.

Quest. Was his conduct different from what it is at other times viz. when he is sober?

Ans. It was although I have seen him at other times in the same situation or perhaps worse.

Quest. By Mr Hamilton. Did you see Mr Allison on that day drinking spiritous liquors?

Ans. I did not. It was only from his appearance I formed my opinion.

Quest. Do you recollect the date or was it within the space of one year?

Ans. I do not recollect the date but it was within a year & I only recollect it by the removing of the trough.

Quest. Is there any difference between you and Mr. Allison?

Ans. Not to my knowledge. I have no antipathys at him & if he has toward me he does not show it."

Another witness — Henry Large was examined after which Session voted on the question.

"Is the charge against Mr Allison supported it was unanimously answered in the affirmative.

"Resolved therefore that as the crime of intoxication is established against Mr William Allison by his own confession as well as by competent witnesses & as he has contumaceously refused to obey the citations of this session he ought to be & is hereby suspended from the communion of the church until he give evidence of his repentance for intemperance & contumacy & manifest his reformation.

Adjourned
Concluded with Prayer"

2. RECORDS OF BELLEVUE PRESBYTERIAN CHURCH,
WASHINGTON COUNTY, CALEDONIA, MISSOURI, 1833[3]
[The oldest Presbyterian church with continuous
existence west of the Mississippi River]

Feb. 16th 1833

At the call of the Moderator, the Church session of Concord met and was constituted by prayer. Members present

[3] MS. Records at the Historical Foundation, Montreat, N. C.

Revd Thomas Donnell, Moderator, Joseph McCormick, Wm Carson, John P. Alexander, and. A. T. Alexander, Elders. A charge of unchristian conduct preferred against Mr. James Robinson upon the grounds of Public Fame, by the church session of Concord this 16th day of Feby 1833. Specification, 1st for abusing his wife, 2d for using unchristian language. Witnesses to support the above specifications Messrs Saml Henderson, Archibald Robinson and wife: Feb — 16th 1833 also a charge preferred against Mrs. Tabitha Robinson, wife of James Robinson for using unchristian conduct both in words and actions toward her Husband. Witness to support this charge, Sam'l Henderson Archibald Robinson and wife. At the instance of common fame, a charge was also preferred against Mr. Alexander Gregg for unchristian conduct, exhibited both in words and actions. Witnesses to support this charge, Mr. Archibald Robinson and Mrs. Eliza Aitkins. Resolved by the session that the stated clerk issue citations to the persons stated in the foregoing charges with the witnesses to support them respectively. Adjourned to meet on Friday the 1st day of March, 1833 at 11 o'clock to investigate the foregoing charges. Concluded with prayer.

THOS. DONNELL, Mod.

March 1st. 1833; The Church Session of Concord met pursuant to Adjournment. Members present Revd Thomas Donnell, Moderator, John P. Alexander, William Carson and A. R. Alexander, Elders. absent Joseph McCormick. Constituted with prayer. The session then took up the charge against Mr. James Robinson as recorded, page 80th. The specifications embraced in this charge were admitted as true by Mr. Robinson. The further consideration of this case deferred until Saturday 9th March. The session then called the charges against Mrs. Tabitha Robinson, as recorded on page 81 of this book. She not being present was notified to attend on the 9th of March to answer to the same. The session then proceeded to take up the charge preferred against Mr. Alexander Gregg as recorded on page 81st of this book. The charge of unchristian language admitted as true by Mr Gregg, but the charge of unchristian conduct denied. Mr. Wm Carson excused from acting in the case now pending by the residue of the Session. Mrs. Eliza Aitkens was then called forward to give evidence in the case, and after being sworn, testified as follows, viz; that she, the said Mrs. Aitkens was at the house of the aforesaid Alexander Gregg sometime in the month of January last, and that he, the sd Gregg, in her presence with his hand struck, or shoved his wife so that she fell across a chair, and continued in that situation for several minutes. She further stated that upon her coming to the back door of the house that she saw the affsd Gregg dragging, or leading his wife across the floor and about midway of the floor gave her a sling and cast her upon a bed; she furthermore states that he, sd. Gregg shoved her, the sd Mrs Aitkens out of his house and shut the door against her, further she said not. The session then adjourned to meet in Concord Meeting house on Saturday the 9th of this Inst at 10 o'clock. Concluded with prayer.

THOMAS DONNELL, Modr.

The foregoing cases continued to page 120 of this book.

3. RECORDS OF THE FIRST PRESBYTERIAN CHURCH OF EAST BATON ROUGE, LOUISIANA, 1838
(Pp. 18-22)[4]

Baton Rouge July 1838.

Session met & opened with prayer — Present James Purvience Minister. P. A. Walker, Ch[s] W. Crawford Jno Kennon, James Cooper, Rul[g] Elders —

Reports unfavorable to the moral and religious character of Andrew Black, a member of this church, having been wildly circulated and believed by many, — the session of the church have deemed it their duty to invistigate said report,

Andrew Black is accused by common fame of

[4] Original MS of Hist. Foundation, Montreat, N. C.

Intoxication. —

Specification In this that the said Andrew Black some time in the month of June last, in the town of Baton Rouge did become intoxicated from the use of some drink or drinks to the session of this church unknown — and then and there did expose himself to the observation and remarks of sundry persons thereby bringing reflection on the Church of Christ of which he is a member.

Charge 2ᵈ *Using profane language*

Specification — In this that the said Andrew Black sometime in the month of June last, in the Parish of East Baton Rouge did then and there use language of a profane nature, to the reproach of the cause of Jesus Christ, and to the mortification of the members of his church.

Wednesday, 30ᵗʰ August 1838. The session met at 11 o'clock A. M. in the Church. Opened with Prayer. — Present James Purvience Minister; P. A. Walker, John Kennerd, Chas W. Crawford, and James Cooper, Elders.

Andrew Black the person accused in the foregoing charges and specifications being had to him he plead guilty to each and all of them.

Before passing sentence the following facts in substance operated upon the minds of the session.

Andrew Black is now about 70 years of age; for the last two years he has been a member of this church — Previously to that time he had lived in all the indulgencies of a worldly life. — Now he is a weak enfeebled old man. When it has become necessary for him to make an exertion he has sometimes thought it equally necessary to use stimulants to enable him to make that exertion.

Owing to this he fell into the grevious sins for which he now stands charged to which he now pleads guilty. — and for which he now expresses himself deeply ashamed and sincerely penitent; — He has come to the solemn resolution of never again using intoxicating liquor of any kind or in any quantity. He feels the propriety of Church discipline hopes it will be blessed to him — and humbly submits to whatever action the session shall take in his case.

After mature deliberation the session were unanimously of the opinion that it would tend most to the promotion of the purity & general edification of the Church — and also the benefit of the offender himself, to suspend him from the privileges of the church, until he gives satisfactory evidence of repentance.

Whereupon it appearing most for edification to publish the sentence only in the judicatory, the Moderator solemnly advised Andrew Black that he was suspended from the privileges of the Church, until he give satisfactory evidence of repentance. The session closed with prayer —

JAMES PURVIENCE Modtr.

4. APPLE CREEK PRESBYTERIAN CHURCH, CAPE GIRARDEAU COUNTY, MISSOURI, 1839

Sept 28th 1839
Session then proceeded to take a vote whether or no they take up an existing charge made against James R. Little, deeply implicating his Christian and moral Character, brought by common fame; all members voted the affirmative except John Wallace. Session then proceeded to order a copy of the charge, with the names of witnesses to substantiate the same. . . .

Oct. 10th
Session met etc. . . .
Mr. Little then comes forward and declares himself not ready for trial. At his request, trial put off till Friday, Nov 8th. . . .

Nov — 8th
Session met, members present James Stevenson, A. Baldwin, James Wallace, John Wallace. Opened with prayer. The charge read — Mr Little consented to go to trial, witnesses called and qualified by the Moderator. Witnesses present. Louisa Clodfelter, Sarah Mathews, Margaret Stevenson, Jane L. Smith, Leah E. Smith; Proceeded to examine Mrs Clodfelter, who testified as follows: a few days after his youngest child was born I went with mother

and sister Martin to see his wife. When they insisted on us to stay all night which we did. During the night Mr Little came to the bed and acted in a very unbecoming way, and at another time in riding behind him, he acted that same way and at another time when I was sick he lay on the bed. On her cross examination, states that he waked her by laying his hands on her. Q. Was there any person in bed with you? Ans——. There was one of his sisters, and one of mine. Q. Was there any light in the house? A. Very little. Q. Where did he put his hands? A. Replies that it was where decency forbids answering, and riding from Sunday School he acted in like manner, so that it was necessary for one to resist his invasion.

Mr. Little then had liberty to ask questions. Replies he has none. Miss Sarah Mathews was called and testified as follows; some four years ago sister Catherine and I were at James R. Little['s] all night and in the night some time, said Little came to the bed, where they were lying and commenced pulling off the bed clothes, and I spoke to sister and she turned over: he then stayed out some time before he came in again. When he came in he came round the foot of the children's [bed] and came back to the bed where we lay and commenced pulling the bed clothes as before; I spoke to sister twice before she spoke, and when he found [we] were both awake, he left the bed and went to his own where his wife lay. At other times he had similar conduct. One night Jane L. Smith and I were at his house all night; we were lying on the flour by the fire, and Mr. Little got out his bed came to the fire, and put his hands under the bed clothes where Jane's feet were. I waked her, she was asleep and knew nothing of it till then. She told me that he had his hand on her when she awoke. He then left the bed and went to his own. Q. Did he put his hands on you in any improper place, or about you? A. He had. Q. Have you not frequented the house of Mr Little since? A. I have, but he has frequently interrupted me, and states that when lying with his children, she had to resist his hands and that she did not go to Mr. Little's when she knew he was at home. Mr Little has no questions to ask. Margaret Stevenson called, knows nothing. L[eah] E. Smith called, and states as follows; Sometime in the spring of 1837, Mr James Little came to my father's house late in the evening with his two oldest boys to stay all night. He and his sons were put on a bed together to sleep. I lay on the floor near a back door. In the night sometime I was awaked by said Little feeling over the bed where I lay. I drew the clothes close around me and he returned back to his own bed again. Q. Was it dark in the house? A. It was not very. Q. Have you not visited Mr. Little's since? A. I have in his absence, but not when I knew he was at home — only as compelled by my parents. Q. Did your parents know of it? A. Not till of late.

Mr George Fleming called and sworn, states as follows; About eight or ten months before the death of his father, his father had a severe spell of sickness and required attention day and night. On a certain night Little and several others came in till there was tolerable plenty of company. After supper we concluded to divide the time sitting up. As my wife and I had watched all night before, some one named that we had better sleep all night, or at least till we were needed. Geo. A. Stevenson and myself went up stairs where there were two beds, one on each side of the room. My father needing some little attention about that time, and being not unlike almost every sick person thought my wife could do it better than any body else. She stayed up till she had done whatever it was and came to bed to me. Some time after that James R. Little came up and waked me and told me that he wanted to lie down and wished me to sit my turn. I had just slept enough to make me want to sleep more, but I complied with his request and got up, he said something about not knowing where to sleep. I told him that Thomas was in bed by himself in the other side of the room, he could sleep with him; but I heard him up, sometime walking on the floor, sometimes spitting out at the windows, that was close to where my wife lay, she being so fatigued and sleepy, payed not attention to him. I became a little agitate, thought he was using my wife impolitely, and that he ought at least to have been at his own window. I went up stairs to my wife that she might come down; he was standing somewhere near the foot of my bed, as I went toward it he walked toward his own. I asked him what was the matter that he could not sleep. He replied that he had the toothache. Q. Was there light in the room? A. None but moonlight. Q. Was there any person present? A. None but the said Stevenson. Q. Did he lay his hands on your wife? A. He did not touch the bed to my knowledge. Mr Little has no questions to ask. Jane L. Smith called and states as follows: Some years ago I was at the house of James R. Little with Sarah Mathews. We were sleeping on the floor by the fire and in the night sometime Sarah Mathews woke me and Mr Little had his hand under the bed clothes on my feet and legs, but when he found we were both awake, he left the bed and went to his own. Another time I was at James R. Little's with sister Leah C. Smith and in the night, Mr Little came to the bed where we were lying and wakened us by feeling over us. After we awaked he left us and went to his own. Q. What year was it? A. I do not recollect. Q. Was there any light in the house? A. There was little. Q. Were there any children in the beds. A. None, there were two other persons. Mr Little has liberty of asking questions, but says he has none. After finishing the examination of witnesses, a deposition was read as follows; Hillsborough, Illinois — Oct 28th. James Stevenson and John Wallace, at the house of Harry Stevenson's appointed, proceeded to take the deposition of Mrs. Catherine Stevenson; opened with prayer; she was then sworn and states as follows: "That James r. Little was at the house of my mother during the winter that my father died. I went to bed with my sister Nancy on the floor, and when I waked she had got up and the said person was in her place and the said person had his hand on my privates. I then arose and left the bed. Again riding behind him on the same beast from his mother's, I was going home and so was he, and on the way he turned around his hand and put it on, or as near my privy parts as he could get it, and I could not get it off my lap until he saw fit to take it off, or till I got off the beast, I do not exactly remember which. This was since the death of my father, the year I am not certain of. At another time soon after their son Hiram Alexander was born, I was at their house one night. There were several people there that night among which was one of his sisters, I believe Margaret: she, L. E. Smith, Nancy Jane, his daughter and myself lay on the floor, the said person lay on the floor or hearth and floor, as there was no fire in the house that night. Sometime in the night I waked and there was the same person at the bed and had his hands on my legs up to my knees. I called to his sister, the person moved off toward the place where he lay down. There was but one other man in the house that night, that was Mr Ross who with his wife lay in a bed in the back part of the same room. Mrs Little asked Mr Little to sleep with her that night, his reply was, that it was too warm. Concluded with prayer."

Mr Little has liberty of making his defense. Says he has none to make. Session then retires, and after deliberating unanimously agree to sustain the charge of unchristian conduct and decide to suspend James R. Little from Church privileges until he gives evidence of repentence. Adjourned, concluded with prayer.

JOHN WALLACE, T. Clerk.

5. TRIAL OF A MINISTER BEFORE THE PRESBYTERY OF TOMBEEBEE, STARKVILLE, MISSISSIPPI, APRIL, 1839.[5]

Charges preferred

The Committee to whom was referred the case of the Rev. Thomas Davis, made a report, which was received, and after being amended was adopted and is as follows. To wit —

"Common fame" charges the Rev Thomas Davis with a

[5] MS Records, Tombeebee Presbytery, II, pp. 48-54 at Hist. Foundation, Montreat, N. C.

long series of conduct entirely inconsistent with the character of a minister of the Gospel.

Charge first, Duplicity.

Specification 1st. Mr. Davis stated that he had been at
Waterword with the brethren Gray and McCullum on a
certain Sabbath, (which was the 3rd Sabbath in March,
1839) which statement seemed evidently designed to make
a false impression.

Witnesses
Mr James Colbert
Mr John B. Clauselle

Specification 2nd Some time in the fall of 1837, Mr
Davis asked permission to leave his daughter with Mrs
Margaret Allen untill he could ride a few miles on some
business and return: after which he left his daughter one
whole week, and for which conduct he rendered no satisfactory apology.

Witnesses
Maj. J. L. Allen
Mrs. M. Allen

Specification 3rd. Mr Davis rendered as a reason for
absence from the session of the Presbytery of Tombeebee
at Starkville in April 1839, inability to attend from sickness in his own person and family through out the last winter and the present spring when notwithstanding he was able
to travel hundreds of miles for the benefit of land specu-
lations.

Witnesses
James Gardner
Hezekiah Gardner

Charge 2nd. Fraudulent transactions.

Specification 1st Several years ago Mr Davis purchased
Books from the Rev. John B. Warren, then of Mobile,
which books have never been accounted for.

Witnesses
Rev. J. B. Warren
Jas. S. Crieg

Specification 2nd In the spring of 1838, Mr Davis gave

his note to K. Clark & Co. of Paritotac Mississippi, for a store acct. created with them at that place, which account had been previously thereto submitted to Mr. Davis and carefully inspected corrected and acknowledged; and shortly afterwards, in a suit founded on said note, instituted in the Circuit Court of Lafayette County, Mississippi made affidavit that such note was not given for a valuable consideration, which he could prove by two witnesses absent from the State and Mr. Davis afterwards did not avail himself of the aforesaid defence.

Witnesses   Kinneth Clark
                Norman Clark.

A certified copy of the record of the suit founded on the note aforesaid, embracing a copy of said affidavit now remaining in the clerks office of the Circuit Court of Lafayette County Mississippi.

Specification 3rd   Mr. Davis attempted to defraud Mr — John Black by making an unexpected and extravagant charge for having shown him lands, some 4 or 5 miles distant, and for having loaned him a mule: which charge was made, apparently for the purpose of canceling a just debt.

Witness   John Black

Charge 3rd.   Sabbath Breaking.
Specif. 1st   Searching for land lines on the Sabbath day in 1834 & 1835.

Witnesses   Drennen Love
                Rev. T. C. Stuart. —

Specif. 2nd   Going after Ponies on the Sabbath day in the fall of 1837.

Witnesses   John L. Allen
                Margaret Allen

Charge 4th   Neglect of ministerial duties and character.

Witnesses
Drennan Love
Rev. D. Wright
Rev. T. C. Stuart

Specif. 1st He has not for several years, attended to regular preaching on the Sabbath.

Specif. 2nd He has resided within the bounds of this Presbytery eight years, and in that time has never attended Presbytery but twice to give any account of his labour; and within that time has been transiently at its meeting not more than 2 or 3 times.

Witness   Tombeebee Presbytery

Specif 3rd Mr Davis was frequently seen in company and associating with a man of infamous character, who kept a grocery establishment: and after the same man was indicted for stealing cattle, spent a night at his house as at the house of a friend.

Witnesses
Rev. T. C. Stuart
Col. Wm. H. Duke.

After the above charges were made out the following citation was issued

Rev. Thomas Davis,

You are hereby cited to appear before the Tombeebee Presbytery at its nest sessions to be held at the Camp Ground in the bounds of the Ebenezed Congregation in the County of Lafayette and State of Mississippi commencing on the Thursday before the first sabbath in October 1839, then and there to answer to the above and foregoing charges and specifications.

Issued this ninth day of April in the year of our Lord one thousand eight hundred and thirty nine by order and in the name of the Presbytery of Tombeebee.

[The trial was held at the next session of the Presbytery and the Rev. Thomas Davis was "solemnly deposed from the sacred office of Bishop; and further" he was also "suspended from the Communion of the Church."]

6. EXTRACTS FROM THE RECORDS OF THE MISSOURI PRESBYTERY, 1817-1820

CONSTITUTED DECEMBER 18 ANNODOMINI 1817[6]

Order of the Synod of Tennessee. Extracts from the minutes of the Synod of Tennesee [*sic*] at their sessions in Nashville Octr. —— 1817.

The synod having had a recess, the Presbytery of West-Tennessee presented the following request, namely, that the Revd John Matthews, Salmon Giddings, Timothy Flint and Thomas Donnell be erected into a Presbytery, to be known by the name of the Missouri Presbytery, to hold their first meeting on the third Thursday in November next at St Louis, that Mr Matthews, or in case of his absence the senior minister Present, open Presbytery and preside untill a new moderator is chosen, and that the line of division between that Presbytery and the West Tennessee Presbytery be the Missisippi [*sic*] River.

This request upon due consideration was accordingly granted

A true copy

Nashville   Test   CHARLES COFFIN Std. Clk.
Octr 4th 1817

.   .   .

The following Members, viz., the Revd Thomas Donnell, the Revd Salmon Giddings and Mr. John Cunningham Elder and delegate from the Church in Bonhomme met according to the order of Synod on the third Thursday in Nov.; but the Revd Messrs Matthews and Flint not having received information and being absent, there was not enough to transact busines, they therefore appointed the third Thursday in December to meet for the purpose specified by the Synod and sent information to the absent members.

On the 18 of December the Presbytery met and the meet-

[6] From the original MS in the Missouri Historical Society, Columbia, Missouri.

ing was opened with a sermon from Matt. 13,52 by the Rev[d] John Matthews. The Presbytery was then constituted with prayer. Present the Rev[d] Messrs Matthews, Donnell & Giddings. Absent Mr. Flint. Present Mr. S. Hempsted Elder of the church in St. Louis. The Presbytery then proceded to the choice of Moderator and clerk, when the Rev[d] John Matthews was chosen Moderator and the Rev[d] S. Giddings clerk.

On motion resolved that the Presbytery hear a statement, from the members, of the state of religion in their vicinity.

On motion resolved to attend to the [mat]ter of supplying destitute churches and congregations. When according to arrangement the Rev[d] S. Giddings agreed to spend the one half of his time at discretion in the settlements of Bonhomme, Florasant and that near Belle fountain during the winter, the other half by engagement in St. Louis.

The Rev[d] Thomas Donnell agreed to spend his time at Belleview and Mine A—rton according to previous engagement. The Rev[d] John Matthews agreed to spend one half of his time at Buffaloe and the other half at discretion in the neighboring settlements.

The Rev[d] Mr Flint was to spend his time in St. Charles and the neighboring settlements at discretion.

On motion adjourned till 9 oclock tomorrow morning. Concluded with prayer.

Friday Dec 19th Presbytery met according to adjournment and constituted with prayer. Members present as above. The minutes of the last session were read.

On motion, resolved that a season be spent this day, in prayer for the advancement of the Redeemers Kingdom, commencing at 2. oclock in the evening.

On motion resolved that this Presbytery recommend to be observed in the churches the following regulations respecting communion. That previous to communion the Pastor with the Elders appoint a day for conversing with and examining the members of the church and that previous to the meeting those of other denominations, which hold to the essential doctrines of Divine revelation, who are in regular standing in their own church and wish to commune to be invited to attend, and be examined in the same manner as our own members and if approved, admitted. and that our communicants receive Tokens — That members of Sister churches, and those of other denominations above mentioned who may happen to be present on the day of communion and not having an opportunity of being examined if they desire to commune be admitted on certificate from their own church or the testimony of persons in ours respecting their membership and moral character.

On motion resolved that the Revd Messrs Flint and Giddings be a committee to draft an address of the Presbytery to the public and request the Printers in St. Louis to publish it. ——

On motion resolved that Presbytery adjourn to meet on the fourth Thursday in April next at Belleview. Concluded with prayer.

                    ALBERT SALMON GIDDINGS Clk.

April 23^d. — 1818 Presbytery Met acording [sic] to adjournment at Belleview. A sermon was preached by the Rev. Timothy Flint from James 5 19-20. . Presbytery was then constituted with Prayer by the Moderator. Present the Rev. Messrs John Matthews, Timothy Flint, Salmon Gidings [sic], and Elders Stephen Hempsted & Robert M.Stephenson — — — — — — — Absent Rev^d. Thomas Donnell — — The Minutes of last Session of Presbytery were read.

Found on enquiry that members had fulfilled their appointments.

On Motion resolved that the same arrangement for the supply of destitute Congregations be adopted as at the last session.

A call from the Concord Church & congregation in Belleview was presented to Presbytery for the installment of the Rev. Thomas Donnell as their Pastor.

On Motion Resolved that This Presbytery recommend

to the Churches in their jurisdiction and to all professing
Christians who wish for good order in society, for the
spread of religion, and its growth in their own hearts —
in their families and in society generally, to observe strictly
the sabbath, and use their influence with their neighbors
and others for the same purpose.— — — —

On motion adjourned to meet at Mr. W^m. Sloans tomorrow morning at 7 oclock   Concluded with prayer.

April 24th Met according to adjournment, & constituted
with Prayer, Members present as above & present Rev. T.
Donnel who then signified his acceptence of the (sic) Concord Church and Congregation.   On Motion, Resolved
that Presbytery proceed to install the S^d. Thomas Donnell
tomorrow at 10, oclock A.M.

On Motion adjourned to meet at the meeting house at
ten oclock   Concluded with p.   Presbytery Met according
to adjournment and constituted with prayer — — — —

Whereas it is of the highest importance that houses for
public worship should be built for the accommondation of
settlements forming themselves into religious Congregations, and whereas the most unhappy divisions are apt to
arise in such attempts with respect to the Location of such
houses Therefore resolved by this Presbytery that we do
earnestly and affectionately recommend in such cases of
dispute, that, after such neighborhoods find themselves unable to determine this point harmoniously They do refer
the said point of the decision of disinterested persons
chosen from without their settlement, who before entering
upon their duties shall pledge themselves that they are
disinterested, and who shall proceed to determine the point
where such houses shall be Built, and further resolved that
we shall view with regret an unwillingness in any members
of such settlement to submit a point of such vital importance to the gospel to a mode of decision equitable impartial and sanctioned by the experience of all ages and
Countries,

On Motion adjourned to meet at Mr. W^m. Sloans to
morrow morning at 10 oclock.   Concluded with prayer.

April 25th Met according to adjournment and constituted with prayer. Then proceeded to the Installation of Mr. T. Donnell Sermon was preached by the Rev. S. Giddings and the charge to the Pastor & Congregation was given by the Rev. Timothy Flint. —

On Motion resolved that Presbytery adjourn to meet at St. Charles on the fourth Thursday in august. Concluded with Prayer.

Attest.   Salmon Giddings

Meeting of Presbytery Aug. 27 — 1818

August 27, 1818   Presbytery met according to adjournment at Rev. Timothy Flint's St. Charles,   A sermon was delivered by the Rev. S. Giddings from Ezekiel 12.2 —

Then constituted by Prayer. Present the Revd Messrs. Matthews, Flint, & Giddings. Elder S. Hempsted, Absent Rev. Mr. Donnell.

On Motion resolved to Proceed to elect officers for the ensuing year. The Rev. T. Flint was chosen Moderator and the Rev S. Giddings clerk.

On Motion adjourned to meet tomorrow morning at nine oclock A. M.   concluded with Prayer —

Aug 28   Presbytery meet [sic] according to adjournment, and constituted by Prayer. Members present as above — — — — — —

On Motion the Rev. S. Giddings was chosen delegate from This Presbytery to attend the next meeting of the general Assembly at Philadelphia.

On Motion adjourned to meet at Buffaloe at the home of the Rev. Mr. Matthews on the last Thursday in april. 1819   Concluded with Prayer.

Attest SALMON GIDDINGS Clk.

Lousiana

April 29. 1819

Presbytery met according to adjournment at the house of Rev. J. Matthews.   The Rev. David Tinny & the Rev. Charles Robinson Joined Presbytery — being invited   Present John Matthews S. Giddings, David Tinny Charles Robinson, Elder— James Watson.

Absent. Messrs. Flint & Donnell

The application of Rev. T. Flint for a dismission from this Presbytery on account of his having removed from the country was taken into consideration.

On Motion resolved that the Rev. T. Flint. Be dismissed from this Presbytery according to his request so soon as he shall have joined some other Presbytery or association of Clergymen — & that a letter be prepared & sent to him —

On motion resolved that this Presbytery deem it expedient to form a Missionary Society within their bounds and that the Rev. Messrs Giddings Robinson & Tinny be a committee to prepare a constitution & report to-morrow

On motion adjourned to morrow at 9 oclock A.M. concluded with Prayer

April 30. Presbytery met according to adjournment — constituted by prayer

Members present as above

The committee appointed to prepare a constitution for a Missionary Society which was red [*sic*] & accepted — —
— — — — —

On motion adjourned to meet at St. Louis on thursday 23ᵈ of Sept. 1819. Concluded with prayer —

Attest S. GIDDINGS Sect — —

The Presbytery of Misouri met according to appointment in Union Church (composed of rich-woods & Dry creek) the first of Deᶜ. 1819 — and was opened with a Sermon by the Revᵈ J. Matthews from second Cor. IV. 18.

Constituted by prayer —

Members present the Revᵈ Messrs Salmon Giddings, John Matthews & Thos. Donnell Elders — Thos. Garvin & Mical McKee Absent the Rev. Charles S. Robinson, The revᵈ David T nny deceased.

The minutes of last Pres.y were read.

Then took up the charges of John McKean & Mrs Chatherine Horine against William Graham & Miss Phobe McKee.

A coppy of the charges ———

To the Revd Presby of Missouri Territory your Petitioner begs leave to show that one called a Brother named William Graham & one called a sister Named Phobe Mc Kee Members of the Union Church of Richwoods & dry creek — have behaved wickedly and uncharitably towards your Petitioner — Thus s^d Graham has slanderously and falsely spoken words meaning to create a belief that your Petitioner should have attempted to seduce his wife to break her Marriage vows — also hath reported a slanderous tale invented by the s^d Phobe McKee meaning to create a belief that your Petitioner held & maintained an unlawful intimacy with Catharine Horine wife of Mr Benj Horine and s^d Phobe McKee also having spoken and then making oath to certain words meaning a charge of actual adultery committed by your Petitioner with the s^d Catharine at your Petitioners own home in May 1818 and in the bed with s^d Phobe, and in the Room with your Petitioners wife — all of which reports suggestions, words & oaths, being false & malitious, and contrary to the good of our Redeemers cause and the Rules of our Church your Petitioner pray they may be dealt with accordingly — and your Petitioner will as in duty bound ever pray.

Witnesses to prove the above, Benj. Horine, Catharine Horine his wife, Eleazer McKee, Benjamin Johnston. —

To the Revd Presbytery of Missouri Territory, your Petitioner begs leave to inform your reverend body of some wicked and uncharatable conduct of one called a Brother named William Graham and one called a Sister named Phobe McKee — the s^d. Phebe has uttered slanderous words and had them committed to writing & made oath to the same said words, the purport of which words went to charge your Petitioner with the act of Adultery, all of s^d. words uttered, spoken, written, & sworn are false, therefore your Petitioner prays that the the s^d. Phebe may be dealt with according to the rules of our Church disipline.

— S^d. W^m. Graham has industriously circulated s^d. Phebe's slander — and your Petitioner shall as in duty bound ever pray. —

Catharine Horine

Witnesses names Benjamin Johnston Esq. John McKean Eleazer McKee. —

Witnesses were then called for in order to support those charges. Mr. Eleazer McKee appeared, and being duly sworn, deputed, and said — that Mr. Graham gave him to understand in a certain conversation that took place between them that Mr. John McKean had used such words to his wife, as induced her to believe that he wished to seduce her. — also s^d Graham told him, that he saw s^d. Mr. McKean & Catharine Horine both siting at a Table, one on each side talking in an imprudent manner — that s^d. McKee went round to s^d. Catharine — set down on a pallet beside her — laid his head upon her feet, and clasped her legs in his arms — and farther your deponent saith no[t].

Presbytery adjourned to meet tomorrow morning at W^m. Grahams half after 8 o'clock. — — Concluded with prayer.

Dec. 2^d. Presby met according to appointment. — Members present as on yesterday — constituted with prayer — — —

Mrs. Peggy Graham was called upon, and being duly sworn deposed and said, that in some time in October 1818, Mr. John McKean, when the deponent was at his house, and no other person being present, asserted that the most virtuous Women had been seduced — that the crime was small if they did not publish it to the world and many other things of the same import, which lead your deponent to conclude that the s^d. J. McKean had designes of seduction. — — —

Miss Betsy Deen being already sworn, deposed and said — that on the night in which Madam McKean lay a corpse, she was there with Mr. Graham & when she retired to rest she fell asleep — and some time in the night she awoke & saw no body in the room except M^r. McKean & Mrs. Horine & that Mrs. Horine was siting [*sic*] by the Table & M^r. McKean siting on a pallet beside her — with his head leaning on her — & with his right arm across her legs — she also saw him the same night with his head reclining upon her lap, in a [like] manner. —

After hearing the evidence brought forward to substantiate the charges alledged against W^m. Graham & Phebe McKee now Phebe Castleman, Presbytery on motion unanimously were of oppinion & determined accordingly.

1. That the charges alledged by Catharine Horine against Phebe Castleman were not substantiated and that she be acquited.

2. That the charges alledged by Catharine Horine against s^d. Phebe Castleman were found on a writing and oath which was not legally taken: therefore resolved that the charges be rejected without criminating s^d. Catharine. — —

3. That the charges alledged against W^m. Graham do not amount to an [act] of slander as he proved in his justification that the s^d. McKean had said and done those things which s^d. Graham had reported in substance.

4. Presbytery on the proof of those things being done and said by the s^d. J. McKean which he alledged against the s^d. Graham as an accusation of slander which proof was adduced hath hereby suspended the s^d. McKean from all Church privileges until he shall clear himself of the charges, or manifest repentance. — — —

Presbytery appointed the Rev^d. Salmon Giddings as their commissioner to the next general Assembly. —

Concluded with prayer.

Attest THOS. DONNELL, S. C.

27th 1820
Concord Church — Belleview April

Presbytery met according to adjournment, and was opened with a sermon by the Rev^d. Charles S. Roberson from 11. Timothy IV. 7, 8. —

Members present the Rev^d. Messrs John Matthews,

Charles S. Roberson & Thomas Donnell. — Absent the Rev^d. Salmon Giddings. Elder William Sloan — — — Constituted with prayer.

Owing to certain circumstances Presby. adjourned by prayer to meet tomorrow morning at the Rev^d. Thos Donnells at 7 oclock. Concluded with prayer.

April 28th. Presbytery met according to adjournment. Constituted with Prayer. Members present as on yesterday.

In consequence of the absence of our Moderator the Rev^d. John Matthews was chosen Pro. tem.

The minutes of the last sessions of Presby. were read. — —

The Rev^d. John Mathews reasons for not attending a former meeting of Presby. were sustained.

The Rev^d. Charles S. Roberson's reasons for not attending our last meeting of Presby. were sustained. —

Upon enquiry it was found that the members of Presby. had generally, as far as practicable attended to the business of schools & supplies —

Adjourned to meet at W^m. Sloans at   oclock in the eavning [sic]. Concluded with prayer.

Presbytery met according to adjournment, members present as above.

Upon the subject of supplies

The Rev^d. John Matthews is appointed to complete the organization of a Church in the settlement of Turkey-hill — state of Illinois & to administer the Lords supper — also to spend a month or six weeks in the settlements of [Boars Lick] — all at discreation. —

The Rev^d. Thos. Donnell is requested to obtain information by letter respecting the state of the infant Church in Jackson — whether they are supplied — and if not — whether, they are desir[ous] to have preaching, and the Lord's Supper administered amongst them, & if so, attend to that business if practicable.

Adjourned to meet tomorrow morning at this place 7 Oclock. Concluded with prayer. —

April 29th. Presbytery met according to adjournment — members present as on yesterday. Constituted by prayer. —

Presby. adjourned to meet the 14th of next September in St. Charles. — —

Concluded with prayer. — —

Attest.   THOS. DONNELL, S. C.

7. EXCERPTS FROM THE

RECORDS OF KENTUCKY PRESBYTERY,

ASSOCIATE REFORMED PRESBYTERIAN CHURCH,

TOUCHING THE

CASE OF

MR. JOHN SNODGRASS, 1801–1802[1]

Cynthiana   Tuesday 29.Sept.1801.

. . . The Presbytery then took up the case of "John Snodgrass, charged by Hannah and Nancy Summers, with being the father of their two children illigetimately [sic] begotten", and proceeded to read the depositions formerly taken before the Session of the congregations of Kinkson and Bethsaida After which the subsequent witnesses viz. William Holliday, Nathan Sellers, Henry Hall and William Kirkpatrick being called appeared before persbytery [sic] and were duly sworn. . . .

. . . The case of John Snodgrass &c. having been considerably progressed in; on motion agreed to defer the farther consideration of it till next meeting of presbytery. And that the Session of Cynthiana be as they hereby are appointed to take all the testimony that may cast light upon this subject, previous to the next meeting of presbytery. . .

At Mr. Thompson's, Tuesd.9.o'Clock

May 11th, 1802.

. . .On motion; Entered on the consideration of the case relative to John Snodgrass and the Summers'. The pres-

[1] From MS Record, Vol. 1801-1877, pp. 6, 8, 10, 11, 12; Hist. Foundation, Montreat, N. C.

bytery having made some progress in the investigation of this subject. — Adjourned . . . (see Record,Vol.1801-1877,p.7-8.) . . .The presbytery proceeded, in the consideration of the case of Snodgrass and the Summers', and having made considerable progress therein. — Adjourned. . . .

Wed.12th May 1802.

. . .The presbytery then resumed the consideration of Snodgrass' case &c. and having seriously and deliberately examined the whole of the Testimony with regard to that case — have not clearness to determine thereon — and therefore they will and hereby do refer it, to the meeting of presbytery at Hephzibah.

On motion, agreed, that Mr. Craig and one of his Elders be, as they hereby are appointed to deal seriously with John Snodgrass' conscience relative to the case of himself and the Summers', previous, to the meeting of presbytery at Hephzibah. On motion agreed that the presbytery cite Mr Jno.Snodgrass to attend their next meeting. . . .

Tuesday 7th Sept. 1802.

. . .Motioned and agreed, that, on account of Mr.Snodgrass' non-attendance, according to citation, his case be, as it hereby is deferred till the next meeting of presbytery — Ordered, that Mr.Snodgrass be again cited to attend that meeting.

On motion agreed, that Mr. A.Craig and one of his Elders be, as they hereby are appointed to deal seriously with John Snodgrass' conscience, relative to his case, depending in presbytery, previous to their next meeting. . . .

Cynthiana. Tuesday 14th, December 1802.

. . . The case of Mr.Snodgrass' having been referred to this meeting of presbytery — On motion, Resolved that the presbytery now take up said case — which having investigated at at (sic) considerable length — Agreed to hold a private conversation with said Snodgrass. — which having done. Adjourned . . .

Wednesday 15, Decr. 1802.

. . . The presbytery continued the farther consideration of and after a lengthy investigation of the subject. On motion, Resolved, that a member be employed in prayer, for direction previous to its final decision; Accordingly Mr. Rankin prayed. The question was then put "Acquit, or not acquit Mr. John Snodgrass of the charge exhibited against him by Hannah Summers". And it was unanimously carried: "Acquit." — A similar vote was taken with regard to Nancy Summers and it was carried "Acquit." Accordingly Mr. Jno. Snodgrass stands judically acquitted from thes [sic] charges by the sentence of this court.

At the request of two members the votes with regard to Nancy Summers were recorded — which were as follow.—

"Acquit."	"Non-liquet"
Adam Rankin.	John Steele
Thomas Meek.	Thomas Shaw.
Thomas Stewart.	

Adjourned. . . .

CHAPTER XII

DOCUMENTS RELATING TO PRESBYTERIAN EDUCATION IN THE EARLY WEST

1. Reports concerning Transylvania Seminary, 1795.
2. Subscription Lists for Kentucky Academy, 1794-1797.
3. Letters concerning the Founding of Lane Theological Seminary.
4. Subscription List for James H. Logan's School, 1837.

[Original MSS in the Shane Collection]

1. REPORTS CONCERNING TRANSYLVANIA SEMINARY, 1795

Report of the state of Transylvania Seminary in the month of April 1795, submitted to the consideration of the Board of Trustees, in compliance with their standing order, by H. Toulmin.[1]

Gentlemen,

In obedience to your directions I now inform you that the number of pupils with which the session has closed is twenty-one. The studies in which they have engaged are similar to those which were stated to you at your October meeting. Some of them indeed, have entered upon a course of lectures on rhetoric & the belles lettres,— and others have been paying some attention to the use of the terrestrial globe, & to the first principles of Astronomy, or of optics, — or to some leading facts comprehended under the head of Natural history.

The names of the pupils who have attended since Christmas, or who are at present, in the seminary, are J. Bledsoe, N. Nelson, J. Moss, T. Barr, M. Harding, W. Brashear,

[1] The Rev. Harry Toulmin was chosen by the Board of Trustees in 1794 to succeed James Moore as head of Transylvania Seminary. After two years he left this position to become Secretary of State for Kentucky. He was born in England, and was opposed by the Presbyterian members of the Board of Trustees as a disciple of Priestley and an admirer of Jefferson. See Davidson, Robert, *History of the Presbyterian Church in Kentucky*, p. 290.

J. Bradford, Wm Logan, E. Warfield, J. Cape, Wm Downing, W. Gist, Robt Barr, H. Lewis, A. Lewis, A. Linear, R. Nicholas, T. Gist, J. D. Craig, W. Wilkins, J. Chambers.

The number of pupils, you will perceive, is less than it was, at the last meeting of the board; — but I have the satisfaction to inform you, that I have received from the parents of almost all the pupils who have lately discontinued their attendance, the most friendly assurances of perfect satisfaction as to the attention which has been paid to their improvement, but that the great difficulty of procuring proper places for them to board at, or the great expence of boarding youth in Lexington, has induced them to keep their sons at home. I have myself received numerous opportunities of observing the trouble and perplexity which almost every one has who brings his son to the seminary. A gentleman of Washington some time since informed me that there were five or six at that town, desirous of coming forward when that difficulty could be removed.

It was out of my power to afford much encouragement, as to the prospect of obtaining places for boarding: and I have since learnt that the gentlemen of that town are using some efforts to establish a seminary there, — and I understand that arrangements are making with a similar intent in some other counties.

Far would I be from mentioning these things as subjects of regret. They evince the growing prosperity of the country, and will promote the respectability of this seminary in particular, when the productiveness of its funds shall enable the board to carry into full effect that comprehensive system of education which was contemplated in a resolution passed by the trustees at their October session. They forcibly express, at the same time, the necessity of some steps being taken, if any can be taken, to render it more easy & less expensive to parents, to place their sons at Lexington. But there is another circumstance, which concurs in demanding some public establishment for the boarding of the pupils. In such a town as Lexington, the present mode of having them scattered about through a variety of houses, is by no means compatible with strict morals, & regular discipline. Many irregularities must necessarily pass undetected: their attendance at the seminary cannot be uniform, whilst their distance from the house makes any inclemency of weather a sufficient excuse for absence: nor can it be expected that the hours of business should be strictly observed whilst the pupils are dispersed among families whose hours for meals are various & uncertain. At the same time I conceive it to be impossible, in a town where house rent is so high, to procure a person properly qualified to undertake the boarding of any number of youth at a lower price than the most advanced one which is now given. May I be pardoned, therefore, in intimating a wish that the board would take it into consideration whether any means can be devised for rendering this building capable of accommodating from 12 to 20 pupils. A third floor I conceive may be laid, and a room fitted up, capable of loging some such number, — the lower school room, would, without interfering with the school, answer the purpose of a dining room,— so that no additional building might be absolutely necessary, to accommodate a family without children, but a kitchen and a room above, with some little convenience. The advantage of having a house rent free, & some part of the lot as a pasture,— would unquestionably enable a steward provided by the trustees, to board the youth for somewhat less than the common price. There are, however, two difficulties. The first is, the means of obtaining the sum requise to make the necessary improvements: but I would remind the board that there is a lot of 100 acres, originally intended to be leased, which is still undisposed of,— the price of which for three lives or for the term of 21 years, would probably be nearly competent to the business: and it may be worthy of consideration whether an additional £100, if necessary, might not be borrowed on interest to be paid by the resident, till the board is able to extinguish the debt. The other difficulty, is that of obtaining a proper person to undertake the business. As to the probability of obviating this difficulty, you who are acquainted with the neighbourhood, are more competent judges than I can be. For my own part, I can see that I feel a disposition to do any thing in my power, which will be beneficial to the institution:— but as I have a family of children, — I should, were I to think of undertaking it, probably stand in need of more room than the improvements I have contemplated would afford.

At the October session the board adjourned to some day in November in order to consider of the propriety of appointing an assistant. A sufficient number however did not assemble, to constitute a board,— and the meeting was again adjourned to some day in December. The appointment was then entirely forgotten:— but having an opportunity of procuring some assistance on low terms, and finding an occasion for it, at that season of the year; I ventured to engage Mr. Bledsoe for one quarter, for the sum of 12 dollars & ½, besides his tuition: & must now request the board to determine whether the trustees can take the contract upon themselves.

I would take leave to remind the board, that they deferred determining upon the time of the year at which the vacations shall in future take place: as the prevailing practice of making a holy day at christmas, and the favourableness of the months of April & October to the business of students, seems to render some alteration advisable.

Will the Board likewise be pleased to inform me whether attendance at the Seminary on a saturday be expected: for the general practice of schools to do nothing on that day, makes it difficult to assemble any number of pupils on a saturday morning.

I could likewise wish that the board would endeavour to adopt some species of literary encouragement, in order to promote regularity and permanency in the attendance of the pupils. The idea of sending a raw youth to a college for the space of six to eight months, with the view of improvement, is altogether rediculous;— and it is impossible that such abortive scholars should do any credit to their instructors, or answer the expectations of their parents.

I am happy to inform you that the books belonging to the seminary are lodged in the library room, & I have the pleasure of presenting you with a catalogue of the books arranged according to the subject. I must request your instruction respecting, occasionally granting the use of the books to persons not attending at the seminary.

I am, Gentlemen
Your humb. Servt.
H. TOULMIN

Lexington.—
April 6th, 1795

2

SUBSCRIPTION LISTS FOR KENTUCKY ACADEMY, 1794-1797

We who have hereunto subscribed our Names, Do severally promise to pay or cause to be paid unto the Board of Trustees of the Kentucky Academy or to its Order, for the Use and Benefit, of the said Academy, the Sums of Money and the Quantities of Land annexed to our respective Names: Provided however, and on Condition that the said Board of Trustees doth before the first day of October next, fix the Seat of the said Academy at or within One Mile of the place, in the County of Woodford, called and known by the Name of Pisgah Meeting House: Also on the further Condition that the said Board of Trustees doth, before the said first day of October next, enter into a Covenant with the said Subscribers not to remove the said Seat within the Period of Twenty Years from the day on which it shall be thus fixed: and more over that if within the Period of Thirty Years after the expiration of the said Twenty Years the Seat of the said Academy shall be removed, Then each of the said Subscribers and their Legal Representatives shall have a right to demand and recover from the said Board of Trustees, the Price now set on the Land they shall convey and the sums of Money they shall pay thereto. The Lands subscribed to be conveyed with

General Warrantee at any time when demanded after the above Conditions are complied with, and the Monies to be paid, the one half before the first day of January next, and the other half on or before the first day of January following; except in the case of such subscribers as shall expressly specify a different manner of Conveyance, or times of Conveyance and payment. In witness whereof we have hereunto set our Hands and Seals.

April 17, 1797.

(Seal)   Robert Scrogin About Ten Acres and Sixty Poles of Land, Beginning at a Buckeye and two Hiccories the South West Corner of the Tract on which he resides and to extend North 18 degrees East 83 poles, and Eastwardly at right Angles from the said line Twenty poles. Rated at Four pounds the Acre —————————£41 10 0

(Seal)   Moses M'Ilvain about Twelve Acres and an half of Land, To begin at a Box Elder Buckeye and Mulberry in the above named Scrogin's line, Thence with the same North Eighteen degrees East 115 poles to a Hackberry Sugar Tree and White Ash, Thence North 83 degrees West Thirty Eight poles to a Hiccory Corner to Samuel Stepenson and thence to the Beginning. Conveyed with Special Warrantee, Rated at four pounds the Acre. Ten Acres to be given the rest to be paid for ————— £40 0 0

(Seal)   Samuel Stephenson A certain quantity of Land to begin at his Corner Hiccory mentioned in Moses M'Ilvain's Subscription, Then North Seventy Degrees West Sixty poles, and thence South Eighteen degrees West to a Line of a Survey made for Marshall and Chritendon, And then from the said Hiccory with the said

M'Ilvains line and a line of M'Conalds Military
Survey to the said Marshall and Chritendon's
Line.   Ten Acres of which he gives, and the re-
mainder he engages to sell to the Above named
Trustees at four pounds the Acre Except Two
Acres Thereof including the 40   o o above men-
tioned Meeting House and the Grave Yard which
I reserve for the Use of the Pisgah Congregation,
and also the privilege of the Use of the Spring.

SAML. STEVENSON

(Seal)	Caleb Wallace Sixty Pounds	60 0 0
(Seal)	Tunstal Quarlie Sixty Pounds	60 0 0
(Seal)	Robt. Parker — Sixty Pounds	60 0 0
(Seal)	John Brown Fifty Pounds	50 0 0
	in addition to Forty five Dollar heretofore paid	
(Seal)	Lewis Craig fifty dollars	15 " "
(Seal)	Will Phillips Twenty Dollars	6.00

Marquis Calmes Ten Acres of Land part of Fifty
Acres Lately purchased of Alexander Dunlap adjoining the Tract on Which Samuel Stephenson resides.
To Begin at the South Eastwardly End of the said
Fifty Acres and to Extend North Westwardly so far
as will Include the said Ten Acres.   Rated at Four
pounds the Acre.

Marquis Calmer   £   412 10 0

A Plat of the Lands Subscribed as a Seat for the Kentucky Academy.

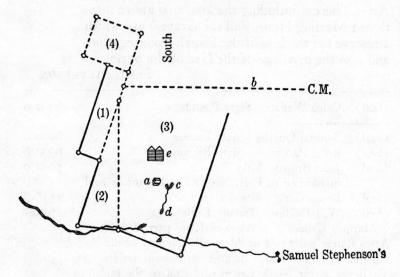

(1)   10 Acres and 60 Poles subscribed by Robert Scrogin.

(2)   13 Acres subscribed by Moses M'Elvain.

(3)   70 or 80 Acres subscribed by Samuel Stephenson.

(4)   10 Acres Subscribed by Thomas Sthreshly.

a   The Meeting House called Pisgah.

b   The supposed situation of a line of a Survey made for Chritendon and Marshall.

c   The Meeting House Springs.

d   Other Springs.

e   An elevated Situation.

N. B. Marquis Calmer has Subscribed Ten Acres of Land,
for which Samuel Stephenson will give Ten Acres
of what he has agreed to Sell

Plat of the Lands Subscribed as
a Seat for the Kentucky Academy.

We the subscribers do severally promise to pay or cause
to be paid unto the TRUSTEES of the Kentucky Academy,
and their successors, or to their agents or assigns, at any
time when required in the month of December, one thousand seven hundred and ninety-seven, the sums annexed to
our respective names, for the use of the said Academy: one
third part thereof to be paid in Cash, and the other two
thirds in Live Cattle, Pork, Flour, Hemp or Cotton, at
the then cash prices, delivered at such convenient places in
the counties where the subscribers severally reside, as the
said Trustees or their agents or assigns shall appoint. For
the due and faithful performance of which, we do severally
bind ourselves, our heirs, executors and administrators unto
the said Trustees and their assigns in the penalty of double
the sum annexed to our respective names as aforesaid. In
Witness whereof, we have hereunto set our hands and seals.

SEALS.	NAMES	S.D.			SEALS.	NAMES.	S.D.
Seal	Robt Todd	9	0	0			
Seal	Jacob Todhunt	3					
Seal	Francis Allen	8	10	0			
Seal	James Raneck	5	0	0			
Seal	James Marton	2	0	0			
	James	1	10	0			
Seal	G ^{os}. Robb	1	0	0			
Seal	Wm. Ellott	1	0	0			
	John Bell	3	0	0			
	Robert Thon	1	0	0			

Pisgah Congregation

We the subscribers do severally promise to pay or cause
to be paid unto the TRUSTEES of the Kentucky Academy,
and their successors, or to their agents or assigns, at any

time when required in the month of December, one thousand seven hundred and ninety-six, the sums annexed to our respective names, for the use of the said Academy: one third part thereof to be paid in Cash, and the other two thirds in Live Cattle, Pork, Flour, Hemp or Cotton, at the then cash prices, delivered at such convenient places in the counties where the subscribers severally reside, as the said Trustees or their agents or assigns shall appoint. For the due and faithful performance of which, we do severally bind ourselves, our heirs, executors and administrators unto the said Trustees and their assigns in the penalty of double the sum annexed to our respective names as aforesaid. In Witness whereof, we have hereunto set our hands and seals.

SEALS	NAMES	S. D.	SEALS	NAMES	S. D.
Seal	Wm. Renick	1 10		James Crawford	1 10 0
	Saml. Scott	6— 0 0		Clement Hill	1 0 0
Seal	John Welsh	4 0 0			
	George Scott	5—0—0			
Seal	Alex Eliot	3		11—15—0	
Seal	Sam Montgomery	3			
	Andrew B Sh	1			
	Nathan Linmie	3			
	Charles ———	3 12			
	James M Graham	2 0 0			

S D

15—12 0

	Wm. Brown	3 0 0

Seals	Names	S. D.	Seals	Names
	John Voreis	3 0 0		
	Rachel Downing	2 5 0		
	Moses Dooley	5 0 0		
	Mary Rice – –	0 12		
	Benjamin Spielman	0 9 0		
	George Doglas	3 0 0		
	Jno. Floyd	1 10		
	Raba Brown	2 5 0		
	James Sellers	1 10 0		

Cornealius Bontea	1 0 0		– S D
			23–11– 0
			11–15– 0
			15–12– 0
			50–38– 0

Memm. of Subscribers names Anext to a Subscription
Returnd to the Board of Trustees Towit

		Sh	D
James Thompson	10	00	00
John Lapsley	10	00	00
Henry Pawling	5	00	00
William Lamme	5	00	00

Forks of Dicks River – 2
53 – 8 – 0

3. A SUBSCRIPTION LIST OF THE WALNUT HILLS CHURCH FOR KENTUCKY ACADEMY[2]

We the Subscribers, for the purpose of promoting learning and useful knowledge, do subscribe the following sums annexed to our names, for the use of a Public Seminary, as agreed on by the Transylvania Presbytery: one third of which shall be paid in Cash, and the other two thirds in the following specific articles, viz. live Cattle, Pork, Flour and Hemp: the Cash to be paid on or before the first day of November next, to the collectors appointed for that purpose: And the Property shall be payable on demand, any time after the first day of December next, to be delivered at some convenient place, and to some proper person, who shall be appointed in each county respectively: For the due and faithful performance of the above, We the subscribers (each for himself) do bind ourselves, our Heirs, Executors and Administrators (unto Col. John Caldwell, Col. Robert Patterson, Col. James Smith, Col. Joseph Crockett and Mr. James Thompson surveyor; in trust for said Seminary until Trustees are appointed thereto) in the penal sum of

[2] Shane Collection, Presbyterian Historical Society, Philadelphia.

One hundred Pounds each: As Witness our Hands and Seals, this   day of May, One Thousand, Seven Hundred and Ninety Four.

£.			
	15.	James Crawford	fifteen pounds
	10.	A. McNabb	ten pounds
	3.	William Dunlap	three pounds
	6	J. Bell	six pounds
	6	John Gray	six pounds
	2	Lozann Rogers	two pounds
	6	John Morrison	six pounds
	10	Bryan Ferguson	Ten pounds
	3	John Wallace	Three pounds
	3	Samuel McCroskey	three pounds
	3	John McNary	three pounds
	3	Hgt. Logan	three pounds
	3	Alexn. Hall	three pounds
	2	Jno. Hall	two pounds
	3	Theo. Barr	three pounds
	3	Wm. Campbell	three pounds
	1	Samuel Wilson	twenty shillings
	1	William McNary	twenty shillings
	1	Alexander Campbell	one pound

£   84

Amt. brot over   £ 84

William	one pound	1
David Campbell	one pound	1
Richard M. Sanns	1 pound	1
Michael McKee	1 pound	1

£ 88

4. LETTERS CONCERNING THE FOUNDING OF LANE THEOLOGICAL SEMINARY

Copy of a Letter on the Subject of a Theological Seminary in the West.   (Circular)

Cincinnati Sept. 1822

Rev^d. and Dear Sir,

From the present state and opening prospects of our country, and from the remoteness of our Eastern Seminaries, it must, I think, be obvious to you that, a "School of the Prophets," well founded and amply supported, is a great desideratum in the western section of the Presbyterian Church.   The partial and premature efforts recently made in the North East corner of the State of Ohio and the circumscribed measures of some of our brethren in Tennessee have only served to evince a zeal worthy of a more enlarged policy and exite alarm in the hearts of those who have contemplated a more extensive plan.   On this subject we may adopt a political maxim "United we stand, divided we fall." So far as human means and measures are concerned, nothing can better secure the dignity and utility of a Theological Seminary in the West than the cordial union and energetick co-operation of those Synods which Divine Providence has spread over this fair portion of the New World.   This subject has been deemed of sufficient important to find a place in the deliberations of the Synod of Ohio.   Attempts have been made to open an official correspondence with the other Synods in the West and new efforts are anticipated at their next meeting, which is to take place in this city the 17th of next month.   Is not this subject of sufficient moment to gain the attention of the Synod of Kentucky?   And will not the Synods of Pittsburgh and Tennessee unite in the accomplishment of a grand scheme?   Shall we ever have the mortification, of beholding Ministers, of the glorious gospel, influenced by that narrow policy which too often divides and distracts neighbourhoods when the seat of empire for a common pedagogue is the subject of discussion?   Might not a committee be appointed from each Synod to form a joint committee to draft a plan, devise the ways and means, and select a suitable site for an extensive and permanent institution?   It is not my province, it is far from my design, to dictate.   My wish is to bear some humble part in accomplishing a great and good work.   On the influence of your talents I place great reliance and a communication from you on this subject will be duly appreciated by your friend and brother in the gospel.

J. L. WILSON[3]

[3] Cf. article on Joshua L. Wilson, ff.

Cincinnati Oct.28. 1823

My dear George,

My horse being lame and my gig crazy I did not arrive in Chillicothe until late on Friday the 17th inst. I found several of W. Carlisle's family sick and proposed taking my board in another family but they would not suffer me to leave them during my stay at Synod.

Having no private room and being constantly engaged in business or sorrounded with company I found no opportunity of writing you.

The Sessions of Synod were solemn, harmonious and marked with brotherly love. The public religious exercises were edifying and impressive, Several of our Ministers were absent and four have been called to give an account of their Stewardship — The Rev^d — Robins, Boyce, Prescot B. Smith and Joseph S. Hughs. If these men were faithful as well as professed Ministers of Christ they have received crowns of glory infinitely more desirable than all the kingdoms of this world and the glory of them.

After an absence of eleven days I arrived at home having enjoyed good health and pleasant weather, I found Henry at Home and all well. We have had the pleasure of a letter from D^r. — and one from you since your arrival in Lexington but before yours came to hand the one you mentioned from M^r. Hall was returned by mail. The innumerable blessings of a kind Providence ought to excite our warmest gratitude and lead us to repentance. Permit me my dear son to exhort you in the language of wisdom "Remember *now*, thy Creator in the days of thy *youth*." Now — Tomorrow may be too late — — — .

I was much pleased with the information you gave us respecting the discourses of Messr. Hull and Beckenridge as it affords me an opportunity of repeating to you the words of Solomon "He that walketh with wise men shall be wise"; When youth habitually prefer wise and good companions it is a hopeful indication of prudence if not of piety.

By the intercourse with such good principles are cherished and confirmed, good habits formed and a maturity of

wisdom attained.   But they who select bad company are in
the way of learning and practicing all the evils which lead
to temporal and eternal ruin, and therefore Solomon adds
— "A companion of fools shall be destroyed."

I wish you to ascertain the state and prospects of the
College at Danville and give me information.   Give my
best respects to M^r. Hall and family, Mr. Blair & family,
D^r. Blythe & family, Dr. Drake and family, Mrs. Russel
& family, Mrss. Hurt & C. & C.   Tell Mr. Hall that the
Synod of Ohio have appointed the Rev^d. James Gilliland,
John Thompson and myself a committee to confer with a
committee of the Synod of Kentucky on the Subject of establishing a Theological Seminary in the West.   Your
Mother, Grandmother brothers and sisters unite with me
in love to you.

Farewell,

J. L. WILSON

Rev. J. L. Wilson [To his son]

Lexington   Sept. 2, 1825

Rev^d & dear Sir.

I crave your attention to our object of the deepest interest to our western Churches, and of no small interest to the
City of Cincinnati.   It is the location of the contemplated
Theological School of the West.   It must have occured to
you in looking over the list of the names of the Commissioners and Board of Directors who were appointed to hold
their late meetings so far east as Chillicothe that there is a
desire, at least among the Pensylvania brethren to have the
School located in the western part of that State.   To me it
is probable that the friends in the eastern parts of Ohio
united in this wish and that Washington or Connisburg was
had in view.   I have thought much on this subject within
a few weeks, and have come to this conclusion: that your
City presents the only favorable site for this location of the
contemplated Seminary.   Kentucky is more central for
the western country than Ohio or any other state.   But the
existance of Slavery among us is an insuperable objection,

and as an individual I respect too highly the principles that give birth to the objection, to urge very warmly our claim arising from our location. Cincinnati must be the place. It is highly probable that the Synods of Tennessee and Kentucky will cooperate heartily in this thing, provided the location of the school be not farther eastward than your city, if farther east the people will not be induced to lend their aid. Measures have been taken to bring this matter definitely before these two synods, and I have little doubt of its success. You have much in your power on this subject. When Dr. Drake was in Lexington I mentioned the subject to him. I understood from him that in your town the people had almost abandoned the idea of succeeding in the establishing of a College proper in Cincinnati, and he thought they would be disposed to present your College buildings to the Board, provided the school were located in your town. If this be a fact, and if your wealthy people would otherwise exert themselves I have little doubt of your success. Located permanently, as I am in Kentucky, I would naturally wish to have the school in my own state, this I believe to be impossible notwithstanding our central situation as an individual I feel disposed to give all my little influence to Cincinnati; and unless my views should greatly change I will advocate this location if I go to the general Assembly this spring, as I hope to do. You are well aware, my dear Sir, that the people of the West are a high minded free thinking people. We, like the inhabitents of Athens of old, are ever seeking for something *new*. Now I hold it to be a self evident truth that if we have a Theological School in the West, unless it be one of the very first character, conducted by men of the first character, who shall be in the prime of life and be wholy devoted to their work, and be supported by all the authority and aid of the General Assembly, we had a thousand times better have none. More than one we shall not need for half a century. If we are to have an *Hopkinsian Manufactory* in one corner of our country, and an *Antinomian* in another, you and myself tho' old men may live long enough to lament the day that ever a Theological School was thought of by our Church.   There is nothing I view with so much dread as the *multiplication* of Theological Schools.   The (owning) opinion of my brethren in the west seems to say we must have a school among us.   I own that I am not convinced.   I feel willing to give a portion of (the) little energy of my declining days to the promotion of this object, but I am willing publicly to declare that one prime object with me, will be, in the *location* as well as the organization of the School to make it such, as to have no pretext for the formation of another in a few years.   Would you not think proper to bring this matter before your Synods of Ohio, Tennessee and Kentucky unite about Cincinnati it will fix the thing.   I think I can assure you of the cooperation of the Synod of Ky.

   With sentiments of great stress
           I am dear sir your

                          JAMES BLYTHE[4]

Mrs. Blythe and I present our kindest respects to you and Mrs. Wilson, and our sincere condolence for the loss of your son.   We need not say to you that nothing can bind up the broken hearts of bereaved parents, but the Gospel. You have found I trust, that this can.   You will find in the Post Office a letter directed to our friend Mr. Thompson it is directed to your care.   I did not know how to finish this endorsement.   You will have it forwarded.

To the Moderator of the Session
The First Presbyn. Church in Cinn.
   Rev. Sir.
       The Committee appointed by the meeting held in the Church on the evening of the 23[d] of August on the subject of the location of the Western Theological Seminary of the Presbyterian Church, having obtained from the Trustees of the Cincinnati College a Grant of One half of the Col-

---

[4] Cf. James Blythe, ff. to Joshua L. Wilson (Durrett collection).

lege Lot & Edifice and having made application to the Trustees of the Church to unite [with] the Trustees of the College in [gift] to said Theological Seminary [of] liberal and suitable donati[on]. Are sorry to say that the Trustee[s] refused to comply with their request and moreover refused to submit the matter to a vote of the people. The Committee therefore respectfully request the session to call a meeting of the Congregation as soon as convenient, in order that the proposition may be laid before them for their consideration and decision.

W. NOBLE
P. YOUNG
SAMUEL LOWRY
CALVIN FLETCHER } Committee
JOHN B. ENNESS
JOHN MAHARD
JOHN F. KEYS

Cincinnati Sept. 30th 1825.

Rev. J. L. Wilson
Moderator of Session
1st. Presbyterian Church.

Original Constitution
of
Lane Seminary

Adopted at a meeting held in the Session Room of the 1st Presbyterian Church in Cincinnati, Oct. 10.1828[5]

Extract—

Article 7.
A majority of the members of the Board and of the Executive Committee, as well as all the instructors employed in the Theological department of the Seminary shall be members of the Presbyterian Church Under the care of the General Assembly in the United States, in good standing.

[5] Extracts from Original Constitutions and Minutes.

Formula

The Committee, on that subject reported a formula to be adopted by the Professors in the Theological department on their inducted into office, which was approved and is as follows — viz.

Every Theological Professor previously to entering upon the duties of his office shall make and subscribe the following declaration to wit: "In the presence of God and of the Trustees of this Seminary I declare my belief in the Scriptures of the Old and the New Testament as the word of God and the only infallible rule of faith and practice. I receive also and adopt the Confession of Faith of the Presbyterian Church in these United States and to be Zealous and faithful in my endeavours to maintain the purity and peace of the Church and to qualify those young men who may be under my care to explain, defend and apply the truths of the Gospel." Adopted and Subscribed at the Inauguration of Dr. Beecher & others. (or at least one more not named in the minutes) — Dec. 26, 1832.—

Extracts from the Charter

"An act to incorporate the Lane Seminary in the County of Hamilton"

Section 3ᵈ   That the officers and members of the Executive Committee shall reside in the City of Cincinnati or its vicinity; a majority of whom, together with the Professors, Tutors, Teachers and Instructors, in said Institution, shall be members of the Presbyterian Church, in good standing, under the care of the General Assembly of that Church, in the United States

Passed Feb. 11. 1829

Office of the A.H.M.S. 144 Nassau St.
New York July 22. 1829

Rev. J. L. Wilson D.D.
Cincinnati, Ohio
   Rev. & Dr. Sir.
      I am happy to address you by the hand of Rev. Mr. Coxe who returns to Ohio in answer to your solicitation to

engage a short time, if you still desire it in the service of the Lane Seminary. The importance of that object, in our view is so great, & his qualifications for the service proposed so peculiar that we dare not detain him from it, though we have other work of importance for him to do. And I weep when I think of New Orleans, But at this present time & perhaps for a year to come, Br. Coxe may be of more service in your State. I am happy to commend him to your advice, which he will highly value. We have lately appointed Br. Pomeroy as Agent for the Home Miss Society in Ohio & Indiana for one year. & I rejoice to inform you that we have a prospect of sending to Ohio this year a greater re- enforcement than in any former year. Some 10 or 12 young men are already engaged to go to that State in the fall, & others we hope may yet direct their course to that interesting portion of the West.

With the leave of Providence I expect in a few weeks to take a journey to your State, & hope to be in Cincinnati in Sept. When it will be my wish to confer with you and other friends of the cause in your vicinity on the subject of our operations at the west, & shall hope to learn the will of God in relation to what this Society may do to bless & multiply the churches in the great field to be occupied by our denomination towards the going down of the sun. —

With grateful acknowledgements for the blessings of your ministry the last year & on the churches in your city, I am

Very truly Your Friend & Br.

ABSALOM PETERS

Cor. Sec. A.H.M.S.

Cincinnati January the 5th 1830

Dear Sir.

I had the honor to receive your note of this morning inviting me to attend a meeting of the friends of Lane Seminary to be holden this evening at the first Presbyterian church

I understand the invitation to be a conditional one; that

is, if I approve the plan of the institution I shall accept it as such, and in doing so, circumstances seem to require that I should state the light in which I approve the plan & designs of the institution, and how I consider myself its friend,

As a citizen of the West and especially of Cincinnati I regard it in the most favorable light in which its projectors and particular friends would have it estimated. Its local importance to us cannot be questioned. Its bearing on Cincinnati both in a pecuniary & moral point of view must be obvious to all.

As it relates to the preparatory school in which it is calculated to qualify students for the Colleges of the country I deem it of great importance. Such a one is greatly wanted. In such matters experience is worth a thousand arguments, & every one must know that such a school would be free from those scenes of vice and objects of temptation that a city or town school must always present to the minds of youth

There is one point of view (& perhaps that is the only one in which I should think of it) in which I consider myself the friend of the institution. As a point at which sound & practical knowledge may be obtained & from which well instructed & virtuous men may be sent forth to spread the glad tidings of great joy & publish throughout all nations the *revelations of God to man* I feel the warmest solicitude for its prosperity & shall contribute my feeble aid to its establishment

Perhaps I shall ever remain as I now most certainly am a thorough dissenter from many of the peculiar or sectarian views of religion that will most probably be taught in this Institution; but these are matters peculiarly my own & to be accounted for only to him who has pleased to give us those revelations on which are based all of our high hopes of immortality. A difference of opinion on those matters does not however stand in the way of a hearty cooperation with the particular friends of the Seminary.

In reflecting on this subject I think I have brought my

mind to ask the question, does the institution promise to be a medium through which, the moral, intellectual, civil & religious condition of my fellow beings can be ameliorated? If it promises the accomplishment of these high & charitable ends (and that it does to a considerable extent I have no doubt) it presents strong claims for the liberal aid of the phylanthropic of all denominations.

If it shall be the means through which the *word* shall be spread & the light made to shine in & illumine the minds & warm the hearts of the thousands who are now destitute of that knowledge which comes alone through the Bible, it certainly cannot be a matter worthy of cavil whether it be affected through the instrumentality of Presbyterians, Baptists, Methodists or of any other denomination who profess to know the only true God and Jesus Christ whom he hath sent.

With these views of the Lane Seminary I wish to be regarded as one of its friends,

I have the honor to be
with great respect
Your obt. Sevt —

J.D.GARRARD[5a]

Rev. J. L. Wilson
Cincinnati

For the Cincinnati daily Chronicle[6]

Lane Seminary
E. D. Mansfield Esqr.
Dear Sir,

In the Chronicle of the 8th an article appeared written by Doctor Stowe, calling public attention to the right ownership of Lane Seminary. The question stated and discussed by the Doctor appeared to me to be irrelevant. The question is not, "Who *endowed* Lane Seminary?" — but, *for*

[5a] J. D. Garrard was a prominent lawyer of Cincinnati, and the grandson of ex-Governor James Garrard of Kentucky.

[6] An open letter for the *Cincinnati Daily Chronicle* about Lane Seminary and the New School Party. Harriet Beecher, the daughter of President Lyman Beecher, became the wife of Professor Calvin E. Stowe in 1836.

what Society and *for what purposes* was Lane Seminary
founded. Ought we not to look at the foundation of a public Institution when we attempt to settle the question of
ownership or rightful posession? The question, who gave
lands, money, books, or anything else, for the purpose of
carrying on the Seminary is of no importance compared
with the question, *for whom,* and *for what,* were these contributions made. If the Episcopal Bishop of the diocese
of Ohio founds an institution of learning for his own denomination and secures an endowment from Lord Gambier
does that prove that his Lordship can put into the College
dissenting Professors and that when they are in they become the rightful owners?

Doctor Stowe says, that Mr. Elnathan Kemper gave land
to Lane Seminary and "he was New School, an Elder in
Lane Seminary Church." Very well. But what has that to
do with the question of ownership?

Did Dr. Stowe intend to make the public believe that
Lane Seminary Church was in existance and that Mr. Kemper was a ruling Elder there when he gave the land? If
so, it is a sheer imposition. I prefer however to look more
at Dr. Stowe's argument, than his history of Mr. Kemper.
It is this — — Lane Seminary was endowed by Ebenezer
Lane, A Baptist, — by Gen¹ Van Rennsalear, of the Dutch
Church, — by John Tappan, Congregational Church, —
and F. Y. Vail was one of the agents, — *therefore* the New
School are the rightful owners of Lane Seminary! Verily,
if Dr. Stowe's Biblical learning is no better than his logic
it will be of little value to his disciples. But further, any
attempt to "disturb" them aught to be looked upon "with
indignation." Perhaps this attempt to disabuse the public
mind may be looked upon in the same way, but I will bear
"the indignation" for the sake of discharging a duty. If
Dr. Stowe had intended to afford the Public correct information — why did he not inform them that the Original
Constitution of Lane Seminary was adopted at a meeting
held in the Session Room of the First Presbyterian Church
in Cincinnati, — that this Constitution, the Act of incor-

poration, and the covenants in the deed for the sixty acres of land require "That a majority of the Officers and members of the Executive Committee, together with all the Professors, Tutors, Teachers, and Instructors, shall be members of *the Presbyterian Church*, in good standing, under the care of the *General Assembly of that Church, in the United States.*

This was the designation of a Society then existing, which distinguished it from all other societies in the world, as much as the name Lane Seminary distinguished the Institution founded by them, from all other public Seminaries.

The New School of whom Dr. Stowe speaks were never known as an organized body for ten years afterward. They organized in 1838 and ratified their form of Government in 1840 — which, in some of its features is widely different from the Form of Government of "The Presbyterian Church" for whose benefit Lane Seminary was founded. But how did the New School get this institution into their possession?

The answer is furnished by the whole tenor of Dr. Stowe's Publication. The names F. Y. Vail, Arthur Tappan, Ambrose White, J. H. Groesbeck, N. Wright, J. C. (Finis) Robert (Boal) and Elnathan Kemper as New School contributors to the Institution. When the Lane Seminary was founded and when these "New School" contributers made their donations what did they profess to be? They professed to be members of the Presbyterian Church described in the deed and charter. They professed to be exactly what the Revd James Kemper, P. H. Kemper, J. Baker, Robert Wallace, Wm Schillinger, & many other worthy brethren, who aided in founding Lane Seminary professed to be. And we lived and laboured together as brethren. But Dr. Stowe has shewn that there was, as far back as 1828, an organized party at work in the Presbyterian Church, to subvert her interests and hold her funds and Institutions, and the Dr.'s view is proved to be correct by the history of their proceedings in 1838 — when they made a secession, organized a New General Assembly and immediately brought Suit for the Corporate Powers and all permanent funds of the Presbyterian Church. There probably never was a more secret conspiracy against the welfare of any denomination. It was long after Lane Seminary was founded before we ever heard of the name New School. And when some became alarmed with new doctrines and new measures and expressed their fears that the Presbyterian Church was endangered every allegation was denied and continued to be denied for eight years, till the General Assembly of 1836 when they thought them-selves triumphant and all disguise and concealment were thrown off. They were however defeated the next year by the Presbyterian Church rising in the majesty of her strength and the party being unmasked seceded in 1838.

The rightful owners of Lane Seminary did not attempt to reclaim the Institution while the Great Church Case remained undecided. But now the New School are ad-judged by the Supreme Court of Pensylvania *not* be the legitemate Assembly of the Presbyterian Church. It re-mains to be seen whether the Board of Trustees will place in the Institution such men as the Charter requires, without further trouble or expense, or whether they will wait for compulsory process. If they delay, they may rest assured the rightful owners of the Seminary will compel them to execute their trust notwithstanding the threat of "indigna-tion" uttered by Dr. Stowe.

Very respectfully

J. L. WILSON

May 1839

5. SUBSCRIPTION LISTS FOR JAMES H. LOGAN'S SCHOOL, 1837

[Original MS in Shane Collection, Philadelphia.]

April 7 — 1837

I James H. Logan of the one part agree to continue the School in the same house, or in the house which is in prog-ress of preparation, for the purpose, in case it be fitted up:

and obligate myself to give instruction, to the best of my abilities, in such branches of Education as are usually taught in a common Academy: and pledge myself to use dilligence to promote the progress of pupils, committed to my charge, in a knowledge of those branches.

TUITION

For a term of five months and a half —
The Latin and Greek Languages, Mathematics &c.
per term $15.00
English Grammar, Geography, advanced Rules in
Arithmetick &c.   10.00
Spelling, Reading, Writing, and first principles in
Arithmetick &c.   6.00
The second term to commence on Monday the 17th April 1837 and to continue for five months and a half, ending on the last of September next.

The School to be open five days each week, from 8 o'clock A. M. untill 5 o'clock P.M.

April 7th 1837.   JAMES H. LOGAN

We whose names are hereunto subscribed obligate ourselves to pay to James H. Logan tuition on the number of scholars subscribed by us severally, according to the terms above specified, to furnish a comfortable house for the school in a suitable location, and to provide the necessary fuel.

Subscribers' names	Number of Scholars –
Reuben Hall ———	4
Mary Allison	3
Hugh Allison	2
A.& I.C. Brown	1
Lee Bird	1
James B. Buford ———	1

CHAPTER XIII

DOCUMENTS ILLUSTRATING THE WORK OF PRESBYTERIAN INDIAN MISSIONS

1. Extracts from the Records of the Western Missionary Society, 1804-1825.
2. Extracts from the Records of Missionary Work among the Choctaw and Chickasaw Indians.
    (A) The Association of Missionaries, 1827-1828.
    (B) The Tombigbee Presbytery, 1829-1830.
    (C) Sessional Record of the Presbyterian Church, Monroe, Chickasaw Nation, 1823-1824.

1. EXTRACTS FROM THE RECORDS OF THE WESTERN MISSIONARY SOCIETY

[The Synod of Pittsburgh, composed of the Presbyteries of Redstone, Ohio, and Erie, was erected in 1802. At its first meeting it resolved itself into the Western Missionary Society, the object of which was "to diffuse the knowledge of the gospel among the inhabitants of the new settlements, the Indian tribes, and, if need be, among some of the interior inhabitants, where they are not able to support the gospel."[1] On March 20, 1810, the Legislature of Pennsylvania passed an act constituting the Synod of Pittsburgh "A corporation and body politic, in law and in fact, by the name, style and title of 'The Western Missionary Society,' for the purpose of promoting and spreading the knowledge of agriculture, literature and Christianity among the Indian tribes of America."[2] The Society was permitted to hold property "provided that the clear annual income of all such property shall not exceed five thousand Dollars: and provided also, that the fund of said corporation shall not be employed for any other purpose than the Mechanical arts, or agriculture, and the knowledge

[1] *Records of the Synod of Pittsburgh* (Pittsburgh, 1852), p. 11. See also David Elliott, *The Life of the Rev. Elisha Macurdy* (Allegheny and Philadelphia, 1848), p. 106. *The Centennial of the Western Foreign Missionary Society, 1831-1931* (Pittsburgh, 1931), p. 14.

[2] *An Act of Incorporation,* in the MS Records of the Board of Trust of the Western Missionary Society, 1804-1826.

of the Christian religion among the Indian tribes." A supplementary Act enabled the corporation to extend the use of its funds "to the important objects of distributing Bibles and other religious Books gratis, and sending Missionaries to preach the Gospel in such places as are destitute of the means of instruction, and for the Education and instruction of any of the Indian tribes in such manner as the said society may think proper."[3]

For the "effectual attainment" of their object the Western Missionary Society appointed annually a Board of Trust, consisting at first of seven members and later of nine, "who were charged with the transaction of all missionary business necessary to be done between the annual meetings of the society."[4] The manuscript minutes of the Board of Trust for the years 1804-1826 are in the custody of the Library of the Western Theological Seminary of Pittsburgh. Selections from these records illustrative of one phase of the work of the Society, its Indian missions, follow.]

Records of the Western Missionary Society

Pittsburgh, Oct. 5, 1804

The Board of Trust appointed by the Western Missionary Society on the 4th instant, met agreeably to appointment. Present — The Rev. Messrs. Joseph Patterson, Sam'l. Ralston, and Elisha M'Curdy — with the Elders John Moore & John Duncan. Absent — The Rev. Thomas Marquis & James Dinsmore, Elder. The Rev. Joseph Patterson was chosen Chairman & Rev. Sam'l. Ralston, Clerk. Constituted with prayer. No business being before the Board they adjourned to meet on the 3rd Wednesday of November next at the house of John Couren. Concluded with prayer.

.   .   .

March 27, 1805

A pro re nata meeting of the Board was called. Present — Revd. Jos. Patterson, Thomas Marquis, & Elisha M'Curdy. Constituted by prayer.

[3] *Ibid.*
[4] Elliott, *op. cit.*, pp. 106-107.

The Board received information yt. the Wyandot Indians[5] had agreed to hold a general council on 14th April next for the purpose of considering and determining on the expediency of receiving Gospel ministers among them, & requested that a Minister of ye Gospel should attend the Council.

The Board finding that a Minister could not be obtained to attend the council — thought it advisable to send Hampton Northop the Interpreter with a speech.

A letter was received from the Rev. William Wick informing the Board that he would not fulfil the Mission to the Indians — whereupon Mr. Patterson was appointed to attend the Presby. of Erie at their next meeting in order to obtain a substitute.   Concluded with prayer.

.   .   .

West Liberty, April 17, 1805

Mr. Patterson reported that he had attended ye last meeting of Erie Presby. & obtained the appointment of the Rev. Joseph Badger[5a] as a Missionary in the place of Mr. Wick — and Mr. Badger was accepted by the Board.

A letter was received from the Rev. George Hill of the Presby. of Redstone, informing the Board of his acceptance of the Mission appointed him to the Wyandot Indians.

The Rev. Messrs. Patterson & M'Curdy were appointed a Committee to draught letters to the Rev. Messrs. Badger & Hill — containing directions for the commencement & end of their Mission. — And the Rev. Messrs. Marquis and Ralston to prepare instructions whereby the Missionaries are to be directed in their Missionary conduct.

Adjd. to meet to-morrow morning at 7 o'clock.   Concluded wt. prayer.

.   .   .

[5] The Wyandots were living at this time in northern Ohio, as were most of the Indians to whom the Western Missionary Society sent missionaries.

[5a] Since 1800 Badger had been serving as a missionary under the Conn. Missionary Society, See *Sprague, op. cit.*, III, pp. 473-479.

Pittsburgh, October 3, 1805

The Board met agreeably to adjournment. Present —
Joseph Patterson, Thomas Marquis, Sam'l. Ralston, Elisha
M'Curdy, Mins. John Duncan, Elder, Constituted with
prayer.

The Board heard Mr. Badger's journal of which they approved, and ordered the Treasurer to pay him fifty dollars
for ten weeks services. The Board also heard the Rev. John
Anderson's journal which was approved, and they ordered
the Treasurer to pay him forty dollars for two months
services.

After hearing the reports of the Missionaries, and conversing with them, the Board were impressed with the idea
that there is at present a very flattering prospect of promoting the Gospel amongst the Wyandot Indians, and that
it ought to be prosecuted by the Society with the greatest
assiduity. From a view of the poverty of the friends of
the Society, the Board also beg leave to suggest to the
Society the expediency of applying to the General Assembly to take the Society fund into their hands with the
limitation of the Assembly's always allowing a committee
of this Synod to conduct the business in the interval of the
Assembly's meeting but subject and accountable to the
Assembly.

The Board also recommended to the Society to petition
Congress for a part of the reserve tract at Lower Sandusky
for a Missionary Station. Concluded with prayer.

.   .   .

Cross Roads, Dec. 25, 1805

The Board settled with Hampton Northup, who was employed for five months & three weeks as Interpreter at $20
per Month. Found he had received from Mr. M'Curdy
the sum of $93.63 cents, and ordered the Treasurer to pay
him the balance due, 21.37.

.   .   .

Feby. 25, 1806.

The Board met at the Rev. Mr. Marquis'; at the request of Mr. Badger. Present, the Rev. Messrs. Hughs, Marquis, M'Curdy and Messrs. Rea, Lee and Duncan. Absent, Rev. John Anderson. Constituted with prayer.

The Rev. Joseph Badger met with the Board and agreed to undertake the Mission to Sandusky agreeably to the appointment of the Society, and the Board agreed to allow him 450 dollars for one year, with any extra expense which shall appear reasonable in his report; the year to commence on the first of April, on when he shall set out, and allowing him a reasonable compensation for his time and trouble in making the necessary preparations. The Board also allow Mr. Badger to employ two laborers for seven months at $12 per month ea. — and a black man with his wife for one year at 100 dollars.

The Board gave to Mr. Badger an order on the Treasurer of the Missionary fund for 300 Dollars and also directed Mr. Hughs to forward to him 100 Dollars sent out from Philadelphia.

The Board purchased a horse from Mr. Rea for the service of the Mission at $45 to be paid out of the fund. They deliver the said horse to the care of Mr. Badger. Adjourned to meet at Upper Buffalo on the 17th of April next. Concluded with prayer.

·   ·   ·

Cross Creek, October 1806.

The Board met agreeably to adjournment. Present, Rev. Messrs. Hughs, Marquis, Anderson & M'Curdy. Messrs. Lee & Duncan. Constituted with prayer.

The Rev. Joseph Badger our Missionary met with the Board, and read his journal and gave a particular account of his manner of performing the duties of his Mission, and the appearance of success therein, which gave to the Board a high degree of satisfaction and encouragement.

·   ·   ·

Chartiers, Decem. 24, 1806.

The Rev. John McClain met with the Board and made a report of his proceeding in his tour to Scioto and Sandusky, which was approved, and from which it appeared that he had obtained in Scioto and conveyed to Mr. Badger at Sandusky, fifteen head of cow cattle & twenty-two head of hogs, and he returned to the Board the sum of Seventeen Dollars and fifty cents, which remained in his hands after all the expences were discharged out of the money which he collected in his tour. Mr. McLain would receive no compensation for his services, but made a present thereof to the Mission.

. . .

[Mr. Anderson's, Feb. 3rd, 1807.]

The Board desirous to extend the benefits of the Gospel, agreed to appoint the Rev. John McPherrin to visit Cornplanters Town, in order to obtain information whether there be a disposition among the Indians at that place to receive a Missionary to preach the Gospel to them, and instruct them. To go out as soon as convenient.

. . .

Cross Creek, Sept. 15, 1807.

After prayer Mr. Badger's letter was read, from which it appeared that Mr. Atkins had declined serving any longer in the Mission, and that the horse sent out last spring had proved so bad on fences that Mr. Badger had been obliged to sell him. That two hands and another horse was required for the necessary business of this fall. The Board agreed to hire and send out for two months two hands as soon as possible, and having been informed of a horse offered gratis for the service of the Mission by a friend: they agreed to receive him gratefully, and send him on with the men. And also to send on some tea and coffee for the Mission, and some cloathing & books for the Indians at school.

The Board of Trust received of the Rev. Joseph Patterson one mare valued at $45 forty five dollars, the donation of William Flancken, of his congregation, for the use of the Mission to the Indians.   Adjourned & Concluded with prayer.

.   .   .

Stuebenville, October 20th, 1807

The Board of Trust agreed to employ Samuel Perry and his wife to labor in the Mission at Sandusky for the space of one year, for one hundred and sixty-eight Dollars, and to allow Mr. Badger to employ a young woman for the space of a year at 75 cents per week — 39 Dollars p. year.

.   .   .

Pigeon Creek, June the 20th, 1808.

The Board met and was constituted with prayer.   Present, Messrs. Hughs, Marquis, Anderson and Macurdy. The Board received communications from Gov. Hull and from Mr. Badger, containing statements of complaints forwarded by the Indians to the Gov. against Mr. Badger, and requesting that some of the Society should go out to the Missionary Station in order to inquire into these complaints and investigate the conduct of Mr. Badger.   The Board after deliberating on the matter agreed and appointed Messrs. Marquis, Anderson and Macurdy a committee for that purpose to go out to Sandusky on the 1st of Sept.

Adjourned to meet at Pittsg. 1st wed of Oct.   Concluded with prayers.

.   .   .

Cross Roads, Nov. 29, 1808.

The Board concluded that it might be best to let out Missionary Farm at Sandusky on the shares. . . .

The Board received a report from the committee appointed by Synod to visit the Missisanqua & Chippaway Indians, from which it appears that there is a considerable encouragement to pay attention to them and endeavor to have a school instituted among them.

.   .   .

West Liberty, Oct. 20, 1812.

The Board of Trust appointed by the Western Missionary Society at their last meeting, met agreeably to their appointment. Members present, the Rev. Messrs. J. Hughs, Thos. Marquis, Elisha Macurdy and Joseph Stevenson. Elder, Wm. Hughs.

Mr. Marquis was chosen Chairman & Mr. Anderson Secretary and auditor of account.

Mr. Fia Condit was appointed a missionary for three months, to spend six weeks on the waters of the Muskingum and Scioto, and six weeks on the head waters of Wheeling, Grave Creek and Ten Mile, at $20 per month.

Messrs. Hughs and Stevenson were appointed a committee to visit the Wyandot Indians near Urbana, to inquire into their situation, and the prospect of rendering further Missionary services to them, and to report to the Board on their return.

Mr. Joseph Anderson was appointed a Missionary for one month on the Waters of McMahon's Creek and southerly at $20 pr. month. Adjourned to meet at Cross Creek on the 3d. Tuesday of January next.

Concluded with prayer.

.   .   .

Pittsburgh, Oct. 6th, 1814.

The Western Missionary Society at their last meeting, elected the following members to serve as a Board of Trust for the ensuing year — namely, the Rev. Messrs. Francis Herron, Elisha M'Curdy, James Graham, Thos Hunt, Robert Patterson, Michael Law — with the Elders, Thos. Davis, James Cooper & John Snowden.

The Board of Trust met — & after prayer was organized in the following manner — Rev. Thos. Hunt, Presidt., Rev. Francis Herron, Sect. — Rev. Elisha Mcurdy, Treas. & Revd. Robt. Patterson, Auditor,

Resolved that the Rev. Thos. Hunt be appointed a Missionary for one month to visit Corn Planters Indians & collect all ye information requisite for a Missionary establishment among them — & report immediately to this Board the result of his Mission.

Resolved that Forty Dollars be allowed Mr. Hunt while on Missionary service — to be paid in (?)

Revd. Elisha MCurdy and John Snowden were appointed to draught instructions for Mr. Hunt.

Messrs. Herron, Hunt & Cooper are authorized to make arrangements with the Interpreter.

The Rev. Jos. Stevenson is appointed Missionary for five weeks in the districts of country on the Waters of the Monongahela & Fish Creek.

Adjd. to meet on ye first Wednesday on December. Concluded with prayer.

.   .   .

Pittsburgh, Dec. 7th, 1814.

The Board in consequence of the information laid before them by Revd. Thos Hunt — & after deliberation on the subject — Resolved to establish a school among the Indians — & appoint a Missionary for three months — and to carry this resolution into effect, Messrs. Herron & all besides are authorized to employ a schoolmaster, who shall have ye management of the school — and also an Interpreter for one month to assist in organizing the school.

.   .   .

Pittsburgh, June 17, 1816.

The Board of Trust met agreeably to notice from the President — & was constituted by prayer.

After some conversation with Corn Planter, the Indian chief — & Mr. Oldham the Schoolmaster, on the continuance of the school among the Indians, & the manner of providing for it the ensuing year, the Board adjourned to meet on the Wednesday the 3rd day of July at 9 o'clock. Concluded wt. prayer.

. . .

Pittsburgh, August 29, 1816

The Board of Trust met agreeably to notice from the President — & was constituted by prayer.

Members present — Rev. Thos. Hunt, Elisha MCurdy, Francis Herron, Robt. Patterson, with the Elders James Cooper & Thos. Davis.

On motion, resolved that the Rev. Elisha MCurdy be authorized to inquire — Whether another school can be established among the Indians — & collect such information as will be useful to this Board on his Missionary Tour — & report as soon as practicable.

Resolved that the Rev. Cyrus Riggs be appointed a Missionary for one month to visit the Indian School & adjacent settlements.

Adjourned to meet at Washington on the 1st Tuesday, Oct. 1816. Concluded wt. prayer.

. . .

Pittsburgh, April 21, 1817

The Board of Trust met agreeably to notice from the Secretary. After prayer, it appeared that ye Revd. Messrs. Elisha MCurdy, Thos. Hunt, Francis Herron, Robt. Patterson & Jos. Stockton with the Elders John M. Snowden, Robt. Highlands & Thos. Davis were present.

The Committee appointed for the purpose of preparing & having printed a form of commission for our Missionaries, & instructions for their direction in Missionary labours reported — and their report was accepted & the form adopted.

Resolved that the thanks of this Board be presented to

John M. Snowden for his liberality in printing the above form of commission & instruction for the Missionaries.

Mr. Herron reported that he had obtained a seal for the use of this Board agreeably to instruction.

Resolved that this seal — designated by the inscription, "The Western Missionary Society" — as reported by the Secretary be adopted by this Board & be annexed to such papers of this Society as the Board shall direct.

.   .   .

Pittsburgh, Jan. 12, 1818

The Board of Trust met agreeably to adjourn. After prayer, it appeared the following members were present. — Rev. Messrs. Joseph Patterson, Thomas Hunt & Elisha MCurdy — with the Elders, James Cooper, Thos. Davis & Wm. Guay.

A communication was received from the Rev. Alvin Coe — stating that the Wyandot Indians at Upper Sandusky are anxious to have a school & a Mission established among them.

The Journal of Mr. Fairchild on the Morgan Town Circuit for two weeks was read — his diligence & fidelity was approved by the Board — & hopeful appearances attended his ministrations.

From a view of the flattering appearances in ye Morgan Town Circuit, it was deemed expedient yt. a Missionary for the month of February be appointed in that circuit — & that Mr. Fairchild be appointed to return to Morgan Town on the 1st of March. It was therefore on motion resolved that the Rev. Thos. Hunt be appointed for the month of February in the above circuit. But in case Mr. Hunt cannot comply with the appointment — Messrs. Patterson & Hunt are appointed a Committee to employ a suitable Missionary for one month on the above circuit.

The Rev. Messrs R. Patterson, Michael Law, James Graham & Francis Herron are appointed as supplies for Mr. Hunt's pulpit in case of his compliance with his Missionary appointment.

Adjd. to the 4th Tuesday of April.   Concluded wt. prayer.

.   .   .

Pittsburgh, Sept. 8th, 1818.

The Board of Trust met agreeably to notice.   After prayer, it appeared yt. the following members were present — Revd. Messrs. Joseph Patterson, Michael Law & Francis Herron, with ye Elders Thos. Davis, Wm. Guay & James Cooper.

A letter from Saml. Oldham was received & read — stating several unpleasant circumstances in relation to ye school at Cornplanters Town — & the Board taking into serious consideration ye contents of ye said letter, & after some discussion — unanimously resolved — that Revd. Michael Law be respectfully requested to visit the School at Corn Planters, for ye purpose of obtaining & forwarding to this Board all necessary information in relation to ye school in its present circumstances.   Adjd. to meet as above.   Concluded wt. prayer.

.   .   .

Pittsburgh, April 5, 1820

Whereas a communication was recd. from the Presby. of Portage — stating that an Indian School had been commenced by the Rev. Alvin Coe, of Greenfield — & considerable aid afforded by ye people in that region, but still inadequate to ye support of the School — and also requesting assistance from this Board.

It was therefore on motion resolved that 20 Dollars per month be paid Mr. Coe out of the funds of this Society until the meeting of the Synod in Oct. next.

Ordered that the Treasurer forward money to Mr. Coe from time to time, as the Funds may admit — & that ye Secretary be directed to send a copy of these resolutions to the Portage Presby.

Adjd. to meet on 3rd Tuesday of June.   Concluded wt. prayer.

.   .   .

Pittsburgh, May 20th, 1820.

Resolved that the wages for Missionary labours be reduced from 40 Dollars to thirty three & one third Dollars per month after this date.

.   .   .

Pittsburgh, Oct. 6, 1820

The Board appointed the Rev. Jos. Badger for two months to labor in the settlements on Lake Erie from the State line to Portland.   The Rev. Wm. McLean for three months — his rout to be directed by the Rev. E. McCurdy. The Rev. Mr. Stevenson on his last rout, and in case he cannot perform his Mission — the Rev. Mr. McCurdy was authorized to employ a suitable Missionary, or, to fulfill the appointment himself.   The Rev. Mr. Cove was appointed for one month on his former routs.   The Rev. Mr. Chase was appointed for two months in the settlements on Brokenstraw and Conewango.   The Rev. Hezekiah Woodruff was appointed for one month in the county of Warren and Ashtabula, Ohio.

Mr. Salmon Cowles was appointed to continue his present Mission until the first of April next.   The Board voted to continue their former appropriation of $20 per month to the Indian School under the care of the Rev. Avn. Coe, and such other aid in cloathing, books and stationary as they may from time to time deem necessary.

.   .   .

Pittsburgh, Jan. 2, 1821

On motion

Resolved that Messrs. Herron and Swift be a Committee to address a letter in the name of this Society to the Board of Managers of the United For. Missionary Society,[6] suggesting the propriety of appointing a Board of Agency to act in the name of sd. Society in the bounds of this Synod, and also proposing to them the joint co-operation of this Society in the establishment of a Mission — to some one of the Indian Tribes, and engaging in case such a measure were adopted, to supply such an establishment with all the necessary articles and provisions, cloathing &c. so long as it should continue or as such aid should be necessary.

Adjd.   Concluded with prayer.

.   .   .

Pittsburgh, April 3, 1821

A letter from the Rev. Mr. Coe, Superintendent of the Indian School, having been read, on motion.

Resolved that the Rev. Elisha Macurdy be appointed to visit that part of the country in which the school is located, inquire into the number, state and prospects of the Indians in that country, their condition and disposition, and report upon the expediency of establishing a permanent Mission among either the Wyandot, Chipawas or Ottoway Indians, — and that the Presbytery of Washington appoint supplies for his pulpit during his absence.

.   .   .

Pittsburgh, June 21, 1821

The Rev. Mr. Macurdy made a report of his journey and proceedings in relation to his appointment at the last stated meeting, which was read and accepted.

On motion resolved that the Indian School established in Greenfield, Huron Co., Ohio, be and the same is hereby taken under the direction and patronage of this Society, and

[6] The United Foreign Missionary Society was organized in 1816-1817 by the General Assembly of the Presbyterian Church, in coöperation with other presbyterian bodies, and had for its object the spread of "the gospel among the Indians of North America, the inhabitants of Mexico and South America and in other portions of the heathen and antichristian world." Baird, op. cit. (ed. Philadelphia, 1856), pp. 320-321.

that the Rev. Alvin Coe be appointed to take the charge and superintendence of said school, and report to this Board on account of all the necessities and expenditures of the said establishment, and of all the donations in provisions, utensils, cloathing, &c. which may be made to it, and for the just appropriation of which he is accountable to this Board.

· · ·

Pittsburgh, Aug. 14th, 1821

The Board met agreeably to notice previously given by the Secretary and was constituted with prayer. Present, Rev. Messrs. Patterson, Herron, Stockton, Law and Swift, with the Elders Davis & Cooper.

On motion resolved that the circular letter prepared according to a resolution of the last meeting and in part printed, be for the present deferred. The following preamble and resolution were then proposed and adopted, viz:

Whereas the Board of Trust have contemplated the establishment of a Mission among one or more of the Indian Tribes on the Maumee or Sandusky Rivers, and whereas they conceive that there are some inquiries and arrangements to be made (not comprised in those instructions which were given to the Agent who was sent out in May last) before the Board can feel prepared to adopt any decisive measures on that subject, therefore

Resolved that the Rev. Messrs. Elisha Macurdy, Michael Law and Elisha P. Swift be appointed a Committee to proceed to the Indian country and if after inquiry into the ability and willingness of the churches in that vicinity to aid such an establishment and after making additional inquiries concerning the disposition & wishes of the Indians subject to a further dicision of the Board, supplies were appointed for their pulpits during their absence.

Adjourned to meet during the Sessions of Synod. Concluded with prayer.

· · ·

Pittsburgh, Oct. 8, 1821

On motion

Resolved that the Secretary direct a letter to the Modr. of the Synod of Ohio to meet in Chilecotte on the 16th inst., informing them that this Board is about to establish a Mission among the Ottoway or other Indians in Ohio & respectfully request the co-operation of those ministers and churches of that Body who may find it convenient to aid in the benevolent enterprise.

On motion

Resolved that as far as practicable communications be sent to all the principal settlements of our Missionary ground, and circuit, requesting them to inform the Board what portion of assistance in cash or otherwise, they can engage to afford for the support of Missionaries that may be sent among them.

On motion

Resolved that the Rev. Mr. Coe be authorized if there be vacant & it be practicable, to rent at a reasonable compensation the house or houses occupied by Mr. Montgomery at the Seneca village, until the first of April next, and that in case this can be done, that he remove to that place as soon as practicable and continue his school there.

2. Resolved that in the event this cannot be done, the further operation of the School at Greenfield be suspended until the ensuing spring and that during this period the children be disposed of to the best advantage by Mr. Coe.

. . . .

Pittsburgh, Nov. 1822

A letter from the Rev. Mr. Coe having been read

On motion

Resolved that a commission for two months service in the destitute settlements in his vicinity be sent to Mr. Coe, with permission to fulfil it or not as he shall choose, and that the Secretary write to him, and inform him that the final question of establishing a Mission among the Indians has not been yet decided by the Board, and that he retain in his possession the property belonging to the Society at Greenfield until he receives further directions from the Board.

.   .   .

Pittsburgh, Jany. 15th, 1822.

The Board of Trust met agreeably to notice previously given, and was constituted with prayer. Present, Rev. Messrs. Jos. Patterson, Elisha Macurdy, Jos. Stockton and Elisha P. Swift, with the Elders Messrs. Davis and Hannen.

1. The following resolutions were submitted to the consideration of all the facts and statements laid before them, both for and against such a measure, that this Board are led to the conclusion, all things considered, there does appear to be sufficient encouragement in the Providence of God, for the establishment of a Mission among the Ottoway Indians on the Maumee River in the Michigan Territory.

2. Resolved that the Board proceed to take the requisite measures for the location of a Mission in that vicinity as early as convenient.

3. Resolved that a petition be sent to the Gen.Government, soliciting a donation of one section of land near one of the Indian Reservations of said River to be held in trust as the property of this Board to be sacredly devoted to the object of civilizing and christianizing the said Ottoway Indian, or in case that should ever become hereafter impracticable of any other tribe or tribes inhabiting the U. States the said section of land to be located by his Exc. Lewis Cass, Govr. of the Michigan Territory. Or in case this cannot be bestowed.

4. Resolved that the said petition to Congress solicit the right of pre-emption to one half section of land at the minimum price.

5. Resolved that the Secretary address a letter to his Exc. Lewis Cass, Govr. of the Michigan Territory, appriz-

ing him of the measures taken on this subject by this Board and respectfully soliciting his advice and patronage.

. . . .

Pittsburgh, March 5, 1822

On motion, resolved that the Secretary announce in the 'Pittsburgh Recorder' that the Board are now wanting to complete their Mission-Family, a Superintendent (who must be a clergyman or a licentiate preacher of the Gospel), a Teacher, a carpenter, a blacksmith, a forman and some other person or persons to be connected with the Mission in other capacities, and that applications will be received thro the Secretary from any persons who may feel willing to go to the heathen in one of the above capacities for the benevolent purposes contemplated by the Board, and on the conditions usually entered into by those who devote themselves for life to the cause of Christ among the heathen.

Resolved that the Secretary be directed to address a letter to the Rev. Professors of the Theo. Seminary at Princeton on the subject of obtaining a Superintendent from that Institution.

. . . .

Pittsburgh, April 9, 1822

The Rev. Thomas E. Hughes was unanimously appointed Superintendent of the Mission about to be established at Maumee: and it was resolved that in consideration of the great importance of having that station filled as speedily as possible Mr. H. be requested to give his decision on this appointment as soon as may be consistent with a due and prayerful consideration of so important a question of duty.

. . . .

Pittsburgh, April 22, 1822

This having been the day appointed by the Board to receive the decision of the Rev. Mr. Hughes on his appointment and he having stated that his mind was still per-plexed with doubt and difficulty on the subject of duty, the Board after mature deliberation that Friday coming next be set apart to be observed by them & the friends of Mr. Hughes as a season of special prayer to God for his divine direction.

.   .   .

Pittsburgh, June 11, 1822

The Rev. Messrs. Elisha Macurdy and Joseph Stevenson were appointed Commissioners of the Board to proceed to Maumee, fix upon the site of the Missionary station — purchase 320 acres of land for the said establishment in an eligible situation, and on the best terms they can; and to superintend the erection with as little delay as possible of such buildings as may be necessary for the temporary accommodation of the Mission, provided that on their arrival it shall not appear that God does not evidently close by some unforseen event of his providence the door of en-trance among the heathen in that quarter.

.   .   .

Pittsburgh, August 6, 1822

The Rev. Joseph Stevenson was appointed superintend-ent pro tem of the Mission contemplated, and that during the same time in which he may retain this appointment he is to be considered in the same light as a Missionary in the ordinary service of the Board.

Mr. Isaac Bowers was appointed a member of the Mis-sion Family, and designated to the general superintendence of the carpenter & wheelwright department.

Resolved that the Mission Family be organized in this city on Wed. the 25th of Sept. next.

. . .   . . .

On motion resolved that the Rev. C. Byington, a member

of the Chocktaw Mission be & hereby is appointed superintendent of the proposed establishment.

Pittsburgh, Sept. 3, 1822

The resolution appointing Mr. Byington was reconsidered & postponed. From letters received and other sources the Secretary reported that it was not likely that two or three other persons appointed would be engaged as members of the Family.

.   .   .

Pittsburgh, Sept. 10, 1822

Resolved that the organization of the Family be deferred to Friday the 27th inst.

.   .   .

Pittsburgh, Sept. 17, 1822

On motion resolved that the organization of the W. M. Family be postponed for the purpose of taking the advice and direction of the Synod at their next meeting.

.   .   .

Pittsburgh, Sept. 24, 1822

Information being received that several members of the Mission Family had arrived in this city. Whereupon on motion resolved; that they be invited to remain, and the President of the Board and Mr. James Cooper be a committee to provide them, and such others as may arrive, with lodging till after advice and direction from the Society, and that the expenses be defrayed from the funds of the Society.

.   .   .

Washington, Oct. 3rd. 1822

The Board of Trust met agreeably to an order of Synod. Members elected this year, the Rev. Messrs. Francis Herron, Elisha P. Swift, Elisha Macurdy, Joseph Stockton, John Andrews and Obadiah Jennings, with the Elders, John Hannen, Samuel Thompson and John Duncan.

Constituted by prayer. Members present, — the Rev. Messrs. Francis Herron, Joseph Stockton, Obadiah Jennings, John Andrews and Elisha P. Swift, with the Elders John Hannen & Saml. Thompson.

The Rev. Francis Herron was chosen President and E. P. Swift, Secretary.

On motion

Resolved unanimously that the Synod be requested to appoint the Rev. Sam. Tait Superintendent pro tem of the Mission Family about to be located among the Ottoway Indians on the Maumee River, & that the Synod direct the adjacent Presbyteries to appoint supplies for Mr. Tait's pulpit during his absence.

The Synod having almost unanimously resolved "that there is sufficient encouragement to authorize the Board to proceed without delay in the organization and establishment of a Missionary Family among the Ottoway Indians," —

Whereupon on motion

Resolved that the said Family be organized in Pittsburgh on Tuesday Evening next. — the 8th inst.

Mr. Wm. Porter was appointed a member of the Family to go out in the capacity of Blacksmith. Adjourned. to meet in Pittsburgh on Saturday the 5th inst. Concluded with prayer.

.   .   .

Pittsburgh, Oct. 7, 1822

Resolved that the sum of $100 be put into the hand of the Superintendent for the purpose of purchasing a waggon and rifle for the Mission — & for meeting other expenses incident to the Mission.

.   .   .

Oct. 8th. on motion
Resolved that the Rev. Ob. Jennings be requested to furnish a copy of the Sermon delivered by him last evening in
the 2d Pres. Church on the occasion of the organization of
the Mission Family for publication; & that the expenses
incurred in printing it be paid out of the Funds & the pro-
ceeds arising out of the sale of the same be appropriated to
the general purposes of the Mission.
Oct. 11 — The Mission Family having this morning taken
their departure, the Board proceeded to the completion of
the business of its session.

. . .

Pittsburgh, Oct. 31, 1822
    On motion
    Resolved that the ½ section of land No. 20 adjoining
the tract of 152¾ acres already purchased by the Board,
be, if practicable, entered in the name of the Society & that
the Rev. Mr. Macurdy be appointed to loan money sufficient to meet this payment.
    On motion
    Resolved that the Rev. Thos. Hunt be appointed a Mis-
sionary for one month or more to proceed to Deleware
(Ohio) & enter the said tract — to solicit live-stock in the
district of country between his residence and the Mission
Station, & to drive them on to sd. station; in doing which
he is authorised to employ any assistance which may be
necessary to accomplish his object.

. . .

Pittsburgh, Dec. 9, 1822
    The Rev. Alvan Coe, Assistant in the Missy. Family at
Maumee, having formerly expressed a wish & by letter recently renews it, to be permitted to engage exclusively in
the study of the Indian language, the Secretary was directed
to refer him to his instruction & inform him that the Board
deem it at present entirely inadvisable.

. . .

Pittsburgh, Feb. 5th, 1823

An application from Mr. Isaac Barnes in behalf of himself & family for a dismission from the service of the Board having been received and read, — the Board after mature and prayerful deliberation unanimously adopted the following preamble and Resolution, Viz. —

Whereas Mr. Isaac Barnes did offer himself to this Board to be by them employed for life as an Assistant Missionary among the heathen, & was in consequence thereof taken under their care as such, and in Oct. last solemnly set apart to that service and sent forth in connection with his brethren to the heathen: — and whereas it appears that some parts of his conduct soon after his arrival at Maumee were justly deemed by his brethren very exceptionable & improper, & that now without assigning any reason or adequate cause for such a change of opinion and desire to contravene his solemn vows & engagements to & with this Board he has now applied for a discharge from the Missionary service, — Therefore

Resolved. 1. That this Board highly disapprove of the conduct of Mr. Barnes & consider the course which he has adopted as entirely repugnant to his high and solemn engagements with this Board at the time he was taken under its care.

Resolved. 2. That in view of this and his application now laid before them, this Board considers it inexpedient, undesirable & improper that he should continue longer in connection with this Board as their Missionary or with the Family as one of its members; and that the said relation between this Board and the said Mr. Barnes & Family be and the same is hereby dissolved.

Resolved. 3. That all the property made over to this Board by Mr. Barnes at the time of his reception as an Assistant Missionary, and the clothing particularly designated by the Board for his use, or that of his family, be retained by & transferred to him, on condition of his refunding — & when he shall refund to the Society, the amount paid by the Board in cash on his account, and the liquidation of debts contracted previously to his reception,

& the money belonging to the Board which may have been in his hand on or since the 1st of Nov. last, & which has not been applied to the use of the Mission.

. . . .

Pittsburgh, April 24, 1823

On motion resolved that the Revd. Obd. Jennings be authorized during his attendance at the Genl. Assembly to seek a permanent Superintendt. for the establishment of Maumee.

. . . .

June 3, 1823

On motion resolved that the Report of the Rev. Saml. Tait, late Superintendent of the Mission of Maumee of his services for seven months on that Station be approved, and that the Board entertaining as they do, a high sense of his diligence & fidelity in their employment, return him their sincere thanks for the important services which he has rendered.

. . . . . .

Resolved that Messrs. Jennings, Macurdy & Swift be appointed a Committee to use all proper exertions between this and the next meeting of the Board to seek information on the subject of a proper Superintendent for the Maumee Mission.

. . . .

Pittsburgh, July 9, 1823

On motion resolved that after solemn prayer to God for his gracious direction & blessing, the Board proceeded to the Election of a Superintendent for the Missionary establishment. — Whereupon the Rev. Ludovicus Robbins, a member of the Presbytery of Washington, was unanimously chosen. Mr. R. being apprised of declared his acceptance of & his acquiecence in this appointment.

On motion resolved that the Superintendent and his family be publicly received and by prayer set apart to the work of their appointment at Washington on Tuesday the 2d of Sepr. next at 2 o'clock P. M.   The Rev. Andrew Wylie was appointed to preach on the occasion and the Rev. John Anderson, D. D. to give the Charge & the Secretary was appointed alternate to the former & the Rev. Francis Herron alternate of the latter.

.   .   .

Oct. 11, 1823

On motion resolved that a warrant amounting to $57.00 be issued to pay for 3 Ten plate Stoves purchased & sent to the Missy. Family, — Mr. Coe having appeared before the Board, the President in the name of the Board, stated to him that the Board had never designed to prevent him from preaching the Gospel to both the white people and the Indian, or of acquiring a knowledge of the Indian language as speedily as his situation shall allow. — Nor have they ever designed to allow such a use of ardent spirits at the Station as should ever even render this a matter of grievance to any member, nor have they any evidence that this has ever actually been the case, after which the President intimated to Mr. Coe that the Board expected him openly, honestly & unreservedly to declare his real, final and fixed determination on this question now to be put to him.   The President then inquired of Mr. Coe, Are you or are you not willing to acquiesce in the conditions stated by the Board in their last communication to you? — The Board before asking an answer of Mr. Coe, resolved to address the throne of Grace — after which having made some observations, Mr. Coe answered this question in the negative, declared that the only alternative of his remaining was that the Board should now engage to allow him to leave the Station for the study of the Indian language, and declined the offer of permitting him to continue until next Spring with the Family leaving the question until then undecided.

The Board being satisfied that Mr. Coe cannot be reconciled to a continuance in the Solen Sevice in which he is engaged; & feeling unwilling to disclose to the world what they deem the irregular & highly reprehensible conduct of Mr. C. in this office, —

On motion

Resolved that he and his family be & they hereby are dismissed from the care & patronage of the Westn. Missy. Family & their relation to the Missy. Family be dissolved.

. . .

Pittsburgh, Jan. 22, 1824

On motion.resolved that Mr. John Glocester, a licentiate preacher of colour, resident in Philada., be appointed to labour as a Missionary among the people of colour in this city & the Town of Washington & their vicinity for 3 months provided the Board of Missions of the Gen. Assembly shall consent to sustain one half of the expenses of the same.

. . .

Pittsburgh, Oct. 27, 1824

Resolved that the request of the Mission Family to be permitted to engage in doing work upon the lands of the Indians on a reasonable compensation — to have the Superintendent released from secular concerns — & to take out a license for the sale of imported goods — & to allow the Superintendent to engage in the study of the Indian language, be & are hereby postponed for future consideration.

. . .

Pittsburgh, Dec. 9, 1824

The Rev. Mr. Macurdy stated to the Board that he had employed Mr. John Rennels assisted by four young men to drive the sheep out to the Station, and that he had exhibited the following statement, viz., that he had lost 12 sheep on the way — sold 101 which became unable to travel, for good notes at 120 days credit, and delivered at the Station 303 — that the expenses amounted to $70.73 — the wages of himself and son to $29.50, and those of the other men to $30.00.

·   ·   ·

Pittsburgh, Jan. 12, 1825

A communication from the Board of the United Foreign Missionary Society, Proposing certain questions on the subject of the overture made to them by the Synod; when after some conversation it was

On motion Resolved that the Secretary be authorized and directed to reply to the above mentioned communication & to answer the several inquiries therein contained.

·   ·   ·

Pittburgh, April 12, 1825

The Rev. Dr. Herron, or in case of his failure, the Rev. Mr. Macurdy was appointed to visit the Station during the succeeding summer & inquire into the State of the Mission — give any necessary directions concerning its operations & report on the same to the Board.

The Rev. Mr. Robbins having requested the Board that he might be dismissed from the Superintendancy of the Family & having expressed his desire to resign the same provided the Board should not grant his request, it was after due deliberation

Resolved that under existing circumstances it is expedient that the request of Robbins be granted and that Mr. Robbins be and hereby is dismissed from the Superintendency of said Mission from & after the First day of May instant.

·   ·   ·

Pittsburgh, June 27, 1825

Mr. Swift on behalf of the Committee appointed to confer with the executive committee of the Board of the U. F. Missionary Society, report that they had duly attended to that appointment — the U. F. M. Society did engage to take the Missionary Station at Maumee under their care & exclusive direction, and pay the Board of Trust of the W. Missionary Society $1000 — in cash provided the Synod of Pittsburgh shall duly & legally convey & transfer to them the said Station with all the real & personal property of the Board of Trust of said Society thereunto belonging, to be the property and employed for the use of said U. F. Miss. Society; and that, in the confident anticipation of the assent of said Synod to these stipulations, they are willing to assume from this time the care, management and direction of said Mission, provided that the Board of Trust of the Western Missionary Society shall engage faithfully to refund to the U. F. M. Society all monies which shall have been expended on said Mission by said U. F. Missionary Society antecedently to the next meeting of the Synod of Pittsburgh, in case & on condition that the above mentioned agreement & transfer shall not then be duly ratified by them.

On motion resolved that the above stipulation, and transfer therein contained be approved by this Board — that the said stipulation, so far as it respects the direction of the Mission until the next meeting of Synod be accepted — and that it be and hereby is recommended to the Synod of Pittsburgh to accept & ratify said proposition of the M. F. M. Society.

The Secretary directed to communicate a knowledge of these proceedings to the Corresponding Secy. of the U. F. Missionary Society, and through him to inform the said Committee that the arrangements are to be understood as extending to the property taken to the Station by and belonging to the Ministers of the Mission Family, and the adjustment of which is to be a matter of mutual contract — between the said committee & the members of the Mission themselves — and further that it is understood that all formal & legal ratification of this transfer between the U. F. Miss. Society be deferred until after the meeting of the Synod at which time it is hoped that some commission agents representing that Board will then be present duly commissioned to close the contract.

It appearing from letter received from the Rev. Mr. Robbins, late Superintendent of the Mission at Maumee, that the design of his application to the Board was not understood, and that it was his object to be released rather from the superintendancy of the secular concerns of the Mission than from membership in the Family itself; the Secretary was directed to inform him that, in as much as the duties of the office to which he was appointed are one & indivisible, according to the plan of the Board, they could not understand a request of the kind which he made to be released from the superintendancy of the Mission, as implying anything less than an entire discharge — and that on the presumption that this was his meaning, he was accordingly dismissed, without censure and with their implied approbation of his diligence, integrity and faithfulness while in their employment, and this was the state of the matter when the Committee left home for N. York to confer with the Board of the U. F. Miss. Society, and as since that period a conveyance of the Mission to the U. F. M. Society has been entered into, it is now entirely out of their power to take any measures in relation to the management of the Mission, and consequently renders it impossible for them to correct the mistake which seems to have been committed in relation to his application, but that the Board cherish towards him the most kind and respectful feelings, and entertain the fullest confidence in his piety & devotedness — & that, as the measure in question originated entirely in his own communication, and was based upon it, he be, should he feel disposed, in existing circumstances, to continue in the Mission, affectionately advised to submit the whole matter to the Board of the U. F. Miss. Society, to whom, as the only proper organ, he is now respectfully referred.

On motion

Resolved that Mr. Van Tassell and Dr. Clarke, whose applications for a dismission have never been acted upon, be and the same hereby are referred to the Board of the U. F. M. Society.

The male members of the Family were appointed a Committee to settle up the accounts of the Mission, so far as relate to the Station, up to the 1st of July next and transmit the same duly balanced to the Society, after which date all accounts are to be kept in the name of, and all drafts & communications made to the Board of the U. For. Miss. Society through the Rev. James C. Crane, Missionary Rooms, Cedar St., N. York.

.   .   .

Washington, Oct. 20 ,1825

On motion resolved that, in conducting domestic Missions, it be considered as a leading object of this Board to secure the settlement of ministers in those destitute settlements to which their Missionaries are sent — to secure the aid & cooperation of the people themselves to the full extent of their ability; and to continue their operations somewhat regularly in all those circuits to which their attention & their efforts have been once directed. That it therfore be a general rule with this Board in all their appointments primarily to regard this object — that, if possible, all such places as shall subscribe sufficient to pay the expenses of a Missionary be statedly supplied with one under the direction of the Board — and that ordinarily all Missionary stations or circuits be aided with an amount of Missionary labor proportionate to the sum actually paid by themselves.

.   .   .

Washington, October 25, 1825

The Synod having ratified the contract contemplated by the Board in their negotiations with the U. F. Miss. Society, the Secretary was authorized to hand over to the Secretary of that Board now present all papers in relation to the

Mission at Maumee & to that part of the operations & funds of this Society which respect Indian Missions generally.

· · ·

2. EXTRACTS FROM RECORDS OF MISSIONARY WORK AMONG THE CHOCTAW AND CHICKASAW INDIANS

[The Choctaw and Chickasaw Indians, living largely in the region west of Georgia and east of the Mississippi River, were the objects of much Presbyterian missionary endeavor. The missionaries to these Indians, at first united in an Association, were constituted in 1828 as the Tombigbee Presbytery by the Synod of South Carolina and Georgia. Original MS in the Historical Foundation, Montreat, N. C.]

(A) THE ASSOCIATION OF MISSIONARIES, 1827–1828

At a meeting of the Association of Missionaries in the Choctaw & Chickasaw Nations holden at Mayhew in the Choctaw Nation Oct. 11th 1827.

Present, Rev. Cyrus Kingsbury,
    Brn. Loring S. Williams,
      John Smith
      Calvin Cushman
      William Hooper,
      Anson Dyer,
      Anson Gleason
      David Wright &
      Timothy Butler.

The meeting was opened with prayer by Br. Kingsbury.

Rev. Cyrus Kingsbury was chosen moderator,

Bro. Anson Dyer was chosen Scribe.

Voted, that the meeting be adjourned until half past one o'clock P.M. when the Brethren will assemble to give a relation of the situation & prospects of the particular stations to which they are attached.

That a signal be given in all instances for meeting & that but ten minutes be allowed after the signal before opening the meeting. That all our meetings be opened & closed with prayer.

Br. Smith closed the meeting with prayer.

Met according to adjournment.

Rev. John Bell a missionary in the Chickasaw Nation was introduced.

Br. Smith gave a general statement of the station at Eliot. Br. Cushman made a statement of the plan & prospects of his intended station. Rev. Mr Bell also related the situation &c. of his station among the Chickasaws. Meeting adjourned to the 12th instant at 2 oclock, P.M.

Today 12th. Met according to adjournment. Adjourned until 9,oclock P.M. M⁄t accordingly. Adjourned until Saturday 1, oclock P.M.

Saturday 13th. Met according to adjournment

Voted that we propose to the Brn of the Chahta Mission such a division of S. Mission as shall place those members who are devoted to the study of the language preparing & printing books, preaching or teaching in the native language under the immediate direction of the Pru. Com of the A.B.C.F.M. drawing their funds from the Treasurer of the same & unconnected with the English schools or with the general government. That Brn Kingsbury, Hooper, & Dyer acting as a Committee, communicate this resolution together with its reasons to the absent Brn for their consideration & if approved by them that the said Committee forward the same together with the signature of the Brn to the Pru.Com; adjourned until 9 oclock, P.M.

Met according to adjournment. Br. Kingsbury asked to be excused from acting as one of the Committee on the above resolution

Voted that our next annual meeting be holden at Eliot, on the Thursday preceding the third Sabbath in Sept. 1828, meeting dissolved —

Extracts from the minutes of the meeting kept by the Scribe

CYRUS BYINGTON Clerk

Religious meetings

Preaching . Friday evening, Saturday afternoon, Sabbath morning & afternoon

Prayermeeting Thursday forenoon, Friday afternoon, Sat. Forenoon Sab. morning

Conferences Thursday evening, & Saturday evening, & Sabbath evening.

Manuscript Sermon read Saturday forenoon.

Examination of condidates for admission to the church Sat. afternoon.

Admission of Wesson, Folsom, Hunt, & Hadley to the church, Sab.

Baptism of Mr. Nathaniel Folsom, children of D. Hunt, child of Br Gleason, & child of Sister Ward, Sabbath.

Sacrament of the Lords Supper administered to Sisters Gleason & Macomber on the Sabbath, (in their home I suppose)

Sacrament of the Lord's Supper administered in publick to about 40 members.

1828

At a meeting of the Association of Missionaries in the Choctaw & Chickasaw Nations holden at Eliot Sept. 19, 1828,

Present.   Rev. Cyrus Kingsbury
Alfred Wright
Cyrus Byington &
William C. Blair

The meeting was opened with prayer by C. Kingsbury

The Rev. Cyrus Kingsbury was chosen Moderator,
Cyrus Byington was chosen Scribe.

Voted to invite Brn L.S.Williams, John Smith, Joel Wood & Zechariah Howes to sit with us as members of this Association.

Voted to correct the minutes of the meeting held at Mayhew in Oct. 1827, so as to correspond with the articles of this Association.

Voted that the clerical Brn & Br.Wood be a Committee to make arrangements in regard to publick & social religious exercises during the term of the meeting.

Br. Blair arrived & took his seat.

Voted that we meet tomorrow at 2.P.M. for prayer & for the purpose of attending to reports from the Evangelists of their labors & of the state of the churches.

At 2 oclock P.M. met & conversed upon various subjects, which being concluded as not properly coming before this Association were not acted upon.

Voted to appoint a Committee to correspond with the Pru:Com: to learn their views relative to the subject of having the pastoral relation regularly constituted, between any of the ministers of our association & their respective Mission churches.

Voted that Brn Blair & Byington constitute this committee.

Adjourned till tomorrow at 8 oclock,A.M.

Closed with prayer by Br.Blair.

Met according to adjournment, Meeting opened with prayer.

Voted that the opening of each daily Session the names of the members of this association shall be called.

Voted that it is expedient to take some preparatory measures with reference to the formation of a Presbytery within our own bounds.

Voted to hold our next annual meeting at Monroe in the Chickasaw Nation on the Thursday next suceeding the third Sabbath of Sept. 1829.

Voted that the Brn residing in each district in the Choctaw Nation chose [sic] & send a delegate to meet the association at the time & place above mentioned.

The following appointments were made by the moderator for the next annual meeting, viz,

A sermon for criticism by Br Kingsbury.

Exegesis of Phil.2.ch.5-11.v. by Br.H.Wilson

Exegesis of 1 John4th ch: 19 v. bq Br.L.S.Williams.

Dissertation on the importance of high attainments in piety to the Missionary character, by Br. Byington.

Sermon for the edification of those engaged in the missionary work by Br. Stewart, or by Br. Blair as his substitute.

Saturday at sundown adjourned after prayer by the Moderator.

Other exercises

Preaching, friday afternoon, Saturday morning, & on the Sabbath three sermons besides the administration of the Lord's Supper, Monday one sermon.

Prayer meetings   Friday half past ten oclock A.M.   Saturday morning, Sat. evening, Sab. morning.   Br Hoopers funeral sermon was preached Sab. morning.

(B) RECORDS OF THE TOMBIGBEE PRESBYTERY, 1829–1830

Extracts from the minutes of the Synod of South Carolina and Georgia at their Session in the City of Columbia S.C. commencing the 11th of Dec. 1828.

"By request, from the Presbytery of South Alabama the Synod constituted a new Presbytery including the territory North of the Lipse river in Alabama & embracing the Choctaw & Chickasaw Nations of Indians.   The Presbytery to hold their first meeting at Mayhew, one of the missionary stations, in the Choctaw Nation on the Friday preceding the first Sabbath in June 1829.   The meeting to be opened with a sermon by the Rev. Alfred Wright."

Agreeable to the above act of Synod the Rev. Messrs Thomas Archibald, Alfred Wright and Cyrus Kingsbury members of the Presbytery of South Alabama met at Mayhew this 5th day of June 1829, & constituted a new Presbytery to be called the *Tombigbee Presbytery*.

The meeting was opened with prayer by the Rev. Alfred Wright.   The Rev. Alfred Wright was chosen Moderator and the Rev. Cyrus Kingsbury Clerk.   Maj. William H. Craven ruling Elder of the church at Columbus took his seat, as a member of this Presbytery.   The Rev. Robert W. B. Kennedy a member of the South Alabama Presbytery, was invited to take a seat with the Presbytery, as a corresponding member.

Presbytery adjourned to meet at the camp ground near Fuli honimas tomorrow at 3 oclock P.M.

June 6th Presbytery met according to adjournment. The Rev.Cyrus Byington, having given satisfactory evidence of his dismission from the Presbytery of Cincinnati & of his having been recommended by that Presbytery to this requested to be received as a member of this Presbytery. His request was granted.

The Presbytery voted that their next meeting be held at Yoknokehaya on Thursday preceding the first Sab. in November next. Presbytery adjourned with prayer.

C. KINGSBURY Clerk.

Yoknokehaya   Oct. 29th 1829.

A quorum not being present, Presbytery was not constituted. Oct.30th a quorum having arrived Presbytery was constituted with prayer by the Rev. C. Byington, the moderator of the last meeting being absent.

Present the Rev T. Archibald, C. Byington & C. Kingsbury.

The Rev. C. Byington was chosen moderator, & C Kingsbury Clerk. The minutes of the last meeting not being present & no business being before Presbytery, Presbytery adjourned to meet at Mayhew on Wednesday the 11th of Nov. next. Concluded with prayer.

C. KINGSBURY Clerk.

Mayhew Nov.10th 1829.

Presbytery met according to adjournment & was constituted with prayer.

Present	*Elders*
Rev. T. Archibald	Wm. Wright of Unity
C. Byington	Church
C. Kingsbury	Isaac Toomer of Beer-
Alfred Wright absent	sheba Church

The Rev. William Montgomery, Rev. Jacob Rickhow & Rev. Benj. Chase being present were invited to sit as corresponding ing members.

Messrs Loring S.Williams Moses Jewell & David Wright, Licentiates from the Mississippi Presbytery, having obtained a dismission & recommendation from that Presbytery, were, at their request, rec. under the care of this Presbytery. They having been licensed by that Presbytery as "extraordinary cases".

Mr. David Wright having requested ordination as an Evangelist, resolved that his application be rec. & that he be directed to prepare a popular discourse on Eph:5.14, also a Lecture on Heb.1-1-8, as parts of his trial preparatory to his ordination.

Mr. Loring S. Williams having requested ordination as an Evangelist, voted that his application be received & that he be directed to prepare a popular discourse on Eph.1.7, also a Lecture on the Parable of the Sower the latter to be written both in Choctaw & English & both to be presented at the next semi annual meeting of Presbytery.

On motion resolved, that the next Semiannual meeting of Presbytery be at Aiikhuna the friday preceding the last Sab. in March, 1830 at 9 oclock, A.M.

Adjourned to meet at Columbus the Friday preceding the second Sabbath in Jany. 1830, at 3 oclock P. M.

Columbus Jany.8th 1830.

Presbytery met according to adjournment, opened by the delivery of a Sermon by the Rev. Harrison Allen & was constituted with prayer by the moderator.

Present.   Rev. T.Archibald
                       C.Byington
                       C.Kingsbury
    Rev.Alfred Wright absent
Elders   Henry W.Hunt from the church at Columbus,
              Isaac Toomer from the church at Beersheba.

The Rev. Messrs Joseph P. Cunningham & John H.

Gray from the South Alabama Presbytery & Rev. Harrison Allen from the Newburyport Presbytery were invited to sit as corresponding members.

The Rev. Thomas Archibald was chosen moderator & Rev. Cyrus Byington Clerk (recess till 7,oclock P.M.) Br. David Wright, Rev. C. Kingsbury, & Br. Henry W. Hunt were appointed a Committee of arrangements.

Proceeded to examine W. D. Wright with reference to his receiving ordination as an Evangelist, as to his acquaintance with experimental religion, the Greek language & theology in part.

The report of the Committee of arrangements was read & accepted.

On motion adjourned till tomorrow morning at half past 8 oclock. Concluded with prayer.

Jany 9th. Met according to adjournment

Members present, as on yesterday. Mr. Toomer absent.

Prayer was offered by Rev. C. Kingsbury.

Examined the candidate on his views of the Sacraments & church Govt.

On motion voted that the examination of W. D. Wright be sustained

On motion voted that his excuse for not preparing a written Lecture be sustained. (Recess till after sermon by the candidate)

On motion voted that the sermon as a part of the trials of the candidate be sustained. Recess till 2,oclock,P.M.

The ordination Sermon was delivered by the Rev. Joseph P. Cunningham (from 1 Thess.2d,8-9 v). The Rev. T. Archibald addressed the congregation upon the nature of the ministerial office & read the questions to the Candidate pointed out in the Discipline. To all which he answered in the affirmative. The consecrating prayer was offered by Rev. C. Byington when the Presbytery imposed hands upon the candidate & afterward gave him the right hand of fellowship. Rev. C. Kingsbury delivered the charge & Rev. J. H Gray addressed the people. Rev. H Allen offered the concluding prayer, after singing had a recess till after the delivery of sermon in the evening.

Rev. David Wright was invited to sit as a member of this Presbytery.

Rev. C. Byington was chosen Stated Clerk.

The Rev. Hillery Patrick presented a Certificate of dismission & recommendation from the Union Presbytery to join the Mississippi Presbytery. But it appearing from statements made, by Mr. Patrick that there was a mistake in the name of the Presbytery to which he had been recommended, it being that of Miss. when it should have been Tombig [sic] bigbee, on motion resolved to receive him as member of this Presbytery.

The Rev. Hillery Patrick was chosen a commissioner to attend the meeting of the next General Assembly.

On motion adjourned to meet at Aiikhuna on the Friday previous to the last Sab of March, at 9 oclock A.M. Concluded with prayer by the moderator. Doxology sung at the close.

      Attest   CYRUS BYINGTON Stated Slerk.

    Aiikhuna Chahta Nation March 24th, 1830

Presbytery met according to adjournment, opened by the delivery of a Sermon from Matthew 28th ch.18,19,20,v, by the Rev. C. Byington, & was constituted with prayer by the Moderator.

Present. Rev. Thomas Archibald
             Cyrus Kingsbury
             Alfred Wright &
             Cyrus Byington.

Absent, Rev. David Wright, & Hillery Patrick.

Elders present. William Givens of Unity church.

Calvin Cushman an elder in the Mayhew church presented a petition from that church to be rec. under the care of this Presbytery, which was granted. And he took his seat as a member of this Presbytery. Rev. Alfred Wright presented a petition from the Goshen church to be rec.

under the care of this Presbytery, which was granted. Ebenezer Hotchkin an elder in the Goshen church took his seat as a member.

Rev A. Wright, rendered an excuse for his absence at the last meeting, which was sustained.

On motion resolved to correct the Records of the meeting held at Mayhew on Nov.11th 1829, by inserting on the 6th & 7th lines from the top of page 4th the following words "They having been licensed by that Presbytery as Extraordinary cases." And the Records of the meeting held at Columbus in Jany last, by inserting the words "as an Evangelist", between the 5th & 6th lines from the top of page 6th.

Brn. Williams, Byington, & Cushman were appointed a Committee of arrangements.

Ebenezer Hotchkin having presented a request to be rec. under the care of this Presbytery, as a candidate for licensure in the Gospel Ministry, resolved to examine him, as to his acquaintance with experimental religion, & his views in wishing to become a preacher of the Gospel.

On motion, resolved that the examination be sustained,& that he be rec. under the care of this Presbytery.

Rev.Harrison Allen having produced a letter of dismission & recommendation, from the Presbytery of Newburyport, on motion resolved to receive him as a member of this Presbytery.

Mr. Hugh Caldwell a Licentiate, having produced a letter of dismission & recommendation from the New Brunswick Presbytery; on motion resolved to receive, him under the care of this Presbytery.   Recess till 2 oclock, P.M.

On motion resolved to examine Mr.Hotchkin in English grammar & Geography.   The examination was sustained.

On motion resolved that Mr.Hotchkin prepare himself as portions of his trial, to be examined in Astronomy Natural & Moral Philosophy, at the next meeting of this Presbytery, & that he also write a discourse from the Gospel according to St John 4th ch.24th v.   On motion resolved

that Mr. Williams deliver a popular discourse at 4 oclock
this afternoon as a part of his trial, preparatory to ordination.

Mr. Hugh Caldwell having requested ordination as an
Evangelist upon motion resolved that his application be
rec. & that he deliver a popular discourse this evening at
7 oclock as a part of his trial preparatory to ordination.
Proceeded to examine Messrs Caldwell & Williams, as to
their acquaintance with experimental religion, and as to
their views in wishing for ordination as Evangelists.

The Stated Clerk was directed to prepare a Presbyterial
Report of the state of the churches & forward the same
to the next General Assembly.

Mr. Williams delivered the popular discourse, previously
assigned him by this Presbytery, at 4 oclock, P.M.   On
motion resolved that this part of his trial be sustained.

Rev. A. Wright & H. Allen were appointed a Committee to examine the Records of the churches at Beersheba
& Unity.

At 7 oclock P.M. Mr. Caldwell delivered a popular discourse from the first Epistle of John, 3 ch.2 v.   On motion
resolved that this part of his trial be sustained.

Rev. David Wright was chosen Treasurer of this Presbytery.

Proceeded to examine Messrs. Williams & Caldwell, as
to their knowledge of Theology.   Adjourned till tomorrow
morning at 8 oclock.   Prayer by Rev. A. Wright.

March 27th.   Presbytery met according to adjournment.
Prayer by the moderator

The report of the Committee of arrangements was read
& accepted.

On motion resolved, that the examination of Messrs.
Williams & Caldwell, as to their piety, motives of engaging
in the work of the Ministry, knowledge of philosophy theology, church history, & church government be sustained.

The examination in languages for special reasons was
omitted.

Brn. A. Wright, C. Byington, H. Caldwell, were appointed a Committee to draw up a report of the state of religion within the bounds of this Presbytery to be forwarded to the General Assembly.

Mr. Williams delivered his Lecture in Chahta.

On motion resolved, that the examination & the trials for ordination be sustained, & that we proceed to the ordination of Messrs. Williams & Caldwell.

Rev. T. Archibald preached the sermon, from the Epistle to the Coloss. 4th ch. 19. Rev. A. Wright offered the consecrating prayer. Rev. C. Kingsbury delivered the charge & the Rev. C. Byington addressed the people in Chahta.

Rev. L. S. Williams & Hugh Caldwell, were invited to take their seats in Presbytery as members.

The Rev. Hillery Patrick was chosen Commissioner to the General Assembly, & the Rev. Hugh Caldwell as his alternate. On motion resolved that the Tr. of this Presbytery be requested to pay over to the Rev. Hugh Caldwell the amount of money for the Commissioners' fund, that he may deliver the same to the Treasurer of the General Assembly.

The Report of the Committee on the Sessional Records of Beersheba & Unity churches was made & accepted.

Missionary labors were assigned to the Rev. Cyrus Kingsbury west of Mayhew so as to include Twin Cave, & East & South as far as Ititapa. Missionary labors were assigned to C. Byington in Bokpalaia, Wika Shobaba Apokta Chito, Nerha & Okayanali.
Missionary labors were assigned to L. S. Williams in connection with C. Byington, south of Oknakahobi.

On motion resolved that the next meeting of Presbytery be held at Goshen, on the friday previous to the last Thursday of Oct. 1830, at 4, oclock, P.M.

On motion resolved that the following Brn attend to the following subjects in examining candidates for licensure or ordination, viz.

Rev. D. Wright, English Gram. & the Languages.

Rev. T. Archibald, Geography & Nat. Philosophy

Rev. A. Wright, Moral Philosophy & Astronomy

Rev. C. Kingsbury Church Government.
C. Byington, Church History
H. Allen Natural Theology,
L. S. Williams, experimental religion.
Moderator, Theology.
On motion resolved to adjourn. Prayer by moderator
singing of doxology at close.
Attest.   CYRUS BYINGTON Stated Clerk.

(c) SESSIONAL RECORD OF THE PRESBYTERIAN CHURCH
MONROE, CHICKASAW NATION, 1823–1824

The Rev. Hugh Dickson,[7] of the Presbytery of So. Carolina, having been commissioned by the missionary Society
of the Synod of So. Carolina and Georgia, to visit Monroe
for the purpose of examining into the state and prospects of
the mission, arrived on the 29 of May 1823. The mission
family, having a desire to be united in a church capacity
that they may regularly enjoy the privilege of the sealing
ordinances of the gospel, expressed the same to Mr. Dickson. Accordingly on the 7th of June 1823 a church was
organized; consisting of the following members, viz—
Hamilton V. Turner
James Wilson
Nancy Turner
Mary Ann Wilson
Ethalinda Wilson
Prudence Wilson (not a member of the mission)
Susan Stuart
Owing to our peculiar situation, the usual, mode of requiring certificates of dismission and good standing from
the churches to which the members had respectively belonged, was dispensed with. The Rev. Thomas C. Stuart,
superdt [sic] of the mission was nominated as Stated Sup-
ply. After the exercises of the day, a Session consisting of

---

[7] Hugh Dickson (October 15, 1772-July 9, 1853) was licensed to preach
in 1800. He was ordained and installed pastor of Greenville Church, Abbeville District, S. C., November 11, 1801, which pastorate he held until his
resignation in 1846. Howe, George, *History of the Presbyterian Church in
South Carolina*, 2 Vols. (Columbia, S. C., 1833), II, pp. 750-753.

the Rev. Messrs. Blair and Wilson, assisted by Father Dickson, convened in the prayer hall. A black woman, named Dinah, belonging to Mr. James Gunn, applied to be received into the newly organized church. After a careful examination the session felt satisfied with her christian experience, and accordingly admitted her to the privileges of the household of faith.

Rindah, a black woman, belonging to Mr. Turner, was debarred from church privileges for improper conduct.

August 3. 1823. Dinah, having previously expressed a desire to have her children baptised, and having given us satisfactory evidence as to her knowledge of this holy ordinance, presented her three children Chloe, William and Lucy and dedicated them to God in baptism.

August 6. 1823. Margaret Ethalinda, daughter of Rev. H. Wilson & Ethalinda Wilson, was baptised.

May 15th. 1824. Abram, a black man belonging to an Indian, and husband to the woman received at our last communion, applied for church privileges. His examination was satisfactory and he was accordingly admitted. Rindah, who was suspended from the communion of the church at our last, made application to be restored. On her professing sorrow for her offence, and promising amendment, she was reinstated.

May 16. The ordinance of baptism was administered to Abram.

Nov. 9. 1824. Mr. James Holmes, a member of the presbyterian church in Carlisle, Pennsylvania, was added to our number.

Decr. 4. Mr. Barnard McLaughlin, Mrs. Tennesses Bynum, a native, and Esther, a black woman belonging to Mrs. Colbert, having given satisfactory evidence of a work of grace upon their hearts were admitted as members of the church. Esther was baptised.

Decr. 19. The ordinance of baptism was administered to Br. H. Wilson's infant daughter Rachel Clementine; Mrs. Bynum's two children Turner & Elizabeth; Rindahs son Moses, and Esthers daughter Patsy.

Decr. 26. Dinah's infant daughter Patsy was baptised.

CHAPTER XIV

AMERICAN HOME MISSIONARY SOCIETY
CORRESPONDENCE

INTRODUCTION

1. Executive Committee of the American Home Missionary Society to friends of home missions. New York, December, 1831.
2. H. Chamberlin to the Secretary of the United Domestic Missionary Society. St. Louis, Missouri, March 22, 1826.
3. Wm. S. Woodruff to the American Home Missionary Society. Little Rock, Arkansas, July 15, 1826.
4. DeWitt Clinton to Absalom Peters, Corresponding Secretary of the A. H. M. S. Albany, New York, August 3, 1826.
5. James Eels and others to the American Home Missionary Society. Auburn, New York, August 16, 1826.
6. Jas. H. Schuster, Corresponding Secretary of the Indiana Missionary Society, to Absalom Peters, Corresponding Secretary of the A. H. M. S. Madison, Indiana, August 30, 1826.
7. Moses Fisk and others to the American Home Missionary Society. Fort Covington, Franklin County, New York, February 25, 1827.
8. Aaron Foster to the Corresponding Secretary of the A. H. M. S. Abbeville, South Carolina, December 20, 1827.
9. John H. Rice to Absalom Peters, Corresponding Secretary of the A. H. M. S. Union Seminary, Prince Edward, Virginia, October 31, 1828.
10. Michael G. Youse, Treasurer of the Synod of Kentucky, to Absalom Peters, Corresponding Secretary of the A. H. M. S. Danville, Kentucky, December 2, 1828.
11. Absalom Peters, Corresponding Secretary of the A. H. M. S., by Charles Hall, Assistant Secretary, to Michael G. Youse, Danville, Kentucky. New York, January 2, 1829.
12. Absalom Peters, Corresponding Secretary of the A. H. M. S. to Joshua L. Wilson, Pastor of the First Presbyterian Church, Cincinnati. Undated.
13. Knowles Taylor, Treasurer of the A. H. M. S. to the friends of home missions. New York, August 20, 1830.
14. Communication relative to the "Central Committee for Home Missions in the Western States."
15. D. C. Blood to the Corresponding Secretary of the American Home Missionary Society. Covington, Kentucky, February 2, 1832.

16. Nathaniel Hood to the Corresponding Secretary of the American Home Missionary Society. Granger County, Tennessee, January 9, 1832.

17. "A lady in Magnolia, Florida, to her sister in Providence, Rhode Island." Magnolia, Florida, April 27, 1831.

18. A. N. Cunningham to Absalom Peters, Corresponding Secretary of the A. H. M. S. Montgomery, Alabama, September 7, 1831.

19. Fielding Pope to Absalom Peters, Corresponding Secretary of the A. H. M. S. Athens, Tennessee, December 4, 1832.

20. Absalom Peters, Corresponding Secretary of the A. H. M. S. to Benjamin H. Rice, Associate Secretary of the A. H. M. S. Mississippi River, bound from St Louis to New Orleans, January 10, 1833.

21. Absalom Peters, Corresponding Secretary of the A. H. M. S. to Benjamin H. Rice, Associate Secretary of the A. H. M. S. Florence, Alabama, February 28, 1833.

22. A. Savage to Absalom Peters, Corresponding Secretary of the A. H. M. S. Tallahassee, Florida, May 3, 1833.

23. Thomas Brown to Absalom Peters, Corresponding Secretary of the A. H. M. S. Kingston, Tennessee, September 16, 1834.

24. D. A. Campbell to Absalom Peters, Corresponding Secretary of the A. H M. S. Beattys Bridge, North Carolina, September 15, 1834.

25. A. Hale to Absalom Peters, Corresponding Secretary of the A. H. M. S. Jacksonville, Illinois, September 27, 1836.

26. Levi H. Evans to Absalom Peters, Corresponding Secretary of the A. H. M. S. Near Charlestown, Maryland, October 11, 1836.

27. Milton Badger, Associate Secretary of the A. H. M. S., to Levi H. Evans, Charlestown, Maryland. New York, October 16, 1836.

28. Charles Hall, Assistant Secretary of the A. H. M. S., to friends of home missions. New York, May 30, 1837.

29. A. Hale to Absalom Peters, Corresponding Secretary of the A. H. M. S. Galena, Illinois, August 22, 1837.

30. Milton Badger, Associate Secretary of the A. H. M. S., to J. G. Simrall, Carlinville, Illinois. New York, June 20, 1837.

31. J. G. Simrall to Absalom Peters, Corresponding Secretary of the A. H. M. S. Carlinville, Illinois, July 7, 1837.

32. W. W. Woods to Absalom Peters, Corresponding Secretary of the A. H. M. S. Putnamville, Indiana, July 17, 1837.

33. Robert Holman to Absalom Peters, Corresponding Secretary of the A. H. M. S. Mardisville, Alabama, July 27, 1837.

34. S. W. Magill to Absalom Peters, Corresponding Secretary of the A. H. M. S. Bryan County, Georgia, September 21, 1837.

35. H. Reid to Milton Badger, Secretary of the A. H. M. S. South Carolina, August 30, 1839.

36. C. Washburn to Milton Badger and Charles Hall, Secretaries of the
   A. H. M. S.   Benton County, Arkansas, September 8, 1846.
37. A. Williams to Milton Badger, Secretary of the A. H. M. S.   Grand
   River, Arkansas, November 8, 1848.
38. Milton Badger, Secretary of the A. H. M. S. to A. Williams, Grand
   River, Arkansas.   New York, December 8, 1848.

[The American Home Missionary Society was organized as an
interdenominational home missionary agency on May 12, 1826 at a
meeting in the Brick Presbyterian Church in New York City.[1] The
major motive in forming the Society was to unify, through voluntary
consolidation, the efforts of a number of home missionary agencies.
The largest single agency coöperating in the formation of the Society
was the United Domestic Missionary Society which had been formed
in New York in 1822 to consolidate home missionary work in that
state.

The American Home Missionary Society was the first home missionary agency organized on a national scale and it soon became the
principal agent in carrying out the Plan of Union, though by no
means did it confine its activities to those regions where Presbyterians
and Congregationalists were in coöperation, but soon extended itself
over the entire nation.   It immediately assumed responsibility for
the eighty-one missionaries of the United Domestic Missionary Society and by the close of the first year of its operations it had 169
missionaries laboring in 196 localities in fifteen states and had affilia-
tions with 124 home missionary auxiliaries in widely scattered parts
of the country.[2]   The letters received annually by the Society were
often in excess of 5,000.   The correspondence between the Corresponding Secretary in the Society's New York office and the missionaries, auxiliaries, donors, friends and communities requesting .mis-
sionaries furnish a vivid picture of religious, moral and general social
conditions on every frontier.

From the beginning portions of the letters received were published
weekly in the *New York Observer*, and after 1828 in the Society's

[1] Spring, Gardiner, *Personal Reminiscences of the Life and Times of.* 2
Vols. (New York, 1866) II, pp. 265ff.   Gardiner Spring was the pastor of the
Brick Presbyterian Church at this time.   See also *The Congregational Home
Missionary Society.   One Hundredth Annual Report,* 1926 (New York,
1926), p. 7; also Gillett, *op. cit.,* II, pp. 227-228, 448-449.
[2] *First Report of the American Home Missionary Society presented by the
Executive Committee at the Anniversary Meeting, May 9, 1827* (New York,
1827), pp. 42, 52.

own paper *The Home Missionary and American Pastor's Journal,*
which was made up largely of excerpts from the correspondence.
These letters were published under such captions as "Destitute Regions and Applications for Aid," "Interesting News from the Borders
of the Northwest Territory."

Until 1833 the Society received its largest support from the Presbyterians. In a *Circular* prepared by Absalom Peters, the Corresponding Secretary of the Society and published in the *Home Missionary* for April, 1829, he states that the American Home Missionary Society is composed principally of Presbyterians and that up to
that time it had derived "more than four fifths of its income from
Presbyterian Churches."[3]

The entire correspondence of the American Home Missionary Society consists of more than 70,000 original letters besides 150 volumes of "press" copies of letters written by the officials of the Society.
The entire collection is deposited in the Library of the Chicago Theological Seminary. The letters here presented have been selected from
this large collection to illustrate the work carried on by Presbyterians
particularly, and emphasis has been placed upon those sections of
the country in which other denominations aided by the Society were
not particularly active.]

[Extract from a letter issued from the Office of the A. H.
M. S. in December, 1831, and signed by the members of
the Executive Committee.]

This Society, as you are probably informed, was instructed by a large Convention of the friends of Missions
assembled in this city, [New York] May 1826, from thirteen of the United States & Territories, & from the Presbyterian, Congregational, Reformed Dutch & Associate Reformed Churches. Its object, as defined in its Constitution,
is "to assist congregations that are unable to support the
gospel ministry, & to send the gospel to the destitute within
the United States." This object has been pursued with un-
anticipated success, the operations of the Society have been

---

[3] *The Home Missionary,* April, 1829, I, No. 12, p. 210. Gillett, *op. cit.,* II,
p. 448, states that till 1833 more than half of the funds of the Society came
from New York state alone. On the other hand A. E. Dunning in *Congregationalists in America,* states that "From the beginning . . . Congregationalists were much the most prominent in gifts and in labors." This seems to
be the tradition held among Congregationalists but is evidently not supported by the facts.

signally blessed, as a means of advancing the moral & religious interests of our country, especially within the widely extended bounds of the Presbyterian Church. In the five years & seven months, since its organization, it has aided in the support of 821 ministers in congregations & missionary districts, which, without such assistance, must have remained but partially or not at all supplied with the preaching of the gospel. These ministers have reported 1170 years of ministerial labor performed in the service of the Society. Sabbath School & Bible Class instruction have been pursued with great success in most of the congregations aided, numerous & interesting revivals of religion have been enjoyed, & not less than 15,000 souls have been reported as the hopeful subjects of renewing grace under the labors of our missionaries.

Of the whole number of ministers, in whose support aid has been granted, 232 have been located & employed west of the Alleghany Mountains, which is nearly one half of the present number of Presbyterian ministers on that whole field; thus furnishing religious instruction to many of the new & rising settlements in those frontier States & Territories, of which they must otherwise have remained destitute.

In the prosecution of an enterprise so extended, it is —apparent that large means are required. Yet the Society has no permanent funds, but is dependent entirely on the yearly contributions of the benevolent. Until the two last years, these contributions were sufficient to sustain its operations, but of late they have not increased in proportion to the necessary expenditures of the Society. At the last Anniversary the number of Missionaries reported was 403, the amount of expenditures, during the year, was $47,247. But the receipts of the year, from ordinary sources, fell short of this sum more than $4000, & would have left the Society so much in debt, had it not been for the very providential & timely reception of a Legacy of $5000, leaving in the Treasury $877, at the end of the year, in May last. Since that time 63 new appointments have been made, mak-

ing the whole number of ministers, in whose support the
Executive Committee is pledged to render aid within the
current year, more than 500. These, at an average of $100
each, will require an annual expenditure of more than $50,-
000. For this amount we have endeavored to provide by
the appointment of Agents to solicit funds in different parts
of the country, & by other means. But notwithstanding
these provisions the payments of the Society to meet the
current demands of the Missionaries have greatly exceeded
its receipts. The Treasury is now overdrawn nearly $12,-
000, for which individuals of our own number are personally responsible. This responsibility we have assumed only
from the necessity of the case. We have conscientiously
observed the strictest economy in our appropriations, pledg-
ing in each case the smallest amount which, after due examination appeared sufficient to answer the object of the
Society. But, after every possible retrenchment, we have
been obliged to borrow the above amount.

St. Louis, March 22ᵈ '26

Dear Sir,

I am happy to address you, as the Secretary of the U. D.
M. S.[4] & to make known to you my situation & prospects.
Your predecessor, Mr. Bruen, in a letter, which I received
since my arrival, requests me to state particularly the manner in which my time has been employed. This from the
notes, which I have kept, may be easily & summarily done.

I left New York the 20ᵗʰ of October & arrived at Wheeling, on the Ohio, the 10ᵗʰ Nov. On my way I preached
in Philadelphia & Washington, & endeavored to excite an
interest in favour of a National Domestic Missionary Society.[5] From Wheeling I went to Marrietta, 80 miles,

[4] The United Domestic Missionary Society. This Society, which was the
immediate predecessor of the American Home Missionary Society was conducted in a manner very similar to the latter. The correspondence of the
United Domestic Missionary Society forms a part of the collection in the
Chicago Theological Seminary.

[5] The American Home Missionary Society was the result of such agitation
for a national domestic missionary society.

where I arrived in seven days.   This was owing to the
very low state of water.   Did not leave Marrietta untill the
18th of January, 62 days from the time of my arrival.   A
little more than two weeks of this time I was confined by
sickness.   The remaining time was spent in labouring
among the destitute in that county in such a manner as I
thought would best promote the cause of Christ.   Some of
the fruits of that labour are already reported.   The 21st
of Jan. I arrived in Louisville, nearly four days from
Marietta.   There I was under the painful necessity of remaining five weeks & one day.   At Louisville I supplied the
pulpit of Rev. Dr. Blackburn who is afflicted with a cancer
on his lip.   There was no destitute congregation in that
neighbourhood, where the Dr. thought I could be so use-
fully employed.   Left Louisville on the 26th Feb. & arrived
at St. Louis the 8th March — eleven days.   The boat
which brought me was the first which left Louisville after
my arrival.   While on board this boat I had religious exercises, preached to cabin & deck passengers on the Sabbath,
& did all in my power to prevent vice & promote religion.
This is the brief history of my journey.   But the painful
feelings which I have experienced by such an unexpected &
unavoidable delay are known & *can be known only to God*.
In choosing a public conveyance I acted according to the
best advice I could obtain.   Had I taken a private conveyance I might have come to St. Louis in six weeks.   Had
I been alone I should have come sooner.   For my labour I
have received four dollars & fifty cents only.   We have been
treated with kindness & our board, where we have stoped,
has cost nothing.   Our expenses have been *great*, very
great, amounting to more than two hundred & fifty dollars.
This renders my pecuniary circumstances a little trying.   I
suppose the year commenced when I left New York.   In
your committee I have the fullest confidence, that they will
do right, in this matter,   If they should think it expedient
to make some deduction for so long a delay, I beg the
favor that my situation may be known to some friend of
Zion who may have the power & the *heart* to afford some

relief. Pecuniary sacrifices I have made, in coming to the West, greater than are known to any of the committee. I however have a confidence in God that I shall not suffer.

The wish of your Committee that I should remain in St. Louis, produced some uneasiness at first in the mind of Mr. Giddings supposing such an event might depreciate his usefulness. But the result has been very happy indeed. I proposed these, as the only conditions on which I could, consistently with the interests of the Society & the feelings of my own heart, remain in St. Louis:

1st That I have Mr. Giddings' approbation.[6]

2d That the people desire it.

3d That I cooperate with him in the labour of the ministry.

4th That the people defray the expense of my board, & contribute anything further which they may please.

These proposals met the minds of all as soon as made; the Presbytery then in session expressed their sense of the importance of such a measure; Mr. Giddings was pleased; & all the arrangements most harmoniously made. I am to labour jointly with Mr. Gidings, preaching *in* & *about* St. Louis. The door of usefulness is wide — very wide. An inteligent judge of court has said, "A blow struck here will be felt by more than two millions." My responsibilities are then great, *very great*. It is probable I shall receive little more than my board during the present year. St. Louis is an expensive place to live in. The results of the Committee's deliberations on the subject of compensation I shall be pleased to know soon, if convenient. In this letter, I have omitted many considerations of importance. But it seemed necessary to say this much. — I remain, sir, with considerations of greatest respect,

Yours,

H. CHAMBERLIN

. . .

[6] Rev. Salmon Giddings organized the first Presbyterian Church in St. Louis on November 23, 1817, with only nine members. He was installed as pastor upon completion of the church building eight years later. Gillette *op. cit.*, II, p. 428.

Little Rock, July 15th, 1826.

Dr Sir,

Your favor fr last mail (the letter is not before me, but in the hands of Mr Newton to whom I sent it, to be shown to his friends, & I forget the date) did not come to hand until last Saturday, in consequence of a mistake being made at the P. O. in giving out my letters on the evening of its arrival.

.   .   .

You are pretty well acquainted with the principal men of this place, & from the conversations I have had with you on the subject, I think you know well what description of a Minister will suit the people. — One who would study their disposition, & endeavor to *persuade*, rather than *drive*, them from their immoral habits, & lead them by mild & conciliatory means into the paths of virtue, would become popular — while one of a contrary turn, would soon become the object of slander & detraction, & be made a subject for the ridicule of every ungenerous & immoral person in our little town — to[o] many of whom move in circles which their vicious practices do not entitle them to.

For my part I most sincerely hope you will succeed in procuring a Minister for us, of some respectable denomination, & shall cheerfully contribute my mite towards his support, as will also each of the gentlemen to whom you referred, & I have no doubt, the people generally.

Very truly,
Y^r friend,
WM. S. WOODRUFF

.   .   .

Albany 3 August 1826

Revd Sir,

In answer to your letter announcing my election as one of the Vice-Presidents of the American Home Missionary Society, I have the honor to state that I accept the appointment and shall derive much gratification from promoting a cause so closely connected with the best interests of humanity.

Accept the assurance of the high respect of
Your most obed^t Servt
DeWitt Clinton

Revd Absalom Peters
Corresponding Secretary, &c., &c., &c.,

.   .   .

[Views of Convention at Utica Explained]

Having understood that impressions are existing in the minds of our brethren in New York, who are connected with the Amerⁿ Home Miss^y, Soc^{ty}. that the convention at Utica, which organized the Westⁿ. Dom. Miss^y Soc^y. Auxiliary to the A. H. M. S. were influenced, in doing this, by feelings unfriendly to the Parent Institution, — we think proper to make the following statement: viz. — That the object of the Utica Convention was to form an Auxiliary Society for the purpose of determining by experiment, the effect of a plan, which has, for years, been conversed upon with deep interest in this section of country, the leading feature of which is that the country be divided into districts, each including as much territory as can be superintended by one man, whose business it shall be, as a District Agent, to effect the settlement of ministers over connected Societies formed for this purpose; — to preach in rotation in all those places, that remain without a pastor, finding as many preaching stations within . . . his limits as he can for this purpose; & to do all that can be done to prepare the way for pastors to be thus settled, & to continue his operations on this ground till the whole shall be bro't, as far as may be, into a state of religious organization, — It was the opinion of this conversation that, upon this plan aid would be afforded to a great number of small & feeble congregations, that would, otherwise, be destitute of preaching, & be given up wholly to sectarian influence; — that more would be raised in these destitute places, to support the Gospel among themselves; — that more ministers would be settled, & probably many more within the same limits; & consequently more good would be accomplished in the work of Domestic Missions. — So far was this convention from indulging any hostile feeling towards the A. H. M. S. that, at their 1st meeting in March, at which the above stated was unanimously approved,— it was judged important to send a commissioner to New York, to lay this plan before the Executive Committee, & ascertain whether the formation of such an Auxiliary would meet their approbation. — The convention then adjourned to the 1st week in June, to hear the report of their commissioner; & having thus obtained the approbation of the Executive Committee of the A. H. M. S. this Auxiliary was organized, with a view of carrying into effect the above plan, to embrace as many counties in this section of Country as may be disposed to unite in this measure. —

We do exceeding regret that any apprehensions should be indulged, whatever cause may have led to them, that this Auxiliary cherishes feelings unfriendly to the Parent Institution. Such apprehensions, we are very confident, do not accord with the facts.— So far from indulging hostile feelings, we do as we always have done, feel a deep solicitude for the prosperity of the A. H. M. S. — We regard it as one of the richest blessings to our country ! — & we cannot see that the plan of this Auxiliary will at all interfere with any of its operations. — Our brethren in New York cannot be more impressed than we are with the importance of maintaining feelings of cordiality, & of uniting in our measures so far as this can be done, while laboring to build up the waste places of Zion. — This, we trust will be uniformly manifested in all the future operations of the Western Domestic Missionary Society.—
Auburn, Aug. 16, 1826

JAMES EELS
MOSES GILBERT
ABIJAH CRANE
JOHN F. SCHERMERHORN

The Subscriber was not present at the convention holden at Utica; but he cordially agrees in the opinions and feelings above expressed.

HENRY DAVIS.

.   .   .

Madison [Indiana], August 30th 1826

Rev. Absalom Peters
Cor. Sec. of A. H. M. S.
Dear Sir,

Agreeably to my promise I now forward to you the report of the Standing Committee of the Ind. Mis. Soc^y. which has just come to my hands—

The Standing Committee of the Missionary Society of Indiana Auxiliary to the A. H. M. Society,[7] with thanksgiving to the Great Head of the Church, for the smiles of his kind providence upon our feeble efforts, during the past year, respectfully submit the following report.

Your Committee have employed seven missionaries in the course of the past year, but some of them have not sent us their reports.   From those who have reported we make the following statement.

[7] The Constitution of the American Home Missionary Society provided for auxiliary societies in the following manner:

Art. 7.   Any Missionary Society may become auxiliary by agreeing to pay into the Treasury of this Society the whole of its surplus funds, and sending to the Corresponding Secretary a copy of its Constitution and Annual Reports, mentioning the names of its Missionaries, and the field of their operations.

Art. 8.   Every Auxiliary Society which shall agree to pay the whole of its funds to this Society, shall be entitled to a Missionary, or Missionaries, to labour in such field as it may designate; at least to the amount of its contributions; provided such designation be made at the time of payment.

Art. 9.   The officers of all Auxiliary Societies shall be, ex-offico, Directors; and annual contributors to their funds shall be members of this Society. [*First Report of the American Home Missionary Society, presented by the Executive Committee at the Anniversary Meeting, May 9, 1827* (New York, 1827), p. 4.]

The Indiana Missionary Society was organized in 1822 and amended its constitution in August, 1826, so as to become auxiliary to the American Home Missionary Society. [*The Home Missionary and American Pastors Journal,* I, No. 2, pp. 28-29.]

Mr Reed spent 26 days, rode 500 miles, preached 15 sermons, attended 3 communions, received 6 persons to the privileges of the Church, & baptized one adult.

Mr Dickey spent 2 weeks, preached 13 times, baptized 7 infants, received 3 persons to Communion, administered the Lord's Supper twice, formed one Sabbath School Society, & rode 156 miles.

Mr Brown spent 5 weeks, rode 416 miles, preached 29 times, attended two communions, received to communion 11 persons, baptized one adult & five infants, & formed 5 Sabbath Sch^l Socities.

Mr. Bush spent 9 days, preached 8 sermons, administered the Lord's Supper once, & travelled 114 miles.

Mr Williamson spent 2 months, preached 50 times, baptized 13 infants, administered th^ Lord's Supper once, & travelled 480 miles.

Mr Holman, a licentiate, spent 2 months, preached 60 times, & travelled 555 miles.

From the reports received by your Committee, it appears that your Missionaries have spent, in the service of the Society 196 days, preached 175 times, attended 9 communions, received 20 persons to communion, baptized 2 adults & 25 infants, formed 6 Sabbath Sch^l Societies, & travelled 2221 miles.

In a review of the operations of the Society, the last year, we are constrained to say that goodness & mercy have followed us thus far, & the grand aim of the Society, the glory of God in the Salvation of souls, has been promoted. The destitute in many parts of the State have been visited & refreshed, by the means of grace. We have become more particularly acquainted with the moral wastes of our country, & the pressing Spiritual wants of its numerous & destitute inhabitants. "The harvest truly is plenteous, but the labourers are few." May the Lord of the harvest speedily send more labourers into his harvest. By the labours of your Missionaries, public attention has been aroused from the long sleep of death, & made to enquire after salvation.

The change in the Constitution, which makes this Society auxiliary to the A. H. M. Society, we consider important to the interests of Missions in our State; & to that Society we look, as an instrument in the hands of the King of Zion, for breaking the bread of life to our perishing & destitute citizens, & for opening springs of the water of life in this parched land.

Trusting in the promises of God for success, let the friends of missions go forward with alacrity, in the cause of God our Savior. It is an enterprise of mercy, to publish the gospel of the grace of God— those glad tidings of great joy — to the solitary & forlorn inhabitants of the wilderness. And finally let the honour of being fellow-workers with Christ, in his Kingdom of grace, & the hopes of meeting, at last, the martyrs & missionaries of the cross, with all that have come out of tribulation & have washed their robes in the blood of the Lamb, excite us to increase in these labours of love, knowing that they shall not be in vain in the Lord. —

The funds belonging to the Society at present amount to about three hundred dollars.

Hoping that we may be permitted ere long to hear from you, & to see more missionaries sent from your Soc^y to our State, I subscribe myself yours, in the bonds of the Gospel,

JA^s. H. SCHUSTER

Cor. Sec. of Ind. Mis. Soc^y

(To Rev. Absalom Peters)

. . .

To the Secretary of the American Home Missionary Society— Fort Covington— February 25th 1827

Rev. & Dear Sir

We the Session of the Presbyterian Church of Fort Covington beg leave to petition your Society for aid during the present year— The Church for which we solicit your aid is at present attached to the Associate Ref. Synod of New York — For some years past we have been destitute of a

Pastor, and the Church seemed to be dwindling— During three or four months past we have enjoyed the labors of a young man who was ordained in this place on the 12th inst. by the Washington Presbytery whose labors we feel desirous of having continued among us— The liberality of the inhabitants of our Small village and its vicinity has been loudly called upon by subscriptions for the erection of a convenient house for public worship which is already in progress, When the house shall have been completed, We do not doubt but that we shall be abundantly able, under the blessing of the Head of the Church to maintain the ordinances among us— The peculiar pressure upon the people at the present time renders it difficult to procure a sufficient support for the minister and has led us to request if it is consistent that your Society would grant us for this year One hundred and fifty Dollars, which will greatly assist us in our present embarrassed circumstances— And which we hope, if we are blessed and prospered by him "who is over all God blessed forever" to be able in some future time to contribute again to the funds of your Society—

If this our humble petition is thought worthy of acceptance will you have the goodness to give us as early information as possible, and direct your letter to Mr. Ransom Hawley the Clerk of the Session— Fort Covington— Franklin Co. N. Y.—

MOSES FISK
DAVID MCMILLEN   Session
WM. CRIGHTON
RANSOM HAWLEY, Clerk

.   .   .

[Extract from a letter by Aaron Foster to the Corresponding Secretary of the American Home Missionary Society. Abbeville, S. C., Dec. 20, 1827.]

Most of our Clergymen are unreasonably inveterate against northern missionaries, but I have stayed so long as to change all their prejudice *towards me* to warm friendship, — *men must stay who come or they will undo all that I have done.*

Our chhs. are not prepared to apply for your Missionaries nor to receive them as Missionaries like the people of the West because they have not yet been made to see the good done by them. By the particular enquiry of your letter respecting Sallary I hope your committee do not mean to send a man only when I can find a place where the people will send their obligations signed & delivered to support him. *Let a beginning be made that the people may learn to appreciate* the value of Missionaries & know where to send for them. How can you reasonably expect a more encouraging beginning than the representation I have now given? or where do you Expect an inviting field for your Societies operations if not where the people have invited again & again when they cannot obtain & have been these 20 years stationary as to the advancement of religion *only for want of active & zealous ministers?*

.   .   .

Union Seminary [Prince Edward, Va.] 31 Octr 1828
My Dear Sir

I have just returned home, from a long excursion to our Presbytery & Synod, and only on yesterday received your letter about Mr. Saxton. Mr. Nettleton is now in Staunton, beyond the Blue-ridge, one hundred miles from this place, and I can do nothing but send your note to him by the first opportunity.

Allow me, however, to say that in this southern region, we do not want any body, who thinks that he has made new discoveries in religion; or that he can account for things, which none before him ever could account for. We hold here that the religion of the Bible is a religion of facts; and that it is the part of the Christian to receive the facts which God has revealed, because He has told us of them, and He knows. *How* things are, we do not pretend to explain; and we do not want any body to perplex the people by attempts to do what we are assured cannot be done. In a word, the people here know nothing of the *Isms*, which have plagued you all to the North; and we do not wish them to know. But a man, who will just preach the Bible honestly and faithfully; and endeavour to make the people understand its meaning, and obey its precepts, will be well received, and we hope supported. We should like to receive many such. The country does need most exceedingly many such preachers. For want of them, the people are greatly misled by Arminians and high Churchmen. . . .

JOHN H. RICE.[7a]

[To Rev. Absalom Peters.]

· · ·

Danville Kentucky Dec[er]. 2nd 1828

Rev[d]. and dear Sir.

At the last session of the Synod of Kentucky, in this place, a resolution passed by that Boddy, enjoins it upon me, as their Treasurer, to apply, through you, to the American Home Missionary Society, for the privilege of appropriating to their own destitute Churches the Missionary Money in my hands as their Treas. which was donated to them by Synod in the amount in my hands, heretofore donated to the A. H. M. Society by the Synod of Kentucky is, One hundred, Ninety Seven dollars 27½ cents, to which may be aded, one dollar note, payable at the Bank of Cape fear, not currant in this section of country. Will you have the goodness, as early as practicable to lay this petition before your honorable Body — and advise, me, or some member of this Synod of the result.

Very Respectfully,

Rev[d]. A. Peters   Your Ob. & H. Servant,
   Corg. Secretary   MICHAEL G. YOUSE, Trea[s].
   A. H. M. Society   of the Synod of Kentucky.
      New York

· · ·

[7a] At this time Rice was Professor of Theology, Union Seminary, Prince Edward, Va. *Dictionary of Am. Biography* XV, pp. 541-542.

Office of the A. H. M. S.
141 Nassau St.,
New York January 2, 1829

Michael G. Youse, Esq.,
  Danville, Ky.,
    Dear Sir,

Your letter of December 2nd is now before me & has received the consideration of the esecutive committee. The request presented by the Synod of Kentucky, as we understand it, is that $197.$\dfrac{27\frac{1}{2}}{100}$ granted by the Synod to the A. H. M. S. be left in your hands to be appropriated according to the wishes of the Synod to the Missionary work in their bounds. Your letter does not inform us whether the Synod wished to take the management, or only wish to have us appropriate it in their bounds. The Executive Committee therefore resolved, that monies in your hands be appropriated to Missionary purposes in the bounds of the Synod of Kentucky, the selection Missionaries & their field of labor to be made by the Synod or their committee appointed for that purpose.

Permit me now respectfully to suggest, in compliance with the desire of the committee, that on several accounts it is desirable that as this sum has formerly been placed by the Synod at our disposal, it should be reported by us in our Annual Report. We would therefore request — either that the commissions be issued by this Committee to such persons & in such fields as the Synod shall designate — or else, when the Synod shall have expended the sum in their own way, they make report of the appropriations made by them as auxiliary to the A. H. M. S. These plans are submitted for the decision of the Synod, the Executive Committee not having chosen to trammel their vote of acquiescence to your request with any conditions.

Very respectfully yours, &c,
A. Peters, Cor. Sec., A. H. M. S.
By Charles Hall, Assist. Sec.

.   .   .

[Extract from a letter by Absalom Peters, Corresponding Secretary of the A. H. M. S. to Rev. Joshua L. Wilson, Pastor of the First Presbyterian Church, Cincinnati. Undated, probably 1830.]

We have delayed to forward you the foregoing longer than I anticipated when I left Cincinnati Decr last — The reason has been our wish to mature our plan as far as possible before submitting it to your consideration — We have deliberated on the subject of submitting this plan to the consideration of the Presbyteries of the West, with a view to have their delegates to the Genl Assembly instructed in relation to it, but on the whole this Com^{ee} have decided that it will not be expedient for us to be instrumental in procuring such instructions. Such a measure it is supposed might subject us to the charge of having wished to forestall the opinion of members of the Genl Assembly, & we wish to avoid even the appearance of evil — We have therefore determined, if necessary, to make our proposition directly to the Genl Assembly, without taking any previous measures with the Presbyteries — Again we are now deliberating on the question, whether we shall make our proposition first to the Board of Missions, previous to the meeting of the Assembly, & ask them to unite with us in bringing it before the Assembly, or whether we shall present it to the Assembly first — Which of these will be likely to result the most favorably, we are not able yet to decide — but hope that an interview which I expect to have with the Professors at Princeton, in a few days, will afford us the means of determining what is best — In the mean time, we have yet to confer further with the Princeton brethren on the subject of a general union of our Society & the Board of Missions — but from what we have already gathered from a brief interview with them, on my return, & other conversations we have held, I am sorry to say that the General Union does not seem likely to succeed — We have therefore taken our measures with regard to the Cincinnati Committee, as if the Genl Union were already abandoned[8] — We shall, however, pursue the object as far as is thought prudent, & shall relinquish the prospect of effecting it with deep regret — But the proposed cooperation of the two Boards in the appointment of the Agency at Cincinnati is regarded by the Princeton brethren & all others of whom we have proposed it, as entirely practicable & desirable.

.   .   .

[Extract from a form letter issued from the Office of the American Home Missionary Society, August 20, 1830, by order of the Executive Committee and signed by Knowles Taylor, Treasurer.]

During the first year of this Society's operations, aid was extended to 190 Congregations and Missionary districts. In the second year, 244 were assisted; in the third, 401; & in the fourth nearly 500. In the second year of the Society' labors, we reported with joy, *one thousand souls* added to the Churches. The last year, our missionaries have reported *nearly two thousand*! Add to the immense indirect benefits which the preaching of the Gospel has exerted on such a vast number of people, in edifying the pious, restraining the wicked, and in teaching 19,000 S. S. Scholars, the things that belong to their peace.

The importance of this work is as great as the importance of the Salvation of Souls. Look at that single section of our country called the "valley of the Mississippi." In twenty years if it should continue to increase as it has done

[8] The General Assembly of 1828 reorganized and enlarged the scope of home mission work of its Board of Missions. The dangers involved in an attempt to carry on home missionary work in the same territory by two independent agencies was immediately apparent. Consequently the corresponding secretaries of the two agencies, the American Home Missionary Society and the Board of Missions, worked out a proposed plan of union. Opposition to this plan was such that the executive committee of the Society declined to submit the plan to the annual meeting in May, 1829. This failure of proposed union, however, did not prevent steps looking to union in western work, which were taken in 1830. "Proposed Union of the Board of Missions of the General Assembly with the American Home Missionary Society," in *The Home Missionary and American Pastor's Journal*, I, No. 12, pp. 206-211.

in population, it will contain a majority of the people of the
United States, & also have a majority in the halls of Congress. The destinies of the Union will be in their hands.
If that portion of the country be not brought under the
influence of religion *now*, it cannot, to human view, be done
at all. Already the infidel is there, — the *Socinian*, the *Universalist*, the *Roman Catholic* is there. *Now or never* — is
the watchword of all the benevolent Societies in reference
to that region. Every Agent that goes there to explore; —
every Missionary, every intelligent Christian layman —
writes back — *What you do for this Country, do Soon.*
We see the urgency of the Case; we feel the moment is critical. We are assured the people are ready to receive ministers, — Ministers are ready to go. Hundreds of Congregations might be gathered; many already organized
might have the bread of life Secured to them, were the
necessary funds at our disposal.

There is one fact that is in danger of being overlooked
by the Christian public, — and that is — the importance
of Home Missions to the Success of other benevolent efforts. No enterprise for the spread of Christian principles
can be carried on without *men*, and, in most of the new
settlements, men who will take hold of these valuable objects are not to be found. Just so far as ministers are there
does the Bible effort succeed; — they are also the main dependence of the Tract operations; & without the constant
supervision and encouragement of the ministry, the Sunday
Schools which it is proposed to establish throughout the
West, will languish and die.

And now, what shall be done? It rests with the Christian public — with our Auxiliary Societies — to decide
whether any more souls shall be converted through the labours of this Society. Just as far as our patrons assist the
Society, it can assist the destitute, and no farther. The usefulness of the institution, Christian friends, will wax or
wane with your liberality. We have done all we could, and
gone to the extent of, & even beyond the means put at our
disposal. If the Churches say we must stop, or contract our

operations, we must submit; but what will then become of the Souls that are ready to perish?

For the remittances which you have generously made to the Treasury of the A. H. M. S. you will please to accept the hearty thanks of the Committee. We hope you will by no means forget this institution in your future Charities and prayers; — we need them both, especially at the present time when the Treasury is largely overdrawn, and the calls for assistance increasing in number and urgency.

. . . .

CENTRAL COMMITTEE FOR HOME MISSIONS
in the WESTERN STATES[9]

It having been duly ascertained that the separate action of the American Home Missionary Society & the Board of Missions of the General Assembly of the Presbyterian church is attended with evils in all cases where the operations of both are conducted on the same field, & these evils being especially apparent & alarming in the western states, where there is danger that they will increase & be multiplied in proportion to the extension & efficiency of the operations of the two Institutions above named; & it being manifest to all acquainted with the details of the work of Home Missions in this country, that west of the Alleghany Mountains,

[9] The action embodied in this document was taken February 22, 1830. The General Assembly of 1830 declined to endorse the proposal for a joint agency. Consequently, the American Home Missionary Society then proceeded independently, organizing the Central Committee for Home Missions in the Western States late in the Autumn of 1830. The matter of cooperation in the West between the two agencies was again presented to the General Assembly in 1831. On this occasion the matter was referred to the synods and presbyteries in the area concerned. Divided opinion among these western groups, as expressed in a convention held in Cincinnati in November, 1831, led to a recommendation to continue the *status quo*, which left the Board of Missions and the Society free to follow their independent, and often competitive, courses. *The Fourth Report of the American Home Missionary Society, Presented by the Executive Committee at the Anniversary Meeting,* May 12, 1830 (New York, 1930), p. 55. Baird, Samuel J., *A Collection of the Acts, Deliverances, and Testimonies of the Supreme Judicatory of the Presbyterian Church, Etc.* (Philadelphia [1859]), p. 356. *The Home Missionary and American Pastor's Journal,* IV, No. 2, p. 34. Baird, *op. cit.,* pp. 356-357.

the operations of either of the above Institutions, both in the collection & appropriation of funds on that field, may be conducted by a Committee or Agency established at some central point on the field itself, much more conveniently, intelligently & efficiently, & with less expense, than by either of the Communities of the above Institutions located in New York or Philadelphia;

Therefore the *Executive Committee of the American Home Missionary Society*, deeply impressed with the importance & the increasing magnitude & difficulty of their work in that portion of the United States above alluded to, & with a view to increase the cooperation of the churches on that field, & partially to prevent the above evils, *have resolved to appoint, & do hereby appoint, the following individuals*, (leaving two blanks hereafter to be filled,) *a Committee of Agency for this Society,* one year from this date, or until the same shall be superseded, as herein after provided, or renewed by another appointment; said Committee to act under the rules which follow, excepting such portions of them as relate to the Board of Missions of the General Assembly; viz. —

Committee of Agency

Rev.	Joshua L. Wilson, D. D., Pastor of the First Presby. Ch., Cincinnati.				
"	David Root, Pastor of the Second	Do	Do	Do	
"	———— Pastor of the Third	Do	Do	Do	
"	Lewis D. Howell, Minister of the Fourth	Do	Do	Do	
"	Amos Blanchard, Editor of the "Christian Journal"			Do	
Mr.	Henry B. Funk, Elder in the	First Presby. Ch.,		Do	
Mr.	John Baker, Do	Do	Do	Do	Do
Dr	James Warren, Do	Second	Do	Do	Do
Mr.	John H. Groesbeck, Do	Do	Do	Do	Do
"	Robert Baal, Do	Third		Do	Do
"	Jabez C. Tunis Do	Do		Do	Do
"	Samuel Newell Do	Fourth		Do	Do
Rev.	———— Corresponding Secretary			Do	

But being aware that the above appointment, without the expressed concurrence of the Board of Missions of the General Assembly in the same, may not secure the entire union & cooperation of the western churches in conducting their missionary operations, & being deeply impressed with the importance of such *entire union* & cooperation, & cherishing feelings of the most fraternal regard to the said Board of Missions; Therefore,

The *Executive Committee of the American Home Missionary Society have resolved to instruct, & do hereby instruct*, the above Committee of Agency to suspend the commencement of their operations, for the present, for the purpose of waiting the result of such overtures as may be made by this Committee to the next General Assembly of the Presbyterian church.

And the said Executive Committee of the A. H. M. S. have further resolved that, unless otherwise advised, or unless some more effectual remedy shall be found for the evils alluded to in the introductory paragraph to this article, it is their intention to make the following requests & propositions to the General Assembly of the Presbyterian Church, next to be convened in Philadelphia in May next, viz.

1. They will request the General Assembly to concur with this Committee in the appointment of the above Committee of Agency, with such alterations in the same as shall be mutually agreed on by this Committee & the said General Assembly.

2. They will request the said General Assembly to instruct its Board of Missions to transact its business within certain limits, through the said Committee of Agency, & to cooperate with the same in the manner prescribed in the following rules.

3. Should the General Assembly agree to comply with the above requests, then the appointment of the above Committee of Agency by this Committee, as heretofore announced in this article, shall become void, & this Committee will proceed, with the concurrence of the General Assembly, to appoint a Committee at Cincinnati, composed of the above individuals or others, as shall be mutually agreed on, which shall be the mutual organ of the American Home Missionary Society & the Board of Missions of the General Assembly for the transaction of their business within

prescribed limits, & who shall act under the following rules with such alterations as shall be mutually agreed on by this Committee & the Geneeral Assembly.

[Ten Rules are given, followed by a letter to the proposed chairman of the Committee of Agency.]

.   .   .

[Extract from a letter by D. C. Blood to the Corresponding Secretary of the American Home Missionary Society. Covington, Kentucky, February 3, 1832.]

Your Com. at Cincinnati saw fit to locate me, for the winter at least, at Newport & Covington, Ky. I found no Presb. Church or place of worship in either of these places. But on being assured that places would soon be provided in both villages, I consented to preach for a short time in private houses, & occasionally in rooms occupied by the Baptist & Methodist Societies. I had been doing this about two weeks, when I was informed that a Mr. Jones was in Covington and soon after, as I was on my way to preach a lecture in Newport, I was informed that Mr. Jones had a lecture at the same hour in the Meth. Meetinghouse—& that it was the understanding that my lecture was given up. I tho^t it best to leave the village without correcting the mistake. After possessing myself of some facts which I have not time to relate, I met your Com. & made a full statement of the case. It was their opinion that the good of the cause required me to confine my labors for the present to Covington. Mr. Jones preached in N. a short time & left for the purpose of bringing on his family. He has been absent about two months. But I am informed that he intends to come to N. early in the Spring. I have been requested to preach occasionally in N. & shall do so for the present. Br. Jones acts under the high authority of the Gen. Assembly's Board, tho when he was sent to N. & C. they did not know that you had a missionary on the ground, nor was he apprised of the fact, till he came on. *Newport is a very desirable village—we must have it.*

I found in Covington no preparation for a Presb. minister, no Presb. Ch. & only four Presb. professors. After waiting several weeks for a place of worship to be prepared, I took upon my self to provide one. I obtained a room large enough to seat some 75 or 80 persons. For one or two of the first Sabbaths the cold was so severe that none would turn out to hear a Presb^n. But by visiting & distributing Tracts &c. I excited a few to attend my meetings. Just at this time I was taken sick of the Measles, But by the blessing of God I was confined only about two weeks. Since my recovery, which is about five weeks I have visited from house to house, preached three sermons each week, established a Sab. School, which promises much usefulness, & made arrangements to commence a Bible Class next Sab. Our S. S. embraces only about 35 scholars. There is another S. S. in the place which has about the same number. We shall probably be able to increase our school to 80 or 100 when the weather becomes mild, & the Measles have subsided, as many who will attend our S. S. are now confined by this disease. Our Bible Class will embrace many persons of influence in the place. . . .

Respecting this place I scarcely know what to say. *Covington* in the region about is but another name for the dwelling place of every thing that is irreligious, low & wicked. To not more than nine hundred inhabitants, there are at least 15 & probably 20 places where spirituous liquors can be had. There is no Meetinghouse in the place. We have almost no Sab. B[u]t you can scarcely meet a boy without hearing an oath. This last named vice I have opposed with a strong hand, reproving without respect to the titles, Esqr., Dr., Gen., et cet., & said a lady to me, "There has been quite an improvment in this place, in regard to profane-swearing, since you came here."

. . .

[Extract from a letter by Nathaniel Hood to the Corresponding Secretary of the American Home Missionary Society. January 9, 1832, Granger County (Tennessee).]

Rev. and dear Sir, This day closes the third quarter

of my Missionary appointment, and it again becomes my duty as your Missionary to lay before you a list of my labours during the quarter. From the date of my last, I proceeded, as instructed, to attend the meetings of Presbytery & Synnod, which occupied my time until the 20th of Oct. At each of these Meetings, the Spirit of the Lord was evidently present. The Presbytery was held in a country Church to which many families moved in waggons and remained four days without any apparent concern about their worldly affairs and domestic concerns. During the meeting hundreds wept under the weight of conscious guilt and many of those before the meeting closed were rejoicing in the hope of pardoned Sin, a more general feeling I never witnesed. At one time it was ascertained in quite a large assembly, that there was not a single individual present, who was not a professor of religion or on the anxious Seats asking the prayers of the people of God and inquiring what they must do to be saved. The meeting of Synnod was one of deep interest, many of every age and sex from three-score and ten down to the Sabbath School child of Seven were made to partake of the blessings of that meeting. At one time during the meeting (which continued Seven days) it was published by the minister that every Sabbath School Schollar & teacher, who was present, were either professors of religion or on the anxious Seats. At the Meeting of Synnod, Much was done in favour of the A. H. M. S. One half of the public collection (which was $58) was given to it and the other half to the Genl Ass^y board but a few individuals gave $36 to the A. H. M. S. making in all for that Society More than $60. and for the Genl Ass^y board about $26. From this Meeting I returned to my own field of labour feeling that I was and had been an unfaithful Servant to my covenant God.

.   .   .

[Extract of a letter from a lady in Magnolia, Florida, to her sister in Providence, R. I. The letter bears the date of April 27, 1831 and this extract was received by the American Home Missionary Society on May 13, 1831.]

Had I been sure of your remaining with Mamma this winter I should have urged sister Ann to have accompanied us. How active she might have been here among the heathen: the Sabbath here is only regarded as a day of frolic; the stores are open all the morning; there is not a place of worship; nor a school of any kind in the place.

My daughter Delia, with myself, commenced a Sabbath school on the 13$^{th.}$ of March; we had but seven pupils; some of the parents told me in the presence of six or seven children, when I requested their attendance, they might go if they had a mind to; the children said, they did not want to know how to read. You can scarcely imagine a more savage place, one of the Children asked me if God was a Black, or white man; she knew he was ugly, because he had made a Hell. Attempts have been made to erect a building for a Church, but in vain; the very few who care to have one cannot afford the expense; and say if we had a Church we could not support a minister. I think it would be well if the missionary societies looked to such little settlements; and furnished them with a minister, as no part of Hindostan needs one more than this does.

.   .   .

[Extract from a letter by A. N. Cunningham to Rev. Absalom Peters. Montgomery, Alabama, September 7, 1831.]

I arrived upon my designated field of labour on the 14th of Jan 1831. In compliance with the advice of several of the clergymen of this Presb. & the solicitations of the people of this place, I located for the year in the Town of Montgomery. This town consists of 800 or 1000 inhabitants. It is situated on the Ala. River, nearly at the head of Steam boat navigation, in the county of the Same name. It is surrounded by a very fertile soil, covered with a comparatively dense & wealthy population (principally planters). The population of our Town is of a mixed order; made up of

emigrants from the north & the South.   Perhaps more
than one half is of northern extract.   The general character of the people is marked for intelligence, hospitality,
and independence.

When I commenced my labours here, there were a few
Presbyterians, a few Baptists, & a few Methodists, organized into three different churches, all worshiping in the
same building.   But seldom have I seen so much intelligence
and so little piety existing together.

.   .   .

[Extract from a letter by Fielding Pope to Rev. Absalom
Peters.   Athens, Tenn., December 4, 1832.]

In September, I held a four days' (or Sacramental) meeting in this Church, at an encampment which we have in the
vicinity of this place and such were the presence and power
of God that, instead of concluding the meeting on the
fourth day, it was not concluded until the seventh, and then,
not because the people wished to depart, but because we had
to commence another four days' meeting in one of my other
churches on the next day.   During the meeting from 35 to
100 persons at different times came forward to the *Anxious
seat*, about thirty professed to have been born again, and
fifteen then united themselves to the Church for the first
time. . . .

You have learned that we are a divided community.   Baptists, Methodists, & Cumberland, all claim the soil as original proprietors, and their grants are so old, and their
entries so well made (as they think) that they will not give
up one single tenement [*sic*] and household without *suit*,
and not then, untill a mandamus is issued from the Supreme
Court and served upon them by the proper officer.

.   .   .

[Extract from a letter by Absalom Peters, Corresponding Secretary of the American Home Missionary Society,
to Benjamin H. Rice, Associate Secretary, Mississippi

River, bound from St. Louis to New Orleans, January 10, 1833.]

When the A. H. M. Society was organized, in May 1826, there were in these two states (Illinois and Missouri) eight Presbyterian Ministers. Of these five were in Missouri & three in Illinois, & five of the number, viz. three in the former & two in the latter State, were Missionaries of our Society under its former organization. Two of the above, viz. the Rev. Messrs Giddings of St. Louis & Robinson of St. Charles, have since been called to rest from their labors, having with great faithfulness & self denial accomplished the work which was given them to do. Two others, one from each state, have removed to other fields of labor, leaving only four of the original eight, who, six years & six months ago, constituted the whole strength of the Presbyterian ministry in Missouri & Illinois; & the Holy Ghost which was with them constituted *their* strength & laid the foundation of the unexpected success which has attended their labor. The number of Presbyterian ministers now laboring in these states is 51, of whom 37 have been sent here or aided in their support by the Home Missionary Society. These now constitute two Synods under the care of the General Assembly. The first is the Synod of Illinois, constituted in 1831, embracing three Presbyteries & 33 ministers, 24 of whom are or have been Missionaries of the A. H. M. S. The other is the Synod of Missouri, constituted in 1832, embracing 18 ministers, 13 of whom are or have been Missionaries of our Society. . . .

. . .

[Extracts from a letter written by Absalom Peters, Corresponding Secretary of the American Home Missionary Society, to Benjamin H. Rice, Associate Secretary. Florence, Alabama, February 28, 1833.]

My last dated Jan. 10th, & written on the Mississippi river was mailed at New Orleans, where I arrived on the 16th of the same month, & I trust reached you. My passage down the river was rapid, & it was with much regret that I felt obliged by the short time allotted to the performance of my long tour to pass the states of Tennessee, Mississippi, Arkansaw (Territory), & Louisiana, with only a brief stop at a few places, as suited the convenience of the Boat, & an interview with only two or three ministers of those states. In the first viz. Tenessee, with a population of 700,000, there are only 68 Presbyterian ministers, which is less than *one* to *ten thousand*. Mississippi has a population of about 145,000 & only 20 Presbyterian ministers, which is about *one* to *seven thousand*. Arkansas Territory, with a population of perhaps 40,000 has only one minister of our denomination, excepting such as are engaged as missionaries to the Indians within its bounds. The population of Louisiana is not less than 230,000, & yet there are not more than seven or eight Presbyterian ministers within its limits, which is about *one* to *twenty-eight thousand*. . . .

There is perhaps no city on the globe whose position, character, commercial prospects, & prospective influence on the souls of men should be regarded with more intense & fearful interest by the Christian community, than those of the city of New Orleans. It is the grand emporium of the great valley of the Mississippi, & if war or pestilence, or some other scourge from the Almighty do not arrest its prosperity, the time is not far distant when it will be the principal depot of the commercial wealth of a hundred million people & the point through which they will hold intercourse with all parts of the world. Its influence will be direct & immense upon this mighty mass of mind & enterprise which will spread the savour of its religious or irreligious character round the globe. On the ascendency of pure religion in the hearts & lives of the citizens of New Orleans, therefore, may depend the immortal destiny of many millions of souls. At present however it is known & lamented that the restraints & the controlling influence of religion are but partially & feebly felt in that city. . . .

As my face is now set homeward I deem it proper to remark that unforeseen circumstances have determined me to change my purpose, expressed in a former letter, of returning through the southern Atlantic states, & I am now waiting the departure of a Boat to take me down the Tennessee river to the Ohio, by which I hope to reach home through Pittsburgh, &c. as early as the first of April. Permit me then to close this correspondence with a few general remarks. It has long been familiarly understood in our Committee, as a general fact, that our missionary operations, in proportion to the number we have induced to plant themselves south of the slave-holding line, have been more expensive & less successful in securing for the gospel a permanent & steady influence here than north of that line. The reasons of this fact we have never fully appreciated. It is no doubt to be attributed principally to the different modes of cultivating the soil which prevail. North of the line above named farmers usually conduct their business on a smaller scale, depending more or less upon their personal labour in raising their crops & the produce of their labour is generally not sufficiently large to justify them in the expense of conveying it to a distant market. The consequence is that they usually make their sales & purchase their supplies at the nearest village. This encourages the country merchant and mechanic, & the consequence is that a little village is built up & sustained in every township, & each of these villages becomes a permanent centre where houses of worship may be erected, ministers located & all the fixtures of religious society established to act on the surrounding community, as far at least as the intercourse of business extends its influence. Thus, as fast as townships become in a considerable degree settled, the materials exist of forming in each a compact religious society. But it is not thus generally in the southern states. Here the richest portions of the country are owned in plantations of 640 to 5,000 & even 10,000 acres. These are cultivated by negroes in companies of tens & fifties & hundreds under over-seers, some planters owning & employing several hundreds. Thus each planter possesses a little empire of his own, & productions of his land are so abundant as to make it for his interest to do business directly with the large cities. He of course affords but little encouragement to the country merchant & mechanic, & the consequence is that country villages are few in such communities, & generally of slow growth, being sustained almost wholly by the trade of the poorer classes, who are thinly interspersed among the plantations of the rich. Thus there are prevented, in these states, comparatively few points where compact religious societies can be formed. This, to say nothing of mistaken fears of unhealthiness, & nothing of the adverse influence of slavery as a system upon the religious conscience of the people has doubtless contributed much to produce that unequal supply of ministerial service which now exists in the northern & southern sections of the great western valley. Thus in the state of Alabama, for instance, which possesses perhaps double the commercial wealth & nearly double the population of Illinois, there are fewer ministers than in the latter state, the number of Presbyterian ministers in Alabama being only *thirty*, which is less than *one* to *ten thousand* of the population.

I make these remarks, my Dear Bro., not to discourage the efforts of our committee on behalf of the South, but to make them the ground of urgency for increased exertions in these states. If the points of efficient religious influence are fewer here, than in the northern states, they are comparatively more important; & if they are more difficult & expensive, they demand our more vigilant & prayerful attention. The same considerations evince the immense importance of maintaining the institutions of religion in our southern cities. In proportion as they act directly upon the planting population of the country & absorb the business, which, in the northern cities, is divided with the country villages, they ought themselves to be made the centers of that religious influence, which in the north, emanates still more propitiously from the numerous & flourishing smaller towns.

.   .   .

Tallahassee, May 3, 1833

To the Rev. Mr. Peters,

Dear Sir:

I am happy to introduce to your acquaintance Mr. John Atwater, who is a member of our infant church, a subject of the revival here. He was a fellow passenger with me to this place and at that time a N. York infidel a follower of R. D. Owen. He is now I think a sincere Christian. . . .

We need very much some missionaries in this Territory to go out on circuits that might be formed. But if possible get good Southern Men. The prejudices against anything nothern are strong and even good people partake of them. . . .

Affectionately,

A. SAVAGE

[Extract from a letter by Thomas Brown to Rev. A. Peters, Corresponding Secretary of the American Home Missionary Society. Kingston, Tennessee, September 16, 1834.]

The friends of the temperance reformation are Still increasing, tho the contest on that Subject is yet considerable. This is, chiefly, owing to the fact that Some Ministers of the gospel belonging to a denomination of [professing] Christians,[9a] numerous here, are engaged largely in making and selling whisky; and from their own interest they spare no pains, so far as possible, to excite prejudice against the temperance cause by charging its friends and advocates with being hostile to civil liberty, and with having a deSign to destroy both Church and State with temperance Societies. The Same men, in their wisdom, I am told, deSided Some time ago, that the Bible and Tract Societies were the great evil[s] which brought upon our happy land, that deSolating Scourge, the Cholera. This might appear to be great ignorance, but I fear it is greater wickedness than igno-

[9a] The denomination here referred to is the Primitive (Hard-Shell) Baptists.

rance. The question is now Shortly to be decided by their ecleseastical court whether, or not, a member of their church Shall be excommunicated from their communion for the crime of joining a temperance Society. This Subject has been agitated there for Sometime past, and the decision, let it be as it may, will, I believe, promote the Temperance Cause.

. . .

Beattys Bridge, N. C. Septr 15th 1834
Direct your letters (except one
to Mil.) to Collumbus when you
think I have got there.

Dear Brothers Peters
   Sir. For some months back I have determined to leave N Carolina, or at least my present charge and go to some of the more Southern States, and while I was endeavouring to fix upon some place, I came accross some letters, which were directed to you, from a correspondent in Missippi [sic], and published in the *Home Missionary*, which letters have induced me to write these few lines to you. Now Dear Brother, if you have not yet obtained a suitable minister for Columbus, and its neighbourhood; you may write to them that I am on my way to that place, for before this letter will have reached you, unless prevented by the Providence of God, I will be some distance. And when I arrive there I will be better able to Judge, whether I can be useful among them as a minister of the Gospel, Or if you think proper, you may give me some short appointment, according to their directions. . . .

You may ask — Why leave poor N. Carolina? It is indeed a destitute field; but Dear Brother I feel that I must go somewhere else for these reasons — I have been labouring in connection with a Dear Father in the ministry and we both only get $400 between us. This we find is entirely too small to support both of our families in this country for, you will understand that in the lower part of N. C^a. the people confine themselves mostly to Lumber —

Tarr, Turpentine and consequently provisions are high. As, therefore the place is too strait for us, it is but right that one of us sh^d. go. My only wish is, that your efforts may enable me to be more useful in the ministry. You will very much oblige me if you will write to me soon and direct to Milledgeville, G^a. I am dear Brother Yours in Gospel Bonds,

D. A. CAMPBELL.

You may publish this little note which is below as a fact:
I hereby certify, that, so far as my own Knowledge extends, the Southern people are not opposed to the Preaching of the Gospel to their slaves, but on the contrary, are willing, and many do sincerely desire that their servants should be orally instructed by intelligent ministers; But they are opposed to those ignorant preachers who endeavor to work more upon the Passions and Sympathies of the Negro by loud unmeaning bawling instead of truth. I have preached, for two years, to large assemblies of them and many have been converted.

D A CAMPB

.   .   .

[Extract from a letter by A. Hale to Absalom Peters. Jacksonville, Illinois, September 27, 1836.]
My journey was principally in the lead mine district & east of the Mississippi River. Br. Kent[10] & myself visited the principal villages & settlements. We found no ministers of our denomination & very few of any other. Indeed, we have no missionaries N. West of Rock River except Br. Kent, at Galena, & Br. Watson, who I suppose has returned to DuBuque. In the Wisconsin Ter^y. with a population

[10] Aratus Kent was the first Presbyterian minister in northern Illinois. Galena, the center of a rich lead mining area, was the base of his missionary operations. The American Missionary Society sent Kent there in 1829 in response to requests from inhabitants of the community for a minister of the gospel. Riegler, Gordon Arthur, "Aratus Kent, First Presbyterian Minister in Northern Illinois," in *Journal of the Presbyterian Historical Society,* XIII, No. 8 (December, 1929), pp. 363-380.

25,000, there are not more than 4 Or 5 ministers of all denominations— i.e. not more than that number that we
could hear of— Br. Kent has long been calling for aid, &
if men of the right sort can be had his call ought to be immediately attended to.   The population of the Terʸ. is somewhat peculiar.   A far greater portion of them are *foreign-
ers*, than of the people of Illinois.   They are as a body
more intelligent.   There is more open *wickedness*, such as
intemperance & gambling, &c., more *infidelity*, or rather it
is more bold & open, & there is more *money*.   We need
immediately, *two* Missionaries to plant within 40 miles of
Galena — but they must be *men* — men of sound minds &
warm hearts — men who can meet opposition & bear insults, & are willing to labor hard & bear reproach for
Christ, men who might do well in many parts of this state,
I am persuaded could not succeed there.   I hope you will
be on the lookout & as soon as you can find the men send
them to Br. Kent & he will go with them to their places of
destination.   It must not be forgotten that churches in
Wisconsin are as scarce as ministers — all is new — a few
professors of religion scattered over the field panting for
the bread & water of life & a large number who once were
enrolled among the people of God & are now twice dead &
among the most formidable obstacles to the progress of
religion.

Near
Charlestown, Cecil County, Md.
Octo. 11ᵗʰ 1836

The Rev'd Absalom Peters
          Dr Sir,
                    We wish to obtain a Pastor for a
small Presbyterian Congregation at Charlestown, and as
the congregation is limited in means it will be required of
the clergyman that he teach a ~~select~~ number of students
preparatory to their entering College, say about 12 or 15.
          salary
The perquisites will be for both about $500. pr. An: be-

lieving your society able and willing to assist in procuring such a person I have taken the liberty of requesting your friendly aid. As it will be important to know something of our prospects before the commencement of the winter sessions at the different Academies an early answer is respectfully requested.

Yours very respectfully,
LEVI H. EVANS.

.　　.　　.

Office of the A. H. M. S. 150 Nassau St.
New York Oct. 16, 1836

Mr. Levi H. Evans,
　　Dear Sir,
　　　　　　Yours of the 11th instant has been received; and it would give us great pleasure to name to you such a minister as you desire, if there were any one within our knowledge that you would be likely to obtain immediately for that station. The demands for well qualified ministers of the Gospel are numerous & pressing. We are not able to supply but a small proportion of those that we are constantly receiving. The probability is so small that we shall be able to render you any efficient aid in [illegible] to meet your wishes, that we have thought it best to apprise you of it at once, that you may lose no time in seeking for a supply elsewhere.

Respectfully yours,
MILTON BADGER,
Asso. Sec. A. H. M. S.

.　　.　　.

Office of the A. H. M. S.
150 Nassau Street
New York, May 30th 1837.

Dear Sir,
　　From the public journals and from other sources, you will have heard much of the embarrassment and distress prevailing in our Commercial cities, and affecting the prosper-

ity of the country generally. To those in comparative retirement it is difficult to convey a just estimate of the changes which a few months have produced. Riches have truly taken themselves wings and have flown away. Embarrassment and prostration have succeeded to the highest prosperity with astonishing rapidity. Many of those who love the cause of Christ, and contributed liberally to its promotion, are among the sufferers. So general and severe are the effects, that our Benevolent Societies are involved in serious difficulties. Our beloved Society does not escape: And we believe you will sympathise in its difficulties, and as far as practicable, will cooperate in measures of relief. It has ever been our privilege to meet with promptness the drafts of our Missionaries. When the treasury has been exhausted, the Committee, from their private resources, or on their responsibility, have been enabled to Command all needed funds, — even to many thousands. In the present juncture they fear that this will be impracticable. They therefore ask you to favor the Society, by witholding your drafts on its treasury, until the Committee shall apprise you of their ability to meet them, or shall remit to you a check for the amount due. Every effort will be made by the Committee, and they trust a few months will give them the satisfaction of proceeding with their payments as usual.

It would be a very grateful assistance, if under existing circumstances your people could be stirred up to do something for the A. H. M. S. either by the formation of an auxiliary society, or the increased activity of one already existing, or if this is impracticable, by taking up collections and subscriptions in behalf of this object. We leave this to your judgement. Whatever may be raised may be applied on account of the sum guaranteed to you in our Commission.

By order of the Executive Committee, —
Yrs. in the Gospel,
CHAˢ HALL, Assisᵗ Secʸ
A. H. M. S.

.   .   .

[Extract from a letter by A. Hale, Agent for the Society, to A. Peters, Corresponding Secretary. Galena (Illinois), 22ᵈ August, 1837.]

And now another question of interest is how shall I remit the money I have on hand? To obtain a draft is impossible & to get hold of Eastern bills except small bills of 5 or 10 dollars is in most cases equally impossible, I shall leave this place in a few hours for Chicago. I am personally acquainted with W. H. Brown, Esq., Cashier of the Bank in that place, thr'o whom I hope to obtain money to remit which will go in N. York, — but all is in doubt. I trust also the Church in that place will add to the amᵗ. — Probably you will hear from me again at Chicago. The thoᵗ has occurred to me that the Socʸ. might draw on me for the amᵗ. in favor of Missionaries in this state & in that way till some convenient mode of exchange is found money can be paid over without the cost or trouble attendant on our present *means* of remittance. If that way should be adopted the Comᵉ. will say so. I shall be in Jacksonville by the 20ᵗʰ Sepᵗ. & in the meantime shall collect what I can & if I can obtain current money in bills of suitable amount I shall forward without delay. Notwithstanding the pressure, my mind is made up that Illinois will do more the present year for Home Missions than on any previous year. All we want is the spirit of self denial & the work is done.

•   •   •

Office of the A. H. M. S. 150 Nassau St
New York Jun 20ᵗʰ 1837

Rev. J. G. Simrall
    Carlinville, Ill.
        Dear Sir,
. . . You speak of a renewal of your commission for the current yr. It is in accordance with our rules, that there should be an application from the people in order to have the request come regularly before us. If your people are really needy, I doubt not our committee would readily comply with their request in extending to them continued aid.

But we cannot forbear to express the hope that they will find their own resources, the current year, adequate to their necessities. We cherish this hope from the very liberal collections they have made the last year to benevolent Societies the amount they have raised for their house of worship, and the amount they have pledged for the Theological Seminary. . . .

Those nearer by can judge of the circumstances in the case better than we can & our committee have referred the matter to our agency at Jacksonville, Ill. If your people will forward their application to Rev. Albert Hale at that place it will receive the action of that Board & we shall then be prepared to act intelligently & rightly, I trust, in regard to it. . . .

MILTON BADGER
Asso. Sec. A. H. M.S.

. . .

Carlinville, Ill.
July 7th 1837 —

Rev. Dr Peters
Dear Sir,
    I received on yesterday the letter of your Assistant Secretary— in relation to my Commission for this year— I am glad you have not sent it— as I should have had the trouble to return it— I determined after seeing the proceedings of the Convention and Assembly to have nothing more to do with your Society[11]— and informed my church here to that account— I have received a commission from the Assembly board— you need not therefore consider me in any way connected with your Institution— although I

[11] The Old School group favored the Board of Missions of the General Assembly to the American Home Missionary Society as the proper channel through which home mission work should be carried on. The General Assembly of 1837, which was controlled by the Old School group, passed a resolution requesting the American Home Missionary Society to "cease to operate within any of our Churches." The author of this letter quite evidently belonged to the Old School party. Baird, Samuel J., *A Collection of the Acts, Deliverances, and Testimonies of the Supreme Judicatory of the Presbyterian Church, Etc.* (Philadelphia [1859]), p. 754.

believe it has done much good— yet under all the Circumstances — and in view of the State of Our Church at large — I am satisfied with my present views I cannot again Sustain it.

Yours respectfully

Jn. G. Simrall

[Extract from a letter by Wm. W. Woods to Absalom Peters. Putnamville, Indiana, July 17, 1837.]

There are great hindrances to revivals in this part of the country:

1st A general want of intelligence among the people, and particularly about the doctrines and precepts of the Bible.

2 Worldly mindedness among the renewed, the true Israel of God, and as a consequence of want of faith and holy fervent, prayer.

3. Isms— these are numerous— Parkerites, Mormanites, Campbellites, Newlites, &c. &c. but lately we have heard of other ites, viz. Conventionites,[12] if their sentiments and practice are what they were at a protracted meeting in Philadelphia not long since. I would dread to have them added to the list of hindrances already around me. It is said of them, to make men feel quickly their obligations to love God, repent of sin & believe to salvation in the son of God— they teach that men have no ability in any sense to do these things (mirabile dictu). In practice they adopt the strange notion that the end sanctifies the means — to bring peace they . . . use discord— to make strong, dismember— to honor law, trample upon it— to prevent in-

[12] The writer here undoubtedly refers to the convention which met in Philadelphia on May 11, 1837, one week before the meeting of the General Assembly. This convention was called by a committee appointed by the Old School members of the Assembly of 1836. A memorial containing the Old School proposals for action was drawn up and presented by the convention to the Assembly. Since the Old School, or convention, group was in the majority, it is not surprising that the memorial was so nearly in accord with the subsequent acts of the General Assembly. Baird, Samuel J., *A Collection of the Acts, Deliverances, and Testimonies of the Supreme Judicatory of the Presbyterian Church, Etc.* (Philadelphia [1859]), p. 710.

novation, innovate— rather than not have public fame
for prosecutor make public fame— rather than have light
admit of no discussion— to fill the churches with an enlightened & pious ministry, keep them retarded, or stop the
means of support. To sustain the Gospel throughout the
feeble Churches, dry up the streams of benevolence by
which this work has been most effectually carried on— there
are but few amongst us of this sort— if they were numerous I would loose hope of having revivals soon.

．　．　．

Mardisville, Ala., July 27th 1837

Rev. & dear Brother—

The Lord hath been pleased to pour out his Spirit & revive his work in one of my churches. In the Hatchet-
Creek Church, twenty-five miles distant from this place, I
commenced a sacramental meeting on last Thursday— the
meeting was numerously attended from the beginning, but
no special indication of the divine presence, untill Sabbath
evening— before the close of Service the influence of God's
Spirit was manifest in every part of the Assembly— no
noise, *it was the still small voice*—a deep & solemn feeling
more resembling a death bed scene than anything else—
All kinds of temporal business was suspended— & all classes
came to the meeting— the interest increased untill the close
— we were compelled to close on monday night— I had no
assistance except an eminently pious & efficient Elder.

Thirteen were added to the Communion of our church.
Some will join other churches & multitudes went away
uncomforted— O that the converting & saving grace of
God may go with them—

So you see, my Dear Br., the good work will go on— notwithstanding all the obsticles thrown in the way by Ecclesiastical war.

I feel assured that there never has been a period in the
history of the Church demanding so much fidelity & agoniz-
ing prayer. How good is to come out of our church diffi-

culties I know not— yet I wish to believe that it is all right
— as God allows it—

I was much pleased that the minority of the last Assembly did not break off— Surely there is redeeming power
enough within the bosom of the Presbyterian Church to
correct the unconstitutional proceedings of the Majority—

I love the name Presbytery, I love my confession of
faith— & I love the American Institutions—

So far as in me lies I will try to have the whole Presbyterian Church represented in the next Assembly—

Then if the Doing of the last Assembly are not reversed
I will submit.

But *I had not intended* to say one word about these
things— but to give a short account of what the Lord is
doing in my churches—

Please send me the *Journal* — & write if you have time.

Your Br. in the best of bonds,

ROBT. HOLMAN

Rev. A. Peters, D. D.

. . .

Bryan Co., Geo, Sept. 21st, 1837

Rev. Absalom Peters

Dear Sir

A few weeks since I read to my people, an account
of the embarrassments, which have existed of late, in the
pecuniary concerns of the Home Missionary Society, which
had the effect to awaken their interest considerably to draw
from them a contribution to the funds of your Society,
which, tho', small in amount, was, I trust, acceptably to the
Society & to the God of Missions, as an indication of our
interest in the work of the Lord—

Since then, an old gentleman in my congregation, a super-
annuated Presbyterian Minister, has imbibed a prejudice to
the Society & to yourself— on the ground that you are an
Abolitionist[13]— the idea, he has taken from some one of the

---

[13] In reply to this letter (the reply is for the most part illegible), Absalom
Peters, Corresponding Secretary of the Society, called attention to the fact

religious papers, tho' I cannot say, which, as I have seen no indication of the kind, in any paper, which has come under my eye— It exists, however, with the strength of a prejudice, in his mind, & he has infused the same, into the minds of other individuals in the community. And the report may spread, until many persons, here at the South, have imbibed.

You are aware, that no charge against your Society, could act more prejudicially, among the people of the South than this, of being Abolitionists—

I regret exceedingly the effort, which some in the Presbyterian Church are making for the breaking down of Voluntary Societies, especially of the H. M. S., at least of hindering the action of those Societies, within the bounds of the Presb^n church— Such an effort, should it be successful, must have the effect to increase sectarianism & bigotry among Christians— An evil earnestly to be deprecated & which has always very much paralised the energies of the Church—

It really seems like an attempt to bring back the bygone days of Christian Indifference & inactivity — when anything is done to retard the efforts or at all impair the influence of such Societies as the A. B. C. F. M.[14] & the A .H. M. S. — the Education Society, &c.

I am anxious to have it in my power to correct any detrimental impression which may exist in the mind of any individual or be floating about— the community— I have therefore in this letter to ask, not your views on the great subject of Slavery, but simply, whether you allow the charge of your being an Abolitionist, & whether there is anything in the principles of the A. H. M. S. or of its leading men, calculated to excite uneasiness in the minds of *Southern* Christians & make them fear the action of your Society, South of the Potomac—

that the American Home Missionary Society had never neglected missionary work in slave states and had never taken any official position on abolition. The close relationship of the Society to the New School group in the Presbyterian church, which was decidedly opposed to slavery, however, could easily lead one to associate the society with the abolitionists. See Barnes, Gilbert H., *The Antislavery Impulse, 1830-1844* (New York, 1933).

[14] The American Board of Commissioners for Foreign Missions.

If your answer to my inquiry is such as is calculated to allay any suspicion & prejudice which may exist at the South, in reference to the A. H. M. S., it would undoubtedly help the cause of Missions & of Southern Activity, to have your statement published in some Southern religious paper, Say the *Charleston Observer*— Let me know in your answer, if you authorise me to do so—

You will excuse the liberty I take & believe me, Yours with highest esteem & in the fellowship of the Gospel,

S. W. MAGILL

P. S. Please to direct to me care of R. Habersham, Esq. Savannah—

. . .

South Carolina. 30th August 1839

Revd Milton Badger,
            Dear Sir,
                    When in New York a few weeks ago I mentioned to yourself or Mr. Hall that I thought it was time to establish a home mission in the Republic of Texas, and that it was probable I would be willing to undertake such mission. My mind is now fully made up on the subject, I am willing to go, provided my little family can be sustained, Mrs Reid, our Daughter and myself make up the number. With respect to my qualifications for such a station you can enquire of Dr MacCauley, Mr Whittlesey, Mr Brighem. . . . Texas is an important station, and it would certainly be a matter of christian prudence that we as Presbyterians should occupy the province immediately. That Country must fill up rapidly, and that too with men of great enterprise; they must be met with the gospel in its purity. We believe that the doctrines, government, and discipline of the Presbyterian church as they are laid down in our Confession of Faith are nearer the scriptural model than any other branch of the christian church, with which we are acquainted; and thus believing, we ought to make an effort to bring them to bear on every part of the whole world.

I shall be in Columbus, Mississippi about the first of October, at which time I should like to hear from you definitely on the subject, as I should like to reach Houston, Texas by the middle or 20th of November. I hope the Committee will take the subject under serious and prayerful consideration. What we do in Texas as Presbyterians must be done quickly, the eyes of other denominations are fixed upon it, as [a] very desirable spot. We as a denomination, have lost much in Georgia, Alabama, Mississippi and Louisiana because in them we did not take time by the forelock, we suffered others to be pioneers, while we unwisely followed after, to gather up the scraps. Let us in the new Republic make an effort with the first, and an effort it will take; it will require much self denial in the Missionaries; and much liberal contributions by the friends of the cause at home. As an individual I have nothing to fear from the climate, being a Southerner by birth, and having spent almost the whole of my life in a Southern Latitude. I leave the matter with you. I pray that you may be enabled to decide in the power of God.

Yours in the bonds of Christian affection,

H. REID.

.　　.　　.

Benton Co.　Ark^s. 8th Sep^t. 1846

Rev. Messrs. Badger & Hall
　Sec^s. A. H. M. S.
　　　　Dear Brethren,
　　　　　　　Though no longer one of your missionaries, I feel it to be my duty to address you in reference to the spiritual condition & wants of Arkansas. The principle of your society, "To help those, who try to help themselves," tho *just* &, as I doubt not, in most cases, *wise,* should, as I think, be modified in respect to such communities as Arkansas. If there were no ministers at all in this State, there would be no difficulty in supplying the State by the A. H. M. S. The people are as truly desirous of enjoying the institutions of christianity as any people, &

would be ready to sustain these institutions according to their ability, if there were no counteracting influences. The true state of Arkansas is not known. It is a delicate subject but I feel it duty to make it known to you. Of course it could not be wise or useful to spread it before the public. In developing to you the true condition of this field for Missionary labor, it will be necessary for me to speak of the different denominations.

I. The Cumberland Presbyterians. These are the most numerous & the most intelligent denomination that may be regarded as standing in the way of the operations of the A. H. M. S. In the ministry of this denomination there are several men of good native talents, of good English education & are good preachers. All their ministers I would fain hope are truly pious — some of them devotedly so. The defects of this sect are, 1. They are strongly & decidedly sectarian & especially prejudiced against the "Blue stockings" or Presbyterians, (whether "Old" or "New School"). 2. They are all Arminian in doctrine except in the single article of the "Saint's Perseverance" & on this point they are Antinomian. Their Arminianism is of the school of "Watson's Institutes." 3. They are the strong champions of "Camp-meetings," strong excitement of animal passions, shoutings, noise & disorder. They could hardly believe it possible for a revival of religion to exist where there was not much noise & confusion, or that a sinner could be converted but at a campmeeting. 4. Their converts are always hastily taken into the church at the time & place of their supposed conversion. 5. Religion is made to consist, almost entirely in the strong excitement of feeling, & of course, is pereodical and spasmodic. 6. They depend entirely upon contributions taken up at their campmeetings to sustain the ministry & all christian institutions. These contributions are generally regarded as a matter of *charity* & not as a debt, or a binding christian duty. They are also very small. One wealthy farmer in their church when called on to contribute for the support of the "Circuit preacher" refused to give. "He blessed GOD that his re-

ligion was free. He had been a christian fifteen years &
his religion had cost him only one bit," that is, twelve & a
half cents. 7. They practice only the Itinerating system in
opposition to settled pastors. 8. They introduce men into
the ministry who are wholly incompetent. In this respect
there is quite an improvement going on. They have now
several young men training for the ministry that I fervently
hope will be respectably furnished for the sacred work.

II. The Methodists. These are the next numerous sect.
They are well known to you. They are now in Arkansas
what they were forty years ago in the northern & middle
states. Most of the preachers are deplorably ignorant,
bitterly sectarian, & wildly fanatical. Their tone of piety
is very low, except when the fit is on them. They have all
the defects of the preceeding. The promulgation is some
portions of our country of "Oberlin perfectionism" seems
to have greatly revived the "Methodist doctrine of christian perfection." This is the most frequent theme of their
declamation & ranting. Among their preachers are some
very intelligent & pious men & in their church are some most
lovely Christians. As a denomination they are more faithful to maintain true gospel discipline than those above
named. The whole denomination are staunch friends & advocates of Temperance.

III. The Campbellites. These are all going to heaven
by water. The cold assent of the head to the proposition
that "Jesus is the Christ" & immersion in water constitutes,
in their view, a full qualification for a title to eternal life.
They are rapidly increasing in some parts of the state. As
a denomination they are opposed to creeds, to S. Schools,
to Temperance Societies & to supporting the ministry & sus-
taining any religious institutions with money.

IV. The Baptists. These are all "Hard shells." They
oppose all Missionary, Bible, Tract or Temperance Societies & all Sabbath schools. In a word they are opposed to
every institution that costs money, or, as themselves express
it, that "moves on silver wheels." They look upon learning

as death to all religion. Many of their preachers are unable to read intellibly. This sect are increasing.

V. Protestant Episcopalians. There are but two or three ministers of this denomination in the State. These, I believe are good men & are trying to do good. But their whole system of worship is inconguous to the genius of the people of Arkansas. They have too much of formalism ever to do much good or harm here.

VI. The Romanists. These are coming in in considerable numbers & are bringing in ample funds & means to build & sustain their institutions. They are laying deep & broad foundations. My only hope that they will not succeed in establishing their soul destroying systems of idolitry & iniquity is in GOD.

The foregoing is an outline of the religious sects who may be regarded as standing in the way of your society. The C. Presbyterians & Methodists are those who are more immediately and actively occupying the ground. *After a minute examination & mature & prayerful deliberation I have come to the settled conviction that it would be decidedly for the religious interests of Arkansas if every minister & preacher of the above denominations were out of the State.* Among the C. pres[ns]. & Methodists are a good many ministers who are men of piety & intelligence. They are good preachers. They do good. Sinners I doubt not are converted & saved thro' their means. But the souls are saved at too great an expense. The aggregate of evil vastly preponderates over the good. The most intelligent & devoted & useful still give their whole influence to sanction & perpetuate the system of fanaticism & confusion which uniformily attends their meetings. The consequence is, that all their members look upon religion as consisting wholly in the strong excitement of feeling & that to give utterance loudly & boldly to these feelings & zealously to defend this fanaticism is the sum total of christian duty. I can name scores of individuals in those churches who scarcely afford any other evidence of piety than to "get happy" & "shout" & 'sing' about twice a year. These are thriving farmers who

have an income over & above their expenditures of from
100 to 500 dollars per annum.   And yet the whole amount
of their contributions to sustain & spread the gospel does
not exceed from twenty five to fifty cents a piece annually.
They manifest just as much of the spirit of the world as
those who do not profess religion.   When the fit is on them,
they will pray & exhort, be zealous in the cause of Temperance and sab. schools; but alas the fit soon cools & then
they are alive only to their farms & shops.   Such my dear
brethren is the general standard of Arkansas piety.   Such it
will continue until a different ministry & a different style of
preaching is bro't to bear upon the hearts of the people.
Now it seems to me to be the appropriate work of Home
Missions to carry the pure gospel & true standard of piety
to such communities as this in Arkansas.   If it were not for
the influence of such preachers as now occupy the ground,
ministers of the right stamp would be immediately sustained
by the people.   As it is, the ministry needed in Arkansas
must be sustained by missionary funds until by a divine
blessing upon their labors, the present state of things shall
be counteracted.   The little church of which I am acting
pastor have put forth all the effort they can to sustain me
here & I have labored, on my little farm, as hard as I could
to make a living.   The amount subscribed towards my support is some what increased but still is inadequate; & if I
can get no aid from your Society, I must abandon Arkansas.
In my youth, in obedience, as I believe, to the call of duty I
left father, mother, brethren & sisters, christian privileges
& native land to labor for Christ among the heathen; but
if I must abandon Arkansas, it will be with more regret &
deeper sorrow than I then felt.   To leave Arkansas myself,
if others were here to occupy this great & needy field I
should not regret.   But if I go there is none left.   In looking over the field marked out by your Com. I see Iowa &
Texas & Oregon are remembered, but Arkansas is forgotten.   Here are 165000 precious souls for whom Jesus
shed his blood.   Can you not at least afford them one missionary.   Send one & if need be, I will cheerfully go else-

where.   The College faculty is appointed & I shall not probably be in any way be connected with the board of instruction.   It is my highest wish to be in some portion of the great field where I might be able to devote my self wholly to the work of the ministry.   The Old School general Assembly's Board have appointed several missionaries for this state, but none of them have come on & I believe none are now expected from that source; O may the great Lord of the harvest send forth laborers into this part of his harvest.

With respectful & fraternal regard,

I am, dear brethren,

Yours in gospel bonds,

C. WASHBURN.

·   ·   ·

Grand River Arkansas Nov 8, 1848

The Revd. Milton Badger, D. D.

Rev. Sir:

I offer myself as a missionary in your employment to labor in Arkansas, Mississippi, Louisiana, or Texas, or all the three. [The word *Mississippi* had been inserted.] I am ready to commence now if you would employ me. I am a Presbyterian minister, have been connected with the Old School openly since the division. But have but little preference for Schools. In fact, I hardly know the difference, I have been frequently asked the question what difference the two schools And have scarcely ever been able to give a satisfactory answer. When I preach the gospel brethren I try to know nothing but Jesus Christ and him crucified. I am cordially willing to labor in your employment and to be instructed by you. Please let me know speedily whether you will employ me and what support you give and oblige your brother in the gospel

A. WILLIAMS

Direct to Grand Prairie, Arkansaw

·   ·   ·

New York Dec. 8th 1848

Rev. A. Williams,
           Dear Brother,
                     In answer to yours of the 8th

Nov. I would say, in the first place, that we have not that knowledge of your qualifications for usefullness in the missionary field that is requisite for our action in the matter you propose. Then we have no mission at present in the district which you name, & do not think that we could organize & establish one, to advantage, this season. Again, our funds are exceedingly low at this note. We are greatly in arrears to our brethren for service rendered; & are obliged to be exceedingly cautious in reference to assuming new responsibilities. For these reasons our committee think it not expedient for them to give you any encouragement of an appointment.

                     Yours truly,
                     MILTON BADGER,
                     Secty. A. H. M. S.

CHAPTER XV

CERTIFICATE OF LICENSURE, CALL AND SUBSCRIP-
TION PAPERS OF FRONTIER PRESBYTERIAN
MINISTERS, AND PERSONAL
CORRESPONDENCE

1. Certificate of Licensure of Joseph P. Howe, by the Presbytery of South Carolina, April, 1793.
2. Petition of the Congregation of Little Mountain and Springfield, Clarke County, Kentucky, asking for the services of Joseph P. Howe, October 4, 1794.
3. The Call of Joseph P. Howe by the Congregations of Little Mountain and Springfield, March 17, 1795.
4. Subscription papers of Little Mountain and Springfield Congregations.
5. Articles of agreement between Joseph P. Howe and certain Subscribers for the conduct of a school.
6. Correspondence between the Associate Reformed Presbyterian Church of Ebenezer, Jessamine County, Kentucky, and Mr. R. H. Bishop regarding a call, February, 1804.
7. Letter from the Bethesda Church, Kentucky, asking for an adjourned meeting of the Presbytery at that Church to ordain a minister, April 22, 1836.
8. Correspondence of James Welch: Welch to James Blyth, February 23, 1792; March 8, 1792; Andrew McClelland, Junr. to Welch, July 3, 1792; Robert Marshall to Welch, August 27, 1792.

INTRODUCTION

[The frontier presbytery often licensed men as preachers to work beyond the bounds of the presbytery, as was the case of Joseph P. Howe. After having supplied vacant congregations these licensed preachers were, in many cases, called to become regular pastors. The call was sent to the presbytery, together with the subscription paper, and the call was then either approved or rejected by the presbytery.

The personal letters illustrate the type of correspondence carried on among the young missionaries working in the early West.

The original MSS used in this Chapter are in the Archives of the Presbyterian Historical Society in Philadelphia and constitute a part of the Shane Collection.]

April 1793.

This is to certify that the bearer Mr. Joseph [P] How[e][1] having passed through the usual trials preparatory to Licensure, was licensed in October 1792 by this presbytery to preach the Gospel of our Lord Jesus Christ. As he signifies an intention of travelling out of the bounds of the presbytery he has our permission to do so, & is hereby recommended to any christian Society where providence may order his lot, as a Licentiate in good Standing.

Given in open presbytery ⎱ THO⁵. REESE Mod⁵.
at Bullocks creek church ⎰ FRANCIS CUMMINS S. Clk.

[On back of paper]

Certificate from
Presbytery of
South carolina.

Oct. 4th 1794   Clarke County   Kentucky

We the Inhabitants of Little Mountain & Springfield Congregations, being destitute of the Regular & Stated means of Grace have felt ourselves Reducd. to A Dilemma Under the Prospect of Raising Our familys on Such a Situation, having had Some Opportunity of the Labours of the Revrd. Joseph Howe a Candidate from the Presbytery of South Carolinea, & thinking that his Ministry Under the Blessing of Heaven might be Useful to us & our familys, We humbly Pray & Petition your Revrd. Body for his Labours for one year amongst us, for which that we may be Delivered from the Inthraldom of the World we promise

[1] Joseph P. Howe was a native of North Carolina and was licensed by the Presbytery of South Carolina. He is described as a "devoted man" of moderate abilities. He had a prominent part in the great Kentucky revival and was the Moderator of the Commission of the Synod of Kentucky appointed to deal with the Cumberland Presbytery. Later he became Professor of Ancient Languages in Transylvania University. (*Gillett, op. cit.*, I, p. 417.)

to pay him the Sum of One hundred Pounds one third Part in cash the Other two thirds in Marchantable Produce, Or if Mr. Howe Should Incline to Reserve one third of his time to himself, We Promise to Pay him for the other two thirds of his time in proportion at the Rate of one hundred Pounds Pr. Annum for his Whole Labours, On Condition that Mr. Howe Settles with his family in the bounds of our two Congregations, In hopes that the Lord may Direct you, bless you in all your Consultations, & Prosper Sion under your Care is the Earnest Prayer of your humble Petitioners . . .

THE Congregations of Springfield and Little Mountain

Being On Sufficient Grounds, Well Satisfied of the Ministerial qualifications of you Joseph Howe And having good hopes, from Our Past Experience of your Labours, that your Ministrations in the Gospel Will be profitable to Our Spiritual Interests, Do Earnestly Call, and desire you, to Undertake the Pastoral Office in Said Congregations, Promising you in the Discharge of your Dutys all proper Support, Encouragement, And Obedience, in the Lord, And that you may be free from Worldly Cares and Avocations, We hereby promise and Oblige Ourselves, to pay to you, the Sum of One hundred Pounds in Regular Yearly payments One Third part in Cash The Other two thirds in Marchantable produce, During the time of your being, and Continuing, the Regular pastor of these Churches, In testimony Whereof, We have Respectively Subscribed Our Names this 17th Day of March 1795.

> Attested by
> I Poage   Who
> Presided at the Meting

Wm Nobington	Hugh Forbes
Wm meteer	Joseph Simpson
Jᵃˢ Trimble	Robert Patten
John Kenderson	Matthew McClung
John Lochrodge	Walter Smith

Jas . Magill
Robert Woods
Wm Willson
John Robinson
Wm Moffets
Robert Walker
James Lorhedg
Fsngie [Forgis?] Graham
James Crooks
Andrew Shanklin
Th^{os} McClune
Jas Hawthorn
Robt Trimble
Abraham Miller
Andrew Hodge
William Ashmore
In°. Hamilton Hodge

Robert Stevenson
William Golding
Samuel Downey
Jas Wade
John Judy
James Crawford
Robert Moore
ABner Hamilton
Abner Dooley
Patrick McCollum
Alex^r. Rhea
David Beadle

We the Subscribers of Little Mountain Congregation do Oblige Ourselves to Pay the Sums Annexed to Our Names One third Part in Cash the Other two thirds in Marchantable Produce for the Support of a Minister in Conjunction With Springfield Congregation for his Labours for One year Or in Proportion for any Shorter time . . .

	£	S	D		£	S	D
I^{as} Poage	3	0	0	Allison	0	6	0
Wm Meteer	3	0	0	Robert Stinson	0	6	0
Andrew Hodge	1	0	0	John See	0	10	0
James Ward	2	0	0	Conrad See	0	15	0
Samuel Downey	1	10	0	Robert Brown	0	12	0
James Magill	2	0	0	Thos McClure	2	0	0
Thomas Dale	0	12	0	Saml Miller	1	10	0
William Nelson	1	10	0	John Smith	0	15	0
Mathew McClurg	1	10	0	Winepark Judy	9	8	0
John Judy	1	0	0	Robert Moore	0	15	0
James Gray	0	10	0	Samuel Spurgin	0	10	0
Arthur Conally	1	0	0	Porter Fourt	1	0	0
Nathaniel Logan	1	0	0	William Allison	0	6	0
Joseph Simpson	0	10	0	James Walker	0	6	0

	£	S	D		£	S	D
John McGlauchlam	0	6	0	Paral Hubs	0	6	0
John Henderson	1	10	0	Robert Walker	0	6	0
William Wilson	1	5	0	John McKee	0	18	0
Joseph Turner	1	0	0	William Kelso	0	1.2	0
Moses Lacy	0	4	0	James Evans	0	12	0
Robert Wood	1.	0	0	Mabey Evans	0	12	0
Christopher Wolls	1	0	0				
Walter Smith	0	10	0		13	5	0
William Frame	1	10	0		40	8	0
James Clarke	0	12.	0				
Hugh Forbish	1	0	0		53	13	0
Henry Cooper	1	0	0				
Robt. Pattan	0	6	0				
John Scott	0	6	0				
Forge Baty	0	12	0				
John Calbrath	0	10	0				
Robert Walker	3	0	0				
William Frame	2	0	0				
James Hind	2	0	0				
Abraham Miller	0	15	0				

40 8

page 2

We the Subscribers of Springfield Congregation Do Oblige Ourselves to Pay the Sums Annexed to Our Names One third Part in Cash the Other two thirds in Marchantable Produce for the Support of A Minister in Conjunction With Little Mountain Congregation for his Labours for One year Or in Proportion for any Shorter time . . .

	£	S	D		£	S	D
Wm. Robinson	1	5	0	James Hurley	0	12	0
John Robinson	1	5	0	Robert Crochett	0	12	0
Thos. Gill	1	5	0	Wyett Rucker	0	12	0
Wm Moffett	1	5	0	David Beadel	0	12	0
Ritc^h. Crooks	1	5	0	James Higdon	0	6	0
James H. Lane	1	5	0	William Spence	0	6	0
Abner Hamilton	1	5	0	James Downing	1	0	0
Daniel Dean	1	5	0	And^w. Downing	1	0	0
And^w. Shanklin	0	18	0	Abraham Switzer	0	12	0
Robert Trimble	1	0	0				
Abraham Dick	0	15	0		5	12	
Thos. Bradshaw	0	18	0				
William Berry	0	15	0	John McCollum	1	5	0
~~James Will~~	~~0~~	~~15~~	~~0~~		31	8	0
Saml. Brinton	0	6	0		5	12	0
Den Deson	0	6	0				
Abner Dooby	0	15	0		37	0	
Ja^s. McClenathan	0	10	0				
Hugh Robinson	0	12	0				
John Lochridge	1	10	0				
James Harrow	0	13	0				
James Knox	0	12	0				
Ja^s. Braken	0	6	0				
James Wilson	0	6	0				
Henry Davis	0	6	0				
William Yardley	0	12	0				
James Trimble	2	0	0				
Forgis Graham	1	10	0				
Thos. Montgomery	1	10	0				
William Lansdale	1	-0	0				
Alex^r. Rhea	0	15	0				
John Hamilton	1	0	0				
William Young	1	5	0				
William Forguson	0	12	0				

31 8

[On the back of sheet]

A Suppteration for the labors of Mr Howe —

ARTICLES of agreement Made and entered into between Joseph [P.] Howe of the One Part, And the Subscribers hereunto of the Other, witnesses, As follows. The S^d. Howe On his part is to teach reading, writing and Arithmetic to the best of his Skill and art for the Space of One year, from the   day of   in the Year. i.e. five days for each week except Sickness or necessary business prevents him, in either of which Casses he is to make up time so lost

The Subscribers, hereunto agree to pay S^d. School by Subscribing their names hereunto. The employers Also agree On their part to furnish a convenient house for the purpose of a School, and further Oblige themselves to furnish S^d. School with fire-wood And their Scholars with books and other Necessaries for their tuition. In testimony Wherof we have hereunto Set our hands Nov. 1807

Subscribers Names	No Scholars	Subscribers Names		No Scholars	
John Young	1	William Sanders		1	
Hugh Helso	3	John Harry; March 28		1	
Joseph Simpson	3	Wm Ferguson		/4	
Jeremiah Davis	2	Mr French		1	
John B Fisher	1	Wm. Roberts began March 21			
Madnn Bron	1	Jo^s Yongue	May 1	1	
Grace Forbis	1	Mr Helm	June 8 pd	1	
Polly Hend	1	Sally McDoogle	June 8	1	
Wm McSwain	1	Rollen Gains	August 8		
I S Magawon	1	Mr. Hutson	8 Ditto	2	
James Milney	1/2	Mr Riggs	August 1	1	
Wm. Johnston	1				
Andrew Rigg	1	H Kelso	5	0	
Jno Peebles	3	Jo^s Simson esq	8	0	
Jno Erwin	3	Wm Orare esqr	3	0	
Geo Black	2	Enoch Smith	14	0	
John Crawford	1	Jno Fisher	1	25	
M Harrison	4	Jo^s Simson	5	0	
William Tipten	2/1	Wm Johnston	0	75	
D Trimble	1	Erwin & Peoples	24	62	1/2
John Mason Jr	1				

Subscribers Names	No. Scholars		Subscribers Names		No. Scholars
John Henderson	1			61	62 1/2
Saml Downey	2			45	—
Samuel Spurgin	1				
Enoch Smith	2			16	62 1/2
Will Prear	1			1	50
James Ward	2				
			settled I pay Mr.	18	12 1/2
			Fumster		

Jessamine Co^y. Feby. 1804

We whose names are hereto annexed members of the Associate Reformed Church of Ebenezer, having in the course of last year subscribed according to our different abilities for the one half of the ministerial labours of Mr. R.H. Bishop, and our call having been regularly presented unto the said R.H. Bishop, and Mr. Bishop, having declined accepting of our call and having with the approbation of Presbytery resolved to divide his time, for a few months longer as equally as possible betwixt us, and the congregation of Madison, and Salt River *Wherefore* we hereby engage, that the whole of our forsaid subscription shall be paid for the years following the year [illegible] shall be devoted to the use of our congregation in the following manner:

1. The money of the aforesaid subscription shall be paid into the hands of the trustees of the congregation to form a fund for discharging the necessary expence attending those supplies of sermons, which may be procured in the course of the year.

2. The cash part of the aforesaid subscription shall be paid at the end of every three months, and the property part at the end of every six months.

3. Whatever of this fund is not needed for supplies of sermon[s], at the rate of five dollars for each sabbath, shall be applied to the finishing off of our church.

4. At the end of the year the trustees shall call a

meeting of all the subscribers, and lay before the meeting an exact account of the money collected, and of the manner in which it has been used.

	Cash	Trade		Cash	Trade	
	Dollars			Dollars		
Thomas Woods	8	8	R. H. Philips	3	3	
William Garett	8	8	William Kinning	1½	1½	
Wm. Evans	8	7	John Ramsey	1½		
David Steele	7	8	Wm. Ramsey	?	?	
Ephraim January	5	7	J S Garrett	5		
Thomas Reed	4	4	William Hopkins	8	8	
Robert Black	5	5	John Stitt payd	10	Gon	
						A.C.-[?]
Robert Lowney	2	3	Joseph Thompson	5	3	2.50-
						2.50
			John Sellers	6	8	
James Dunn	2	1				
John Scott	4	3				
Alexander Dunn	1	1				
William Dicks	2	0				
James Livingston	2	0				
David Dennis	1	0				
W. L. Steele	2	3				
Walter Cunningham	2½	2½				
~~John Sellers~~	~~6~~	~~7~~				
George [illegible]						
John Paul	4	4	1 of March 180	2	2	
Hugh Garet	1	1				
Joseph Kennedy	1	1				
John Yong	1	3				
James T. McCoun	~~ ~~	~~ ~~	Recd for two & half years	$10-	—	
~~Preston Brown~~						
Joseph Sellers	1	2				
Robert I. Sorbet	1	2				
[Twelve other names illegible]						

To the members of the Associate Reformed Church of Ebenezer —

Dearly beloved

I take this method of shortly stating unto you why I did not accept your call which was presented unto me at last meeting of Presbytery. It is well known to all of you that there were also at that time two other calls presented unto me. I cannot say that I have any particular attachment to one place more than to another; and I am equally at a loss to determine which of all the places in question is the most needy. This being the case, I judged it in the present circumstances of our church to be of most advantage for all parties, to divide my labours for a few months longer as equally as possible among you all at which time (it would be) acceptable (and under proper management, you may all have comfort (and blessing) of worship provided and become a little stronger in some other respects, and thus be in a better situation for a stated ministry. It is also pretty certain that in that time you shall all have an opportunity of hearing several other preachers, so that in the issue none shall fail of obtaining a settlement to their mind.

Along with this I beg leave to submit to your consideration plans for disposing of, to the good of the congregation that money which you have subscribed for the support of a stated ministry. Upon the supposition you had at this time obtained a settlement, all the money and also all which you may have otherwise subscribed for the building of the meeting house, must have been paid in the course of a year — The plan proposed, therefore does not put you to any more expense than what might be reasonably expected. I shall endeavour to make my arrangements so that I shall visit you once every month — you may also expect some supplies from others, which at a moderate calculation shall amount to other eight sabbaths — 20 sabbaths at 5 dollars each is only 100 Dollars — This I suppose is only about the one half of what you have subscribed for the one half of my labours which to the plan proposed will afford you nearly as much sermons as you could have expected had I at present accepted your call — Thus you will have 100 Dollars more to expend upon your meeting house — which being added to what you have otherwise provided cannot fail to procure you a good comfortable house —

From the knowledge which I have of the good sense and public spirit which pervade your society I presume I need say no more. Go on brethren, in the same deliberate steady manner in which you have hitherto proceeded and there is

not the smallest doubt but that at the end of another year
you shall have fresh occasion to set up your Ebenezer,

                    I remain
              with sentiments of esteem and affection
                              sincerely yours
Feby 1804   R. H. BISHOP

Circular
To the members of the
A.R. Church
of Ebenezer

[The letter addressed to Rev. Andrew Todd, Flemingsburg, Kentucky.]

                    Bethesda Church, April 22, 1836
To the Ebenezer Presbytery;
                    Beloved Brethren;
                              The undersigned,
(members of the Bethesda Church & congregation) would
request of the Presbytery an adjourned meeting at this
church for the purpose of ordaining the Rev. John H.
Condit as an Evangelist — We believe this people are perfectly united in Rev. Condit, yet the state of feeling in regard to settling a minister at present, is such, that it seems
impracticable to take measures for making out a call — One
prominent obstacle, is the enfeebled state of the congregation — But whilst we are not prepared to settle a minister,
we do feel desirous of having the ordinances of the Gospel
regularly administered and we are deeply solicitous that
Rev. Condit should be ordained, that he may fulfil all the
duties of the ministerial office — We are far removed from

any ordained minister, the nearest being seventy or eighty miles distant, & it is but seldom we are visited by one — Neither of the *sacraments* have been administered here for nearly one year past — There are children to be baptized & the people of God feel very anxious to enjoy the privilege of regularly sitting down at the Sacrament Table — In addition to this, the interests of this Church are suffering deeply for the want of wholesome discipline — And we feel that the discipline of the church cannot be effectually attended to, until we have an ordained minister among us — We wish the ordination to take place here, as many of the people have never witnessed such a solemnity & we cannot but hope that the exercises which would be connected with the occasion will prove a blessing to this people —

JOHN POAGE

ROBT. POAGE	Eldr.	GEORGE POAGE	Elder
JOHN H. POGUE	Elder	E.T. CARTER	Elder
THO. H. POAGE		H. A. POAGE	Elder

Dear Brothers;

Will you not if any way practicable attend the meeting of Presbytery & see that this business is attended to — We as a people are very solicitous on the subject — We cannot bear the thought of being deprived of the labours of an ordained minister for six months & perhaps for a year to come, should the Presbytery decide not to ordain Mr. Condit — Our situation is peculiar and it is a critical time with us as a church — If you cannot attend Presbytery yourself, will you not see Bro. Garrison & other members if possible & urge the matter — We feel deeply indebted to you & other members of Presry. for the kind interest you have hitherto taken in this church & this encourages us to urge our plea in this case —

Your brother in Christ

ROBT POAGE

Answd. May 30, HBB.

Persons Names	Pr. Names	Persons Names
William Poage		
Benj. Lambert		
W.B. Brey		
John Brubaker		
Elizabeth Brubaker		
Harriet Castle		
Nancy A. Poage		
Linnett Frame		
Catherine Waugh		
Ann Poage		
Margeret Poage		
Mathy Chentwood		
Mageret McCrosky		
Margart Poage		
Sarah Ann Pogue		
Ann Poage		
Elizabeth Poage		
Catharine Paull		
A. Paull		
George Tanner		
Elizabeth Tanner		

[To Mr. James Blyth, Crab—— Cumberland.]
Very Dr. Sir   Mr. Rice's Feby. 23 . 1792
I am now at Mr. R[ice's] Presbytery and embrace this opportunity of writing to you. I am in tolerable health of body but in a great perturbation of mind — I have some thoughts of joining Presbetery but know not what is duty — I received your letter from Mr. Rice's, am much obliged to you for your kindness, and attention to that matter nevertheless I am hard put to it, to know what to do — The prospect that lies before me, makes me shrink — Dr. Sir, I could not have believed that I should have felt so timorous of fellow mortals as I do — however, could I know the mind of God, see my duty and find his aid therein it would not be so much matter about other things — My own dead-

ness, is my greatest difficulty; — & my greatest hold back. Alas! I know not what I should do, were I in the ministry, unless I get clear of it I long to hear from you, & how you get through ye Wilderness — Colonel Pattersons family were all well yesterday morning — We want you back much; I fear all will be settled on the[ir] Lees, before you come — I grow sick of Lexington & wish I was ready to leave it — I hope the Lord is with you where you are & will manifest the riches of his grace to you, in fitting you for doing all his will amongst that People; — And that in the day of our Lords coming & the light of a vast eternity, it may appear that the Lord has blest your labours abundantly — May you then, as more than a conqueror stand at the head of a goodly company, & in immortal triumph march with your Dr. prince emanuel before to ye kingdom of his glory, to shout his praises on eternally. Forget not your Unworthy friend in your addresses to *you* to the thron[e] of grace——I am very, Dr. Sir Unfeignedly yours, etc . . .

JAMES WELCH[2]

Cr.N.B. fail not to if opportunity serves.

[2] James Welch was sent out by the Synod of Virginia as a missionary to the frontier settlements and after supplying vacant congregations for a number of years became the settled minister of the Lexington and Georgetown Congregations (1796-1804) in Kentucky. In 1810 he became the pastor of the Presbyterian Church at Dayton, Ohio. He was also one of the first three professors in Transylvania University. (Gillett, *op. cit.*, II, pp. 125, 151, 155, 302, 397; Davidson, *op. cit.*, p. 296.)

James Blyth was a native of North Carolina and was educated at Hampden-Sydney College, where he had been one of the student leaders in the great revival of 1787. He graduated in 1789 and was licensed by the Orange Presbytery in 1791 for missionary work in Kentucky. Two years later he became pastor of two congregations, Pisgah and Clear Creek, and soon was recognized as one of the most influential Presbyterian ministers in the West. He had a large part in the establishment of Transylvania University and was appointed professor of Mathematics, Natural Philosophy and Astronomy, later serving as acting President for twelve years. When Dr. Holley was elected President in 1818 Blyth was transferred to the professorship of Chemistry. (Sprague, *Annals of the American Pulpit*, III, pp. 591-599; also various references in Davidson, *op. cit.*, and Gillett, *op. cit.*, Vols. I and II.)

[To Mr. James Blyth.   Preacher of the Gospel at Cumberland For^d by Mr Clark]

Lexington March y.e.8th 1792

Very Dr. Sir —

An opportunity offering for the conveyance of a letter to you; I have endeavoured (though in a poor state of health) to write a little — A variety of things at present seem to conspire together to damp my spirits, and Render this vail of tears more gloomy — I am sometimes dubious whether I shall ever get safe through it or not — I enjoy but little sunshine on my path (if I ever enjoyed any, I may justly adopt the language of Great Dr. Watts But oh how soon my joys decay, How soon my Sins arise, And Snatch the heavenly Scene away, From these lamenting eyes — O for the time when these Robbers will be put to death, when victory will be obtained over them, When this bewitching world & its gay Scenes will no more draw away this deceitful heart, & these wild affections from precious Jesus, Where they ought still to center — I long to hear from you, and expect you will write if opportunity Serves — Your Parents are just started home from this place they have been with us two nights and a day are in health as also the family except one Sister who complains sometimes — I wrote to you from Presbetery but doubted whether you might receive it — I have joined Presbetery A God only knows what will be the isue — I am in great trouble about it; want of health & several other things bring me into many difficultys — I would be very glad at present of a while of your company — I am appointed a Lecture on Titus 2nd Chap. & 11.12 & 13 verses, for the next Presbetery; and I fear I shall make a sad hand of it — Dr. (Bro) try to help me by your prayers — Please let us know (if you write) what the Lord appears to be about to do at Cumberland; — Hasten back, for death Temporal, & Spiritual Reigns here, and it is to be feared greatly, that death eternal will close the same. — I am Dr Sir yours etc.

JAMES WELCH

NB. If my friend Mr. Robinson be with you at Cumberland please to give my kind respects to him and tell him from me that I have reason to believe his family were all in health not longe since —

[To James Welch, Lexington, Kentucky: For favour Mr. Jn. Flennken.]

Muddy Creek, July 3ᵈ 1792

Dr. Sir.

I have had the pleasure of Seeing a letter you wrote to some young people on Georges Creek. I believe they are sensible of and would wish to acknowledge their obligations to you, for your friendly and excellent advice, and Cautions. I think I can feel myself obliged to you for your friendship — They seemed much effected with reading your letter and I trust it was a means of rouseing to a greater diligence and making some serious impressions which will not wear of. — — — There is great cause to mourn for the deadness which is too apparent in our Congregations, (and in none more than Muddy Creek and no individual appears so insensible as myself.) O the Amazing patience of God, that we are not cut down as fruitless cumberers of Ground, we have been highly privileged. God has done great things for us but we remain unthankful. The Revᵈ. Mr. Jennings, came to this country in the winter and at Spring Presbytery accepted a Call from the now United Congregations of Dunlaps Creek and Muddy Creek each one half his Labours. — The divisions about Psalmody seems rather to increase, many have entirely quit coming to meeting. And that party went so far in opposition that on the Sabbath that the Lords Supper was administered at Dunlaps Creek, they had Mr. Henderson preaching at old Mr. Frames, — Georges Creek and Morgan Town are vacant. Apparently from an Division among about a Minister, some were, for a certain Mr. Cooley from Carolina. Others for Mr. George Hill, and could not come to an agreement and so miss'd of both.

Your acquaintance here are well as far as I know and there appears to be a considerable engagedness in a number of old and young — there were six in our Congregation made Application for privilege before the Sacrament at Dunlaps Creek. Our places of publick worship are not so thronged as the[y] were last summer, although we believe Mr. Jennings to be really a wellwisher to the cause of Christ and is a warm preacher. But not so great an orator as some. — — — The few lines I have written are not what they should be, I do but grovel in the dust and seldom if ever get higher, but I could not bear to be raised. There is such a wreched proud heart. I think when you wrote the letter I mentioned you had got quite above the World, — do sir try to remember a poor Wretch sometimes when you get near the Mercy Seat, That the Lord would bless and direct you in you[r] undertakings. I think I desire should be the prayer of your Unworthy though I trust your Sincere friend and

Honb¹. Servt.
ANDREW McCLELLAND JUNᴿ.

Mr. James Welch, Candidate for Min.
Lexington,
by Mr. Lockridge   Kentucky.
Green ——— August 27th. 1792.
Dr. frd.,

Yours of the 8th ult. came to hand about the middle of this month — I was much revived at the refreshing news it contained. My thoughts were anxious to know whether those we left under impressions when we departed from you were still pursuing the way to Xt. You satisfied me in this. & gave me an account that others were still willing to attend public & social means. I find by a letter from another hand, that the uproar among the R[an]k[i]nites is not ceased Ignorance, biggotry, blind zeal & pride will carry men a great length; will make a great noise & shew, when true piety & humility lie in a great measure concealed, or more softly, & unobserved — The State of many in that land is truly a deplorable one, & very likely to remain so.   But we have certainly reason to bless God for his abounding grace to some whom he hath plucked as brands from the burning; & for his apparent willingness to be gracious to more — I think long to see you, & to visit those once more among whom I have gone preaching the gospel; but my return to Kentucky will be attended with greater difficulty than my departure from it, as I have now a second self to carry with me.   Yet I hope, if Spared, to suit in the month of Octr.   I do not expect to go out by the way of Redstone, but by the Kinaway — I have had no further account from that country since I came in than what I had before I left you —

When I last wrote I appeared to be in a melancholy situation; my hopes of heaven were all gone; I have had some since, but what sort they are, or were, I am uncertain — I feel exceedingly dead at this time — Whether my everlasting state will be good, or bad I know not — My deadness seems very inconsistent with a State of grace; but I believe, if I am now without grace I shall continue so.   "O if my soul is formed for woe,

"How would I vent my sighs,

"Repentance should, like rivers flow

"From both my streaming eyes."   This would be the case if such a State were consistent with my present feelings — But I must try to have recourse to X^c for I know of no other refuge, & if I perish I will perish there — I have not seen Mr. Allen since June last, nor heard from him since, I then had hopes that he would return to Kentucky this fall —

"Uxorem habeo, quae religionem possidet, naturam que bonam, vero non fortunam"

Please to present my compliments to Col. Patterson & his lady, to Mr. Boswell, & inquiring friends —

Pardon my brevity, it is a fault that may be forgiven, as I am very seldom guilty of it. —

I am, Dr. Sir, your friend as before,

ROBT. MARSHALL[3]

P. S. My wife would
doubtless compliment
you, but I am at this time
40 miles distant from her

[3] Robert Marshall and Carey H. Allen were the first missionaries sent out by the Synod of Virginia in 1790. Marshall was a native of Ireland and was a licentiate of Redstone Presbytery. He had been a Revolutionary soldier. After the War he joined the Seceder Presbyterians, but under a sermon of Dr. McMillan professed conversion and entered the ministry. He studied at Liberty Hall and under John McMillan. (Gillett, *op. cit.*, I, pp. 406-407.) Allen was a graduate of Hampden-Sidney College and was converted in the revival which took place in the college in 1787. Marshall became the pastor of Bethel and Big Spring churches in Kentucky, while Allen returned to Virginia in 1791. (*Ibid.*, p. 408.)

CHAPTER XVI

EXTRACTS FROM THE JOSHUA L. WILSON PAPERS AND CORRESPONDENCE

INTRODUCTION

[Joshua L. Wilson (1774-1846), a native of Virginia, was taken with his family to Kentucky in 1781 and grew to manhood with few opportunities and little education. He entered school in his twenty-second year and began preparation for a professional career. Although working under the frontier handicaps of poverty and disease he became in a short time one of the best trained ministers of the West. He was licensed by the Presbytery of Transylvania on October 28, 1802, and on June 8, 1804, he was ordained over the churches of Bardstown and Big Spring in Kentucky. On May 28, 1808, he entered upon a period of service at the First Presbyterian Church of Cincinnati which continued until his death on August 14, 1846.

Wilson was one of the dominant characters of the Presbyterian church. A master of the polemics of his day, he employed his powers in support of a rigid Calvinistic theology. Following the division of the Presbyterian church in 1837-38 his colleagues of the Old School elected him moderator of the General Assembly of 1839.

The following correspondence has been selected from the manuscripts of the Joshua L. Wilson Papers. They are a part of the collection of the late Colonel R. T. Durrett of Kentucky, and are deposited in the libraries of the University of Chicago. As the Wilson Papers number more than 2,000 documents those published in this volume exclude others of equal importance. The letters included, however, will throw light upon the man, his church and his times.[1]]

Let this certify that Joshua L. Wilson lived some time in this congregation, was admited to full communion with us,

---

[1] A discussion of the life and work of Joshua L. Wilson may be found in Raymond L. Hightower, *Joshua L. Wilson, Frontier Controversialist,* [Typed] Ph.D. Thesis, University of Chicago, 1933.

and now leaves us free from any cause of church censure know to us, and is hereby recommended to any society where God may cast his Lot.

Pisgah Church,[2] give this 14 of April, 1796

JAMES BLYTHE V. D. M.

. . .

Livingston County February 2nd 1803

Dr Sir

Yours of October 9th came safe to hand, for which I thank you. You say you intend to pay a visit to our part of the country: I should be glad if you could find it convenient so to do; preaching among us for some time past is much more acceptable, and much better attended upon than formerly, and I hope you would find that your labour would not be in vain. There is a vacancy about 14 miles below where I live that is somewhat promising, there has been a stir of religion among them for some months and a number I hope have got true religion. There is a prospect of another vacancy forming a few miles below that, so as to fill up the space between that and the Ohio River, these two vacancies if prospered would be able to call a Minister. If you would visit and preach among them, perhaps after acquaintance it might suit both you and that people to settle among them. I should be glad if such an event should take place; and if you are not yet ingaged I hope you will take the matter under consideration.

While the Lord has been raining down righteousness upon other churches in our western Country, he has in mercy caused a refreshing shower to fall even upon us. The first visible appearance of a stir of religion among us took place something more than a year ago, and still increased along more and more, until in the latter part of the Summer, and Fall it became very considerable. I hope there

[2] Wilson had been getting his first schooling at Pisgah. See his *Memoirs* in the Joshua L. Wilson Papers.

are a considerable number who have experienced a change of nature, and I trust will be useful members of religious society.   There is a considerable difference in the face of families, neighbourhoods, and these congregations, when compared with what formerly appeared.   But as is the case I suppose in all revivals of religion so in this; while the good seed is sowing the wicked one is sowing his tares; and in some instances transforms himself into an angel of light; and while we are with caution and prudence endeavouring to [illegible] thing that is enthusiastick or disorderly; we [illegible] some time have cause to be thankful that there is so much of that prevailing which we hope is genuine religion.   May the religion of Jesus more and more prevail among us, in its poise and purity, and have its transforming influence upon the hearts and lives of many.

Please to write me the first opportunity you have.   Give my compliments to Mrs. Wilson.

Dr Sir, I ever remain yours in affection unfeigned

Terah Templin[3]

Joshua L. Wilson

Preacher of the Gospel in Jefferson County.

.   .   .

Rev^d and Dear friend,

Your highly esteemed favour of Jan 17 was handed to me by Colo. Smith, for which I sincerely thank you.   I have often wished to write to you but have hitherto met with no opportunity when I had time to prepare a letter.

I here feel disposed to write a line or two of sincere compliment but remembering that we have no rules to distinguish true compliment from real flattery I content myself by observing that I believe you to be my real friend[4] and

[3] Terah Templin, being the son of John Templin, was the step-brother of Joshua L. Wilson.   At this time Terah was a member of the Cumberland Presbytery.   This letter was written at the time the great Cumberland revival was in progress.

[4] It was due to "seasonable counsel" from Archibald Cameron that Wilson

am sorry that I so little deserve your attention and esteem. From the time I returned from the Ohio State till within a week or two past I felt myself declining and was a little apprehensive, from a violent cough which I had, that I should fall into a decay. But having for some time past kept pretty close at home and preaching none except on Sabbath days, I find my bodily strength increasing, and my voice assuming its usual force. I have been endeavouring for some time to take the advice given in the latter part of your letter. But how can I preach persuasively without feeling the importance of the subject? And how can I feel without vociferation? This perhaps is a habbit which may be overcome, the which, I am more ready to believe, when I consider that loud preaching is not always powerful preaching. I have sometimes thought that if our trust was in God, we would not use such exertion, but to trust *him* without exertion is tempting *him* which we are commanded not to do. I read with a little surprise your observation respecting real friendship and would just observe that tho nature be curious yet I think the chagrin we frequently experience may arise from the frame of our own minds or from a want of a thorough knowledge of the intentions or situations of others, so as but a small share to originate from evil designs toward ourselves. I join heartily with you in your sentiment respecting Jonathan's friendship. The older I grow the more I sincerely despise sycophancy. The reproof of a friend has been far more sweet to me, than all the adulation I ever received.

I am very sorry to say that religion appears at a low ebb with us at present. Some who have seemed affected are becoming worse, yea, threefold more the children of the devil than before. I have been treated worse lately by Capt Sweets than I ever was by a man, the particulars of which I cannot here relate.

began the study of theology in preparation for the Presbyterian ministry. The two men were friends until Cameron's death on December 4, 1836. (See Wilson's *Memoirs*, in Joshua L. Wilson Papers; also article on Cameron in *Dictionary of American Biography*, Vol. III.

By last mail I received a letter from Mr. Lacy[5] in which is the following interesting paragraph. "Some weeks ago I received a letter from a friend in Philadelphia, in which he mentioned that he was informed by a Christian brother in the East that Mr. Gerrick one of the missionaries sent to that part of the world by the London Missionary Society had been very successful in preaching among the heathen. That he had Baptized 2700 on the coast of Malabar. Also that Mr. Cary had met with considerable success at Serampore, and had baptized a number among which were two Hindoos, one of them a Brachmin, the first of that cast that has ever embraced the Christian religion." Thus it appears that the blessed Redeemer's Kingdom is spreading even in the dark corners of the earth.

Our friend Jno. McGee has been bitten by a mad dog, but as the skin in not broken so as to draw blood he appears under no apprehension of danger. But when I recollect that the infection of the Kine-pock can be communicated by an infected lance without drawing blood I consider his case truly alarming. O that we may all be prepared for every event of God's Providence.

I have quite forgotten whether Pby meets the first or second tuesday in April. I wish you to inform me as soon as possible. Likewise let me know whether you think I can then be ordained or not.[6] I have obtained License to marry and as the court mistook my license for preaching for credentials of Ordination I would rather be ordained at Pby than in these congregations.

I have taken the charge of a Grammar school here consisting at present of 22 scholars eight of whom are studying the Latin language. I wish you would amuse yourself by

---

[5] Rev. Drury Lacy was the brother of Wilson's mother. He won a wide reputation as a preacher in Virginia and was chosen moderator of the Presbyterian General Assembly in 1809. He died in Philadelphia on December 6, 1815. Foote, W. H., *Sketches of Virginia* (Philadelphia, 1850), p. 491.

[6] Wilson was ordained on June 8, 1804. See *Minutes of the Transylvania Presbytery*, Part II, Chap. VI.

coming over and spending two or three weeks at my house or at least in Nelson and B. Town.

My Dear unites with me in wishing you real happiness and prosperity. May we all grow in grace here and meet in heaven hereafter. I am your sincere friend

JOSHUA L. WILSON

Bardstown Feb. 6 1804

[To] The Rev^d Mr. Archibald Cameron
Shelby County

. . .

Chillicothe 17th Feby 1808

Revd Sir

I write to inform you that Cincinnati is now a vacancy. Mr. Davis who lately supplied that place is dead & an Elder from that Church informed me yesterday they had no pastor in view.

I think the minister who fills this church with acceptance & dignity must possess talents of piety — the people profess to be able and willing to give a liberal support to their Pastor : such as will enable him to devote his time to regular preparation for public duties — To a young man possessing talents piety & a constitution to bear the labor this is indeed a desirable situation. In Cincinnati a University is incorporated — The minister of that place will doubtless find employment there if disposed to accept of it. — If your engagements will permit I hope you will immediately visit that place — that your Lord & mastr may place you in a sphere of more extensive usefulness to the world & to yourself; & employ all the energies of your mind in his service.

There are some respectable vacancies in my neighborhood — which (I think) I mentioned to you at Synod — We lament the want of life in religion in all our churches in this quarter of the vineyard — but we serve a faithful God who has promised that the gates of Hell shall not prevail against

Zion.   Accept my best wishes for your welfare & believe me to be your friend and brother in the Gospel of Christ.

ROBERT G. WILSON[7]

[To] Rev. Joshua L. Wilson, Bairdstown, Kentucky.

.   .   .

Cincinnati April 3ᵈ (1808) Sabbath night

My loving Wife,

I am happy to have it in my power to acknowledge the receipt of a letter from you.   Yours of March 15 arrived this evening by mail.   So soon as you receive this you may desist from writing as I expect to leave this place before your letters could arrive.   The matter is not decided but I feel almost certain of moving to this place if the Lord permits.   You need not look for me at home till toward the last of the month.   I have not been to Dayton but saw Colo. Patterson on his way thro' this place to Lexington with his family they perhaps will be at Bardstown before me.   I write this for my friend Goodlet as I have not time to write to him by this mail.

There are difficulties attending a settlement in this place which I cannot fully communicate till I see you but there are prospects of usefulness here which I have seen nowhere else but my mind must determine before I leave the country.   Had I an opportunity of consulting you, my dear, It would greatly ease the weight of responsibility which I now feel.   May the Lord direct our footsteps right.

Tell our dear children that their father remembers them daily.   Give my kind respects to my mother.   Tell doctor Goodlet (if he has not done it) that I want my mare exchanged for a good horse.   If the sheriff should call before my return get him to wait if possible till I come.   If the doctor has a good opportunity of disposing of either or both by lots let him do it.   I want no obstruction to our removal

---

[7] R. G. Wilson was unrelated to Joshua L. Wilson but both had belonged to the Transylvania Presbytery.   R. G. Wilson later became President of Ohio University (Sprague, *Annals,* IV, pp. 122-126).

should that be the result and I had rather sacrifice my property than come away embarrassed.[8]

My dear pray for us for we are needy. Pray for our little ones for their souls are precious. Pray for the advancement of the redeemer's Kingdom.

With my usual flow of health and spirits I subscribe myself your loving husband.

J. L. WILSON

[To] Mrs. Sally M. Wilson   Bardstown   Ky.

.   .   .

Cincinnati Ohio April 3[d] A. D. 1812

Very dear Brother

Your communication of January 25 and March 5 are both before me. Earlier attention should have been paid to them but the precarious state of my health and pressing concerns domestic and professional I hope will form a sufficient apology.

I sincerely thank you for the first no. of the Evangelical Record and herewith transmit names of subscribers most of whom have been obtained since it came to hand. Before people saw it some objected to the price and others feared with regard to the performance, for the editors were concealed from their view. Those whose names are on the inclosed subscription will expect the work from the commencement forwarded by mail.

I believe no steam boat will be running from this place to Pittsburgh this Spring.

I send you Mr. Burke's Vindication &c. hoping you will do him the same impartial justice which you think you have done me.[9]

[8] His income having become insignificant Wilson was involved in debt and was in danger of losing his property at this time. His friends came to his relief. See his *Memoirs*, Joshua L. Wilson Papers.

[9] During the sitting of the Western Conference of the Methodist Episcopal Church at Cincinnati in 1811 some of its members had reprinted in pamphlet form a piece of satiric doggerel against Calvinism, entitled, *The Dagon of Calvinism or the Moloch of Decrees*. Wilson replied to it with an attack on the Methodists in, *Episcopal Methodism: or Dagonism Exhibited.* This

I am not determined what course I shall pursue with respect to it. I only received it a few hours ago and have barely given it a glance. My heart's desire and prayer to God is that a stumbling block may not be cast before the blind by our pamphlets. (Mine and Burks)

You request copies of my pamphlet for distribution. The pamphlets remain entirely at the disposal of the printer. 1000 copies were printed 100 of which the printer offered me for my manuscript but I accepted of 50 only, which have been sent in different directions by mail to my brethren. The greater part of the others are sold but as some are yet on hand the no. wanted in your bounds will no doubt be forwarded if an order be directed to Carpenter & Co. accompanied with the money price 2 dollars per dozen 25 cents single.

Our prospects in religion are more flattering in Cincinnati than they have ever been since I have lived in this place. Not a few are I believe seeking the Lord. Some are perplexed with the present disputes but more are excited to search the scripture daily. There has been a greater spirit of inquiry excited here by the publication of "Dagonism exhibited" than has ever been produced before in Cincinnati.

May the Lord enable us to walk humbly, to Labour faithfully and be more solicitous for his glory than for our own tempered ease, fortune or fame.

My dear Brother pray for me that my strength may be equal to my day. I am surrounded by a host of enemies. Infidels and Arminians who act in Co. No less than 10 methodist preachers live in Cincinnati! But great is truth and must prevail tho' hand join in hand against it. For all that I have thought spoken written, or acted amiss may I

was answered by Rev. William Burke, then the most prominent Methodist in Cincinnati. His tract was entitled, *The Methodist Episcopal Church, Their Doctrines and Discipline, Together With the Characters of Certain Individuals, Vindicated From the Unjust Representations of Joshua L. Wilson.* These pamphlets received extended reviews in the *Evangelical Record and Western Review*, which was edited by Rev. John P. Campbell and Rev. James G. Blythe, and published in Lexington, Ky., in 1812-13. See Raymond L. Hightower, *Joshua L. Wilson, Frontier Controversialist, op. cit.,* pp. 113-122.

lie humble, abhor myself and repent in dust and ashes. But if I am even cast down to the dust I shall not be in dispair, for

> "Christ is my life my joy my hope
> How can I sink with such a prop?"

My wife unites with me in Christian love to you and Sister Campbell.

J. L. Wilson

J. P. Campbell's letters Jan 25 March 5. 1812.
My answer April 3 do.

. . . .

Walnut hill Oct. 3rd 1814

Dear Brethren

Your errand at my house to-day, notwithstanding it opened with something like professions of Christian friendship, appeared to me very different from that, when you had fully opened it — This indeed provoked my resentment, however just, was expressed with an irritated temper, and in language, which under certain circumstances might have been proper, was, under existing circumstances very improper. — If other men should act imprudently, or even manifestly from an evil design, I not only know — but now, to each of you as I have done to two of you already, very sincerely acknowledge to you all that even in the above case, — I *am not released* from my sacred obligation to prudence, wisdom and forbearance — And for having suffered any irritation of mind, or expressed myself in any degree inconsistant with the spirit of the gospel, I am very sorry—

I hope the Lord has forgiven me — and further, that you will also do so, when I say, I will for the future endeavour to guard against improper irritation and all improper expressions of resentment and further, that I desire another interview with you on the subject if you say so — and for this purpose I will give myself the trouble of meeting you at Mr. Wade's any day this week if you will give me timely notice. This I will do with no other view, than the most prudent mode of accomodating any existing jars which seem to have taken place. —

All old matters, on the first proposal of an accomodation, and casting them into eternal oblivion I cordially and cheerfully agreed to — but you are to understand that I never did and hope I never shall, give or sell indulgences to commit the same or similar offenses with impunity.

I am dear brethren
very sincerely yours in the Gospel —
JAMES KEMPER SENR.[10]

Revd Joshua L. Wilson and Messrs David E. Wade and Jesse Reeder.

. . .

Cincinnati, May 12ᵗʰ, 1818

Mr. R. Boal junr
Dear Brother,
As you are Secretary of the 1st Presbyterian Congregation in this place, I address to you and through you to the Elders and Trustees a few lines which are extorted from me by justice and necessity.

I need not inform the officers of the Church of the great change which has taken place in the enlarged circle of my acquaintance, the augmentation of my family, and the increased price of our markets — nor need I state that I am greatly involved in debt — for these are things so obvious that they must be generally known — But I will state that my debts are annually increasing — that my house is decayed so as to be uncomfortable and I have not the means of paying the former nor repairing the latter — Besides I am left in a state of painful suspense from year to year — Last year not a word was said to me about remaining in the Congregation nor was there any subscription circulated untill the fall Presbytery and what was still worse the representative who applied for my labours had no instruc-

---

[10] For an account of Kemper's relationship to the Presbyterian Church in Cincinnati, see Chapter IX in this book.

tion to do so from the Session, nor from the Trustees nor from the people but from an individual only — I do not mention this by way of complaint but simply state it as a fact which was calculated to produce in me a tedious and painful suspense.

My gratitude is greatly excited by a recollection of past kindness from the Session, Trustees and people and by recurring to the many seasonable supplies they have already afforded me — But my circumstances are such at this moment as to induce me to request a speedy answer to the following questions. — Are you willing after ten years trial to settle me permanently as the Pastor of the 1st Presbyterian Church in Cincinnati? Are you able and willing to make arrangments for the gradual discharge of my just debts which amount to upwards of [$] 1600? And can you afford an adequate support for myself and family so as to keep me free from worldly cares and avocations so long as I continue to be your minister?

I wish it to be distinctly understood that I consider the congregation under no obligation to do any of the above mentioned things — But unless something is done and that speedily for my relief Justice and necessity will compel me to sell what property I have to pay my debts and seek other quarters where I can live in greater obscurity, and with less expense. I should prefer making this communication verbally were it not for one consideration, that is, I think it better not to be present when you deliberate on my case — I wish your deliberations to be free. — If you wish me to converse with you on any points contained in this letter or on any other topicks I will wait on you with pleasure whenever requested. I wish it to be recollected that my term of service will terminate on the 27th Inst. unless a new engagement be made — It may not be improper also to remark that the defalcation on the subscription for the year ending May 28, 1816 amounted to $250 and for year ending May 23 1817 $150 making a defalcation of $400 in the two past years what will be the deficit for the year ending this month cannot be ascertained as yet.—

May the Lord direct you to that course which may be most for the peace and edification of the Church. For myself I can say "I am troubled but not perplexed, cast down but not in despair" for my trust is in HIM who feeds the ravens and clothes the grass of the field. With much esteem I am dear brethren affectionately,

J. L. WILSON

. . .

Cincinnati Sept. 12, 1828

My dear Brother Cameron,

In your kind letter of Aug. 27 past marked Sept 9th and received yesterday morning I have a fresh token of brotherly kindness which is like a cordial to my heart. I am pleased to find that the people where you labor patronize the Calvinistic Magazine and other religious publications; and the publisher of the The Pandect, Mr. R. Robbins very thankfully acknowledges the favour conferred by the list of subscribers contained in your letter. In my undertaking to edit a paper, the obstacles thrown in my way at first by friends and enemies constrained me to relinquish all expectation of profit to make sacrifices both of time and money — and to associate with me as a co-editor one who will allways be an encumbrance (inter nos) — But a decided religious News Paper was so much needed here and the City and country were so much deluged with infidel & political journals that I at least determined to have a religious vehicle of intelligence let it cost what it would.

You think I have promised too much. If I promised to exemplify the whole plan in every paper it would have been impossible. But this you know was never designed by me nor expected by anyone. As to talents and acquisitions, they need not be those of ——? The only one talent that is of much importance is good judgment in selection. Our resources are inexhaustible. We obtain between 30 and 40 of the best publications and always have on hand twenty times more matter than we can publish. Yet we prefer some old things to new publications. Old wine is better than new. — And some men of older times were giants compared to modern scriblers who garble and mangle and spoil their works to make out something they call original. I witnessed a thing of this kind some time ago. A piece was published as original from Andover on the question whether Peter was ever at Rome which was on reason of my publishing the Modest Inquiry of the Antiquarian in the Pandect. Another reason was to show the people here that the lofty pretentions of the Pope stood upon nothing. The Roman Catholicks here are in great agitation and the priests in wrath. But then time is now short and it will not be many years till the "Beast and false Prophet and Satan" will all go into perdition and these fine Cathedrals will be cleansed of their idols and be converted into evangelical sanctuaries. This is not prediction but inference from prophecy and promise. As to the old Psalm business its crescent is on the wane too as well as that of Mohomet.

I do not expect to keep the Pandect free from hay and stubble yet I hope now and then you will find something in it more desirable and valuable. It seems you have not heard the Brethren Ross & Gallaher preach.[11] If you were to hear them you would hear two men of very different talents and acquirements whom God had just fitted to labor together. They both in one point are alike — plain, evangelical, unaffected simplicity of matter and manner. Nothing below the dignity of the pulpit — nothing above the capacity of a child — Ross excells in a Sermon — Gallaher in exhortation —

Affectionately,

J. L. WILSON

I doubt whether the man ever lived who had more pith, point, tact and power in exhortation than James Gallaher. My paper ends when my story is just begun. But farewell.

[11] Frederick A. Ross and James Gallaher were conducting revivals together in the Mississippi Valley at this time. They were also the editors of the *Calvinistic Magazine*, published at Rogerville, Tennessee. (For an account of the activities of Ross and Gallaher and their relation to Wilson see Hightower, *op. cit.*, pp. 152-155.)

And do give my love to brother Singleton and tell him that I never pass a day without remembering him & his family.

Revd. A. Cameron   Shelbyville, Ky.

. . .

Cincinnati March 17, 1830

Rev^d and dear Brother,

In reply to your interesting communication of Feb. 23^d which has already remained too long without an answer — I can say that I do not expect to be a member of the next Assembly. I have long been of opinion that we ought to have a Western Assembly.[12] Our present Genl. Assembly is so connected with the New England Associations and with almost all the anniversaries of the great benevolent institutions of the present day and the affairs of Princeton — to say nothing of the difficulty of removing their books and papers any great distance: and the probability that few of the eastern sages would be willing to cross the mountains — that I think it would hardly be good policy to change the time or place of meeting. But if a meeting were appointed on this side the mountain we should rejoice to have it in Cincinnati.

But we need a Western Assembly. The line between us and our eastern brethren is not so broad and deep as the Atlantic Ocean but it is more prominent. The western churches cannot be represented at Phil^a. nor could the eastern at Cincinnati. The Genl. Assembly is not as it ought to be "the collected wisdom and the united voice of the whole church." An eastern and western Assembly might harmonize by a delegated correspondence and by holding their meetings at different seasons of the year. We should prob-

[12] In his letter of February 23, Rev. Samuel Steel, of Hopewell, Ky., requested Wilson's advice on attempting to have the General Assembly of 1831 meet in the Mississippi Valley, preferably in Cincinnati. He mentioned the fact that in the early years of the Church in the United tates it had met twice in Carlisle, Pa., and once in Winchester, Va. MS of Steel's letter contained in *The Joshua L. Wilson Papers*.

ably gain the attendance of corresponding members and afford them an opportunity of seeing what we are. Two assemblies need not be considered two heads any more than the Assembly at Phila. and that in Scotland are two heads. Jesus Christ is the head of the Church and ecclesiastical bodies are only members. No one can tell what an impulse might be given to religion in the West by a western Assembly.

With my present views and feelings I advise that the Western Presbyteries, or some of them, say, Cincinnati and West Lexington petition the next Assembly for a division by altering the Form of Church Government so as to admit of two assemblies in amicable correspondence and let the proposed alteration be sent down to the Presbyteries for their approbation or rejection. Let nothing be done in haste. Let everything be done prayerfully & harmoniously. Our Presby. will meet the 1st Friday in next month and I shall bring the subject up. After the meeting of your Presbytery I shall be pleased to hear from you again.

With Christian affection I am
Yr. Br. in Xt.
J. L. WILSON

Reply to Rev. Mr. Steel.

• • •

Cincinnati Feb. 12, 1834.

Revd R. J. Breckinridge,
      Dear Sir,
            Your favour of Jan. 9. has been duly received and as I did not consider my letter of Nov. 15 an answer to yours of June 19 I have laid your communications both before me and now ask your kind, candid and patient attention to the following reply.

You "consider the condition of our Church decidedly better than it was last year or the year before, and decidedly improving." — To support this opinion you appeal to facts. 1. *To the exclusion of committee-men from the General*

Assembly.[13] I ask, what is gained? A. B. appears in the Assembly with a commission certifying the truth, namely, that he is a committee man and you reject him. C. D. appears with a commission certifying a falsehood, namely, that he is a ruling elder, when he is in fact a committee man, and you permit him to sit, deliberate and vote. There are two kinds of false commissioners, as I understand, one, where the man is certified to be a ruling elder, when he never was elected nor ordained to that office — the other, where the man has been elected and ordained with the express understanding that everwhere else except in the Assembly he is to *be* a committee-man. Does this afford any relief to sound Presbyterians? Does the nominal elder appear in the Assembly a better Presbyterian than the committee-man? And think you that men who have long professed Presbyterianism, whilst inimical to the faith and order of our Church will boggle at a pious fraud like this? To reject a committee-man while the unconstitutional agreement with Congregational Churches remains in force is like clipping the twigs of a noxious plant while the roots are invigorated by cultivation and the branches spread with more luxuriance.

2. *To the history of the catechisms.* This history is quite curious. The assertion that the catechisms and directory for worship made no part of the standards of our Church had been made and often repeated but it could not bear the light of investigation. I was wonderstruck when I saw how the New School party in the Gen. Ass. quailed before the report of the committee on that subject. Their boldest champions had not the temerity to vindicate in the Assembly what they had so often asserted elsewhere. But do they love the catechisms any better than before? Do they preach the doctrines of imputed sin and imputed righteousness, or human inability and effectual calling, of vicari-

[13] Numerous churches in central and western New York and in the Western Reserve of Plan of Union or "Accommodation Plan" origin having no elders had sent committeemen to the General Assembly. (See Baird, *op. cit.* (1855), pp. 574-579.)

ous atonement & the Spirit's quickening power any better than formerly? Are they not as decidedly hostile to our standards as ever?

When they have some special purpose to answer, to promote their ultimate views, by present measures, they can preach orthodox sermons on a few subjects, but it is now, as in days of old, "by good words and fair speeches they beguile the hearts of the simple." The account you have given me of the labours and pledges of some conspicuous men brought to my mind the words of the Lord Jesus, "if it were possible they would deceive the very elect."

3. You say, *In the soundest of the middle men there is a greater approximation to us.* By *us*, I suppose you mean Old School men. The fact, I think, is the other way. There is a greater approximation to *them*. The Old School men have gone down to *them*! In some instances *below* them! Look at this downward approximation in the change of the Editor of the Presbyterian. See it again, in the Presbytery of Carlisle in the Duffield Case. In the Cincinnati Synod on a question of order, which became a test question, the New School fell into the minority. But when Mr. George Beecher's doctrine became the subject of consideration many of the old school sank down to a level even with New Haven. The Indiana Synod is chargeable with a similar fault in the case of Wheelock. I can derive no consolation from approximations of this kind.

4. You appeal to *Dr. Miller's Writings.*[14] Dr. M. is one of the most unsubstantial props you could have selected to support an opinion. On some subjects he writes well. But what signifies his writings? Look at his conduct. Can a bad state of things be made better by the writings of a man who captivates and misleads at the same time? Who proves that men are ecclesiastically base as swindlers, counterfeiters and perjured persons and yet takes them by the hand and cries *peace, peace!* Sir, I have no confidence, no com-

---

[14] Samuel Miller was professor of Church History and Government at Princeton Theological Seminary and was a voluminous writer. He was usually regarded as an Old School man. (*Dict. of Am. Biography,* Vol. XII.)

fort, in such men. They are broken reeds which will pierce the hand that rests on them for support.

5. You refer to *the increase of Dr. Green's popularity and the disgrace of Dr. Beman.*[15] I doubt whether a majority of the next Gen. Ass. will think of the Doctors as you do. Some men think with you but the number is small. After looking at all the facts you have stated I cannot see that the condition of our Church is better in regard either to doctrine or order. I believe it is decidedly worse.

Next you say, "we are getting worse in respect to the administration of discipline." This is true. But the cause you assign for it, namely, that discipline has become a party matter, is taking the effect for the cause. That which makes the parties in the Church is the cause. Difference in doctrines makes the parties and is the true cause of all our troubles in the church. When the doctrines of our Standards were believed and taught, generally, in the Church, was there any difficulty in the administration of discipline? Could not men be put out before they became as heretical and wicked as Theodore Clapp?[16] The histories of Balch,

[15] Dr. N. S. S. Beman was an outspoken member of the New School while Ashbel Green was a recognized leader of the Old School party. Beman was a native of New York state and educated in Williams and Middlebury Colleges. After serving as minister of several churches in Portland, Maine and Troy, New York he became President of Rensselaer Polytechnic Institute in 1845 where he remained until 1865. He was recognized as a leader of the New School party in the Presbyterian Church and was chosen Moderator of the General Assembly in 1831. He was noted for his pulpit eloquence and was an able advocate of the abolition cause. (*Dictionary of American Biography,* II, pp. 171-172.)

[16] Theodore Clapp was a New Englander, born at Easthampton, Massachusetts, in 1792 and died in Louisville, Kentucky, in 1866. He was a graduate of Yale (1814) and studied at Andover Theological Seminary in 1818-19. In 1822 he was called to the pastorate of the First Presbyterian Church in New Orleans where he remained until 1857. In 1834 he adopted Unitarian views and organized the Church of the Messiah, a congregation made up of a large proportion of the members of his former Presbyterian congregation. He was conspicuous for his aid to the sufferers in twenty yellow fever and cholera epidemics which devastated New Orleans during his residence there. In 1857 he resigned his church pastorate because of failing health and settled in Louisville, Kentucky, where he wrote *Autobiographical Sketches and Recollections of a Thirty-Five Years Residence in New Orleans* (Boston, 1857).

Davies, Craighead, Stone and the Cumberlanders furnish a conclusive answer to this question. Latterly, cases by no means doubtful, purely personal and strictly disciplinary have failed! Why? Because the majority is against the truth, or have such an elective affinity for errour that nothing but compromise can be effected.

You have warned me agaist secession. For this you have my thanks because it was done kindly and from a good motive. But I never thought of secession as long as there is hope of reformation. When that hope fails I will come out if God permit. Yes, come out, not from Presbyterianism, but from a corrupt majority, from men who say they are Presbyterians and are not but do lie. Did Luther and Calvin leave the Church of God by *coming out* from the Church of Rome? Reformation and not secession is my object, and has been from the time I wrote the four propositions. For reformation the Standard was unfurled and I trust its pages shall never be disgraced by downward approximation.

You tell me that I may look for a better state of things in this region. Your opinion is formed from statements made to you by Dr. N. and Mr. G. I am not surprised at your good opinion of Dr. N. I trusted him too,[17] before I knew him. There was a time when I had equal confidence in Mr. G. in the days of my ignorance. But I consider your confidence in Mr. G. now altogether inexcusable after what you witnessed in the Cincinnati Convention and then in the Gen. Ass. of 1832. And they have really made you believe that N. is *off* and G. is neutral in relation to the A. H. M. S.! We in this region know better. We have not forgotten the recent efforts made by Mr. G. in behalf of that Society at the quasi-anniversary. What! did they not know that the A. H. M. S. spent large sums every year in support of Congregationalism before that flag was raised in Indiana?

[17] Dr. David Nelson and Rev. James Gallaher had assisted Breckinridge in a revival at his church in Baltimore (*Letter, Breckinridge to Wilson*, Joshua L. Wilson Papers, Jan. 9, 1834).

Did they not know that the Confession of Faith was to be altered when they obtained a sufficient majority? Did not Dr. N. say to me after the Cincinnati Convention,[18] "in less than 20 years there will be no Confession of Faith containing more than 3 articles? And Mr. G. is cooled from his Lane Seminary friends!"[19] Indeed! and yet left his church in the hands of a Professor who has sustained heresy to the extent of his power both in the case of Barnes and Beecher! To cap the climax they have given to you a pledge that their *great* Missouri affair shall not fall into the hands of unsound men! Who are unsound men in their estimation? Is Professor Biggs? The 3ᵈ Ch. was committed to him in Mr. G.'s absence. Is Mr. Sawtell? He has been invited to take the professorship at Marion. Is F. A. Ross? Dr. N. has lately made a speech to build up his reputation. Is any man calling himself a Presbyterian unsound? Dr. N. being recently asked, by a respectable and serious inquirer "what is the difference between the old and New School Presbyterians?" replied, "the difference is as much as between an old cocked hat and a cocked old hat" — and left the man under the impression that the church had been uselessly agitated by a few old men who wanted to govern. — When I read that part of your letter about the pledge and the 4000 dollars, it reminded me of the saying of an old French Doctor I once knew, "some say he good doctor, some say he bad doctor, he don't care so he get de money." I am informed they have collected considerable sums from among their New

[18] As a result of an order of the General Assembly of 1831 the Cincinnati Convention was called in November in an effort to agree on a plan of conducting missions in the Mississippi Valley. The Presbyterian papers of the West carried reports of the meeting, *The Standard* (Cincinnati), beginning with the issue of January 6, 1832.

[19] Following the revival in the First Presbyterian Church of Cincinnati in 1828 the Third Presbyterian Church was formed. James Gallaher was brought to Cincinnati as its pastor largely through the influence of Wilson. As Gallaher sided with the New School and Lane Seminary under the presidency of Lyman Beecher, the friendship between him and Wilson became more and more strained until they dwelt in opposite camps. See Raymond L. Hightower, *op. cit.*, pp. 152-155.

School friends in this city. What sort of pledges do you think they gave them?

I must notice here a seeming incongruity in your senti-ments — in your letter of June — you say, "the wildfire is running out — the application of true principles is break-ing up the men and modes of doing these things and the things are growing into contempt — May I ask what men, modes, things and wildfire you meant? In your letter of Jan. you highly commend Dr. N. and Mr. G. You go the whole for camp-meetings, anxious seats and hasty admis-sions, that is, admissions of all instanter who convince you *"by words"* that God has converted their souls. I per-ceive, Dᴿ Sir, you are on the same slipping path in which I unhappily trod before you and you are conducted exactly by the same guides. If you are a faithful minister of Jesus Christ, these movements will yet give you unspeakable dis-tress and much trouble. But no man is prepared to take warning while he is in a fit of blind zeal. There must be time to cool and come to himself. You talk of sanctifying forms to save men's souls. If forms are scriptural they must not be sacrificed — if unscriptural they must not be adopted. Scriptural forms, like essential truths, are un-changeable. In finding fault with the Standard, you say, "I am strictly and thoroughly a Presbyterian of the old School" — and yet you affirm, "I reject and *ever did*, the doctrine of the limited atonement." This surprises and alarms me more than anything you have written. Is it not declared in the Standards of our Church that God elected *some* to everlasting life? — that he entered into a covenant of grace to redeem *them*? — that the elect only are re-deemed by Christ? — that God *passed by* the *rest* of man-kind and ordained them to wrath for their sin? — If so, then you "reject and ever did reject" a cardinal doctrine of the Presbyterian Church. Atonement. What is it? Is it not that which removes the offence and reconciles the par-ties at variance. Is anything atonement that does not pro-duce reconciliation? Is not reconciliation made by the death of Christ? — by the blood of the Cross? Is not this the ransome? — the price of redemption? Was the price paid for devils? Was it for the non-elect whom God passed by and ordained to wrath for their sin? Then verily Jesus can never "see of the travel of his soul and be satisfied" unless universal salvation be true. The doctrine of an unlimited atonement is the very quintessence of those errors which you profess to abhor — it is the hearts-core of all the wrong systems which are abroad under the name of *liberal Christianity*. The saints in heaven better understand this subject, They say to Jesus, "Thou hast redeemed us to God by thy blood *out of* every kindred." Christ understood this subject. He said, "I lay down my life for the sheep" — "All that the Father hath given me shall come to me" — "Ye believe not because ye are not of my sheep." — On this subject I had much rather be a "double and twisted Covenanter" than a slack twisted semipelagian who can talk about the atonement securing the salvation of no one yet made as much for one as another or tell us about the atonement being a governmental arrangement by which faith and partial obedience are accepted for the sinner's justification instead of perfect obedience to the divine law.

The number and importance of the subjects embraced in your communications form some apology for the tax I have imposed upon your time and patience. I shall expect to hear from you again when you have duly considered our memorial.

With much esteem and affection your unfeigned friend and fellow laborer in the great harvest of souls — Present my kind and Christian regards to Mrs. B. and your dear children —

J. L. WILSON

P. S. You think Lane Seminary will fail. I know not what God intends. It is now a Mammouth establishment. Three professorships well endowed — 60 acres of first rate land in two miles of the Cincinnati market — tuition fees and manual labour at low prices — extensive buildings — 6 printing presses in operation — a system of popular theology and 4 out of 6 churches in this city in its favour. Sir, it is the *Bohon Upas* of the West. Since I commenced writing this letter Mr. G. has returned and 1 am told is labouring busily and cordially with his Lane Seminary friends — *ut semper*.— The heads of Marion! The heads of Lane! Heu pietas! par nobile fratrum! —

The circular of the Presbytery of Onandago affords a gleam of hope but if they do no better than the "Pastoral Union" of Connecticut I can expect but few beneficial results — a pastoral union professing to *come out* from *error* and still retaining in their creed the two radical and prolifick tenets of almost all heresy — human ability and indefinite atonement can afford but little ground of hope for the truth. Dr. Tyler too placed at the head of their new Seminary whose faith sermon was the *sound* of which Fred. A. Ross was the echo! O tempora!

Answer to R. J. Breckinridge's letters of June '33 & Jan. '34 Feb. 12, 1833.

.   .   .

Cincinnati, Jany. 21, 1836

The Hon. Belamy Storer,[20]

My much esteemed friend,

Your communications of the 6th Inst. did not reach me until the 18th owing to the failure of the mails. I take the earliest opportunity in my power of expressing to you some of my thoughts and opinions on the interesting subject to which you have invited my attention.

As a citizen of these United States I cannot feel indifferent to any subject in which are involved the great principles of civil and religious liberty; nor look without concern to any movements which threaten the integrety of our Union.

Being born in one slaveholding State (Va.) and educated

[20] Belamy Storer, a member of the House of Representatives from Ohio (?), wrote to Wilson on January 6, 1836, requesting his views on slavery, and also sending him a "protest" which had been laid upon his table in the House. *Letter of Storer to Wilson* in the Joshua L. Wilson Papers.

in another (Ky.) where slavery assumed the mildest aspects
I spent the first thirty years of my life under the blind belief that the word of God and sound policy justified both
the principle and practice of domestic slavery.   Hence I
have a strong sympathy and an almost indomitable affinity
for slave-holders who are yet in bondage themselves to the
delusive and dangerous prejudices of education and interest.
But by careful investigation my own mind has under the
divine blessing been emancipated from these fetters of darkness and for the last thirty years I have had not a solitary
doubt that slavery is alike unscriptural and unwise.   A just
comparison between the states of Ohio and Kentucky forms
a striking commentary on this whole subject.

I consider slavery in these United States sinful, impolitic, contrary to the revealed will of God, as unfolded in the
supreme law of love, contrary to reason, which speaks
loudly against oppression, repugnant to our declaration of
independence, to our bill of rights; and a foul blot upon
our national escutcheon.   But it is a national evil.   The
North, South, East and West have consented to its existence.   Nor do I blame the great and good men, who framed
the Federal Constitution, considering the critical situation
of the emancipated colonies, and the danger they were in,
without a bond of union, of falling into anarchy or sepa-
rating into pety despotisms, for incorporating slavery in
our form of government and making it the basis of wealth
and representation.   The evil has augmented with progress
of population contrary to the forethought of the wise and
good; and while the foreign trade is wisely prohibited
agreeably to constitutional provisions; there is no provision
of this kind made for putting an end to the domestic traffic
in human beings.   The North have become rich by the foreign trade — the South by the domestic labour.   In existing
circumstances the North has no more right to say to the
South give up your wealth than the South to the North
give up yours.   What then?   Is the evil of slavery with all
its atrocities and abominations to roll on its demoralizing
and desolating tide forever?   No.   He who "rideth upon

the Heavens by his name *Jah*" bringeth out those who are oppressed and unjustly bound in chains. God has no perfection in his nature which can take sides with oppressors. Like the great Jefferson, "I tremble for my country when I remember that *God is just*." Shall we wait for the colonization Society to put away the national sin? That Society may benefit Africa but can do no good to the United States. Shall we look to the schemes of Abolitionists for a remedy? Alas! I can bear them record that they have a good motive but their zeal is not according to knowledge! To whom then are we to look for a cure of this great national evil? I answer to the nation itself. "Phisician heal thyself." If the body politic is so diseased that there is no energy to throw off the disorder then death must ensue. But I hope better things under God. The nation incorporated the evil with our civil institutions. It exists by common consent. It is incorporated in the federal compact and all must abide by it until the compact is changed. Begin at the right place. Let the South agree to give up the slave trade and the slave labour and let the North give up the Slave wealth, the ill-gotten gain in their hands to indemnify the South. Let the constitution be amended and the evil put away by consent & proper legislative action. Neither the North nor the South can live without servants — but let them be free and serve voluntarily for wages — The white hireling can stand the cold — the blacks the heat — but if they choose to exchange situations let them all be free to live and labour where they can get the best homes and secure the best wages. I am confident it would be the making of the South both in wealth, security and happiness if their plantations were cultivated, as our farms, in Ohio, by free labour.

The South and the North should confer on this subject in the spirit of kindness and agree to amend the Constitution so as to abolish slavery and bring the surplus revenue of the nation or some other means to bear on this subject for the purging of our land from the crime of oppression.

"Behold, the cries of the oppressed have entered into the ears of the Lord of Sab'aoth."

What are the representatives of the nation to do while this amendment of the Constitution is regularly made to prepare the way for legislative action? I answer. They must support the present Constitution in all its parts. Domestic slavery must be sustained — the freedom of speech and of the press must be preserved — the right of petition, dissent, protest and even remonstrance must be admitted. The petitions of the humblest individuals in society, on all subjects of grievances when expressed in proper language must be treated with attention and respect. One of our complaints against Great Britain was that our petitions were disregarded.

The wreckless sentiments expressed by Governor McDuffee and the attack made by our chief magistrate upon the Abolitionists, if persevered in, may bring on not a servile, but a civil war. Mistaken zeal on the one hand and violent measures on the other are alike impolitic and unless checked must lead to desparate collisions — oppose them both — but never admit for a moment that slavery is right or that the evil is irremediable.

Men cry out against the slave trade on the coast of Africa and denounce it as piracy. How is it piracy for an owner of slaves on the coast of Africa to sell them to a merchant from Cuba any more than for an owner in Washington City to sell them to a merchant from Louisiana? Some talk and write very finely about abolishing the slave trade on the coast of Africa who kindle into fury if you speak of its abolition in the District of Columbia. But all the laws and all the navies of the civilized world can never abolish the slave trade. Nothing but the abolition of slavery — universal emancipation can do it. So long as slavery exists the trade will be carried on and I have as good a natural right to buy a slave from an African factory as from a factory in Washington — from an African Prince as from a Virginia Nabob. Open a market for white slaves and there will be buyers and sellers as readily as for black men. Destroy the market and the traffic ends.

There is another thing about which men deceive themselves, namely, preparing slaves for freedom. Men can not be prepared for freedom while kept in bondage.

But, sir, I forbear, the subject is like Congressional debates, interminable. The construction of some of my sentences may appear like dictation. They are not so intended. I have only meant to give my opinion, for the perfection of which I set up no claim to infallibility —

Give me leave to say I have great confidence in your integrity, philanthropy and political wisdom and the more so because I believe you seek wisdom from above and endeavour to cherish the spirit of Him who has given a perfect specimen of moral painting in the parable of the good Samaritan.

Though I have greatly taxed your patience I cannot persuade myself to close this letter without asking about your spiritual health, while breathing the atmosphere of Washington? The religion of Jesus Christ is called "saving health." Some moral as well as natural regions are pestiferous. When called in Providence to reside and transact business in unhealthy climes we must take the more care. I never was at Washington — but I have formed an idea that there are many scenes of dissipation — many temptations — which become "the [illegible] time and poisin the mind." When Christ [illegible] his followers he said "I pray not that thou shouldest take them out of the world but that thou shouldest keep them from the evil." I trust this intercessory prayer will be prevalent for you, my dear sir, and that you like Colo. Gardner in the Army and Surgeon Mickle in the Navy will always find some sweet moments of pious solitude in the midst of all your faithful labours for the good of this nation.

I am with much esteem your very
sincere & affectionate friend —

J. L. WILSON

The Hon. B. Storer, Washington City, D. C.

• • •

Cincinnati July   1839

Miss Rebecca,

Since my return from Phila. I have had a good deal to say and much to do. Among other things I have been trying to pay some of my literary debts.

I had on hand a large number of unanswered letters among which yours of May 12 (received while I was absent) pressed itself on my attention, but I still put it down to the bottom of the file, hoping for an opportunity of answering it verbally. But now I think it will be several weeks before I can visit Beechwood and possibly I may be deprived of that pleasure for months to come.

What I write must be principally in relation to your remarks on my Lecture. You wish I had pursued the subject further, in an appendix or somewhere else, and loudly condemned slavery as held in the U. S. &c.

My object was, not to be influenced by my sympathies or prejudices, but concisely and clearly to take up the subject where the inspired writers began it — dismiss it as they presented it and end where they were silent.

If I have departed from the scripture of truth, my defect, redundancy, misinterpretation, or misapplication, or erroneous deduction, let the departure be pointed out and it will greatly oblige me. I thought however that my lecture was secure against misconception on the subject both of the slave trade and American slavery. But you assure me that some scruple not to say that I justify slavery throughout. To this I have only to say that some, on hearing the discourses of Christ did not scruple to say, "he hath a devil and is mad why hear ye him?" — You think no pious reflecting Christian ought to keep a fellow mortal in bondage. Now I think that depends entirely on the circumstances of the case, and I believe many pious, reflecting Christians do hold slaves — first because they have no way of making them free and second because they are not fit for freedom. The golden rule is easily prevented by sympathy and if the text, "God has made of one blood" &c proves that all slaves should be set free without regard to consequences — it equally proves that there should be no landmarks and that A may settle down on the land of B. because he has a right "to dwell on all the face of the earth." The golden rule rightly understood is that I should treat another as he ought to treat me if our circumstances were changed i. e. the judge ought to condemn the criminal, because, if he were in the box and the criminal on the bench of justice the criminal ought to condemn him — And the text "God made of one blood" &c. — simply proves that the whole race of man descended from one original stock and reflects the false philosophy which affirms that there were more Adams and Eves than one — and that the red, black and white men are not varieties of the same family but distinct and separate species of one genus. That text might be urged also with great force against compulsory emigration or force used to prevent emigration — and yet in some cases it is right to compel people to go away and in others to compel them to stay. The truth is man in his fallen state has no right to anything, — liberty, property, nor life — and it is just as God pleases under his Providential arrangements how much of each may be enjoyed. But you say — "I believe God permits slavery — that he approves it I never can."

Now I believe he approves *slavery* as he does *war*, as one mode of punishing sin in the world. So far as God's will is revealed to us on this subject, he allows human governments to manage these two modes of punishment under his Providential government. So that where the powers that be say there shall be slavery or war, every soul under that government is commanded to be subject not only for wrath but for conscience sake. Under such governments relations are formal between officers and soldiers, masters and servants, out of which relations, grow important reciprocal duties. As long therefore as the government stands thus, these relations must be admitted as lawful, and the relative duties performed. The Government may be altered and when that is done those relations may be abolished — war and slavery may cease. God has not put other modes of punishing sin under the power of human Governments — such as, pestilence, famine, earthquake & conflagration, by fire from heaven. None of these modes of God's punishment of sin will exist when all nations become righteous. When the kingdoms of this world become the kingdoms of our Lord and of his Christ and *he* shall reign (Rev. xi.15) — then the nations shall learn war no more and slavery will cease — for the nations being righteous there will be no national sins, nor punishments. But remember, this happy state of things will not be brought about by the American Anti-slavery Society — but by the everlasting gospel — Rev. xiv. 6.

  Very kindly and respectfully your friend —

        J. L. WILSON

P. S. I learn that my book is hated by abolitionists and slaveholders. — surely this letter is long enough.

     Miss Rebecca C. Clopper

Care of   near Cumminsville

 J. C. Clopper, Esqr.   Ham. County, Ohio.

CHAPTER XVII

RECORDS OF PREACHING TOURS OF FRONTIER PRESBYTERIAN MISSIONARIES

1. Plan adopted by the Synod of Virginia for sending out missionaries, 1789.
2. Extracts from the Journal of William Hill, Virginia, 1790-1791.
3. Kentucky and Tennessee preaching tours, 1813-1814.

INTRODUCTION

[An interest in missions has characterized the Presbyterian church from the earliest period of its establishment in this country. Only two years after the first presbytery had been formed every minister was urged "to supply neighboring destitute places where a minister is wanted, and opportunity of doing good offers." From this time till the period of the Revolutionary War the needs of destitute communities demanded the attention of presbyteries and synods. The missionary work of the church suffered somewhat during the war, but when the General Assembly was formed in 1789 the subject of missions assumed a large place in its deliberations. The need of pastoral care in those frontier settlements which sprang up rapidly after the war was known to be great. At first little more was done than to send occasional assistance to such people as requested it, but soon the "duty of sending the gospel without solicitation to destitute regions was more sensibly felt" and synods and presbyteries appointed ministers to itinerate among the frontier settlements.[1]

The first General Assembly adopted a minute to the effect "that the state of the frontier settlements should be taken into consideration, and missionaries sent to them to form congregations, ordain elders, administer the sacraments, and direct them to the best measures for obtaining the gospel ministry among them."[2]

In 1790 two missionaries were sent out by the Assembly, but it

[1] A brief history of the missionary activity of the Presbyterian church till 1820 is given in *A Digest Compiled from the Records of the General Assembly of the Presbyterian Church in the U. S. A.* (Philadelphia, 1820), Part VII, "Of Missions," Chap. I, "Domestic Missions."

[2] *Minutes of the General Assembly*, 1789, p. 10.

soon became evident that in the more distant fields of the church the Synods of those areas were best fitted to direct the laborers who were sent out.   The synods of Virginia and the Carolinas (1791) were allowed to manage the missions within their bounds.[3]   The matter was not, however, left solely in the hands of the synods, and the missionary interests of the Assembly became so numerous that in 1802 a Standing Committee of Missions was appointed.   This became a Board of Missions (1817) clothed with full power to carry on the missionary business of the church.

Two types of missionary work were undertaken by Presbyterian ministers: first, they were often directed by their presbyterys to preach a certain number of times annually in churches without regular pastors;[4] second, they were appointed by presbytery, synod, or Assembly to itinerate through the "destitute" settlements performing the functions mentioned in the minute quoted above which was adopted by the Assembly in 1789.   The preaching tours described in the following pages were made in connection with the latter type of service.]

I. PLAN ADOPTED BY THE SYNOD OF VIRGINIA FOR SENDING OUT MISSIONARIES, 1789.[5]

2nd meeting — held Lexington — beginning Oct. 21, 1789[6] —

Report of the committee for preparing a draught of a plan for sending forth missionaries was resumed and agreed upon which is as follows.

The Synod taking into serious consideration the State of the vacant congregations within their Bounds and seeing with much concern the miserable state of multitudes who have none to break the bread of life amongst them and are perishing for lack of knowledge; and being affected with the situation of the youth upon whom the hope of the Church in future seems to depend; who are likely to be brought up in in [i]gnorance and profanity: desirous to remedy these evils as far as practicable in dependence upon

[3] Gillett, *History of the Presbyterian Church,* II, p. 279.
[4] Refer, for example, to the mention of "supplies" in the Session Records of the frontier presbyteries.
[5] MS Records of the Synod of Virginia, in the Library of Union Theological Seminary, Richmond, Va.
[6] Ibid, Vol. I, pp. 14-16.

the great head of the church have resolved to adopt the following plan —

proper

1. That we will take all possible care to seek for men of Knowledge Integrity and piety who may travel throughout our bounds as Missionaries to preach the Gospel, to chatechise and interest the youth and to discharge such other parts of Ministerial Duty as they may be authorized to perform —

2. That there shall be a Committee of Synod appointed, consisting of four ministers and four Elders who shall be called the Commission of Synod to receive the recommendations of such men from the respective Presbyteries, to examine into their credentials and fitness for the discharge of such an office and who shall give them such directions and instructions as the exigencies of different places may require that they shall meet annually and oftener if thought necessary; and that any two Ministers and as many Elders of the Commission as shall be convened at the place appointed shall have sufficient power to proceed to business. —

3. That it shall be recommended to the different presbyteries to raise such contributions as they may be able in their respective bounds: which be put into a general fund for the support of such missionaries. —

4. That there shall be a Treasurer appointed in whose hands the money raised by the different Presbyteries shall be deposited who shall keep a fair book of Accounts, give and take receipts for all money received or paid away by him and shall make a return to the Commission of Synod or to the Synod as often as may be required. And that he pay out such sums upon the order of the Commission to the different Missionaries as may be appropriated to them. —

And all those collections or donations that may be received by the different Missionaries from the Societies shall be accounted for by the said Missionaries to the Commission of Synod.

The Revd Messrs Graham, Scott, Sweet & Mitchel Ministers. and Messrs. Charles Allen, Benjamin Rees, John Lyle and John Wilson Elders are appointed to be the Commission of the Synod. Mr. William Alaxander of Lexington is appointed Treasurer of the Synod.

JOHN TODD, Mod^r.   JOHN McMILLAN, Cl.

2. EXTRACTS FROM THE JOURNAL OF WILLIAM HILL, VIRGINIA, 1790–1791.[7]

[A few years before William Hill began the Journal from which the following Extracts are taken he entered Hampden-Sydney College as a student. At that time the College was spiritually at a very low ebb. Hill was of a devout nature and continued his private devotions, though in secret. For several years he pursued studies preparing him for the practice of law. In 1788 he was one of the students who had a prominent part in the remarkable revival which broke out in the College and exerted its influence on the churches of Virginia and Kentucky. Several of the ministers and missionaries mentioned in this journal were converted at that time. William Hill was instrumental in the conversion of James Blythe, who became the leader of the little group of students whose devotion changed Hampden-Sydney.[8] William Calhoon, who became a missionary to Kentucky, was also converted through the influence of Hill and became a member of the College group, as did Clement Reed and Cary Allen. The short, but remarkable missionary activity of the latter in Kentucky, led many young men to enter the ministry of the Presbyterian church.

Hill abandoned his study of the law and, after his graduation in 1789, entered the Presbyterian ministry. He was licensed to preach by the Hanover Presbytery (July, 1790). For some months he itinerated under the direction of this Presbytery. In September of 1790, along with his schoolmate Cary Allen, and with Robert Marshall he was appointed a missionary of the Synod of Virginia. His

---

[7] To be found in the Library of the Union Theological Seminary, Richmond, Virginia. For a more complete biography of Hill, see W. B. Sprague, *Annals of the American Pulpit*, III, pp. 563-570. Parts of this Journal and a sketch of the early life of William Hill are found in Foote, W. H., *Sketches of Virginia, etc.*, Second Series, Philadelphia, 1856, pp. 169-190.

[8] Blythe visited Kentucky as a missionary in 1791, was ordained as pastor of Clear Creek and Pisgah Churches in 1793, remaining pastor of the latter for nearly forty years, after which he became President of Transylvania University, and subsequently President of South Hanover College, in Indiana. Gillett, *op. cit.*, I, p. 415; Sprague, *Annals*, III, pp. 591-599.

experiences while on this missionary tour are recorded in the extracts
of his Journal quoted below.

In 1792 Hill was ordained by the Hanover Presbytery and called
to the pastorate of the Charlestown and Hopewell Churches. When
the Presbytery of Winchester was erected in 1794 he became a
member of that body. In 1800 he commenced his prolonged pastorate at Winchester, where he served till 1836, when he was called
to Second Church, Alexandria. His pastorate here continued for
only two years. During the years of his fruitful ministry he served
on important boards and commissions of his synod and of the General
Assembly.

From this record of the first preaching tour of a young Presbyterian minister one gains a vivid impression of the life and labors
of early frontier preachers.]

A Journal, kept by William Hill, beginning July 1st 1790

This Journal, was commenced, while I lived at Majr.
Edmond Reads, near Charlotte Court House, where I was
furnished with a home, from April 1st 1789 till July 9th
1790; when I was licensed to preach the everlasting gospel
of Jesus Christ. During my residence in this hospitable
family, I pursued my classical course of studies privately,
while my class was pros[e]cuting their studies in College.
I was forced to do this, because my Uncle, who was my
guardian, became offended with me, for not complying with
his wishes, in studying Law; for which he had made all the
necessary arrangements. Being on this account displeased
with me, he withheld from me every cent of my little patri-
monial inheritance for nearly two years. A comfortable
home being thus afforded me, clear of expense, I prosecuted
my studies in the best manner I could, and obtained permission from the Board of Trustees, of Hampden Sydney
College in Sept. 1789 to stand my examination with my
class, for the degree of Bachelor of Arts;— which examination was sustained, & I was permitted to graduate with my
class.

After I had graduated, I continued to reside with the
same kind family and prosecuted the study of theology, in
the same private manner, under the general direction, of

my Dear and beloved Friend: Dr. John B. Smith, who resided near the College, in Prince Edward, about 22 miles off.[9] All the time I had for the study of divinity thus privately was from the 1st of Oct. 1789 when I graduated till July 9th 1790, when I received license to preach the gospel, being a little over 9 months. During all this time I held meetings of one kind or another, and exhorted in the best manner I could in various destitute neighbourhoods in Charlotte County which county had no regular clergyman settled in its bounds at that time.

These were all the advantages which those dark times afforded me in preparing for the ministerial office. But my trust was in him, who said "A man is accepted not according to that which he hath not, but according to that which he hath". If the superior advantages which are now enjoyed (1836) could have been had, most gladly would they have been embraced & diligently improved. But I felt it my duty to use my one talent, & not hide it in a napkin & bury it in the earth, because I did not have five or ten talents, which others might enjoy, committed to my care.

The following Journal begins July 1 1790 Just before I was licensed.[10]

Saturday Agust 14th 1790. This morning was much quickened by conversing with a young man under deep concern about the salvation of his soul — he told me that he had led a very thoughtless life, until three days ago, & that my poor unworthy efforts were the means of opening his eyes. Not unto me O Lord, but unto thy name be all the glory.

While on the road today, I fell in with Mr. Southall a

---

[9] John Blair Smith exerted a remarkable influence on the young men of Virginia. From his pulpit he exhorted them to join the ranks of the Revolutionists, and himself organized and led a company as captain. He succeeded his brother as President of Hampden Sydney College, and had a large part in the revival of 1788-89. He followed Dr. George Duffield as pastor of Third Church, Philadelphia. Five years later he was invited to the presidency of Union College. Sprague, *Annals,* III, pp. 397-404.

[10] The entries from July 1 to August 14, 1790, and occasional subsequent entries have been omitted because they do not relate to the preaching tour.

Methodist preacher, who had an appointment on the road I was travelling. I called in to hear him, & afterwards addressed the people myself, but it was cold work. There were but very few present, & they as well as their preacher appeared stupid & dead. Rode that afternoon to Capt Thos Smiths on Sandy river.

Sab. 15— Preached to a very large congn at Sandy river Meeting House. Good attention was given to the word— & some few affected— when I closed Wm Elliot a Baptist preached— & my good friend Robert Stockton another baptist exhorted.

Mon. 16th Remained all day at Capt Smith's a member of the presbyterian church, & one who professes considerable zeal, but who is somewhat eccentric in some things, — tried to spend the day in study — prayer, & religious conversation — but found myself in a very dead & lifeless frame & at a distance from God.

Search me O Lord, & try my ways & whatever is the cause of thy withdrawing, & of my present deadness, let me see it, & then remove it from me, if it is as dear as a right hand or a right eye?

Tues. 17— Preached at Capt Smiths house— the people generally attentive — felt shut up in the fore part of my discourse but the Lord gave me liberty toward the last, & the people became generally affected.

Wed. 18. In the morning felt some little engagedness in family prayer, but was afterward posessed by a very dead & lifeless frame, & had no liberty or delight in any duty. In the evening held a society meeting at the Widow Smiths, but felt very dead & heartless.

Thurs. 19 — Augt. Preached at Sandy River Meeting house had much liberty this day in speaking, & there seemed some effect produced among the people. In the afternoon rode to Mr. Zac Mortons who removed to this neighbourhood lately from Prince Edward; but had a gloomy solitary evening of it — felt much dejected this night, as I found nothing from within or without to cheer me.

Frid. Augt. 20th 1790. In the morning still gloomy—

could have scarce any liberty in private duties. Preached to day at Strawberry Meeting House — had some enlargement while speaking — but in the afternoon my much dreaded frame returned felt a great dejection of mind, & my spirits much sunk — could find no delight in my duty or any thing else. O it was a wretched time with me indeed. I could scarcely get any sleep during the night, & what was still more distressing, I could not fix my mind upon things of a serious nature. I had awful fears about myself— sometimes fearing I never had any religion — or if I had, that I had basely some how or other, backslidden from God. But the thoughts that such a creature should attempt to preach the gospel was still more distressing. Sometimes I wished that I never had harboured one thought that way, from the first — or that I should now be forced to quit it — O wretched man that I am, who shall deliver me from the body of this death! Oh! that God would search my heart & shew me the cause of my distance from him — I feel willing to part from every sin, & to comply with every duty I know to be such. Create within me a clean heart, & renew a right spirit within me O Lord — My God!

Sat. 21. My melancholy frame still continued, & I could have no peace or satisfaction in anything I did. Found no relief in anything — but so much sin, with such a backwardness to duty, that my duty became almost an entire burden & task to me; — & yet a much heavier burden to neglect it, so that I could do nothing else but cry to God to be merciful to me a poor worthless sinner.

Sab. 22nd. In the morning thought I felt a little liberty in prayer to God, though still at a great distance from him, but began to hope that matters were about taking a turn for the better.

Preached today at Tommahock Meeting house, but was never so entirely forsaken since I professed religion. I was shut up in every sense of the word. It was a poor jumbled performance indeed, — felt heartily sorry for the people that they should turn out to so little purpose, that I had only hurt their feelings through sympathy for me. — I was afraid I had disgraced the cause of God, & subjected it to ridicule— I was really ashamed to look the people in the face, could have wished to have hid myself & been seen by none of them. This thickened my gloom still more & my sorrows & distresses ran very high this evening.

Mond. August 23rd 1790. Rose early & betook myself to the lonesome woods, & was something assisted in prayer, & comforted. This consideration relieved me much, "That the work I was engaged in, was not my own, nor to be performed by the strength of man, but that it was the Lord's work, & that he was able to see it done". I tried to preach again at Tommahock. I was really surprized to see so many come out again to hear me after what they had witnessed from me before; — but there was a considerable gathering and I do not remember that I ever had greater liberty given me in my life. I felt strong in the Lord & and in the power of his might. O it was a time of sweet refreshing to my soul, & what sweetened it more, was, that it came after such a heavy gloomy night. O the Lord was with me this day of a truth — the people very solemn & attentive, & many were deeply affected.

Tues. 24. I preached at Widow Hodges, & had also much liberty in speaking — my mind much comforted & refreshed. Felt unusually concerned today for poor sinners. The thoughts of their dreadful situation — their blindness, & deadness, truly affected my heart. O that my head were waters, & my eyes a fountain of tears, that I might weep day & night over poor perishing sinners.

Wed. 25. Preached this day at Pittsylvania Old Court house & was enabled to speak with some life & power— had a very serious & attentive audience — & believe the Lord is at work with this people; O that he would carry it on with great power and glory!

Thurs. 26th. Preached no where to day, but spent it chiefly in private prayer, & reading Bunyan's Barren Figtree — felt a great calm & peace of soul, though no very *extraordinary* exercises any way. But feel much determined to follow Jesus where ever he may lead me, & whatever duties he may call me to perform. Lord set my face like a flint!

Fri. 27. Preach at Tommahock M.H. and blessed be the Lord if ever I was happy in the Lord, it was this day. My stammering tongue was set at liberty, & the house seemed filled with the glory of the Lord. Several were constrained to cry aloud, & many were deeply affected. I felt loath to leave the place for fear something would intrude itself into my heart, & rob me of my joys.

> O that day when freed from sinning
> I shall see thy lovely face
> Clothed then in blood washed linnen
> How I'll shout redeeming grace

Sat. August 28. 1790. I rode up to Snow creek in Franklin County to a Methodist Quarterly meeting, & after one of their ministers had preached, I gave an exhortation. I believe this day proved a blessing to many.

Sab. 29. In the morning the sacrament was administered by the Methodists, I partook of it with them, but had very little satisfaction therein — they do it in such a slight & hurried manner, that I am sure, that sacred ordinance can be but of little benefit to them; at least this was the case with me. It is a solemn thing to partake of the sacrament of the Lords supper in my apprehension. One of their ministers preached after the communion, & I was much quickened under the sermon — He preached well, a few thing[s] excepted. After he preached — by invitation, I preached, & was assisted in speaking & felt my soul enlivened while describing the loveliness of Jesus & the happiness of those who love the Blessed Saviour. I could cry out with the spouse, He is the chief among ten thousand, & altogether lovely. This is my Friend & this is my Beloved O Daughters of Jerusalem.

Mon. 30. I spent this day very agreeably with my good Baptist Brother Stockton. Was the most of the day in private reading a little book containing the experiences of some of the most eminent Saints of God — felt some liberty in prayer & freedom of thought.

Tues. 31 — I preached at Beever creek M. H. to a very small congn — was in poor ardor for preaching — & much shut up to the faith. — Spent the evening more agreeably in singing conversation & prayer with my friend Stockton.

Fri. 24th Sept. 1790 The Commission of the Synod of Virginia appointed by the Genl Assembly of our church to conduct missions, & employ missionaries within the bounds of the Synod met in Lexington[11] & here I was engaged for the first time to ride as a missionary under their direction, having itinerated till now under the direction of the Presbytery of Hanover. Messers Cary Allen & Robert Marshall were appointed missionaries at the same time.[12] I preached this day at New Monmouth Meeting near Lexington Rockbridge County before the Commission of Synod, but felt shut up & insensible except to shame & regret at my conduct yesterday, — felt ashamed to look at the pulpit, much more so to enter it.

Found upon conversing with my friend Turner, he had

[11] The "Plan for Sending Forth Missionaries" which had been adopted by the Synod of Virginia in October, 1789, is printed in full above. The Committee of Synod for Missions met in April, 1790, and appointed Nash Legrand as its first missionary. Legrand had been at Hampden Sydney with William Hill and had also felt the influence of the revival. At the time of his appointment he was a probationer of the Presbytery of Hanover. (See Gillett, *op. cit.*, I, p. 282; Sprague, *op. cit.*, III, p. 564.)

[12] Cary H. Allen, the son of a Virginia planter, was one of the group of Hampden Sydney students who entered the Presbyterian ministry in 1790. With Robert Marshall he was sent to Kentucky as a missionary. His methods, though most unusual (see Davidson, *History of the Presbyterian Church in Kentucky*, pp. 108-110) were very effective, and his services were greatly in demand. Sprague *op. cit.*, III, p. 563.

Robert Marshall, a native of Ireland, came to Pennsylvania in his twelfth year. His experiences in the army and his narrow escape from death somewhat sobered his impetuous nature. As a probationer of the Redstone Presbytery he was sent to Kentucky. Here he became a leader in the extravagant type of evangelism which led to the secession of five ministers from the Presbytery of Kentucky, and the formation of the Springfield Presbytery. This movement was at first called Marshallite, but when Marshall again joined the synod, the adherents were called Stonites. (See Gillett, *op. cit.*, II, pp. 169-77; Davidson, *op. cit.*, pp. 105-108.)

spent just such a night as I did. We both resolved that we would be more watchful & circumspect for the future.

Sat. 25 — Sept. 1790. Mr. Robert Marshall, one of the missionaries just appointed by the Commission of Synod preached an excellent Sermon— felt a deep sense of great unworthiness before God & man— My relenting, were enkindled for while, but presently returned to a state of great insensibility.

Sab. 26th. In the morning Mr. Graham preached an excellent sermon but did not move my insensible heart. The Administration of the Holy Supper then came on, I still continued unmoved as to feeling — but think I gave myself unreservedly away to the Saviour — not wishing to have one sin spared & heartily willing to accept Christ Jesus just as he is offered in the terms of the gospel.

Mon. 26 Rode to Staunton, where I heard Mr. Smith preach in the evening, but my heart was yet unmoved, & I felt myself at a great distance from God — & could find little or no satisfaction in any duty.

Tues. 28 — Rode constantly all day. Tarried at night at a tavern in Rockingham County. Felt no relief for any thing in the world; & yet could not enjoy religion itself.

Wed. 29. Rode as far as Newtown in Frederick County. But by riding all day through the rain, till late at night, by the fatigue of a long journey, & the dejected state of my mind, I went to bed quite sick.

Thurs. 30. The Synod of Virginia met to day in Winchester. I made out with difficulty to ride that far— & was obliged to get to bed immediately, seriously indisposed. Friday & Saturday I kept my bed, quite ill.

Sab Oct 3rd 1790 Still continued sick, but by a great effort I got to the place of worship, & once more attempted to commemorate the death & sufferings of our Lord Jesus Christ. But a more stupid soul, I suppose never handled the symbols of a crucified Saviour. But the Lord taught me a necessary lesson by this sickness, which I much needed. For sometime past, I do not remember ever to have enjoyed such perfect health as I did; I began to conclude that if I should be visited by sickness, I should feel the impressions of divine things more forceably upon my mind, & that sickness would rather be a blessing than otherwise. By this means I thought I should be more deeply humbled & view death as just at hand. I expected to feel the importance of eternal things, & be entirely dead to the world & all its enjoyments, & if I lived to get well I should feel abundantly more for poor sinners. This was the plan I had laid out for the Almighty to work by; & forgot to be thankful for the health I enjoyed. But when sickness came, an awful hardness of heart & insensibility of soul came with it, so that my plan completely failed me; for I could neither pray, nor read, nor think, nor converse, with any satisfaction at all, — but my mind was shut up, & dark; & Satan himself at times, seemed to be let loose upon me with temptations of infidelity & blasphemy, so that I became awfully afraid at times that I should at last be a cast way.

By this I see God can bless health as well as sickness, & that no affecion of itself, notwithstanding its natural adaptation to awaken serious reflection would every prove a real blessing without its being sanctified by the grace of God. I saw also what a blessing, & precious jewell, health is; & that no one can appreciate it duly, until deprived of it. It is both our duty & happiness to be content in whatever situation it shall please God to place us, for he knows better what is good for us, than we do.

Mon. Oct. 4— 1790. Set off from Winchester for Prince Edward in company with Mr. Smith, & Mrs. Smith and Mrs. Read. As I was very weak I was favoured with a seat in Mr. Read's carriage. Mr. Smith preached by the way at New town, — but I continued in a very insensible state of mind.

Tues. 5. Rode very constantly all day, found that I recovered strength of body, notwithstanding the fatigue of riding. We lodged at a public house kept by a man named Wickliffe, in Culpeper County at a place called Gaine's cross-roads. But from the disorderly house that he kept, we came to the conclusion, he bore a very distant relationship to that great morning star of the reformation, of the same name.

.   .   .

Sat. 20th Nov. 1790.   Rode constantly all day, & after being lost & perplexed, in finding the right road, arrived at night, at Col James Gordans in Lancaster County. I hope I was not altogether left to barrenness this day & felt my mind unusually drawn out in family prayer at night.

This is the only county in the lower part of the state, where it was known that any presbyterians were to be found.   Presbyterians were introduced in this region by some Scotish merchants who settled upon Rappahanoc & Potomac rivers.   When Whitfield visited this country they dispatched a mesenger after him & induced him to visit, & preach, in Lancaster County about the year 1740.   A congregation was organized here some time afterward which was visited occasionally by Mr. Davies & others & after some time Mr. James Waddell was induced to settle here & built up a flourishing church, which continued in that state until he left them & removed over the mountain. They have continued vacant ever since, without once being supplied by a presbyterian minister, till this visit of mine. The congn had nearly become extinct.   There were about a dozen members when I arrived — the rest had died— removed— or joined other denominations of christians. The Methodists & Baptists used their meeting house at pleasure.   We arrived at Col. Jas. Gordons some time after night.   I gave him a letter of introduction which I took which procured us a very cordial reception.   His house was full of company, relations, & other friends, when we arrived.   They were generally persons who moved in the higher circles, & appeared unusually gay & shiney in their dress & manners.   The Col. took me & my young friend Smith in sucession around the room & introduced us to each of his guest & members of his family one by one in the most formal & stylish manner.   This placed us rather in an awkward situation as we had both of us been accustomed to the plainest manners & used to see religion in its plainest & simplest dress. So that we were a little disconcerted when we were received in this manner by Col Gordon, whom we had expected to find a very plain & pious man, from the accounts we had heard of him.

After supper we were conducted to bed without having an opportunity of forming much acquaintance with any except from what we saw. After we had got to bed my young friend Smith proposed that we should be off in the morning, as he supposed they were only the gay fashionable people of the world who cared very little about religion & among whom he supposed there was little prospect of doing good. But I told him we would try them awhile & see what could be done.

Sab. Nov. 21st, 1790. I found in the morning, the Revd Mr. Hit a Methodist minister had an appointment to preach at the Presbyterian Meeting house near the Court house. We both however preached. I felt my own mind much impressed with eternal things & spoke with some liberty & freedom & was very much pleased with the appearance of the audience, which was a very large one.

.   .   .

Wed. [Dec] 12. I rode with Friend Sutton to York river, where we were detained by high wind till night, before we could cross. We crossed a little after night, after being heartily sick & disgusted with the thoughtless creatures we were thrown among the greatest part of the day.

We entered Williamsburg some time after night entire strangers. When about leaving Lancaster Col Gordon gave me a letter of introduction to Mr. Holt who, he said, was a very pious presbyterian, & brother in law to President Davies. Without further ceremony we stopped at Mr. Holt's door, & asked a servant if Mr. Holt was at home. He said he was. I told him to tell him that I wished to speak to him. After considerable delay he made his appearance at the door. I told him who I was, & that I was a presbyterian minister, & held a letter of introduction in my hand to him. He asked me, from whom the letter was; I told him from Col James Gordon of Lancaster County— he replied that he knew no such man. I told him Col G— said he had served with him in the Virginia Assembly. Without saying any more or taking the letter which I reached toward him, he turned about & shut the door, & left us standing in the street. I was now left in an awkward situation. Fatigued with my days work — in a cold winter's night— in a land of strangers — the disappointment was great, but the incivility & rudeness with which I was treated were worse. We left the house not knowing where to find a tavern or having any one to direct us. We soon however came across a negro man in the street. I asked him if he knew of any religious man, a good christian in Williamsburg. After studying awhile he said, he did not know any such man in town, but there was a very good old man about a mile from town. I told him I would give him a quarter of a dollar if he would conduct us to his house, which he did much to our satisfaction and comfort. This good old man, was a Mr. Wilkerson, living about a mile north of the town, whom we found just such a man as the poor negro took him to be; a plain, artless unaffected, hospitable pious methodist, who received us very cordially & treated us with every possible kindness.

Thurs. 13— I made application for permission to preach in the episcopal church, as I was told the methodists were permitted to use it sometimes. This was promptly refused. I applied for permission to use the Court house, & after being referred first to one magistrate & then to another, this was ultimately denied me. I was requested by Mrs. Ball of Lancaster, who had a poor unfortunate son in the Mad house to call & see him & let her know something about his situation. The Keeper said I could not be admitted until he had consulted some of the visitors. That I must call again, & he would let me know. I did so, & he told me he had positive orders not to admit me, for that it was such persons as I was, who sent so many persons to bedlam, so that I was not admitted at all.

I examined the old Capitol, which was a mere desolation, & used at pleasure by the beasts that went at large in the streets — I found one room more decent than the rest, & made an appointment to preach there the next day & got the favour of my good friend Wilkerson to circulate notice about town.

During the course of this day, a servant of Mr. Holts called upon me, to inform me that his master was very desirous of seeing me at his home. I told him to go & tell his master that I had given him an opportunity of shutting his door in my face once, & I should be careful how I gave him another. That if he had more business with me now than I had with him, I thought he might come to see me. The servant soon returned & said his master was in great distress, — was sorry for what he had done, & insisted upon seeing me. I told him to tell his master where I was, & he might come to see me if he was so desirous of an interview. But my old friend Wilkerson, who, I think had more of a christian spirit than I had, or else knew more about his situation, interfered, & intreated that I would go & see what the man wanted. So I went, & was truly glad I did. He met me at the door, asked a thousand pardons for the treatment he gave me & with a flood of tears said he had spent the greatest part of the night upon his knees before God, & had slept none, & exclaimed "My God has it come to this, that the only presbyterian minister who had been at his door for about forty years, should have been rudely turned away in a cold winters night. He then explained the whole mystery to me, which was this. He had been both unfortunate & imprudent in the management of his property. And having entered into a second marriage with a wife of an extravagant turn, & fond of display — he was now reduced from affluence to bankrupcy. Executions were then out, to take him to jail & the sheriffs had laid many schemes to get him out of his house that they might secure him, but he had hitherto eluded them, & was forced to keep himself closely shut up in his own house. He supposed when we called at his door it had been a trick of the sheriffs to entrap him. He is a poor unhappy man, who has been hurled from affluence to poverty & indigences; he has experienced a complication of misfortunes & distresses, & is scarcely himself at present. He was deeply distressed as soon as he discovered his mistake which caused him to treat us as he had done. He asked a thousand pardons — which were granted most sincerely — & I commiserated him from my heart. I still hope he may be a christian. But alas! what will not pride & the sorrow of the world bring a man to!

Friday 14. My baptist brother Sutton, & myself & Mr. Wilkerson's family set off at the appointed hour to the Court room in the old Capitol to preaching; but when we got there we formed the whole of the congregation. We found it would be in vain to wait. I asked Mr. Sutton to join me in singing a while, this attracted the attention of the boys & others passing the street, which when reported in the families near at hand brought out a few from curiosity to see what it meant. I asked them as they came in to be seated, & in a few minutes we would say something to them. Thus we collected a small congn. of a very miscellaneous & loose character. We both gave them a short sermon & dismissed them. The inhabitants of Williamsburg appear to be so entirely careless about religion, or are so wedded to the old church of England, that they will hear no others preach the gospel, & it is much to be feared that from the style of preaching which they now have, that their empty forms of worship may do them more harm than [good].

I obtained an interview this day with some of the students of William & Mary College, some of whom were formerly my fellow students in Hampden Sydney College, the particulars of which from motives of delicacy I shall pass over. If this was a fair specimen of the influence which this institution exerts over the youthful mind, I should pronounce it a grand nuisance which ought to be suppressed. But their rudeness, infidelity & ribaldry might have proceeded from mere youthful folly & indiscretion.

Sat. Jany. 14 —1791. Finding there was no probability of my being permitted to preach in Williamsburg, & hearing that the methodists had a quarterly meeting about eight miles, off in James City at an episcopal chh I took leave of my baptist brother Sutton, & set off for this methodist meeting. On the road I feel in company with one of their preachers. We made ourselves known to each other. He asked me to preach for them that day. I agreed to do so. But says he, as I suppose you are a calvinist you must promise not to preach these doctrines, or we cannot suffer you to preach. I told him, if I preached at all, I should preach what I believed to be the truths of Gods word, & I would suffer no man to control me in matters of that kind, but would act as duty & prudence might seem to prompt me. He told then plainly that I should not be suffered to preach; otherwise they should be obliged to oppose my doctrine. This led us directly to controversy, & it is probable we were both too much exasperated for the occasion. I considered that I was very rudely treated, for he was a very rough man & said many provoking things — such as that the doctrine which I preached was forged in hell & beat out upon the Devils anvil, & Poor man, if his heart is not better than his head (which I hope is the case) I fear he knows but little of the religion of the Bible. Their presiding Elder Mr. Cole preached, & Messrs Brown & Roswell exhorted. It was poorly calculated to awaken devotion in my heart. At night I attended their meeting again, & being in a more brotherly manner, I preached among them, without calling forth any opposition.

.   .   .

Mon. 31st. Being invited I preached at Mr. Stephen Hills in Surry County— & Mr. Hill & friend Spencer both exhorted after me. I felt some enlargement of soul in preaching. At night a congre[g]ation met of their own accord, at the same place; — I preached to them again, & it seemed to be a time of refreshing from the presence of the Lord.

Tues. February 1st 1791. In the morning when about to part from my old acquaintance Spencer, I asked him for an introduction to some of his Methodist brethren in & about Petersburg, that might assist me in getting an appointment for preaching there. This he declined doing, and gave me plainly to understand that he did not think I need expect to be invited to preach any more among the methodists, as they were not at all pleased either with my doctrine or manner of preaching. Poor man, I am afraid he knows not what kind of spirit he is of. I rode through excessive cold weather through Prince George to Petersburg. But having no acquaintance in the place & no letter of introduction I met with a cold reception here. There was not a member of the presbyterian church that I could hear of in the place, & I could find no one who was willing to receive me & lend a helping hand. I asked permission to make an appointment to preach in the Episcopal church, & also in the methodist meeting house, the only places of worship in the town, & was peremptorily refused in both instances. I then went through the different taverns, & asked permission to use their public or ball rooms for an appointment to preach, but failed even in this. Concluding there was nothing that I could do in this place, I rode just before night to a tavern in Dinwiddie County about 8 miles from Petersburg, & there spent the night with a parcil of as swearing & drunken wretches as I ever was constrained to keep company with.

Wed. Feby 2—1791. I went this day to visit to Revd Devereaux Garrett,[13] an aged, respectable & pious minister of the gospel living in Dinwiddie County. This clergyman was formerly an intimate friend & associate of the Revd Archd McRoberts, both members of the episcopal church, & both zealous & successful ministers of the gospel, by whose labours a very extensive revival of religion took place in Chesterfield Dinwiddie Amelia & some other coun-

[13] The reference is to Devereux Jarratt. The story of this interesting figure is told in his autobiography, *Life of Devereux Jarratt* (Baltimore, Warner & Hanna, 1806). See also Sweet, W. W., *Men of Zeal* (New York, 1935), Chap. I, Devereux Jarratt, Forerunner.

ties before the revolutionary war. But they were sorely
persecuted by the rest of the episcopal clergy for the zeal
and piety. Mr. McRoberts felt constrained to withdraw
from the episcopal church & joined the Presbyterians. Mr.
Garrett for a while attached himself to assorted with the
Methodists. But not agreeing with them on several points,
he returned to his old church where he stood solitary &
alone, without the countenance or fellowship of any of the
very loose & unprincipled clergy of the church. Such was,
his situation when I called upon him. "Faithful among the
faithless was he found." I felt much edified & comforted
by his company & instructive conversation.

Thurs. 4. I heard Mr. Garrett preach a very excellent
sermon upon a funeral occasion at Mr. Davis' & was richly
feasted under his sermon, then rode with him to a marriage
where we dined, but the light and trifling behaviour & conversation of the company badly comported with the employ-
ments of the fore part of the day, or compensated the loss
of his edifying conversation which I should otherwise have
enjoyed. We spent the night together at Mrs. Stauntons,
where I had the pleasure of meeting with my very dear
friend Little Rae Morton from Charlotte, whose company
& conversation were truly refreshing to my mind, for by
him I heard from my numerous friends & acquaintances in
Charlotte & Prince Edward from whom I had heard nothing for many months.

Sat. Feby 5. 1791. I heard Mr. Garrett preach a warm
& affecting discourse at Mr. Wiley's, & was sweetly refreshed by his sermon. Blessed be God for the strength he
this day afforded to me. I felt quite dead to the world &
the flesh was effectually bowed in subjection to the will of
God, while the Devil, the lying tempter, was kept at a distance. Bless the Lord O my Soul!

Sab. 6. I preached at Mr. Meridith's in Dinwiddie to a
respectable & attentive congregation, felt my own heart
much engaged in the duties of the day, & hope it was not
altogether labour in vain.

At night I had the happiness to meet with my good

friend & companion in travel David Smith whom I had
left in Lancaster a cripple by a fall off his horse about a
month ago. He had followed my track, & overtook me this
day. What a comfort would his presence & conversation
have been to me in some of the rugged scenes which I have
passed through almost friendless & alone.

.   .   .

Mon. April 4. 1791. The Presbytery & Commission of
Synod still continued their Sessions at Briery. Mr. Cary
Allen missionary preached, & Mr. Ja Turner,[14] candidate
for the ministry exhorted.

Thurs. 5. The Presbytery & Commission both adjourned to meet this day at Hampden Sydney College.
The Revd Devereaux Garrett an episcopal minister from
Dinwiddie County being present & still as a corresponding
member in Presbytery, was invited to preach which he
cheerfully complied with, & gave us an excellent evangelical
sermon. Mr. Legrand then preached a trial sermon preparatory to ordination — which with other parts of his
trial being sustained, he was then solemnly ordained to the
full work of the gospel ministry.

Wed. 6th Aprl. Cary Allen & myself rode down to
Great Guinea in Cumberland, to visit our friends & relatives there & spend a few days where before we set out
anew, upon missionary excursions, through different parts
of the state. We visited a sick woman by the way & hope
Jesus was with us while engaged in prayer with her.

Thurs. 7. Spent with friends & relations in this neighbourhood chiefly engaged in transacting some of my worldly
business.

Fri. 8. Services preparatory to the communion commenced this day at Cumberland Meeting house. Messers
Allen & Marshall preached — my heart felt as cold &
senseless as a rock of sin.

[14] Probably Rev. James Turner, who was licensed by the Presbytery of
Hanover in 1791, and ordained the following year. Sprague, *op. cit.*, III,
pp. 581-587.

Sat 9.   Myself & Mr. Legrand preached, but I fear it was winter with our souls.   In the evening we held a society meeting at Mr. Ja Allens, a venerable old father in our Israel.

Wed. June 1st, 1791.   I had the curiosity this day to ascend Chestnut mountain in this vicinity, & take a view of the surrounding scenery & the wonderful works of God, & I did not at all repent of it, although at first I felt like it was triffling & a mis-spending of time.   My mind was greatly elevated with the prospect, & prepared to adore the God of nature.   In the afternoon, I had the unexpected pleasure of meeting with my old friend & college mate John Lyle,[15] who has just been licensed by Lexington Presbytery, & sent by the Commission of Synod to join me in this tour of missionary labours over the frontiers of Virginia.   Our Blessed Lord sent the primitive Heralds of the gospel by two & two.   Two is better than one.   The company counsil & assistance of such a companion might have saved me from some of the deep plunges of gloom & discouragement I have heretofore gone through while alone.   I was much refreshed with my colleagues company, & felt like thanking God & taking courage.   was rejoiced to hear from him what a cloud of Witnesses the Great Head of the church was sending out by Lexington Presbytery.   O that God would raise up and send forth many labourers into his vineyard, for the harvest truly is great, but the labourers are few & that he would stir up the hearts [of] old ministers from their luke-warmness & formality.

Thurs. June 2nd 1791.   I preached at Mr. John Martins to an attentive assembly, & my friend Lyle preached after me.   I hope God will carry on his own work in this neighbourhood.   How desirable that some one should stay with them to nurse the impressions that have been made.

[15] The reference is probably to Reverend John Lyle, who is well known in Presbyterian history because of the prominent part which he played in helping to check the extravagances of the Kentucky revival of 1800. The statement that he had "just been licensed by the Lexington Presbytery" is obscure, since Gillett and Sprague both record the date of his licensing as April 21, 1796. Gillett, *op. cit.*, I, p. 417; Sprague, *op. cit.*, IV, pp. 178-185.

But from our instructions & the extent of the bounds prescribed to us, we are constrained to pass on.

Fri. 3. We had an appointment to preach at Mr. John Dickinsons, on Pig river — very few came out, we turned the appointment into a sort of prayer meeting, & both of us exhorted, a hardened & careless company of sinners.

Sat. 4 was to me a singular & distressing day. In the morning I suffered some triffling occurence to ruffle my temper far beyond any true cause & it really seemed as if Satan used it very successfully against me all day, for my mind, which had become agitated, like the surface of a lake gave back every image, that was reflected from it, crooked & distorted, so that I continued in a fretful mood all day & I could not reason nor shame myself out of it, by all the exertions I could make. At Snow creek heard Mr. Anthony a baptist minister preach, but I could neither pray hear nor perform any other duty with any satisfaction. "The good that I wd I do not, but the evil that I would not, that do I." O wretched man that I am.

Sab. 5. After Mr. John Aspland,[16] a Swiss baptist had preached an excellent sermon, I attempted to preach, I began with some liberty, but soon became shut up & embarrassed. Oh! my wretched pride of heart. Mon. 6. I went to Franklin Court, & transacted some worldly business, & felt a cold hard heart all day.

Tues. 7. Preached after Mr. Lyle at Mr. Turners on Towns-creek with much light, ease, & liberty. I preached at the same place again at night, with not so much liberty as in the day, though I trust I was not altogether left to perform duty in my own strength.

Wed. 8. Mr. Lyle preached at a meeting house near Capt Hairstows, I then exhorted— & was followed by exhortation from a Mr. Blanton a methodist, & a Mr. Hall a baptist, — but it was cold work all round.

Thurs. 9. I preached the funeral of old Capt. Hairstow. Had a large congregation, — felt in pretty good tune for

[16] The author of the well known *Baptist Register.*

preach[ing]—& Bror Lyle was as happy at exhortation. A solemn impression was made upon the people. Fri. 10. We rode to the head of Smith river in Patrick County to Mr. Ia Turners. In the evening I felt much of a spirit of prayer — was dead to the world. And experienced that, which I believe no hypocrite ever felt. Bless the Lord O my soul. Sat. 11. I set apart this day for prayer & fasting— but had not the liberty or comfort I had yesterday. Preached at Mr. Pilsons, but was cold and dead. The people seemed in the same state. Mr. Lyle preached after me.

Sab. June 12th 1791. Mr Lyle & myself both preached at the head of Smiths river — In the afternoon, I preached again. In the fore noon I was sorely afflicted with my constitutional malady. the head-ach which I found is almost sure to follow a day of fasting, & whenever it occurs it is sure to unfit me for duty— but in the afternoon I was much favoured both in body & mind in preaching to the people. The Lord loosed my poor stammering tongue, & I felt that the Lord was with us of a truth. O that the whole world would love & serve the Lord, for he is a good Master.

Mon. 13. My headach, that thorn in my flesh returned with violence. In the morning we visited a family where the old man died last night & laid a corpse before us, while we sung prayed & exhorted the family & neighbours. We then crossed the Allegany mountain into Montgomery County, & lodged with Majr Eason. Tues. 14 we continued at Mr. Easons & I had to lament a lukewarm heart, & an indifferent state of mind.

Wed. 15. I preached at Majr Easons to a large & attentive congregation was a good deal in the dark myself. Friend Lyle preached after me. The people here seemed as if they would hear preaching if they could have it, but it is an out of the way place, where they seldom hear preaching of any kind.

Thurs. 16. We rode as far as Capt Ishams where we expected to preach but notice had not reached the place of our appointment. We however gathered a few of the neighbours & Mr. Lyle preached & I exhorted, but they were a hardened ignorant set, entirely unaccustomed to anything of the kind. We rode in the afternoon, & arrived at nightfall, at a miserable cabin where we were obliged to tarry— but they were so poor that they could afford us scarcely any thing for man or beast. After cutting a sheaf of green Rye spieu for our horses, & eaten our supper of a Rye ash pone & sour milk we slept in an open uncovered pen designed when finished, for a sort of barn with our saddles for our pillows, & our great coats for our covering, but we found ourselves all safe in the morning, except a hoarseness, caused by a thick fog which came over us before day.

Fri. 17. I preached at Mr. Whitlocks in Wythe County on little Read Island creek to a decent & attentive little congregation, many of whom seemed seriously impressed. Mr. Lyle also preached— in the afternoon we rode to Mr. Sawyers where we spent the night. We found Mr. Sawyer a stiff bigoted old side Scotch Irish presbyterian, a bitter enemy to new lights & enthusiasm & I am afraid to all revivals & vital relgion. We were however received & treated hospitably, but in a very rough style.

Sat. 18th June 1791 We rode to the Lead mines in Wythe, where digging & smelting of lead was carried on to considerable extent. We were receive & treated very hospitably by Mr. Frisbie the superintendent of the works but no friend I fear to religion. We visited & inspected the mines & works.

Sab. 19th Mr. Lyle & myself preached at the lead mines, to a very large & to us very unexpectedly very attentive congregation— who appeared eager to heard the word of God. This makes preaching & every other duty easy. We rode in the afternoon to Mr. Baxters, with whom we spent the time comfortably for there is reason to hope he was a pious good christian, & it is not a common thing to find pious presbyterians in some parts.

3. KENTUCKY AND TENNESSEE PREACHING TOURS, 1813, 1814.

[MS in the Shane Collection, at Philadelphia, Pa.]

[That the missionary activities of the Presbyterian church became very large in the early years of the nineteenth century is shown by the fact that in 1814 the General Assembly alone commissioned more than fifty ministers to undertake missionary tours. Ten of these were directed to carry on their work within the bounds of the Synod of Kentucky.[17]

The following extracts are taken from the Journal of a Presbyterian minister, describing preaching tours in Kentucky and Tennessee during the years 1813 and 1814. The Journal is a part of the Shane Collections, and has been attributed to Reverend William Dickey. But from internal evidence it is clear that it cannot have been written by him.[18] The records of two preaching tours are given

---

[17] Rev. William Hodge, for two months, within the limits of the Presbytery of Muhlenberg, in the counties of Robertson, Montgomery, Tennessee, and Christian, Kentucky.

Rev. William Dickey, for two months, in the counties of Livingston, Caldwell, Muhlenberg, Ohio, Henderson, Hopkins, and Union, with the adjacent settlements along the Ohio river.

Rev. James M'Gready, for three months, within the bounds of the Presbytery of West Tennessee. His route to be prescribed by Rev. Gideon Blackburn, and Rev. Robert Henderson.

Rev. John R. Moreland, for three months, within the counties of Knox, and Rock-castle, Kentucky; and to continue his route through the back part of those counties adjoining the line that divides Kentucky and East Tennessee.

Mr. —— Crowell, for six months, in Tennessee. His route to be prescribed by the missionary society of East Tennessee.

Rev. Joseph P. Howe, for two months, in the lower part of Kentucky, and in the counties of Stewart, Dixon and Montgomery, West Tennessee.

Rev. John Lyle, for four months, in the counties of Bourbon, Harrison, Nicholas, and Fayette, Kentucky; and in his mission he will pay particular attention to the blacks.

Rev. William W. Martin, for three months, in the counties of Clark, Estil, Montgomery, Nicholas, etc. Kentucky.

Rev. Nathan Hall, for three months, within the bounds of the Transylvania Presbytery.

Rev. Joseph B. Lapsley, for two months, within the same bounds.

[18] The writer of this Journal was probably Rev. Joseph P. Howe, who was one of the missionaries commissioned by the General Assembly in 1814. (*Extracts of Gen. Assem. Min.*, p. 122). The author lived in Kentucky (*cf.* entry for Dec. 1, 1813), about thirty-six miles from Lexington (*cf.* Dec. 15, 1813) and twelve or thirteen miles from Winchester, Kentucky (*cf.* Sept. 20

here. The first took place during the closing weeks of 1813 and carried the missionary into Southern Kentucky and West Tennessee. The body under whose commission he went out is not expressly stated, but it was probably the General Assembly. During the second tour, which occurred during September and October, 1814, the missionary visited a number of Presbyterian communities lying within the bounds of the Transylvania Presbytery which, in most cases, were not being served by regular pastors. The commission for this tour was given by the General Assembly in May, 1814.]

I left Home on Monday the 11th of October 1813 &

and Oct. 18, 19, 1814). This description fits the location of the community at Mt. Sterling, Montgomery Co., in the West Lexington Presbytery, where Joseph P. Howe was stationed from 1795 to 1830. (Gillett, *op. cit.,* II, p. 155). From the fact that the two tours here described originated and terminated near Lexington, Kentucky, it seems probable that the writer was a member of the West Lexington Presbytery. Three men from this body were appointed missionaries by the Assembly in 1814: John Lyle, serving at Cane Ridge and Concord; William W. Martin, a licentiate; and Joseph P. Howe. The first of these seems improbable as the writer of the Journal because of the location of his residence and the nature of his commission: "to pay particular attention to the blacks," and the second would have been unable to administer the sacraments, a function which the writer of the Journal did perform.

The problem may be approached from another angle. The missionaries appointed by the General Assembly in 1814 to carry on work in Kentucky and Tennessee may be briefly considered (*cf.* note 15). Hodge was living in Tennessee (Shilo, Sumner Co.), and was probably referred to in the entry of November 30, 1813; Dickey is referred to in the third person (October 27, 1813), and so was Nathan Hall (December 9, 1813); Moreland was a licentiate of the Transylvania Presbytery and was to work exclusively in Eastern Tennessee. Lapsley was pastor at Bardstown, in the Transylvania Presbytery, which place was visited by the author on October 14, 1813. Lyle and Martin have already been mentioned. McGready was a member of the Muhlenburg Presbytery, serving at Sharon Church, in Logan County. This county was included in the 1813 tour.

Four of this same group had been commissioned in 1813 by the Assembly: McGready, Moreland, Hall and Howe. McGready's commission was to travel in the bounds of the Muhlenburg Presbytery; Moreland was to work in Knox and Rockcastle Counties, Kentucky, and in East Tennessee, while Hall was to travel in the limits of the Transylvania Presbytery. Howe's commission was "for two months, in the lower part of Kentucky and West Tennessee," which exactly defines the territory described in the preaching tour of 1813. For some unexplained reason the 1814 tour was confined largely to territory lying within the bounds of the Transylvania Presbytery, and did not extend into the "counties of Stewart, Dixon, and Montgomery, West Tennessee" as included in the Assembly's commission (*Extracts Gen. Assem. Min.,* p. 122).

rode 29 miles to old Mr. Grahams, Tuesday the 12th passed thro Lexington to old Mr. Black's, 16 miles & there lodged being a wet Evening —

Wednesday 13th passed on thro' Versailes to a Mr. Grey's Beaver Creek intersecting the Delany road 28 miles there pd. half a Dollar for my lodging — thence —

Thursday 14th rode to Bards Town 30 miles — & attended Synod[19] — preached on Friday Night, availed myself of every Opportunity of receiving Information from such Members as could afford it of the most suitable missionary Ground in the bounds assigned me in my commission, but found myself considerably disappinted by reason of the total absence of both the presbyteries in W. Tennessee.[20]   I had not opportunity of preaching more than once during my stay at Synod, as the appointments had been designated previous to my arrival, on

Tuesday 19th — rode twenty-five Miles to Elizabeth Town in Harden County and preached at the lighting of the candle to a considerable number of the Citizens tho as far as I could learn scarcely a professor among them yet an apparent serious attention was given —

Wednesday 20th — rode six Miles to a Missus Morrisons & preached to 40 or 50 People where there appeared to be a solemn attention given by most of them & some affected — rode in the Evening after sermon four Miles to a Mr. Haycraft's a Baptist professor, on my way to Litchfield.

Thursday 21., rode twenty miles to Litchfield in Grayson County preached to 30 or 40 Persons among whom were perhaps about half a dozen presbyterian Professors who gave a serious attention and most of them were considerably affected there was in general an apparent solemn attention & some whom I expected were professors in other churches were affected — but I left the place shortly after

[19] The Synod of Kentucky. Lexington and Versailles were both in the Presbytery of West Lexington, which was connected with the Synod of Kentucky.

[20] Reference is here made to the Presbyteries of West Tennessee (erected in 1810) and of Union (erected in 1797).

sermon, & rode thirteen miles to a Mr. Bryants a Baptist professor & preached after night to about twenty or some more persons, being after dark when I arrived, I was informed several had left the place expecting there would be a disappointment the people gave (what I might call) an approbating attention to what was said — but I could not learn that there was a Presbyterian present except a Man who rode with me from Litchfield — nor any in that neighborhood except one Man & his Wife, who had left the place before I arrived & they were only by Education attached to the presbyterian tenets.

Friday 22 — rode twenty seven miles to Hartford in Ohio County & preached to 25 or 30 Persons a few of whom appeared gladly to receive the Word, a general decent attention was given — there was a person after sermon solicited private conversation with me desiring counsel what he should do, he told me, he trusted the Lord had had Mercy upon him some time before, that he most cordially approved the Doctrines of Grace held by the presbyterian Church, but that he had no opportunity of enjoying the public & instituted means of grace in that way, he wished to know whether I thought it would be advisable for him to connect himself with any other church. I told him I thought not, recommending him to be attentive to the private Means of Grace particularly to make the Word of God the man of his counsil, availing himself of the aid derivable from other good Books, he desired my counsil in a selection of Books, I mentioned a few he told me he had adopted a plan of private Devotion in his Family, & modeled after the Example of the psalmist David on the Lord's Day; I recommended him to persist in his course, humbly looking to, & waiting with God till he would provide better things for him — Then stated to him the Missionary Institution, stating the benevolent provision made thereby for his & similar situations; & the Directions I had to receive from any, disposed to contribute to the Fund of that benevolent Institution reporting the sum together with the persons contributing; He observed he had not Money with him, but that he would be very willing to give twenty five or thirty Dollars, if he had an Opportunity of putting it into my hand, but had no desire his Name should appear annexed to it; I have been thus particular, being much pleased, as he appeared to feel himself bound to do something for the Savior, who had done so much for him. Thus far I had proceeded in fulfilling appointments previously made by a Member on his way to Synod, but they were so distant from each other as my Journal will show, that it was with considerable Exertion I could reach the places in time, & could do nothing more than barely preach & pass on; The appointments terminating at Hartford; & having no opportunity of forwarding any other appointments, I rode on.

Saturday Morning 23 rode toward Greenville in Mulinburg County got into the bounds of Mount Zion Church a vacancy of the Presbyterian Order distant from Hartford fifteen Miles, had notice circulated for sermon on the Lord's Day. This church, I understand, is united with that at Greenville — about 9 or 10 miles distant from each other.

Sab. Octr. 24th. Preached at Mount Zion, it was a very wet day, which prevented a good many from attending, however there were more attended than I expected considering the state of the weather, & the time for giving notice, there appeared to be an anxiety for enjoying the Means of Grace by this People There was a serious attention given, & in a few instances affection — rode after sermon three miles to a Mr. Glenn's on my way to Green-ville, & had an appointment forwarded there for preaching on Tuesday finding it impracticable to have it sooner, I also had an opportunity, & forwarded an appointment to Maddisonville in Hopkins County —

Tuesday 26th — rode [7 miles (?)] to Green-ville Mulinburg County & preached to a few People part of a Presbyterian Ch^{ch}. known by the name of Carmel, but owing to the want of general notice — the wetness of the Day, & a regimental muster including part of the Congregation, there were but few present, in this Church there are several respectable presbyterian Professors, but having a appointment before me I could [not] stay longer at this place, rode after sermon six miles to Mr. Hugh Martins —

Wednesday 27th rode 15 miles to Madison-ville — preached in a private house to a large room-full of People, but perhaps most of the professing part of the audience were Baptists & Methodists, nevertheless there were a few Presbyterians — Mr. Wm. Dickey one of our Preachers who had overtaken me on his way from Synod, preached also, there appeared to be a decent & in some instances an interested attention given forwarded appointments for each of the two following days at a Major Downey's ten miles distant from this place, who had been for 12 or 15 years a member of one of my own charges — the churches under my own care

Thursday 28th — rode to Downey's — it was a very wet day but very few attended. I had Mr. Dickey to preach as he would not be present the Day following —

Friday 29th — preached at the same place — the audience was not large but considerably more so than the preceding day — Maj^{or} Downey & his wife had their youngest child baptized — —

Sat., 30th. rode three miles to Alexander Rhea's & preached to 40 or 50 people had general attention, 2 or 3 presbyterian professors were affected —

Sab. 31st rode 7 or 8 miles to Madison-ville where I had left an appointment — preached to a considerable number people. I delivered a very lengthy discourse, yet love, & unremitted attention was given, such as had not been witnessed in that place, as I was informed — particularly by the non professing part of the audience the great majority of professors in this county are Baptists, also a considerable number of Methodists, presbyterians are but thinly scattered, — rode after sermon 7 or 8 miles to Mr. Harrison Davis's on my way to Hopkins-ville Christian County.

Monday Novem. 1st —rode twenty eight miles to Hopkins-ville expecting to preach the day following, but found

my appointment had not reached the place for that purpose, found the Court of Claims was sitting at that time,
& it was thought it would not be expedient to make an appointment for that day, being also informed that Mr.
Blackburn[21] had forwarded an appointment for administering the Sacrament of the Supper at that place the ensuing
Sabbath, I concluded to attend with him — on the Occasion, but in the interim determined to visit a destitute
neighbourhood or two, in each of which there were a few
presbyterian families, therefore

Tuesday   2nd — rode 19 miles to a Mr. Garvins being
near to the publick road from Hopkin's-ville to Russelville in Logan County, appointed to preach the day following —

Wednesday 3rd — preached to a small but apparently
attentive collection of people, some of the young people
were in tears.   The same evening at the lighting of the
candle attended a social meeting, about a mile from this
place, gave an exhortation, & united in prayer & praise
with a few praying members of society. —

Thursday 4th — rode about 8 or 9 miles to a Mr. Hay-
good's had an appointment made, &

Friday 5th preached to a few, there appeared due attention paid; I had not ventured to say any thing to them at
this place, nor had I at any former place publicity on the
propriety of contributing to the support of the missionary
fund, yet from a very few, who had long since been impressed with the propriety of supporting the Gospel Ministry, gave me three dollars; after sermon I rode eleven

[21] Gideon Blackburn had been a pupil of Doak and Henderson, and was
licensed by the Presbytery of Abingdon in 1792. He became the pastor of
the Maryville congregation (1794) which was placed in the Presbytery of
Union in 1800. In 1811 he removed to Franklin, taking charge of Harpeth
Academy, and preaching in rotation at five different places within a range of
fifty miles. At each of these he organized a church. It was while engaged
in this work that his path crossed that of the writer of this Journal. Blackburn is perhaps best known for his fine work in organizing the mission
among the Cherokee Indians. He served as President of Centre College
from 1827-1830. Gillett, *op. cit.*, I, p. 429; II, pp. 202-204, 308.

or twelve miles, toward Hopkins-ville, to attend the Sacramental Occasion —

Saturday 6th rode ten miles to Hopkins-ville. Mr. Blackburn had preached there the preceding day. I preached on Saturday, to a considerable audience — Mr. Blackburn then ordained four Elders, & constituted a church to be known by the name of Hopewell — & afterward preached at the lighting of the candle —

Sab. 7th. Mr. Blackburn preached — I introduced the Ordinance & served two tables. Mr. Blackburn one. I preached at the lighting of the Candle.

Monday 8th — Mr. Blackburn preached; afterward I administered the Ordinance of Baptism, baptizing two children, then gave a concluding address, inculcating a careful attention to the discharge of relative duties I received at this place five Dollars seventy five cents for the Missionary Fund — the presbyterian interest appeared in a detached, unorganized state in this part of the Country, however there appears the Prospect of another church being formed in this County — it appears that several have been led off from the presbyterian church by that part of the old Cumberland P.b.y. who had been declared by Synod as having no authority derived from the presbyterian Church to preach the Gospel; which appears to have been done in several instances by their giving a very uncandid and fallacious representation of the conduct of Synod & its commission toward them — after they had been dissolved — they recreated themselves or constituted a P.b.y., progressed in licensing & ordaining Preachers,[22] until they have amounted to 12 or 13 ordained preachers — with several licentiates & candidates — they have divided themselves into three Presbyteries — Logan P.b.y. Cumberland P.b.y. & Elk River P.b.y.— & constituted themselves into a Synod — rode from Hopkins-ville this evening 14 or 15 miles on my way toward Nashville had appointments forwarded by

[22] Further details of this interesting movement will be found in the extracts from the Minutes of the Cumberland Presbytery (1802-1806) printed in Chapter VII of this volume.

Mr. Blackburn toward Nashville — lodged at Jnº. Gilmore's —

Tuesday 9th — went two miles to a Capt. Jno. Davis's it being a very wet evening there were but few convened, I preached & baptized a child —

Wednesday 10th rode 14 or 15 miles to a Mr. Mitchels on the Sulphur Fork of Red River; here, had just entered the Tennessee state, but it being a very wet day, found but two or three persons collected exclusive of the family. I did not preach —

Thursday 11th, I rode fifteen miles to Springfield, in Robison County, found their Court sitting, had no other opportunity but to preach in a new open House, I did so, the day was considerably cold, there were but few ventured to attend, I do not know that there was a single Presbyterian present, the Professors in this county are chiefly Baptists & Methodists, after sermon rode 7 or 8 miles to a Mr. McMurry's —

Friday 12th — rode 9 or 10 miles to Squire Watton's, but found my appointment for preaching at that place had not circulated (this is about 2 miles from where Mr. Stone lives) I did not preach, but rode on 13 miles to Nashville, lodged at Mr. Grundy's a member of Congress, finding Mr. Blackburn would preach in the place the ensuing Sab. I rode on Saturday the 13th to Judge Stuarts within two miles of Franklin Williamson County, this town is about 18 miles from Nashville, it was late in the evening when I arrived, but the Judge was officious in circulating Notice for sermon the ensuing Day.

Sab. 14th. preached at the Court House in Franklin rode after Sermon three miles to a Mr. Hamilton's.

Mon. 15th. returned to Mr. Blackburns within a mile of Franklin, & then rode 16 miles to Mr. James Lockridge's on my way toward Columbia in Maury County.

Tuesday 16th rode 5 miles to David Longs, preached there at the lighting of the candle to a few of his near neighbours —

Wednesday 17th — rode ten miles to Columbia from

there 7 miles across Big-bay to the Revd. Jas. Stephenson's in Frierson's Settlement had given partial notice for preaching on the next day, but Thursday morning was so inclement that it was thought proper to countermand the appointment, I did not leave this place until Friday morning the 19th I rode 18 miles to a small Society on Big Creek a Water of Elk-river, in Giles County to which place together with Pulaski the seat of Justice of s'd county, I had endeavoured to forward to each of these places from Columbia, but found when I arrived the appointments had failed in reaching each of them, however had an appointment circulated on Friday Evening, & preached on Saturday at Big-spring to a much larger collection of people than I expected, they appeared serious and attentive, but nothing remarkable — rode the same Evening 7 or 8 miles into the Neighbourhood of some Presbyterians on Robison's Creek —

Sab. 21st rode between ten & eleven miles to Pulaski & finding my appointment had not reached the place, had notice speedily circulated thro the town, the inhabitants of the place were shortly convened. I preached to them pretty lengthily they appeared to give an apparently more serious attention than is usual for the Inhabitants of little towns on the Frontiers; returned ten miles the same evening & fulfilled an appointment I had left for preaching in the morning, the evening being very wet, there were but few attended but some of them appeared to hear the Word gladly the preaching here was in the Night — In this part of the country like most other there is considerable diversity, some adhering to the Presbyterians, some to the Baptists, some to the Methodists, & some to the irregular & unauthorized part of the old Cumberland P.b.y., however there are a few Presbyterian societies in this part regularly organized, & others have it in prospect — staid Monday at Wm. Prices

Tuesday 23rd. rode twenty miles to old Mr. Baldriges on Globe Creek a branch of Fountain Creek, had no opportunity of having People collected for preaching, it being a wet day and night.

Wednesday 24th rode ten miles to a Mr. Allen Liefers living on the S.W. Fork of Rock-creek, it rained exceptionally hard upon me the greatest part of the way The creek was swimming. & no opportunity of passage, I was courteously invited to tarry. I did so. I found myself in the bounds of a regularly organized congregation, where Mr. Morrison[23] a member of W. Tennessee P.b.y. had been preaching as an hirling or supply for eighteen months or more, but was informed there was no prospect of his regular settlement among them; there are two other small congregations in connection with them; there were a few of the neighbours convened at the lighting of the candle. I preached to them, there was a solemn attention given, & a few affected. It was concluded that the water would be impassable the next day and the people appeared very anxious to hear more preaching — I appointed to preach at the same place the next day — as extensive notice was given as could for the state of the waters —

Thursday 25th preached to a considerable number of people, it appeared to be a very affecting, & refreshing time to many, much the most so that I had witnessed in my missionary tour — a considerable number shed many tears, & a few exclaimed aloud in accents of joy; I understood after the assembly had been dismissed that there were several in conversing among them who were wondering whether there was any probability I would leave my own charges, etc—

Friday 26th rode 18 miles to the waters of Spring-creek on the South side of Williamson County, lodged at Wm. Ligates —

Sat. 27th rode twenty seven miles to Jefferson, in Rutherford County, crossed Duck River, & the W. Fork of Stone River, had an appointment made for preaching in Jefferson the ensuing day.

[23] Rev. Andrew S. Morrison, who had become a member of the West Tenn. Presbytery shortly before this. He was located at Bethesda. *Min. of Gen. Assem.*, 1814, p. 209.

Sab. 28th preached to the inhabitants of the town with some few others, altho the day was cold there was a more than usual attendance by the inhabitants of that place, & considerable attention given but nothing farther worthy of being particularized — Monday 29th rode 25 miles to a Mr. Ross's on my way toward Shiloh, in Sumner County — Tuesday 30th — crossed the Cumberland River, called on Mr. Hodges, passed thro' Gallatine, & arrived at Henry Neils, riding this day 18 miles, had an appointment made for preaching at Neils the ensuing day —

Wednesday *December 1st* preached to 40 or 50 persons, the audience was attentive — When passing thro' Nashville I had opportunity of forwarding a few appointments into Kentucky to be fulfilled on my way homeward — the 1st was at a Mrs Bibb's [?] meeting house about 6 or 7 miles from Russelville which was on the first day of December, but owing to obstructions by high water & otherwise, I was unavoidably prevented from being able to reach the place, of course was hurried on to reach my next appointments.

Thursday *2* — rode 30 miles to a Mr. Joshua Owings in Logan County Kentucky, a part of the country in which there are no Presbyterians —

Fri. *3* rode twelve Miles to Sam.Evans's near Judge Skiles in Warren County —

Sat. *4*th rode eight Miles to a Widow Reeds near Shaker Town, on the Waters of Gasper River, but the Day being wet there were very few attended, there are scarcely any Presbyterians in the Neighbourhood, no Shakers present,[24] I preached on the subject directly opposed to a part of their scheme

Sab. *5*th preached at Judge Skiles to a numerous, but mixed multitude, there was a decent & close Attention given, a few gave Evidence of their feeling themselves interested in the subject — from a few having expressed a Desire, they could have preaching in the evening, I appointed to preach at Mr. Abner Evans, who lived in sight of Skiles,

[24] For an interesting account of this movement see the article in *The Pageant of America*, p. 243.

at the lighting of the Candle — I did so, there were not very many present, owing probably, to the Appointment being made somewhat dubiously, together with its being in the Night, & the roads being in a slouhy state; out of the few present there were some affected — I likewise appointed to preach in Boling-Green on Monday Evening at the lighting of the Candle, it was thought the most proper time as it was their Court Day —

Mon, 6th   rode between 4 & 5 miles to Boling-green, the Streets being in a very muddy state there were but very few females present, the principal part of the Audience were Lawyers, Storekeepers, & Mechanics men as I supposed of corrupt Minds — I preached and had unexpectedly, a decent, & marked Attention —

Tuesday 7th — rode fifteen Miles to Sqr. Wallace's at Pilot Knob —

Wednesday 8th   preached at Do. the day being wet, & there being no Presbyterians in the Neighbourhood but one family except Wallace's, there were enuf present, however I preached, there was an interested attention given, some affected.   after sermon rode eight miles to a Mr. Gatewoods living on the Lexington Road from Boling Green —

Thursday 9th rode thirty-five Miles to my Brother's at Green Town in Green County, there tarried until Saturday Morning; rode that Day twenty six miles to Mrs. McElroy's in Hardin's Creek Congregation, where I found Mr. Hall[25] had an appointment for the next day —

Sab. 12th   preached to a considerable Assembly that appeared serious, & attentive — rode after Sermon eight Miles to a Mr. Cunningham's —

Monday 13th   rode twenty two miles to Harrodesburg where I had intended to have preached that Night but the Evening being cold, & withal no moonlight, it was thought there could be but very few collected   I declined therefore making the attempt —

[25] Nathan H. Hall was licensed by the Transylvania Presbytery in 1805 and was serving as pastor of the Springfield and Hardin's Creek Churches in 1813. *Min. Transylvania Presby.*, IV, p. 59; *Extracts Gen. Assem. Min.*, 1814, p. 202.

Tuesday *14*th   rode rode 28 or 30 miles to Lexington, as the ordinary time of preaching in this place exclusive of the Lord's day is on Wednesday Night   I made no attempt of preaching—

Wednesday — rode Home being 36 miles, & thro' the tender Mercies of God, found my Family in Health, after an absence of sisty-six days.

[Second Preaching Tour].

1814

Tuesday the *20*th of *Sept. 1814* — I set out to fulfill a Month of a Missionary Tour assigned me by the Genl. Assembly of our Church last May — rode 25 miles to a Mr. McChords on the Waters of Muddy Creek, Madison County, south side of Kentucky River, had an appointment made & on

Wed. *21*st preached to a small assembly chiefly of the presbyterian Persuasion, there was a decent & solemn Attention given, after Sermon baptized 4 children, rode this Evening 18 miles to Colo' Barretts on my way to Paint Lick —

Thurs. *22*nd.   rode 8 miles to Paint Lick Church a vacancy in our Connection, in Garrett County   The Morning being wet, but few attended — I preached, & I trust not unprofitably — I appointed the Administration of the Sacrament of the Supper to be at this place on the 3rd Sab. of October, lodged this Evening at Mr. Jno. Henderson's, one Mile from the Meeting House —

Fri. *23*rd rode 7 or 8 Miles to Lancaster, the Seat of Justice of this county, for want of general Notice & being the time of Court, but few attended — I preached in the Seminary there was a decent & respectful attention given — there is no church regularly organized in this place, but a prospect that there will, there are a few Friends to Presbyterianism, in, & around this place, they have instituted a subscription paper & raised about a thousand Dollars for building a Meeting House, I left an Appointment for preaching at this place on Friday the 14th of October; rode to Mr. Jno. Lapsley's —

Sat. 24th rode 9 or 10 Miles to Buffalow Spring, Lincoln County, near Stanford — preached to a considerable Congregation, an interested Attention was given by a goodly number — having in prospect the Administration of the Supper on the ensuing Day —

Sab. 25th I delivered a Discourse appropriate to the Occasion, to which there appeared in general, a close solemn, & in some Instances an affectionate Attention given, after which (Mr. Finley[26] being present) he introduced the Ordinance, & served the first table I the second, & afterward giving a short Address closed the publick Solemnities of the Evening, lodged this Evening with Mr. Finley about 5 miles from the Meeting House —

Mon. 26th — rode 10 or 11 Miles to Mr. Jas. McGills on my Way to Pulaski County, & had Appointments forwarded.

Tues, 27th rode 11 Miles & preached at a Mr. Beaties in Pulaski C[i]t[y], the Notice being short, the audience was but small, there are but few Presbyterians in this place, there was however respectful attention given in the general & a few affected lodged here this Night.

Wed. 28th rode 9 miles to Somersett, preached a considerable Number of People, the Audience was attentive but nothing remarkable appeared. Here the majority of Professors are Baptists, there are a few presbyterian Families, in, & around the place, after Sermon rode 10 miles escorted by Col°. Newel's to his House, who had attended sermon partly for this Purpose, where I had forwarded an appointment for preaching the ensuing day —

Thurs, 29th preached at Col°. Newel's in Wayne County the audience but small, owing in a measure as I was informed to the shortness of the warning, & previous arrangements of a domestic nature; the people were attentive but nothing remarkable appeared — there are but very few

[26] Rev. Samuel Finley (not to be confused with Dr. Samuel Finley, Principal of the Nottingham School and later President of Princeton) was a member of the Transylvania Presbytery, and was pastor of the Buffalo Spring Congregation in 1814. *Min. Transylvania Presby.,* IV, p. 59.

Presbyterians in this Neighbourhood — tarryed this night also at this place

Fri. *30th* rode 10 miles to Golston's meeting house which belongs to the Baptist Society, but found when I arrived that either for want of disposition, or opportunity the appointment had not circulated, of course did not preach, but being informed that a monthly meeting of the Baptists would be at that place on the ensuing day, I went to Mr. Simpson's a Presbyterian, about two Miles from the place, & lodged that night, returned the next day, & being pressingly, tho, politely, invited, by the stated Preacher of the church, I preached to a considerable audience, had a general close attention, yet nothing appeared worthy of remark, unless it was the friendly respect there was paid to me, I did not learn there was more than one Presbyterian family present; returned to Mr. Simpsons this evening

the Cty Town of Wayne

Sab. October 2 — rode 5 miles to Montecello & preached to about 60 or 70 people but owing to the stated monthly meeting of the Baptists at Golston's about 5 miles from this place, together with knowledge of the appointment not having sufficiently circulated, were the reasons suggested why the audience was not larger, there were but very few of presbyterian sentiment present, there was general attention but perhaps in no instance a more than ordinary evidence, by any, of their feeling themselves interested in the subject discussed — left an appointment at this place for the administration of the Sacrament of the Supper on the ensuing Sabbath — rode 12 miles to a Mr. Jno. Duffey's —

Mon. 3d. preached at a Mr. Turners, about a mile from this place, on the leading road from Montecello to Stockton's Valley, in Cumberland County, the Audience was small but some affection appeared, lodged this night also at Duffey's

Tues, 4, rode ten miles to a Mr. Robt Poage's in Stockton's Valley, Cumberland County — There was here a respectful & in some instances an interested attention given, appointed preaching again at this place the ensuing Friday, tarried here until Thursday Morning — then rode 9 miles to a Misses Campbell's whose Husband deceased last spring, & preached to about 70, or 80 persons they were attentive, & some apparently solemn, Mr. Hall arrived during Sermon & preached after I had done, tarried here this night —

Fri. 7th. We rode 9 miles to Mr. Poage's, & both preached to about 40 persons they were generally attentive & some affected after sermon I baptized a child for a widow Prowl, we then rode 10 or 12 miles to a Mr. Duffey's our way to Montecello where I had appointed the Administration of the Sacrament —

Sat. 8th   rode 12 miles to Monticello we both preached to about 40 people   there was a solemn attention given

Sab. 9th   I preached to a considerable assembly of people on a subject appropriate to the occasion.   Mr. Hall introduced the Ordinance & administered at the 1st table, and I at the second, there were about 28 or 30 communicants, there was in general a solemnity — & in some instances affection, I understood there were a few Methodists communed, there are but few Presbyterians in this part of the country   the Professors are chiefly Baptists, & they chiefly of the separate & socinian Party —

Monday 10th — Mr. Hall preached & supported the Divinity of X^t, & baptized infants & evinced at considerable length his right of doing so, I had intended an address on the relative Duties of religion, but the day being considerably elapsed, & having a considerable distance[,] 10 miles[,] to ride this evening, I found it impracticable, therefore declined — I received at this place $2.87½ — rode 15 miles to Colo. Newelles —

Tues. 11th at Colo. Newelles preached to about 25 or 30 persons there was a decent and solemn attention given, I baptized an infant for Mrs Evans a Daughter of Colo. Newelles, I then rode 8 or 9 miles to a Mr. Jones in Pulaski County & preached at the lighting of the candle to, about

40 persons there was a very close, & in some instances an apparently interested attention given —

Wed, 12th, rode 5 miles to Somersett, I preached to a considerable audience there was a decent & respectful attention given, I afterward baptized 3 children for a Mr. Palmer, I here received a compliment of $2.25 — after Sermon I rode 9 miles to Mr. Beaties & preached to between 40 & 50 persons, there was generally solemnity, & a few affected — lodged here —

Thurs, 13th rode 11 miles to Mr. McGills & preached to a small audience of about 30 persons they were attentive but nothing notable appeared, after sermon rode 10 miles to Mr. Findley's —

Fri 14th rode 14 or 15 miles to Lancaster in Gerrard County & preached to about an 100 persons there was a decent & very close attention given, after Sermon rode 7 miles to Mr. Jas. Henderson's, two miles from Paint Lick meeting house

Sat. 15th, preached at Paint Lick to a considerable audience there was a general, solemn, & in some instances an interested attention given, the assembly was then dismissed & chiefly removed to a Mr. Reid's about half a mile from the meeting house, & Mr. Findley preached a sermon after which I baptized 3 children for a son of Mr. Reids whose wife lately died — there were several considerably affected during the Administration of the Ordinance —

Sab., 16th, preached to a numerous, attentive, & solemn audience previous to the communion — The Ordinance was afterward by the Rev. Saml. Findley — the Table was filled 3 times, there were about 75 communicants, it was a solemn, and & many instances an affectionate communion

Mon 17th I preached again at the same place to a considerable, & very attentive audience afterward there was a contribution made, out of which I recevied $7.62½ for the Missionary Fund — rode this evening 15 miles to Richmond in Madison County, & preached at the lighting of the Candle to a few of the inhabitants of the place & its vicinity, I was informed that the knowledge of the Appointment had very imperfectly circulated, I could not learn that there was a Professor in the Village, tarried here this night Tues, 18th rode 10 miles to old Mr. McChords, & preached to a small but very attentive audience, they were chiefly of the Presbyterian persuasion, after sermon rode 12 miles to Winchester in Clark County — & on

Wed. 19th rode Home, and thro, the good Providence of God found my Family in Health —

CHAPTER XVIII

TWO PRESBYTERIAN FRONTIER AUTOBIOGRAPHIES

1. The Autobiography of Peter Van Arsdale.
2. The Autobiography of J. Allen.

1. THE AUTOBIOGRAPHY OF PETER VAN ARSDALE

[Peter Van Arsdale, whose brief autobiography[1] follows, was of Dutch ancestry, the first of his family in America having settled on Long Island in 1653. On the death of Van Arsdale's father in Mercer County, Kentucky, in 1802 the family was left destitute and Peter was bound out at fifteen to a blacksmith where he remained until his twenty-first year. During these bitter years of legal bondage Peter developed a fierce hatred of slavery which later led him to take his family from Kentucky to Illinois. The autobiography tells the story of a young Kentucky blacksmith of serious mind, who became prosperous, joined the New Providence Presbyterian Church and soon was a leading man in the community as well as an elder in the church. His son, James Harvey Van Arsdale, describes his father as "a great reader and deep thinker, and ever ready to act out his conviction . . . and as the peer of any member of the Session of that Church, in business or ecclesiastical proceedings."[2] At this time (about 1825) the New Providence congregation was worshipping in a large country church building 65 by 40 feet, with a large gallery for colored folks. The pastor, Dr. Thomas Clelland, lived on a farm within a half mile of the church, and served the congregation for forty years.]

1844) As I expect my children and other Relatives to begin the world poor, as I have done. I have thought proper to make a record of a few facts and circumstances connected with my beginning in early life. In order that they may not be discouraged because they happen to have

---

[1] The original manuscript of this autobiography is in the Indiana State Library and is published with the consent of Mrs. S. V. Helliwell of Milwaukee, Wisconsin, a granddaughter of Peter Van Arsdale.

[2] From a letter written by James Harvey Van Arsdale, only son of Peter Van Arsdale, to his daughter, Mrs. Harlan Page Carson, Huron, S. D., August, 1890.

but little of this worlds goods.   Peter Vanarsdall.   My
Father died in Mercer County Kentucky a short time before
I was fifteen years old.   he left no property not even a
home for my widdoed Mother, this was in the fall.   during
the winter I remained with my Mother working for her
benefit, and part of the time for my oldest brother to pay
him for sometime spent for my benefit as my guardian. —
the next Spring by order of court. I was bound an Apprentice to the blacksmith business, till I should be twenty one
years of age, wich would be nearly six years. — for that
sirvise I was to have Schooling including the single rule of
three, and a suite of clothes, and also a hors saddle and
bridle with one hundred dollars, — the Schooling and clothing I never got, the hors & saddle, and some pay for the
lack of Schooling, I got after a good deal of delay, and
difficulty.— — The man to whom I was bound became de-
rangd and I worked out the last year of my time with another man. — — My time was up as an Aprentice on the
20th day of December 1808. — I then spent a Month or
two with my Brotherinlaw Cornelious Demaree. and went
to School a short time. at the Stone Schoolhous on Harrods
run, to Dr. Samuel R. Demaree. — — — during the winter.
I made an agreement with my oldest Brother, Cornelious,
to build a Shop and other cabbins on his land. on the then
main road from Frankfort to Harrodsburgh, three miles
from the latter, this I was to keep for Six years. — — Accordingly I borrowed an ax and commenced work on the
20th day of Febuary 1809.   I cut logs built a Shop, cut coal-
wood and burnt coals, had a bellows made hired some tools
borrowed some. and began to work as a blacksmith on the
20th day of March   I then set in a rule not to go in Debt
however needy I might be unless it was for materials to
work on that I could turn into money; that Sumer I was so
destitute of clothing. and not able to buy that my relatives
pityed me. and my old mother and two youngest Sisters
made me a Suit of cotten, I was not even able to buy molds
for buttens, but made them myself.   I continued to work
hard late and early. the Same fall the 16th of September

I was married. and in about Six weeks after I got my cabbin ready and moved my wife home. Our property then consisted of one hors beest, two cows given to my wife by her father, he also was so good as to give her a table a beadstead, and some other houshold furniture so that we could begin on a very Small Scale, to keep hous. When I began to keep hous, I found that I needed so many things that I had not the means to buy. that I remember well that I then thought that if I only had what was necessary to keep hous with conseenscience. I would not want to own land. But I have long since found that I was mistaken for I was no nigher being sattisfied when I owned near five hundred acres of land and lived in a good brick hous. — — — — — —
But I continued to work hard, and to lay by every dollar I could Spare. till about the first 1813 I had loaned out two hundred and sixty dollars and had gethered some property, and was out of debt. — — — I was very fond to read and during the year 1810 myself and two others took a news paper, "the Kentucky Reporter", and I have continued to take a paper of some kind and sometimes two or three ever sinc. — my good Brotherinlaw John Curry also took pleasure in furnishing me with books to read and borrowed for me Bishop Newton on the prophecies wich I read with considerable intrest. I went through it 2 volumes 500 pages each in one winter season although I worked every night in my Shop till 8 oclock accept Saterday night. I have reason to hope that the reading of that work was of servis to me.
The beginning of the year 1813 I found that I had work enough to employ two hands beside myself. I then hired another set of tools and had Clarkson E Randolph and John Adams as apprentices. — — — — during the Summer I worked very hard. and had a good deal Standing. out and about the first of August I was taken sick with the feaver and entirely confined for five or 6 months and unable to do any work, till the next Spring 1814. And when I was able to get about I found myself crippled by a Swelled leg. occasioned by the feaver. wich afterwards brok out into a sore, from wich I have Suffered very much at different times ever-

sinc. —————— When I first got able to work after the spell of fever and I became very much dissatisfied where I was living we having then two children living and having already buried two. I began to look about for a State of Society where I would like to rais my children. And I finaly bought an old farm 197 acres on Salt river for wich I pd $656 in the neighbourhood of New providence meeting hous. I moved to that place the fouteenth day of September 1814. and left it the fourteenth day of September 1836 having occupied it just twenty two year. —— this place had for a long time belonged to orphan hiers, and been rented out untill there was scarcely any fenc on it and very much grown up with briars and besides it was very rockey. So that it had obtained the name of Stoney Batted. ———— Here we began by moving some old cabbins and building others. and fencing, and clearing up the old fields & etc & etc from September 1814 till September 1816. I had built a cabbin to live in a kitchen a hardlog smoke hous, a long log Shop. and a Stable and also a long Stone Spring hous over a good Spring — that fall in September I left my Shop in the care of C. E Randolph and James Anderson, the latter an apprentice) and took a journey to Missouri in company with the following persons (viz) James McAfee James Buckhanan Robert McKamey and Jacob Banta, we took a pack hors to carry provison and laid out all the time we traveled through Indiana and Illinois and about two hundred miles up the Missouri river, and then back almost the same rout that we went out. In 4 years ater James McAfee and Robert McKamey removed to Missouri. James Buckhanan had some time before removed to Indiana; Jacob Banta sometime after removed to Illinois. and I settled in Taswell County. After I got home I was much discouraged about living on poor land but could not think of moving out with my family to a new and unsettled region where there would not for a long time be any prospect of good Society. I according went on to improve my place by making a paling round my garden planting trees & etc. I had before in the Spring 1815 planted a small orchard wich supplyd us with plenty of good fruit while we remained on the place. — The year 1818 was an important era in our history. we had for several years before been reading and thinking on the Subject of Religion. as I have before remarked, I had read Newton on the prophesies and it had led me to believe that the Scripturs were of divine origin About the year 1814 Dr. Cleland began to circulate among the congregation at new providen a great many good books. he enduced them to buy books by selling them at cost and carriage. I got at that time the Village Sermons. and Village dialogues, and a good many others, among them "Simpsons plea for Religion this latter work made an impresion on my mind that I could not get clear of. — I continued to read various things on the Subject of Religion, among others Ridgleys Body of divinity. from all of them I cam to the conclusion that the moderate Calvinistic view of the Subject was the correct one, and I thought nearest the Scripture in general. Accordingly in August 1818 myself and wife united with the presbyterian church at new Providence and had out four children baptized, (viz) Ida Phebe James Hervey and Jane. we finally had all our children baptized by the same man.

1818 During this year I began to be so pleased with the Society around me that I concluded to build and remain where I was. I accordinly that fall put up a small fram dweling hous, with a view of building larger afterwards. and then using that as a kitchen, which we afterwards did, for want of means and other reasons I did not finish the small frame hous for seven years afterwards, for some time past I had been perplexed about the subject of Slavery Expecially now when I saw nearly all the different Religious denominations owning Slaves, but more of that hereafter. In the year 1819 my self and wife went on a visit to Indian[a] to see a Brother of my wifes Daniel Demaree. who had settled in Switzerland County not far from the mouth of the Kentucky River at that visit we spent a week or more. I mentioned my journeys and visits to show that we were not unsociable amid all our efforts to get along in the world. —— In 1820 I built a larg frame Smoke hous, and continued to make improvements on my farm by making new fields fencing etc. —— I had for a long time wished to live in town on account of being in the midst of society and social intercours. but I could not think of living in a town in a Slave State. therefore I was constantly looking for some suitable place in the free States that were then settleing to get a location. — during the Summer 1821 the town of Indianapolis was Advertized for sale. About the first of October, a number of us concluded to attend that Sale, accordingly we made up a larg company of the Smocks Demotts and etc. and we took a waggon to carry our provision, and other lugage, we had a company of ten. Six were connected with the waggon four rode on horsback, and campd together every night — but when we got to the town site, the Sale was postponed for a few day. Some of the company looked about the country and entered land, on wich they afterwards Settled. as I was disappointed in the sale of the lots, and not being prepared to buy land, I concluded to go with another company to visit the Wabash Country, that company consisted of the following persons (viz) John Smock, John Comingore, Cornelious Demaree, George King, Simon Covert a Mr Hannah & a Mr Shannon. We traveled north west from Indianapolis till we struck Sugartree creek. then we divided into two compannies, four went on the north side of the creek, and four on the south side with an agreement to meet at the mouth on the Wabash River, and there report what each compan[y] had seen. the four on the south (viz) Smock Comingore Demaree and myself again divided, Comingore and Demaree went on to meet the other company at the mouth of Sugartree creek Smock and myself turned south untill we struck the head water of little Raccoon then down that stream till we came to the Settlement During that journey we saw no inhabitants from tuseday morning early near Indianapolis till friday evening when we came to a solitary family on Sugar Creek near the Wabash. —— — But as I have left a journal of all that journey among my

paper I will refer to that we finaly all got together on big
Raccoon Creek at the hous of old Samuel Adams. there
we spent a night together, and then again separated. King
Covert Hannah and Shanon took the nearest rout through
Indiana to Madison on the Ohio, and then home The
others (viz) Smock Commingore Demaree and myself took
down the Wabash to Vincennes thenc through the country
to the main White River into Dubois County to some Relatives and acquaintenances, where we spent a few days, and
then took the rout by Louisville home; having been gone
over or about Six weeks. At that time I dont recollect
who I had in the Shop or on the farm to work. — — During the year 1822 I was busily engaged having shingles
made, and hauling timbers to the sawmill and geting materials ready for building, wich I intended to do so soon
as the limber should seasoned. during this year I finished
myself a new waggon. that was the first I had ownd a
waggon, having always hired my hauling done or hired a
waggon, although I had now kept hous for thirteen years.
My Brotherinlaw Isaac Smock who lived near to me furnished some horses, and I furnished some and waggon, and
he was the driver. with this arangment I felt quite Independent, and we made a good many trips to Louisville
with our own produce and for others — — — This year
also my Brotherinlaw John Curry spent a good deal of
time at my hous making shingles for me. he had lost his
wife (my wifes oldest sister.) and had rented out his farm.
He was an excellent man perty well read, Especialy on
doctrinal points in Religion the same fall he married the
second time, to my Niece Timmy Smock. — —
1823 Early in the Spring of this year My Brotherinlaw
Isaac B Smock sold out a small farm he owned near me
determining to move to Indiana somewhere in the Region
of Indianapolis. As we had been raisd together, and had
been long very intimate, and he had Married my wifes
younger sister and as our wives were very much attatched
to each other, we all found that it would be very hard to
separate. According Smock proposed to loan me two hun-

dred dollars of his sale money, in order that I might go
out with him, and if we could be suited to settle near each
other.— According to this arangment we made prepera-
tions. And started to Indiana some time in May My
Nephew John B Smock also went with us. he had sold his
farm in Mercer County near Harrodsburgh. — — We
went first to Brookvill on whitewater, where the Land
Office was then kept. we there got a plat of the Country
from Indianapolis sout, taking several townships on the
Road leading to Madison on the Ohio. We then went
and selected pieces of land. Isaac Smock and John B Smock
found land to pleas them on the main road then just being
opened. I selected a piece of land adjoining Isaac Smock
on the west, on account of a very fine spring on it. We
then had to go back to Brookvill to make the entries and
then back home having been gone three or four weeks. I
then intended to move to that part of Indiana, as my Brotherinlaw John Curry had also exchanged his land on Salt
River for land in the same Region in Indiana. And we
thought again to live Neighbours in a free state. But how
uncertain are all human calculations. — — That fall John
Curry Died and his only son a very promising Boy. About
the same time Isaac Smock and some others of the Smocks
moved to Indiana. And at the Request of the widow of
John Curry I Administerd on his estate which gave me
considerable employment and trouble as it was the time
of the Cominwealth Bank of Kentucky.
1824 this year was one of considerable interest to me.
My Brotherinlaw John Smock, Husband of my oldest sister died in August, and at the Request of the widow and the
family Cornelious Demaree and myself Administered on the
estate. As soon as the property of Smocks estate was disposed of, Myself and wife started on horsback on a visit
to our Friends in Indiana, carrying with us our daughter
Susan then about Six months old. — — In that visit I
began to look more seriously at the difficulties of Making
a farm in a very heavey timbered country such as the one
in wich our friends had settled. My wife also seeing the

difficulties that those had to encounter that had settled
there. it very much abated our anxiety to move to a new
country. Especialy as I had no help of boys as we had but
one son than only seven years old. — — — In this state
of mind we returned home, begining to think of fixing up
some more buildings to accomodate our family as we then
had six children the oldst more than twelve years old during
the winter 1824-5 nothing of intrest occurd that I can remember. — — — 1825 this Spring I gethered up some
lumber and finished the frame hous that I had put up seven
years before, making it into Rooms above and having it
plastered, and whitewashed and I had also built a kitchen
ajoining it, some time before. — — this fall Isaac Smock
and wife from Indiana paid us a visit, and we then engaged
a season of kind social intercours long to be remembered. — —

1826 — In the fall of this year My old Fatherinlaw Cornelious Demaree, Clarkson E. Randolph, and myself took
a trip to Indiana as far as Indianapolis. and among our
Relations in that Region My object was to induc or persuade Clarkson E. Randolph to get a good situation on the
main Road, and engage as a Blacksmith as he had to land
in Kentucky. On the way Back we visited our Relations
in Switzerland County and spent a few days among them
including the Sabbath. — — nothing of intrest occured
during the remainder of that year that I Recollect. — —

1827) During this year in August my friend and Neighbour Clark McAfee died. he was an Elder in Providence
Church. during that fall I was elected an elder in his
place. — The situation of the church at that time was very
prosperous in our Neighbourhood and as some of our children had already joined the Church I began to think I
had better give out moving from so good a state of society.
Especialy as we had generly a school in that Region. And
I was anxious to give my children an education. — — From
all these considerations, and also the sickness that obtained
among our Relatives in Indiana, and the difficulties that
they had to encounter in various ways in the region where

we had intended to settle. we began again to make prepartions to build a good dwelling hous. during that fall and winter I gethered up lumber and made arangements to built the next Summer. — — — —

1828) The Spring of this year I employed a man to make brick and burn them, and got all the meterials ready to build a hous thirty six feet long by twenty wide. And during the Spring Sumer and fall I had the brick made and burnt and the walls put up, and the carpenters work done so far as to enclose the whole. And two rooms finished so far as to winter in them. this I had done, and at the same time made a crop on the farm, and kept my shop a going also. At that time I had Samuel Black Son of old Mr John Black as an Apprentice. I now had my hous under way so that I could use it, and finish it as I might be able. Nothing more occurd this year to notice. —

1829) This Spring and Summer I began again to have my hous worked on, but did not finish and found it would involve me in Debt. During this fall my wife took a journey to Indiana, to see her sister and other Relatives. She went in company with Cornelious Covert and wife. I remaind at home. they stayed away some three weeks and would have stayed longer, but for the sickness of Coverts family which obliged him to return sooner than they intended. — — that fall the weather was very wet and the roads very heavy, the whole country where we intended to have moved to looked very discouraging, and my wife was again discouraged from Moving to Indiana, and I had determined not to move to any place where she would be dissatisfied.

1830) This year I finished my hous had it painted planted trees around the year[d] and etc — — during this fall of this year we had a visit from Henry Smock, and wife Isaac Smock and wife from Indiana, Robert McKamey from Missouri. this fall also was a time of considerable Revival in the Church at Providenc.

1831) During the Spring of this year our daughter Phebe was married to Thomas Derr — in the fall a company of

us consisting of the following persons again took a trip
to Indiana (viz) Daniel A Breeder Abraham Vanarsdall
Thomas Derr and myself, we started late in November,
and had a dredfull muddy time when we went, and a very
severe cold time when we returned.   At that time I entered
a fraction of land adjoining what I had there before.   I
had before in 1826 entered a simeral [sic] fraction all adjoining each of them containing 56 or 57 acres. — — —
On my Return home I brought with me my wifes half sister Sally Demaree.   And we had great difficulties getting
home on account of the Ice in the rivers.   Especialy in the
Ohio we found we could not cross at Madison, we then
went and spent a few days in Switzerland County among
our Relations.   And finaly crossed the Ohio river at Vevay,
and then could not cross the Kentucky River for the ice, and
had to travel over the Eagle Creek hills to Frankfort to the
Bridg — then home.   thus closed this year.

1832)   This Spring, our oldest daughter Ida was married
to George W. Cardwell.   And the same fall they moved
to the State of Missouri in company with William Smithey
and family one of our kind neighbours, thus that discription
of persons that we valued very much were leaving our
Region.   And greatly weaning or loosing our attatchments
to the neighbourhood.   Our Brother Isaac Smock had left
in 1823; our kind neighbours, the best of men with their
families the two McKameys had already removed to Missouri one in 1826; the other in 1828. — the Voorheeses,
and the Coverts, and many others had left our Society. —

1833)   Nothing occured in our familyes this year worth
noting that I now recollect.   In the Church and neighbourhood the Subject of Slavery began to be a good deal talked
of as this year the first Anti Slavery or Abolition Society
was formed at Philadelphia. — — — — — Before that
I had been attached to the Collonization Society hoping
that it would remove Slavery at least from the church
— — — — — in this year Jenk McAfe a member of Session of Providenc Church and Clerk of Session went as minister or Charge de Affairs to South America under General

Jackson. I was then appointed Clerk of Session in his stead in wich capacity I continued to act till I left the neighbourhood. — — — —

1834) As the Subject of Slavery had occupied a good many of our mind in the churches of Harrodsburgh and Providin[c]e and some of us became anxious to move to a free State with our families. Accordingly Cornelious Demaree of Harrodsburgh Church and myself then of Providinc concluded to take another journey through Indiana and Illinois, to see if we could ascertain where we ought to settle. Demaree already owned a good deal of land in Indiana, and I owned some. We left home about the first of April, traveled through Indiana, crossing the Wabash above Rankvill, and above the mouth of Sugartree Creek, thence through the State of Illinois, crossing the Illinois River at Peorie, and there into what is called the Military tract for some distance, where Demaree had some business with his Relation Denis Bice. we had also in company Samuel Demaree, son of Cornelious who went with us from Johnson County Indiana where he had engaged teaching School. — here we separated, I had determined to go over into Missouri to see my daughter Ida and family and other friends there. — Before we parted we agreed to meet again in I think two week at Dr. Blackburns at what is called Spring Cove on Macaupin Creek in Macaupin County. — I then traveled on through Knox County, McDonough Ct. Warren Ct. Handcock and Adams Counties to Quincy on the Missispy, here I crossd and traveled int Missouri as far as Paris in Monroe County. here I spent a few days with my Relations and old acquaintances. And then started back to meet my fellow travelers at Spring Cove. I traveled by Bowlingren to Clarksvill on the Missisipy River here I crossd and traveld through the counties of Pike and Calhoun to the Illinois River at the mouth of Apple Creek here I crossed over into Green County and between the River and the County Seat Carrollton I saw that discription of country that first determined me to settle in the State of Illinois. — — — — — I traveled on to

Spring Cove and arrived there the very day we had agreed
to meet each other; this was on Thursday, I then found
that Demaree had left there the Satterday before by way
of Springfield for home, as I then had no company I concluded to take a different rout home. I then traveled towards Alton, stopped at Brighton that night with Mr.
Griggs — then to Edwardsvill and then to Greenvill there
I spent the Lords day with some of my old acquaintances,
the Blacks. — — — —
from there I traveled on to Vandalie and to Vincenns
on the Wabash, then on to Louisville and so on home
having been absent from home about six week. my fellow traveler C. Demaree got into the same Region where
I lived the same evening I got home and got home the
next day. — — — the fall of this year there was a great
deal of discussion in our region on the Subject of Slavery.
In October the Synod of Kentucky met at Danville. I
attended as a deligate from Providenc Church. at this
Synod the Subject of Slavery came up, and there was a
great deal of Debating. And preparations made for considerable action, by appointing a larg Committe with John
Browers of Frankfort as Chairman and John C Young as
Secretary, but it all died away before the frowns of slav-
holders. — Here at Danville I first got acquainted with
James G Birney, and heard him give an anti-slavery lecture
in the old Presbyterian Church, while preaching was goin
on in the new church, there was a larg attendance to hear
Birney. But the rich slaveholding professors of religion
I think did not attend to hear the lecture, but rather gave
it the *Cold Sholder*. — — at that meeting of Synod, old
Archabald Cameron (from Shelby County) made a long
speech in favour of the practice of Slaveholding and tryd
hard to prove it to be right *from* the *Bible*.
1835) the beginning of this year there was a great deal
of debating in our region on the Subject of Slavery. Mr.
Birney came into the neighbourhood, spent a night or two
at my hous and debated the subject of Slavery at Providenc with Dr Cleland and others, on two different occations

at considerable lenth.   And very considerale impression
was made on some in the Neighbourhood, as Peter. R.
Dunn Esquire soon afterwards free[d] his slaves, and refused to hire any more Slave labour in his hemp factory or
otherwise. — — — —

During this fall my wife and son Hervey went on a visit
to Indiana, and spent some time there. and not being very
well pleasd with Indiana, on account of the difficulties of
opening a farm in that heavey timberd country. — I therefore began to think about moving to Illinois, and accod-
ingly offered my farm for sale that winter. — —
This far I written these sketches in July 1844, wile con-
find to the hous with a very sore ankle. I will therefore
begin where I then left off, it is now Febuary 1857, great
changes in 13 years.
In the begining of the year 1836 I sold my farm on Salt
river Mercer County Ky. to James P. Vanarsdall for
$2650.00, $2000 to be paid by the first march, $500 before
he got possession, the ballance to be paid in June 1837,
and I was to keep and have the use of the place till the next
October. — — in March 1836 the 20 day I started to Illinois in company with Dr William Robertson of Harods-
burgh. We left my hous early monday morning, had a very
cold stormy day went on horsback to Frankfort. there
we took the Stage to Louisville, then took a Steam boat
passage to St. Louis, there we took the Illinois Boats, the
Dr for Alton. I took passage to Columbiana on the Illinois river, I arived there in the night in company with
Capt Henry Merriwether, who had come on board the
Steamboat I was on at the mouth of the Comberland river.
The day was very rainy. I came on with Mr. Meriwether
and spent the night at his hous, the next day I went to my
Brother Simon M Vanarsdall — — I then looked about the
country a little, bought a hous and lot in Carrollton, and
80 acres of land a few miles east of Carrollton, and I will
just here remark that I gave for the hous & lot $750.00
& for the land $200.00   I kept the hous & lot some 12 or
15 years & sold it $250.00 and the land sometime after for

$250.00: after determining to move to that place I returned back to Kentucky and made preparations to move in the fall. during the Sumer George W. Cardwell his wife & child came from Missouri to Kentucky, and remaind with us till fall, and then we all came together to Carrollton Illinois. I then sold to Cardwell a waggon and two horses, and him and his family went on to Missoury. — We had left Kentucky the 22nd day of Septembr, had very wet & bad roads. it took us some three weeks to get to Carrollton. — — the Same fall in November 1836 I entered into partnership with David Peirson in a Store. Paid into the concern for half the stock some $3000, continued in the business about a year and a half during that time in 37 the great break up took place in the commercial world, and as I had a larg family & provisions, and every thing els was very dear. So that when I sold out to my partner & settled up I found I had about $1000 less than when I came to the Country. In the winder 1837 & 8 I bought a farm ajoining the town lands of Carrollton and moved out on to it in March 1838, having before that sent my son Hervey to Indiana with power of an Attorney to sell some land I had there and he did not return till after we had moved out on the farm. — —

When we commenced on the farm we did not adhere to the rule we had set in with when we began houskeeping. we bought on Credit in the store and made but little on the farm, till in a year or two we found ourselves several hundred dollars in debt. the price of Property had gone down very much about Carrollton so that I found it necessary some time in 1843 or 44 to borrow some $400.00 and give a Mortgage on part of my farm. I soon after sold part of my farm to a german and paid of the Mortgage. I still had some land in Indiana that was sold by my friend and relative Isaac Smock who still lived ajoining the land I had there. it was sold in 1842 or 1843, but I had not got any pay for it yet. In 1844 I concluded to visit our relatives in Indiana and collect my money that was due there, and also to pay a visit to our friends & relatives in Ken-

tucky. during the Sumer 1844 in July I was again so badly
afflicted with my sore leg that I was entirely confined to the
hous for a lenth of time, during that confinement having
nothing els that I could do I began writing these sketches.
—— In August 12th of that year we started in a two hors
carriage for Indiana, myself & wife and daughter Sarahh
and my son Herveys wife & her two children. It took us
a week to go to Waveland in Indiana. after stay there a
few days we went on to Greenwood to see Isaac Smock
& family and other friends and relatives in that region, and
to collect my money that was due me there, having spent
some time there we went on to Kentucky to see my wifes
Father my oldest Brother, and other friends & relatives in
the region where we had been raised. we came back by
way of Greenwood & Waveland, and arived at home on
the 9th of November.—during our absence our Son Hervey
& our daughter Susan kept hous for us, and managed our
affairs. —— the begining of the year 1845 we received letters from Missoury from Cardwells family inviting our
daughter Susan to come over to that region and teach
school, and as she wished to go and try it I went with her
in a carriage starting the last day of January 1845. took
her to Cardwells and returned by way of Louisana where
I was detained a day or two on account of the ice. Nothing more occurd worth noting till May of that year, when
I was coming from Spring Cove in a one hors buggy with
my wife and daughter Jane, when in String Prairie near
Taylors Creek the Buggy got turned over, and in the fall
I had my hip put out of place. I was then about ten miles
from home, and it was a half a day before I could be got
home, and the doctor that was calld in to attend to the case
was so *ignorant* that he thought the joint was not out of
place. and it continued so for some time when other doctors were calld in and examined the case, and they said the
hip joint was out of place and the socket had filled up so
that the joint would not stay in place if it were put in. —
So it has remained and I am cripple. — during that Sumer
I had to hire as best I could, my Hervey gave us a great

deal of assistanc at harvest and otherwise. In the fall of
that year our daughters Ida & Susan came over from Mo
and brought with them a young man by the name of Powel,
who set in to work for me for a year, but did not continue
more than 6 or 8 months. after that I hired a hand for a
few months in the Spring each year and then the ballanc of
the year I would do my own feeding and geting of fire
wood & under great difficulties. *So much so* that we began
to look about for some small place to buy where we could
live without trying to farm. — during the Sumer 1850 our
daughter Sarah was engaged teaching a school at Jersey-
ville, and our daughter Susan was teaching a school under
the Bluffs, and Almeda was at home with us, that.Sumer I
had George Colley hired to work on the farm. the same
fall our daughter Sarah F went to Montecelio Semenary
and the same fall our dauter Susan went with our relations
to Indiana and spent a year there. during the winter 50
& 51 we heard that a small part of the Brighton farm with
a good hous could be bought, I accordingly went there and
and bought twenty acres and, the hous that I now occupy.
I was to have posesion in March 1851. I then rented the
hous & ground to Dr Brown, and we remained on the
farm at Carrollton untill the next fall, during the Sumer
51 Sarah H spent her vacation teaching a school at Rhoads-
point in Macoupin County, and when the time came for
her to go back to the Semenary Almeda wished to go with
her and spend one term at the Semenary. they proposed to
board themselves and accordinly we made preparations for
them to go. We also expected to leave the place in a month
from the time. I cant tell how sorrofull I felt that morning in September when we took breakfast together for the
last time where we had then lived together for more than
13 years: Susan had not yet returned from Indiana. we
had our grand daughter Ellen Derr with us at that time.
She remaind with here grandmother; and I went with the
wagon and took Sarah & Almeda to Montecelio with their
things for houskeeping. Susan got back home sometime
in October. I then made a sale the 18th of that month,

Sold of my stock tools & etc and we then went to Brighton the last of October, having rented the farm to Clarkson E Randall, we then boarded with Dr Brown till the first of December 1852. —— In May 1852 we paid a visit to our relatives the Bantas in Woodford county; and spent some three weeks away from Brighton. —— In December Dr Brown moved onto his place, and we commenced houskeeping again, there was then only myself & wife & daughter Susan, and we had plenty of housroom, good society & good neighbours, and Susan was so good & neat a houskeeper and of such good judgment pertaining to everything that made for the *comfort* of her *parents* that the time from December 1852 till Febuary 1856 was the most pleasant part of my life till the death of that beloved daughter wich took place Febr. 27th 1856. —— I will now go back a few years to relate some family occurences that took place; in the winter 1850 I had several letters from George W. Cardwell proposing to leave his wife and children with us in Illinois, while he would go to California, and try to make money for a year or two; we acceded to his prosials, and in June 1850 I went with the waggon to Missouri and brought the family to our home in Ills. during the time that Cardwells family remained at my hous he remained in California, and for some time after they went back to Missouri, for they went back to Mexico, Mo. some time in the fall of 1851. the Same fall Susan came back to Illinois from Indiana and we left the farm at Carrollton on the 28th day October 1851. the next year after Dr Brown & family moved out of my hous to their own place, in the fall of 1852, we gave an invitation to all our children and grandchildren to pay us a visit on thanksgiving day in that fall wich took place in Nov. According to that arangment they all came to Brighton, children grandchildren & 2 great grandchildren, amounting in all to forty three persons. we all took a thanksgiving diner together for the last time, as it was then perdicted and as it has turned out, for now 1857 there have gone from that family circle the following persons — Susan H. Vanarsdall wife of James H. Vanars-

dall, and their infant child, Charls Albert Brown Son of
Dr Brown, Susan B Vanarsdall, Ann Jane Johnson daughter of George & Ida Cardwell and Febuary 5th 1857 Charity Vanarsdall.

2. EXTRACTS FROM THE AUTOBIOGRAPHY OF J. ALLAN
HUNTSVILLE, ALABAMA, 2 JULY, 1828

[The author, John Allan, here gives a brief account of conditions
at the new University of Georgia, his early religious experience and
the beginning of his career as a western school master. Later Allan
became a member of the North Alabama Presbytery. The autobiography has a particular interest because of the description of the effects
of the earthquake of 1811 upon religion in the West. The following
extracts were secured through Dr. Geneva H. Drinkwater.

"Beginning on December 16, 1811 and continuing for weeks, the
central Mississippi region was rocked by a series of earthquakes, the
like of which the white man had never known before nor since in
that region. . . ." During the succeeding three months 1,874 distinct shocks were recorded of which eight were violently severe, ten
were very severe, and thirty-five generally alarming. It is not surprising that the earthquakes brought thousands into the church, nor
is it surprising that the gain was hardly more than temporary.[3]]

Huntsville   2 July, 1828.   J. Allan
[Pp. 17-18.]

In the spring of 1803 my father and myself went to
Athens [Georgia]. He was engaged in building there and
went before the rest of the family in order to get things
in readiness for their removal. After keeping a sort of
Bachelor's hall for some time, very much to my dissatis-
faction we were joined by my mother and sisters. We had
a comfortable two story framed house of our own, which
we were pretty well prepared to appreciate having been
so long under the roof of another. My mother and sisters
opened a school for young ladies which was quite flourish-

---

[3] Posey, Walter B., *The Development of Methodism in the Old Southwest,
1783-1824*, pp. 50-51. Also Sampson, F. A., "The New Madrid and Other
Earthquakes." *Proceedings of the Mississippi Valley Historical Association*,
VI, pp. 218-238 (contains bibliography).

ing for some time. Athens is pleasantly situated on the river. It was very judiciously selected as a suitable site for the university which had just gone into operation before we removed. We were now much better situated as it respected society. There were a few genteel intelligent families who had settled there at this early period. M. [Josiah] Meigs[4] was at that time President of the university. He had been Professor of Mathematics in Yale College. He was subsequently Surveyor General of the U.S. and Commissioner of the General Land Office. He was a man of handsome acquirements, and had he held the reins of government with more firmness, the institution would have flourished — but unhappily he was skeptical in his religious views and of course did not use those efforts to check the propensities of the vicious, which he would otherwise have done. The youth who resorted to College were generally sons of the rich, had been accustomed to every indulgence and were consequently impatient of restraint. Vicious habits became strengthened in proportion as their number increased, but little attention was paid to study — the reputation of the college was seriously affected by these things. Mr. Meigs was entirely too lenient — he laid too much stress on the efficacy of mere advice — strict discipline was therefore neglected. I entered college soon after our removal to Athens. Commencing with [illegible] I read through this book in three weeks without however passing at all. This was a most unhappy commencement, the effects of which I felt many years afterwards. I began indeed at the same time to learn grammar but it was only a by business instead of being made as it ought to have been the principal object of attention. I learned to construct with as much facility as I could under existing circumstances. In addition to my classical studies I kept up a course of English reading. Hume's History of England, Rollin's Ancient History and Plutarch! This I read with considerable

[4] For a sketch of Josiah Meigs see *Dictionary of American Biography*, Vol. XII; also Meigs, W. M., *Life of Josiah Meigs* (1887).

interest. I joined a Debating Society which tho' often badly managed I found to be a source of improvement.

But while I was making some advances in intellectual knowledge I found the ill effects of bad company on my morals. There was not at that time a single serious student in college. Indeed there were but very few who were not grossly immoral. One however I found who tho' not religious was strictly moral, with him I formed an intimate friendship — this lasted during the time of his stay at College, and after his leaving there, for he graduated before me, we kept up a constant epistolary correspondence for some years. It was finally dropped without any particular cause. I still look back upon the period of our acquaintance and intercourse with some degree of pleasure. He was a great admirer of nature and something of a Botanist. We used to take many a pleasant ramble through the woods together. His name was James Jackson. He was the son of a General Jackson — a gentleman of considerable distinction among the Politicians of Georgia. James married and settled near Louisville in that State.

After he left college I had no very intimate associate until some time after my acquaintance with the Rev. Jno. Hodge who came to reside at my father's. This event was the occasion of a new era in my life, to which I hope I shall ever look back with adoring gratitude to that Being who ordereth all things after the counsel of his own will. This gentleman was a cousin of your Mama's. He was well educated, deeply pious, and of a most amiable natural disposition. He had gone to Georgia on account of his health. He commenced preaching stately at Athens and at some other places in the neighborhood. He and I occupied a room together in my father's house. The college building was not yet in readiness to receive students. I was much pleased with the amiableness of his disposition and the cheerfulness of his manners, and after some weeks acquaintance was congratulating myself on his silence, that is in his conversation with me, on the subject of religion. The event however proved to me that he did not intend leaving me at my ease on this subject. He was probably studying my disposition with a view to make his approach to the best advantage. To my shame be it spoken I had not the most distant idea of making religion a practical concern. On a certain occasion he was about going into the country for the purpose of catechising one of his congregation, he asked me to accompany him. I shall never forget the wicked contempt with which the proposal was heard. This feeling however was concealed from him, and I gave him some evasive answer. Sometime after this he asked me what profession I intended to study. I replied "Either law or physick." He then asked what I should think of Divinity? I told him I had not the necessary qualifications. He observed "You have the natural qualifications and the moral ones you *must* have." This made a deep and lasting impression on my mind, tho' I said but little at the time. I began to think I had been counting without my host or in other words making erroneous calculations when I supposed this amiable minister would say nothing to me on the subject of religion. Soon after this Mr. H. was appointed Principal of the Preparatory School attached to the college. The scholars being numerous it was necessary to have an assistant — to which office I was appointed. I began to feel in some degree the necessity of becoming more steady, viewing it important in order to maintain the dignity of my new station. The relation which Mr. H. and myself sustained as fellow teachers served also to bring us into a still closer intimacy than before. We took a room together in College.

About this time I began to accompany him in his excursions into the country where he used to preach. During our rides he often entertained me with an account of the Western country whither his parents had removed some years before. He gave me also particular details of the great revival that had prevailed there. I now began to converse with him on personal religion. I remember particularly inquiring of him whether prayer was necessary. Of this I was convinced before, but I wished to hear what he could say on the subject in order to have the duty more deeply impressed on my mind. I had formerly been in the habit of attending to that duty, that is of saying my prayers — but even this had been omitted for some time past. Having now some sense of the importance of religion, I resumed the practice. I was by no means under what is usually called conviction — but acted from a sense of duty. I remember well the confusion of my thoughts the first time I attempted to pray in my own words. I went out into the woods for this purpose after night. I felt discouraged but continued to persevere.

[Pp. 35–39.]

It was during this winter [1810] I received an invitation to take charge of the Lebanon Academy in Christian County, Kentucky. After considerable deliberation we determined to accept the offer, accordingly removed. The situation was worth about 400 per an, and as we had no rent to pay, a house being furnished, and as we lived in the practice of a most rigid economy we were enabled to save about 300 at the end of the year. Our mansion was of a very humble grade, a small cabin, one story high with a wooden chimney and no windows. The floor was of rough planks laid down loose. The situation was a very pretty one. It was on the edge of the open in a beautiful grove of thrifty young timber — sufficiently elevated yet not hilly. In a hollow near by was a delightful spring. It was quite secluded from the neighboring plantations none of them being in sight, and far enough from the Academy to be free from all annoyance from that source, this building which was spacious, one story high built of brick was designed as well for a meeting house as an Academy. The night after our arrival at our little secluded cabin, the pork which had been engaged was brought in. We had neither smoke house nor kitchen, so the hogs must needs be laid down in our parlour without much danger however of spoiling our carpet. The mighty task of cutting them up of course devolved on me, for which I was totally unprepared. I had no bench to cut

on and nothing but a dull case knife to cut with, and what
was perhaps worse than all I was absolutely ignorant of
the manner in which it was to be done. Nothing daunted
however I went to work. For a bench I laid two planks
upon two chairs and thus badly equipped with a dull knife
I proceeded under your Mama's directions and finally with
much fatigue and trouble I accomplished the Herculean
task. We had at that time no servant but Abbey and she
was only a child of eight years of age. I used to cut all
the wood and make the fires. We lived then as comfortably I believe as have done at any period since. At the
close of this year I bought Phil who was then about 10
years old. He proved to be a very worthless fellow and
on this account I parted with him perhaps in the year 1815.
The school I had there was much more respectable than
any I had had in Summer County. There was a much
larger proportion of classical scholars. The second year,
viz. 1812, of our abode in Kentucky was distinguished for
those memorable earthquakes which shook a vast extent of
the country. The first shock occurred in the night when
we were asleep, the noise awoke us. I got up immediately
to see what was the matter. I noticed the door rattling
and opened it to see if any one was there, but could see
nothing. I then noticed the floor above which was composed of loose planks to be shaking — I supposed something to be the matter then. Your Aunt Katharine was
then on a visit to us, she slept upstairs, i. e. up the ladder
for small as our cabin was we contrived to have a bed up
in the roof. The thought occurred to me that she had
either got up in her sleep and was dancing or had fallen
into a fit. I immediately called out to her and found from
her answer that she was in bed perfectly quiet. The real
cause of the commotion then for the first time occurred to
me and I observed to your Mama — "It is an earthquake
and we shall probably have another shock in a few minutes." This accordingly took place, tho' I have myself no
distinct recollection of it. I felt perfectly composed hav-

ing satisfied myself as to the cause of the disturbance I slept soundly till daylight.

Soon after we rose and were standing in the door talking about the occurrence of the preceding evening I was expressing a strong desire to witness another shock, my wish was instantly met. The distant lumbering was heard, the house began to shake and everything that was in it. I could see the fence in the yard most distinctly waving back and forth. The foundations of the earth were terribly shaken. I was then quite satisfied and had no desire to see any more shocks. Still I did not feel any alarm because I did not apprehend much danger. I knew that shocks of earthquakes were frequently in places without being accompanied with any injury. After breakfast I repaired to the Academy as usual and was not a little astonished to learn that the whole neighborhood was in a state of exceeding alarm. Several families had met together and spent the night in prayer. Some of the most irreligious had through fright been brought to cry out for mercy. I made some remarks to the students on the subjects of earthquakes — the tendency of which to allay their fear. During prayer with which I was accustomed to open school another shock occurred. It was with some difficulty I could maintain the composure of my mind. I went on however as usual with the business of the day. At night the people assembled in crowds at the Academy which was also a meeting house for the purpose of worship. From this time for many weeks religious meetings were frequent and numerously attended. They were accompanied with a great deal of noisy excitement. Multitudes appeared for a time to be serious, many made a profession of religion. Far the greater proportion of these, so far as my observation went, threw off their concern as soon as the earth ceased to shake. There is reason however to hope that some few sought and found the pearl of great price during the religious excitement that then prevailed.

About this time the winter vacation occurred and we embraced the opportunity of visiting our friends in Sum-

mer County. Here we found the religious excitement quite
as great as in the place of our residence. Prayer meetings
were held almost every night somewhere in the bounds of
the congregation of Shiloh. My own mind after having
for some time speculated on the interesting phenomenon
of the earthquake, was now more intensely turned to religion than at any former period with one exception. The
exception alluded to occurred the year before my marriage.
I went that year in company with a Mother in Israel to a
sacramental meeting on Red River about forty miles distant from Shiloh. At this meeting I went up to be prayed
for. It was common at that period 1808 to assemble immediately round the pulpit or stand. The platform occupied by the ministers when the meeting was held out of
doors, those persons who felt any anxiety about the salvation of their souls. I had then never been accustomed to
anything of this sort, indeed the prejudice of my education
was against it. But I overcame this prejudice without much
difficulty. I wanted as I thought religion and was willing
to seek it in any way. Accordingly I engaged in prayer
aloud in conjunction with those around me as was the cus-
tom. My feelings became most intense, I thought at times
the blessing was just at hand and that I could almost reach
it. I was looking out for some miraculous change.—a confidence that should put all doubt to flight and a joy that
should be overwhelming. The burden of the directions
given me by the ministers attending was "Believe". They
were good men but did not according to my present views
give just that sort of instruction which my case demanded.
It seems to me they should have insisted more on repentance — should have told me plainly that notwithstanding
this anxiety I manifested I was not willing to come to
Christ. This I have no doubt was the true state of the
case and is with every unconverted sinner whatever may be
his anxiety. I thought I was willing to have religion and
that in this way it was to be obtained. What I desired was
not so much holiness as a confidence that my sins were pardoned. I was not indeed consciously acting the hypocrite

but my views of religion were exceedingly indistinct. My animal feelings were enough up. I literally labored in prayer until my physical nature was completely exhausted. As I remarked before I was at times in my own view just on the point of receiving the blessing for which I was praying. From what I learned subsequently I suppose my countenance was lighted up with hope. The good old lady with whom I had gone to the meeting and who was now watching me with intense anxiety and no doubt praying for me, told me afterwards, she thought she saw at one period during the struggle that smile on my countenance which usually preceded those high demonstrations of joy common with persons making profession of religion under those circumstances. The fact is I believe I was precisely in that state of high wrought excitement in which hundreds and thousands have been deceived. And for many years I have thought that I ought to feel most grateful to God that he did not permit me at that time to become the subject of a delusive hope. I returned from that meeting with the deepest feelings of solemnity. I was then and had been for some time in the habit of secret prayer. And when we went housekeeping I always maintain family worship. These exercises though not attended to in a proper manner had some tendency to increase my knowledge of the corruption of my heart. During the visit before alluded to in the month of January or February 1812 I was at a prayer meeting in Shiloh congregation. My mind was deeply exercised on the subject of religion. I became despondent almost ready to conclude there was no mercy for me. A very pious and sensible man, Mr. Richard King an Elder in that congregation, conversed with me. On reviewing the exercises of my mind during that conversation I have some reason to believe that I then realized for the first time something like unconditional submission to the will of God. I felt that God might justly cast me off forever. This was not attended however with any sensible comfort. After the meeting was dismissed we went, if I mistake not, to Uncle Wm. Hodge where we spent the night. Sometime during the night we were waked up by one of the most fearful shocks of the earthquake that had yet occurred. The voice of lamentation and prayer was heard in every direction. The first and prevailing desire of my heart was that this fearful visitation might be blessed to the salvation of souls. I lost in a great degree my personal fears, I seemed to lose sight of my individual interests feeling a deep concern for the glory of God, willing that judgments should come, provided that object was promoted. A morning or two after that while engaged in secret prayer in the woods at the foot of old Shiloh hill on which the meeting house [stood] — I was blessed with such views of the divine character as I never had before. The holiness of God appeared in the view of my mind with a peculiar lustre, altogether new, it seemed to me ineffably bright and infinitely interesting; — I was lost in wonder and devout admiration. I had a deep sense of its intrinsic excellence and glory. The characteristic of it which seemed most prominent was its spotless lustre. My imagination pictured it before me as a boundless sea of spotless light, irresistibly attractive — unmixed goodness. I have often attempted to describe the scene as it presented itself to my mind then and my feelings accompanying it but it ever seems to beggar all description. I can find no language adequate to the task. The impression then made seemed in a sort as vivid now as they were then though an interval of more than twenty years has elapsed since. The next object which presented itself to the view of my mind at the time of which I speak was my own character as a sinner. It appeared to me in contrast with the glorious character of God as a spot of perfect darkness without the relief of a single ray of holy light — totally depraved — evil and only evil, altogether ill-deserving and utterly destitute of all claim on the divine goodness. My mind was next directed to the character of God in Christ, the Glorious Mediator he appeared indeed "the chief among ten thousand and altogether lovely." I thought with pleasing wonder and delight on his amazing love to sinners, it seemed wonderful and glorious that a being of such exalted dignity should lay down his life for sinners. I had a distinct view of the all-sufficiency of his atonement. My heart went out in strong and ardent affection. I was filled with holy delight. But still I did not then think this was the exercise of religion. The fact was I thought but little of myself — my mind was almost exclusively taken up with the ineffably glorious character of God. After spending some time in these delightful meditations I returned to the house where we had spend the night. It was then the hospitable mansion of Mr. and Mrs. Motheral two venerable saints, many years since called home to their Father's kingdom. I was requested to lead in family worship, which I did with feelings such as I had not experienced before. I presume there was something in my manner of praying somewhat peculiar and different from what I had at any time manifested before as I learned afterwards from your Mama, that Mrs. M. remarked afterwards she did not think any one could pray as I had done and be a stranger to religion. I had said nothing to any one about the remarkable exercises of which I had been the subject in the morning nor do I remember to have mentioned it to any one for some time after. The report however was soon in circulation that I had professed religion. For many weeks after the memorable scene which I have been attempting to describe I was favored with similar views as often as I engaged in prayer. This duty was indeed a delightful employment.

The vacation in my school drawing to a close, we began to think of returning to Kentucky. Not willing yet to admit that I had undergone a change — I determined on my return to retain my old attitude of a seeker of religion — not supposing that any of my Kentucky friends would know anything of what had transpired. But here again I was mistaken for the report of my new views and feelings had preceded me. However, I adhered to my resolution and at the first meeting I was at after my return took my place among the anxious. Engaging in prayer as usual, I found myself rather unexpectedly praying most earnestly for the unconverted around me. I began at length to suspect that I might be wrong and that if I had undergone the great change, why it would be better for me to avow it than to conceal it. I was the more slow to admit a hope of this sort because the process had not been such as I had prescribed to myself I had calculated too much on a confidence that was never to be shaken by a single doubt — and on a holiness of character approaching to perfection. Another circumstance which seemed rather mortifying was that I might subject myself to the reproach of having merely an earthquake religion. For it was quite obvious that multitudes that evinced great concern many of whom bid fair to be religious lost all concern and gave up their professions when the occasion had passed by which excited their fears. My case however differed in some respects from theirs. I had been more or less serious for several years. In view of these circumstances I felt some reluctance in admitting that I had been received. I was almost wholly secluded from the company of intelligent Christians — the instructions of such would no doubt have been beneficial. I now began to think seriously of making a public profession of religion. I then lived in a congregation of Cumberland Presbyterians — in essentials we were agreed and I habitually worshipped with them in public. I had no idea of connecting myself with that branch of the church however, and therefore began to look out for an opportunity elsewhere. Hearing of an appointment for a sacramental meeting in the Presbyterian church at Nashville, then supplied by Dr. Blackburn — I determined on attending. The fame of the Dr's eloquence had reached me long before this and I was very desirous of seeing him. I had already opened a correspondence with him. I was led to this in order to ascertain his views on certain theological points, having heard opinions attributed to him which I supposed he did not hold.

CHAPTER XIX

DOCUMENTS RELATING TO THE OLD SCHOOL-NEW SCHOOL CONTROVERSY AND SCHISM

1. Secret Circular of 1831.
2. Minutes of the Convention by which "The Cincinnati Memorial" was published, 1833.
3. Address of the Presbytery of Indianapolis to the Pittsburgh Convention, May, 1835.
4. Letter from the Presbytery of Chillicothe, Ohio, to the Presbytery of Ebenezer, Kentucky, on the Question of Slavery, 1836.
5. Action of the North Alabama Presbytery on the Controversial Issues, 1831-1838.
6. Resolutions adopted by the Presbytery of Louisville on the action of the General Assemblies of 1837 and 1838.
7. Resolutions adopted by the Tuscaloosa Presbytery approving the action of the General Assembly of 1837.
8. Action of the Synod of North Carolina justifying the action of the General Assembly of 1837.
9. Report of the Committee on the State of the Church, Concord Presbytery (North Carolina), October, 1837, and Report of the Committee on Minutes of the General Assembly, Concord Presbytery, October, 1838.
10. Action of the Holston Presbytery declaring the Exscinding Acts of the General Assembly of 1837 unconstitutional.
11. Action of the Old School minority of the Holston Presbytery relative to the division of the Presbytery into Old School and New School bodies.
12. Resolutions adopted by the Eaglefork Presbyterian Church, Missouri, relative to the Acts passed by the General Assemblies of 1837 and 1838.

1. SECRET CIRCULAR OF 1831[1]

[The Secret Circular of 1831 was issued by a committee of the Old School minority of the General Assembly of 1831 in their attempt to defeat any possible plan for continuing Presbyterian relationship with the American Home Missionary Society.[2]]

[1] From the Baird MSS in possession of the Historical Foundation, Montreat, North Carolina.

[2] Baird, "History of the New School," *op. cit.,* pp. 287-391.

Dearly Beloved Brethren

You must already have been in some measure apprised of the hazard to which the vital interests of our beloved church were exposed, at the last meeting of the Gen.Ass. For a time it seemed as if nothing less alarming was likely to ensue than the mutilation, if not the subversion of the whole Presbyterian system. In these circumstances, a number of the Brethren held meetings for prayer, and for conference on the measures which they might adopt, with the best prospect, under the Divine blessing, of averting the evils apprehended; and the Great Head of the Church did, as they believed, remarkably interpose to suspend for a time the impending calamity. The Gen. Ass. was dissolved without carrying into effect the most injurious of those measures which had been projected, and one of which — the entire change of the Missionary Board — had been proposed and urged. Thus another year is afforded us to live under the unmutilated standards and institutions of the church in which we were born and nurtured. But this is the last year, it is our solemn conviction, in which our church will remain without essential changes, unless her children shall [awaken] to a sense of their danger, and call into vigorous action their united energies in her defence. It was under this impression, that the brethren who were instrumental in preventing the threatening evils to which we have alluded, did, after much and prayerful deliberation, appoint the undersigned a Central Committee, to correspond with other Committees in the several Synods of our connexion; and it was their judgment that the Synodical Committees would do well to appoint and correspond with committees in such of their Presbyteries as they might believe to be friendly to their views, and disposed to co-operate in giving efficiency to their plans.

You cannot be ignorant, Dear Brethren, that during the lapse of several years, cricumstances have not unfrequently occurred, which seemed to prognosticate evil to our church; and which awakened in the minds of some, the apprehension that an important crisis was approaching. But, with many of our ministerial and lay brethren, throughout the country, we cherished the hope that the danger had been magnified by fear, and that no serious interruption to the safety and peace of the church would ensue. This illusion of hope was dissipated by the last Assembly. We cannot pretend to give a detail of the proceedings of that Assembly; but having been near and attentive observers of them, we are prepared to say, that the spirit and purpose unequivocally manifested by a majority of the members, did impress on our minds the conviction, — that our Theological Seminaries are in danger of being revolutionised (*sic*), and perverted from the intention of their orthodox founders: that the property & endowments of our church are in danger of passing, for application and disposal, into the hands of those who have contributed little, if any thing, to their amount: that our doctrinal standards are in danger, either of total disregard, or of a revision and alteration that will essentially change their character; that our supreme ecclesiastical judicatory is in danger of being controlled by delegates unconstitutionally appointed and commissioned, and destitute of every legal claim to membership; and finally, that our Boards of Education and of Missions, are in danger of being wrested from the hands of those who wish to make them the sources of supply to the wants of our church in an uncorrupted state, and of being rendered subsidiary to the plans and purposes of voluntary associations, subject to no ecclesiastical responsibility, and adopting no formula of faith by which their religious tenets may be ascertained.

But although we believe, Dear Brethren, that our beloved Zion is in danger, and that the danger is exceedingly imminent, yet we are far from thinking her situation hopeless. Our peril, we verily believe, arises chiefly from the want, in the sound part of our church, of a due sense of the danger which exists; and a consequent security and inactivity, *apathy* may we not call it — while those who are seeking to innovate, are all life and energy — prompt and united in their measures and movements, and combined in their operations. We have not a doubt that if the orthodox part of our church had been as fully represented in the last Assembly as its opposers were, the majority would have been with us and not with them; and when we consider the interposition of God's good providence — for to this it must be attributed — to save us from fatal innovations for another year, we cannot but consider the language of the dispensation to be — "You shall have another year to make it manifest, whether you have a sufficient love to the pure and holy truths of your Confession of Faith and Catechism, and to the sacred institutions of your fathers, to awake to their defence and preservation; or whether, with listless indifference, you will suffer them to be invaded and destroyed, and you and your children deprived forever of a birthright, which you ought to value more than life itself."

Are we asked then, what ought to be done? We answer briefly,—

First of all, look to God for his guidance and blessing. Let there be much prayer, that he who has the hearts of all men in his hands, may incline his people of our denomination to think of the preciousness of those divine truths which, drawn from the pure fountain of divine revelation, have been collected in our doctrinal standards, as into a sacred reservoir, and which every Presbyterian ought, without hesitation, to make every necessary sacrifice to preserve and pepetuate in their purity. To think, too, of that invaluable form of church government and order, derived from the oracles of inspiration, which they have received from their progenitors, and under which our church has prospered, flourished, and extended, in a degree altogether without a parallel.

Let us, also, both pray and labor to promote vital piety. Those who oppose us, love to represent themselves as the friends, and us as the enemies, of revivals of religion. Let us convince the world that this is, what it certainly is, a totally false representation. While we leave to others all those *new measures* for promoting revivals, which are merely of man's divising, and keep close to the guidance of the divine word, and recognise as indispensable the special agency of the Holy Spirit in the conversion of sinners, let us, in prayer, in preaching, in holy living, and in zealous activity in doing good, and in striving to win souls to the Saviour, demonstrate that we are not less, but more the friends to genuine revivals of religion than those who slander us.

2. Let all lawful measures be used to rouse our brethren, both clergy and laity, to a just sense of their situation and their duty. With this view, we advise that you correspond with Presbyteries, as stated in the beginning of this communication. Make, also, a free but discreet use of the press; and encourage liberally, and circulate as widely as possible, those publications which maintain the real doctrines of our church, and advocate the support of her institution. Our opponents, who wish a continuance of the existing apathy and baneful security of the orthodox part of our church, cry, "peace, peace, when there is no peace." Expose this artifice. Peace indeed! Would God, our peace had not been disturbed by innovations which threaten our ruin. Would God that peace and safety were compatible. But, at present, they are not compatible. We are called to "contend earnestly for the faith once delivered to the saints", and for an inheritance of inestimable value, which we are in danger of losing. Let us pursue our object with a Christian spirit, and by no other means than those which are lawful. Bet let us do it firmly, resolutely, perseveringly. Let no smooth words or soothing propositions turn us from our purpose. We have been credulous and hoodwinked too long already.

3. Our Board of Education, and Board of Missions, must both receive a liberal patronage and a decided support. This is essential — without this we are undone. The voluntary associations that seek to engross the patronage of our church, and have already engrossed a large part of it, have taken the start of us in the all important concerns of education and of missions. They now labor to get the whole of these into their own hands; well knowing, that if

this be effected, they will infallibly, in a very short time, govern the church. For education furnishes missionaries, and missionaries become pastors, and pastors with their ruling elders, form church sessions, Presbyteries, Synods, and General Assemblies. The whole, it is seen at once, is traced back to education, as to a salient point; and from this it springs and rushes forward, through every channel of influence, till it reaches the highest fountain of power in the General Assembly.

At the present moment, our Board of Missions is experiencing a very distressing and embarrassing want of missionaries. The destitute churches are crying, in the most affecting manner, to the Board, for the supply of their necessities; but how can the Board satisfy their importunate demands? The Board can furnish funds, but they cannot create missionaries. Nor can they take them of all characters and descriptions, as the voluntary associations may, without regard to the correctness of their theological sentiments and teachings. The Board want men of knowledge and soundness in the faith, as well as of piety and zeal. Our churches ask for such, and are unwilling to receive any other; and the Board are equally unwilling to send any other. But where are they to be found? They cannot be had in number at all adequate to the demand, till they are educated. Our Education and Missionary Boards, therefore, we repeat, must be sustained; must be promptly, and liberally, and efficiently patronised, or our church is gone. Yes, dear Brethren, whatever other benevolent institutions we favor, and we wish well to all that are truly benevolent, our Boards of Education and Missions must share most largely in our charitable contributions. We must take from others, so far as it is necessary, to give to these; and we ought to regard it as a sacred duty to withhold our aid from all institutions, that seek to supplant or to rival these. These are the sheet anchors of our church; which must enable her to ride out the fearful fluctuations by which she is now agitated, and in jeopardy of [being] wrecked and lost, amidst the quicksands and whirlpools of theological error and heretical innovation.

Finally — That several judicatories of our church must be carefully and punctually attended by every orthodox man, whose right and duty it is to hold a seat in them. This is another item of vital importance. It may happen, and sometimes has happened, even in Presbyteries, that by reason of the absence of some of the members, measures of great importance have been adopted, contrary to the mind of a real majority — measures, sometimes which a majority could not correct. This is more likely to take place in the election of commissioners to the General Assembly than in any other case; and in no case, at the present time, can a Presbyterial error so deeply injure the general welfare of our church. Every Presbytery that by the attendance of every minister and every elder entitled to a seat and a vote, has it in its power to send an orthodox delegation to the next General Assembly, and fails to do so, may justly be regarded as incurring a criminal responsibility of no ordinary character. The neglected duty may occasion a wound to the church that can never afterward be healed. Nor was it ever so important in our church as at the present time, that orthodox Presbyteries should choose wise men, and firm men, to represent them in the Assembly. But it is most of all important that every man elected, whether minister or elder, unless prevented by invincible hindrances of a providential kind should attend that body at the next meeting. For the want of this, at the last meeting, we were left in a minority. We are fully aware, beloved brethren, of the difficulty of a general attendance, by the distant members; and we sympathise with them deeply. But truly it is at present a question of existence. The life, so to speak, of the Presbyterian Church, is, under God, in the hands of distant members; and are they not ready, for the preservation of that life, to make every necessary sacrifice? We trust they are, and that they will not fail to do it. Should it be found, in the General Assembly of 1832, that every orthodox commissioner — minister and elder — is in his place, we have not a doubt that the formularies, government, institutions, and endowments of our church will be preserved; but we shall not be surprised if they shall all be swept away, or materially changed, if the neglect in attendance shall be as great in the coming year, as in that which is past.

Thus, brethren beloved in the Lord, we have endeavored to acquit ourselves of a trust confided to us by those members of the last Assembly, whose exertions, under the Divine blessing, were made instrumental in arresting measures of fearful import to our much loved Zion. We have laid before you honestly and without exaggeration, our views, apprehensions, and wishes. We pretend not to dictate. We have no right and no inclination to do so. Adopt such measures, on our suggestion, as you deem expedient, and no more; and devise other measures for yourselves. A solemn duty to the Savior and to his church is incumbent on us. If we neglect it, we have a tremendous responsibility. If we perform it with fidelity, and put our trust in our covenant God, he will prosper the work of our hands; we shall rejoice in his mercies, and the Presbyterian church to the latest generations, reaping the fruit of our exertions and our sacrifices, may rise up and call us blessed.

ASHBEL GREEN.
GEO.C.POTTS.
WM.M.ENGLES.
SAMUEL G.WINCHESTER.
MATTHEW L.BEVAN
SOLOMON ALLEN.
FURMAN LEAMING.

Philadelphia,July 21st,1831.

2. MINUTES OF THE CONVENTION BY WHICH "THE CINCINNATI MEMORIAL" WAS PUBLISHED, 1833

[The Convention which met at Monroe, Butler County, Ohio, represented the effort of the Old School party in and around Cincinnati to form a definite organization to combat their opponents. There were present at this meeting about a dozen ministers and as many elders. The meeting was held outside Cincinnati because of the prevalence of cholera in the city. The Memorial drawn up by this convention demanded abrogation of the Plan of Union; the restraining of presbyteries from ordaining ministers who are to serve outside the bounds of the presbyteries where they are ordained; that the General Assembly conduct its own missions; and that the General Assembly take action against the many errors creeping into the church. The Convention adjourned to meet in Cincinnati in October.]

Monroe,Butler County,Ohio
July 31,1833.

In consequence of the fearful decline of sound doctrine and faithful discipline in the Presbyterian church, and the apprehension of its entire subversion; and with a humiliating sense of the divisions and broken peace of the church, already abounding and producing dismay, certain brethren, being fully persuaded that some remedy ought to be applied, in reliance on the head of the church, to remove these evils, and avert impending ruin, opened a correspondence with many brethren in the ministry, inviting their counsel in the case, and their attendance at a Conference to be held at the house of Elder John Monfort, in the township of Monroe, to take the subject into prayerful consideration.

At the time and place above mentioned a Conference was held, and the following persons were present: Francis Monfort, David Monfort, Thomas Barr, Robert B.Dobbins, Peter Monfort, James Coe, John L.Belville, Simeon H. Crane, Sayrs Gazlay, Reuben Frame, and Adrian Aten, Ministers:— and John Monfort, Jonathan Whittaker, Samuel Clendenan, Moses W.Carr, John Bigger, William King, Charles H. Spinning, William Lowrie, Frederick A. Kemper, and Archibald Campbell, Elders. The Rev. Francis Monfort was chosen Moderator, and the Rev. Sayrs Gazlay, Clerk. The Conference then held a season of devotion, and the Brethren in repeated addresses to the Throne of Grace implored the Divine favor and guidance.

It being announced that several letters were on the table, addressed to the Conference, and several others addressed to individuals, relating to the subjects that would occupy the attention of the meeting, it was resolved that these communications be read. Letters were accordingly [read] from the following persons, viz: Rev. John Burtt, Rev. J. F. Crowe, Rev. Robert Stuart, Rev.John Howe, and Rev. James Blythe, D.D., when the Conference had recess for an hour and a quarter. After recess, communications were read from Rev. Joshua L. Wilson,D.D., Rev. John McArthur, Rev. Mr. Archibald Hanna, Rev. John Matthews, Rev. Robert J.Breckinridge, and Rev. Ashbel Green,D.D. After reading the above communications, Messrs. Barr, Coe, and D. Monfort, Ministers; and C. H. Spinning, S. Clendenan, and W. Lowrie, Elders, were appointed a Committee to take into consideration the communications which had been read, and to take notes, during the calling of the roll, and embody the suggestions in the communications, and the views of the members of the Conference, and report to this meeting as soon as practicable after the calling of the roll.

The roll was then called; and every member had the opportunity of expressing his views in relation to the business of the meeting, to enable the Committee, before appointed, to ascertain and report the views of the members. The Rev. John L. Belville was appointed additional Clerk. Adjourned until tomorrow morning at 8 o'clock. Concluded with prayer.

Thursday Morning, 8 o'clock.

The Conference convened and engaged in prayer, reading the Scriptures, and singing: and continued their exercises until 10 o'clock; then had a recess for half an hour.

After recess, the committee reported, and recommended that a memorial be addressed to the next General Assembly of the Presbyterian Church; and presented a draught of such memorial. The report was accepted, the memorial read, and taken into consideration. After considerable progress in reading it by paragraphs for amendment and adoption, the further reading was arrested by the adoption of the following resolutions:

Resolved, That the draught of a memorial which has been read, expresses the sentiments of this Conference, as to its general features; and that it be committed to T. Barr, J. L. Wilson,DD., and J. Burtt, ministers; and Henry B. Funk, S. Clendenan, and J. Bigger, Elders; to be by them revised and reported to the next meeting of the Conference.

The Committee were instructed not to add any other subjects, but to confine themselves to those already embraced in the aforesaid draught.

Adjourned to meet during the Sessions of Synod in the First Presbyterian Church in Cincinnati, on the 18th October next, at 7 o'clock,P.M. Concluded with prayer.

FRANCIS MONFORT, Moderator.

SAYRS GAZLAY } Clerks
JOHN L.BELVILLE }

The Conference convened, pursuant to adjournment, in the First Presbyterian Church, in Cincinnati, October 18, 1833, Mr. Monfort in the Chair, and Mr. Gazley Clerk. The meeting was opened with prayer. After reading the minutes of the former meeting, the Committee appointed to revise the memorial reported it, as revised.

Conference had a recess until the next evening at 7 o'clock, when Conference met, and accepted the report of the Committee, and then had recess until Monday noon. After recess, proceeded to consider the memorial by paragraphs for adoption. After some progress, had a recess until 7 o'clock in the evening. After recess, the Conference assembled, and, having finished the reading and amending of the memorial, adopted it as amended; and appointed Rev. J. L. Wilson,D.D., Rev. J. Burtt, and Mr. Samuel Lowrie, a Committee to present it to the Synod of Cincinnati through their Committee of Bills and Overtures. Had recess until the recess of Synod tomorrow noon. At which time the Conference convened. The Committee to present the memorial to the Synod, reported, that the Committee of Bills and Overtures declined presenting it to Synod, on account of its length, and the amount of business on the docket of Synod. The report was accepted and the Committee discharged. A Committee was appointed to procure the publication of one thousand copies of the memorial, and furnish each member of the next General Assembly with a copy. The Conference then adjourned, and the meeting was concluded with prayer.

3. TO THE CONVENTION OF PRESBYTERIAN MINISTERS AND ELDERS, TO MEET IN PITTSBURGH, ON THE 2D THURSDAY OF MAY, 1835[3]

[The Old School minority in the General Assembly of 1834 after having been defeated in their efforts to pass certain resolutions condemning errors in the abstract met together and drew up a paper called *The Act and Testimony* which "in startling tones" described the many dangers confronting the church and called for all those who approved these statements to give public adherence to this position. The leaders in this movement also called a convention to be composed of those favoring this position to meet in Pittsburgh previous to the meeting of the General Assembly in 1835 and there adopt such measures as should be "best suited to restore the prostrated standards." The following is the response of the Indianapolis Presbytery to this appeal addressed to the Convention of Presbyterian Ministers and Elders to meet in Pittsburgh on the 2nd Thursday in May, 1835.[4]]

The Presbytery of Indianapolis respectfully address you, Brethren, as those to whom is committed the solemn and deeply interesting concern; viz: that of devising and concurring in such measures to be laid before the next General Assembly, which, if adopted by them, may ultimately eradicate from our beloved *church*, the evils that now distract & divide us, and prevent their future increase and recurrence. To aid your counsels, we have sent two of our number, brethren in whose intelligence, soundness in the faith, and fidelity to the cause, we have entire confidence. Nevertheless, we deem it our duty and our privilege, at this eventful crisis, to present in this formal manner, some measures in

[3] Baird MSS: *Presbytery of Indianapolis to the Convention of 1835*, pp. 59-64, Historical Foundation, Montreat, N. C.
[4] Gillett, *op. cit.*, II, pp. 486-488.

our estimation indispensibly necessary to be obtained, or peace, unity, and purity, can never be restored to, or preserved in, the Presbyterian Church. The 1st is an abrogation of the Plan of Union between Congregationalists and Presbyterians, adopted in 1800 (Digest p.277.) and as a part of the same policy, the Plan of Union and Correspondence between the General Assembly and the several ecclesiastical Associations of New England. In the first named compact provision is made for the introduction of men into all our church judicatories, to deliberate and vote, who are not entitled to this privilege by our Form of Government, and by the same compact ecclesiastical tribunals unknown, and repugnant to the Constitution of the Presbyterian Church, have been established. This compact ought to be totally set aside. And in the "Plan of Union and Correspondence," the way is opened for the too hasty admission of Congregational ministers and licentiates to full standing in the same character within the Presbyterian church. This plan ought to be repealed, and in future the same order to be observed in securing ministers and licentiates from Congregationalists and any other different denominations, as is prescribed for "foreign ministers and licentiates," in Digest, pp.280,& 285.

Another, and second necessary measure is, "That the General Assembly resume the full exercise of their own functions in conducting missionary operations within the Presbyterian church," and take the necessary measures to have it so arranged, that any Missionary laboring any where within the said denomination, be there as commissioned and directed, by the Assembly or some other constitutional organs of the Presbyterian *church*, and bound to render to them a regular report of his labors. The Presbyterian church will never be safe from the inroads of error, and will alway [*sic*] be open to the aggressions of designing and ambitious men, so long as a non-ecclesiastical, irresponsible Association is permitted to select, introduce and control a large number of her officiating ministers. We, here, in the west, have had long and bitter experience of the evils resulting from the combined operations of the "Compact" "Plan of Union" and the A.H.M.Society. The first two have opened the door for the too ready entrance of Congregational ministers among us. And the H.M.Society takes up and sustains almost the entire class of these New Presbyterians, that come to the west; and they, as it is natural, in return, sustain that intrusive and schismatical associations, (for such it is,) in its continued infringements upon what is the proper functions and due order of the church itself. Towards evangelical Congregationalists, as a distinct christian denomination, we have no other feeling than of respect and affectionate regard; and to the individuals of this class, who come among us in good faith, receive and adopt our creed and our form of Government, we respectfully give the right hand of fellowship, and rejoice in their aid. This we say, and can say truly, that we may not be chargeable with holding an invidious prejudice. We earnestly pray, that wisdom and union may mark your deliberations, in conjunction with the determined purpose not to be satisfied with any thing less than some clear and decided measures of Reform. And should these be denied by the next General Assembly, then we trust the Convention will not adjourn until they shall have solemnly deliberated on the next step, whether further efforts for reform or for a separate union of those who conscientiously adhere to the standards of the Presbyterian church, but who can no longer reconcile it to their sense of duty to remain in an ostensible connection with these, with whom they have no real union. On you, Beloved Brethren, rests a solemn responsibility. If you are wise, firm and united, in maintaining the truth and order of the church, now so grievously assailed, & trampled upon, the blessing of many generations will come upon you. That thus you may act, and be thus blessed, is the desire and prayer of your companions in tribulation of the Indianapolis Presbytery.

A true copy   Signed by order
Done in Presbytery, at   Attest WILLIAM SICKLES
Knightstown, April 10,   Stated Clerk Ind.Pres.
            1835.

4. LETTER FROM THE PRESBYTERY OF CHILLICOTHE, OHIO
TO THE PRESBYTERY OF EBENEZER, KENTUCKY ON
THE QUESTION OF SLAVERY, 1836

Ohio   Jan. 6th   1836

The presbytery of Chillicothe to the presbytery of Ebenezer
Ky.

Dear Brethren beloved in the Lord — Feeling that the cause of Christ is a common cause, in which all the members of his body the church, wherever found are more or less interested, we are induced to address you on a subject deeply involving her purity and prosperity. So close and tender are the ties which bind us together as members of the same church, and as children born of the same spirit that where one member rejoices, or suffers all the members should rejoice or suffer with it. The present time is witness to the saddening truth, that vital godliness is greatly declining, division in some form prevailing, alienation of feeling and affection toward the brethren existing, and but little success attending the means of grace and the efforts of the church for the extension of the Redeemers Kingdom. For all this there is verily a cause and that cause exists in the church. The great head of the church in all these things is saying unto us — "There is an accursed thing in the midst of thee O Israel, thou canst not stand before thine enemies untill ye take away the accursed thing from among you" What then dear brethren is our duty in such a crisis as this? Is it not to enquire diligently after the cause in order to its speedy removal, from the church, that the divine presence and blessing may no longer be with-held from us? Up sanctify the people, is the command of God addressed to all the leaders in Israel; and feeling this to be incumbent and believing that the sin of *SLAVERY* as it exists in the church is the *"accursed thing"* we as a presbytery have been impelled under these Convictions and a love to the souls of men, to adopt measures for its exclusion from the churches under our care. "The following resolutions, expression of our views as a presbytery touching this subject, we have adopted, and they are hereby laid before you that you may as a presbytery consider them, and if you approve any or all of them that you may adopt them, or something similar which shall go to exclude slavery in due time and in a proper manner this crying sin from the churches under your care viz.

1st.   Resolved That the buying, selling, or holding of a slave for the sake of gain, is a heinous sin and scandal requiring the cognizance of the Judicatures of the church ————

2nd.   Resolved that giving or bequeathing slaves to children or others as property, is a great sin and whenever committed by members of the church, ought to subject them to church censure.

3rd.   Resolved That to sell a slave his own Liberty, except when the slave was purchased at his own request, and has failed to remunerate his master for the price paid is a great injustice and ought to be made a term of communion ————

4th.   Resolved That to offer a slave his freedom only on the condition that he will leave his country and go into a foreign land, is unjust and cruel, and ought to subject a church member to censure.

5th.   Resolved That when a slave is emancipated whose services have been of much value to his master refusing to give him a reasonable compensation for his labor, when the master is able to do it; or turning him out to the world when he wishes to stay as a tenant or a hireling is a great sin and when committed by a church member ought to subject him to suspension until he repent.

6th.   Resolved That when a master advertises a reward for a runaway slave against whom no other crime is alleged than escaping from slavery, he is guilty of a scandalous sin and forfeits his right to the sealing ordinances of God's house.

7.   Resolved That to apprehend a slave who is endeavoring to escape from slavery with a view to restore him to his master is a direct violation of the divine law, and when committed by a member of the church ought to subject him to censure.

8th.   Resolved That any member of our church who shall

advocate, or speak in favor of such laws as have been or may yet be enacted for the purpose of keeping the slave in ignorance and preventing them from learning to read the word of God, is guilty of a great sin, and ought to be dealt with as for other scandalous crimes.

9th. Resolved That should any member of our church be so wicked as to manifest a desire to exclude colored people from a seat in the house of God, or at the Lord's table with white people he ought on conviction thereof to be suspended from the Lord's table untill he repent.

Believing as we do, that every Christian church, or union, or association of particular churches, is entitled to declare the terms of admitance into its communion and the qualifications of its ministers and members as well as the whole system of its internal government, which Christ hath appointed; we can see no good reason why the church or any branch of it, should hesitate to exclude in a regular way this sin, merely because we find it involved in our political relations. If any man chooses to hold slaves under the constitution of any slaveholding state, we as a church infringe not upon his constitutional rights. But has he a right to enforce a claim upon the grant of church communion, while chargeable with a sin in itself so peculiarly heinous in the sight of God? Certainly not. If our government should establish and protect by Law a system of the grosest Idolatry, would it be the duty of the church on that account to admit those who practice it into her communion? Certainly not. In such a case while rendering obedience to God we would only claim the exercise of our own rights, without infringing on any man's civil rights. Every man, in such a case and also in the case of slavery would have his election, and although he might be dissatisfied, yet certainly he could have no just cause of complaint, especially if the church should be acting in a way consistent with the word of God, as we verily believe would be the case while aiming at the speedy and entire removal of this sin from our beloved Church. Say not the work is too great, nor this deadly enemy to our peace and prosperity too powerfull to be resisted. It

is a sin that loves the darkness and cannot endure the light.
An enemy that cannot stand before the sword of the spirit
and the remnant of God's people, girded with the panoply
of heaven and trusting in the God of Zion for victory.
Prayer and consistent effort in this matter will bring to our
aid the resources of OMNIPOTENCE.

Praying that the great head of the church may by his
spirit and his word guide you on his own right way we
remain

Affectionately
Yours.

Signed by order of the JNO P. VANDYKE S. Clerk
Presbytery.

5. ACTION OF THE NORTH ALABAMA PRESBYTERY ON THE CONTROVERSIAL ISSUES, 1831-1838[5]

[1831[6]]

Resolved that it be recommended to all churches within
our bounds to take up a monthly collection in aid of the
funds of the American Board of Commissioners for Foreign Missions.

[April 5, 1832[7]]

The committee appointed to take into consideration the
minutes of the Convention in Cincinnati, & the report of the
minority, made the following report, viz.[8]

Whereas, the minutes of the convention which met in Cincinnati in 1831 by recommendation of the last Genl. Assembly to consult on Missions, and also the report of the
minority of said convention have been sent to this Presbytery with the design that they may express their views on the
subject, Resolved that this Presbytery severely regret, that

[5] MS. *Minutes of the North Alabama Presbytery* in the possession of the
Historical Foundation, Montreat, North Carolina.

[6] MS. *Minutes,* p. 121.

[7] MS. *Minutes,* pp. 128-129.

[8] For an account of the Cincinnati Convention see Baird, "History of the
New School," *op. cit.,* pp. 376-391; see also brief statement in Chapter V
of Part I; also Hightower, *op. cit.,* pp. 160-170.

the evils occasioned by the collisions of Assembly's Board
and the Board of the American Home Missionary Society
from their separate action in the valley of the Mississippi
appear not likely to be removed by the measures adopted
by that convention.

Resolved that the measures proposed by the minority of
the convention to request the next Genl. Assembly to form a
Separate board in the west were in the view of this Presbytery made in the spirit of compromise, and would in their
opinion be the most probable means of removing the evils,
complained of, & producing peace in the church.

Resolved, that although in view of the feelings of a large
portion of our church on this subject, a union of the two
boards is not now to be expected, yet this presbytery do approve of the organization & rejoice in the operations of
the American Home Missionary Society. This report was
adopted by the following vote, viz. 9 to 7.

[Sept. 7, 1837, Moulton, Ala.[9]]
Saturday morning, 8½ o'clock.
Presbytery met and was constituted with prayer.

The committee appointed to draft a resolution or resolutions expressive of the views of this Presbytery in regard
to the doings of the last assembly in reference to the attempted excision of the Synods of Western Reserve, Genessee, Geneva & Utica etc. Reported, which report was accepted, and, is as follows, viz.:

The Committee appointed to draft a resolution or resolutions expressive of the views of this Presbytery in reference
to the doings of the last Gen'l. Assembly in regard to their
attempted excision of the four Synods of Western Reserve,
Geneva, Genessee, and Utica, and also their attempted effort
to dissolve the third Presbytery of Philadea — beg leave to
present the following report —

Resolved, 1st Th[at] the Presbyteries of our Church
being the appointed guardians of its constitution it is at
once our duty and privilege as a Presbytery to review the

[9] MS. *Minutes,* pp. 222-223.

proceedings of the General Assembly and to express our approval or disapproval of any measures adopted by them.

Resolved 2d. that the attempted excision of the four Synods above mentioned is highly unconstitutional. The following reasons are offered in proof of this position.

First, These Synods were regularly constituted by the Gen'l. Assembly whose province it is to form Synods. These Synods were not created by the Plan of Union of 1801, and did not depend for their original existence or continuation upon that plan. Were we to admit the propriety of the act of abrogation, it can do no more than take away the privileges it conferred, among these may be enumerated as most objectionable the provision which admitted a committee man to have a seat in the Presbytery, now the act of abrogation takes away this privilege, and the committee man has no longer a seat —

Bow [but] how this feature in the plan of union or any other which it contains goes to vitiate the entire structure of Presbyteries & Synods formed by the Assembly itself your committee cannot see.

Secondly, whatever may be the gentle language of the friend of excision, denying that it is excision — it appears to us most manifestly a judicial act of the utmost severity cutting off from the church a very large number of ministers and laity without giving them the opportunity of a hearing.

Now our Book of Discipline points out carefully the method to be persued toward those who err. — Definite charges must be made out, witnesses summoned etc. etc. See Book of Discipline, Chap. 4 throughout.

But again Chap. 7 — Sect. 6 — When any important delinquency or grossly unconstitutional proceedings appear in the record of any judicatory, or are charged against them by common fame, the first step to be taken by the judicatory next above is to cite the judicatory alleged to have offended to appear at a specified time and place & to show what it has done or failed to do in the case in question, after which the judicatory issuing the citation, shall remit the whole matter to the delinquent judicatory with a direction to take it up & dispose of it in a constitutional manner, or stay all further proceedings in the case as the circumstances may require.

The Genl. Assembly in their course of action toward the afore mentioned Synod did it appear[s] to us violate most grossly the very letters and spirit of that portion of the Book of Discipline just cited.

Resolved 3d. That the Third Presbytery of Philad. has just cause of complaint against the last Genl. Assembly in their effort to dissolve that Presbytery — The resolution purporting the dissolution of that Presbytery was manifestly unconstitutional because it virtually condemned them without accusation or citation — It was an assumption of power not authorized by the Book of Discipline See Bk. of Dis. Chap. 12.

Resolved 4. That we do hereby cordially sympathize with the so called ejected Synods and with the third Pres. of Philada. and that we concur in the opinion expressed by a large number of the brethren, that the Presbyteries comprising those Synods together with the Pres. of Philada. should go on to elect commissioners to the next Genl. Assembly as heretofore regarding the action of the last Assembly, in reference to them as entirely unconstitutional —

Preamble & first Resolution unanimously adopted —
Second Resolution adopted
Third & fourth Resolution lost

[Oct. 6, 1838[10]]

The committee to examine the minutes of the Assembly, reported, which report was accepted and the resolution which it contained adopted, and is as follows —

They recommend to the attention of the Pres. the acts of the Assembly on the State of the Church, pps. 34,35, and would recommend the adoption of the following resolution in regard thereto, viz. —

Resolved that while it is known that there exists a difference of opinion among the members of this Presbytery in

[10] MS. *Minutes,* p. 243.

regard to the regularity or expediency of some of the acts
of the Assemblies of '37 and '38, They do nevertheless
hereby declare their cordial adherence to the body which
met in the 7th Pres. Church in the city of Philadelphia and
continued its session there until its close as being the true
& only Gen. Assembly of the Presbyterian Church in the
United States of America.

Adopted 9 for
   5 against

6. RESOLUTIONS ADOPTED BY THE PRESBYTERY OF LOUIS-
VILLE ON THE ACTION OF THE GENERAL ASSEMBLIES
OF 1837 AND 1838[11]

[Sept. 12, 1837]

. . . Resolved that this Pby approve the acts of the last
Genl Assembly

1 In the abrogation of the plan of union of 1801 be-
tween Presbyterians and congregationalists. The yeas and
nays on this item being called for stand thus. Yeas W.L.
Breckinridge, N.L.Rice, H.H.Hopkins, J.Hawthorn, C.P.
Humphrey, A.H.Kerr and D.G.Stuart, ministers — and
Danl Rizer, Jno. Berniss, J.C.Bayless, J.B.Locke, Wm.
Robison W.Q.Morton, Geo.Bergen Wm.Smith Thos Pax-
ton, Jno Park Henry Cummins, H.R. Tunstall, A.Logan,
Robt Hamilton C Obannon and S.Wilson ruling elders 23.
Nays A.A.Shannon, D.C.Banks and M.A. Remley minis-
ters; and J.N Weaver ruling elder 4

2 In disowning, in consequence of the abrogation of
said plan the Synods of Western Reserve, Geneva, Utica
and Genessee, as being entirely constitutional — Yeas
Breckinridge Rice, Kerr, Hopkins, Hawthorn, Stuart, Wilson Rizer Berniss, Bayless, Robison, Morton, Bergen,
Smith, Paxton, Park, Cummings, Tunstall, Logan, Hamilton and Obannon — 21 Nays Banks, Shannon, Remley,
Humphrey, Locke & Weaver 6. Non Liquet D.C. Proctor.

3. The Pby. also approve of the proceedings of the

[11] Records of Louisville Presbytery, Sept. 12, 1837, pp. 159-160. MS. in
possession of the Historical Foundation, Montreat, N. C.

Assembly in reference to the A.H.Missionary and the A. Education Societies. Yeas precisely as on the preceeding resolution, Nays Banks, Remley, Humphrey, Locke and Weaver, 5. Non liquet A.A.Shannon.

4   The Pby also cordially approve of the establishment of a Board of Foreign Missions by the Assembly. This was adopted unanimously.

5   The Pby also approve of the act of the Assembly in dissolving the 3rd Pby of Philadelphia. Yeas as on the second resolution. Nays Shannon Remley, Banks, Humphrey, Locke and Weaver. . . .

PROTEST AND ANSWER, LOUISVILLE PRESBYTERY,
SEPT. 12, 1837[12]

Protest

The undersigned in reference to the resolutions of Pby approving the acts of the genl.Assembly disowning the Synods of the Western Reserve, Genessee, Utica & Geneva, and dissolving the third Pby of Philadelphia hereby enter our protest against the said resolutions and for the following reasons, viz—

1   Because with respect to the Synod of the Western Reserve, that Synod we think was not formed in pursuance of the plan of Union of 1801, inasmuch as the only effect of that plan was the formation of *individual churches* of a peculiar character. The abrogation of that plan, therefore, could only affect the mixed churches so called, and could not impair the existence of the Synod nor, especially the ecclesiastical standing of regular Pbn Ministers, and regularly organized Pbn. churches.

2.   In regard to the synods of Geneva, Genesse, and Utica, we observe in addition that the act disowning them is based on the assumption "that they were formed & attached to this body (i e the Genl Assembly) under and in execution of said plan of union" of 1801 — whereas we be-

---

[12] Records of the Louisville Presbytery, pp. 162-167.

lieve that this plan *was never adopted*, to any considerable extent, within the limits of the three Synods. The assumption on which the Assembly proceeded being groundless the acts based upon it are void. The plan of union of 1808 in operation in the three Synods has not been abrogated, or annulled by the Assembly.

3 In regard to the third Pby of Phila. we protest because the Pby was dissolved on the ground of heresy vaguely charged but without being accused, cited, tried or condemned, and that too without suitable opportunity of defence contrary to the dictates of natural justice as well as the provisions of our book of Discipline.

Finally we protest against all the proceedings herein noticed, because, they endanger the existence of the Synods of Albany and New Jersey in which are great numbers of churches formed on the plan of union of 1801. We fear that consistency will require future assemblys to cut off these large and pious Synods. Moreover as great numbers of Presbyteries in different sections of the church were formed by the assembly, the reasons urged against the constitutional existence of the 3rd Pby of Phila. may be hereafter employed to destroy other Presbyteries.

For these reasons we would respectfully but solemnly record our protest against the resolutions of Pby approving these proceedings. And we do hereby *Protest* & *Remonstrate* against them as unconstitutional as subversive of the principles of sound Presbyterianism, and as distructive to the spiritual interests of our beloved Zion. Signed by Danl C.Banks, A.A.Shannon, M.A.Remley, G.P.Humphrey, J.B.Locke and J.N.Weaver.

Answer

In reply to the above protest Pby remark —

1 That the plan of Union of 1801 was obviously unconstitutional, that it was therefore the imperative duty of the Assembly to abrogate it. If the plan was unconstitutional

all the acts based upon it were null and void. We believe it to be a fact that the Synod of the Western reserve was formed upon that plan.

"A Pby consists of all the ministers and one ruling elder from each congregation within a certain district" and "A Synod is a convention of Bishops and elders within a larger district, including at least three Presbyteries". Book of Discipline Chaps 10 & 11. But it is an admitted fact that the very large majority of the churches in the Western Reserve are congregational, and not Presbyterian, consequently the ch.sessions, Presbyteries and Synod consist to a great extent of congregationalists. The sessions, Presbyteries and Synod were therefore unconstitutionally formed. Besides the constitution of the Presbyterian church never contemplated that Presbyterian ministers should become the Pastors of congregational churches, therefore the ministers of the W.Reserve being principally either congregationalists or Presbyterians who were pastors of congregational churches had no right to seats on the floor of the Genl Assembly. For many years we have had the anomaly of congregational churches represented by their ministers and laymen in the general Assembly. The protestants are therefore obviously in error when they say "the Synod of W.Reserve was not formed in pursuance of the plan of Union of 1801".

2.   In relation to the Synods of Geneva, Genessee, and Utica we respond that if it be admitted as the protestants aver that they were formed on a plan of Union adopted in 1808, it will not follow that the act of the Assembly disowning them was null and void. The Genl Assembly abrogated the plan of 1801 as being unconstitutional because it allowed our church sessions, Presbyteries, Synods and General Assembly, to be constituted in part of congregationalists. The principle of both the plans, if we regard them as independent, is the same; and the declaration of the assembly that the one is unconstitutional, necessarily implies that the other is of the same character.

Moreover the Assembly disowned the said Synod because

their connection with the Presbyterian church was based on an unconstitutional arrangement. It matters not therefore, whether that unconstitutional plan was formed in 1801 or in 1808.

3. The objection of the protestants to the dissolution of the 3rd Pby of Ph[iladelphia] is, we believe, not well founded. The act of the Assembly, by which the Pby was dissolved, was not of the nature of discipline; and therefore there could have been no propriety in citation and trial. If the Assembly believed it to be conducive to the prosperity of the church that the 3rd Pby of Phila. should be dissolved and that its ministers and churches should become connected with other Presbyteries; they had the right to dissolve it, without calling on the Pby to make any defence; and in doing so they interfered with no constitutional right of its members. It is not important to inquire now whether the reports of heresy, referred to by the protestants, are true or false; because it is not essential to the validity or the propriety of the acts of a judicatory, that *all* the reasons by which its members were influenced, be correct.

Finally this Pby do not believe that the proceedings of the Assembly in relation to the disowned synods endangers the Synods of Albany and New Jersey; because the church sessions and Presbyteries constituting those synods are strictly Presbyterian. But if it be true that they are not; it is believed, that it would be for the good of the church that they should be excinded

Moreover, if it be true, that other Presbyteries have been formed by the Assembly contrary to the constitution of the church and to the earnest desires of the Synods to which they belong, we can see no evil arising from the dissoluton and constitutional formation of such Presbyteries. This Pby however is not aware of the existence of Presbyteries formed as was the third Pby of Philadelphia.

For these reasons and others which might be mentioned the Pby regard the objections of the Protestants as wholly unfounded. . . .

RESOLUTIONS ADOPTED BY LOUISVILLE PRESBYTERY
SEPT. 11, 1838

. . . Whereas the Presbyterian church in these United States has been greatly agitated for some years by questions of doctrine and order — and whereas this agitation has resulted in a division of the church by the secession of a portion of the commissioners to the last general Assembly and the adherence to them of many persons throughout the church, — and whereas in such an exigency it is proper that each Pby. distinctly express its views and intentions, therefore

Resolved That this Pby does hereby recognize and adhere to the body which met and continued to sit in the 7th Pbn. church, Philadelphia, in May last, as the General Assembly of the Presbyterian church in the United States of America. And we do hereby repudiate every other body claiming to be the General Assembly — believing that those ministers and ruling elders alone who sat in the 7th church were properly organized as the Genl Assembly of the Presbyterian church.

Resolved 2nd. That this Pby expects all persons in its connexion to adhere in good faith to the General Assembly as above recognized — to abstain from all acts designed or adapted to disturb the repose of the church — to avoid the introduction and countenance of all sentiments and measures which are at variance with the standards of the Pbn. church, — to encourage and sustain according to their ability the several institutions of the General Assembly, and to decline the support of those institutions of which the Pby. the Synod of Ky, and the General Assembly have expressed their disapprobation.

Resolved 3rd. That this Pby. deem union of counsel and of effort, and mutual confidence as of more importance than numbers, and indispensible to the honour and prosperity of religion :— and while we desire none of our members to separate themselves from us unless they prefer to do so, we are deliberately of opinion if there be any persons united with this Pby. who are unwilling to adhere to the General Assembly as above recognized, to submit to its acts, to support its policy, to encourage & sustain its institutions and to abstain from the encouragement of all other measures and institutions which are hostile to its policy and influence; that candor, brotherly kindness, peace, and the welfare of Zion, as far as its interests are committed to us, require that such persons should no longer seek to maintain a connexion with this Pby.

Resolved 4th. That this Pby. does hereby solemnly express the conviction that the American Home Missionary and the American Education societies have exerted a vast influence in agitating and corrupting the Presbyterian Church.

Resolved 5th. That we recognize a very special duty now to support the Assembly's board of Education and her Boards of Missions; and in particular at this juncture the Board of foreign missions recently commencing its glorious work. The Presbyterian church has been too long either slumbering over this dying world or directing her energies when exerted at all, through channells not furnished by her own organization, nor subject to her control And now that our own board is in successful operation we do affectionately urge upon our own people to unite in its cordial and liberal support and no longer to divert their contributions into other societies of irresponsible and insecure organization, and in no degree subject to their control.

The first and third of the above resolutions were adopted unanimously. The second was adopted mem con — The fourth and fifth with one dissenting voice, Brother Shannon was excused from voting, and Bro Humphrey presented the following protest which was ordered to be entered on the minutes as containing nothing demanding a particular reply.

The undersigned not having concurred in some of the resolutions adopted by Pby. in relation to the proceedings of the last General Assembly asks leave to submit in respect to them his humble protest.

1. He does not concur in approving those proceedings of the last Assembly which go to affirm the acts of 1837 disowning certain Synods, Because (1) Those acts were in his judgment unconstitutional in that by them were separated from us large numbers of regularly ordained and confessedly sound and orthodox ministers and ruling elders together with many churches duly organized according to our form of government. (2) These acts if not unconstitutional are at least extraordinary, and being such are adapted to create the impression that in the judgment of the church its system of discipline does not in its regular ordinary working furnish a remedy for error and disorder. This impression, especially when countenanced by our highest judiciary, your protestant regards as of exceedingly pernicious tendency.

2. Your Protestant cannot concur in the opinion that the commissioners from the Presbyteries within the disowned synods were justly excluded from their seats in the last Assembly, since the acts disowning them were, as he judges, unconstitutional and therefore void.

3 Your Protestant submits the following objections to the three acts so called of the last Assembly. (1)st they seem in the judgment of many to present the approval of the acts of 1837 & 1838 as the test of good and regular standing in the Presbyterian church; whereas no such test of membership or good standing is known to the form of government. (2) Your protestant discovers in these acts a tendency towards an assumption of power by the Genl. Assembly, not delegated to that Judicatory, & towards encroachments on the just prerogatives of inferior judicatories, threatning thereby an alarming centralization of ecclesiastical power. (3) Your protestant moreover discovers in them the development of the alarming doctrine that the constitution so far as it relates to the Assembly, is a *limitation* not a grant of special powers. This doctrine is plainly fatal to the rights of Presbyteries, which are the fountains of power, not the creatures of the Assembly.

4 Your protestant objects to the resolution of Pby. con-

cerning A.H.Missionary, and the A.Education Societies, for the reasons which are contained in a certain protest relating to those societies signed by B Dickinson and others, and published in the minutes of the Assembly of 1837.

5 Your protestant cannot concur in the resolution of Pby in regard to the subject of foreign missions, because of its unfavourable aspect towards societies having a kindred object. This Pby. while it cherishes our own board of missions, should, it is believed regard with the utmost affection and with gratitude to God the efforts of all societies which are devoted to the holy and blessed work of publishing the gospel to the heathen. Especially should it so regard the operations of the American Board of Commissioners for Foreign Missions.

EDWD P. HUMPHREY.

7. RESOLUTIONS ADOPTED BY THE TUSCALOOSA PRESBYTERY
APPROVING THE ACTION OF THE GENERAL ASSEMBLY
OF 1837

[Session Oct. 3, 1837, New Hope Church, Greene County, Ala.[13]]
The Committee on the minutes of the Assembly made a report which was received, amended and adopted and is as follows —

The Presby. has no disposition to sit in judgement upon the doings of the General Assembly, but simply [asks] the privilege in common with all other similar bodies of declaring freely their views on all subjects of this Kind — We are strongly attached to the Standards of our Church in their commonly received meaning and are determined to be first pure then peaceable — We are persuaded that the evils in our church so threatening in their aspect required prompt and energetic action — therefore

1. Resolved, that this Presby. approve of the abrogation of the Plan of Union formed in 1801, regarding it as unconstitutional in its nature and injurious in its tendency

2. Resolved, that inasmuch as the Synods of the West-

[13] MS., pp. 57-73.

ern Reserve, Utica, Geneva, and Genesee grew out of that plan, we approve of the act of the Assembly declaring them no constitutional part of the General Assembly of the Pres-

(Rev. D. Baker dissents from the 2nd Resolution simply on the ground of his not being in possession of the evidence of the fact here affirmed — entered by order of Presby.)

byterian Church.

3. Resolved that we cordially unite with the General Assembly in condemning certain doctrinal errors existing in our church.

4. Resolved, That inasmuch as the American Education Society and especially the American Home Missionary Society distract the peace and endanger the purity of our Zion, we approve the action of the Assembly recommending that they cease to operate in any of our churches —

5. Resolved, That in as much as we believe the Third Presbytery of Philadelphia to have been unconstitutionally formed we approve of its dissolution —

6. Resolved, That in relation to Foreign Missions while the Presby. cherish the most cordial affection for the American Board of Foreign Missions they nevertheless rejoice in the formation of a Presbyterian Foreign Missionary Society

(Note The Moderator Rev. W. W. Williams obtained permission to enter his dissent to the above resolution.)

8. ACTION OF THE SYNOD OF NORTH CAROLINA JUSTIFYING THE ACTION OF THE GENERAL ASSEMBLY OF 1837

[September, 1837]

The committee, therefore, recommends the following resolutions: viz.

1. Resolved that, in the opinion of this Synod, the Plan of Union of 1801 was unconstitutional, at first; & as long as the constitution remains unaltered, in its fundamental principles, must continue to be unconstitutional.

2. Resolved, that we hail its abrogation with satisfaction, as a signal triumph of principle, over that common frailty

of our nature, which lends us to desire to increase numbers, at the expense of truth.

3. Resolved, that the separation of the four Synods from our connexion, was an act, which naturally & properly followed such abrogation; & that, as they were separated from our connexion, with their organization complete, & ministerial character untouched, this Synod cannot but regret such act as combining tenderness to Christian brethren with faithfulness to the truth.

4. Resolved, that this Synod regards the attempt to give Abolition a principal influence in bringing about that result, as making a false issue; & as it was not alluded to in the debate, they believe it had little or no influence in bringing about the decision, but they believe the question was honestly debated, & decided on its own merits.

5. Resolved, that the language of reproach & invective, which has been used against the late Assembly, & which charges on the majority & their adherents insidious & seductive strategems, false pretences, & the ambitious thirst of power, is uncharitable & unwise; & until those charges are proved, we must regard them as not justified by any act of the majority.

6. Resolved, that the right & duty of the church to educate those who are to minister in her sanctuary, is unquestionable; & we believe it to be both unwise & improper to give up the control of this matter to another denomination, while the church has the ability to do it; & we believe it to be unsafe to instruct the management of the missionary operations in the church, to men who have made such societies extensively, the engines of party. This Synod, therefore, approves of the recommendation of the General Assembly, in relation to the "American Home Missionary Society," & the "American Education Society."

7. Resolved, that, inasmuch as the formation of Presbyteries, on the principle of Elective Affinity, is manifestly unconstitutional, & that, as many evils have grown up from the formation of the Third Presbytery of Philadelphia; & as any Body is competent to repeal its own acts, the Synod

hereby expresses its cordial approbation of the dissolution of the Third Presbytery of Philadelphia by the last General Assembly.

8. Resolved, that while the necessity of certain measures which were adopted, is deeply deplored, the Synod regards it as a solemn duty, to sustain to the full extent of its influence, the whole action of the Assembly, believing it to be important to the preservation of our Ecclesiastical order, doctrine, & discipline; & with the blessing of God, happily calculated to arrest existing evils; &, ultimately to restore, to our beloved Zion, purity, peace, harmony & fraternal confidence.

Signed by Committee of Nine.

9. REPORT OF COMMITTEE ON THE STATE OF THE CHURCH, CONCORD PRESBYTERY (NORTH CAROLINA), OCTOBER, 1837[14]

Statesville, Oct. 12th 1837.

. . . The Committee on the State of the Church reported, and their report was accepted and adopted. The vote on adopting was taken by Ays and Nos & was as follows:

Ays — John Robinson D.D. Samuel Paisley, Walter S. Pharr, John M. Erwin, Stephen Frontis, Samuel Williamson, Henry N. Pharr, Daniel A. Penick, Samuel L. Watson, Patrick J. Sparrow, A. Y. Lockridge, James D. Hall, J. M. H. Adams, J. M. M. Caldwell — Elders Col. Wm. Allison, Thomas Allison, Francis Beattie, W. M. Stitt, Thomas Stephenson, A. Davis, J. Sloan, G. Andrews, Wm. Flemming, J. Silliman, Benj. Phifer, John McNeely, Daniel McIver, Richard Hall, Laird Blair— 29

Nos — None.

The following is the report adopted viz:

The committee on the State of the Church in reference to the action of the last General Assembly recommend the adopting of the following resolutions viz:

[14] MS. *Records of Concord Presbytery,* October 12, 1837, IV, pp. 56-59, Historical Foundation, Montreat, N. C.

1st.   Resolved that this Presbytery after mature deliberation do fully approve of the act of the Gen. Assembly of 1837 abrogating "the plan of union of 1801, for the accommodation of churches in the New Settlements," —the said plan having been from the beginning "unconstitutional & void."

2. Resolved that we approve of the resolutions of the said Assembly, declaring the Synods of the Western reserve of Utica, Genesse, & Geneva "to be out of the Ecclesiastical connexion of the Presbyterian church in the U.S.A. & that they are not in form or in fact an integral portion of said Church."

3. Resolved that we approve the act of the said Assembly dissolving the Third Presbytery of Philadelphia, which Presbytery was unconstitutionally formed; and has been the fruitful source of Strife and vexation from its beginning.

4. Resolved that we fully approve of the resolution of said Assembly concerning the American Home Miss. and the American Education Societies being fully persuaded that associations formed for the spread of the gospel, should be held responsible for their doings to the Church.

5. Resolved that we approve the act of said Assembly, Organizing a Board of Foreign Missions, and recommend to our churches and to all our members to sustain said Board.

6. Resolved that we fully approve of the resolution of said Assembly bearing testimony against errors in doctrine & irregularities in practice.

Finally, Resolved that we as a Presbytery, loving the purity, peace & order of the Church are solemnly bound fully to sustain to the extent of our influence the whole action of the last General Assembly; confidently believing that it was in accordance with the will of God; and that His blessing will rest on all lawful efforts to purify his own Church.

S. WILLIAMSON
P. J. SPARROW   } Committee.
GEORGE ANDREWS

Ordered that the Stated Clerk forward a copy of the above resolutions to the "Southern Christian Herald," and to the "Watchman of the South," for publication. . . .

REPORT OF THE COMMITTEE ON MINUTES OF THE GENERAL
ASSEMBLY, CONCORD PRESBYTERY, OCT. 15, 1838[15]

Mocksville, Oct. 15th 1838

. . . The Committee on the minutes of the Gen. Ass. reported in part and their report was accepted and adopted and is as follows viz: For years the conflicting and unhappy state of the Presbyterian Church, has been manifestly and rapidly approaching a crisis, to which no friend of her interest could look with indifference.

That her true members should sit in passive silence, and see her pure doctrines and order continually assailed and supplanted by her professed adherents, *was not to be expected*, — and yet when the needed and faithful warning against encroaching & dangerous errors was given, the friends of truth were charged by the New School party with an intollerant Spirit and uncharitable rigor.

In this humbled state of our church; whilst a strong, foreign influence was bearing down with fearful effect on her dearest rights and interests; and whilst new and dangerous doctrines were publishing from many of her pulpits; and teaming from the press; the church felt it to be her right, as it was her most sacred duty to arise in the strength of her Redeemer and reform encroaching abuses.

For this arduous work the Lord was graciously pleased to interpose for the defence of our beloved Zion; in a manner demanding our lasting gratitude.

When it appeared that the disturbers of our peace had the fixed determination of adhering to their erroneous doctrines, and still holding a place in the Presbyterian Church that they might rule and revolutionize it, the Lord evidently confused their counsels and delivered his Church in the day of her adversity.

[15] MS. *Records of Concord Presbytery,* Oct. 15, 1838, IV, pp. 116-119, Historical Foundation, Montreat, N. C.

That the Gen. Assembly of 1838 which held its sessions in the 7th Presbyterian Church of Philadelphia was the true and only Gen. Assembly of the Presbyterian Church in the U.S.A. we hold to be an obvious fact to every unprejudiced mind.

Therefore Resolved that we highly approve the dignified and christian manner in which the true Gen.Ass. of 1838 acted during the strange and willful disorder of the Seceding party.

Resolved that we fully approve the action of said Assembly for the reform and pacification of the Church; and that we will sustain to the extent of our ability, this noble struggle for the peace and purity of our Zion. . . .

10. ACTION OF THE HOLSTON PRESBYTERY DECLARING THE EXSCINDING ACTS OF THE GENERAL ASSEMBLY OF 1837 UNCONSTITUTIONAL

[Throughout eastern Tennessee the New School party were in the majority. The following is the action taken by the New School majority of the Holston Presbytery in reference to the exscinding Acts of the General Assembly of 1837.]

[New Providence Church, Saturday, September 30, 1837.]

The committee appointed to take into consideration the report of their commissioner to the last General Assembly, brought in a minute, which was accepted.

It was then moved that said minute be adopted. But after some discussion thereon, Presbytery took a recess until after divine service.

Presbytery met.

The discussion of the minute, of the committee, on the report of our commissioner to the last General Assembly, was continued; and, after some debate, it was moved that each resolution, of said minute, be taken up separately.

The said resolutions were then discussed separately, and adopted; and are as follows:

The committee appointed to take into consideration the report of our Commissioner to the last General Assembly, present the following minute:

Whereas the last General Assembly did abrogate the "plan of union", formed in eighteen hundred, an[d] one, between the General Assembly of the Presbyterian Church, and the General Association of Connecticut, and, consequent upon that act, did declare four Synods, viz. the Western Reserve, Utica, Genesee, and Geneva, neither in form, nor fact, an integral portion of the Presbyterian Church of these United States; and, whereas, the said General Assembly did declare the action of the American Home Missionary Society, and the American Education Society, injurious to the interests of the Presbyterian Church; and did discountenance their influence within the limits of our Presbyteries; and, whereas, the said General Assembly did bind its officers not to receive the credentials of certain commissioners to the next General Assembly, denounced by the last General Assembly: And, whereas, it is the duty of the Presbyteries, who are the constituents of the General Assembly, to express their approbation, or disapprobation, of the doings of the General Assembly: Therefore,

Resolved, that we consider the acts of the last General Assembly, herein enumerated, contrary to the Constitution of the Presbyterian Church, and an arbitrary assumption of power.

Resolved, that we believe the "plan of Union" was formed by some of the wisest, and purest men in our Church; and the acquiescence of the Presbyterians, during thirty-six years, has made it obligatory.

Resolved, that the four excinded Synods could never have grown out of "the plan of union"; and, if they had, the abrogation of "the plan of union", could not have affected their ecclesiastical standing, as they were formed according to the Book of Discipline.

Resolved, that the dissolution of "the third Presbytery of Philadelphia", belonged alone to the Synod of Philadelphia: and the General Assembly, in exercising this power, were guilty of a usurpation, gross, and palpable.

Resolved, that we cherish unabated confidence in the American Home Missionary Society, and the American

Education Society; and desire their operations within our bounds, and recommend them to the prayers, and patronage of our Churches.

Resolved, that we consider the acts of the last General Assembly as a mournful exhibition of party-spirit,—five hundred ministers, and sixty thousand members of the Presbyterian Church declared to be, neither in form, nor in fact, component parts of the Presbyterian Church, without the form of trial:— a Presbytery dissolved by a tribunal having no authority to act in the case: Societies, whose benevolent action has been felt to the ends of the earth, denounced: and officers made to promise to carry out doings known to be unconstitutional by some of the leaders of the majority of the last General Assembly:— present a picture of misguided zeal, alarming to every friend of civil, as well as religious, liberty, in our free country.

Resolved, that we approve of the unanimous vote of the Convention at Auburn,[16] viz. to exhort the excinded Synods, and dissolved Presbytery, to claim their constitutional rights at the next General Assembly.

Resolved, that our attachment to the Confession of Faith of the Presbyterian Church is sincere, and unabated; and we earnestly pray that this Confession may continue to be observed in the enlarged, and heavenly spirit of our fathers,— and we love the Constitution of our Church, and will use every proper effort to preserve unfettered the liberty, it has given to us, and to our children, from the effort to secure despotic power, by the majority of the last General Assembly.

On motion, ordered, that the Stated Clerk forward a copy of said report to the editor of the Southern Religious Telegraph, for publication.

[16] A convention of the New School representatives met at Auburn, N. Y., on August 17, 1837, and decided neither to abandon the Plan of Union nor to recognize the validity of the actions of the General Assembly of 1837. In a "Declaration" they set forth their "true doctrines" over against the "errors" charged against them by the Old School. See Thompson, R. E., *A History of the Presbyterian Churches in the United States* (New York, 1895), pp. 118, 357-362. Also, Gillett, *op. cit.,* II, pp. 532 ff.

11. ACTION OF THE OLD SCHOOL MINORITY OF THE HOL-
STON PRESBYTERY RELATIVE TO THE DIVISION OF
THE PRESBYTERY INTO OLD SCHOOL
AND NEW SCHOOL BODIES[17]

[The Holston Presbytery was divided over the action of the General Assemblies of 1837 and 1838, the New School party being in the majority. The following are the Minutes of the Old School minority and illustrates the type of problem faced in those regions where such divisions were created.]

Salem Church,
Oct. 5th. 1838.

A majority of the members of Holston Presbytery having, this day, seceded from the Presbyterian church, by giving their formal votes in favour of adhering to the seceding New School Assembly,— and renouncing the jurisdiction of the true General Assembly of the church to which we have ever belonged,— and having left us in connexion with the church, agreeably to provision made by acts of the last General Assembly: We, therefore, being not a quorum for the performance of the business of Presbytery: adjourned to meet to-morrow, hoping that a quorum may attend.

SAML. W. DOAK ⎱ Ministers.
JAS. A. LYON ⎰

E. L. MATHES ⎫
JOS. BULLEN, ⎪
E. BAXTER, ⎬ (Elders)
J. CARSON ⎪
S. NEILL, ⎪
JOS. DUNCAN ⎭

Salem Church,
Oct. 6th. 1838.

We, members of Holston Presbytery, met according to adjournment, and being not a quorum, and having now no

[17] *Minutes of the Holston Presbytery,* October, 1838 to October, 1839, in volume, January 1st, 1827 to September 28, 1843, pp. 161-226, in possession of Historical Foundation, Montreat, N. C.

hope of the attendance of a quorum at this place, adjourned to meet at Rogersville church on the tenth instant, at which time and place the "Synod of Tennessee" is to meet.

SAMUEL W. DOAK, ⎱ Ministers.
JAS.A.LYON. ⎰

JOSEPH BULLEN, ⎱ Elders.
E.L.MATHES ⎰

Rogersville Church,
Oct 10th. 1838.

The Presbytery of Holston met according to the adjourn-ment of two ministers, and two Elders.   Constituted with prayer.

Members present.

Revd.Samuel W.Doak, Rev.Samuel H.Doak, and James A.Lyon: Messrs. S. Neill, of Rogersville church; Wm.Alex-ander, of New Providence; Jos.Bullen, of Mount Bethel; Alex.N.Wilson, of Salem; Jos.Duncan, of Leesburgh; Wm. Deery, of Blountville; Elders.

Revd.Samuel W.Doak, was chosen Moderator, and Revd.Jas.A.Lyon, Clerk pro tempore.

Revd. Samuel W.Doak was unanimously elected Stated Clerk.

Presbytery adjourned to meet in Rogersville, at such place and time as the Moderator may appoint.

Concluded with prayer.

At Dr.Walker's, in Rogersville,
Oct.12th.1838.

Presbytery met, according to adjournment, at the house of Dr.Wm.A.Walker.

Constituted with prayer.

Members present as above.

A letter from Rev.Andrew Vance, addressed to this Pres-bytery, praying that he might be received as a member, was read.

Mr. Vance was received on his own petition, as a member

of this Presbytery,— it having clearly appeared, from the records of Holston Union Presbytery, read yesterday in Synod, to all the members of this Presbytery, that a majority of that Presbytery, to which he formerly belonged, had seceded with the New School Assembly, and had left him, without a quorum of Presbytery, in good standing in the church.

Revd. Messrs. James A.Lyon, S.H.Doak, and Mr.Jos. Duncan, were appointed a committee to draw up some resolutions, or to suggest some plan for the procuring of our Presbyterial records, now in the hands of those members of Holston Presbytery, that have seceded with the New School Assembly.

A Committee, was appointed to take into consideration the [proceedings] of the last General Assembly, consisting of Revd.Messrs. Samuel W.Doak, Samuel H.Doak, and Mr.Joseph Bullen.

Presbytery had a recess 'till four of the clock,P.M.

4 o'clock,P.M.

The committee appointed to take into consideration the subject of our Presbyterial records,(now in the hands of seceded Holston Presbytery) reported. Their report was accepted, and adopted, and is as follows.

"Your committee, appointed to take into consideration the subject of our Presbyterial records, now in the hands of seceded (Holston) Presbytery, would be[g] leave to report the following resolutions:

"Resolved 1st. That the Rev.Messrs. Jas.King, Daniel Rogan, Frederick A.Ross, Jas.McLin, and Jno.W.Cunningham, having, by a solemn vote, and resolution, renounced the jurisdiction of the true General Assembly, of the Presbyterian church, of which Rev.W.S.Plumer is Moderator, and having adhered to the New School, and unconstitutional Assembly, of which Dr.Fisher was Moderator, are to all intents and purposes, seceders from the true Presbyterian Church, and, *as such,* are no longer members of the true Holston Presbytery.

Resolved. 2dly: That as Revd.John W.Cunningham, the former Stated Clerk of this Presbytery, has, in his hands, the records of this Presbytery, that the present Stated Clerk, (Rev S.W Doak), be, and hereby is required to demand from him, in the name of the Presbytery, said records.

The committee appointed to take into consideration the [acts] of the last General Assembly, reported. Their report was accepted, and adopted; and is as follows:

"Your Committee recommend the adoption of the following preamble and resolutions:

"Whereas, the commissioners from this Pby, unauthorized by the word of God,— by the constitution of the church, or by any instructions from this Presbytery, have united with others in dividing the church, by organizing a secession body, which appropriates to itself the name of "the constitutional Assembly". Believing that the appropriation of descriptive names does not impart nature to things, nor prove that the names are applicable: Presbytery ought, in view of the constitution, and the facts in the case, to adopt the following resolutions:

1. Resolved, that this Presbytery recognize the Assembly, organized, under the presidency of Dr. Elliot, on the seventeenth of last May, of which Rev. W. S. Plumer is Moderator, and, which held its sessions in the Seventh Presbyterian Church, Philadelphia, as organized, and consisting, in all respects, in an exact compliance with the constitution of the church, and the standing rules of the Assembly; and, therefore, the true General Assembly of the Church, and that as such we will adhere to it.

2. Resolved, That this Presbytery recognize that body, of which Dr.Fisher is Moderator,— which calls itself the "Constitutional Assembly," as a body organized, *not* agreeably to the provisions of the Constitution, or of the standing rules of the General Assembly; but, as a body organized in opposition to both,— therefore, as not being the Constitutional General Assembly of the church

3. Resolved, that this Presbytery consider itself as under the jurisdiction of the Synod of West Tennessee, on condition that (said) Synod adhere to the true General Assembly."

Ordered, that the Stated Clerk forward a copy of the above "preamble, and resolutions", to the Editors of the Watchman of the South, and the American Presbyterian, for publication.

On motion, a committee, consisting of Revd. Messrs. Saml. W. Doak, Jas. A. Lyon, and Mr. Jos. Bullen, was appointed to prepare a manifesto, and pastoral letter, addressed to the churches under our care.

Revd. Samuel H. Doak was added to said committee.

Revr. Samuel W. Doak, and Mr. Jos. Duncan were appointed a committee to review the records of Rogersville church.

Presbytery received from Mr. Joseph Duncan, a member of a committee,appointed at our Spring meeting to settle with Jno. Stephenson, Esq. executor of M. Stephenson, deceased, the Treasurer of the Home Missionary society of this Presbytery, eleven dollars, a deficit found due the Assembly's Board of Missions, and receipted him for the same.

Ordered, that the Stated Clerk forward the said eleven dollars, to the Assembly's Board of Missions.

The committee appointed to prepare a manifesto, and pastoral letter, reported, and their report was accepted. (*see pamphlet.*) [*sic*]

On motion, the substance of the said report was approved, and the said report was committed to Rev. Messrs. Samuel W. Doak, and Jas. A. Lyon, who were appointed to amend, and prepare, it, for publication, and to superintend the printing of three hundred copies, and distribute them at the expense of Presbytery. which was ordered.

Presbytery adjourned to meet in the Church tomorrow morning at half past eight o'clock.

Concluded with prayer.

Saturday, half past 8 o'clock.A.M.

Presbytery met according to adjournment. Constituted with prayer.

Members present as on yesterday.

Presbytery proceeded to the examination of Mr. A. Alexander Mathes, preparatory to licensure.

Mr. Mathes read a critical Exercise on Rom.1:16;-22. He was then examined on the Hebrew language, and on Church Government. He read a lecture on Heb.12:1,-3, and the exercise,—lecture, & examination, were unanimously sustained.

The committee appointed to review the records of Rogersville church; reported; and their report was accepted, and adopted, & is as follows:

"The committee appointed to review the records of Rogersville church, report that they have reviewed those records, and found them correctly kept.

"Your committee find in these records an account of the proceedings of the Congregation relative to the [acts] of the last General Assembly, which involve principles of vital interest to the Church.

"In our republican form of church Government, power is delegated to church sessions to transact certain business, defined by the constitution.

"In the present state of the Church something of an extraordinary character; viz. a whole congregation called upon to decide what body will be recognized by them as the supreme judicature of the Church.

"This congregation, your committee believe, has the constitutional right, to declare the connexion in which it stands with the highest court in the Presbyterian church, in the present crisis.—

"If the congregation think proper to speake through her organs, the duly elected church officers; or, if she silently acquiesce in their proceedings, it will be construed into an acquiescence. But the power to transact church business as a *church session* derived from the great Head of the church, is derived from the church. With these preliminary remarks, we ask leave to report the following resolutions:—

Resolved 1st. That the Church of Rogersville acted in perfect accordance with the constitution of our Church; (Chap.15 sec.4,) in the vote they have taken.

Resolved; 2dly. That the congregation of Rogersville, by a majority of their votes have fully, and constitutionally decided in favour of adhering to the only true General Assembly of the Presbyterian church, of which Rev. W. S. Plumer is Moderator

Resolved, 3dly. That this Presbytery heartily concur in the decision, and approve the firm, decisive stand the church had taken for the evangelical, orthodox, doctrines of our Confession of Faith as taught in the Bible; and their strict adherence to the discipline, and order of our church."

Presbytery had a recess until after public worship.

Immediately after public worship Mr. Mathes read, from the pulpit, a popular sermon, on Gal.6:14, which sermon was sustained.

Presbytery had a recess till 3 o'clock,P.M.

3 o'clock,P.M.

Mr. Mathes was examined on Church History, Theology, and the Sacraments; which examination was sustained.

Mr. Archibald A. Mathes having answered, in the affirmative, the questions propounded to Candidates, according to Form of Government, Chapter 14, was licensed to preach the Gospel as a probationer for the holy ministry.

Presbytery had a recess 'till after public worship this evening.

After public worship.

Revd.Samuel W.Doak offered the following resolution, which was adopted:

"Resolved that Presbytery recommend, in case the unhappy divisions now in the Presbyterian church should run generally through any congregation within our bounds, that those who adhere to us as the true Holston Presbytery, show to their seceding brethren all that liberality in respect to property, which equity and charity will admit of."

Ephesians 2:8, "By grace are ye saved,&c." was assigned to Mr.Mathes as the subject of an ordination sermon, to be delivered when the way is clear for his ordination.

Rev. Jas. A. Lyon was appointed to preach a sermon, Rev. Samuel H. Doak, to give the charge, and Rev. Samuel W. Doak to preside at the ordination of Mr. Mathes.

Adjourned to meet at Tusculum Academy at a time, of which the Moderator is to give notice: and in case no notice be given, to meet at Mount Bethel Church, on the first Thursday of April, eighteen hundred and thirty nine. Concluded with prayer.

SAMUEL W. DOAK,S.Clk.   SAMUEL W. DOAK,Modr.
JAS. A. LYON, Clk pr. tem.

Mount Bethel Church.
April 4th. *1839.*

Presbytery met. Constituted with prayer. Members present: Messrs. Samuel W.Doak, Andrew Vance, Samuel H.Doak, and Jas.A.Lyon, Ministers:

Messrs. S. Dobson,   Elder of Mount Bethel;
        Jno. Cowan,   ”   ” Leesburgh;
        Saml. Hodge,   ”   ” New Bethel;
        Wm. Deery,   ”   ” Blountville;
        Wm. Alexander,   ”   ” New Providence;
        Geo. Hale   ”   ” Rogersville.

Rev. Samuel H. Doak was chosen Moderator, and Rev. Jas. A. Lyon, Clerk.

The following paper was presented to Presbytery, and read, viz.

"March 30th. 1839, The session of Baker's-Creek Church met at the call of the Moderator. Members present: Rev. A. Vance, Moderator; Messrs. Wm. Wilson, Jas. Houston, A. M. Wilson, Elders. Constituted with prayer.

"The following preamble, and resolutions were adopted.

"In as much as the minority of Union Presbytery, which

remained after the majority had seceded, was too smal[l] to constitute a Presbytery, this session, and church have agreed, in obedience to the direction of the General Assembly, (of which Mr. Plumer was Moderator), to apply, for connexion to the nearest Presbytery in regular adherence to the General Assembly of the Presbyterian church in the United States:

"Therefore,

"Resolved 1st. that this session will make application to the Presbytery of Holston, at the next meeting of that body, which we have heard is to be held at Mount Bethel, Greene County, to be taken under the care, and Presbyterial supervision of the same.

"Resolved 2dly. that Wm. Wilson be a delegate, from this church session, to attend the meeting of that Presbytery, to represent this church according to the spirit of the above resolution.

Adjourned with prayer.

ANDREW VANCE,
Modr. & Clk. pr. tem.

On motion, Baker's creek church was received under the care of this Presbytery; and Mr. Wm. Wilson, a Ruling Elder of said church, took his seat as a member of Presbytery.

Ewing McClure, an Elder from Salem church, appeared, and took his seat.

Adjourned to meet at Tusculum Academy, at four o'clock, P.M.

Tusculum Academy,
Four o'clock P.M.

Presbytery met. Opened with prayer.

The Stated Clerk reported that he had complied with the injunction of Presbytery in demanding from Mr. Jno. W. Cunningham, the former Stated Clerk of this Presbytery, the records of this Presbytery, which are still in his hands, by addressing to him the following note; but had received no answer.

"March 14th. 1839.

"Dear Sir,

"It is made my duty, by an order of Holston Pres-. bytery, to apply to you, the former Stated Clerk of said Presbytery, for the Presbytery's Book of Records. I hope you will give me an answer, or send me the Book, by the bearer.

"Affectionately Your's &c.

Revd.Jno.W.Cunningham.   Samuel W.Doak,
                                           S.Clk. of Holston Pby."

Ordered that the Stated Clerk procure the records, or a copy of the records of our Presbytery, now in the hands of Mr. Jno. W. Cunningham, (former Stated Clerk of this Presbytery), at the expense of Presbytery.

The committee appointed at the last fall meeting of Presbytery, to revise, and publish a pastoral letter of this Presbytery, reported that they had complied with the injunction of Presbytery; and laid, on the table, a copy of the printed letter: and they reported farther, the expense, of printing, and publishing said letter, amounted to thirty-five dollars, and fifty cents; which sum was raised, and paid by the members of Presbytery.

Mr Sevier Tedlock, an Elder of Providence church, appeared, and took his seat as a member of Presbytery.

The Stated Clerk reported that he had complied with the injunction of Presbytery, by paying over to the "Assembly's Board of Missions", the sum of eleven dollars.

Rev. Samuel H. Doak was appointed a commissioner to the next General Assembly, and Rev. Jas. A. Lyon, his alternate.

Mr. George Hale, an Elder of Rogersville church, was appointed a commissioner to the next General Assembly, — Messrs. Jos. Duncan an Elder of Leesburgh church; an[d] E. L. Mathes, an Elder of Salem church, his alternates.

Mr. Samuel Y. Wyly, a licentiate of New Brunswicke Presbytery, by letter, requested to be taken under our care;

and having produced a regular certificate of his dismission, and good standing, from said Presbytery, he was received.

Resolved, that when we finally adjourn, we will adjourn to meet at Rogersville, on the Friday preceding the second Sabbath in next June.

On motion, Resolved, that Presbytery proceed to the ordination of Mr. Samuel Y. Wyly, at the next meeting at Rogersville; provided they see their way clear. Luke 13:3, was assigned to Mr. Wyly as the subject of a trial sermon.

Presbytery appointed Rev. A. Vance to preside, — Rev. Jas. A. Lyon to preach the sermon, and Rev. Samuel W. Doak to give the charge at the ordination of Mr. Wyly.

Presbytery adjourned to meet at this place to-morrow morning, at eight o'clock.

Concluded with prayer.

Tusculum Academy,

April 5th. 1839.

Presbytery met according to adjournment. Opened with prayer.

Rev. Jas. A. Lyon was appointed the Treasurer of Holston Presbytery.

Presbytery ordered the Treasurer to pay over, to the Commissioners of Presbytery to the next Assembly, the moneys he has received, or hereafter may receive, to defray their expenses.

Presbytery had a recess 'till 4 o'clock. P.M.

A letter, was received from the church of Pleasant Forest, in Knox County, Tennessee, in which they pray to be received under the care of Holston Presbytery; which prayer was granted. The sum of two dollars was received with said letter, of which one dollar and fifty cents was appropriated to the use of our commissioners; and fifty cents to the contingent fund of the General Assembly.

A call, from Salem Church, for the ministerial labours of Mr. Archibald A. Mathes for the third of his time, was laid before Presbytery.

The said call was put into the hands of Mr. Mathes for his acceptance, or rejection.

Mr. Mathes signified to Presbytery his acceptance of said call.

Presbytery resolved to proceed to the ordination of Mr. Mathes to-morrow a[t] eleven o'clock A.M.

Rev. S. W. Doak was appointed alternate of Rev. Jas. A. Lyon, who was appointed at a former meeting to preach the ordination sermon.

Resolved, unanimously, that this Presbytery be auxiliary to the General Assembly's Board of Education.

On motion, unanimously resolved, that Presbytery continue its connexion as an auxiliary to the "Assembly's Board of Missions."

Unanimously resolved, that [this Presbytery], become auxiliary to the "Assembly's Board of Foreign Missions."

On motion, resolved, unanimously, that this Presbytery earnestly request the "General Assembly's Board of Missions" to send to East Tennessee three missionaries,— one of which to be located, and the other two to be itinerants, — all to be subject to the direction of Presbytery.

Rev. Samuel W. Doak, and Rev. Jas. A. Lyon, ministers; and Messrs. Jos. Bullen, and Saml. Neill, Elders, were appointed a committee to direct the labours of whatsoever missionaries may be sent to us from the "Assembly's Board of Missions", between this time, and the next meeting of Presbytery.

Adjourned to meet to-morrow morning, at 9 o'clock, at Mount Bethel church.

Concluded with prayer.

Mount Bethel Church;
April 6th. 1839.

Presbytery met according to adjournment. Opened with prayer.

Mr. Jno. Bell was introduced to Presbytery by Rev. Samuel W. Doak, as a candidate for the gospel ministry,— in full communion, and in good standing as a member of

Mount Bethel congregation, and, as having made considerable progress in the pursuit of a liberal education.

Presbytery examined Mr. Bell on his experimental religion, and his call to the gospel ministry. The examination was sustained; and Mr. Bell was received as a candidate.

Presbytery had a recess for half an hour.

Presbytery proceeded to the ordination of Mr. A. A. Mathes. Mr. Mathes preached a sermon on the text previously assigned him; which was sustained.

Revd. S. W. Doak preached the ordination sermon from 1.Cor.4:5, and presided. Rev. S. H. Doak delivered the charge. Mr. Mathes was ordained by the imposition of the hands of the Presbytery, and prayer. Mr. Mathes took his seat as a member of Presbytery.

Rev. S. W. Doak, and Rev. A. A. Mathes; and Messrs. E. L. Mathes, and David Moore, were appointed an examining committee to examine young men presenting themselves to be taken under the care of the "Assembly's Board of Education."

Resolved, that Presbytery hold its next semi-annual meeting at Salem Church, for the purpose of installing Rev. A. A. Mathes pastor of said church, provided they see their way clear.

Adjourned to meet at Rogersville on Friday, the seventh day of June next.

Concluded with prayer.

| SAMUEL W. DOAK, | SAMUEL W.DOAK, Modr. |
| Stated Clerk. | JAS.A.LYON,Clerk pro tem. |

Rogersville — Court — House
June 7th. 1839.

Holston Presbytery met, and constituted with prayer.

Members present: Messrs. S. W. Doak, A. Vance, Jas. A. Lyon, and Archibald A. Mathes, ministers:

Mr. Jos. Bullen, an Elder of Mount Bethel Church;
" E. L. Mathes, " " " Salem "
" Jos. Duncan, " " " Leesburgh "

Mr. W. Gray,   an Elder of New Providence Church
" Samuel Neill,   "   "   " Rogersville   "
" Wm. Smith,   "   "   " Pleasant Forest   "

Revd. Andrew Vance was chosen Moderator; and Revd. A. Alexander Mathes, Clerk pro tempore.

Revd. Jos. J. Foot, a member of Bedford Presbytery, being present, was invited to sit with us as a corresponding member.

The minutes of the last stated sessions were read.

The Stated Clerk reported that he had attended to the duty enjoined on him relative to the procuring of our Book of Records; but has not yet succeeded in obtaining it.

The examination of Mr. Wyly was made the order of the day for to-morrow morning at half past seven o'clock.

Presbytery complied with the request of the General Assembly, in raising twenty dollars, and seventy-five cents, (our quota,) to defray the expenses of the law suit lately decided by the Supreme Court of Pennsylvania, which was put into the hands of the Treasurer.

Mr. Archibald Alexander Doak, a licentiate of New Brunswick Presbytery, presented a dismission, and recommendation from said Presbytery, and requested to be taken under our care; and he was received.

Rom.V:19, was assigned to Mr. A. A. Doak as the subject of a trial sermon preparatory, to ordination, to be delivered at some future time when Presbytery shall see the way clear to proceed to his ordination: Revd. Jas. A. Lyon was appointed to preside,— Revd. A. A. Mathes, to preach the ordination sermon, and Rev. S. W. Doak, [to] deliver the charge.

Adjourned to meet to-morrow morning [at] half past seven o'clock.

June 8th, 1839

Presbytery met according to adjournment. Opened with prayer.

Presbytery took up the order of the day.

Mr. Samuel Y. Wyly was examined [as to] his experimental religion, and his views in seeking the office of the gospel ministry; and the examination was sustained.

He was also examined [on] Natural Philosophy, the Greek, and Hebrew languages, Ecclesiastical History, Theology, and Church Government; and the examination was sustained.

Presbytery had a recess of half an hour.

Mr. Wyly preached a sermon on the subject assigned him, which was unanimously sustained.

Rev. Jas. A. Lyon preached the ordination sermon from Ezekiel 33:8, Rev. A. Vance presided, and Mr. Wyly,— having answered the constitutional questions in the affirmative, was ordained by the laying on of the hands of the Presbytery, and prayer. After which Rev. S. W. Doak gave the charge

Mr. Wyly took his seat as a member of Presbytery.

Presbytery had a recess until half after 3 o'clock.

Presbytery directed Mr. A. A. Doak, a missionary of the "Assembly's Board," to preach at Blountville, New Bethel, Rocky-Spring, Jonesborough, Elizabethton, Bethesda, Tazewell, Columbianna, McMin County, Hamilton County, Dalas, Ross' Landing, Kingston, Russelville, Greenville, Newport, Rutledge, or locate himself at either, at discretion.

After solemn consideration of the subject, Presbytery adopted the following minute: viz.

Reflecting on the dilapidated state of the Presbyterian Church in East Tennessee, we are Convinced that the propagation of errors subversive of the gospel, and destructive of the order, harmony, and peace of the churches, and the alienations, strifes, envyings, intolerance, and divisions that have existed for many years, must be ascribed, in a great measure, to the general neglect of Catechetical instruction. We are admonished of this when we see evils prevail most where this instruction has been most neglected, and prevail least, where it has been most used.

We, therefore, earnestly recommend to all the church sessions, to see to it, that catechetical instruction be given, regularly, and assiduously, to all their people, [and] especially to the rising generation. We also recommend that the Elders assemble their congregations on their vacant sabbaths, for the purpose of mutually assisting one another in the study of the Bible, and the catechisms of our church, and for prayer and praise. Thus mutual affection will be cherished, knowledge will be increased, and the churches will grow up as well-watered plants, under the fostering care of the Lord of the vineyard.

The following preamble, and resolutions, were adopted:

Whereas, in consequence of the acts of the General Assembly of the Presbyterian Church, in the United States of America, in eighteen-hundred and thirty-seven, and in eighteen-hundred and thirty-eight, a large portion of the ministers and churches in this Presbytery, have seceded from the Church, Therefore,

1. Resolved, that we are humbled in view of the progress of such Theological, and practical principles, and also, of such mis-information amongst us, as have led to this result.

2. Resolved, That while we cherish the most cordial feelings towards Congregational ministers, and churches, in the administration of their own government, and ordinances,— and while we deeply sympathize with such ministers, and churches, (in the four disowned Synods,) as adhere to the doctrines, and discipline of the Presbyterian Church, we cannot approve of any attempt in them, and others associated with them, either by the civil courts, or otherwise, to bring into the Presbyterian Church those numerous Congregational churches, which exist amongst them,— are represented in their Presbyteries, and Synods,— vote for commissioners to the General Assembly,— but refuse to adopt the Presbyterian Form of Government.

3. Resolved, that a misapprehension exists, in this community, respecting the number, and strength of these churches. They are represented as few; but they are numerous in each of the four Synods. They are represented as small, and feeble; but, as a class of churches, they are, individually, very similar to the Presbyterian churches,

among which they are located, — in age,— in the number of their communicants, and in their pecuniary strength.

4. Resolved, that, in our opinion, this fact would have been fully developed, at the Nisi-Prius term of the court in Philadelphia, in the case of Todd vs. Greene, had not the testimony been excluded by the Honourable Judge Rogers.

5. Resolved, That the various attempts to conceal the facts, respecting the existence of these churches, from the Christian community merit our unqualified disapprobation.

6. Resolved, That we express devout gratitude to Almighty God, for the signal deliverance, of our church, from the numerous perplexities into which she has been drawn by some who professed to be her friends; and especially for the wisdom he has given to the "Honourable Court in Bank", and, which is manifested in the recent opinion as delivered by "Chief Justice Gibson".[18]

On motion, resolved, that Rev. Jas. A. Lyon, Samuel Neill, and Rev. Saml. W. Doak, and Jos. Bullen, be continued as the committee of Missions, until the spring meeting of Presbytery.

Adjourned to meet at Baker's Creek Church, on Thursday, the third day of October next, instead of meeting at Salem church.

Concluded with prayer—

SAMUEL W. DOAK	ANDREW VANCE, Modr.
Stated Clerk.	A. A. MATHES, Clk pr.tem.

Baker's-Creek, Church.
Oct. 3. 1839.

Holston Presbytery met, and was constituted with prayer.

Members present: Messrs. Saml. W. Doak, Andrew Vance, and Samuel Y. Wyly, ministers—

Mr. Andrew Cowan, Elder of Baker's-Creek Church,—
" James McNutt " " Lebanon "

---

[18] In a property suit before the Supreme Court for the Eastern District of Pennsylvania the decision favorable to the New School was reversed by the Court sitting *en banc*. See Gillett, *op. cit.*, II, pp. 535-37; also, *The Presbyterian Assembly's Digest*, 2nd Edition (1859), pp. 791-801.

Ministers absent: Messrs. S. H. Doak, Jas. A. Lyon, and A. A. Mathes.

Lebanon church was recognized as one of the churches under our care, on satisfactory evidence, of its adherence to the true Constitutional Presbyterian church, from their representative, Mr. James McNutt, an Elder, who took his seat as a member of Presbytery.

Rev. S. W. Doak was elected Moderator, and Rev. Samuel Y. Wyly, clerk pro tempore.

The Stated Clerk made a report in regard to the Presbyterial records,— that he had been endeavouring to secure the Book, but, as yet, without success.

Resolved, that, from information received from Mr. Wm. Blount Carter, Jr., through a letter addressed by him to the Rev. S. Y. Wyly, of his adherence to the true Presbyterian church, we recognize him as a candidate, under our care, for the gospel ministry.

Resolved, that, as a subject for a Latin Exegesis, we assign to Mr. Carter, "Estne Christus rerus [sic] Deus"? For a Critical Exercise, Romans 5:12. For a Popular Lecture, the 1st. Psalm. For a Popular Sermon, 1st. Corinthians 3:11.

Rev. Mr. Vance, and Mr. Cowan were appointed a committee to examine the minutes of the General Assembly.

Bro. Mathes appeared, and assigned his reasons for tardiness, which were sustained.

Rev. Jos. J. Foot presented his dismission and recommendation from Bedford Presbytery.

The Presbytery proceeded to the examination of Mr. Foot on Christian experience,— didactic, and polemic Theology, and church Government, which was unanimously sustained. Mr. Foot then took his seat as a member of Presbytery.

Presbytery adjourned until to-morrow morning, 8 o'clock.

Friday Morning, 8 o'clock.

Presbytery met, and was opened with prayer.

Resolved that Mr. Foot be appointed to preach the sermon at the ordination of Mr. A. A. Doak.

Rev. N. A. Penland, [a] minister of the late "Union Presbytery", having given satisfaction, in answer to inquiries, that he had not seceded from the Presbyterian church, but continues to adhere to its doctrines, and discipline: Therefore, Resolved that, according to the acts of the Assembly of 1837, and 1838, and particularly the act of 1839, extending the boundaries of Holston Presbytery, he is hereby declared to be a member of this Presbytery.   Mr. Penland then took his seat as a member of Presbytery.

A letter was received by Presbytery from the General Assembly's Board of Missions, which was read, and Rev. Samuel W. Doak, and Rev. A. Vance, and Jas. McNutt, Elder, were appointed a committee to examine this letter.

A Statistical report was received from Salem Church.

Rev. S. H. Doak appeared in Presbytery, and assigned his reasons for tardiness, which were sustained.

Mr. Jas. McNutt was released from the Committee appointed to answer the letter from the "Assembly's Board of Missions", and Rev. Jos. J. Foot was substituted in his place.

Resolved that the subject assigned Mr. A. A. Doak for a Popular Sermon, be reconsidered.

Resolved that Hebrews 2:3, first clause of the verse, be the subject of a trial sermon for Mr. A. A. Doak.

The Presbytery had a recess for one hour and a quarter.

The sum of eighteen dollars, and fifty-cents, was received from Salem Church, for the "Assembly's Board of Missions."

Resolved that this money be paid over to Mr. A. A. Doak, one of the missionaries now labouring under our care, and a receipt taken for the same.

Mr. Penland, and Mr. McNutt, obtained leave of absence for this evening.

The Presbytery proceeded to examine Mr. A. A. Doak on the Greek, and Hebrew languages,— on Philosophy,— Theology,— Church-History, and Church-Government,— which examination was unanimously sustained.

Resolved, that it be the order of the day, on to-morrow

at twelve of the clock, to hear the trial sermon of Mr. A. A. Doak, with a view to his ordination.

Resolved, that the Rev. A. Vance be appointed the alternate of Rev. Jas. A. Lyon, to preside at the ordination of Mr. Doak, and propose the Constitutional questions.

The Presbytery adjourned to meet to-morrow morning at 8 o'clock.

Concluded with prayer.

Saturday — morning.

Presbytery met, and was opened with prayer.

On motion, Resolved, that the Rev. S. H. Doak be ordered to visit Baker's-Creek, Lebanon, and Pleasant Forest, churches, and ascertain what they will do toward the support of their ministers.

Mr. A. A. Doak preached a sermon on the subject assigned him.

Resolved, that the Presbytery proceed to his ordination.

The Rev. Jos. J. Foot preached the ordination sermon from 2d. Tim.4 :22 ; and after Mr. Doak had answered, the constitutional questions, in the affirmative, he was set apart, to the Holy-Ministry, by prayer, and the laying on of the hands of the Presbytery.   The charge was delivered by Rev. Samuel W. Doak.   Mr. Doak then took his seat as a member of Presbytery.

Resolved that the members of Presbytery be called upon and directed to state whether the injunction of our "Book of Discipline," in regard to the public reading of the Sacred Scriptures, had be[en] observed by them.

The Presbytery had a recess for one hour.

Resolved that the next semi-annual meeting of Presbytery be held in the city of Knoxville.

The Committee appointed to examine the Minutes of the Assembly, made a report.

Resolved, that it be earnestly recommended to all the churches, under our care, religiously to observe the "Jubilee", appointed by the General Assembly, on the second sabbath of December next; and, that the contributions made on that day, be for the "Assembly's Board of Missions", and appropriated for the support of domestic missions in East Tennessee.

Resolved that it be enjoined on all the ministers of our Presbytery to use all proper means to promote the objects of the above meeting.

Resolved, that all the ministers, in connexion with this Presbytery, be directed to read the resolutions, in regard to the observance of the Jubilee, in their churches.

Resolved that it be recommended to all the churches under our care, that prayer be made, to Almighty God, for the increase of faithful ministers,— and, that it be recommended to the sessions of our churches, to look out for young men of talents, and piety, who may be educated for the office of the Holy ministry.

Resolved, that our missionary, Rev. S. Henry Doak, be ordered to visit the churches of Baker's Creek, Lebanon, Pleasant-Forest, Knoxville, Rogersville, and New Providence, and ascertain the views of these congregations relative to the formation of the pastoral relation.

Resolved, that the letter from the Assembly's Board of Missions, be referred to the Committee on Missions, of this Presbytery.

Resolved that Rev. S. H. Doak be appointed to preach a missionary sermon at the next [meeting] of Presbytery; and that the Rev. J. Y. Wyly be his alternate.

Ordered, that the Stated Clerk prepare, and forward a Presbyterial report to Synod.

Resolved, that the Rev. S. H. Doak, and Rev. A .A. Doak, be commissioned to organize churches, at discretion, in the bounds of this Presbytery.

The minutes were read & approved. The Presbytery adjourned to meet in the City of Knoxville on the first Thursday of April, 1840, at 11 o'clock.

Concluded by prayer.

J.Y.WYLY, Clerk   SAMUEL W.DOAK,Moderator.

12. RESOLUTIONS ADOPTED BY THE EAGLEFORK PRESBY-
TERIAN CHURCH, MISSOURI, RELATIVE TO THE ACTS
PASSED BY THE GENERAL ASSEMBLIES OF 1837
AND 1838[19]

[July 14, 1838]

At a meeting of the Church of Eaglefork, at the School house near William C. Logans, on Saturday the 14th of July 1838, the following preamble and resolutions, upon mature deliberation, were unanimously adopted, and are designed as their manifesto to all the Churches or to those whom it may concern.

Whereas various and great departures, both in doctrine and discipline, have taken place in the presbyterian Church in the united states to which we belong, for the reformation of which, the General Assembly of 1837 and 1838, passed certain acts and resolutions, as by reference to their minutes for said years will fully appear; and whereas by a persevering opposition to those measures by some, the contest has resulted, during their last Session, in a division of that body into two distinct & independant bodies, each stiling themselves the true and constitutional General Assembly of the Presbtyerian Church in the united States, the consequence whereof is, that as two such coordinate bodies cannot exist in the same Church, diverse in doctrine and discipline, we are reduced to the necessity, and so have been required by the last General Assembly, to take order on this subject, and to say which of those two independant bodies we mean to adhere to, and to hold our ecclesiastical connections with in future.

1. Be it therefore resolved by this Church that we do and will adhere to the Gen.Assembly which met by regular adjournment, in the seventh presbyterian Church, in the City of Philadelphia, the 17th of May last, whereof the Rev. William S.Plumer was Moderator, and the Rev.John McDowell D.D. Stated Clerk; and we do most cordially ap-

[19] MS. Record Book of the Church of Eaglefork, Mo., pp. 5-9, Historical Foundation, Montreat, N. C.

prove of their acts of 1837 and 1838, for the reformation of the Church; and would hereby express our most devout thanks to the great head of the Church, for succeeding their christian efforts thus far in bringing this painful contest to an end.

2. Resolved, that, in our opinion, the other body which held their Session, at the same time, in the first Presbyterian Church in Philadelphia, stiling themselves the true General Assembly, are not such, but a Secession, and that in forming in the presence of the true General Assembly with tumult and violence, and in contempt of that body, departed as we believe, from their duty to God, and to the Church. Wherefore, we do renounce their jurisdiction over us, with all their dependances.

3. Resolved, that we do protest against all the acts and doings of our Commissioner from the presbytery of St Charles to the last Gen. Assembly, in going off with the said Seceding body, and by which he in anywise countenanced, aided or abeted them.

4. Resolved, that our Elder (brother William C.Logan) be our deligate to represent this church in the next meeting of St. Charles Presbytery, provided the majority of said presbytery, taking order upon the subject, agreeably to the act of the last Gen. Assembly as mentioned in our first resolve, and shall adhere to them upon the basis of their acts of 1837 and 1838, otherwise, or failing to take order thereon agreeably to the act of the said General Assembly, we appoint him our deligate to the minority of the said presbytery who shall so adhere, as the only true presbytery of St.Charles to which we belong.

5. Resolved, that the Chairman, and Clerk of this meeting do sign these resolutions, and have them recorded in our Church book; that our Elder present them to the presbytery of St.Charles at their ensuing session, and if he and the Chairman should deem it necessary or proper, to publish them.

W.C.LOGAN Clerk.   JOHN S.BALL Chairman."

BIBLIOGRAPHY

MANUSCRIPTS

American Home Missionary Society Correspondence. Chicago Theological Seminary, Chicago, Illinois. This collection consists of letters and reports written by home missionaries in the field to the Society's headquarters in New York together with 150 volumes of "press" copies of letters written by the officials of the society to the missionaries. The entire collection contains about 70,000 original letters and covers the years from 1825 on.

Draper Collection. Wisconsin State Historical Society, Madison, Wisconsin. Contains much material on Presbyterianism in Kentucky of which the Shane Collection is the most valuable part. See Shane Collection.

Durrett Collection. University of Chicago, Chicago, Illinois. Contains MS materials bearing on western Presbyterianism; particularly the Joshua L. Wilson Papers, about 2,000 manuscripts, letters, diaries, journals, memoranda, sermons, expense accounts, and memoirs. Also *Records of the Board of Trustees of Transylvania University,* 1783-1799.

Montreat Collection. Montreat, North Carolina. The Historical Foundation of the Presbyterian and Reformed churches. Perhaps the largest single collection of manuscripts dealing with the Presbyterian Church in America. Particularly rich in session, presbytery and synodical records covering the region south of the Ohio and as far west as Arkansas and Missouri, for the period covered in this volume.

The MacMaster Papers. Presbyterian Theological Seminary, Chicago, Illinois. Consists of sermon and lecture notes and miscellaneous papers.

New York Manuscripts. Auburn Theological Seminary, Auburn, New York. Session, presbytery and synodical records for Central and Western New York.

Presbyterian Historical Collection. The Department of History of the Presbyterian Church in the U. S. A., Philadelphia. For a list of the MS materials in this collection see *The Journal of the Presbyterian Historical Society,* VIII, 1915-1916, No. 1, pp. 13-22.

Pittsburgh-Xenia Theological Seminary Collection. Pittsburgh, Pennsylvania. MS *Minutes of the Associate Presbytery of Pittsburgh,* 1777-1784; *Minutes of the Second Presbytery, Associate Reformed,* 1793-1803, 2 vols.; and other early MS of the Associate and Associate Reformed churches.

Register of the United Congregations of Cincinnati and Columbia. In possession of the Pleasant Ridge Presbyterian Church, Cincinnati, Ohio.

Records of the Missouri Presbytery 1817—and other MS. Missouri State Historical Society, Columbia, Missouri.

Shane Collection. A large collection of Presbyterian materials consisting of MS, newspaper clippings and other papers collected by Rev. John D. Shane (1812-1864). The collection on Shane's death was sold at auction, the notes and MS being purchased by Draper, who in turn sold a part of them to the Presbyterian Historical Society of Philadelphia. For a detailed account of the Shane Collection see *The History Quarterly of the Filson Club,* Louisville, Kentucky, IV, pp. 1-16. *Shane, the Western Collector,* by Otto A. Rothert.

Transylvania Presbytery, Minutes of. In eleven MS volumes in the possession of Dr. J. Q. S. McDowell, stated clerk of the Synod of Kentucky, Danville, Kentucky.

Union Theological Seminary Collection, Richmond, Virginia. Seventy-two MS, consisting of minutes of early Virginia presbyteries, synods and other MS.

Western Reserve Historical Society Collection, Cleveland, Ohio. MSS relating to Presbyterianism, particularly in the Western Reserve.

Western Theological Seminary Collection, Pittsburgh, Pennsylvania. MS *Records of the Pittsburgh Presbytery,* 1839-1916; *Records of The Ohio Presbytery,* 1793-1870.

Manuscripts in private hands:

MS *Records of the Presbyterian Church, Lancaster, Ohio.*

MS *Minutes of the Reformed Presbytery of America,* 1798-1809; MS *Minutes of Session of Connogocheague,* 1709-1809. In possession of Mr. James Tibbey.

MS *Notes, Papers and Sermons of Rev. Matthew Henderson.* In possession of Miss Mary Henderson.

OFFICIAL DOCUMENTS

Annual of the Board of Education, Presbyterian Church in the United States of America, John Breckinridge (ed.) (Philadelphia, 1835).

Annual Report, American Home Missionary Society, 1827-1844.

Annual Report of the American Tract Society, 1833-1844.

Annual Report, Board of Home Missions, Presbyterian Church in the United States of America.

Annual Report of the Western Foreign Missionary Society, 1833-1852.

Baird, Samuel J., *A Collection of the Acts, Deliverances, and Testimonies of the Supreme Judiatory of the Presbyterian Church* (Philadelphia, 1855; 1859).

Book of Government and Discipline of the Associate Church, Agreed upon and Enacted by the Associate Synod of North America at Pittsburgh, June 6, 1817 (Pittsburgh, 1817).

The Constitution and Laws of the Board of Education of the General Assembly of the Presbyterian Church in the United States (Philadelphia: Russell and Martien, 1831).

The Constitution of the Presbyterian Church in the United States of America: Containing the Confession of Faith, the Catechisms and the Directory for the Worship of God: Together with the Plan of Government and Discipline as ratified by the General Assembly at the Sessions in May 1821; and Amended in 1833 (Philadelphia: Alex. Towar, 1834). Numerous editions.

A Digest Compiled from the Records of the General Assembly of the Presbyterian Church in the United States of America, and from the Records of the Late Synod of New York and Philadelphia, and of their Acts and Proceedings that Appear to be of Permanent Authority and Interest; together with A Short Account of the Missions Conducted by the Presbyterian Church (Philadelphia: R. P. McCulloh, 1820).

Extracts from the Minutes of the General Assembly of the Presbyterian Church, in the United States of America (Philadelphia: Thomas and William Bradford, 1818).

Extracts from the Minutes of the Proceedings of the Associate Reformed Synod of the West, Held in Pittsburgh the 28th Day of May, 1823 — — and in Chillicothe the 26th Day of May, 1824. (Same for 1834, 1836, 1841, 1842.)

Extracts from the Minutes of the Proceedings of the Associate Reformed Synod of the West held at Chillicothe [O.] *Oct. 18th, 1837.* (Hamilton, O., 1837). (Same for 1823, 1828, 1829, 1831, 1856.)

Extracts from the Minutes of the Synod of Cincinnati. Published by Order of Synod at its late meeting in the city of Cincinnati, 1838. (Cincinnati: R. B. Brooks and Co., 1838.)

Minutes of the Associate Presbytery of Pennsylvania, 1783 to 1802. Bound with *Acts and Letters emitted by Synod from 1783-1802.*

Minutes of Associated Reformed Church in North America, 1817, 1822, 1827 to 1841, inclusive.

Minutes of the Associate Reformed Synod of North America, 1783-1813. Bound with *Acts, Letters and Constitutions emitted by Synod from 1783 to 1813.*

"Minutes of the Ebenezer Presbytery" (Kentucky) for the Years 1820 ff., Part V, *Journal of the Department of History of the Presbyterian Church in the U. S. A.*, XVI, No. 3 (Sept., 1934) pp. 126-144. For Part I, see this *Journal*, XV (1933) p. 249 ff. For Part II, *ibid.*, p. 266 ff. For Part III, *ibid.*, XVI (1934) p. 22 ff. For Part IV, *ibid.*, pp. 72 ff.

Minutes of the General Assembly of the Presbyterian Church in the United States of America from the Organization A. D. 1789 to A. D. 1835, inclusive, 2 vols. (Philadelphia: Presbyterian Board of Publication, 1847), Vol. I, 1789-1820; Vol. II, 1821-1835.

Minutes of the General Assembly of the Presbyterian Church in the United States of America: with An Appendix, Published Annually (Philadelphia, 1836, 1837, 1838).

Minutes of the Presbytery of Redstone, 1781-1831 (Cincinnati, 1878).

The Minutes of the Proceedings of the Pittsburgh Convention, Called by the Signers of the "Act and Testimony," May 14, 1835 (Pittsburgh: White and Grant, 1835).

Minutes of the Synod of New York, October, A. D. 1838 (New York: D. Fanshaw, 1838).

Minutes of the Synod of Philadelphia at their Sessions held in Columbia, October, 1833.

The Presbytery of Transylvania to the Churches Under their Care [1802].

A Record of Missionary Meetings Held in the Chahta and Chikesha Nations and Tombigbee Presbytery From 1825 to 1832, edited by John W. Mosely, Jr., Stated Clerk, Tombeckbee.

Records of the Presbyterian Church in the United States of America: Embracing the Minutes of the General Presbytery and General Synod 1706-1788; Together with an Index and the Minutes of the General Convention for Religious Liberty 1766-1775, ed. 3 (Philadelphia: Presbyterian Board of Publication and Sabbath School Work, 1904).

Records of the Synod of Pittsburgh, From its organization, September 29, 1802, to October, 1832, inclusive. Printed by the approbation of Synod, at their meeting in Alleghany City, 1850 (Pittsburgh: Luke Loomis, Agent, 1852).

PRINTED SOURCES

Annual Report of the Kentucky Auxiliary Bible Society, 1818, with an address delivered before the Society by James Blythe, D.D., together with the constitution (Lexington, Ky.: Skillman, 1818).

Barnes, Gilbert H., and Dumond, Dwight L. (eds.), *Letters of Theodore Dwight Weld, Angelina Grimké Weld and Sara Grimké, 1822-1844,* 2 vols. (New York: Appleton-Century Co., 1934).

Beecher, C. (ed.), *Autobiography, Correspondence, Etc., of Lyman Beecher,* 2 vols. (New York, 1864).

Bond, B. W., Jr. (ed.), *The Correspondence of John Cleves Symmes* (New York, 1926).

Broadbury, John, *Travels in the Interior of America in the Years 1809, 1810 and 1811* (Thwaites, R. G., *Early Western Travels*, V, Cleveland, 1904).

Darlington, W. M. *Christopher Gist's Journals* (Pittsburgh, 1893).

Dexter, F. B. (ed.), *Diary of David McClure, 1748-1820* (New York: Knickerbocker Press, 1899).

————*Extracts from the Itineraries and other Miscellanies of Ezra Stiles, 1755-1794 with a selection from his correspondence* (New Haven: Yale University Press, 1916).

Evens, Estwick, *Pedestrious Tours, 1818* (Thwaites, R. G., *Early Western Travels*, VIII, Cleveland, 1904).

Faux, William, *Memorable Days in America; Being a Journal, 1823* (Thwaites, R. G., *Early Western Travels*, Cleveland, 1904).

Flint, Timothy, *Recollections of the Last Ten Years Passed in Occasional Residences and Journeys in the Valley of the Mississippi* (Boston, 1826).

Humphrey, Edward P., and Cleland, Thomas H. *Memoirs of the Rev. Thomas Cleland, D.D.* Compiled from His Private Papers (Cincinnati, 1859).

"The Journey of Lewis David von Schweinitz to Goshen, Bartholomew County in 1831," translated by Adolf Gerber, *Indiana Historical Society Publications*, VIII, No. 5 (Indianapolis, 1923 to 1929). MS Journal is in the Archiv der Bruder-unitat in-Herrnhut, Saxony. Copy of the original German text is in possession of Indiana State Library.

Memoirs of Charles G. Finney (New York, 1896).

Miller, Samuel, *Letters to Presbyterians on the Present Crisis in the Presbyterian Church in the U. S. A.* (Philadelphia, 1833).

Miller, S., *Memoirs of the Rev. John Rodgers* (New York, 1813).

Nuttall, Thomas, *Journal of Travels in the Arkansas Territory During the Year 1819* (Thwaites, R. G., *Early Western Travels*, XIII, Cleveland, 1904).

Purviance, Levi, *The Biography of Elder David Purviance with his Memoirs containing his views on Baptism, the Divinity of Christ and the Atonement,* written by himself (Dayton, Ohio, 1848).

Rankin, A., *A Process in the Transylvania Presbytery* (Lexington, Ky., 1793).

Schermerhorn, John F., and Mills, Samuel J., *A Correct View of that part of the United States, which lies west of the Alleghany Mountains, with regard to religion and morals* (Hartford, Conn., 1814).

A Statement of the Grievances on account of which, that section of the church now called the "Associate Reformed Synod of the West" separated from, and declared themselves independent of the "Associate Reformed Synod of North America" (Pittsburgh, 1828).

Strickland, W. P. (ed.), *Autobiography of Peter Cartwright, the backwoods preacher* (New York: Carlton and Porter, 1857).

————*Autobiography of Rev. James B. Finley, or Pioneer Life in the West* (Cincinnati, 1854).

Sweet, W. W. *Circuit-Rider Days Along the Ohio, Being the Journals of the Ohio Conference from Its Organization in 1812 to 1826.*
———*Religion on the American Frontier: The Baptists, 1783-1830.* A Collection of Source Material (New York: Henry Holt and Co., 1931).
———*The Rise of Methodism in the West, Being the Journal of the Western Conference, 1800-1811* (Cincinnati, 1920).
Thwaites, R. G. (ed.), *Early Western Travels, 1748-1846,* 32 vols. (Cleveland: A. H. Clark Co., 1904-1907).

PERIODICALS

The Alethian Critic; or Error Exposed (Lexington, Ky.: Abel M. Sarjent, 1804).
The Almoner (Lexington, Ky.: Thos. T. Skillman, 1814-1815).
American Missionary Register, Z. Lewis (ed.), United Foreign Missionary Society (New York, 1820-1825, monthly).
American Pioneer, J. S. Williams (ed.) (Cincinnati, 1842-1843).
The American Sunday School Magazine (Philadelphia, 1824-1833, monthly).
Baltimore Literary and Religious Magazine (Edited by Robert J. Breckinridge), Vols. III to VII (1837-1843).
Banner of Truth, Thomas Skillman (ed.) (Lexington, Ky., 1827-1833).
The Calvinistic Magazine (Rogersville, Tenn., 1827).
The Candid Review (Bardstown, Ky., 1807-1810).
The Central Presbyterian (Richmond, Va., 1837, weekly).
The Christian Advocate (Continuation of *Presbyterian Magazine*), Ashbel Green (ed.) (Philadelphia, 1823-1834).
The Christian Almanac (New York: American Tract Society, 1829-1874).
The Christian Baptist, Edited by Alexander Campbell, Revised by D. S. Burnet, From the Second Edition, with Mr. Campbell's last corrections, 7 Vols. in one (Vol. I, 1823) (Cincinnati, 1835).
The Christian Herald, New York, Vol. I (1816)—Vol. VII (1820-1821). With Vol. VIII (1821-1822) title was changed to *The Christian Herald and Seaman's Magazine,* Vol. IX (1822-1823).
The Christian Herald, Samuel C. Jennings (ed.) (Pittsburgh, January 19, 1829-1833).
The Christian Instructor (Philadelphia, 1843, weekly).
The Christian Intelligencer (later *The Christian Intelligencer, and Evangelical Guardian*) (St. Clairsville, Ohio: Associate Reformed Church, January, 1829-1842).
The Christian Monitor, John H. Rice (ed.) (Richmond, Va., 1815, weekly).
The Christian Observer (Louisville, Ky., 1813, weekly).
The Christian Register (Lexington, Ky.: James Blythe, June, 1822).

The Christian Spectator, Andrew Todd (ed.) (New Haven, Conn., 1819-1838).

The Christian's Magazine (New York, 1808-1811).

Church History (American Society of Church History), Editorial Office, Chicago, Ill. (1932-   ).

The Cincinnati Advertiser (Cincinnati, 1818-1841).

The Cincinnati Chronicle and Literary Gazette (Cincinnati, 1827).

The Cicinnati Journal (Cincinnati, 1830).

The Cincinnati Miscellany (Cincinnati, 1845-1846).

Cincinnati Remembrancer (Cincinnati, 1822, weekly).

The Connecticut Evangelical Magazine (1800-1808), *The Connecticut Evangelical Magazine and Religious Intelligencer* (Hartford: Lincoln & Gleason, 1808-1810, monthly).

The Covenanter (Reformed Presbyterian Church) (Philadelphia: David Smith, 1845-1853).

Cumberland Presbyterian (Nashville, Tenn., 1840, weekly).

The Evangelical Guardian (Associate Reformed Synod of the West) Rossville, Ohio, 1843).

The Evangelical Intelligencer (Philadelphia, 1805).

The Evangelical Record and Western Review, J. P. Campbell (ed.) (Lexington, Ky., 1812-1813).

The Evangelical Recorder (Auburn, N. Y., ——).

The Evangelical Repository (Associate Synod of North America) (Philadelphia: William Young, 1842-1885).

The Evangelical Witness (American Evangelical Tract Society), James R. Wilson (ed.) (Newburgh, N. Y.: Gazlay, 1822-1826).

The Evangelist, Joshua Leavitt (ed.) (New York, 1823, weekly).

The Foreign Missionary Chronicle (New York: Robert Carter, 1831).

General Assembly's Missionary Magazine or Evangelical Intelligencer, William P. Farrand (ed.) (Philadelphia, 1805-1809).

The Herald and Presbyter (Cincinnati, Ohio, 1829).

The History Quarterly of the Filson Club (Louisville, Ky., 1926-   ).

The Home Missionary and American Pastor's Journal (American Home Missionary Society) (New York, 1828-1909).

Indiana Magazine of History (Bloomington, Ind., 1905-   , quarterly).

Journal of The Department of History (The Presbyterian Historical Society) of the Presbyterian Church in the U. S. A. (1901-1930 *Journal of the Presbyterian Historical Society*) (Philadelphia, 1901-   ).

Journal of the Illinois State Historical Society (Springfield, 1908-   ).

Liberty Hall (Cincinnati, 1804).

The Missionary Advocate (Pittsburgh: Young Men's Missionary Society of the Reformed Presbyterian Church, 1835).

The Missionary Herald (American Board) (Boston: A. B. C. F. M., 1821-   ).

The Missionary Reporter and Education Register (Missions and Education Boards of General Assembly of the Presbyterian Church in the U. S. A.) (Philadelphia: Geddes, 1829).

The Mississippi Valley Historical Review (Lincoln, Neb., 1914-   ).

The National Crisis (Cincinnati, 1824-1826).

The New York Missionary Magazine, Cornelius David (ed.) (New York, 1800-1803, bi-monthly).

North Carolina Historical Review (Raleigh, N. C., 1924-   , quarterly.)

Ohio Archaeological and Historical Publications (Columbus, Ohio, 1887-   , quarterly).

The Pandect (Cincinnati, 1828-1829).

The Panoplist (1805-1808); *The Panoplist and Missionary Magazine* (1808-1818); *The Panoplist and Missionary Herald* (1818-1821) (Boston).

Pennsylvania Magazine of History (Philadelphia, 1887-   ).

Philanthropist (Mount Pleasant, Ohio, 1817-1836, weekly, 1836-1843, monthly).

The Pittsburgh Recorder [Published under patronage . . . Synod of Pittsburgh], John Andrews (ed.) (Pittsburgh, 1822-1827).

The Presbyterian (Philadelphia, 1831, weekly).

The Presbyterian Advocate (Lexington, Ky., 1830).

Presbyterian Banner (Pittsburgh, Pa., 1814-   , weekly).

Presbyterian Herald (Louisville, Ky., 1831).

The Presbyterian Historical Almanac & Annual Remembrancer (Philadelphia, 1859-1868).

The Presbyterian Magazine (Philadelphia: Littell & Henry, 1821-1823, monthly).

The Princeton Review (Princeton, N. J., 1825-1884).

Proceedings of the New Jersey Historical Society (Newark, N. J., 1847-   ).

Quarterly Theological Review, Ezra Stiles Ely (ed.) (Philadelphia, 1818-1820).

Register of the Kentucky State Historical Society (Louisville, Ky., 1903-   ).

Religious and Literary Intelligencer (Princeton, Ky., 1830-1832, weekly). [Became *Revivalist*, Nashville Tenn., 1832.] [Became *Cumberland Presbyterian*, 1833-   .]

The Religious Examiner (Cadiz, Ohio: Associate Reformed Church, Vol. I, 1827).

Religious Instructor (Carlisle, Pa., 1810, monthly).

Religious Remembrances [oldest weekly religious newspaper], John W. Scott (ed.) (Philadelphia, September, 1813-1823). Became: *Christian Gazette and Youth's Herald* (1823-1825), *The Philadelphian*

(1825-1836), *Religious Telegraph and Observer* (1836-1839), *The Christian Observer* (1840-   , Louisville, Ky.).

The Sentinel and Star in the West (Cincinnati, 1829-1836).

South Carolina Historical Magazine (Charleston, S. C., 1900-   ).

Southern Christian Sentinel (1841).

The Standard (Cincinnati, January 6, 1832).

Tennessee Historical Magazine (Tennessee Historical Society) (Nashville, Tenn., 1915-   ).

The United Presbyterian and Evangelical Guardian (Cincinnati, 1848-1853).

The United Presbyterian Quarterly Review (Pittsburgh, 1860-1862).

The Virginia Evangelical and Literary Magazine, Vol. I, John F. Rice (ed.) (Richmond, Va.: Gray, 1818).

Virginia Magazine of History (Richmond, Va., 1894-   , quarterly).

Weekly Recorder, John Andrews (ed) (Chillicothe, O., 1814-1821).

The Western American (Bardstown, Ky., 1805).

The Western Luminary, J. Breckinridge and C. R. Harrison (eds.) (Lexington, Ky., 1824).

The Western Missionary Magazine and Repository of Religious Intelligence [published under patronage of Pittsburgh Synod] (Washington, Pa., 1803-1805).

The Western Messenger (Cincinnati, 1835-1841).

The Western Presbyterian Herald (Louisville, Ky., 1832).

The Western Spy (Cincinnati, 1810-1822).

SECONDARY MATERIALS:
BOOKS AND ARTICLES

Abbott, J. S. C., *The History of the State of Ohio, from the Discovery of the Great Valley, to the Present Time, Including Narratives of Early Exploration* (Detroit, 1875).

Adams, John Quincy (ed.), "The Diaries of the Rev. Seth Williston, 1796-1800," *Journal of the Presbyterian Historical Society,* VII, pp. 175-208, 234-254; VIII, pp. 40-48, 123-144, 184-192, 226-235, 316-330; IX, pp. 25-40, 368-383; X, pp. 24-35, 130-141.

———— *A History of Auburn Theological Seminary, 1818-1918* (Auburn: Auburn Seminary Press, 1918).

Alexander, J. E., *A Brief History of the Synod of Tennessee from 1817 to 1887* (Philadelphia, 1890).

Alexander, S. D., *The Presbytery of New York, 1738-1888* (New York: Anson D. F. Randolph and Co. [1887]).

Allen, E., *Historical Notices of St. Ann's Parish in Ann Arundel County, Maryland, Extending from 1748 to 1857* (Baltimore, 1857).

An Apology for Renouncing the Jurisdiction of the Synod of Kentucky, To which is added, A Compendious view of the Gospel, and a few remarks on the Confession of Faith, By the Presbytery of Springfield (Lexington, Ky., 1804) (Carlisle, Reprinted by George Kline, 1805).

Arthur, W., *Animadversions on Some Recent Occurences in the Presbyterian Church of Cincinnati* (Cincinnati, 1821).

Ashe, T., *Travels in America, Performed in 1806* (London, 1806).

Averill, W. H., *A History of the First Presbyterian Church, Frankfort, Kentucky Together with the Churches in Franklin County in Connection with the Presbyterian Church in the United States of America* (Cincinnati: Monford and Co., 1902).

Barbour, V. L., *The Slavery Controversy and the Presbyterians* (Typed M. A. thesis, University of Chicago, 1928).

Baird, R., *View of the Valley of the Mississippi; or the Emigrants' and Travellers' Guide to the West* (Philadelphia, 1832).

Baird, S. J., *A History of the New School, and of the Questions Involved in the Disruption of the Presbyterian Church in 1838* (Philadelphia: Claxton, Remsen and Haffelinger, 1868).

Barnes, Gilbert H., *The Anti-Slavery Impulse* (New York: Appleton-Century Co., 1933).

Beecher, L., *A Plea for the West* (Cincinnati, 1835).

―― *Views on Theology* (Cincinnati, 1836).

Beecher, Willis J. and Mary A., *An Index of Presbyterian Ministers, 1706-1881* (Philadelphia, 1883).

Benedict, D., *A General History of the Baptist Denomination in America,* 2 Vols. (Boston, 1813).

Beveridge, Albert J., *Abraham Lincoln, 1809-1858,* 2 Vols. (New York: Houghton Mifflin Co., 1929).

Bishop, R. H., *An Outline of the History of the Church in the State of Kentucky, During a Period of Forty Years, Containing the Memoirs of Rev. David Rice* (Lexington, Ky.: Skillman, 1824).

Blaikie, A., *History of Presbyterianism in New England* (Boston: A. Moore, 1881).

Blake, T. C., *The Old Log House, A History and Defense of the Cumberland Presbyterian Church* (Nashville, Tenn., 1878).

Boyd, Robert, *History of the Synod of Washington, of the Presbyterian Church in the United States of America, 1835-1909* (Seattle, Wash., n. d.).

A Brief and Faithful Narrative of the Various Steps Which Led to the Unhappy Division Which Hath Taken Place among the Members of the Associate Body in the United States, By a ruling elder in the Associate Reformed Synod, 1789 (Philadelphia, 1789).

Briggs, C. A., *American Presbyterianism, Its Origin and Early History, Etc.* (New York: C. Scribners' Sons, 1885).

Brown, Isaac V., *A Historical Vindication of the Abrogation of the*

Plan of Union by the Presbyterian Church in the United States of America (Philadelphia: William S. and Alfred Martien, 1855).

Brownlee, J. T., *History of the Associate and United Presbyterian Presbytery of Chartiers* (Pittsburgh, 1877).

Brownson, J. I., and Snowden, J. H., "Presbyterianism in Washington County," *Proceedings of the Centennial Celebration, 1893.*

Buck, Solon Justus, *Illinois in 1818* (Springfield, Ill., 1917).

Burnet, J., *Notes on the Early Settlement of the Northwestern Territory* (New York, 1847).

Burns, Thomas, *Old Scottish Communion Plate,* 651 pp. (Edinburgh: R. & R. Clark, 1892).

Butler, Mann, *Commonwealth of Kentucky* (Louisville, Ky., 1834).

Campbell, A. D., "The Founding and Early History of the Western Theological Seminary," *Bulletin of the Western Theological Seminary* (October, 1927).

Celebration of the One Hundred and Twenty-fifth Anniversary, University of Pittsburgh Bulletin (Pittsburgh, 1912).

Centenary Memorial of the Planting and Growth of Presbyterianism in Western Pennsylvania and Parts Adjacent (Pittsburgh, 1876).

The Centennial Memorial of the Presbytery of Carlisle, 2 Vols. (Harrisburg, 1889).

Centennial Volume of First Presbyterian Church of Pittsburgh, Pa., 1784-1884 (Pittsburgh, 1884).

Cheeseman, Lewis, *Differences between Old and New School Presbyterians* (Rochester, N. Y., 1848).

Cist, C., *Cincinnati in 1841* (Cincinnati, 1841).

―――― *Sketches and Statistics of Cincinnati* (Cincinnati, 1851).

Cleveland, C. C., *The Great Revival in the West, 1797-1805* (Chicago: University of Chicago Press, 1916).

Coleman, C. B., "Some Religious Developments in Indiana," *Indiana Magazine of History,* V, pp. 57-71.

Collins, L., *History of Kentucky,* Revised and Brought to Year 1874 by R. H. Collins, 2 Vols. (Louisville, 1877).

The Constitution and Standards of 1799, Associate Church in North America, Revised (Pittsburgh, 1832).

Cossitt, F. R., *The Life and Times of Rev. Finis Ewing* (Louisville, 1853).

Cotterill, R. S., *History of Pioneer Kentucky* (Cincinnati, 1917).

Craighead, George, *Scotch and Irish Seeds in American Soil* (Philadelphia, 1878).

Crisman, E. B., *Origin and Doctrines of the Cumberland Presbyterian Church* (St. Louis, Mo.: A. F. Cox, 1856).

Crist, A. C., *History of Marion Presbytery* [Ohio], *Its Churches, Elders, Ministers,* etc. (Delaware, O., 1908).

Crocker, Z., *The Catastrophe of the Presbyterian Church in 1837, In-*

cluding a Full View of the Recent Theological Controversies in New England (New Haven, 1838).

Cumming, William, *The Presbyterian Church Within the Field of the Presbytery of Westchester, Synod of New York, 1660-1889* (Hartford, Conn.: Case, Lockwood and Brainard, 1889).

Cutter, C., *History of Western Reserve College, 1826-1876* (Cleveland, 1876).

Davidson, Robert, *History of the Presbyterian Church in the State of Kentucky; With a Preliminary Sketch of the Churches in the Valley of Virginia* (New York: Robert Carter, 1847).

Dickey, John M., *Brief History of the Presbyterian Church in the State of Indiana* (Madison, 1828).

Dickinson, C. E., "Congregationalism in Ohio before 1852," *Ohio Church History Society Papers,* VII, 1896, p. 41.

Dictionary of American Biography (New York: Chas. Scribners', 1928-1936, 20 vols.).

Dill, J. H., "Congregationalism in Western New York," *Congregational Quarterly,* I, pp. 151-158.

Dow, E. F., *A Portrait of the Millennial Church of Shakers* (University of Maine Studies, August, 1931).

Doyle, Sherman H., *Presbyterian Home Missions: An Account of the Home Missions of the Presbyterian Church in the U. S. A.* (Philadelphia: Presbyterian Board of Publication, 1902).

Drake, B., and Mansfield, E. D., *Cincinnati in 1826* (Cincinnati, 1827).

Drake, D., *Natural and Statistical View or Picture of Cincinnati and the Miami Country* (Cincinnati, 1815).

Eaton, S. J. M., *History of the Presbytery of Erie; Embracing in Its Ancient Boundaries the Whole of Northwestern Pennsylvania and Northeastern Ohio, with Biographical Sketches of All Its Ministers, etc.* (New York: Hurd and Houghton, 1868).

Edson, Hanford A., *Contributions to the Early History of the Presbyterian Church in Indiana* (Indianapolis, 1896).

Elsbree, O. W., *The Rise of the Missionary Spirit in America, 1790-1815* (Williamsport, Pa., 1928).

Esarey, Logan, *A History of Indiana,* 2 Vols. (Indianapolis, Vol. I, 1915).

An Exposition Relating to Some of the Proceedings of the Ohio Presbytery, in the Trial of the Rev. James Welsh, at Vevay in August, 1825 (Vevay, Ind., 1825).

Fairchild, J. H., "The Story of Congregationalism on the Western Reserve," *Ohio Church History Society Papers,* V, p. 19 ff.

Foote, J. P., *The Schools of Cincinnati and Its Vicinity* (Cincinnati, 1855).

Foote, W. H., *Sketches of Virginia, Historical and Biographical* (Philadelphia, 1850 and Second Series: Philadelphia, 1855).

────── *Sketches of North Carolina* [Presbyterian Churches and Ministers] (New York, 1846).

Ford, H. J., *The Scotch-Irish in America* (Princeton, N. J., 1915).

Fowler, P. H., *Historical Sketch of Presbyterianism within the Bounds of the Synod of Central New York,* and Mears, J. W., *The Presbyterian Element in Our National Life and History* (Utica, N. Y.: Curtiss and Childs, 1877).

Galbraith, R. C., *The History of the Chillicothe Presbytery from Its Organization in 1799 to 1889* (Chillicothe, Ohio, 1889).

Gallaher, J., *Western Sketch Book* (Boston, 1850).

Gallandet, E. M., Life of Thomas Hopkins Gallandet (New York, 1888).

Garrison, W. E., *Religion Follows the Frontier: A History of the Disciples of Christ* (New York: Harper and Brothers, 1931).

Gerould, Samuel L., *The Congregational and Presbyterian Churches and Ministers of New Hampshire, etc.* (Lebanon, N. H., 1900).

Gewehr, W. M., *The Great Awakening in Virginia, 1740-1790* (Durham, N. C.: Duke University Press, 1930).

Gibson, W. J., *History of Huntingdon Presbytery* (Bellefonte, 1874).

Gillett, E. H., *History of the Presbyterian Church in the United States of America,* 2 Vols. (Philadelphia: Presbyterian Board of Publication, 1864).

Glasgow, William Melancthon, *Cyclopedic Manual of the United Presbyterian Church of Octorara, June 9th, 1872* (Philadelphia, 1873).

────── *History of the Reformed Presbyterian Church in America* (Baltimore, 1888).

Graham, James R., *The Planting of the Presbyterian Church in Northern Virginia, Prior to the Organization of Winchester Presbytery, December 4, 1794* (Winchester, Va., 1904).

Green, Ashbel, *Historical Sketch of Domestic and Foreign Missions of the Presbyterian Church of the U. S.* (Philadelphia, 1838). (A new edition, with Supplementary notes by John C. Lowrie, 1855 and 1868.)

Green, Calvin, and Wells, S. Y., *A Summary View of the Millennial Church, or United Society of Believers (Commonly called Shakers)* (Albany, N. Y.: Packard and Van Benthuyson, 1823).

Gregory, Parthenia Frances, *The Choctaw Indians.* (Typed M.A. Thesis, Chicago, Ill., 1927.)

Halsey, L. J., *A History of the McCormick Theological Seminary of the Presbyterian Church* (Chicago, 1893).

Hamilton, W. F., *The Founders of the Presbytery of Redstone,* Address at Centennial Celebration, 1881.

Hanna, Charles A., *The Scotch-Irish or the Scot in North Britain, North Ireland, and North America,* 2 Vols. (New York, 1902) [Vol. II contains Extracts from *John Cuthbertson's Journal, Charles C. Beatty's Journal, Dairy of Rev. David McClure, John McMillan's Journal*].

Hayes, Calvin C., *History of the Blairsville Presbytery and Its Churches,* Published by the Presbytery. (n. d.)

Haywood, John, *History of Tennessee* (Knoxville, 1823; reprint Nashville, 1891).

Heinl, Frank J., "Jacksonville and Morgan County: An Historical Review," *Journal of the Illinois State Historical Society,* XVIII, pp. 5-38.

Heiskell, C. W., *Pioneer Presbyterianism in Tennessee* (Memphis).

Higgins, Ruth L., *Expansion in New York: With Especial Reference to the Eighteenth Century* (Columbus: Ohio State University, 1931).

Hightower, R. L., *Joshua L. Wilson: Frontier Controversialist* (Typed Ph.D. Thesis, Chicago, 1933).

——— "Joshua L. Wilson, Frontier Controversialist," *Church History* (December, 1934).

Hill, John B., *The Presbytery of Kansas City and Its Predecessors, 1821-1901* (Kansas City, 1901).

Hill, T., "Historical Discourse," *Presbyterian Quarterly Review* (July, 1861).

Hill, William, *A History of the Rise, Progress, Genius, and Character of American Presbyterianism: Together with a Review of "The Constitutional History of the Presbyterian Church in the United States of America, By Charles Hodge, D.D., Professor in the Theological Seminary at Princeton"* (Washington: J. Gideon, Jr., 1839).

Hinkhouse, J. F., *One Hundred Years of the Presbyterian Church of Iowa* (Cedar Rapids, 1932).

History of Cincinnati and Hamilton County, Ohio; Their Past and Present (Cincinnati: S. B. Nelson and Co., 1894).

History of the Division of the Presbyterian Church in the United States of America, By the Synod of New York and New Jersey (New York, 1852).

History of East Liberty Presbyterian Church of Pittsburgh, Centennial Celebration, 1919.

A History of Education in the State of Ohio, A Centennial Volume Published by the Authority of the General Assembly (Columbus, Ohio, 1876).

History of the First Presbyterian Church of Ithaca, New York, During

One Hundred Years, 1804-1904, John Frederick Fitscher (ed.) (1904).

History of First Presbyterian Church of Pittsburgh (n. d.).

History of the Foundation and Endowment and Catalogue of the Trustees, Alumni, and Students, of the Lane Theological Seminary (Cincinnati, 1848).

History of the Presbytery of Huntington (W. J. Gibson Co., 1874).

History of the Presbytery of Washington, Various authors (Philadelphia, 1889).

History of the Third Presbyterian Church of Pittsburgh, Pennsylvania, etc. (Pittsburgh, 1869).

Hodge, Charles, *The Constitutional History of the Presbyterian Church in the United States of America,* 2 parts (Philadelphia: William S. Martien, Part I, 1839; Part II, 1840).

Hodge, Frederick Webb, *Handbook of American Indians North of Mexico,* 2 parts, Smithsonian Institution: Bureau of American Ethnology, Bulletin 30 (Washington: Government Printing Office, Part 1, 1907; Part 2, 1910).

Hooper, W. S. (ed.), *Fifty Years as a Presiding Elder, By Rev. Peter Cartwright* (Cincinnati, 1871).

Hopkins, Samuel M., "From the War of the Revolution to the Adoption of the 'Presbyterian Form of Government,'" in *A Short History of American Presbyterianism, from Its Foundations to the Re-Union of 1869* (Philadelphia: Presbyterian Board of Publication and S. S. Work, 1903).

Hotchkin, James H., *A History of the Purchase and Settlement of Western New York and of the Rise, Progress, and Present State of the Presbyterian Church in that Section* (New York, 1848).

Howe, George, D.D., *History of the Presbyterian Church in South Carolina,* Prepared by order of the Synod, 2 vols. (Vol. I, Columbia, S. C.: Duffie and Chapman, 1870; Vol. II, Columbia, S. C.: W. J. Duffie, 1883).

Howison, R. R., *A History of Virginia, from Its Discovery and Settlement by Europeans to the Present Time,* 2 vols. (Philadelphia, 1846-1848).

Humphrey, E. F., *Nationalism and Religion in America, 1774-1789* (Boston: Chipman Law Publishing Co., 1924).

Hunt, Gaillard, *The Life of James Madison* (New York: Doubleday, Page and Co., 1902).

Hutchinson, J. R., *Reminiscences, Sketches and Addresses Selected from my papers During a Ministry of Forty-five Years in Mississippi, Louisiana, and Texas* (Houston, Tex.: E. H. Cushing, 1874).

Indian Mission: Conversations on the Choctaw Mission, By the author of *"Conversations on the Bombay Mission"* (Boston, Mass.: Sabbath School Union, 1830).

Indiana University, 1820-1920: Centennial Memorial Volume (Indiana University, 1921).

Indianapolis, Indiana, *First Presbyterian Church Memorial of Indianapolis*, 1925.

Jenkins, W., *The Ohio Gazateer and Travelers' Guide* (Columbus, Ohio, 1837).

Jensen, H. E., *Rise of Religious Journalism* (Typed Ph.D. Thesis, University of Chicago, 1930).

Johnson, Jesse, "Early Theological Education West of the Alleghanies," in *Papers of the American Society of Church History*, Second Series, V, pp. 121-130.

Jones, A. E., *Extracts from the History of Cincinnati* (Cincinnati, 1888).

Jones, Joseph H., *The Life of Ashbel Green, V.D.M. Begun to be Written by Himself in His Eighty-Second Year and Continued to His Eighty-Fourth. Prepared for the Press at the Author's Request* (New York: Carter and Brothers, 1849).

Junkin, George, *The Vindication, Containing A History of the Trial of the Rev. Albert Barnes by the Second Presbytery and by the Synod of Philadelphia* (Philadelphia: W. S. Martin, 1836).

Kemper, Andrew Carr, *A Memorial of the Rev. James Kemper for the Centennial of the Synod of Kentucky* (Louisville, 1899).

Kennedy, W. S., *The Plan of Union: or A History of the Presbyterian and Congregational Churches of the Western Reserve: with Biographical Sketches of the Early Missionaries* (Hudson, Ohio, 1856).

King, R., *Address to the Pioneer Association of Cincinnati, April 7, 1882* (Cincinnati, 1882).

Kirkpatrick, John E., *Timothy Flint, Pioneer, Missionary, Author, Editor, 1780-1840* (Cleveland, Ohio: Arthur H. Clark Co., 1911). The story of his life among the Pioneers and Frontiersmen in the Ohio and Mississippi Valley and in New England and the South.

Koch, G. A., *Republican Religion: The American Revolution and the Cult of Reason* (New York, 1933).

Lane Theological Seminary: General Catalogue, 1829-1899 (Cincinnati, 1899).

Larned, Ellen, "The New Connecticut or Western Reserve," *The Connecticut Magazine*, III, p. 96 ff.

Letters on the Chickasaw and Osage Missions (Boston, Mass, 1833).

Letters and Conversations of the Cherokee Mission (Boston, 1830).

Lexington, Kentucky, *The Celebration of the Centennial of the Organization of the Second Presbyterian Church* (Lexington, Ky., 1915).

Little, A. A., et al., *The History of Steele Creek Church, Mecklenburg County, N. C., Compiled and written by Rev. John Douglass,* Revised and rewritten [Organized 1760] (Charlotte, N. C., 1901).

Lindsley, J. B., "Sources and Sketches of Cumberland Presbyterian History," *Theological Museum* (Nashville, 1877-1878).

Ludlow, A. C., *The Old Stone Church. The Story of a Hundred Years* (Cleveland, 1920).

Ludlow, Mr. and Mrs. A. C., *History of Cleveland Presbyterianism, etc.* (Cleveland, 1896).

Maccalla, W. L., *Case of Maccalla Against Blythe* (Chillicothe, Ohio, 1814).

MacDonnold, B. W., *History of the Cumberland Presbyterian Church* (Nashville, Tenn., Board of Publication of Cumberland Presbyterian Church, 1888).

MacLean, J. P., *A Sketch of the Life and Labors of Richard McNemar.* (Columbus, n. d.).

—— *Shakers of Ohio, Fugitive Papers Concernong the Shakers of Ohio, With Unpublished Manuscripts* (Columbus, 1907).

MacNemar, Richard, *The Kentucky Revival: or A Short History of the Late Extraordinary Outpouring of the Spirit of God in the Western States of America* (Cincinnati: J. W. Browne, 1807; New York: Reprinted by Edward O. Jenkins, 1846).

Mahan, Asa, *Autobiography, Intellectual, Moral and Spiritual* (London, 1882).

Malone, James H., *The Chickasaw Nation, A Short Sketch of a Noble People* (Louisville, Kentucky: John P. Morton and Co., 1922).

Mansfield, E. D., *Memoirs of the Life and Services of Daniel Drake, M.D.* (Cincinnati, 1855).

Martin, Asa Earl, *The Anti-Slavery Movement in Kentucky Prior to 1850* (Louisville, Ky.: The Standard Printing Co., 1918), The Filson Club Publications.

—— "Anti-Slavery Societies in Tennessee," *Tennessee Historical Magazine* (December, 1915).

Martzolff, C. L., *Ohio University: the Historic College of the Old Northwest* (Athens, Ohio, 1910).

Maxson, C. H., *The Great Awakening in the Middle Colonies* (Chicago: University of Chicago Press, 1920).

Maxwell, William, *A Memoir of the Rev. John H. Rice, D.D.* (Philadelphia, 1835).

McCormick Theological Seminary Historical Celebration (Chicago, 1910).

McGhee, R. M., *History of the Red River Presbytery*, MS., in Historical Foundation, Montreat, N. C.

"McGready's Narrative of the Revival in Logan County," *New York Misssionary Magazine* (1803).

McIllwaine, H. R., *Struggle of Protestant Dissenters for Religious Toleration in Virginia* (Baltimore, 1894).

McMaster, J. B., *History of the People of the United States*, 8 vols. (New York: D. Appleton and Co., 1900).

McNaugher, Dr. John, *History of Theological Education in the United Presbyterian Church and Its Ancestries* (Pittsburgh, 1931).

McNeill, John Thomas, *The Presbyterian Church in Canada 1875-1925* (Toronto: Presbyterian Church in Canada, 1925).

——— "Religious and Moral Conditions among the Canadian Pioneers," in *Papers of the American Society of Church History*, Second Series, VIII.

Memorial Volume of the Semi-Centennial of the Theological Seminary at Columbia, South Carolina (Columbia, S. C., 1884).

Miller, A. B., *Doctrines and Genius of the Cumberland Presbyterian Church* (Nashville, Tenn.: Cumberland Presbyterian Publishing House, 1892).

Miller, E. A., *The History of Educational Legislation in Ohio from 1803 to 1850* (Typed Ph.D. Thesis, Chicago, 1918).

Miller, F. W., *Cincinnati's Beginnings* (Cincinnati, 1880).

Miller, James A., *The History of the Presbytery of Steuben, including that of all the other Presbyteries to which the churches of Steuben and Alleghany Counties have belonged, etc.* (New York, Published by Presbytery, 1897).

Miller, James P., *Biographical Sketches and Sermons of some of the first ministers of the Associate Church in America to which is prefixed A Historical Introduction, etc.* (Albany, 1839).

Miller, S., Jr., *Report of the Presbyterian Church Case: The Commonwealth of Pennsylvania, at the Suggestion of James Todd and Others, vs. Ashbel Green and Others* (Philadelphia, 1839).

Mills, Samuel J., and Smith, Daniel, *Report of a Missionary Tour through that part of the United States which lies west of the Alleghany Mountains; performed under the direction of the Massachusetts Missionary Society* (Andover, 1815).

Mitchell, Margaret J., *Development of Religion in Early Ohio, 1788-1820* (Typed M.A. Thesis, University of Chicago, 1914).

Mode, P. G., *The Frontier Spirit in American Christianity* (New York: Macmillan Co., 1923).

Monongahela City Anniversary, 1792-1892 (1895).

Montfort, J. G., *A Historical Discourse, Delivered in the Second Presbyterian Church of Cincinnati, April 9, 1872* (Cincinnati, n. d.).

Moore, C. B., *History of Presbyterianism in Arkansas, 1828-1902* (n. d.).

Moore, E. A., *The Earlier Life of Robert J. Breckinridge, 1800-1845* (Typed Ph.D. Thesis, Chicago, 1932).

Moore, Edmund A., "Robert J. Breckenridge and the Slavery Aspect of the Presbyterian Schism of 1837," *Church History*, IV, No. 4 (December, 1935).

Moore, R. B., *History of Huron Presbytery, showing the working of the*

Plan of Union from its inception in 1801 till after the reunion in 1870, etc. (Philadelphia: Fell and Co., 1892).

Moore, William E., *History of Presbyterianism in Ohio to the Year 1870.* Typed copy in the University of Chicago Library.

Moore, William T., *History of the Disciples of Christ* (New York: Fleming H. Revell Co., 1909).

Morris, Edward D., *A Book of Remembrance; The Presbyterian Church, New School, 1837-1869. An Historical Review* (Columbus, Ohio, 1905).

Murphy, Thomas, *The Presbytery of Log College; or, The Cradle of the Presbyterian Church in America* (Philadelphia, 1889).

Neely, R. L., *Sketches of the Presbytery of Western District* [Tennessee] (1883).

Nevin, Alfred, *Encyclopedia of the Presbyterian Church in the U. S. A.* (Philadelphia, 1884).

—— *Churches of the Valley, or, An Historical Sketch of the Old Presbyterian Congregations of Cumberland and Franklin Counties in Pennsylvania* (Philadelphia: Joseph M. Wilson, 1852).

Nevin, A. C. (ed.), *The Centennial Memorial, A Record of the proceedings on the occasion of the celebration of the One Hundredth Anniversary of the Associate Reformed Presbyterian Church of Little Britain, N. Y., etc.* (New York: Robert Carter and Brothers, 1859).

Nichols, R. H., "The Plan of Union in New York." (*Church History*, Vol. V, No. 1. 1936.)

Norton, A. T., *History of the Presbyterian Church in the State of Illinois* (St. Louis, 1879).

Ohio Church History Society Papers, Vols. I-XII (Oberlin, Ohio, Printed for the Society, 1890-1901).

Osmond, J., *History of the Presbytery of Luzerne, State of Pennsylvania* (Wilkes-Barre, Pa., 1897).

Ozark Presbytery, History of: *Presbyterianism in the Ozarks. A History of the Work of the Various Branches of the Presbyterian Church in Southwest Missouri, 1834-1907* (Published at the request of the Presbytery of Ozark, U. S. A., 1909).

Park, E. A., *Memoir of Nathaneal Emmons* (Boston, 1861).

Parsons, Levi (ed.), *History of Rochester Presbytery from the Earliest Settlement of the Country, Embracing Original Records of Ontario Association, and the Presbyteries of Ontario Association, Rochester (Former), Genessee River, and Rochester City, to which are appended Biographical Sketches of deceased ministers and brief his-*

tories of individual Churches (Rochester, N. Y., Published by the Presbytery, 1889).

Patten, Jennie M., and Graham, Andrew, *History of the Somonauk United Presbyterian Church, near Sandwich, De Kalb County, Illinois, With Ancestral Lines of the Early Members* (Chicago: Printed Privately, 1928).

Pears, Thomas C., "The Foundations of Our Western Zion," *Journal of the Department of History of the Presbyterian Church in the U. S. A.,* XVI, No. 4 (December, 1934).

Pease, T. C., *The Frontier State 1818-1848.* (Springfield, Ill.: The Illinois Centennial Commission, 1918.)

Peter, H. and J. *Transylvania University: Its Origin, Rise, Decline, and Fall* (Louisville, Ky., 1896).

Pierce, Marybelle, *The Establishment of the Associate, Reformed, and Associate Reformed Churches in Western Pennsylvania* (Typed M.A. Thesis, University of Pittsburgh, 1931).

A Plea for Voluntary Societies and a Defense of the Decisions of the General Assembly of 1836, Against the Strictures of the Princeton Review—and Others, By a member of the Assembly (New York, 1837).

Posey, Walter B., *The Development of Methodism in the Old Southwest, 1783-1824* (Tuscaloosa, Ala.: Weatherford Printing Co., 1933).

———— "The Earthquake of 1811 and Its Influence on Evangelistic Methods in the Churches of the Old South," *Tennessee Historical Magazine,* Series II, I, 2 (January, 1931).

Potter, H. N., *Shenango Presbytery, One Hundred Years, 1808-1908* (Published by the Presbytery, September 14, 1908).

Potter, L. D., "Early History of Presbyterianism in the Whitewater Valley," *Indiana Magazine of History,* V, 1909, 28-42.

The Prairie Missionary (Written for the American Sunday School Union, and revised by the Committee of Publication) (Philadelphia: American S. S. Union, 1853).

Presbyterian Reunion: A Memorial Volume 1837-1871 (New York: DeWitt C. Lent & Company, 1870).

Punchard, George, *History of Congregationalism,* 5 Vols. (Boston: Congregational Publishing Society, 1881).

Rammelkamp, C. H., *Centennial History of Illinois College* (New Haven, 1928).

Reed, Andrew, and Matheson, James, *A Narrative of the Visit to the American Churches by the Deputation from the Congregational Union of England and Wales* (London, 1835).

Reigler, Gordon A., "Aratus Kent, First Presbyterian Minister in Northern Illinois," *Journal of the Presbyterian Historical Society*, XIII (December, 1929).

Robinson, Juliette, *The First Presbyterian Church of Kittanning, Pennsylvania, 1822-1922.*

Rodebaugh, James H., *Robert Hamilton Bishop* (Columbus, Ohio, Ohio State Archaeological and Historical Society, 1935). Bibliography.

Rogers, James R., *The Cane Ridge Meeting-house: to which is Appended the Autobiography of B. W. Stone, and a sketch of David Purivance* (Cincinnati: Standard Publishing Co., 1910).

Rogers, Elder John, *The Biography of Elder Barton W. Stone, written by himself with additions and reflections* (Cincinnati, 1847).

Rogers, John, *Works of John Witherspoon, D.D., L.L.D., To which is prefixed an account of the author's life,* 9 Vols. (Edinburgh, 1815).

Roosevelt, Theodore, *The Winning of the West,* 4 Vols. (New York: Homeward Bound Edition, Review of Reviews Company, 1900); 4 Vols. (New York, Standard Library Edition, G. P. Putnam's Sons, 1905).

Ross, A. H., *The Church-Kingdom: Lectures on Congregationalism . . . in Andover Theological Seminary 1882-1886* (Boston and Chicago, 1887).

Rule, Lucien V., *Fore-runners of Lincoln in the Ohio Valley, with historic summaries,* by Rev. Charles R. Erdman, D.D., Rev. Thornton Whaling, D.D., Rev. Henry Van Dyke, D.D., Rev. Warren H. Wilson, D.D. (Louisville, Ky.: Brandt, 1927).

——— *The Light Bearers. Home Mission Heroes of Presbyterian History; Centennial story of an old country church and neighbourhood in the Presbytery of Louisville* (Louisville: Brandt, 1926).

Rupp, I. D., *History of Western Pennsylvania* (Harrisburg, 1846).

Schermerhorn, John F., and Mills, Samuel J., *A Correct View of that Part of the United States, which lies west of the Alleghany mountains, with regard to religion and morals* (Hartford, Conn., 1814).

Schwarz, Julius F., *History of the Presbyterian Church in Nebraska* (1924).

Scouller, J. B., *A History of the United Presbyterian Church.* (American Church History Series, Vol. XI. New York, 1894.)

——— *History of the United Presbyterian Church of Big Spring, Newville, Penna., 1764-1878* (Carlisle, Pa., 1878).

——— *Manual of the United Presbyterian Church of North America, 1751-1887.* Revised edition (Pittsburgh, 1888).

Scovel, S. C., "Presbyterians of Ohio," *Ohio Archaeological and Historical Society Publications,* III, 211-220.

Septuagesimal Celebration of Union Theological Seminary in Virginia, 1824-1894 (Richmond, Va.: Whittet and Shepperson, 1894).

A Short History of American Presbyterianism from its foundations to the Reunion of 1869 (Philadelphia: Presbyterian Board of Publication and Sabbath-School Work, 1903).

Slosser, Gaius J., "A Chapter from the Religious History of Western Pennsylvania," *Journal of the Department of History of the Presbyterian Church in the U. S. A.,* XVI (1934-1935), No. 3, 97-125.

—— "Concerning the Life and Work of the Rev. John McMillan, D.D.," *Journal of the Department of History of the Presbyterian Church in the U. S. A.,* V, (1932-1933), Nos. 3, 4, 5.

Smeltzer, W. Guy, *Racial Migrations into Western Pennsylvania.* (Typed thesis (S.T.B.), Western Theological Seminary, Pittsburgh, Pa.)

Smith, George R., *A History of the First Eighty Years of the First Presbyterian Church of Marcellus, N. Y., etc.* (Canandaigua, N. Y., 1883).

Smith, J., *History of Jefferson College* (Pittsburgh, 1857).

—— *Old Redstone, or Historical Sketches of Western Presbyterianism, Its Early Ministers, Its Perilous Times and Its First Records* (Philadelphia, 1854).

Speer, William, *The Great Revival of 1800* (Philadelphia, 1872).

Spence, Irving, *Letters on the Early History of the Presbyterian Church in America, Addressed to the Late Rev. Robert M. Laird, with a Sketch of the Life of the Author, and a Selection from His Religious Writings* (Philadelphia: Henry Perkins, 1838).

Sprague, W. B., *Annals of the American Pulpit,* 9 Vols., Vols. III and IV: *Presbyterians* (New York: R. Carter and Brothers, 1858-1869).

Spring, Gardiner, *Personal Reminiscences of the Life and Times of,* 2 Vols. (New York: Charles Scribners and Co., 1866).

Stacy, James, *A History of the Presbyterian Church in Georgia.*

Stansbury, Arthur J., *Trial of the Rev. Albert Barnes Before the Synod of Philadelphia in Session at York, October 1835. On a charge of Heresy, Preferred Against him by the Rev. Geo. Junkin. With all the Pleadings and Debate* (New York: Van Nostrand and Dwight, 1836).

Stephens, J. V., *The Cumberland Presbyterian Digest (1899), A Compend of the Organic Law of the Cumberland Presbyterian Church, Together with the Organic Law of its General Agencies, and the Judicial Deliverance of its Supreme Judicatory.* (Nashville, Tenn., Cumberland Presbyterian Publishing House, 1899).

Stephens, John V., *Cumberland University Theological School* (Cincinnati, 1935).

Stewart, D. M., *History of Whitewater Presbytery. Historical Discourses of Whitewater Presbytery, delivered at Lawrenceburg, Indiana, April 12, 1876.*

Stock, H. T.,"Protestantism in Illinois Before 1835," *Journal of the Illinois Historical Society,* XII, 1919, pp. 1-31.

Stoney, Louise C. (ed.), *Autobiographical Notes, Letters and Reflections By Thomas Smyth, D.D.* (Charleston, S. C.: Walker, Evans and Cogswell Co.)

Stowe, Harriet B., *Men of Our Times* (Hartford, Conn., 1868).

Strickland, W. P., *The Pioneers of the West, or Life in the Woods* (New York, 1856).

Summers, T. J., *History of Marietta* (Marietta, Ohio, 1903).

Sweet, W. W., "The Churches as Moral Courts of the Frontier," *Church History* (March, 1933).

—— *Story of Religions in America* (New York: Harper and Brothers, 1930).

Symmes, J. C., *The Trenton Circular, To the Respectable Public of November 26, 1787* (Cincinnati, 1910).

Taylor, Charles B., *History of the Presbytery of Athens* [Ohio] (n.d.)

Tenney, Mary McWhorter, *Communion Tokens, their Origin, History and Use: with a Treatise on the relation of the Sacrament to the Vitality and revival of the Church,* Montreat, N. C., Typed MS, 1934, 319 pp.

Testimony of Associate Church, a Display of the Religious Principles of the Associate Church of North America, 1784, Revised (Philadelphia, 1813).

Tewkesbury, Donald G., *The Founding of American Colleges and Universities before the Civil War with Particular Reference to the Religious Influences Bearing upon the College Movement* (New York: Board of Publication, Columbus University, 1932).

Thomas, D. L., *The Antecedents and Early Years of Centre College.* Typewritten.

Thompson, R. E., *A History of the Presbyterian Churches in the United States* (American Church History Series, Vol. VI).

Tobey, W. L., and Thompson, W. O., *The Diamond Anniversary Volume of Miami University* (Hamilton, Ohio, 1899).

Trial of the Rev. Lyman Beecher, D.D. Before the Presbytery of Cincinnati, on the Charge of Heresy. Reported for The New York Observer (New York, 1835).

Trumbull, Benjamin, *History of Connecticut,* 2 Vols (New Haven, 1818).

Turner, F. J., *The Frontier in American History* (New York: H. Holt and Co., 1920).

University of Tennessee Record (July, 1898).

Van Rensselaer, Cortlandt, *Historical Contributions Relating to the Founders, Principles and Acts of the Presbyterian Church,* etc. (Philadelphia, 1861).

Vander Velde, Lewis G., *The Presbyterian Churches and the Federal Union, 1861-1869* (Cambridge: Harvard University Press, 1932).

Van Voorhis, John S., *The Old and New Monongahela.* (Pittsburgh, 1893.)

Voss, Louis (Compiler), *History of the Presbytery of New Orleans: Presbyterianism in New Orleans and Adjacent Points* (New Orleans, 1931).

Walker, Williston, *A History of Congregational Churches in the United States* (American Church History Series, Vol. III).

Ware, C. C., *Barton Warren Stone, Pathfinder of Christian Union, A Story of his Life and Times* (St. Louis: Bethany Press, 1932).

Warren, Edward L., *The Presbyterian Church in Louisville, From its Organization in 1816 to the year 1896* (Reprinted from *Memorial History of Louisville*) (Chicago, 1896).

Washington: *History of the Presbytery of Washington, including a brief Account of the Planting of the Presbyterian Church in Western Pennsylvania, and Parts Adjacent, with Sketches of Ministers and Elders* (Philadelphia, 1889).

Washington and Jefferson College Bulletin (1932).

Webster, Richard, *A History of the Presbyterian Church in America* (Philadelphia, 1857).

Weigle, L. A., *American Idealism* (*Pageant of American Series,* Vol. X) (New Haven, 1928).

Western Reserve University Catalogue (1893-1894).

Whallon, E. P., *History of the Presbytery of Vincennes* (Indianapolis: W. A. Patton, 1888).

Wilkeson, Samuel, "Early Recollections of the West," *American Pioneer,* Vol. II (Cincinnati, 1843).

Williams, Aaron, *Centenary Memorial of the Planting and Growth of Presbyterianism in Western Pennsylvania and Parts Adjacent* (Pittsburgh, 1876).

Wilson, S. M., *History of Kentucky,* Vol. XII (Chicago, 1928).

Wilson, Joshua L., *Four Propositions Sustained against the Claims of the American Home Missionary Society* (Cincinnati, 1831).

Wood, James, *Facts and Observations concerning the Organization of Churches in the Three Synods of Western New York and the Western Reserve* (Saratoga, 1837).

Woodburn, J. A., *The Scotch-Irish Presbyterians in Monroe County, Indiana,* Indiana Historical Society Publications, IV, No. 8 (Indianapolis, 1910).

—— "Pioneer Presbyterianism" *Indiana Magazine of History,* XXII, No. 4 (December, 1926), p. 335 ff.

—— "United Presbyterian Beginnings," *Bloomington United Presbyterian Church Centennial,* Mimeographed (Bloomington, Indiana, 1934).

Woods, H., *The History of the Presbyterian Controversy with Early Sketches of Presbyterianism* (Louisville, 1843).

Woods, Robert A., "Presbyterianism in Princeton, Indiana, from 1810 to 1930," *Indiana Magazine of History* (Bloomington, Ind.), XXVI, pp. 93-125.

PAMPHLETS

Address to the Presbyterians of Kentucky proposing plan for instruction and emancipation of their slaves (Cincinnati: Taylor, 1835).

Address to the Synod of Kentucky on Slavery, in 1835 (Pittsburgh: United Presbyterian Board of Publication, 1862).

The Associate Reformed Presbytery of Kentucky, to the congregations settled and vacant under their care (Lexington, 1805).

Barbour, L. G., "The Relation of the Presbyterian Church to Education in Kentucky," *Centennial of Presbyterianism in Kentucky* (Harrodsburg, Ky., 1883).

Barton, C. E., *The Founders and Founding of Illinois College* (Jacksonville, Illinois, 1902).

[Bayless, John C.], *Historical Sketch of the Presbyterian Church of Ashland, Kentucky, With Some Notice of Educational Efforts in the Town* (Ashland, Ky., 1871).

Bishop, Robert H., *Discourse occasioned by the death of Rev. James McChord; delivered . . . 1820* (Lexington: Skillman, 1821).

Blythe, James, *A Discourse on the Present State and Duty of the Church: Delivered at the Opening of the Synod of Kentucky, October, 1824* (Lexington: Skillman, 1824).

Boardman, George Nye, *Historical Discourse Preached on the 50th Anniversary of the First Presbyterian Church in Binghamton*, November 24, 1867 (New York, 1868).

Breckinridge, W. L., *Letters Addressed to the Members of the Presbyterian Churches, under the care of the Synod of Kentucky* (Danville, Ky., 1835).

Breckinridge, William L., and Humphrey, Edward P., *Theological Seminaries in the West* (Louisville: Hill and Brothers, 1850).

Brownlee, Rev. W. C., *A Discourse on the Sin and Danger of Opposition to Public Religion Covenanting* (Pittsburgh, 1812).

By-Laws of the Transylvania University, Lexington, Kentucky (Lexington, Ky.: Worsley, 1818).

Caldwell, John H., *Historical Sketch of Holston Presbytery: Presbyterian Church in the U. S. A.* (Rogersville, Tenn., 1923).

A Catechism setting forth the Principles of Public Covenanting as it is practised in the secessions Church (Pittsburgh, 1812).

Centennial of Presbyterianism in Kentucky, 1783-1883, Addresses Delivered at Harrodsburg, Kentucky, October 12, 1883 (Louisville, Ky. [1883]).

Centre College, A Brief History of the Revival of Religion in, and in many of the churches in the bounds of the Synod of Kentucky during the years, 1825, 1826, 1827, 1828 (Frankfort, Ky., 1866).

Certificate of membership, Flemingsburg, Ky. Presbyterian Church (1835).

Circular of the Associate-Reformed Presbytery of Kentucky, to the churches under their care (Lexington, Ky.: Skillman, 1812).

Circular letter to the Churches in Kentucky Presbytery of the Cumberland Presbyterian Church, 1845 (Louisville, Ky.: Hull).

Circular letter, the first historical and doctrinal statement issued by the Independent Cumberland Presbytery, which grew into the Cumberland Presbyterian Church, 1810 (Reprint Nashville, Tenn., 1899).

Circular letter of the Synod of Kentucky (Lexington, Ky.: Charless, 1803).

Clarke, Walter, *Half Century Discourse, The First Church in Buffalo, delivered February 3d, 1862* (Buffalo, 1862).

Cleland, Thomas, *A Brief History of the Rise, Progress and Termination of the Proceedings of the Synod of Kentucky, relative to the late Cumberland Presbytery* (Lexington, Ky.: Skillman, 1823).

Collier, Francis J., *Chartiers Church and its Ministers: An Historical Address: Delivered at the M'Millian Centennial Celebration Held at Chartiers Presbyterian Church, Near Cannonsburg, Washington County, Pennsylvania, August 25th, 1875* (Philadelphia: McLaughlin Brothers, 1875).

Commons, J. R., *The History of Higher Education in Ohio* (United States Bureau of Education Circular, 1891).

[Cressy, B. C.], *An Appeal in Behalf of the Indian Theological Seminary Located at South Hanover, Indiana* (Boston: Pierce and Parker, 1832).

Cumming, W. J., *Historical Sermon, Delivered in the Yorktown Presbyterian Church, August 6th, 1876* (Peekskill, N. Y., 1877).

The Dagon of Calvinism, or the Moloch of Decrees: A Poem, in Three Cantos (Cincinnati, 1811).

Dickinson, Jonathan, *Sermon preached at the opening of the Synod of Philadelphia, September 19, 1722* (Boston, 1723).

Dwight, Timothy, *A Discourse on Some Events of the Last Century, delivered in the Brick Church in New Haven, January 7, 1801* (New Haven, 1801).

God's Providence for Forty Years. Three Discourses at the Fortieth Anniversary of the First Presbyterian Church in Green Bay, Wisconsin (Green Bay: Root and Kimball, 1876).

Hawley, Charles, *The History of the First Presbyterian Church, Auburn, N. Y.* (Auburn: Dennis Brothers and Co., 1869).

Historical and Biographical Catalogue of the Officers and Students of the Western Theological Seminary of the Presbyterian Church at Allegheny City, Pennsylvania, 1827-1885 (Allegheny, Pa., 1885).

Hoge, Moses D., *Memorial Discourse on the Planting of Presbyterianism in Kentucky one hundred years ago* (Louisville, Ky.: Courier [1883]).

Humphrey, Edward W., *Historical Sketch of the Synod of Kentucky, 1802-1902. An address by . . . delivered October 14, 1902, at Lexington, Kentucky, before the Synod of Kentucky, North and South.*

Johnston, James H., *A Ministry of Forty Years in Indiana. An Historical Discourse, Presenting Facts Respecting the Progress of Presbyterianism in that State During that Period Delivered at Crawfordsville, Indiana, February 5, 1865* (Indianapolis: Holloway, Douglas and Co., 1865).

Johnstone, R. A., *History of the Transylvania Presbytery: Historical Sketch* (1876).

Kentucky Presbyterian Education Society, Address (Lexington: Skillman, 1831).

Kentucky Presbyterian Education Society: Constitution (1828).

Kittredge, Abbot E., *Historical Discourses, Centennial Sabbath, July 2, 1876* [Third Presbyterian Church, Chicago] (Chicago, 1876).

Knott, W. T., *History of the Presbyterian Church in What is Now Marion County and City of Lebanon, Kentucky* (Lebanon, Ky., 1895).

Lacy, Drury, *An Account of the Great Revival in Kentucky.* (n. d.)

Little, D. D., *History of the Presbytery of Columbia, Tennessee* (Columbia, Tenn., 1928).

MacLean, J. P., *The Kentucky Revival and its Influence on the Miami Valley.* (n. d.)

McElroy, Rev. I. S., *Some Pioneer Presbyterian Preachers of the Piedmont, North Carolina* (Gastonia, N. C.).

Magill, John, *The Pioneer to the Kentucky Emigrant* (Frankfort, 1832).

A Manifesto Containing a Plain Statement of Facts, Relative to the Acts and Doings of the General Assembly and its inferior Judicatories together with the sentiments of the undersigned Members of the Synod of Kentucky (1840); Thomas Cleland, J. C. Stiles, Dennis M. Winston, Samuel Maccoun. (n. p: n. d.)

Manual for the Members of the Second Presbyterian Church in Madison, Ind. (Madison, Ind., 1845).

McNies, **W. S.**, *History of the Butler Presbytery* (Butler, Pa.: Ziegler Printing Co., 1923).

M'Henry, B., *Remarks on Some Passages in a Periodical Work, Printed in Lexington, Kentucky, Entitled "The Evangelical Record and Western Review"* (Lexington, Ky., 1813).

Minutes of a Temperance Convention of Northern Kentucky, held in Maysville, 1837 (Maysville, Ky.: Collins, 1837).

Mitchell, Arthur, *The Church on the Frontier. An Historical Discourse delivered in the First Presbyterian Church, Chicago, Ill., by the pastor on November 3d, 1878* (Chicago [1878]).

Moffatt, J. D., *Historical Sketch of Washington and Jefferson College* (Washington, Pa., 1890).

Morris, Rev. B. F., *Historical Sketch of Rising Sun and the Presbyterian Church* (Cincinnati, 1858).

Narrative of Mr. Adam Rankins Trial Before the Transylvania Presbytery (Lexington, 1793).

Neill, Edward D., *Early Days of the Presbyterian Branch of the Holy Catholic Church, in the State of Minnesota* (Minneapolis: Johnson and Smith, 1873).

Newton, A., *The Days of Old. A Discourse Preached in the Presbyterian Church, in Norwalk, Sunday, June 24, 1860* (Cleveland, 1860).

Pioneer Presbyterianism in Tennessee: Addresses Delivered at the Tennessee Exposition on Presbyterian Day, October 28, 1897 (Richmond, Va., 1898).

Plan for the Theological Seminary of the Synod of Kentucky, 1829 (Lexington, Ky.: Skillman, 1829).

Proceedings and annual report of the Kentucky Temperance Society, 1832 (Frankoft, Ky.: Hodges, 1832).

Proceedings and Second Annual Report of the Kentucky Temperance Society with an address by Lunsford P. Yandell, M.D. (Frankfort, Ky.: Hodges, 1832).

Proceedings of the Convention of Versailles [Jos. C. Stiles, John H. Brown, John R. Alexander, Committee], March 17, 1840. (n. p: n. d.)

Rafinesque, C. S., *Annals of Kentucky* (Frankfort, 1824).

Rankin, A., *The Transylvania Presbytery* (Lexington, 1793).

—— *A Review of the noted revival in Kentucky, commenced in Kentucky in the year of our Lord, 1801* (1803).

Remarks on the Act of the General Assembly of 1837 Declaring four Synods to be "neither in form nor in fact, an integral portion of the Presbyterian Church of these United States," submitted for the

Consideration of Southern Presbyterians; of a Presbyterian of Virginia (Richmond, 1837).

Rodgers, John, *The Divine Goodness Displayed in the American Revolution, A Sermon preached December 11th, 1783, A Day of Public Thanksgiving* (New York, 1783). (Reprinted in *Patriotic Preachers of the American Revolution.*)

Root, D., *A Sermon Delivered at the Dedication of the New Church Edifice, of the Second Presbyterian Society, Cincinnati, May 20, 1830* (Cincinnati, 1830).

Rules and by-laws of the Presbytery of Ebenezer, to which are added extracts from the minutes (Paris, Ky., 1821).

Rules and standing docket of the Synod of Kentucky (Maysville, Ky., 1823).

Sanford, E. T., *Blount College and the University of Tennessee, 1879.*

A serious address from the Synod of Kentucky to the churches under their care (Lexington, Ky.: Bradford, 1804).

Shane, J. D., *The Bush in the Flame: A Sketch of the Immigrant Church. A Sermon, Preached before the Reverend the Presbytery of West Lexington, at the opening of their sessions at Mount Horeb, September 1, 1858* (Cincinnati: John D. Thorpe, 1858).

Sprague, William B., *A Sermon delivered on Sabbath Morning, January 4, 1846, Containing Sketches of the History of the Second Presbyterian Church and Congregation, Albany, During thirty years from the Period of their Organization* (Albany: Erastus H. Pease, 1846).

Stephens, J. V., *The Story of the Founding of Lane: Address Delivered at the Centennial of Lane Theological Seminary, June 25, 1929.*

A Summary of the Confession of Faith of the Presbyterian Church in the U. S. of America, Drawn up for the Benefit of the Members of the Presbyterian Church on Cherry Valley, N. Y. (Cherry Valley, N. Y., 1854).

Tait, Wilson W., *Historical sermon in which is presented a brief sketch of the history of Ebenezer Presbyterian Church on Cabin Creek, Lewis County, Ky.* (1884).

Tenney, S. M., *History of Churches of Eastern Texas Presbytery* (Minutes, 1923-1924).

A Theological Seminary for the North West (New Albany, 1856).

Thompson, C. T., *History of West Lexington Presbytery.*

Two letters written by a gentleman to his friend in Kentucky: containing a few remarks, tending to develop the causes which gave rise to the late division in the Synod of Kentucky, together with some strictures on the apology of the Springfield Presbytery (Lexington: Charless).

Warren, Edward L., *Kentucky* (New York Board of Home Missions, Presbyterian Church).

Williams, J. L., *Historical Sketch of the First Presbyterian Church, Fort Wayne, Indiana; With Early Reminiscences of the Place. A Lecture before the Congregation October 16, 1881. The Semi-Centennial of its Organization* (Fort Wayne [1881]).

Williston, Seth, *Missionary From Connecticut. Sermon preached at Aurelius (N. Y.) October 6th, 1802, at the installation of the Rev. David Higgins, to the pastoral care of the Congregational Church in that place* (Owego, ——).

Wilson, Joshua L., *Sermons.* From the Durrett Collection, University of Chicago.

Wilson's Plea in the case of Lyman Beecher, made before the Synod of Cincinnati, October, 1835 (Cincinnati, 1837).

Yerkes, Stephen, and others, *A History of Ebenezer Presbytery of the Presbyterian Church in the United States of America from its Organization, April 16, 1799 to March, 1888* (Flemingsburg, Ky. [1888]).

APPENDIX

Key to Map of the Exscinded Presbyterian Churches and Presbyteries of Western New York as They Appeared at the Time of the Schism of 1837.

SYNOD OF GENESEE

Angelica Presbytery

1. Eagle
2. Portageville
3. Ossian
4. Centerville
5. Hume
6. Grove
7. Burns
8. Allen
9. Farmersville
10. Rushford
11. Caneadea
12. Belfast
13. Angelica
14. Almond
15. Black Creek
16. New Hudson; Haight
17. Cuba
18. Friendship
19. Amity
20. Scio
21. Andover
22. Olean
23. Independence

Buffalo Presbytery

1. Clarence
2. Black Rock
3. Buffalo
4. Lancaster
5. Alden
6. East Aurora
7. Wales
8. Hamburg
9. Evans
10. Eden
11. Colden
12. Holland
13. Boston
14. Concord
15. Silver Creek
16. Lodi
17. Springville
18. Ashford
19. Dunkirk
20. Sheridan
21. Forestville
22. Hanover
23. Fredonia
24. East Otto
25. West Otto
26. Franklinville
27. Portland
28. Westfield
29. Stockton
30. Charlotte
31. Villanova
32. Ellicottville
33. Conewango
34. Ripley
35. Mayville
36. Chautauqua
37. Ellery
38. Ellington
39. Great Valley

Buffalo Presbytery (*continued*)

40. Randolph
41. Mina
42. Panama
43. Ashville
44. Jamestown
45. Busti

Genesee Presbytery

1. Alabama
2. Oakfield
3. Elba
4. Byron
5. Pembroke
6. Batavia
7. Stafford
8. Leroy
9. Caledonia
10. Darien
11. Alexander
12. East Bethany
13. Pavilion
14. Attica
15. Covington
16. Bennington
17. Wyoming
18. Varysburg
19. Sheldon
20. Orangeville
21. Warsaw
22. Perry
23. Wethersfield Spring
24. Java
25. Gainesville
26. Castile
27. China
28. Pike

Niagara Presbytery

1. Wilson
2. Somerset
3. Yates
4. Carlton

5. Gaines
6. Porter
7. Lewiston
8. Cambria
9. Middleport
10. Medina
11. Knowlesville
12. Albion
13. Hillville
14. Barre Center
15. Lockport
16. Royalton
17. Niagara Falls
18. Pendleton

Ontario Presbytery

1. Victor
2. Avon
3. Lima
4. West Bloomfield
5. East Bloomfield
6. York
7. Lakeville
8. Livonia
9. Bristol
10. Richmond
11. Geneseo
12. Moscow
13. Mount Morris
14. Groveland
15. Conesus
16. Canadice
17. Sparta
18. Springwater
19. Nunda
20. Dansville

Rochester Presbytery

1. Holley
2. Clarkson
3. Brockport
4. Adams Basin
5. Parma

Rochester Presbytery (continued)

6. Greece
7. Webster
8. Gates
9. Rochester
10. Brighton
11. Penfield
12. Murray
13. Sweden
14. Ogden
15. Chili
16. Pittsford
17. Bergen
18. Churchville
19. Wheatland
20. Henrietta
21. Bushnell Basin
22. Mendon
23. West Mendon
24. Rush

SYNOD OF GENEVA

Bath Presbytery

1. Naples
2. Cohocton
3. Prattsburg
4. Pulteney
5. Barrington
6. Starkey
7. Dundee
8. South Dansville
9. Wayne (another Wayne in Geneva Presbytery)
10. Wheeler
11. Tyrone
12. Hammondsport
13. Kennedyville
14. Howard
15. Bath
16. Hornellsville
17. Cameron
18. Jasper

Cayuga Presbytery

1. Ira
2. Victory
3. Cato
4. Jordan
5. Weedsport
6. Elbridge
7. Montezuma
8. Sennett
9. Marcellus
10. Skaneateles
11. Cayuga
12. Auburn
13. Fleming
14. Borodine
15. Scipio
16. Aurora
17. Moravia
18. Genoa
19. Summer Hill
20. Lansing
21. West Groton
22. East Groton
23. Ludlowville
24. Trumansburg
25. Peruville

Chemung Presbytery

1. Reading
2. Havana
3. Campbell
4. Mead's Creek
5. Hornby
6. Millport
7. Painted Post
8. Corning
9. Big Flats
10. Fairport
11. Greenwood
12. Addison
13. Erwin

Chemung Presbytery (*continued*)

14. Elmira
15. Woodhull
16. Southport
17. Troupsburg
18. Chemung

Chenango Presbytery

1. Otselic
2. Smyrna
3. Sherburne
4. East Pharsalia
5. Preston
6. Norwich
7. South New Berlin
8. McDonough
9. Oxford
10. Guilford
11. Rockdale
12. Smithville
13. Triangle
14. Greene
15. Coventry
16. Bainbridge
17. Masonville
18. Nineveh
19. Harpersville
20. Colesville
21. Windsor
22. Plymouth
23. Pharsalia

Cortland Presbytery

1. De Ruyter
2. Scott
3. Preble
4. Truxton
5. Lincklaen
6. Homer
7. Cortlandville
8. McGrawville
9. Solon
10. Lisle

11. Cincinnatus
12. Freetown
13. Virgil
14. Hartford
15. Marathon

Geneva Presbytery

1. Pultneyville
2. Huron
3. Sodus
4. Ontario
5. Williamson
6. Wolcott
7. Walworth
8. Marion
9. Wayne (another Wayne in Bath Presbytery)
10. Rose
11. East Palmyra
12. Clyde
13. Palmyra
14. Newark (another Newark in Tioga Presbytery)
15. Lyons
16. Savannah
17. Port Gibson
18. Farmington
19. Junius
20. Tyre
21. Phelps
22. Waterloo
23. Seneca Falls
24. Canandaigua
25. Hopewell
26. Geneva
27. Canoga
28. Fayette
29. Gorham
30. Rushville
31. Bellona
32. Romulus
33. West Dresden
34. Ovid
35. Penn Yan

Geneva Presbytery (*continued*)

36. Branchport
37. Hector
38. Mecklenburg
39. Burdette

Onondaga Presbytery

1. Lysander
2. Baldwinsville
3. Cicero
4. Van Buren
5. Liverpool
6. Camillus
7. Syracuse
8. De Witt
9. Chittenango
10. Wampsville
11. Tully
12. Manlius
13. Jamesville
14. Oran
15. Peterboro
16. South Onondaga
17. Lafayette
18. Pompey
19. Pompey Center

20. Cazenovia
21. Nelson
22. Delphi
23. Otisco

Tioga Presbytery

1. Dryden
2. Enfield
3. Ithaca
4. Varna
5. Newfield
6. Danby
7. Caroline
8. Richford
9. Lisle Center
10. Berkshire
11. Spencer
12. Candor
13. Newark (another Newark in Geneva Presbytery)
14. Castle Creek
15. Owego
16. Binghampton
17. Nichols
18. Conklin
19. Veteran

INDEX

Abell, Jeremiah, charges against, 250; investigation of charges against, 251-256; suspension and revocation of suspension of, 254 f.; trial of, 68; withdrawal from ministry of, 256-257

Abolition Society, 807

Abolitionists, 747, 751; Northern, 120

Accommodation Plan, 41, 464, 737 n.

Act and Testimony, The, 838

Adams, John, 5

Adultery. *See* Discipline

Africa, 747

Aitken, Robert, 12 n., 320

Alabama, 678, 691, 695, 815, 856; Montgomery, missionary in, 1831, 676 f.

Albany, N. Y., 40; Presbyterian church in, 41

Alexander, Archibald, moderator of General Assembly, May, 1807, 357

Allan, John, autobiography of, 815-826

Allegheny Mountains, 22, 26, 28, 51, 56, 76; ministers employed west of, 653

Allen, Cary H., 720 n., 755, 773; sketch of, 762, n.

Allison, William, trial of, for intemperance, 551-554

American Anti-Slavery Society, 114

American Board of Commissioners for Foreign Missions, 106, 857

American Colonies, 3, 5, 6

American Colonization Society, 112, 119, 271

American Education Society, 693, 854, 857, 860, 863

American Home Missionary Society, 50 f., 59, 77, 100, 102 ff., 536, 827, 840, 845, 854, 857, 860, 863; correspondence of, 649-701; expenditures of, 653; feeling against, 268 n.; formation of, 652; importance of, in West, 668-670; legacy to, 653; number of ministers aided in first five years, 653; object of, 652; organization of, 651 f.; operations of, 668; request of, to send missionary to Kentucky, 261

American Revolution, 3, 5, 7, 8, 21, 22, 28, 38 f., 752

American Sabbath School Union, request for agent of, 262

Anderson, Alexander, 90; licensure of, 91; ordination of, 91

Anti-revival men, 90

Anti-slavery, agitation for, 118; first phase in United States, 112; lecture, 809; movement, 114; propaganda, 113; sentiment, 111; sentiment in churches, 113; societies in United States, 111

Apology of New Lights, 96

Arkansas, 700; Benton County, 695; Presbyterian ministers in, in 1833, 679; state of religion in, in 1846, 696

Armenian principles, 292, 696

Arsdale, Peter Van, autobiography of, 797-815

Articles of Practice, of Franklin, Ohio, church, 531-532

Aspland, John, 775

Associate Presbytery of Pennsylvania, 20

Associate Reformed Church, assistance of, in forming American Home Missionary Society, 652; in Kentucky, 33

Associate Reformed Synod, 10

Associate Synod, 7

Associate Synod of Edinburgh, 20

Athens, Georgia, 816

Auburn, New York, 124; Congregational Church and Society in, 497; church in, 481, 496; convention at, 864